MASTER VISUALLY®

by Rob Tidrow, David J. Clark, and Michael S. Toot

Windows® XP

Service Pack 2 Edition

Master VISUALLY® Windows® XP Service Pack 2 Edition

Published by
Wiley Publishing, Inc.
111 River Street
Hoboken, NJ 07030-5774

Published simultaneously in Canada

Library of Congress Control Number: *2005923210*

ISBN-13: 978-0-7645-7641-6

ISBN-10: 0-7645-7641-0

Manufactured in the United States of America

10 9 8 7 6 5 4 3 2 1

1K/SS/QY/QV/IN

Trademark Acknowledgments

Contact Us

For general information on our other products and services please contact our Customer Care Department within the U.S. at (800) 762-2974, outside the U.S. at (317) 572-3993 or fax (317) 572-4002.

For technical support please visit www.wiley.com/techsupport.

Sales

Contact Wiley at (800) 762-2974 or fax (317) 572-4002.

Praise for Visual Books...

"If you have to see it to believe it, this is the book for you!"

—PC World

"A master tutorial/reference — from the leaders in visual learning!"

—Infoworld

"A publishing concept whose time has come!"

—The Globe and Mail

"Just wanted to say THANK YOU to your company for providing books which make learning fast, easy, and exciting! I learn visually so your books have helped me greatly — from Windows instruction to Web development. Best wishes for continued success."

—Angela J. Barker (Springfield, MO)

"I have over the last 10–15 years purchased thousands of dollars worth of computer books but find your books the most easily read, best set out, and most helpful and easily understood books on software and computers I have ever read. Please keep up the good work."

—John Gatt (Adamstown Heights, Australia)

"You're marvelous! I am greatly in your debt."

—Patrick Baird (Lacey, WA)

"I am an avid fan of your Visual books. If I need to learn anything, I just buy one of your books and learn the topic in no time. Wonders! I have even trained my friends to give me Visual books as gifts."

—Illona Bergstrom (Aventura, FL)

"I have quite a few of your Visual books and have been very pleased with all of them. I love the way the lessons are presented!"

—Mary Jane Newman (Yorba Linda, CA)

"Like a lot of other people, I understand things best when I see them visually. Your books really make learning easy and life more fun."

—John T. Frey (Cadillac, MI)

"Your Visual books have been a great help to me. I now have a number of your books and they are all great. My friends always ask to borrow my Visual books — trouble is, I always have to ask for them back!"

—John Robson
(Brampton, Ontario, Canada)

"I write to extend my thanks and appreciation for your books. They are clear, easy to follow, and straight to the point. Keep up the good work! I bought several of your books and they are just right! No regrets! I will always buy your books because they are the best."

—Seward Kollie (Dakar, Senegal)

"What fantastic teaching books you have produced! Congratulations to you and your staff."

—Bruno Tonon (Melbourne, Australia)

"Thank you for the wonderful books you produce. It wasn't until I was an adult that I discovered how I learn — visually. Although a few publishers claim to present the materially visually, nothing compares to Visual books. I love the simple layout. Everything is easy to follow. I can just grab a book and use it at my computer, lesson by lesson. And I understand the material! You really know the way I think and learn. Thanks so much!"

—Stacey Han (Avondale, AZ)

"The Greatest. This whole series is the best computer-learning tool of any kind I've ever seen."

—Joe Orr (Brooklyn, NY)

Credits

Project Editor
Sarah Hellert

Acquisitions Editor
Jody Lefevere

Product Development Manager
Lindsay Sandman

Copy Editor
Elizabeth Kuball

Technical Editor
James F. Kelly

Editorial Manager
Robyn Siesky

Manufacturing
Allan Conley
Linda Cook
Paul Gilchrist
Jennifer Guynn

Screen Artist
Jill Proll

Illustrator
Ronda David-Burroughs

Book Design
Kathie Rickard

Project Coordinator
Maridee V. Ennis

Layout
Carrie A. Foster
Jennifer Heleine
Amanda Spagnuolo

Proofreader
Laura L. Bowman

Quality Control
Brian H. Walls

Indexer
Steve Rath

Vice President and Executive Group Publisher
Richard Swadley

Vice President and Publisher
Barry Pruett

Composition Director
Debbie Stailey

About the Authors

Rob Tidrow is a writer and computer consultant for Tidrow Communications, Inc., a firm specializing in content creation and delivery. Rob has authored or co-authored over 30 books on a wide variety of computer and technical topics, including Microsoft Windows XP, Microsoft Outlook 2003, Windows 2000 Server, and Microsoft Internet Information Server. His most current work is *Microsoft Outlook 2003 Bible.* Rob also is the Technology Coordinator for Union School Corporation, Modoc, Indiana. He lives in Centerville, Indiana with his wife Tammy and their two sons, Adam and Wesley. You can reach him at www.tidrow.com or via e-mail at rtidrow@tidrow.com.

David J. Clark has been working with some form of Windows since the beta version of 1.0 and with Windows XP since the early beta while working at Microsoft. He has been explaining how Windows works to others for just as long, with over 15 years experience as an author, editor, translator, and technical editor of computer books, working at major computer book publishers from 1984 through 1994, and then at Microsoft from 1994 through 2002. He now runs DJC Productions and works as a freelance author and editor living in Portland, Oregon with his wife and two daughters. His clients include John Wiley & Sons and Intel Corporation. He hasn't given up hope on finding time to finish that inevitable novel.

Michael S. Toot is a Seattle-based author and consultant. When he's not writing books, customer case studies, or marketing materials for various software products, he is remodeling his 1908 home, reading, sailing, cleaning up cat hair from his two Maine Coon cats, or exploring the great outdoors of Washington state. You can visit his Web site at www.miketoot.com.

Authors' Acknowledgments

Rob Tidrow – I wish to thank the following people for their outstanding commitment to excellence on this book: Jody Lefevere, acquisitions editor; Sarah Hellert, project editor; Jim Kelly, technical editor; David Fugate, literary agent; and the production crew. I would also like to thank my wife, Tammy, and my sons Adam and Wesley, for continuing to give me encouragement and motivation to finish. Now, let's go to the beach!

David Clark – I would first like to thank Lynn Haller, my agent at Studio B, for persevering and matching me up with the right publisher and series. I would also like to thank my coauthors, Rob Tidrow and Mike Toot, for the opportunity to work together. At Wiley, thanks go to Jody Lefevere, our courteous acquisitions editor, Sarah Hellert, our careful project editor, and Jim Kelly, our astute technical editor. Lastly, I would like to thank my wife Janna for her help as reader, editor, and therapist, and my two daughters, Audrey and Olivia, for being quiet when I was trying to write and for putting up with my deadlines.

Mike Toot – Many thanks to Rob Tidrow and David Clark who did all the heavy lifting that made this book possible. Thank you to acquisitions editor Jody Lefevere, technical editor Jim Kelly, and project editor Sarah Hellert, who put all the pieces together. Thanks also to the unsung heroes in production who make the pages so clear and easy-to-read. I've tried to do it; it's a lot tougher than it looks. Last but most definitely not least, thank you, hugs, and kisses to my wife Victoria. Without her love and friendship I would be adrift without a rudder.

PART I Installation, Configuration, and Customization

1) Preparing for Installation
2) Installing Windows XP
3) Customizing and Updating Windows XP

PART II Managing the Desktop Environment

4) Using the Windows XP Interface
5) Customizing the Desktop
6) Managing Users
7) Managing Files and Folders
8) Managing Security
9) Mastering Multimedia with XP

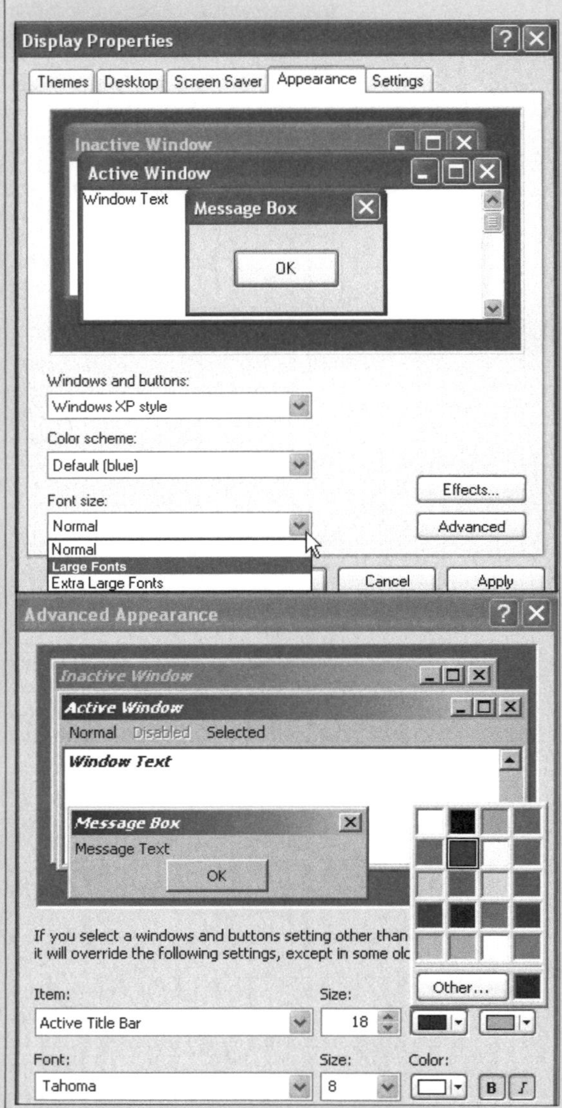

WHAT'S INSIDE

PART III Networking with Windows XP

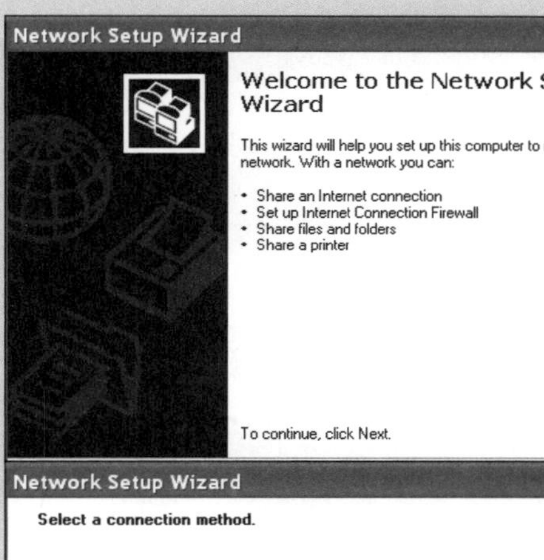

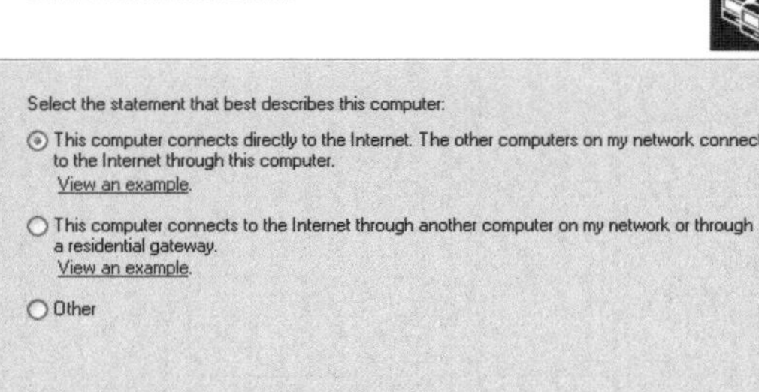

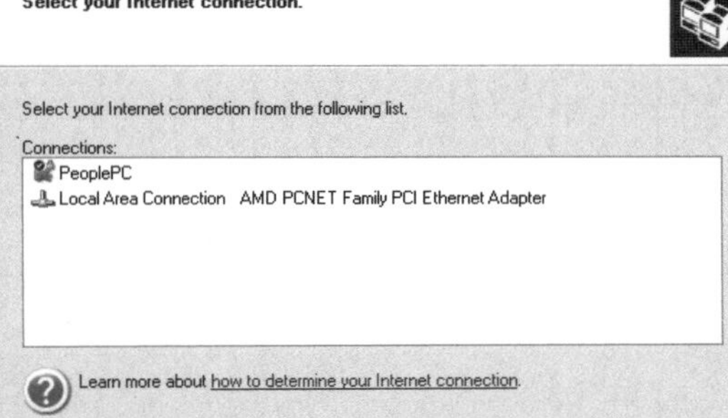

PART IV Managing the Hardware Environment

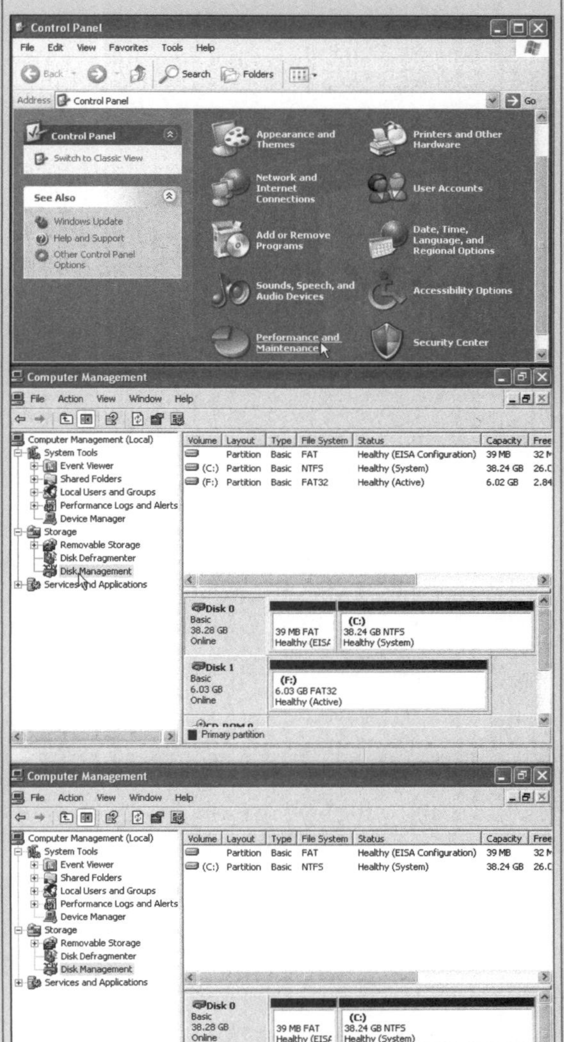

PART I Installation, Configuration, and Customization

1 Preparing for Installation

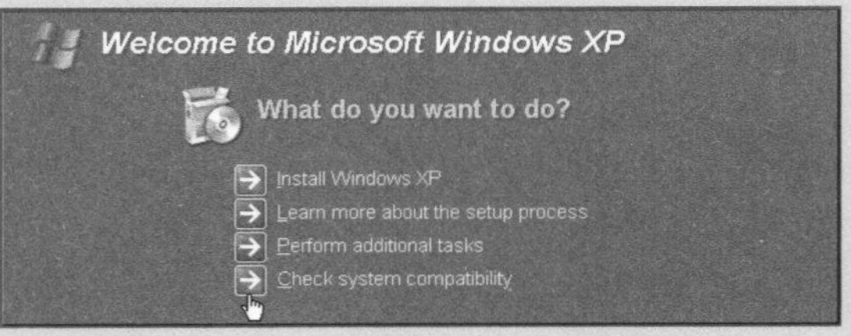

2 Installing Windows XP

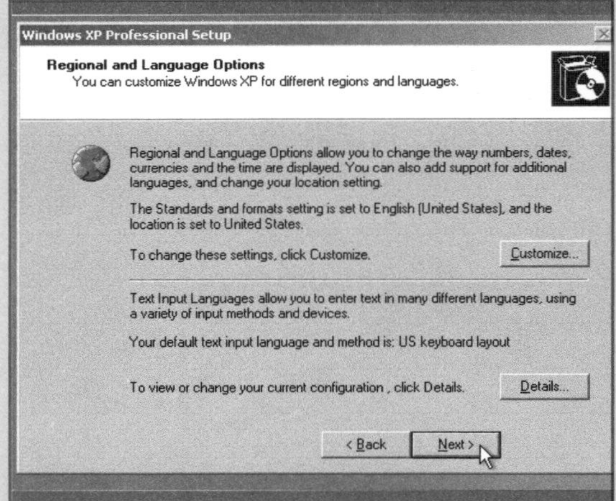

3 Customizing and Updating Windows XP

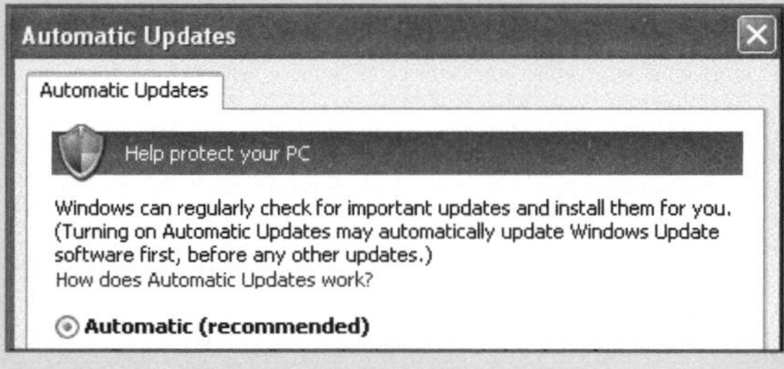

PART II Managing the Desktop Environment

4 Using the Windows XP Interface

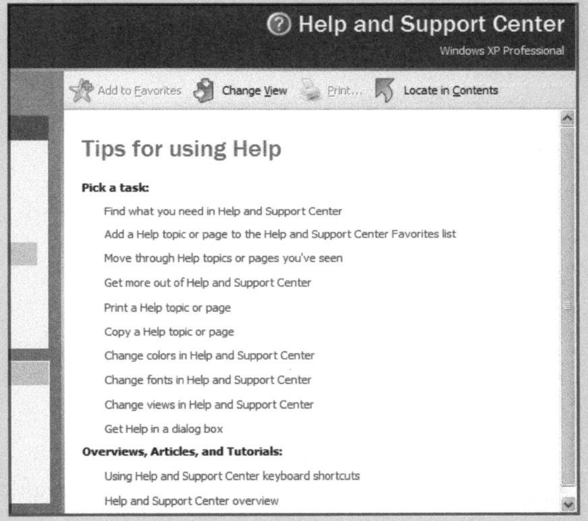

5 Customizing the Desktop

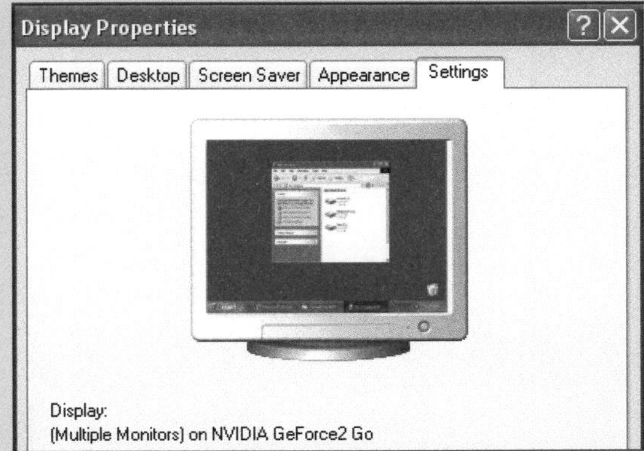

6 Managing Users

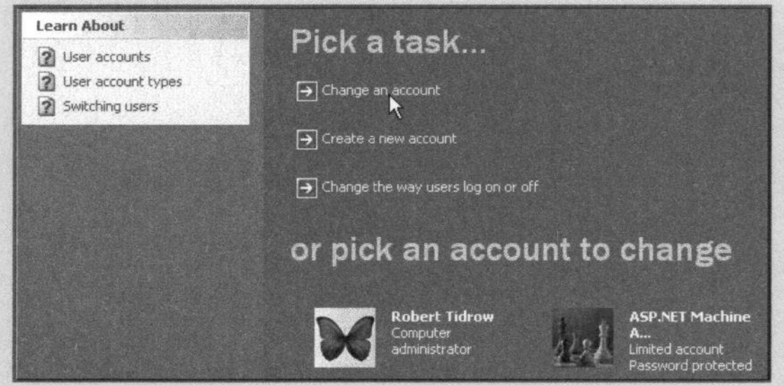

7 Managing Files and Folders

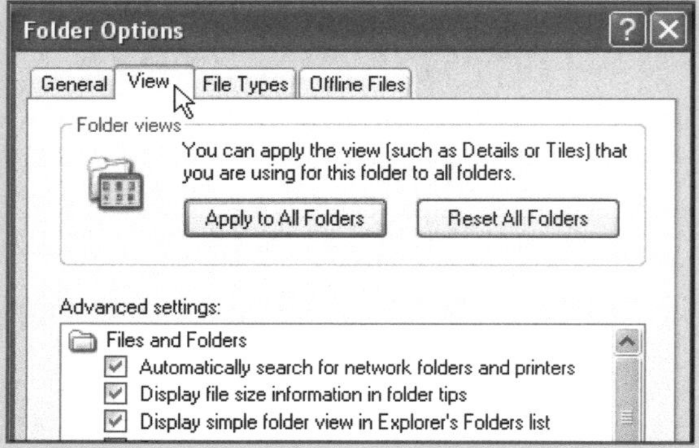

8 Managing Security

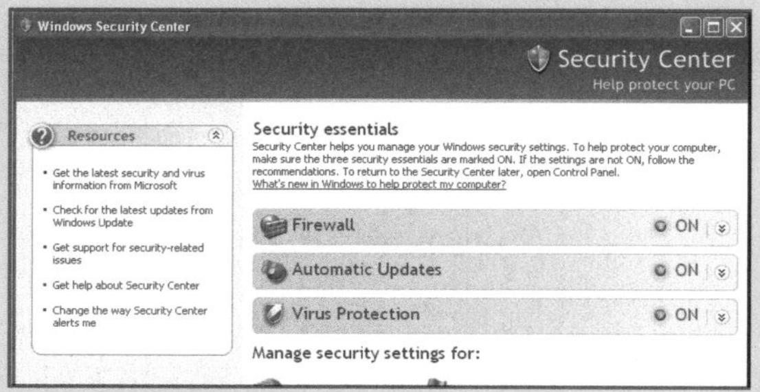

TABLE OF CONTENTS

9 Mastering Multimedia with XP

PART III Networking with Windows XP

10 Networking and the Internet

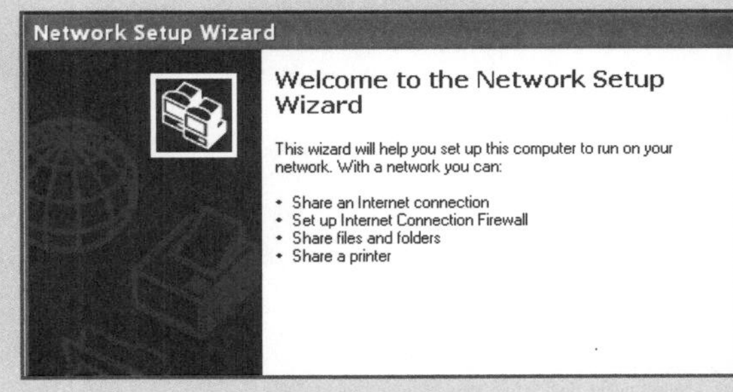

11 Working with Network Services

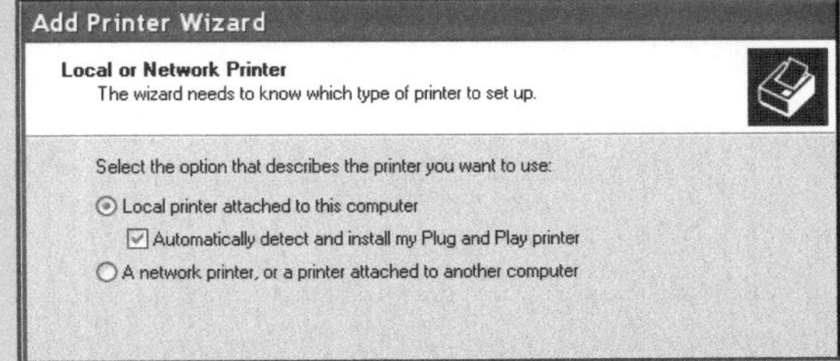

⓬ Working with IIS Components

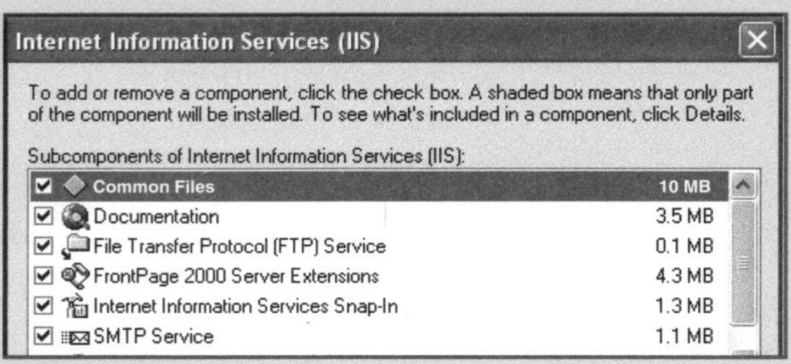

⓭ Integrating with Active Directory

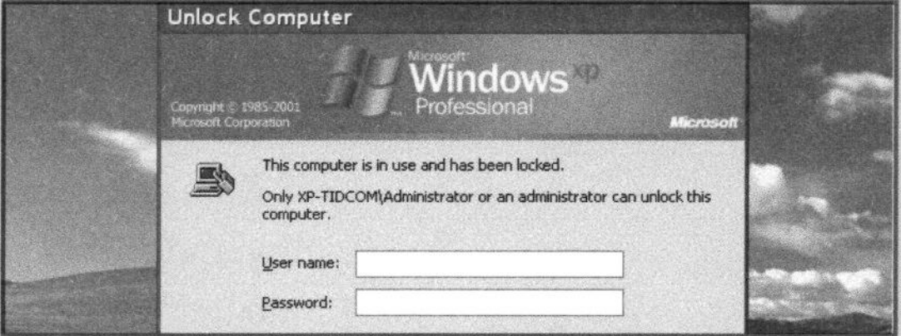

PART IV Managing the Hardware Environment

⓮ Working with Windows Internals

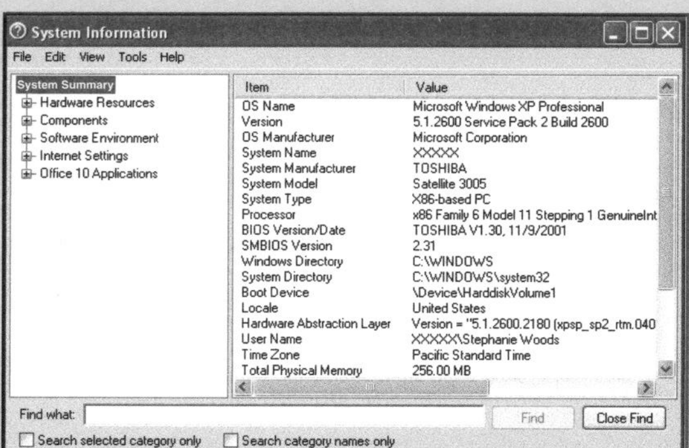

TABLE OF CONTENTS

15 Working with Hard Drives

16 Managing Portable Computers

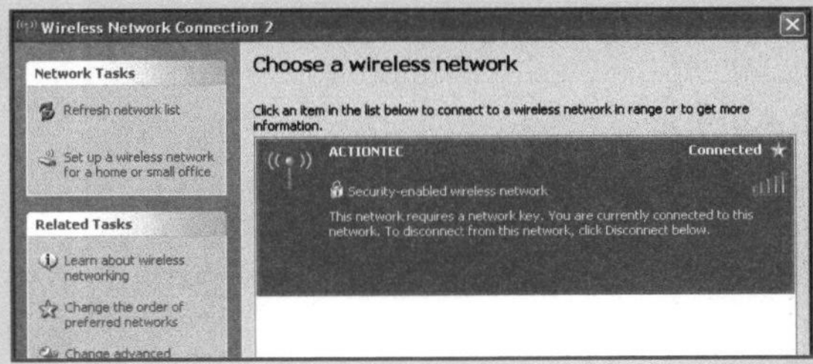

17 Optimizing Performance

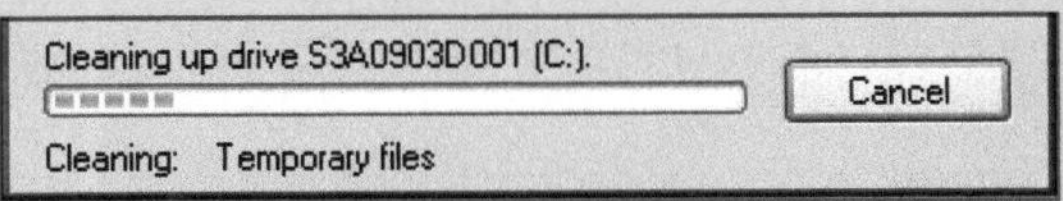

18 Troubleshooting Windows XP

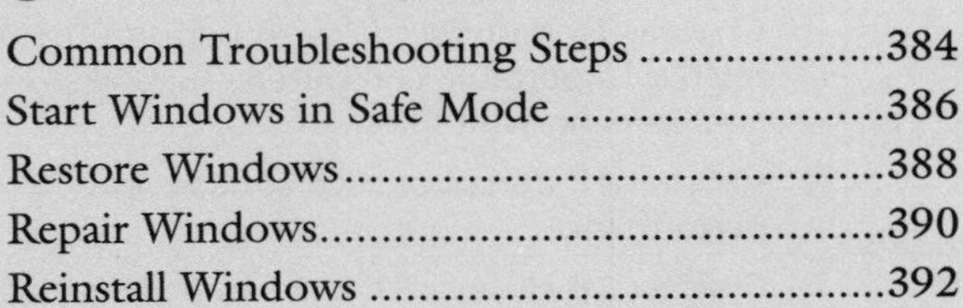

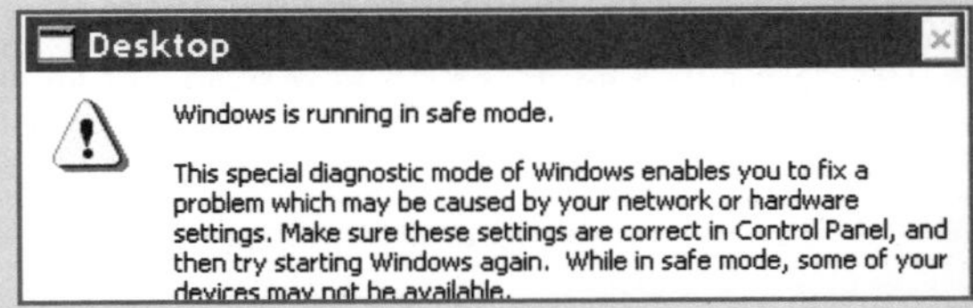

How to Use This Master VISUALLY Book

Do you look at the pictures in a book or newspaper before anything else on a page? Would you rather see an image than read how to do something? Search no further. This book is for you. Opening *Master VISUALLY Windows XP Service Pack 2 Edition* allows you to read less and learn more about Windows XP Service Pack 2.

Who Needs This Book

This book is for a reader who has never used the Windows XP operating system. (Windows novices can also find full coverage of many basic Windows tasks in *Teach Yourself VISUALLY Windows XP*, 2nd Edition.) This book is also for more computer literate individuals who want to expand their knowledge of the different features that Windows XP Service Pack 2 has to offer.

Book Organization

Master VISUALLY Windows XP Service Pack 2 Edition has 18 chapters and is divided into four parts.

Part I – Installation, Configuration, and Customization

Chapter 1 introduces Microsoft Windows XP and helps prepare you for installing or upgrading to Microsoft's desktop operating system.

Chapter 2 walks through the different ways you can install Windows XP and provides some tools to help with troubleshooting if problems arise in the future.

Chapter 3 goes "under the hood" and shows you how to control the fundamental ways that Windows functions on your desktop.

Part II – Managing the Desktop Environment

Chapters 4 and 5 explain the many ways to maneuver through the Windows XP interface, how to get help, and how to customize the desktop.

Chapter 6 covers how to add, configure, and customize user accounts in Windows XP.

Chapter 7 shows you how to use Windows XP's advanced file system to share, compress, encrypt, and customize folders and file properties.

A primary focus of Service Pack 2 is security, and Chapter 8 includes information on the new Windows Security Center, Windows Firewall, antivirus software, and more.

In Chapter 9, you find out how to take advantage of Windows XP's multimedia features, including how to rip, play, and burn music tracks, and how to configure XP for external digital devices such as scanners and cameras.

Part III – Networking with Windows XP

Chapter 10 details how you can connect to networks — local area networks, wide area networks, wireless networks, and the Internet.

You can use Chapter 11 to take advantage of network services, including sharing printers, using Remote Desktop and Remote Assistance, and using Novell and Unix services.

If you want to set up a Web site on your Windows XP computer, Chapter 12 covers Internet Information Service and its accessories — FTP server, SMTP server, and FrontPage Server Extensions.

Chapter 13 shows how to use Windows XP on a Windows 2000 Server or Windows Server 2003 domain.

Part IV – Managing the Hardware Environment

Chapter 14 explains how to perform essential tasks relating to your computer's hardware environment, such as scheduling maintenance tasks and monitoring performance.

Chapter 15 shows you how to work with hard drives installed on Windows XP computers, including changing disks to dynamic disks, creating RAID arrays, and setting disk quotas.

Chapter 16 describes how to perform the most frequent tasks related to portable computers, such as power management, and working with VPNs.

Chapter 17 describes several basic ways to optimize your PC's performance.

Chapter 18 closes with ways to troubleshoot Windows XP, including why and how to run in Safe Mode in case Windows doesn't boot correctly.

HOW TO USE THIS BOOK

Chapter Organization

This book consists of sections, all listed in the book's table of contents. A *section* is a set of steps that shows you how to complete a specific computer task.

Each section, usually contained on two facing pages, has an introduction to the task at hand, a set of full-color screen shots and steps that walk you through the task, and a set of tips. This format allows you to quickly look at a topic of interest and learn it instantly.

Chapters group together three or more sections with a common theme. A chapter may also contain pages that give you the background information needed to understand the sections in a chapter.

Using the Mouse

This book uses the following conventions to describe the actions you perform when using the mouse:

Click

Press your left mouse button once. You generally click your mouse on something to select something on the screen.

Double-click

Press your left mouse button twice. Double-clicking something on the computer screen generally opens whatever item you have double-clicked.

Right-click

Press your right mouse button. When you right-click anything on the computer screen, the program displays a shortcut menu containing commands specific to the selected item.

Click and Drag, and Release the Mouse

Move your mouse pointer and hover it over an item on the screen. Press and hold down the left mouse button. Now, move the mouse to where you want to place the item and then release the button. You use this method to move an item from one area of the computer screen to another.

The Conventions in This Book

A number of typographic and layout styles have been used throughout *Master VISUALLY Windows XP Service Pack 2 Edition* to distinguish different types of information.

Bold

Bold type represents the names of commands and options that you interact with. Bold type also indicates text and numbers that you must type into a dialog box or window.

Italics

Italic words introduce a new term and are followed by a definition.

Numbered Steps

You must perform the instructions in numbered steps in order to successfully complete a section and achieve the final results.

Bulleted Steps

These steps point out various optional features. You do not have to perform these steps; they simply give additional information about a feature.

Indented Text

Indented text tells you what the program does in response following a numbered step. For example, if you click a certain menu command, a dialog box may appear, or a window may open. Indented text after a step may also present another way to perform the step.

Notes

Notes give additional information. They may describe special conditions that may occur during an operation. They may warn you of a situation that you want to avoid, for example, the loss of data. A note may also cross reference a related area of the book. A cross reference may guide you to another chapter, or another section within the current chapter.

Icons

Icons are graphical representations within the text. They show you exactly what you need to click to perform a step.

You can easily identify the tips in any section by looking for the Master It icon. Master It offer additional information, including tips, hints, and tricks. You can use the Master It information to go beyond what you have learned in the steps.

1 Preparing for Installation

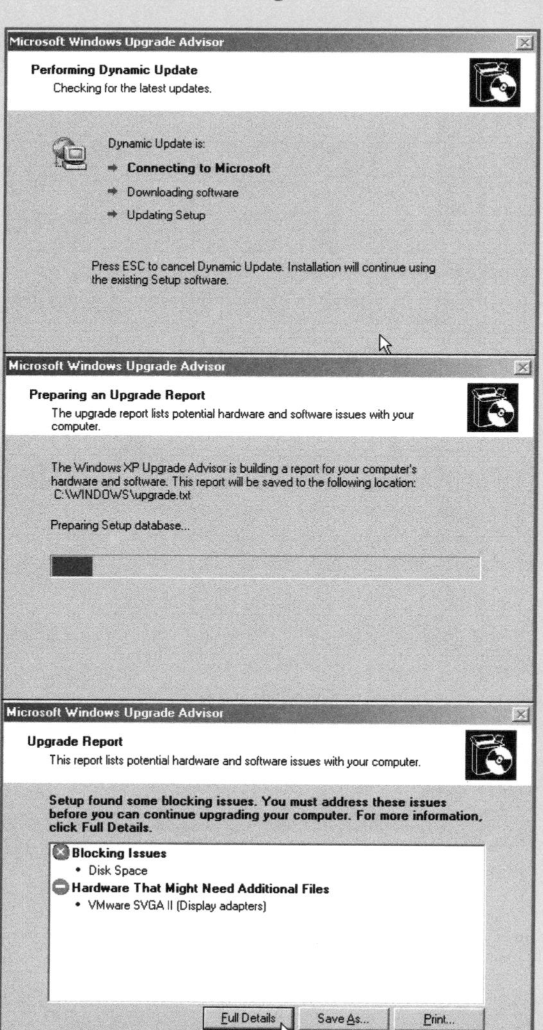

2 Installing Windows XP

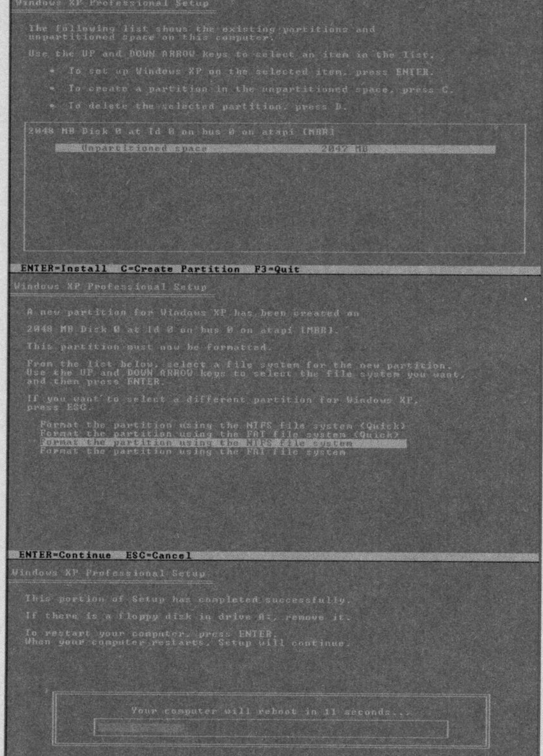

PART I

INSTALLATION, CONFIGURATION, AND CUSTOMIZATION

3 Customizing and Updating Windows XP

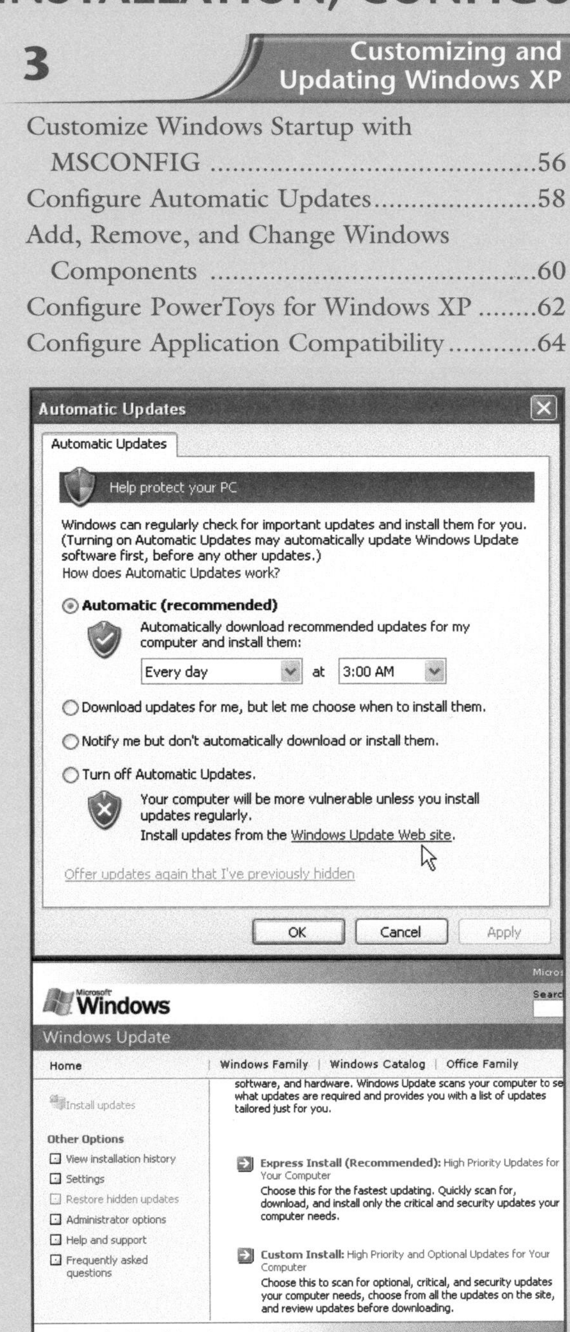

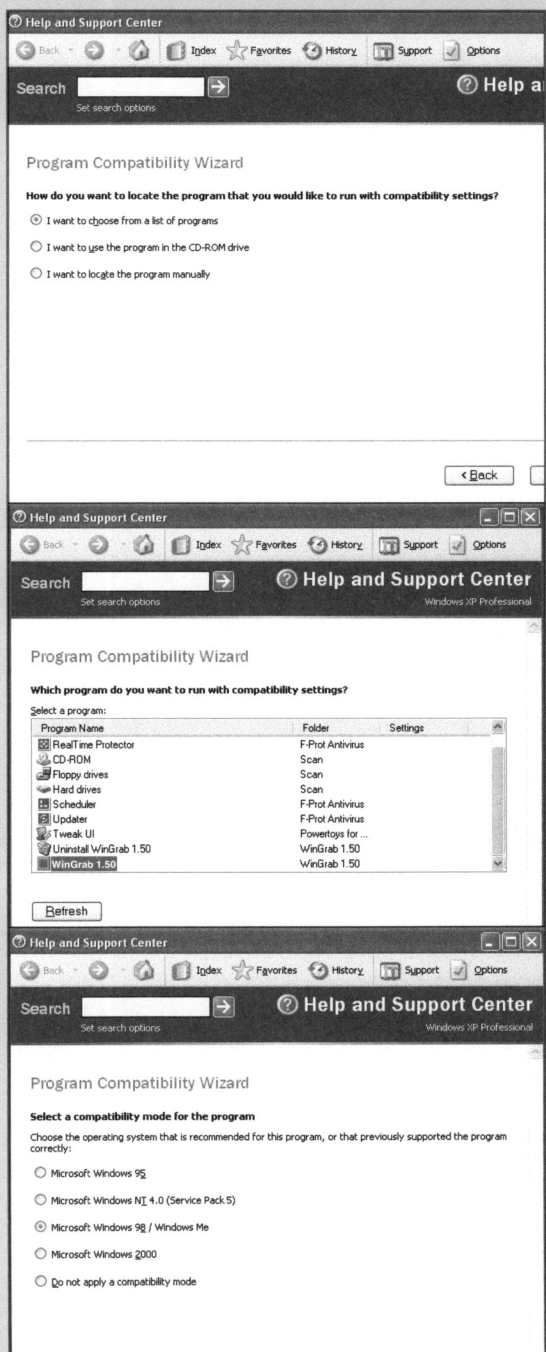

Differences between Home and Professional Editions

Microsoft Windows XP is a desktop operating system designed for both home and professional use. Windows XP Professional provides all the benefits of Windows XP Home Edition, plus additional remote access, security, performance, manageability and multilingual features that make it the operating system of choice for businesses of all sizes, as well as for people who demand the most of their computing experience. It brings together many of the consumer features found in earlier versions of Windows, such as Windows 98 and Windows Me, and business features found in Windows 2000, and merges them into a single, flexible, and powerful desktop operating system.

Offline and Encrypted Files

The Professional Edition includes better support for file and folder management. Improved features include offline file support and encrypted files and folders. Offline files allow users to keep a local copy of files that are stored on a network share, while encrypted files allow users to keep sensitive documents safer through encryption. Both features are particularly useful for laptop users who prefer data on the go but who are also concerned about keeping the data safe when traveling.

Improved File Sharing

Windows XP Home Edition supports only simple file sharing, which is less secure and robust than full-scale user authentication that is used in the Professional Edition. Although most home users may not need more than simple file sharing, business and power users will appreciate the improved security provided by full authentication.

Dual-Processor Support

Professional Edition supports dual-processor computers, while Home Edition supports only a single CPU. If you are using any computation-intensive applications, like video editing or digital photography, dual-processor systems improve your desktop experience and speed up application tasks.

Remote Desktop Support

Remote desktop support allows you to remotely access Windows XP Professional from another Windows computer, so you can control your computer and work with all your data and applications while away from your home or office. The remote desktop functions much like other third-party software that gives you remote control of another computer, but it is built into the operating system.

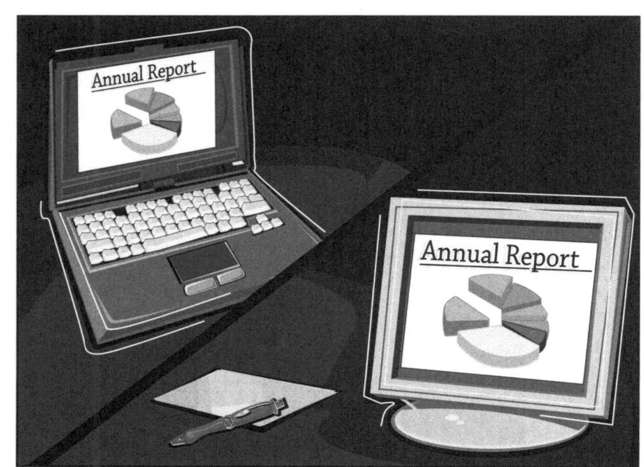

Improved Network Integration

The Windows XP Home Edition leaves out one of the single biggest features found in the Professional Edition: the ability to participate in a Windows 2000 Server or Windows Server 2003 domain. Active Directory support is not included, so features such as Group Policy, centralized administration, roaming user profiles, and access control to files, folders, and applications are not available. Although most homes probably do not have an Active Directory network installed for casual or home use, small office/home office (SOHO) environments or small businesses all the way up to multinational corporations may want to install Active Directory because of the reduced maintenance costs and the degree of control it provides.

Web Services

The Home Edition lacks the ability to run scaled-down Web services. The Professional Edition can be set up to support a Web server, an FTP server, and a Telnet server. These services support a maximum of ten connections, so it is not recommended that they be used for any significant Web traffic. But for users testing and developing Web services for later deployment on the Internet, the Professional Edition is excellent for creating and refining basic Web services.

Multilingual User Interface Support

The Multilingual User Interface (MUI) add-on is available separately from Microsoft for users who need localized Windows desktops, menus, dialog boxes, and help files. This add-on is extremely helpful in regions where users are fluent in different languages but have access to the same desktops or laptops. MUI is used to switch the Windows interface to the language most familiar to the end user. In some cases, separate MUI packs are available for specific applications, such as Microsoft Office or Microsoft Messenger. Contact Microsoft for more information about MUI add-ons.

Additional Versions Available

As Windows XP grew in popularity, additional niche versions were created to support specific hardware configurations. Microsoft also manufactures Windows Media Center Edition, Tablet PC Edition, and 64-bit Edition, which are installed by independent system vendors (ISVs). As of this writing, these additional versions cannot be purchased separately but must be purchased as part of a hardware and software package. Much of this book can be used with those editions, though for functions specific to those editions, consult the online help.

Collect System Information

Microsoft has made great advances in making installation and configuration simpler for end-users and system administrators alike. For the most part, the process can be done with little to no intervention. However, there is still no substitute for knowing the details of what hardware, firmware, and connectivity are being configured on the system. Not only does Windows ask for some of this information during different phases of configuration, but if there are problems with installing new hardware, software, or driver updates, having this information at hand goes a long way in helping to solve the problem.

If you plan on doing a number of installations, or have several computers at home that you maintain, you should collect the necessary information for each computer and keep it in a safe place where it can be referred to when needed — such as in a notebook or on a CD-ROM with the necessary drivers.

Use the SysInfo Utility

If you are running Windows 2000 or Windows XP, you can print out much of the necessary information with the SysInfo utility. Click Start, Programs, Accessories, System Tools, and then System Information. After the window has refreshed, click File and then Print to print out a list of the hardware components, driver information, and other useful details. The report is exhaustive and may take several pages to report. If you have Windows 98 or Me, right-click My Computer, click Properties, and then click the Device Manager tab.

Hardware Model Numbers

If you have purchased a computer from a hardware vendor, make sure you have a list of the model numbers for all the components in your system: motherboard, video card, hard drives, CD or DVD drive, and network card. You will need this information if you have to find and install updated device drivers for your system, or if there are known incompatibilities between some of the devices. In some cases, the only way to find out the particular model number of a component is to open the computer case and look at the component in question.

Firmware Versions

Some hardware devices have device-specific code embedded in them, called *firmware.* Firmware enables features and functions so that operating systems can make the best use of the hardware. Devices that often have firmware are motherboards (basic input/output system, or BIOS), CD or DVD drives, and network cards. Sometimes video cards have firmware as well. Check with each device's manufacturer to see if updated firmware is available for your device. **Caution:** You can completely disable hardware if you flash it with the wrong firmware, such as the wrong BIOS for your motherboard. Follow the manufacturer's instructions exactly, or have a computer professional help you.

Device Drivers

Device drivers are hardware-specific code used by the operating system so that it can interact with, manage, and control its functions. Windows XP ships with device drivers for a large number of hardware devices on the market, and new ones are sometimes made available on the Windows Update site. (See Chapter 3 for information on the Windows Update service.) You should check with the device manufacturer to see if new drivers have been made available since Windows XP's publication.

File System Type

If you are performing an upgrade from an earlier version of Windows, find out the file system type in use: FAT, FAT32, or NTFS. The first two of these are more likely found on Windows 9*x* or Windows Me machines, whereas NTFS is more likely found on Windows NT or Windows 2000 machines. The file system type is relevant, because NT features such as access control, encryption, and compression are not available in FAT or FAT32 file systems.

Internet Settings

Internet connectivity is perhaps the single most important function of any computer today. Whether you are connected to the Internet through AOL, through an independent Internet service provider (ISP), or through your company's service provider, you should have the necessary connection information so that you can set up your new computer properly. This information may already be available on your computer, or you may need to get it from your system administrator. On existing Windows systems, you can find this information by choosing Control Panel and then Network Connections.

Use the Upgrade Compatibility Wizard

The Upgrade Compatibility Wizard is one of the most useful tools available to anyone upgrading an older version of Windows to Windows XP. The wizard takes an inventory of system hardware, software, and device drivers; compares the existing system against a component database; and presents a report of its findings. It lets you know if your system needs a hardware upgrade to meet minimum system requirements for Windows XP or if your hardware is on the Windows Hardware Compatibility List (WHCL). This wizard helps you approach an upgrade forewarned and forearmed, able to correct any potential pitfalls or shortcomings before installation.

Although the Upgrade Compatibility Wizard does not guarantee it will find all known problems or system incompatibilities, it does help you avoid ones that have previously been reported to Microsoft and provides suggestions on how to avoid the problems (for example, install more memory, obtain upgraded device drivers, make more room on a hard drive).

The wizard can be run on any version of Windows, but it provides better results on Windows 2000- or Windows XP-based systems.

Use the Upgrade Compatibility Wizard

1. Insert the Windows XP CD.

   The Welcome to Microsoft Windows XP screen appears.

Note: *You can also browse to the CD drive and click Setup to launch the CD.*

2. Click the option to check system compatibility.

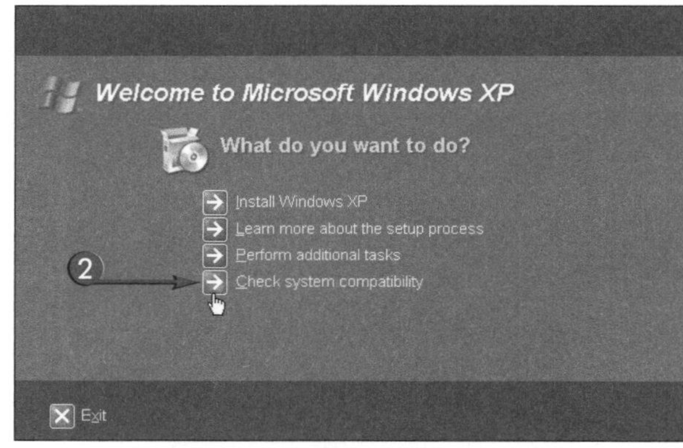

   The next screen asks what you want to do.

3. Click the option to check your system automatically.

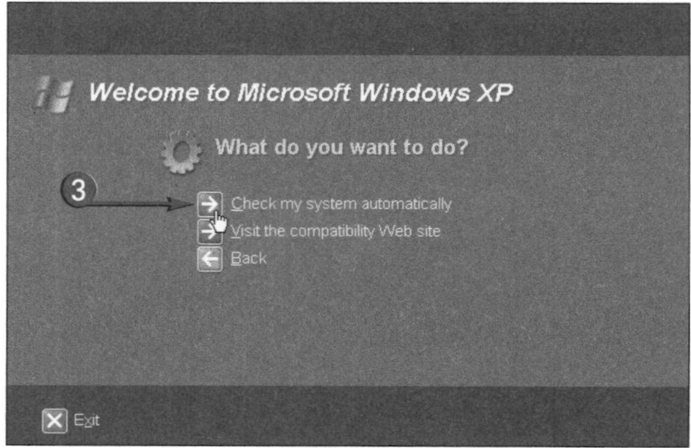

The Microsoft Windows Upgrade Advisor window appears.

4 Click the recommended option to download the updated setup files.

5 Click Next.

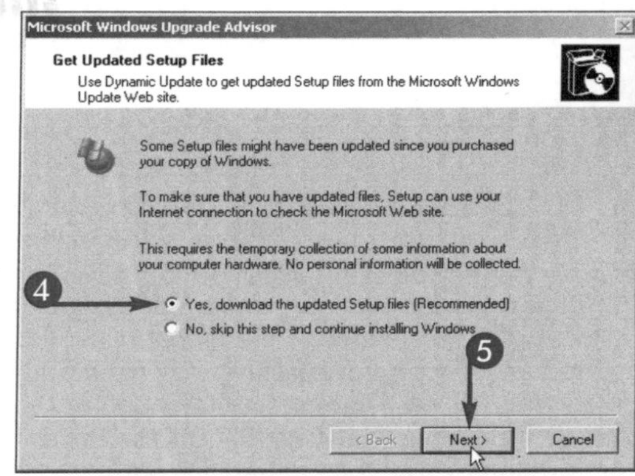

The wizard downloads additional files needed to check your system.

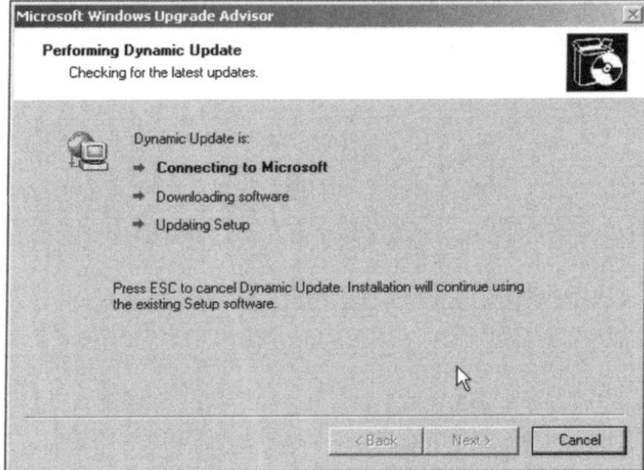

What is the difference between the minimum and recommended system requirements for Windows XP?

- Microsoft uses the term *minimum* for the bare-bones system configuration needed to run an operating system. However, even though you can install Windows XP on a minimum configuration, system performance is barely tolerable, especially if you run any applications that take significant amounts of memory or processing power. The “recommended” system configuration should be considered the bare minimum for minimally tolerable performance. Most blocking issues reported by the Upgrade Compatibility Wizard are based on the minimum hardware requirements, not the recommended ones.

Should I upgrade from the recommended system requirements?

- Microsoft recommends that you have a Pentium-based 300 MHz processor, 128MB of RAM, an SVGA card (800×600 or better), and 1.5GB of hard drive space. In the real world, these requirements provide scant support for all that Windows XP has to offer. Most versions of Windows are RAM-hungry, so you should upgrade your RAM to at least 128MB and preferably 256MB. Next, upgrade your processor to 1 GHz or better (Intel or AMD), and then upgrade your hard drive and video. You will be glad you did.

continued

Use the Upgrade Compatibility Wizard *(Continued)*

The Upgrade Compatibility Wizard generates two types of errors: blocking errors and incompatibility warnings. Blocking errors are ones that prevent you from running the installation program at all, such as insufficient disk space or RAM. Incompatibility warnings are generated either for hardware that may need additional files (marked with the red Do Not Enter symbol) or for software that does not support Windows XP (marked with the yellow warning triangle). The incompatibility warnings do not stop the upgrade process, but the hardware and software may not function properly, or at all, after the upgrade.

The Upgrade Compatibility Wizard bases its findings on the WHCL, which is a list of hardware and software tested by Microsoft and confirmed to work with Windows. The warnings do not mean that your existing hardware or software will not work, only that either there are known problems that have been reported to Microsoft, or that the particular hardware and software has not been tested by Microsoft. In any event, you should check the hardware and software manufacturer's Web site to see if known problems exist, or if updated components are available.

Use the Upgrade Compatibility Wizard *(continued)*

The Upgrade Compatibility Wizard checks your system for potential incompatibilities.

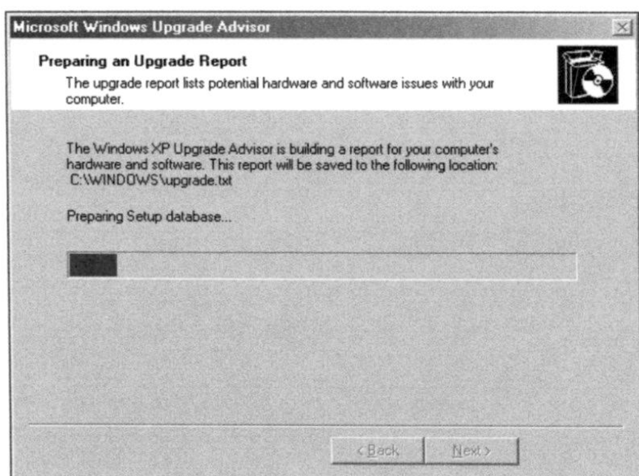

The wizard creates a summary report, showing you problems or potential problems that may occur.

6 Click Full Details.

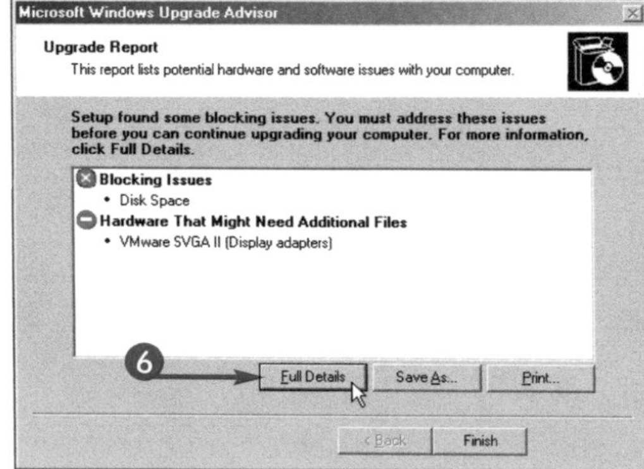

- Review details about the blocking issues or potential problems in the detailed report.
- Click Summary to return to the summary report.

7 Click Finish.

- The wizard reports if there are no problems or potential pitfalls for your upgrade.

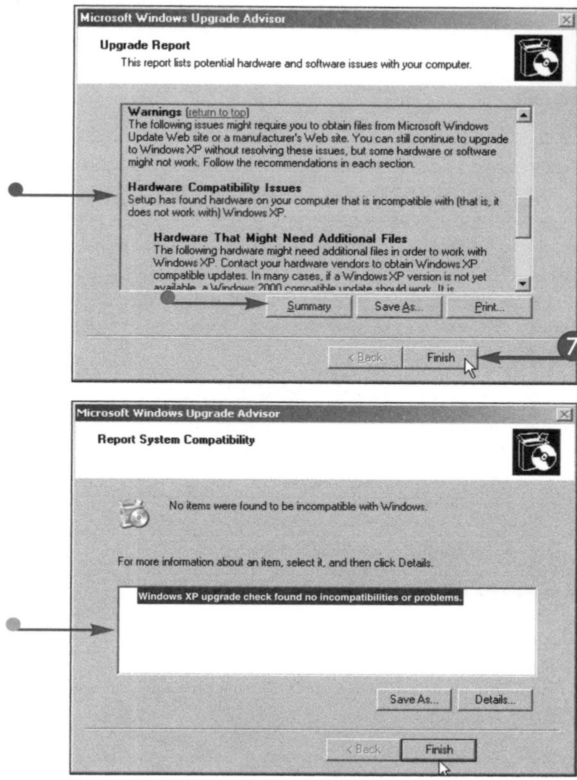

Does the Upgrade Compatibility Wizard work with all versions of Windows?

▼ The wizard does not work with Windows 95 or Windows NT 3.5*x*. You need to upgrade Windows 95 to Windows 98 or later, and upgrade Windows NT 3.5*x* to Windows NT 4.0 or later. If you are running those earlier versions, upgrading your hardware and performing a new install may be easier than upgrading your operating system.

What if I want to check compatibility before I buy Windows XP?

▼ Microsoft provides a downloadable version of the wizard, called the Upgrade Advisor. You can download the Advisor at www.microsoft.com/windowsxp/home/howtobuy/upgrading/advisor.asp and then run it on your computer. Running the Upgrade Advisor helps you determine what upgrades you need to make in order to run Windows XP.

Is there another way to run the Upgrade Compatibility Wizard?

▼ You can run the wizard without launching the initial setup screen. Open a DOS or CMD box, change to <CD drive letter\i386, and run winnt32.exe/checkupgrade only. This launches the wizard and proceeds normally. This method is particularly useful if the source files are stored on a network share and you do not want to carry the installation CD with you.

Transfer Files and Settings

If you are performing a new install rather than an upgrade, you can use another wizard to transfer existing files and settings to Windows XP. The timesaving Files and Settings Transfer Wizard restores personal desktop settings and menu options that you have set up previously in other versions of Windows, including Internet Explorer security settings, bookmarks, and cookies.

Before running the wizard, you should perform some maintenance on your existing system. Run the Disk Cleanup utility to remove temporary files and Internet Explorer cached files; this reduces the number of files to be transferred.

You should also be connected to a network share or have a CD or DVD burner available, because you probably cannot fit all the necessary files onto a floppy disk. You can save the files to a different partition on the same hard drive if you are not deleting or reformatting it during the install process. You can also install the settings directly across a network to the new computer; make sure you have the necessary shares and permissions set up before you do so.

Transfer Files and Settings

1. Insert the Windows XP CD.

   The Welcome to Microsoft Windows XP screen appears.

Note: *You can also browse to the CD drive and click Setup to launch the CD.*

2. Click the option to perform additional tasks.

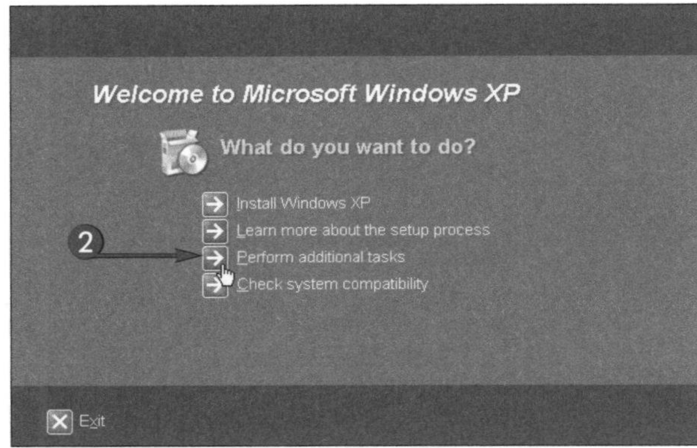

   The next screen asks what you want to do.

3. Click the option to transfer files and settings.

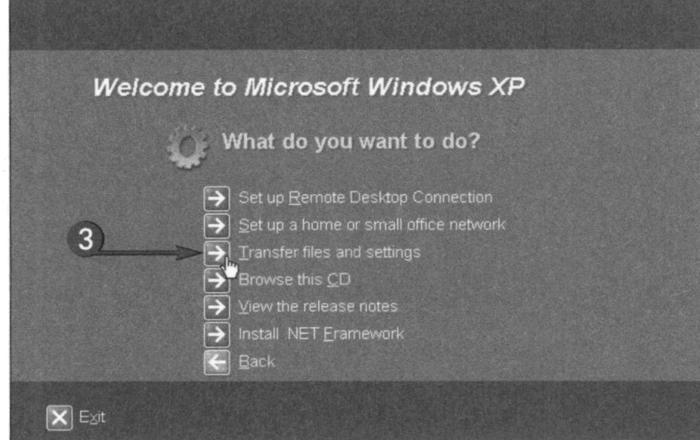

The Files and Settings Transfer Wizard appears.

4 Click Next.

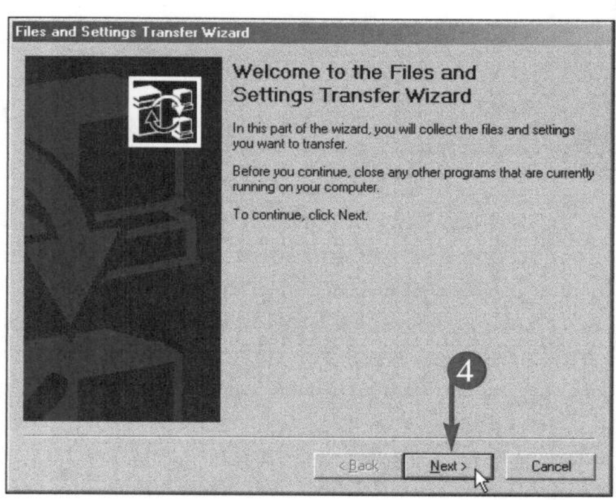

The next screen asks you to select a transfer method.

5 Click the transfer method you want to use.

6 Click Next.

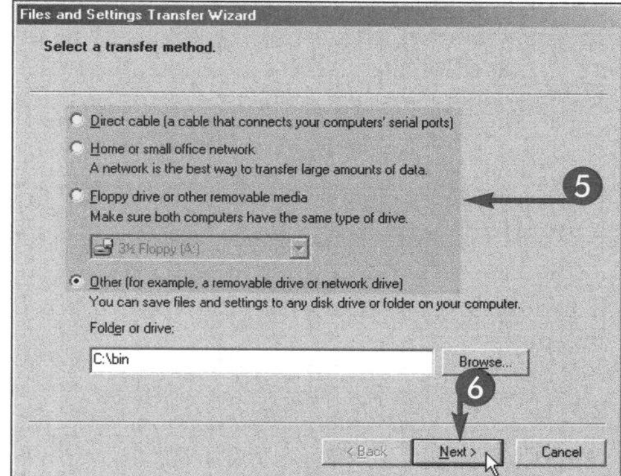

Can I use the wizard to keep my settings in a dual-boot environment?

▼ Yes, you can transfer the necessary settings to the new Windows XP installation if you have installed Windows XP to a different partition. Otherwise, you run the risk of overwriting settings in the shared partition. See Chapter 2 for more information on installation methods and caveats.

Does the wizard transfer any special folders I have set up on my computer?

▼ The wizard packages up any files and folders that you add to it during the transfer process, but it does not always create any special folders or paths on the new computer. If you have a special share that you want to transfer, re-create the share on the new computer before you run the wizard.

I ran the wizard, but when I log in to the new computer, I do not see the files anywhere.

▼ When you import the files and folders to the new system, you must be logged in as the same user. If there are Active Directory policies preventing you from logging in at more than one computer at a time, you need to save the files to an intermediate share first.

continued

Transfer Files and Settings *(Continued)*

The Files and Settings Transfer Wizard moves a large number of files and settings by default. It can also be used to move additional files and folders that can be selected when you run the wizard. You can point the wizard at any folder and move its contents, or you can select files by file type and have those moved to the new system.

Moving only settings does not take up much space. Moving files, especially if you have selected additional files and folders, takes up much more space. Plan on anywhere from 5MB to 600MB of space needed on the target system — more if you choose to move movie, multimedia, or music files such as MP3s.

Although the wizard is good about packing up settings, there are a few caveats for the target system. First, the wizard moves only settings, not entire applications. Second, the specific application should be installed on the target system first, before the settings are imported. Third, the wizard supports only some third-party applications or may only support later versions. An updated list of supported applications can be found at http://support.microsoft.com/default.aspx?scid=kb;en-us;304903.

Transfer Files and Settings *(continued)*

The next screen asks what you want to transfer.

7 Click the option for what you want to transfer: settings, files, or both.

8 Click here to select a custom list of files.

9 Click Next.

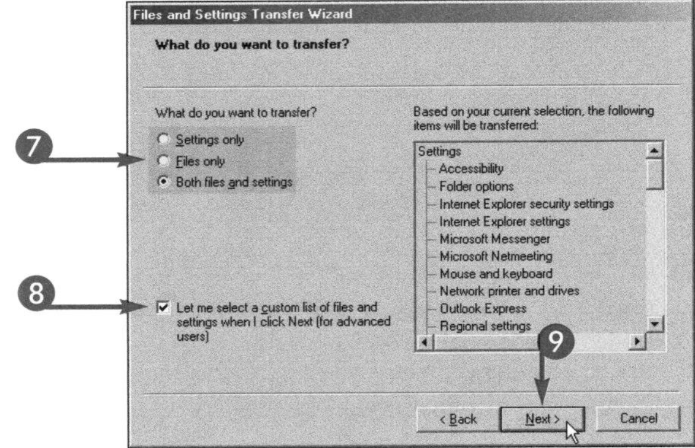

The next screen asks you to select custom files and settings.

10 Click a button to add settings, folders, files, or file types.

11 Click Next.

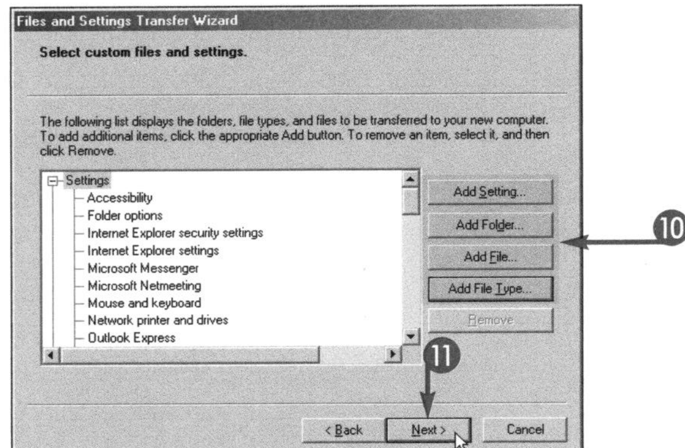

The wizard collects the selected files and settings.

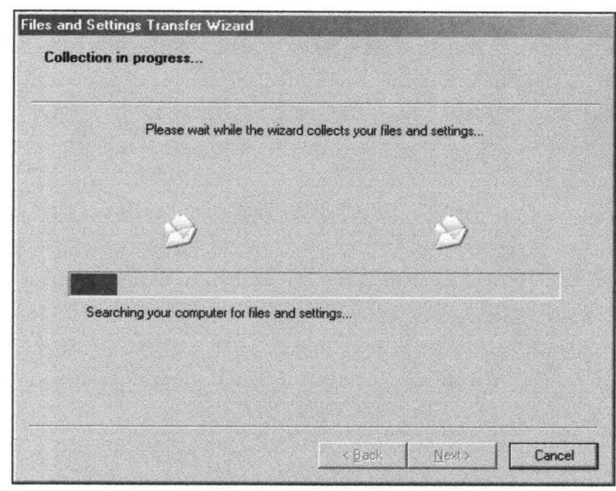

⑫ Click Finish.

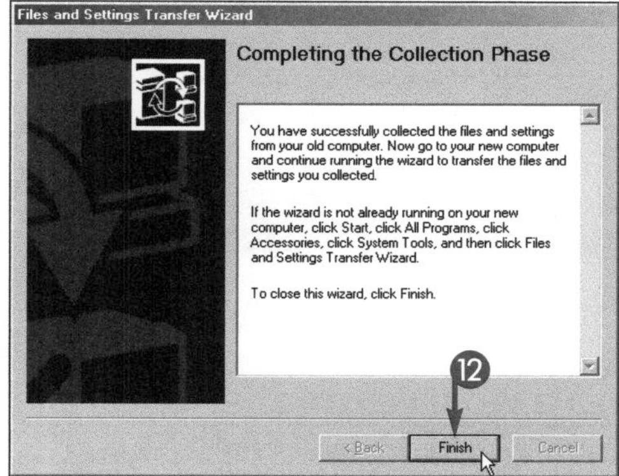

What information is migrated by the wizard?

▼ The wizard is designed to transfer settings for Windows, some Windows applications, and user files. The default settings are listed here.

Hardware settings	Mouse, keyboard, regional settings, network, dialup, and printer driver settings
Desktop settings	Wallpaper, colors, screen saver, menu and taskbar options, folder settings, audio settings
Software settings	Internet Explorer bookmarks and cookies, Microsoft Office settings, Outlook and Outlook Express settings, mail folders and address books, some third-party application settings
Files and folders	Desktop, My Documents, My Pictures, My Favorites, shared desktop, fonts

Restore Files and Settings

After you have collected your files and settings from the source computer, you can import and install them onto the target computer running Windows XP. Only Windows XP natively ships the Files and Settings Transfer Wizard as part of the operating system, giving you easy access to the wizard for any new installations you may be creating.

The Files and Settings Transfer Wizard contains a safety valve: If you are running the wizard from Windows XP, it gives you the opportunity to create a Wizard Disk that you can run on the source machine without requiring the Windows XP install disk. This shortcut is extremely handy and gives you the ability to create another tool for your support toolbox so that you do not have to carry around the Windows XP install disk (which is worth its weight in gold).

The following task assumes you have already run the wizard to collect settings on the source computer. If you have not, see the previous task for more information.

Restore Files and Settings

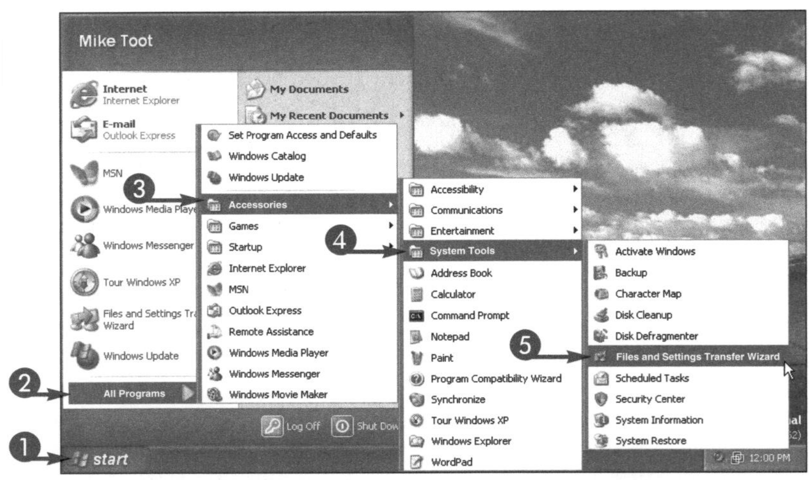

1. Click Start.
2. Click All Programs.
3. Click Accessories.
4. Click System Tools.
5. Click Files and Settings Transfer Wizard.

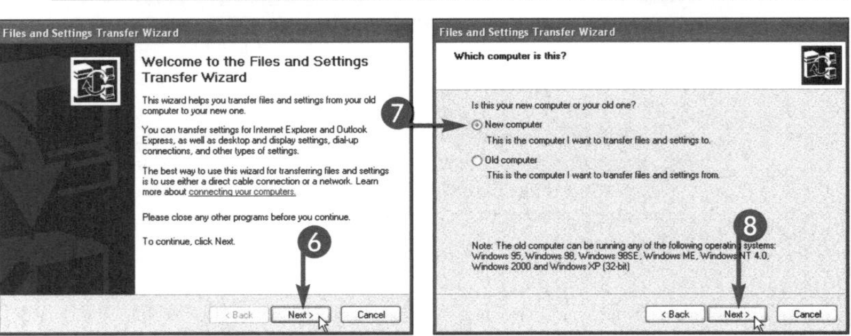

The Files and Settings Transfer Wizard appears.

6. Click Next.
7. Click New computer.
8. Click Next.

Note: *If the Windows Security Alert appears, click Unblock.*

9 Click the option to indicate that you do not need the Wizard Disk.

10 Click Next.

The next screen asks you where the files and settings are.

11 Click Other.

12 Click Browse to browse to the previously collected settings.

13 Click Next.

The source files and settings are applied to the new system.

14 Click Finish.

Note: *After applying the settings, you need to log off and log on again for the new settings to take effect.*

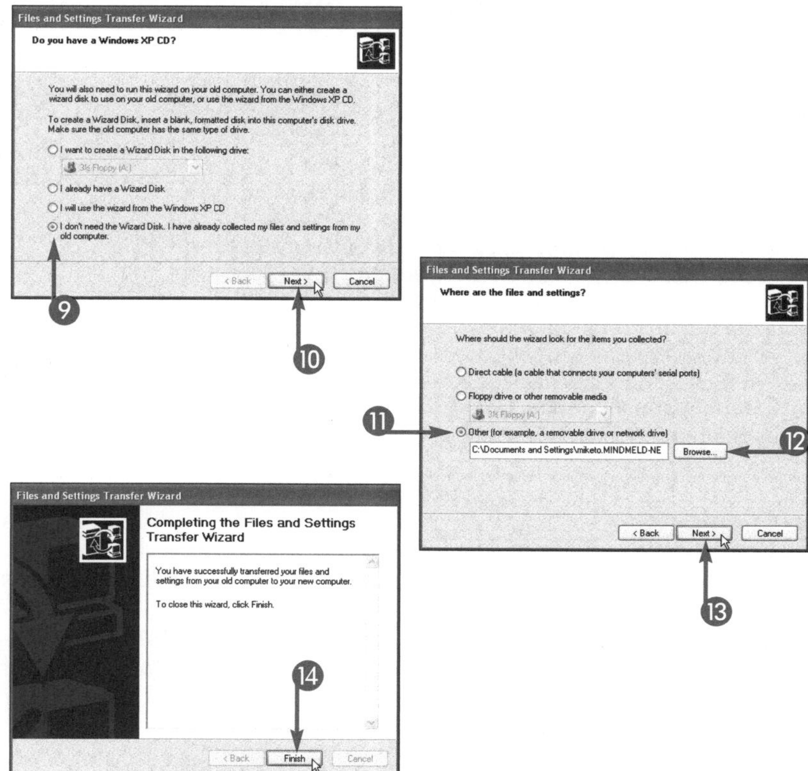

I have several users I need to migrate to new computers. Should I use the wizard for all of them?

- The wizard is an ideal tool if you only have a few users that you need to migrate to Windows XP, such as in a home or a SOHO environment. If you are using Active Directory, there may be easier ways to migrate users. See Chapter 13 for information on working with Active Directory.

Why do I get a Security Alert when I try to run the wizard?

- Windows XP Service Pack 2 includes a new Security Console that detects unauthorized attempts to access your computer or its files from across the network. If you are installing on a pre-SP2 installation, you will not see this message.

Why did my game (or other application) not migrate over?

- Most Windows applications modify the Registry in ways not detected by the wizard. Your best bet is to capture any saved game files (or other data files), reinstall the application, and then migrate the files to your new system.

Introduction to Installation Types

Installing Windows XP involves more than just clicking a Setup icon. Depending on the type of installation you choose, you can bring additional functionality to your existing computer. The different types of installation available reflect the different needs of users: Upgrade an existing installation with the latest bug fixes and features; install on a brand-new computer; upgrade an older version of Windows; dual-boot between versions of Windows; install computers across a network; and script the installation so that it takes place automatically, without user intervention.

Your choice of installation depends on what your role is. If you are a home user, you are most likely to use either a Service Pack Installation or an Upgrade Installation. If you are a SOHO or networking professional supporting many computers, you may use all these methods for varying reasons.

In all cases, Microsoft has made it fairly easy for you to get Windows XP up and running, no matter how you plan to install it. For the most part, these installation types vary only in the first steps. After the system has booted into graphical mode, the rest of the installation takes place normally.

New Installation

A new installation is performed on *bare metal,* a hard drive with no other operating system on it. A new installation is most often performed when you want to wipe out everything and start over, or when you have backed up your previous operating system's contents and data files and want to learn about XP from the ground up. If you choose this path, you need to reinstall your applications, such as Microsoft Office, before you can use them again. See Chapter 1 for information about transferring your files and settings from an existing installation to a new installation.

Upgrade Installation

An upgrade installation is used when you want to install Windows XP on top of an earlier version of Windows, such as Windows 2000 or Windows Me. An upgrade preserves your existing applications and settings so that you can be productive more quickly than you can with a new installation. This installation is frequently used by people who purchase an upgrade version of Windows XP at a retail or online store, which costs much less than a full install version. Compatibility can be an issue, so see Chapter 1 for information on running the Upgrade Advisor prior to starting your upgrade.

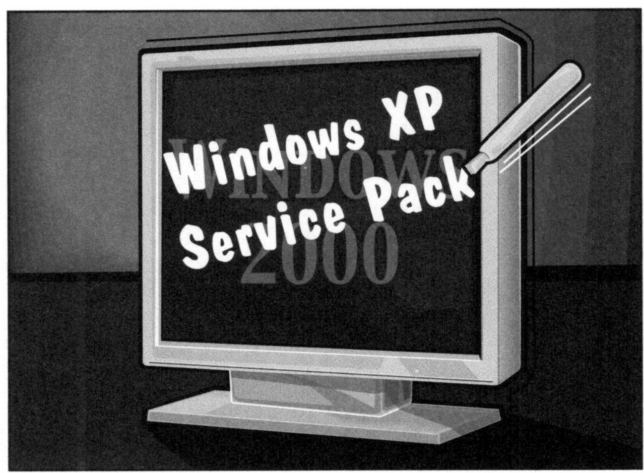

Dual-Boot (Side-by-Side) Installation

A dual-boot or side-by-side install differs from a new installation and is used when you have a spare partition on your hard drive. You can then choose which operating system (OS) to run at boot time, allowing you to preserve the old OS with its applications and settings but giving you a new OS to test, work with, or educate yourself. This installation is most often used for compatibility reasons or when the installation disks for older software are no longer available and you cannot install the application onto a new OS. You need to reinstall your applications into the new partition, rather than use the copy in the existing partition; otherwise, you run into problems with conflicting program settings and possibly corrupted files.

Service Pack Only Installation

If you already have Windows XP installed, with or without Service Pack 1, you can install Service Pack 2 over your existing operating system. This brings you all the bug fixes and feature updates you need without disturbing the underlying OS or requiring you to engage in a lengthy new OS installation. You do not need to reinstall any applications when you do this.

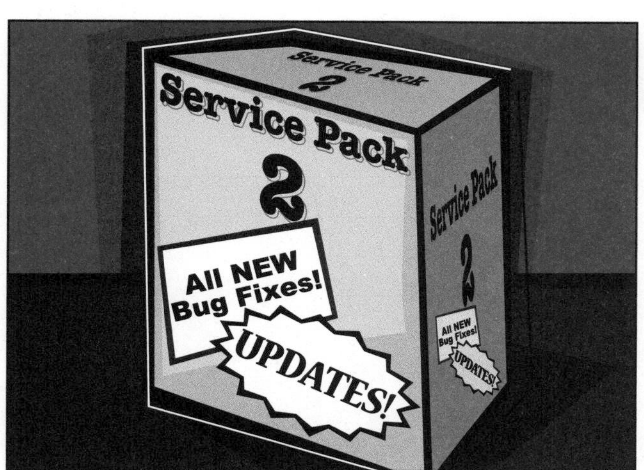

Network Installation

Network installations are used when you have more than a couple of computers on which you need to install Windows XP. With a network installation, the source files are stored on a network share and the setup program is invoked over the network. You can perform either a new installation or an upgrade installation using this method. One of the chief benefits of this method is having the binaries centrally located, rather than being required to take the CD to every desktop. The Network Install section shows you how to "slipstream" Service Pack 2 into the original Windows XP binaries so you can perform a one-step installation process.

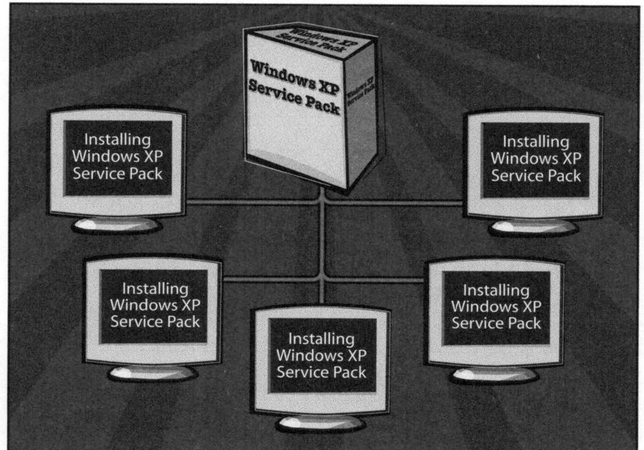

Other Installation Methods

You can use other methods to install Windows XP onto a computer, including *cloning* (using either Microsoft's Sysprep utility or a commercial program like Norton Ghost) and Remote Installation Services (RIS). Both methods are more likely to be used in larger enterprises, though they can be used in SOHO environments. Although these methods are not covered in this book, you can find out more information in both the online help files and the release notes for Windows XP and Service Pack 2, as well as at the Microsoft Web site.

Install Windows XP: New Installation

Performing a new installation is one of the best ways to learn the fundamentals of how Windows is set up for your computer. A new installation wipes everything clean, starts fresh, and lets you configure Windows XP to exactly conform to your environment. After you have run through a new installation a few times, you may want to examine scripting your installation so that user intervention is not required. See the section "Automate the Installation Process," later in this chapter, for more information.

In some cases, you may not be able to perform a new installation on your computer. For example, most systems from major computer manufacturers ship with *restore disks,* CDs or DVDs that contain an image of your operating system and applications that were preselected and preinstalled by the manufacturer. This may not always be what you want, especially if there are applications that are incompatible with the ones you want to install. Your only solution is to go buy a retail copy of Windows XP and install it — but be warned that if you do this, you may void your customer-support agreement with your manufacturer.

Install Windows XP: New Installation

1. Insert your Windows XP CD and reboot the computer.

   The text-mode setup program launches.

Note: *If you have a third-party driver for a RAID array, press F6 when prompted by the setup program and follow the instructions.*

2. Press Enter to continue.

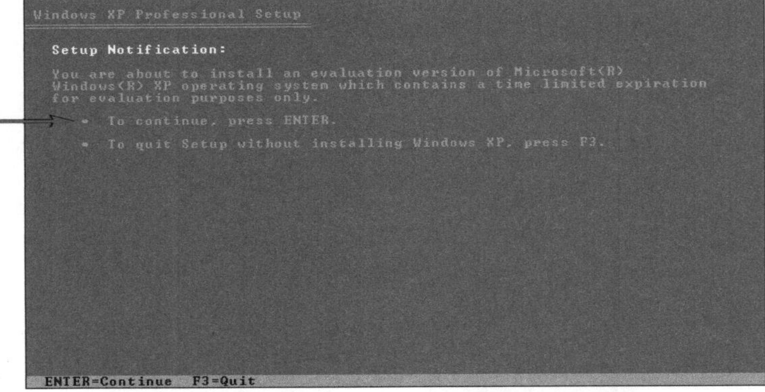

A screen welcoming you to set up appears.

3. Press Enter to continue.

   - Launch the Recovery Console by pressing R. See the section "Install the Recovery Console" for more information.

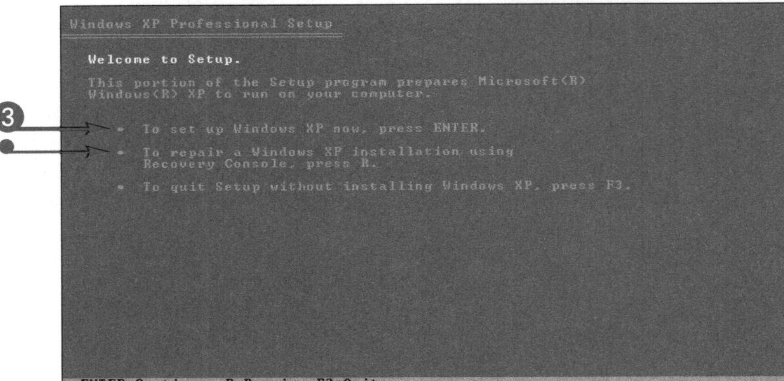

The Windows XP license screen appears.

4 Press the Page Down key to read the license agreement.

5 Press F8 to agree to the license agreement and continue with setup.

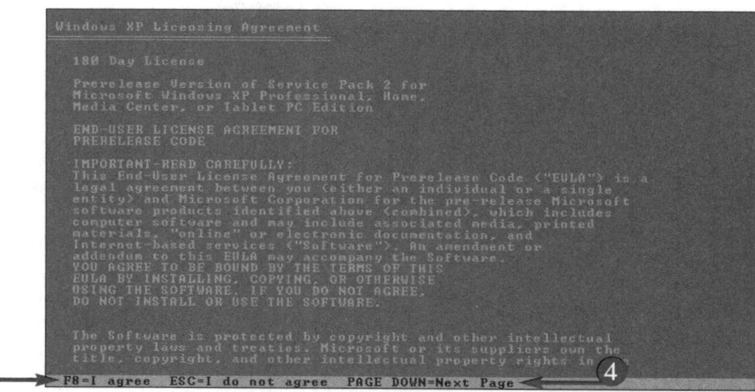

The disk partitioning screen appears.

6 Press Enter to use the entire disk as a single partition.

- You can create several partitions at this screen, or you can create and format partitions after Windows is installed. Press C to create more than one partition, and follow the instructions.

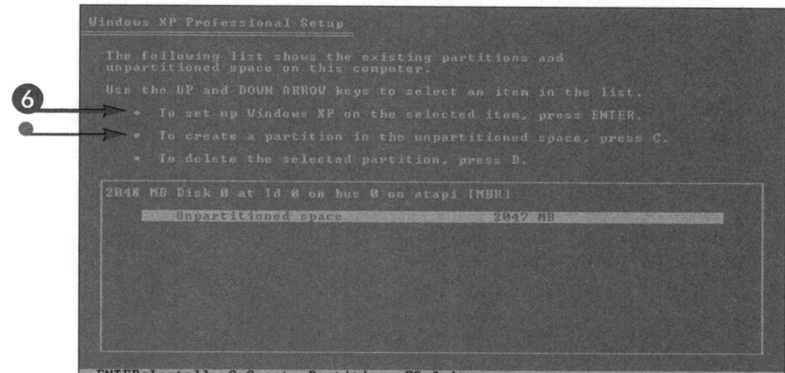

Does the retail version of XP have the service pack installed?

▼ As of this writing, the retail version of Windows XP ships with Service Pack 2 in it and is the most up-to-date version, excluding any hotfixes, bug fixes, or feature updates released subsequent to XP's ship date. Older retail versions may still be for sale, so you should check the retail box to ensure that Service Pack 2 is a part of the product. If it is not, you need to download or purchase Service Pack 2 separately from Microsoft.

Why does my computer not boot from a CD?

▼ Your motherboard's BIOS has either been set to boot from a hard drive, or your BIOS does not support booting from CD, which was common in pre-1998 hardware. Go into your BIOS, usually by pressing the Delete or F1 key during boot time, and change the boot order. Visit your motherboard manufacturer's Web site for information on changing the BIOS or flashing a new version. **Caution:** You can render your computer unbootable if you use the wrong BIOS version, so follow all cautions and instructions from your manufacturer exactly.

continued

Install Windows XP: New Installation *(Continued)*

A new installation will take you anywhere from one to several hours, depending on the speed of your computer, the number of hard drives and amount of drive space you have, and whether you sit by and babysit the computer, ready to click Next or fill in parameters when asked. If you have not done so, you should collect information about your hardware as detailed in Chapter 1. You should also have your Internet connection information handy so you can connect to the Internet during setup.

If you do not currently have an ISP, Windows XP provides you with the means of using dialup connectivity to reach one. You cannot automatically connect to a broadband provider; that requires you to contact a provider ahead of time, install the necessary hardware, and set up your broadband account. It may take several days to set this up, during which you can still install Windows XP. If you bought a new system from a hardware vendor, it may come preinstalled with software to connect to the more popular dialup services, such as AOL or MSN. You should shop around to see if there are better deals from ISPs in your area.

Install Windows XP: New Installation *(continued)*

The format partition screen appears.

7. Use the arrow keys to move the highlight to the file format you want to use (for example, NTFS).
8. Press Enter to continue.

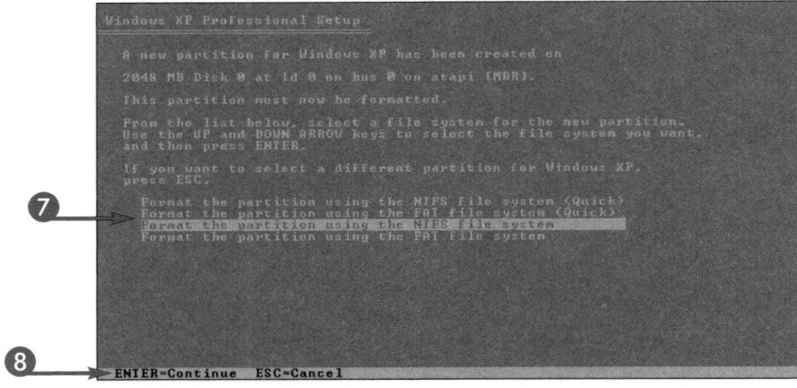

The partition is formatted, and files are copied onto your hard drive.

9. Press Enter to reboot, or wait for Windows to reboot automatically.

Note: *Do not remove the CD from the disk drive; more files are needed during the graphical setup phase.*

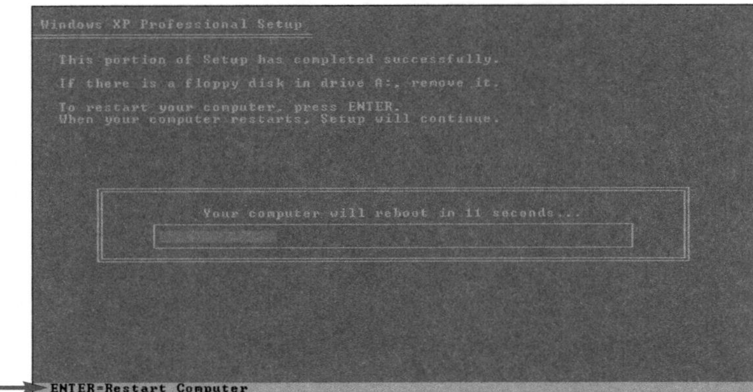

Windows launches the graphical setup.

The Regional and Language Options screen appears.

⑩ Click Next.

Note: *You can change these and all other settings from this point onward by using the Control Panel.*

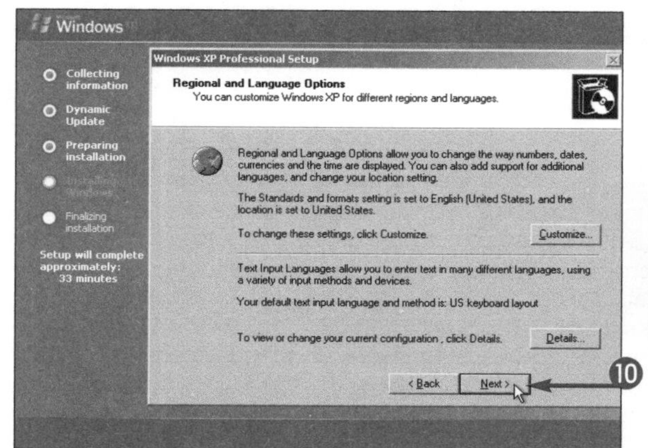

The Personalize Your Software screen appears.

⑪ Type your name and, optionally, your organization.

⑫ Click Next.

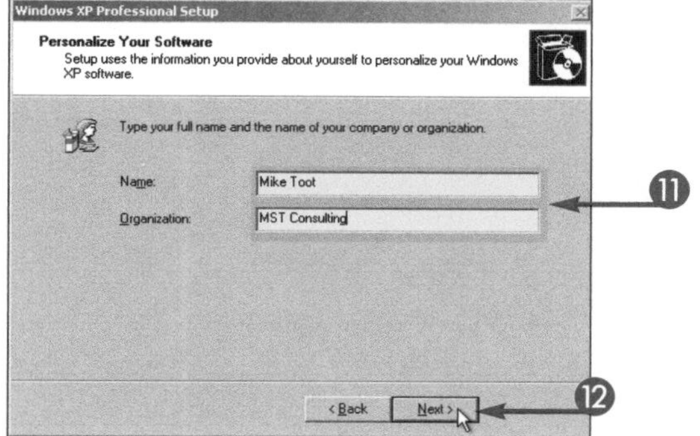

Should I use my entire hard drive as a single partition?

▼ Most admins will tell you that creating two partitions — one for your operating systems and applications, and one for your data and user files — is a good idea. Backing up user data when it resides on only one partition is easier. However, if you are using dynamic disks for all your drives, this is not possible. In that case, you should either have an automated backup in place for your data, or save your user files out to a drive on a network server.

What file format is best for a new installation?

▼ Unless you have an application that requires FAT, you should almost always select NTFS for a new installation. You gain the benefits of access control, encryption and compression, event auditing, and the use of dynamic disks. The only reason to use FAT is if you are dual-booting with Linux or DOS and need access to your Windows XP files; even then, there are Linux drivers you can use to gain access to native NTFS partitions.

continued

Install Windows XP: New Installation *(Continued)*

The Networking portion of setup can be a mixed blessing. You can choose to accept the Typical installation, which installs the Microsoft Network client, TCP/IP protocol, file and printer sharing, and quality-of-service (QoS) management. The Typical installation defaults to using DHCP for retrieving IP addresses and DNS information, which is convenient for most home users and SOHO environments that use DHCP.

However, if you are connected to an ISP or a larger business environment that uses assigned IP addresses, you need to select the Custom installation process and fill in the necessary information that you obtained from your ISP or system administrator. This may include your IP address, the subnet mask, gateway address, and DNS server name or address. All this information is necessary to make connections to other computers on the Internet.

You can always change this information later in the Control Panel under Network Connections. If you have trouble connecting despite using the correct information, you can use the network troubleshooting techniques described in Chapter 11 to help isolate the problem.

Install Windows XP: New Installation *(continued)*

The Your Product Key screen appears.

⑬ Type in the 25-digit Windows XP serial number, found on either your CD jewel case or a separate license with a license sticker on it.

Note: *You may work for a company that has a site license for Windows XP; if so, use the site license key instead.*

⑭ Click Next.

The Computer Name and Administrator Password screen appears.

⑮ Type a name for your computer.

Note: *The computer name should be different from a user's name.*

⑯ Type an administrator password in both boxes. Note that the passwords must match.

Note: *Remember or write down the administrator password and keep it in a safe place.*

⑰ Click Next.

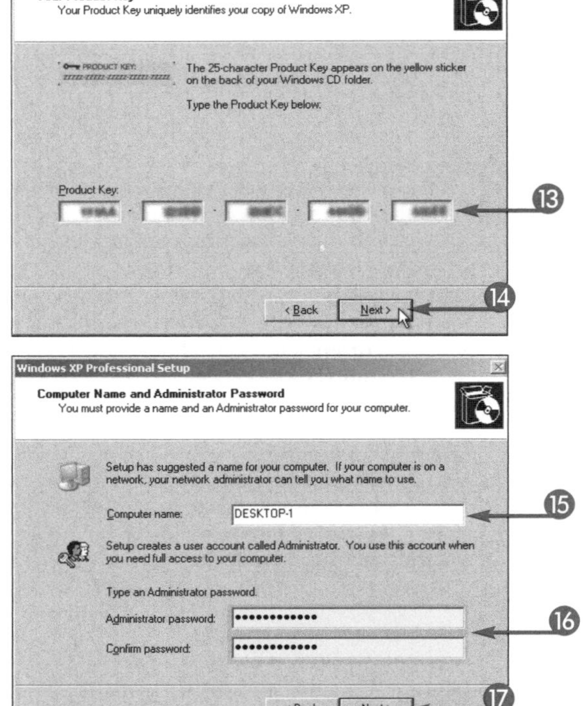

The Date and Time Settings screen appears.

18 Make any adjustments to the date and time, including your time zone and whether daylight saving time is observed.

19 Click Next.

The Networking Settings screen appears.

20 Click Typical settings.

- Click Custom settings if you need to add a network protocol other than TCP/IP, such as IPX/SPX (Novell Networking).

21 Click Next.

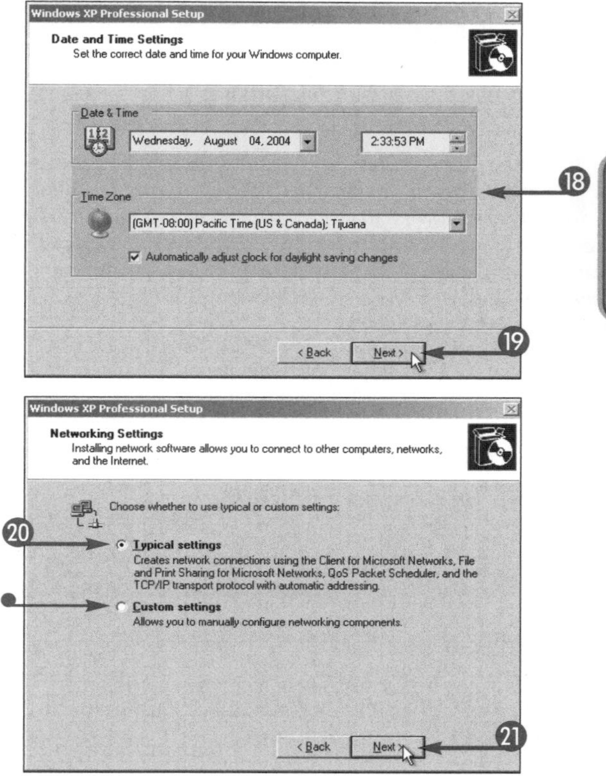

Can I change Windows XP to a different language?

- The Regional and Language Options change only some aspects of Windows XP: the date, time, and currency formats, as well as the kinds of input devices that are different depending on the country. In order to change the menus, dialog boxes, and help files, you need to install the Multi-Language User Interface add-on. You can purchase it separately from Microsoft.

How long can computer names be?

- You can have a computer name up to 63 characters. However, if you are running older versions of Windows on your network, those versions recognize names only to 15 characters. If you are sharing files with older versions of Windows, you should make the names 15 characters or less. Avoid using spaces, periods, or other punctuation marks; dashes are okay.

Windows is asking me for modem information. What should I do?

- If Windows setup detected a modem, you see the Modem Dialing Information screen immediately after the Date and Time screen. Enter your country or region, your area code, whether you dial a number to get an outside line, and whether you use tone or pulse dialing. Click Next to continue.

continued

Install Windows XP: New Installation *(Continued)*

The setup process asks you if you want to join a workgroup or domain. The difference between the two revolves around the centralized authentication, access, and security provided by a Microsoft Windows domain controller. If you are not running a version of Windows Server on your network, then workgroups are appropriate for your setup.

In order to join a domain, you must have a domain controller running on your network, and you need the name and password of an account with rights to add a computer to a domain. Most commonly this is someone who is a member of the Domain Admins account, but it can be any group that has been given rights to join computers to a domain.

If your computer cannot find the domain server, either because you specified an incorrect domain or because you lack the rights to join the computer to a domain, setup asks if you want to try joining a domain later. See Chapter 13 for information on joining a domain.

Install Windows XP: New Installation *(continued)*

The Workgroup or Computer Domain screen appears.

22 Select whether you want to join a workgroup or domain.

23 Type the name of the workgroup or domain you want to join.

24 Click Next.

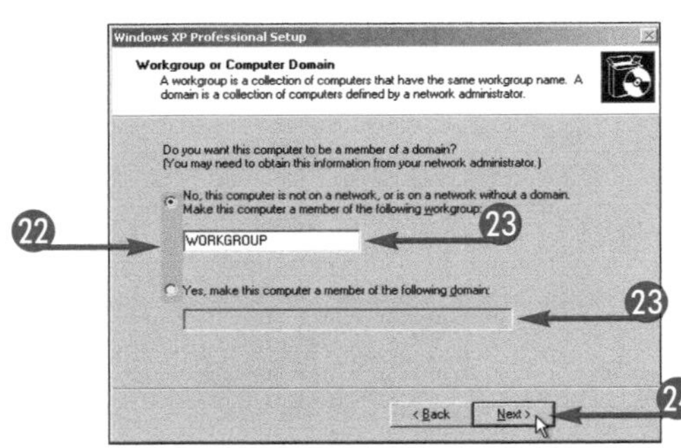

Windows finishes copying files and settings.

25 Click Next.

The Help Protect Your PC screen appears.

26 Click the option to help protect your PC with Automatic Update.

27 Click Next.

Note: *You can turn these settings off again. See Chapter 3 for more information on the Windows Update service.*

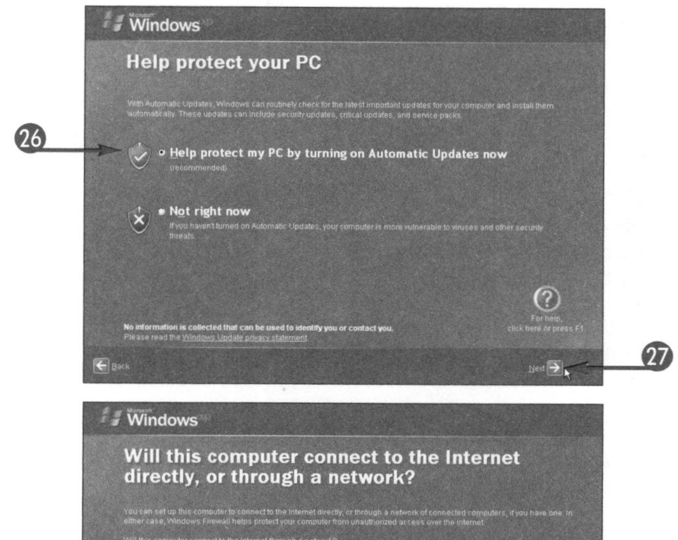

The network connection screen appears.

28 Click the network option that applies to your computer.

29 Click Next.

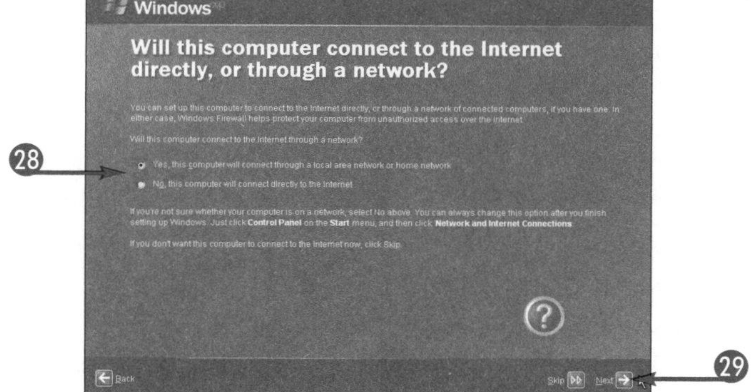

What is the difference between connecting through a LAN and connecting directly to the Internet?

▼ The primary difference is whether you need hardcoded connection information (direct connection) or use DHCP (LAN) to gain access to the Internet. If you use a modem, you are connecting directly; if you connect using a broadband modem inside your computer, you may need to select the direct option so you can enter the proper connection information. If in doubt, check with your ISP or system administrator to see which will work. You can also try the Direct option if you are a SOHO user, because all these settings can be changed later.

Why do I see a modem option?

▼ If Windows XP detected a modem, you see an additional network connection type listed for your modem. You can select it if you connect over dialup.

What do I do if the system hangs during setup?

▼ This is rare, but it happens occasionally. Usually, you can shut down the computer, turn it on again, and setup resumes. If you get error messages after you do this, use the techniques later in this chapter to help you out.

continued

Install Windows XP: New Installation *(Continued)*

Much has been written about Windows Product Activation (WPA). WPA is used to signal whether software piracy is taking place, such as a single retail copy of Windows XP being installed on an entire department's PCs.

WPA does this by creating a hash using the license key and certain identifying characteristics of your hardware, like processor and hard-drive size. It sends this hash back to Microsoft, though no personally identifying information is sent. You can have up to three installations on different hardware configurations, such as when you install a new hard drive or increase the amount of RAM. If you exceed the number of activations, your computer will not let you log in until you contact Microsoft to reset the activation information in its database.

Without WPA, your installation will function for 30 days and then refuse to let you log in.

If you are at a business that has a site license, product activation is not required and you will not see the WPA screen.

Product activation differs from product registration: The latter is not required, and when you register you provide personal information to Microsoft.

Install Windows XP: New Installation *(continued)*

The Windows Product Activation screen appears.

30 Click the option to activate Windows over the Internet now.

31 Click Next.

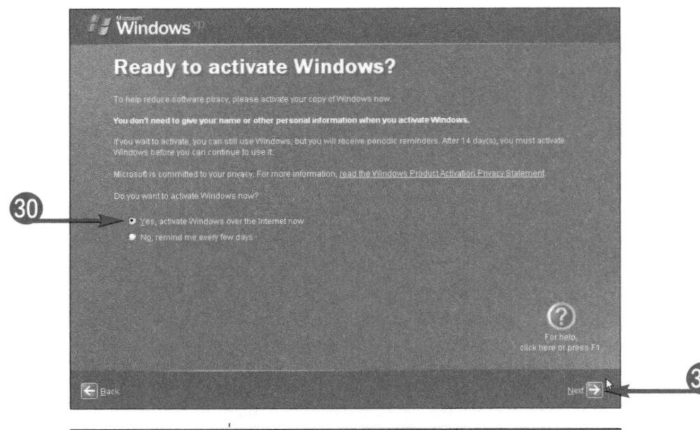

The next screen asks who will use your computer.

32 Type in the user names.

***Note:** At least one name must be entered.*

33 Click Next.

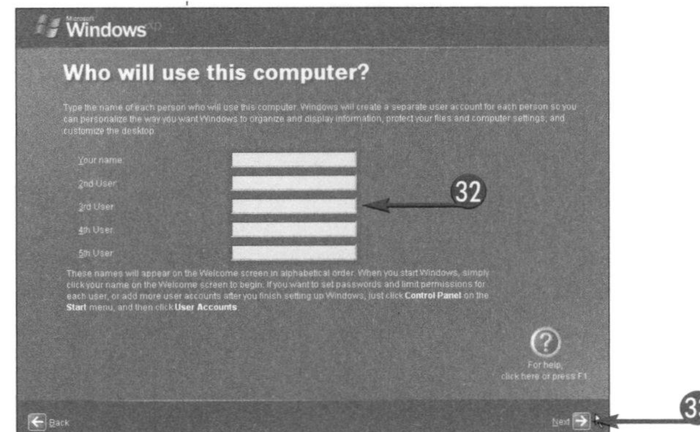

The next screen thanks you for installing Windows XP.

34 Click Finish.

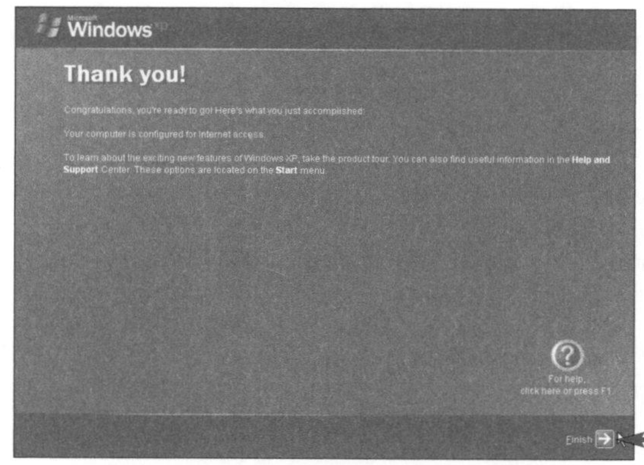

If you have entered only one user name, the Windows XP desktop appears.

- If you have joined a workgroup and entered more than one user name, the logon desktop appears.

If you have joined a domain, the Windows logon dialog box appears.

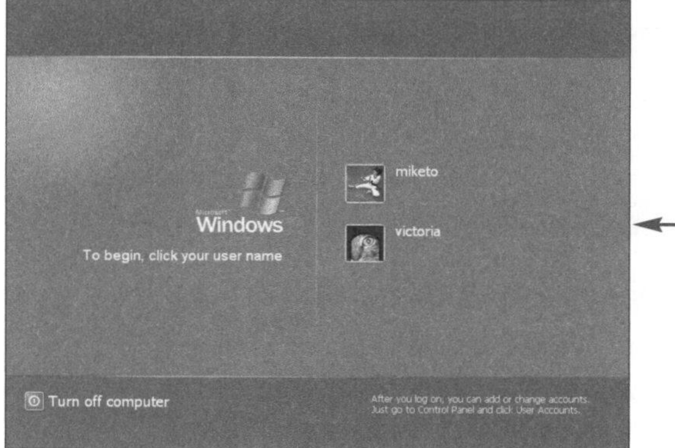

Can I select which components I want to install during setup, like games?

▼ Unlike previous consumer versions of Windows, such as Windows 9*x*, the setup process does not let you pick and choose which programs and applets are installed. This makes the installation process go more quickly and simply for new users but does not provide the flexibility needed by a system administrator. If you need to be more selective about which programs to install, you can investigate the User State Migration Tool, found on the Windows XP CD at <driveletter>\valueadd\msft\usmt. It allows you to be granular about which programs and services are installed.

Do I need to activate Windows during setup?

▼ No. If you choose not to activate Windows, you are notified every few days during the 30-day grace period to activate your installation. If you want, you can choose not to activate Windows until you have all your hardware and software working correctly. Then double-click the Windows Notification icon in the tool tray and activate your copy of Windows XP.

Install Windows XP: Upgrade Installation

An upgrade installation occurs when you move from an earlier version of Windows, such as Windows Me or Windows 2000, to Windows XP. See Chapter 1 for information on checking upgrade compatibility and obtaining any necessary updates so that Windows can install smoothly. Back up your data files to removable media or to a network drive so you can restore them in case the upgrade does not go smoothly.

Plug in and turn on any hardware you want to use with your new installation, such as scanners, PDAs, printers, or USB hard drives. Last, turn off antivirus software and shut down all background applications such as file sharing utilities or PDA synchronization utilities. You can also run the Files and Settings Transfer Wizard to capture your changes to the desktop and vital settings and files. This acts as a safety net in case some settings do not transfer cleanly. See Chapter 1 for information on this wizard.

You can perform an upgrade with either the retail or the upgrade version of Windows; the upgrade version requires you to have your pre-XP operating system disk available.

Install Windows XP: Upgrade Installation

1. Insert the Windows XP CD in your computer.

   The Welcome to Microsoft Windows XP screen appears.

Note: You also can browse to the CD and click Setup.exe.

2. Click Install Windows XP.

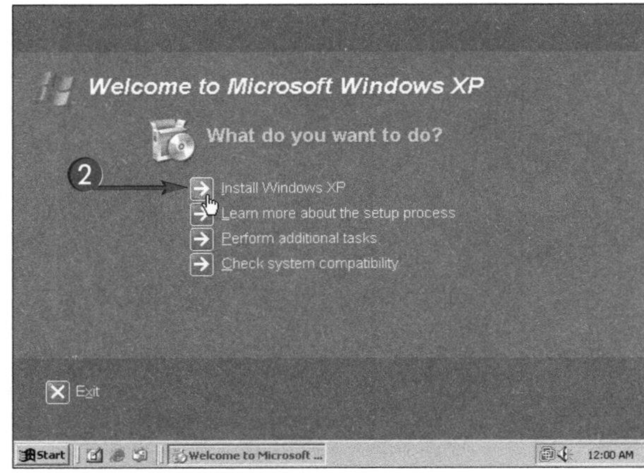

   The Welcome to Windows Setup window appears.

3. Click here and select Upgrade (Recommended).
4. Click Next.

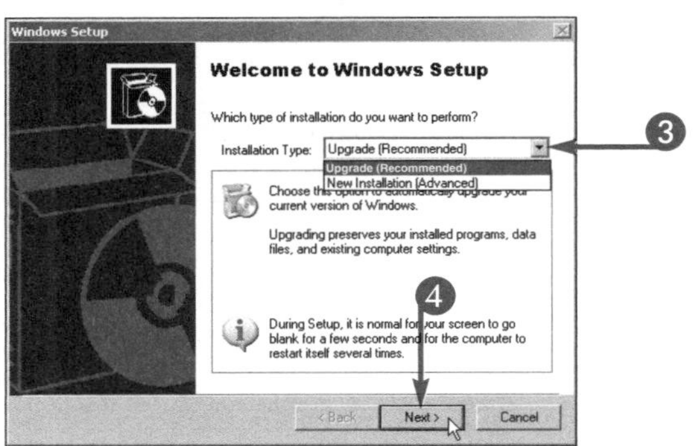

The License Agreement screen appears.

5 Click the option to accept this agreement.

6 Click Next.

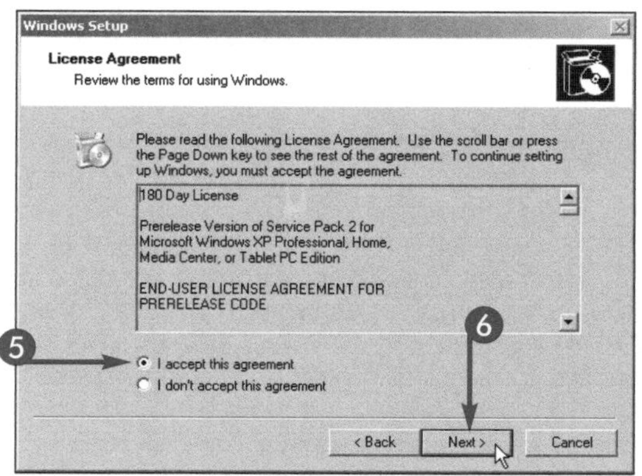

The Your Product Key screen appears.

7 Type the 25-digit Windows XP serial number, found on either your CD jewel case or a separate license with a license sticker on it.

Note: *You may work for a company that has a site license for Windows XP; if so, use the site license key instead.*

8 Click Next.

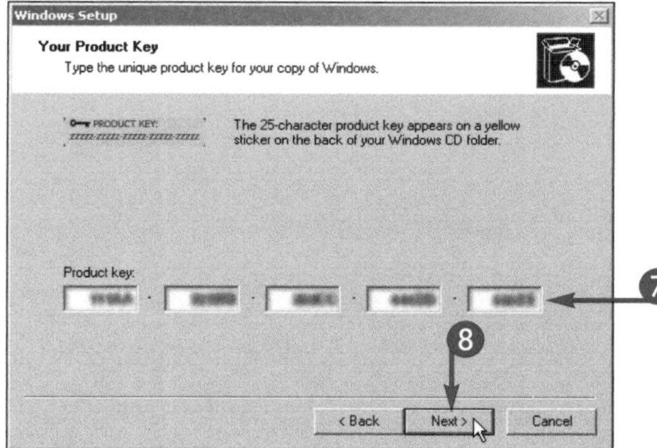

PART I

Will all my older software work under Windows XP?

▼ It depends on which operating system you are upgrading from — the more recent the operating system, such as Windows 2000, the more likely it is that Windows XP has the necessary software support. Older applications that may have run on Windows 98, such as DOS games or applications that wrote directly to the video card, may not natively run on Windows XP. You need to create a custom environment for those applications. See Chapter 3 for information on application compatibility.

Can I convert my partition format without performing a new install?

▼ You can convert a preexisting FAT partition to NTFS during the upgrade. If your partition is FAT or FAT32, the upgrade offers you the option to convert it to NTFS. You can also convert it manually after Windows XP is installed by opening a command prompt and typing **convert** / ?. That gives you a list of commands you can use to manually convert the file format. Back up your data files before you run the convert command.

continued

Install Windows XP: Upgrade Installation *(Continued)*

If you are upgrading from other consumer editions of Windows, such as Windows 98 or Windows Me, you are moving to a true 32-bit operating system and gaining the protection of an enterprise-grade kernel and memory manager. Earlier versions had 16-bit components that were used throughout the product, including the core parts of the operating system, and this caused problems with hardware and applications that tried to write directly to hardware. This resulted in hard locks or sudden reboots.

With Windows XP, the kernel and memory manager are written so that applications cannot write directly to hardware, but must go through managers that keep track of application access and memory management. Hard locks and crashes are drastically reduced and uptime is increased. When you install certified device drivers written specifically for Windows XP, you ensure that those devices will not bring your work or your desktop to a screeching halt.

If you are upgrading from Windows NT or Windows 2000, you are gaining improved performance, reliability, and a much-improved interface that makes your work more streamlined and seamless.

Install Windows XP: Upgrade Installation *(continued)*

The Get Updated Setup Files screen appears.

9. Click the recommended option to download the updated setup files.
10. Click Next.

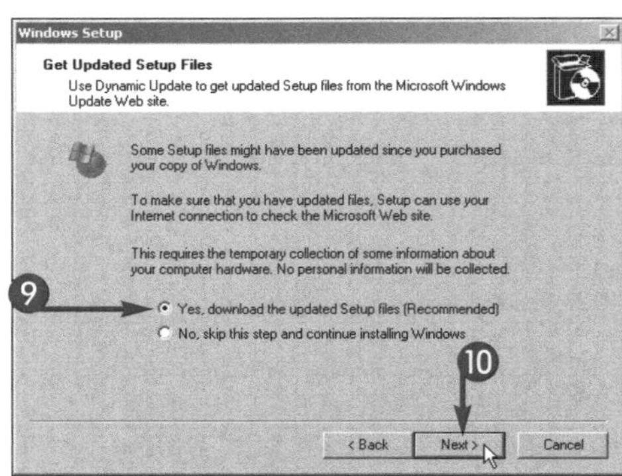

Windows copies the graphical installation files onto your computer before rebooting.

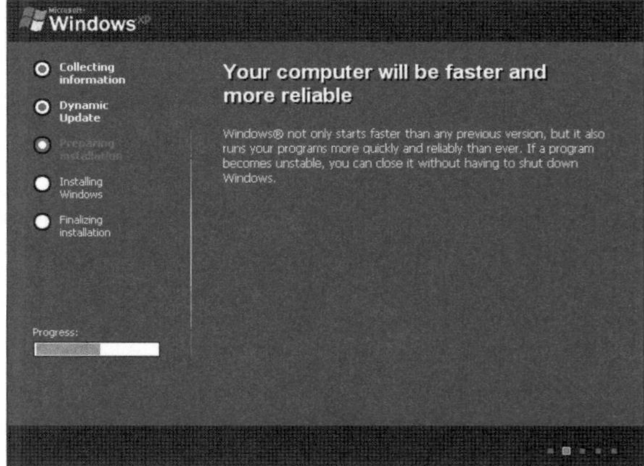

After rebooting, Windows runs the graphical install portion of Windows.

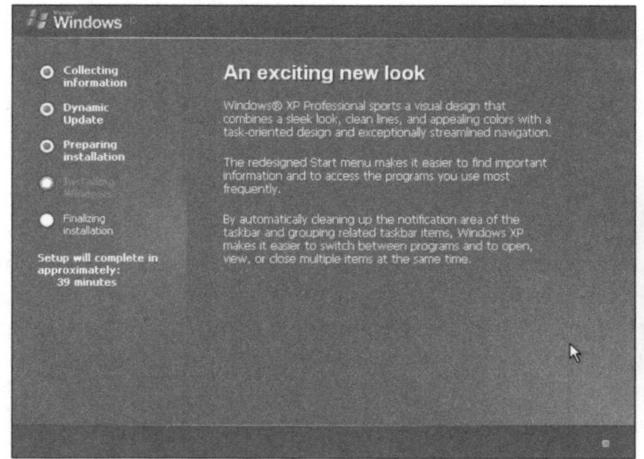

Setup continues in graphical mode.

Note: *The rest of the setup proceeds as described in the section "Install Windows XP: New Installation."*

After I upgrade my operating system, can I remove Windows XP?

- If you are upgrading from Windows 98 or Windows Me, you can remove Windows XP and revert back to your original operating system. This is useful if you find that your old applications or hardware no longer function under XP. See the section "Remove or Uninstall Windows XP," later in this chapter, for information. You cannot remove Windows XP if you are upgrading Windows NT 4.*x* or Windows 2000 Professional.

Can I "upgrade" from an earlier server version of Windows to Windows XP Professional or Home Edition?

- No. The Windows XP setup program does not allow you to upgrade over a server version of Windows. This is done to preserve the domain, security, and services information that is available only to server editions of Windows. If for some reason you want to upgrade, your choices are either to perform a new installation in the same partition, losing all your server information, or to perform a dual-boot installation to a different partition.

Install Windows XP: Dual-Boot (Side-by-Side) Installation

You can install Windows XP in a dual-boot or side-by-side installation so that you can choose which operating system you want to run at boot time. This gives you the ability to test Windows XP with your hardware and software without damaging a working installation. It also lets you keep your old installation in case compatibility issues preclude your moving to Windows XP with all your hardware and software.

There are three ways to create a dual-boot system, two of which are recommended and one of which is not. The first two are to either install Windows XP onto a second hard drive in your system, or to install Windows XP into an empty partition on an existing hard drive. The third way that you can create a dual-boot system — but a method that is not recommended — is to install Windows XP into the same partition as your existing Windows installation. This is not recommended because you end up altering application files when you boot between the two systems, which can cause the application or even the operating system to become unusable.

Install Windows XP: Dual-Boot (Side-by-Side) Installation

1. Follow the steps in the section "Install Windows XP: New Installation" through Step 5.

   The disk partitioning screen appears.

2. Use the arrow keys to highlight your new installation partition.
3. Press Enter.

Note: *You can install into unpartitioned space or create a new partition from this screen as well.*

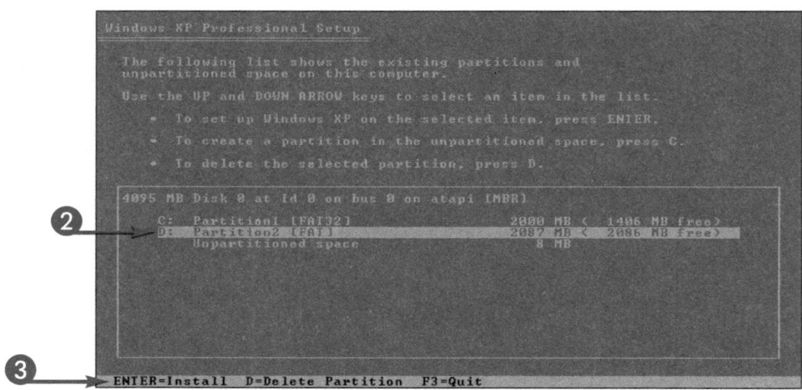

The Format Partition screen appears.

4. Use the arrow keys to highlight the type of formatting you want applied to your new partition.
5. Press Enter.

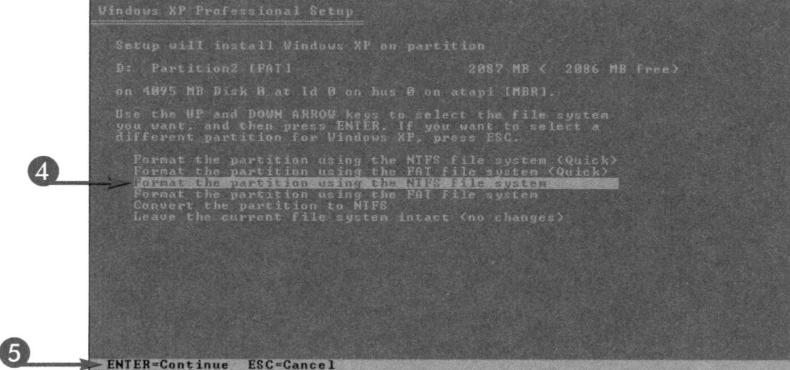

6 If you have chosen a destructive format, press F to confirm the format procedure.

Follow the rest of the steps in the section "Install Windows XP: New Installation" from Step 7 onward.

Windows XP Professional Setup

CAUTION: Formatting this drive will delete all files on it.
Confirm that you want to format:

D: Partition2 [FAT] 2087 MB (2086 MB free)

on 4095 MB Disk 0 at Id 0 on bus 0 on atapi [MBR].

6

• To format the drive, press F.

• To select a different partition for Windows XP, press ESC.

F=Format ESC=Cancel

The next time you reboot, you can select either operating system.

Please select the operating system to start:

Microsoft Windows XP Professional
Microsoft Windows

Use the up and down arrow keys to move the highlight to your choice.
Press ENTER to choose.
Seconds until highlighted choice will be started automatically: 27

For troubleshooting and advanced startup options for Windows, press F8.

What are the differences between the different partition formatting options?

▼ There are four partition formatting types available.

Format	Formatting creates a new (NTFS and FAT) partition table, creates new sectors, and checks the partition for bad sectors. All existing data is wiped out.
Quick Format (NTFS and FAT)	A quick format does not check for bad sectors but otherwise is the same as a regular format. It is available if setup detects that the disk clusters have been formatted before. All previous data is lost.
Convert to NTFS (FAT only)	If the partition has been formatted with FAT or FAT32, you can nondestructively convert it to NTFS. This method preserves any existing data or files that are in the partition.
Leave Intact (NTFS and FAT)	The partition and all data are left intact. This method does not check for bad sectors.

Install Windows XP: Service-Pack-Only Installation

Service-pack-only installation is available for anyone running Windows XP, with or without Service Pack 1. The Windows XP Service Pack 2 is *cumulative,* meaning it contains all the fixes and features found in Service Pack 1 and most of the interim fixes issued by the Windows Update Service.

One of the key features of Service Pack 2 is the creation of the Security Advisor, which turns on the Windows Firewall by default, monitors your antivirus software and its updates, and lets you automatically turn on and install updates issued by the Windows Update Service. For home and SOHO users, this hands-off management and monitoring capability is a blessing, because it no longer requires users or system administrators to visit each PC and make sure the necessary security protections and virus definitions are installed and working.

The Service Pack also includes Movie Maker 2, an upgrade to the multimedia editing program that shipped in Windows XP, so that you can edit your movies and pictures on your own computer. See Chapter 9 for more information on Movie Maker 2.

Install Windows XP: Service-Pack-Only Installation

1. Double-click the Windows XP Service Pack 2 executable.

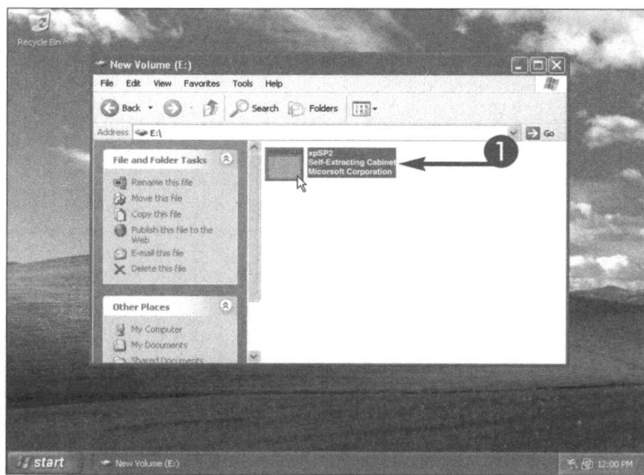

The Welcome to the Windows XP Service Pack 2 Setup Wizard appears.

2. Click Next.

- Read the license agreement by scrolling through the window.
- Click Print to print a copy of the license agreement.

3 Click the option to accept the license agreement.

4 Click Next.

The Select Options screen appears.

- Click Browse to change to another directory to store the backup files.

5 Click Next.

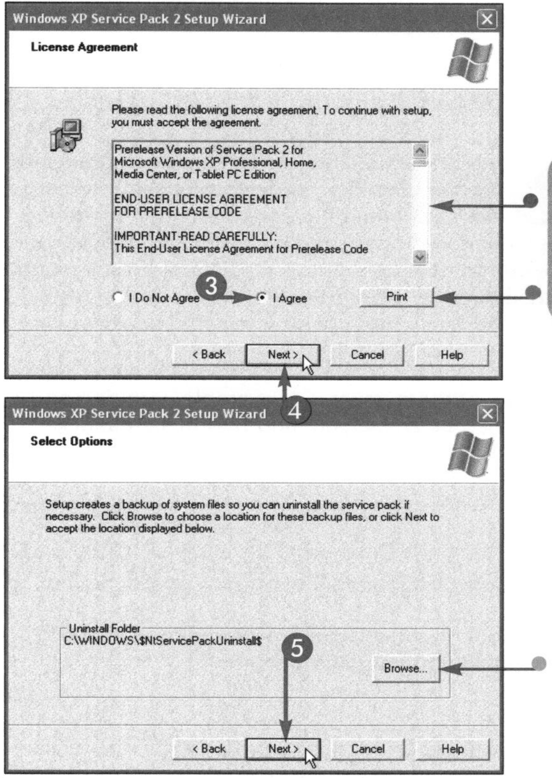

What are the ways I can obtain Service Pack 2?

Service Pack 2 is available as a download from Microsoft, as a CD you can purchase, and as part of a TechNet or MSDN subscription. It is also available "slipstreamed" into retail versions of Microsoft Windows XP that you can find at various retail and online outlets. If you have Automatic Update turned on in Windows XP, the new service pack is downloaded in the background for installation onto your computer.

What is the network install version of the service pack?

The network install version is a complete set of service pack binaries designed to be stored centrally on your network. It differs slightly from the version used by Automatic Update but contains the same core files. If you are a system administrator with a number of machines that you need to update, you can reduce the load on your Internet connection by downloading the network install version and storing it on a server, or slipstreaming it into the Windows XP binary files. See the section "Install Windows XP: Network Installation," later in this chapter, for details.

continued

Install Windows XP: Service-Pack-Only Installation *(Continued)*

Service Pack 2 also includes major upgrades to Internet Explorer. Older versions of Internet Explorer were lax when it came to security; by default, everything was open, and scripting and ActiveX were allowed to operate without restriction. It took manual intervention by users to define secure zones, restrict Web sites, and block pop-ups or unwanted cookies.

In Service Pack 2, updates to Internet Explorer address a number of these issues. For example, scripting and ActiveX are turned off by default, and pop-ups are blocked. These updates fix two of the most annoying (and insecure) aspects of Internet Explorer: reducing the exposure to malicious scripting bugs, and shutting down the ability of Web sites to generate seemingly endless pop-ups and referral windows without user permission.

An additional security feature includes an Attachment Manager that is used by Internet Explorer, Windows Messenger, and Outlook Express. It acts as an intermediary during file downloads and pops up a warning dialog box, identifying attachments that could be harmful, such as EXE or PIF files. These updates go a long way toward helping to stop the accidental opening of attachments that may contain viruses.

Install Windows XP: Service-Pack-Only Installation *(continued)*

The service pack files are decompressed and installed to your computer.

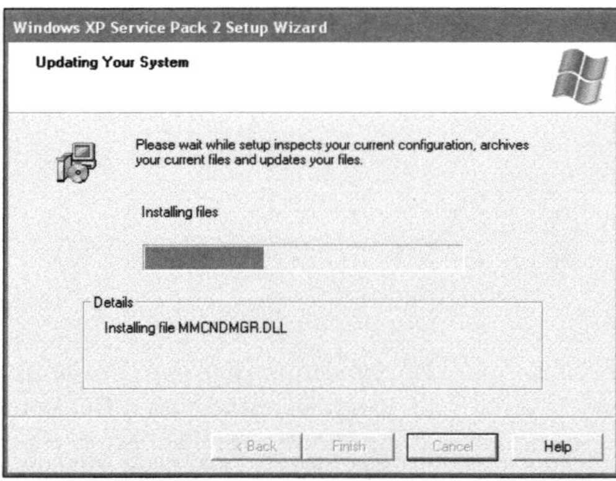

The wizard completes the upgrade.

- Click here if you do not want to reboot at this time.

6 Click Finish.

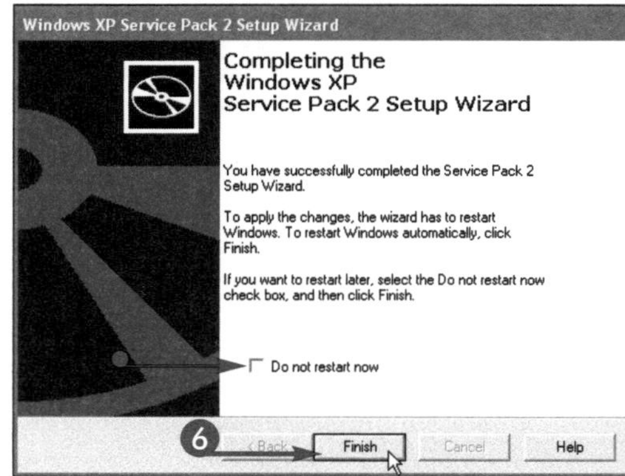

Windows reboots and the Automatic Updates screen appears.

7 Click the option to help protect your PC with Automatic Updates.

8 Click Next.

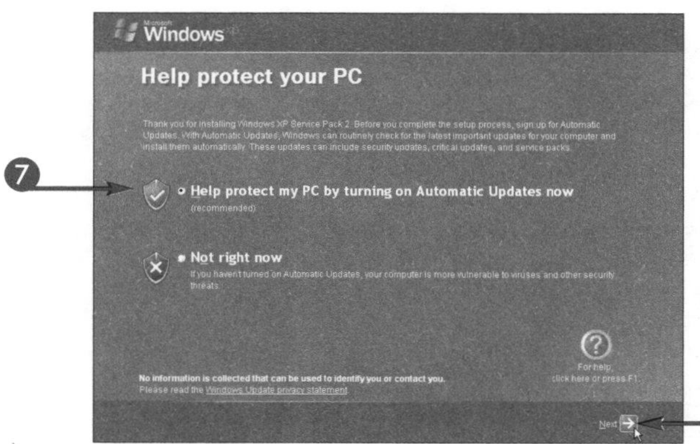

The Windows logon screen appears.

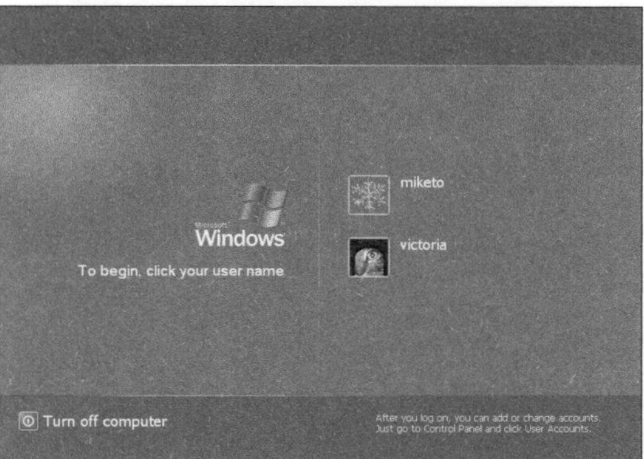

What other updates are included in Service Pack 2?

▼ Microsoft includes upgrades to Windows Media Player 10, with support for additional codecs; upgrades to DirectX 10, with additional support for the most recent video rendering functions and 3-D graphical applications; and additional networking support and compatibility add-ons for Tablet PCs and Media Center Editions. For a complete list, visit http://microsoft.com/windowsxp/default.mspx.

Can I uninstall Service Pack 2?

▼ Older versions of Windows service packs let you select whether to back up the updated files so you could uninstall the service pack. With Service Pack 2, the backup is mandatory, and the older files are kept by default in the Windows directory. You can uninstall the Service Pack by going to the Control Panel and then selecting Add/Remove Programs, Windows XP Service Pack 2, and then Remove. Note that you cannot uninstall the service pack if it is part of a slipstream install.

Install Windows XP: Network Installation

A network install uses a share on the network to store the Windows XP setup and installation files. If you are managing several computers, you can save time by having the files centrally located, rather than carrying the Windows XP CD from one computer to another.

With a network installation, the setup program is executed and the files are copied across the network to the local computer. This method requires user or administrator input to select options or complete information in text fields such as the 25-digit license key.

A network installation differs from using cloning or Remote Installation Services (RIS) to install a new operating system. With cloning or RIS, a copy of an existing Windows XP installation and its applications is created and centrally distributed to new computers. With a network install, the entire setup program must be run on each machine.

This task shows you how to copy the Windows XP binaries to a network drive and then *slipstream* (integrate) the service pack files into the original binaries. This saves you the step of installing XP and then separately running the service pack setup to bring a computer up to date.

Install Windows XP: Network Installation

1. Copy the contents of the Windows XP CD to a shared folder on the network.

Note: *This folder can be on any share; it does not need to be on Windows Server.*

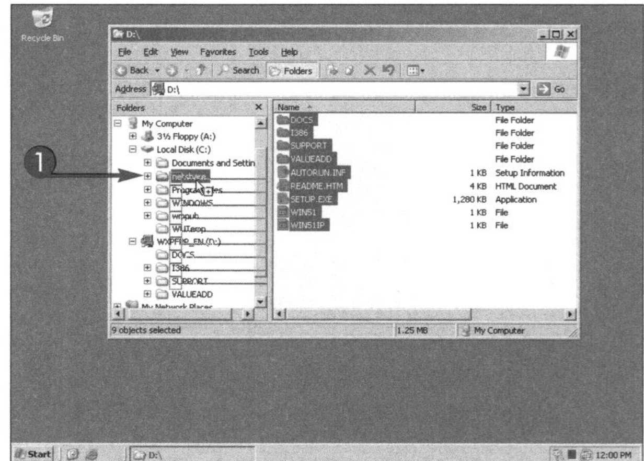

2. Create a temporary folder on the share.
3. Copy the Windows XP Service Pack 2 executable to the temporary folder.

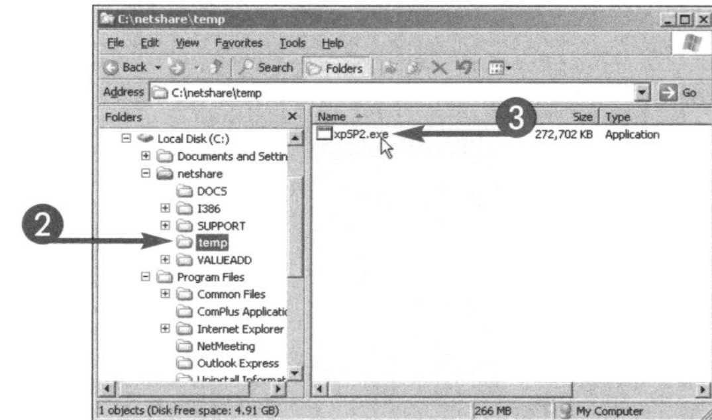

4 Open a command window and change to the temporary folder.

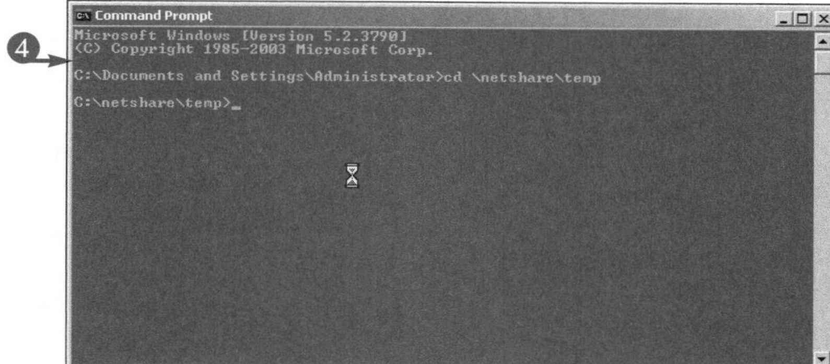

5 Type **servicepackname -s <sharename path>\i386**.

The service pack is integrated into Windows XP.

To run the network install, connect to the share from a computer and type **setup**.

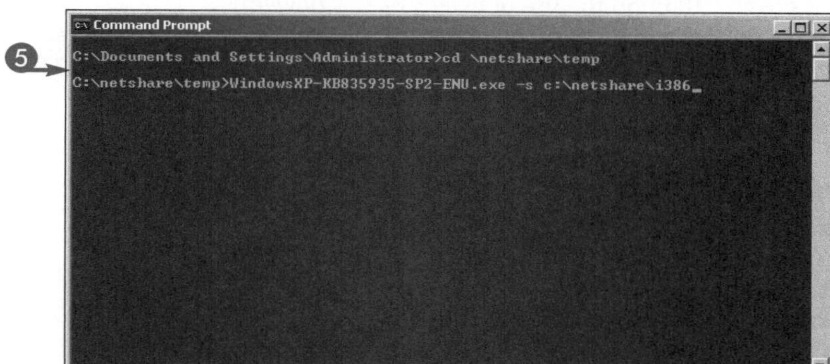

Is there a way to update the network install with Windows Update fixes?

▼ Yes. There is a program called qchain that you can run at the end of the setup process. It chains together the necessary files, works out any interdependencies, then copies the files onto a new installation. This technique is advanced and is more likely to be used in a large organization where advance testing of fixes is needed before rolling them out to all the computers in an organization. You can find more information about hotfix deployment at www.microsoft.com/windowsxp/downloads/updates/sp1/hfdeploy.mspx, and about qchain at http://support.microsoft.com/default.aspx?scid=kb;[LN];Q296861.

Does my Windows license cover multiple installs?

▼ No. Retail, upgrade, or Original Equipment Manufacturer (OEM) boxes are good for a single installation on a single computer. Even if you create a network installation, you are required to have a valid license for every copy of Windows XP you run on your network. If you have more than a couple of machines, you should contact a reseller for information on purchasing additional licenses. You may also need to purchase Client Access Licenses (CALs), which are required for connections to Windows Servers.

Automate the Installation Process

Ever get tired of babysitting a Windows installation, keeping an eye out for the next pause in the process just so you can click Next? Fortunately, you do not need to keep repeating the same behavior. Windows XP includes tools to create an answer file that setup uses to fill in boxes, make selections, and click Next where appropriate.

This is possible through the use of extensive and powerful command-line switches for the core setup executable, winnt32.exe, and to a lesser extent winnt.exe. The command-line switches help control nearly every aspect of installing Windows XP, including location of source files, programs to run after setup completes, and which answer files to use during the setup process.

This task shows you how to use Setupmgr.exe to create answer files and how to use those files with winnt32.exe. Because there are many options available, and many things you can do with option files, this section does not try to cover them all. Instead, it uses the integrated install created in the section "Install Windows XP: Network Installation" as the source files to be used with the answer file.

Automate the Installation Process

1. Extract the deployment files from <share>\support\tools\deploy.cab to a new folder.

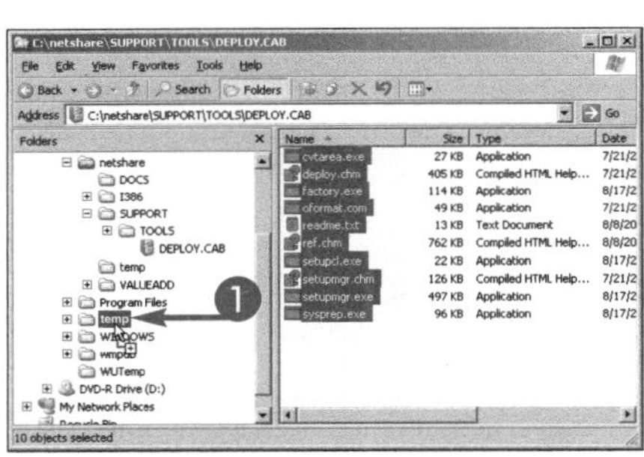

2. Double-click setupmgr.exe.

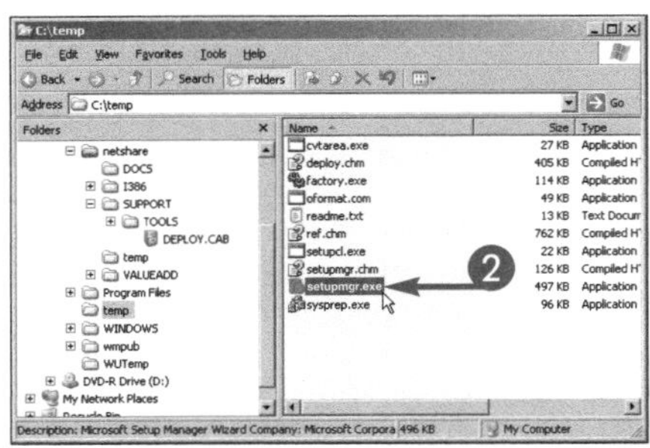

The Windows Setup Manager Wizard starts.

3. Click Next.

The New or Existing Answer File screen appears.

4 Click the option to create a new answer file.

5 Click Next.

The Product to Install screen appears.

6 Click Windows Unattended Installation.

7 Click Next.

The Platform screen appears.

8 Click Windows XP Professional.

9 Click Next.

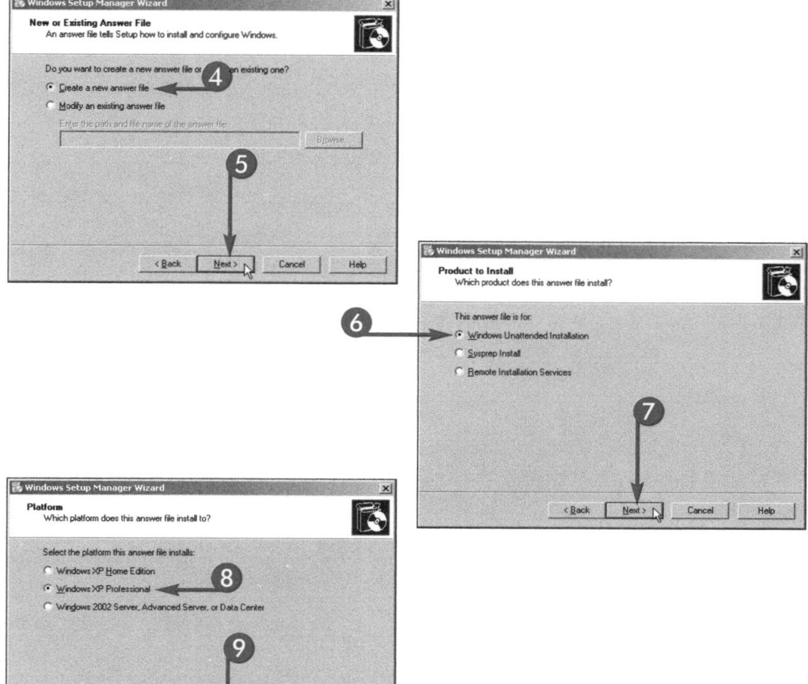

What are the other programs in the deploy.cab file?

- The other programs are primarily used for running sysprep.exe, a cloning or disk imaging utility that Microsoft provides for experienced system administrators. Sysprep is run against an existing Windows XP installation and then the clone is copied to the new computer. Sysprep is used primarily when identical or nearly identical hardware platforms are to receive Windows XP. If they differ significantly, such as having a different video card or processor, Sysprep does not work.

What is the difference between winnt32.exe and winnt.exe?

- These two setup files are run on different versions of Windows. The former is used on 32-bit versions, such as Windows NT Workstation or Windows 2000 Workstation. The latter is used on operating systems that have a mix of 16-bit and 32-bit components in them, like Windows 98 and Windows Me. There are fewer options available when upgrading from these latter two operating systems, so winnt.exe is not nearly as complete or powerful as its 32-bit sibling.

continued

Automate the Installation Process *(Continued)*

You can use the automation process to install Windows XP Home Edition, Windows XP Professional Edition, and Windows Server 2003 Standard, Enterprise, and Data Center editions. The wizard mistakenly refers to the latter as "Windows 2002 Server," though it is fully compatible with the 2003 version. The mistake was likely due to product renaming that Microsoft went through for several months before finally settling on Windows Server 2003. (Remember Windows .NET Server?)

Licensing is an issue you must consider when you use automated installation, no matter which product you are installing. For example, you must have a server license for every copy of Windows Server 2003 you install on your network. In addition, you may need either per-seat or per-server Client Access Licenses (CALs), depending on your environment. In general, if you have more than one server and five desktops that you manage, you should contact a Microsoft reseller to obtain special pricing or volume licensing for your software.

Given that Microsoft employs product activation codes in Windows XP Home and Professional editions, and in Windows Server 2003, it becomes difficult to sneak around the license agreements. Make sure your licenses are in compliance and you will have no problems.

Automate the Installation Process *(continued)*

The User Interaction Level screen appears.

⑩ Click the option to fully automate user interaction.

⑪ Click Next.

The Distribution Folder screen appears.

⑫ Click the option to create or modify a distribution folder.

⑬ Click Next.

The Location of Setup Files screen appears.

⑭ Click the option to copy the files from a particular location.

⑮ Type the location of the i386 folder created in the previous task, or click Browse to browse to it instead.

***Note:** The wizard creates a modified dosnet.inf file, located in the i386 folder.*

⑯ Click Next.

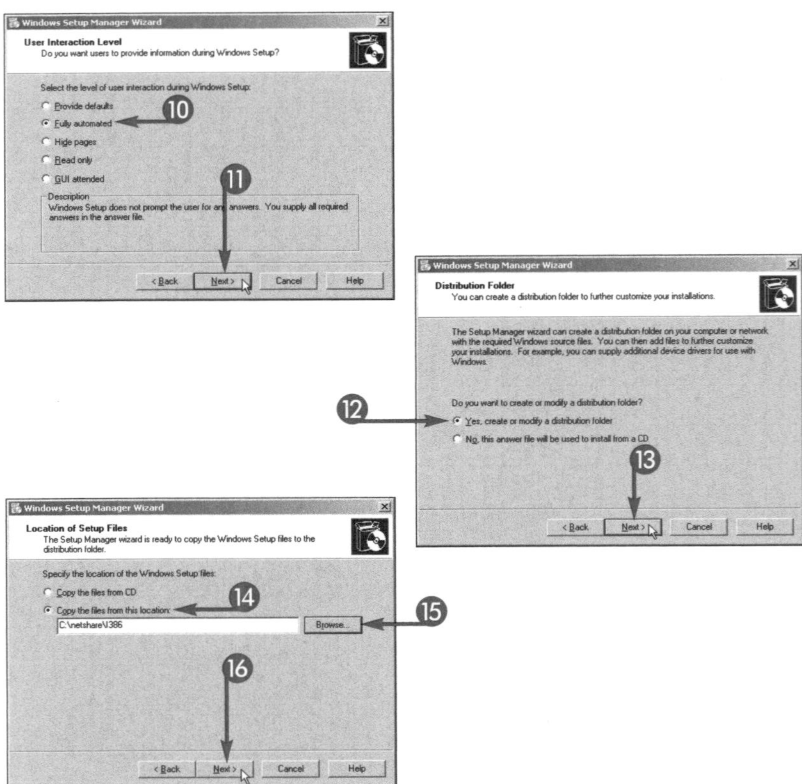

The Distribution Folder Name screen appears.

17 Click the option to create a new distribution folder.

18 Type the location of the new distribution folder or click Browse to browse to it instead.

19 Type a share name for the distribution.

20 Click Next.

The License Agreement screen appears.

21 Click the option to accept the license agreement.

22 Click Next.

The Windows Setup Manager window appears.

23 Type the necessary information in each field.

24 Click Next.

The wizard goes through each item consecutively.

- You can move between settings to change answers.

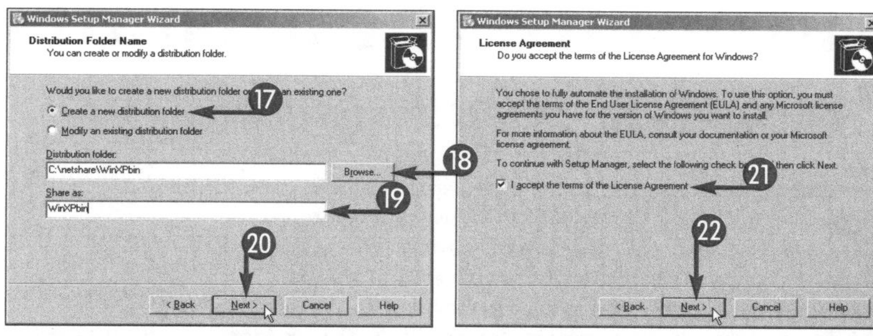

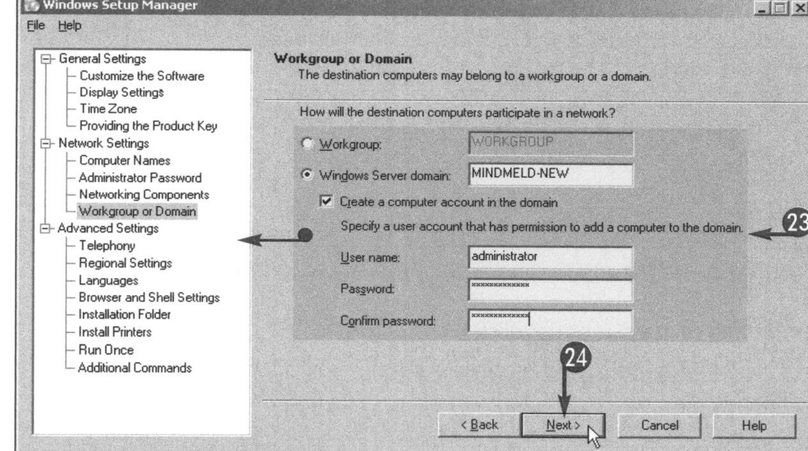

PART I

What do the varying types of user interaction do?

You can change the amount of end-user interaction by selecting one of these options.

Provide defaults	You provide the default answers, but the end-user can review and change any of them.
Fully automated	You provide all the answers. The end-user cannot make any changes.
Hide pages	If you provide all the answers on a dialog box, Windows hides that dialog box from the end-user. The other answers can be reviewed and changed.
Read only	Like hidden, but the end-user cannot make any changes.
GUI attended	Only text-mode (creating or selecting a partition, and so on) is hidden; graphical mode requires answers from the end-user.

continued

Automate the Installation Process *(Continued)*

If you want to use the unattended installation process to install Windows XP across a network to a new computer, the procedure is a little trickier. Because you are working with a computer that has no operating system, you need a way to boot with a minimal OS and connect to a share across the network. This means that you need to create a DOS boot disk that loads network drivers for your network adapter and loads a Microsoft Networking client if you need to connect to an Active Directory server.

This can be a challenge to put together, especially because Microsoft has obsoleted DOS and does not make it easy to create this type of boot disk. Though it can be done, creating an unattended answer file that is used with a CD, and booting from the CD instead, is probably easier.

If you really want to connect across a network for your installs, look into Remote Installation Services (RIS) and using a PXE-enabled (Preboot Execution Environment) network adapter. This combination allows you to connect to an RIS server at boot time and install across the network.

Automate the Installation Process *(continued)*

25 When the wizard is done, click Finish.

The Windows Setup Manager dialog box appears.

26 Click OK.

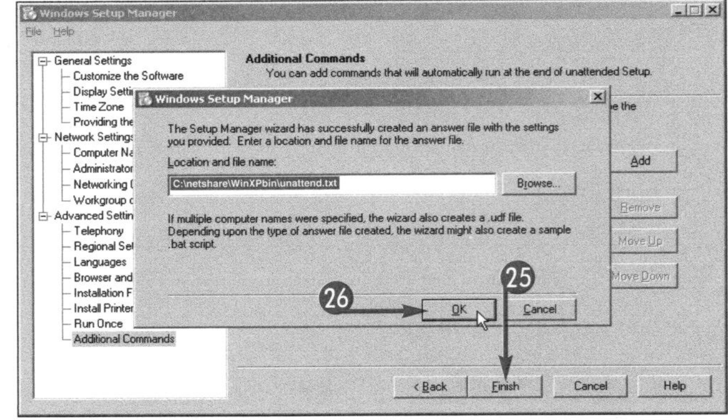

The wizard copies your files to the new distribution share.

The Setup Manager Complete dialog box appears.

27 Click File and then Exit.

The wizard closes.

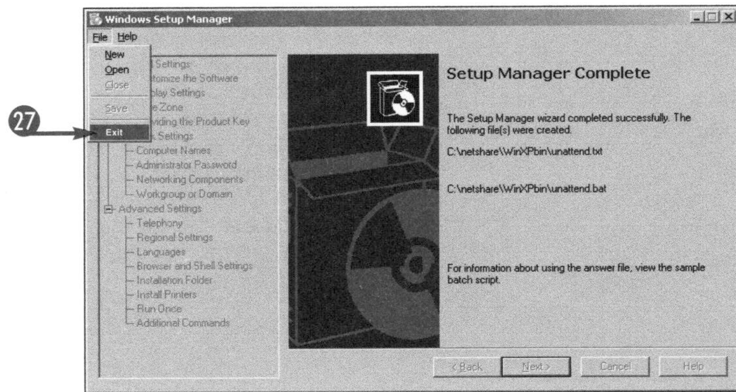

You can view the answers created by the wizard by viewing the unattend.txt file, located in the new distribution share.

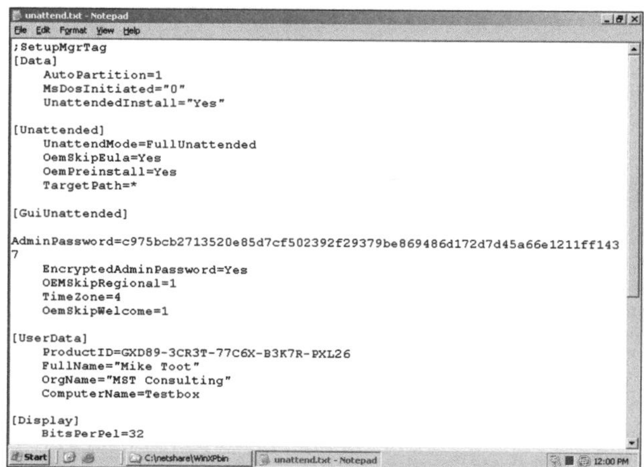

㉘ To run the unattended install, copy unattend.bat and unattend.txt to the new machine and run unattend.bat.

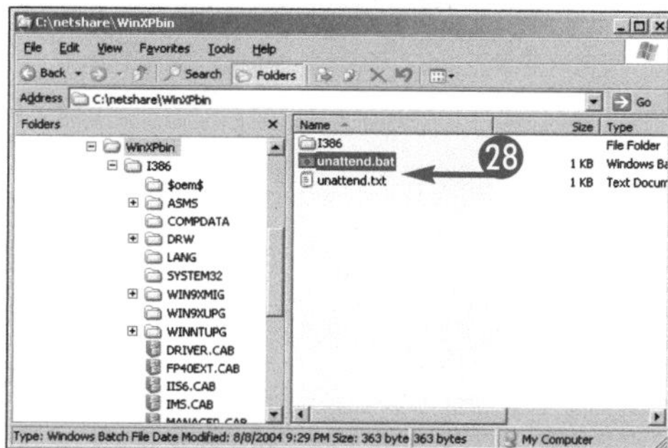

Why can I not run the unattended batch setup?

- There could be several reasons why the unattended setup is not working. Check to see that you have sharing enabled on the distribution folder. If you are using Active Directory, make sure that you log in with an account that has read and execute permissions on that folder. If you are attempting to upgrade a Windows 98 or Windows Me installation, you need to create a separate unattend.bat file that uses winnt.exe. Type **winnt.exe /?** at a command prompt to see the available switches.

What is a UDF?

- A UDF, or Uniqueness Database File, is a text file that is used when you have large numbers of computers that you want to automatically upgrade. Because there are often several unique configuration items for each computer (such as its name on the network, its license file number, and membership in a domain), the UDF allows system administrators to specify the unique entries for each machine.

Remove or Uninstall Windows XP

You can uninstall Windows XP only if you have performed an upgrade installation to Windows 98 or Windows Me. The upgrade process leaves many of the core 16-bit Windows files available on the hard drive for restoring back to the original operating system. This is extremely convenient if you have compatibility issues with your existing applications and need to regain any lost features or functionality you may be experiencing. You cannot uninstall Windows XP if you upgraded from a 32-bit version of Windows, such as Windows NT or Windows 2000.

You can remove Windows XP from a dual-boot installation, though it is not an automatic process. One of the easiest ways is to remove the Windows XP option from the boot loader menu so that only the other installation remains; you can then safely delete the Windows XP files that are in the separate partition. You can remove the boot loader, but only if you reformat the Master Boot Record so that it no longer uses a boot loader, as with Windows 98 or Windows Me, or use the boot loader from other versions of Windows, such as Windows NT.

Remove or Uninstall Windows XP

1. Open the Control Panel and click Add/Remove Programs.
2. Click Windows XP Uninstall.
3. Click Change/Remove.

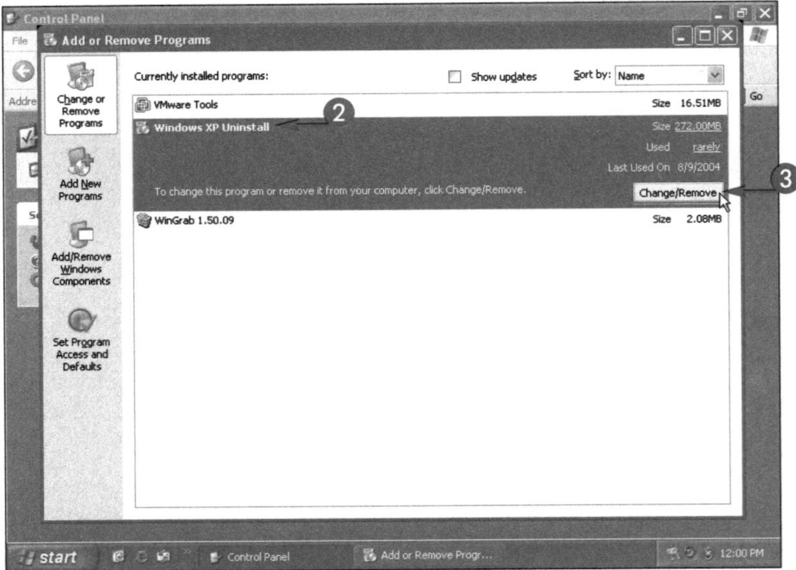

The Uninstall Windows XP window appears.

4. Click Uninstall Windows XP.
5. Click Continue.

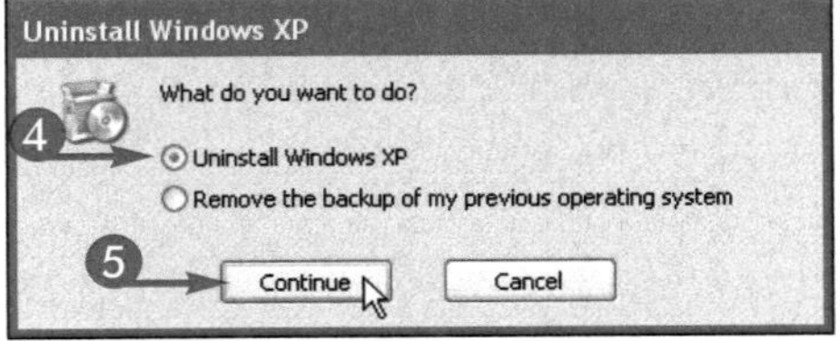

The confirmation dialog box appears.

6. Click Yes.

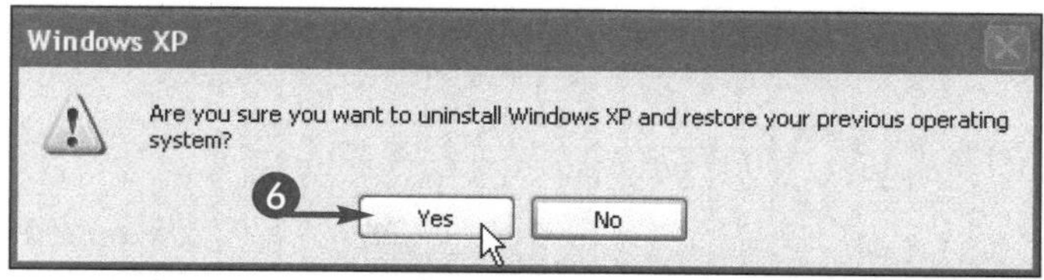

The Windows XP Upgrade is uninstalled from your system.

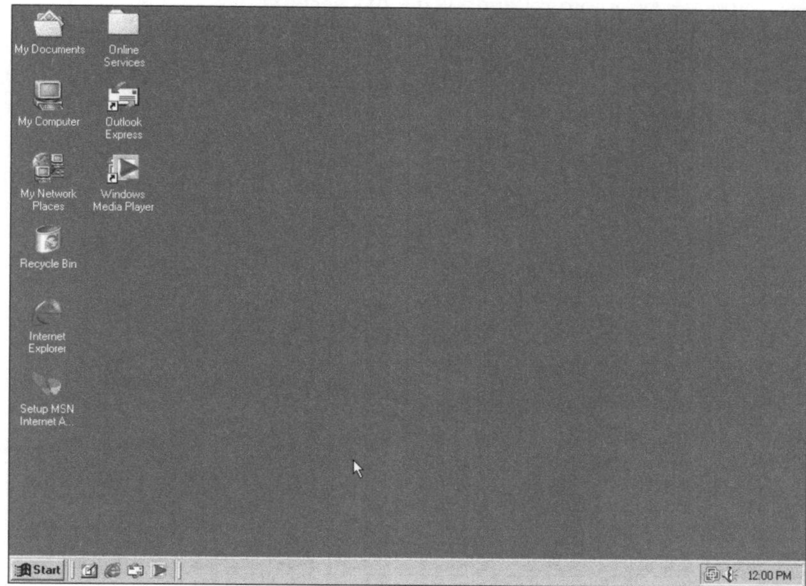

Why can I not uninstall Windows XP from my Windows 98 upgrade?

▼ Although you normally can uninstall an upgraded version of Windows 98, there is a catch. The upgrade process leaves your file system intact. If at some point you used Windows XP to convert the partition to NTFS, either by using Disk Manager or by running convert.exe at the command prompt, you cannot revert back to FAT32. This is due to the additional Windows XP services, security, and permissions that are directly tied to NTFS.

I still cannot revert. Am I missing something?

▼ You need your uninstall files in order to revert. Sadly, the Windows XP Disk Cleanup Wizard prompts you to delete these files 30 days after you upgrade. If you chose to delete these files, you cannot go back; you have to reinstall your earlier version of Windows.

Why do my applications not work after I revert?

▼ Yet another gotcha. After you revert back to your earlier Windows version, you must reinstall your applications. For all these reasons, a dual boot is preferable to an upgrade — or even to a brand-new installation.

Install the Recovery Console

The Recovery Console is a text-mode environment you can boot into if Windows XP has become corrupted and can no longer start in graphical mode. The console provides a minimal environment and some basic file-manipulation tools so that you can effect some basic repairs and get XP working again.

You can install the Recovery Console on your hard drive, creating a boot menu item, so that you always have it available in case of emergency. This is useful if your system has intermittent problems that are difficult to track down and you need access to the Recovery Console on a regular basis.

You can also launch the Recovery Console on an as-needed basis from the Windows XP installation disks.

Install the Recovery Console

1. Insert the Windows XP CD in your computer.
2. Click Start.
3. Click Run.
4. Type **cmd**.
5. Click OK.

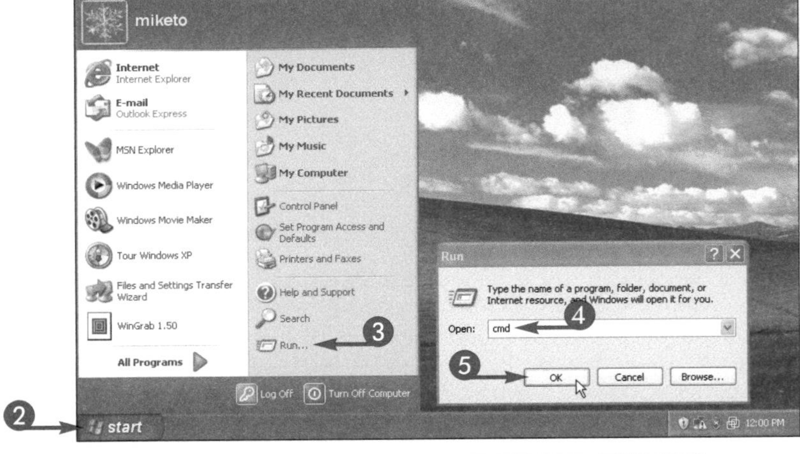

A command window opens.

6. Change directories to the CD drive.
7. Change to the i386 directory.
8. Type **winnt32 /cmdcons**.
9. Press Enter.

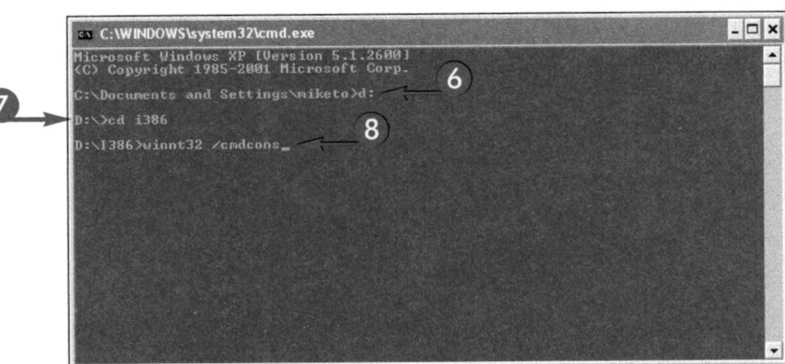

The Windows Setup dialog box appears.

10 Click Yes.

The Recovery Console files are copied to your computer.

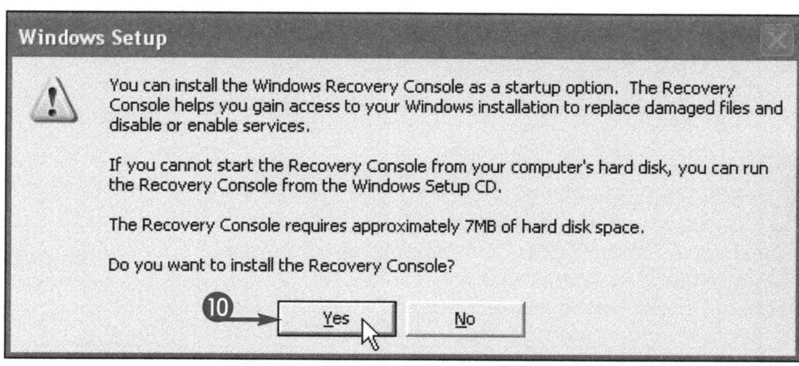

The Setup dialog box appears.

11 Click OK.

The next time you reboot, the Recovery Console is available as a startup option.

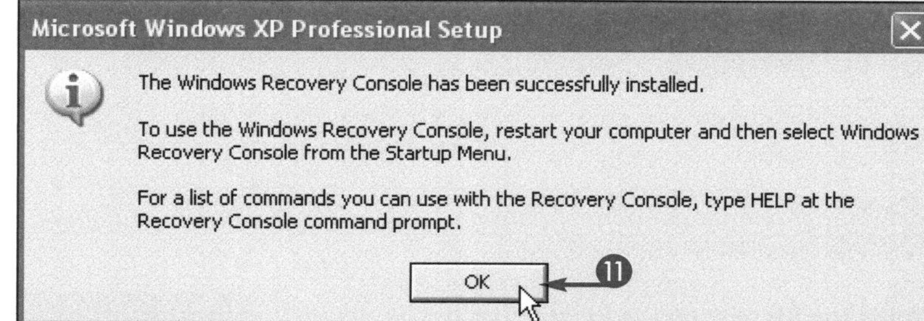

How do I know if I have the latest version of the Recovery Console?

- If you run the console directly from the XP install disk, you will not have the most recent version. Even if you install it on your hard drive, the service pack install does not upgrade the binaries automatically. Although few problems have been reported because of this, working with the latest binaries is always a good idea. You can install the console from an integrated (or *slipstream*) install as detailed in the section "Install Windows XP: Network Installation," and you will have the most recent version available.

How do I load the Recovery Console for just one use, rather than to my hard drive?

- You can load the Recovery Console using the Windows XP CD. Put the CD in the drive and reboot the computer. When prompted, press a key to boot from the CD. At the Setup notification screen, press Enter. At the Welcome to Setup screen, press R to install the Recovery Console. This loads the necessary drivers in memory only, without making other changes to your hard drive. Any changes you make using the Console are preserved, however.

Use the Recovery Console

The Recovery Console lets you gain access to parts of the Windows XP operating system that are normally not accessible to end-users, even ones with local administrator rights. For example, you can gain access to the Security Access Manager (SAM), which contains all the encrypted Access Control Lists (ACLs) for the local computer, including passwords for local logons.

For that reason, the Recovery Console asks you for a local administrator password before giving you access to the system.

You can perform other services-related features using the Recovery Console, such as start and stop services, or set a service to disabled. This prevents a possible troublesome service from causing your system to crash every time it runs.

Use the Recovery Console

1. Install the Recovery Console as detailed in the preceding task, or boot from the Windows XP CD.
2. Use the arrow keys to highlight the Microsoft Windows Recovery Console.
3. Press Enter.

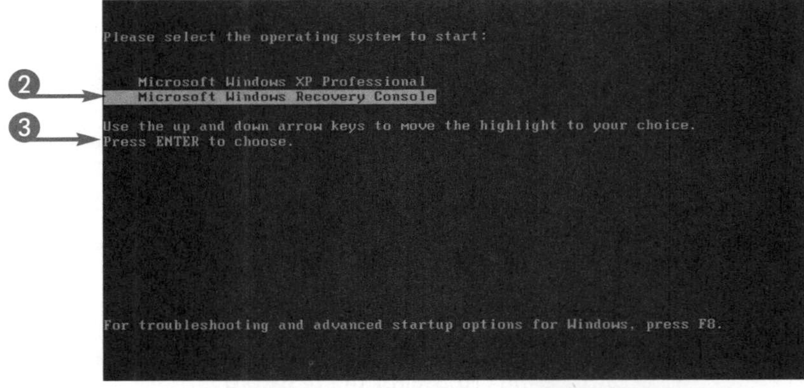

4. Press the number of the installation you want to work with (for example, 1).
5. Type the local administrator password.
6. Press Enter.

   You are logged into the Windows directory.

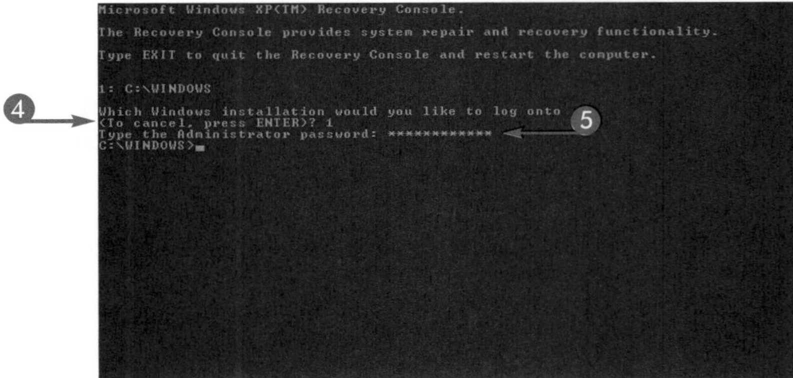

Type **HELP** to see a list of available commands; type **HELP <commandname>** for information about a specific command.

7 To disable the server service, type **disable server**.

The server service is disabled.

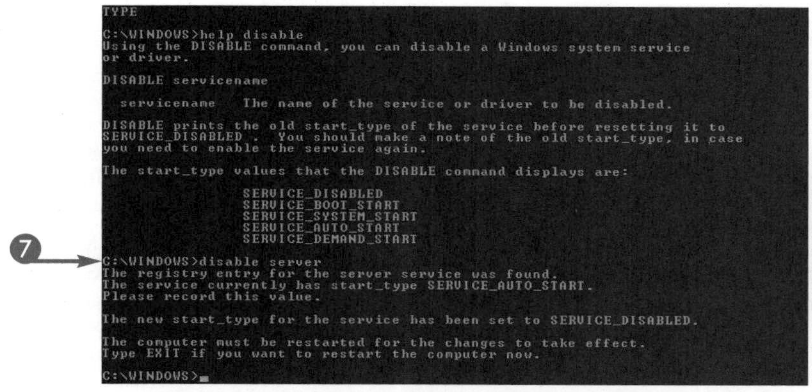

8 To enable the server service, type **enable server service_auto_start**.

9 Type **exit** to reboot the computer.

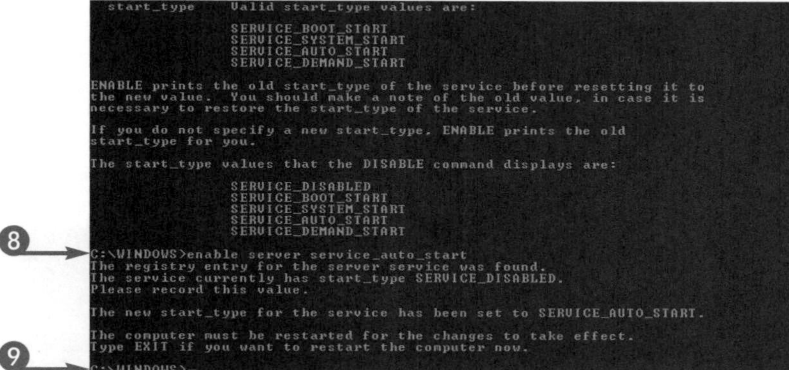

Why can I not log on to Windows using the Recovery Console?

When you type in the adminstrator password, it is authenticated against the password stored in the SAM. If, for some reason, the SAM was corrupted or hacked, then the administrator password may be corrupted and you cannot log on using the Recovery Console. You may need to use Automated System Recovery (ASR) to restore an uncorrupted copy of the Registry. Automated System Recovery is beyond the scope of this book, but you find more information about it in the Microsoft Support Knowledge Base, which is covered in Chapter 4.

If this does not work, are there other nondestructive ways to recover my system?

One of the tricks that is sometimes used to gain access to a system that will not boot is to create a parallel installation of Windows on your computer. This is typically done within the same partition as the failing version, using a different directory than the default of Windows. You can then gain access to the information stored on your computer. This is considered a data-recovery method only, and not a way to fix your system. Get in, get the data, get out, restore the data to a new system, and then decommission the computer and figure out what went wrong.

Launch and Use Safe Mode

All versions of the Windows operating system have stripped-down versions that can be launched to help with troubleshooting a system. This is preferable to wiping the hard drive, reinstalling the operating system and applications, and then copying the relevant data files back onto the user's desktop.

Safe Mode is a bare-bones graphical environment that can be started with or without network support, with or without a GUI, or started in VGA mode. By not installing these various drivers, which tend to cause the most problems with any computer installation, a system administrator can remove the troublesome drivers and back down to a version of stable drivers instead.

Safe Mode often is the only way to uninstall drivers. Some services are still functional in Safe Mode, though if you choose to boot without network drivers, many network-based services are not available. For that reason, if you need to boot into Safe Mode, it helps to have various device drivers and troubleshooting utilities available on a CD so you can use them on the standalone system.

Launch and Use Safe Mode

1. Reboot your computer.
2. Press and hold F8 while the computer reboots.

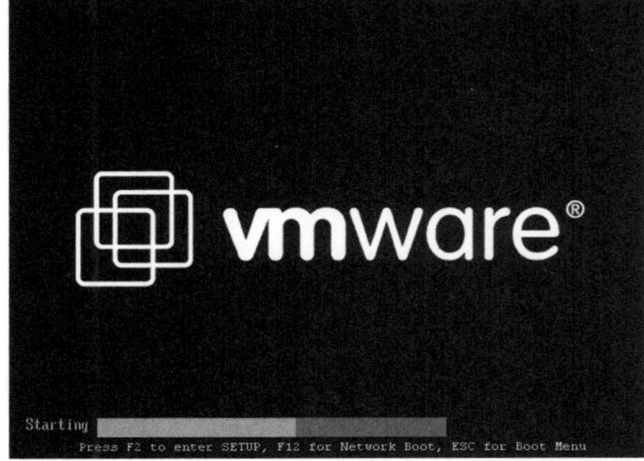

The Windows Advanced Options Menu appears.

3. Use the arrow keys to highlight the mode you want to use.

   For this example, select Safe Mode with Networking.

4. Press Enter.

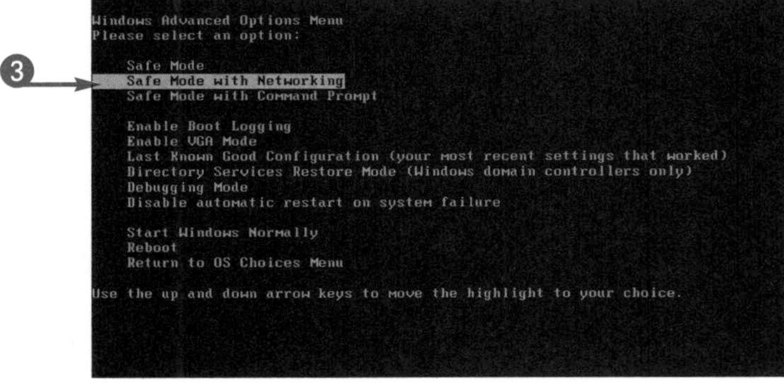

- Windows restarts in the appropriate mode.

5 Log on to Windows.

Note: *You need to use the local administrator account, or an account of someone with local administrator rights.*

- Windows starts in Safe Mode.

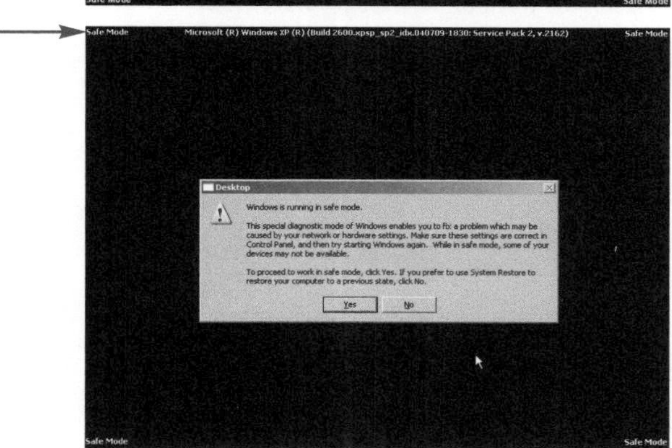

What are the different modes available in Safe Mode?

There are five general categories for Safe Mode that you can use.

Safe Mode	Safe Mode restarts Windows without networking or other common services. By starting with minimal services, you can add services one by one to determine which are misbehaving.
Safe Mode with Networking	Adds network services and Active Directory connectivity to Safe Mode.
Safe Mode with Command Prompt	Restarts Windows at a command prompt.
Enable VGA Mode	Starts Windows using a generic VGA driver, providing 640×480×16 color display.
Last Known Good Configuration	Restores your previous boot settings that successfully started Windows. Note that this does not necessarily restore a working copy of Windows, just one that managed to get to the desktop.

Customize Windows Startup with MSCONFIG

When Windows XP boots, it starts a number of services and applications so that the Windows environment is configured for your optimal use. These may or may not actually be needed; many of them are enabled "out of the box," while others are added by applications or device managers you install.

Microsoft provides a program called MSCONFIG that lets you determine which services and applications run at startup. You can see which programs are starting, find out where they reside on your system, and enable or disable them by clicking a check box. This makes it easy to determine if a particular service or application is needed and lets you edit the configuration files involved without risking a syntax error.

You can also control these programs using the Services Manager and RegEdit or RegEdt32, which provide more granular control and options to restore deleted or modified registry keys. However, if you are experimenting with the boot time and application startup, MSCONFIG is easier to use than the other applications.

Customize Windows Startup with MSCONFIG

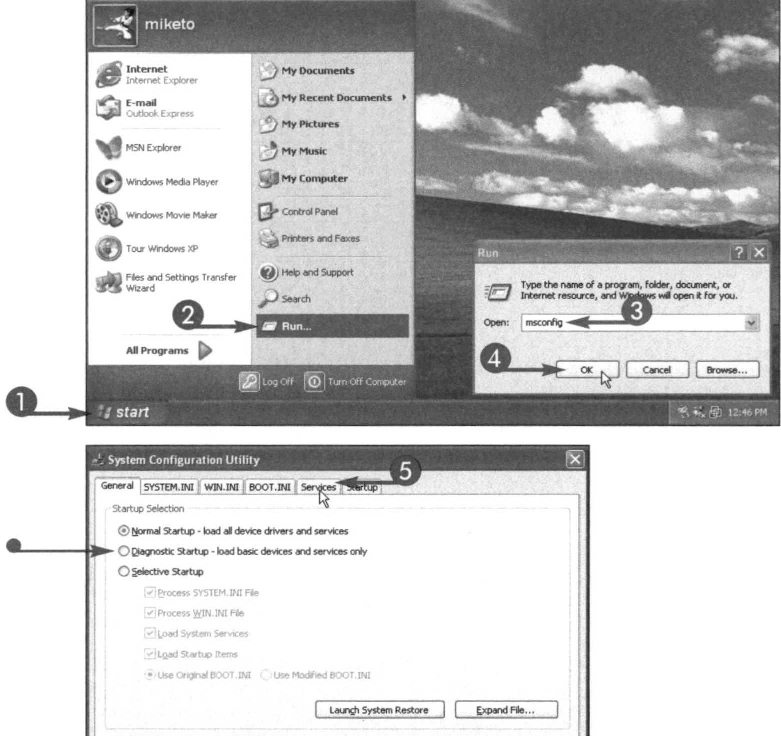

1. Click Start.
2. Click Run.
3. Type **MSCONFIG**.
4. Click OK.

   The System Configuration Utility dialog box, also know as MSCONFIG, appears.

- Select Diagnostic Startup to load with only a minimum of drivers and services available.

Note: *When you reboot, the list of loaded services and applications can be viewed again in MSCONFIG.*

5. Click the Services tab.

The services appear.

- Click next to a service to choose whether it loads on the next reboot.
- Click here to hide or unhide the Microsoft services and list only the third-party ones.

6 Click the Startup tab.

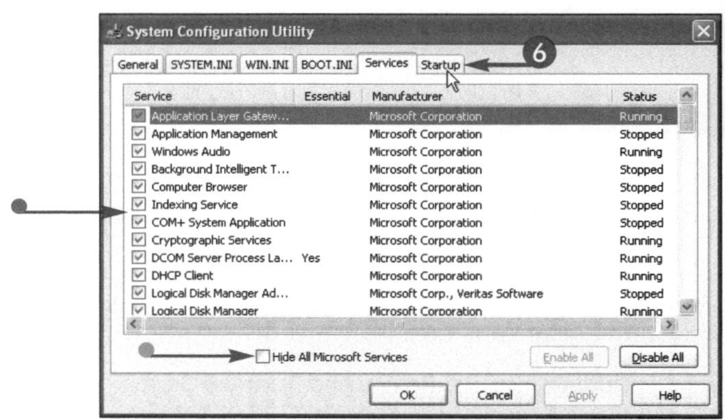

The Startup items appear.

- Click next to an applet to choose whether it loads on the next reboot.
- The Command heading shows from where the applet or application was launched.

7 Click OK to save your changes.

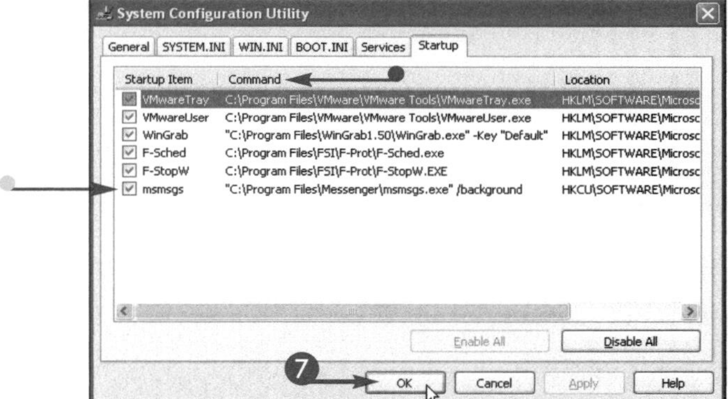

How do I tell which applet is associated with which program?

MSCONFIG usually gives you the path to where the applet originates. By looking at the path, you can usually tell the application to which it belongs. For example, ccApp.exe belongs to Norton AntiVirus.

Why are SYSTEM.INI and WIN.INI listed? I thought they were only for 16-bit Windows?

These files have been present in both 16- and 32-bit Windows for backwards compatibility and for applications that run in the CMD environment. If you have custom applications that have trouble running, you can debug the drivers by not loading them in these files at startup.

Can I edit the BOOT.INI file manually?

It depends on what you want to accomplish. If all you want to do is change the boot order or add some command-line options, you are better off using MSCONFIG to make the necessary changes. If you want to add paths for a new kernel (such as booting into a Linux partition), you will need to use Notepad or some other text editor to make the changes. The disk and drive syntax is tricky, so you should check TechNet or any FAQs on how to modify the BOOT.INI.

Configure Automatic Updates

Automatic Updates is the Windows service that provides bug fixes, patches, and optional features that you can install on Windows. This allows you to keep your system up-to-date, helping defend against hacker attempts and rogue programs that can corrupt or steal data from your computer.

Automatic Updates can still be reached from the Start menu, but it is also part of the Security Center. The Security Center is a central location for configuring updates, firewall settings, and antivirus monitoring. See Chapter 8 for more about the Security Center.

For most users, setting Automatic Updates to download and install new code is the easiest way to keep computers up-to-date. In larger organizations, it is better to use the Software Update Service because it gives you time to test the code for compatibility before rolling it out to the rest of the organization.

You can still manually check for available updates, or disable Automatic Updates if you prefer to have more control over what your PC does in the background.

Configure Automatic Updates

1. Click Start.
2. Click All Programs.
3. Click Accessories.
4. Click System Tools.
5. Click Security Center.

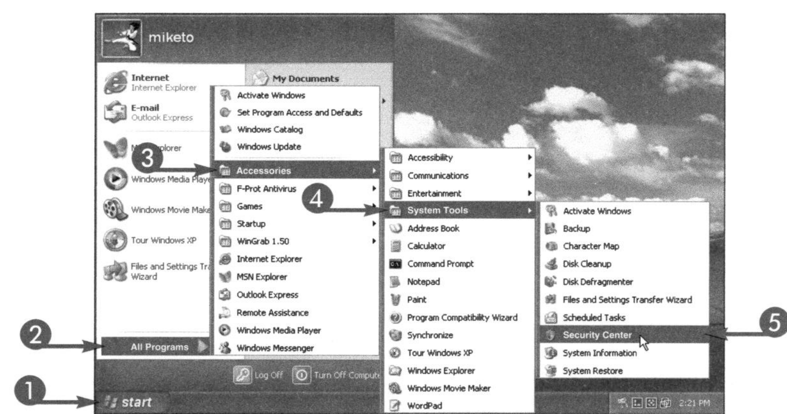

The Security Center window appears.

6. Click Automatic Updates.

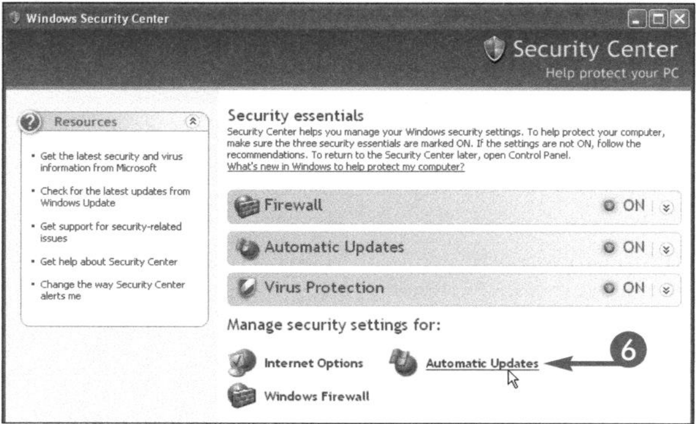

The Automatic Updates dialog box appears.

7. Select which option to use for downloading and installing updates.
   - Click OK or Apply to apply your selections.
8. Click this link to install updates from the Windows Update Web site.

Note: *You can also launch this site by clicking Start, All Programs, and then Windows Update.*

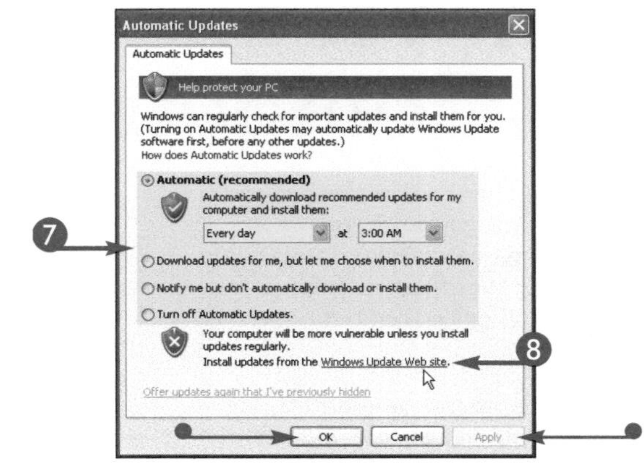

The Windows Update Web site appears.

- Click Express Install to immediately scan for new critical and security-related updates.
- Click Custom Install to scan for critical and optional updates to install.

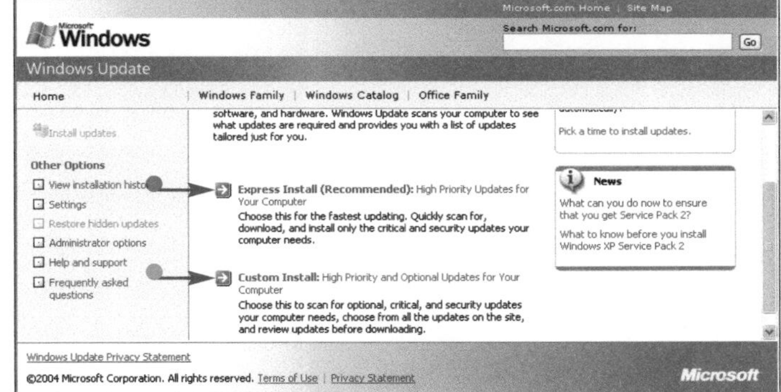

Is there a way to roll back software that gets installed using Automatic Update?

▼ If you know the name or Knowledge Base number, you often will find the updates listed in the Add or Remove Programs section of the Windows Control Panel and can remove it from there. You can also go to the Windows Update Web site and get a listing of what has been successfully installed and what failed. Under Other Control Panel Options, at the left side of the Control Panel, click View Installation History. You will see a list of updates and the status, and the specific name of the update.

Why can I not uninstall a particular update?

▼ There are some updates that cannot be uninstalled. These are most often specific security updates or updates to core system services. For example, Windows Media Player 10 cannot be uninstalled after you install it on a system. Windows Update will tell you prior to installation if that is the case, and you may wish to test the update before rolling it out to the rest of your organization.

Add, Remove, and Change Windows Components

You can add, remove, and change the components that are available to Windows and other applications. These run the gamut from accessibility tools to applets like Calculator and WordPad to services like Internet Information Server (IIS) or Distributed Transaction Coordinator.

Some components, such as additional mouse pointers, are just for fun or add to the things you can do with Windows. Others, like IIS, are meant for heavier-duty use or more extensive use of Windows than as an ordinary desktop PC.

Because many of these components and services are really meant for development usage, not production, there are limits on what you can do with some of them. For example, the version of IIS that ships with Windows XP has a limit of ten concurrent connections. So while you can run a Web server on your desktop, it is more for development efforts than for actual serving of content on the Internet.

Add, Remove, and Change Windows Components

1. Click Start.
2. Click Control Panel.

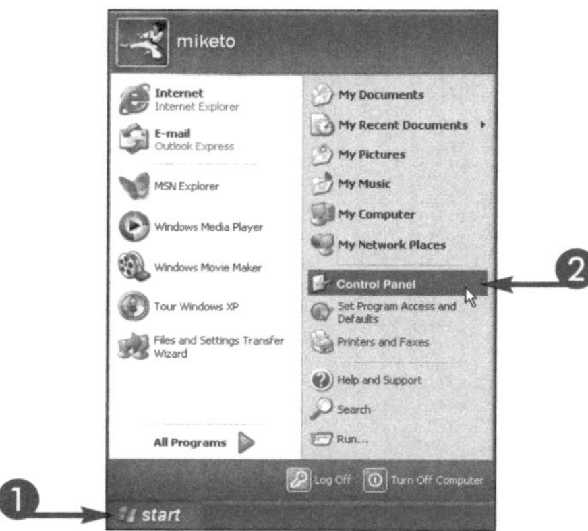

The Control Panel opens.

3. Click Add or Remove Programs.

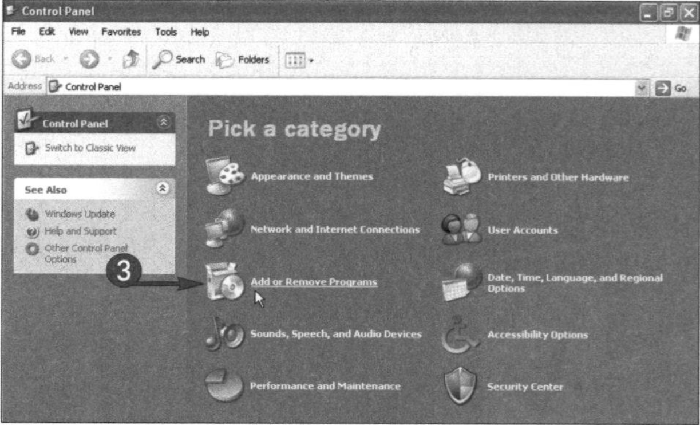

The Add or Remove Programs window appears.

4 Click Add/Remove Windows Components.

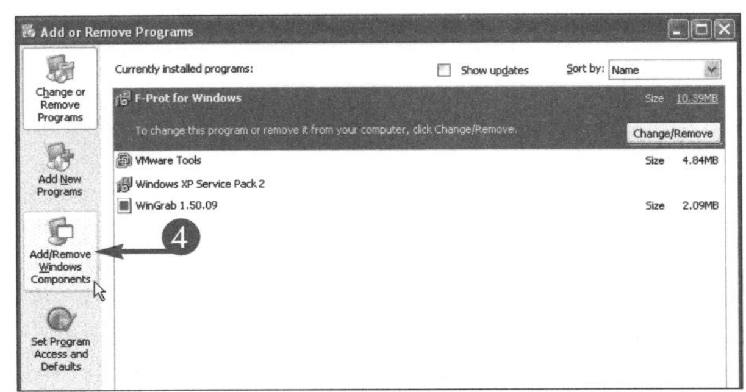

The Windows Components Wizard appears.

Scroll through the list to find the components you want to add or remove.

- Click Details to get a list of subcomponents that can be added or removed.

5 Select a component to add or remove.

6 Click Next.

Windows adds or removes the selected component.

7 Click Finish.

Note: *Depending on the component, you may need to reboot your system.*

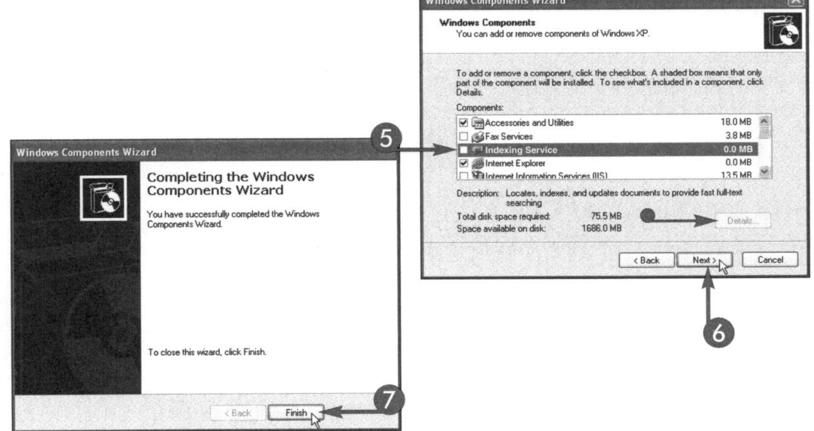

What does the Add New Programs icon in the Add or Remove Programs window do?

The Add New Programs icon can be used to install applications from CD rather than clicking and running Setup on a disk. It also sends you to the Windows Update Web site for updates. However, if you are using Active Directory and Group Policy to manage your network, you can use IntelliMirror technology to provide a list of installable applications under this button as well. It is more common to see this in larger organizations but can be used in SOHO environments as well.

How do I remove components, like games, that are not listed when I click the Add/Remove Windows Components icon?

Older versions of Windows allowed you to select components at installation time. Windows XP installs many components, some of which look like they cannot be uninstalled. But there is a way to list them in Add/Remove Windows Components. Browse to the <windir>\inf folder and use Notepad to open the file SYSOC.INF. Delete the word HIDE from the component you want to appear in Add/Remove Windows Components, and then save the file. Just in case, make a backup of the file first before saving.

Configure PowerToys for Windows XP

Despite all the improvements in the Windows interface, and new usability enhancements, there are many aspects of Windows that are odd, get in the way, or just plain do not work the way most users want them to. Microsoft developers found this was true for them, so some unsung geniuses developed the PowerToys.

The PowerToys collection started out as a user interface configuration application, using check boxes and tabbed dialog boxes to make changes to obscure Registry settings. This would turn off animated menus, for example, or clear all search dialog boxes at logoff.

The recent batch of PowerToys adds useful utilities, not just for the user interface, but for other Windows applications including the command line. Not all of them will be needed by every user, but if you find an annoyance that you want cured, the PowerToys are a good first place to look.

You can download the PowerToys for Windows XP at www.microsoft.com/windowsxp/downloads/powertoys/xppowertoys.mspx.

The PowerToy covered here is Tweak UI, which configures many of the Windows behaviors that are otherwise difficult to control.

Configure PowerToys for Windows XP

1. Download and install Tweak UI for Windows XP.
2. Click Start.
3. Click All Programs.
4. Click PowerToys for Windows XP.
5. Click Tweak UI.

Note: *Older versions of Tweak UI were launched from the Control Panel.*

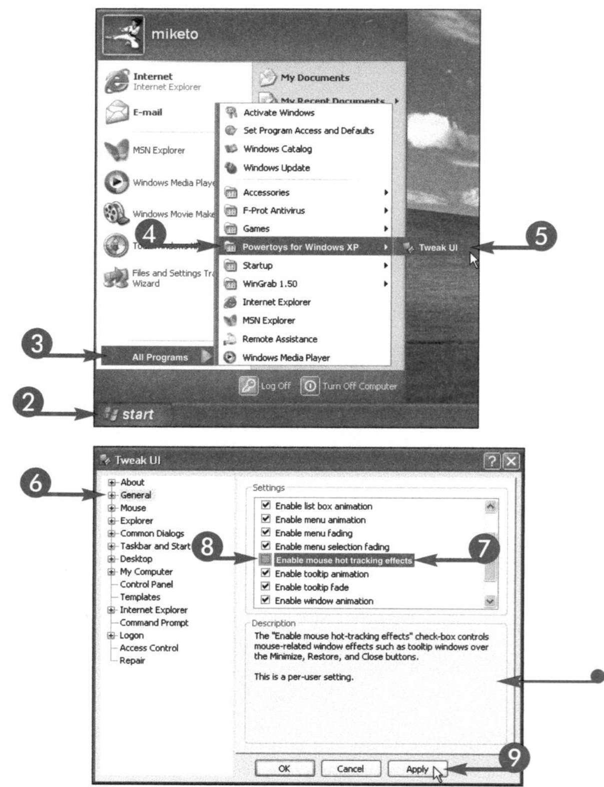

- The Tweak UI dialog box appears.

6. Click General.

   Scroll through the list to an animation item.

7. Select the item.
   - An item description appears.
8. Click the check box to disable or enable the animation.
9. Click Apply.

⑩ Click Explorer.

- Clear file and document history using the Explorer options.

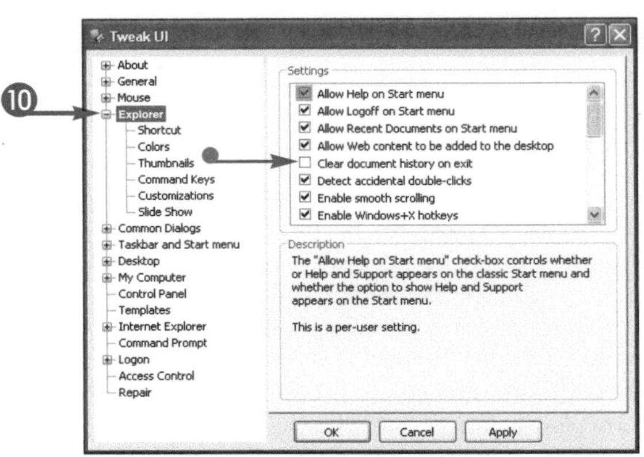

⑪ Click to view the Logon options.

⑫ Click Autologon.

- Click here to set the computer to log on with a user name and password automatically.

Note: *This is most useful for testing and troubleshooting. It is a high security risk and should be disabled as soon as you have finished your testing.*

⑬ Click OK.

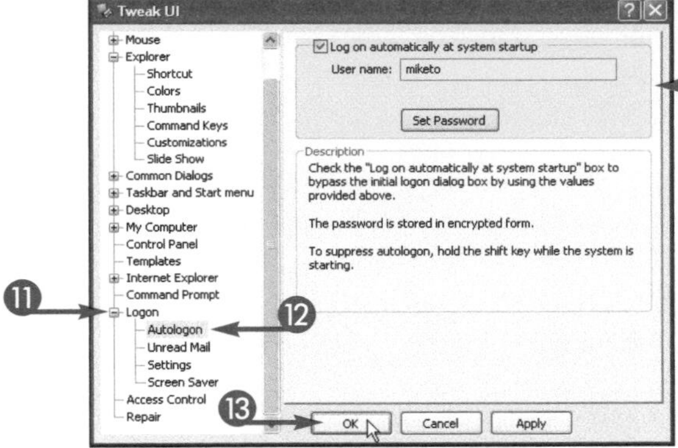

What do the different PowerToys do?

▼ There are several available, depending on what you want to do. The more popular ones are shown here.

Open Command Window Here	Adds an Open Command Window Here context menu option on file system folders, giving you a quick way to open a command window at the selected folder.
Image Resizer	Enables you to resize one or many image files with a right-click.
CD Slide Show Generator	Allows you to view images burned to a CD as a slide show. The Generator works on Windows 9x machines as well.
Virtual Desktop Manager	Enables you to manage up to four desktops from theWindows taskbar.

Configure Application Compatibility

With Windows 2000, Microsoft removed support for older DOS and 16-bit Windows applications found in Windows 9*x* and Windows Me. This code, though well-written, allowed applications to write directly to hardware, causing hard locks, system-level crashes, and the infamous "blue screen of death." Removing the code dramatically reduced the number of crashes, but also made backwards compatibility trickier, especially for businesses that relied on legacy applications or for gamers with several years of older games they wanted to play.

However, Microsoft included *compatibility mode*, a set of software services and database information that provides limited emulation for older applications. For example, some Windows 16-bit applications query for the OS version, and will not run if the version is less than that needed. Compatibility mode provides the necessary information to the application, allowing it to run. This includes re-creating registry structures and other OS-specific variables.

You can invoke compatibility mode using a wizard, or by creating a custom icon that points to your application and modifying its properties.

Configure Application Compatibility

1. Click Start.
2. Click All Programs.
3. Click Accessories.
4. Click Program Compatibility Wizard.

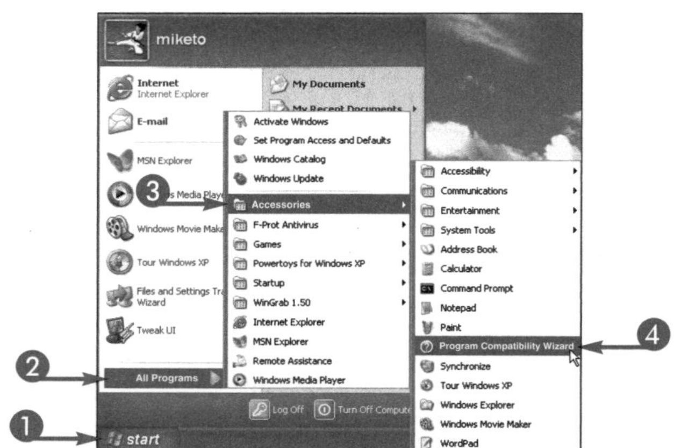

The Program Compatibility Wizard appears.

5. Click Next.

6. Select where to look for your program.
7. Click Next.

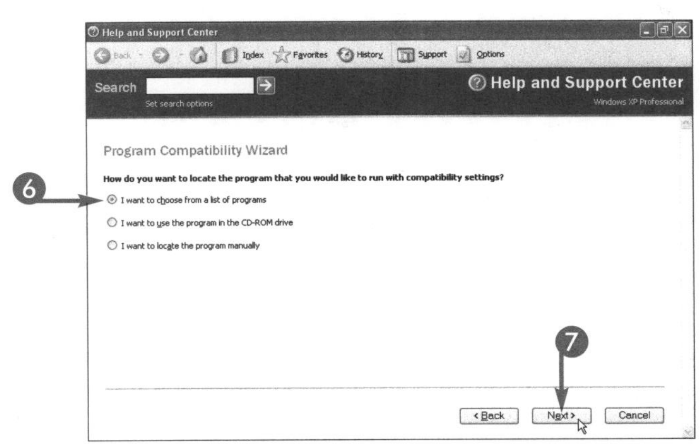

Scroll through the list to find the program you want to configure.

8. Select the program.
9. Click Next.
10. Select the operating system compatibility mode.
11. Click Next.

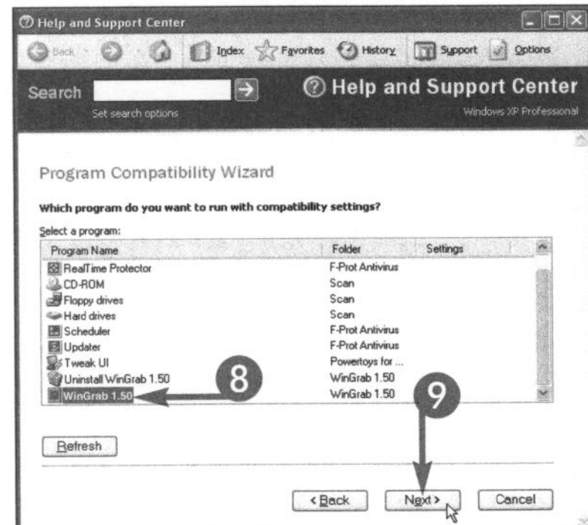

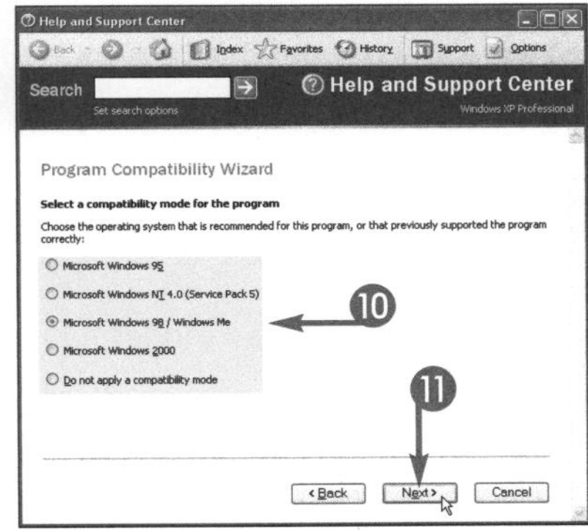

Can I use compatibility mode to run operating system or hardware-management applications?

Compatibility mode attempts to re-create operating system and environment variables from older versions of Windows. If you try to run an application that directly manages hardware or the operating system using compatibility mode, you stand an excellent chance of corrupting your system and making it unbootable. Applications that fall into this category include antivirus, disk defragmentation, registry cleanup, and rescue utilities like Norton Utilities.

Can I configure compatibility mode without using the wizard?

You can set compatibility for any application without using the wizard. Right-click on an executable or a shorcut that launches it, and then click Properties. Click the Compatibility tab to show the compatibility mode options on a single dialog box page, make the necessary selections, and then click OK. Clicking the executable or the shortcut will launch your application using the compatibility mode settings.

continued

Configure Application Compatibility *(Continued)*

If you want to run MS-DOS applications on Windows XP, your course of action is a little trickier. You can run applications in the standard command-line virtual machine, cmd.exe. Or you can run your application in a DOS emulation environment, command.com. Both are managed by NT Virtual DOS Machine (NTVDM). It sets environment variables needed by a program when you run it.

Environment variables can be set two ways: by modifying or creating custom AUTOEXEC.NT and CONFIG.NT files that are run when the virtual machine starts, or by creating a custom .PIF (Program Information File) that creates specific environments for the application in question.

The AUTOEXEC and CONFIG files can be found in <%windir%>\system32 directory. If you were comfortable modifying their analogues in DOS, you can do the same in Windows XP.

PIF files are kept in <%windir%>\PIF, a hidden system folder. You can make one by copying COMMAND.COM to the folder, right-clicking it, and then clicking the Compatibility tab.

All things being equal, it is better to use PIF files. However, because they do not give you as much flexibility, you may need to use AUTOEXEC.NT and CONFIG.NT instead.

Configure Application Compatibility *(continued)*

12. Select optional display modes for your application.
13. Click Next.
14. Click Next to test the compatibility settings.
15. Click the result that applies to your compatibility tests.
16. Click Next.

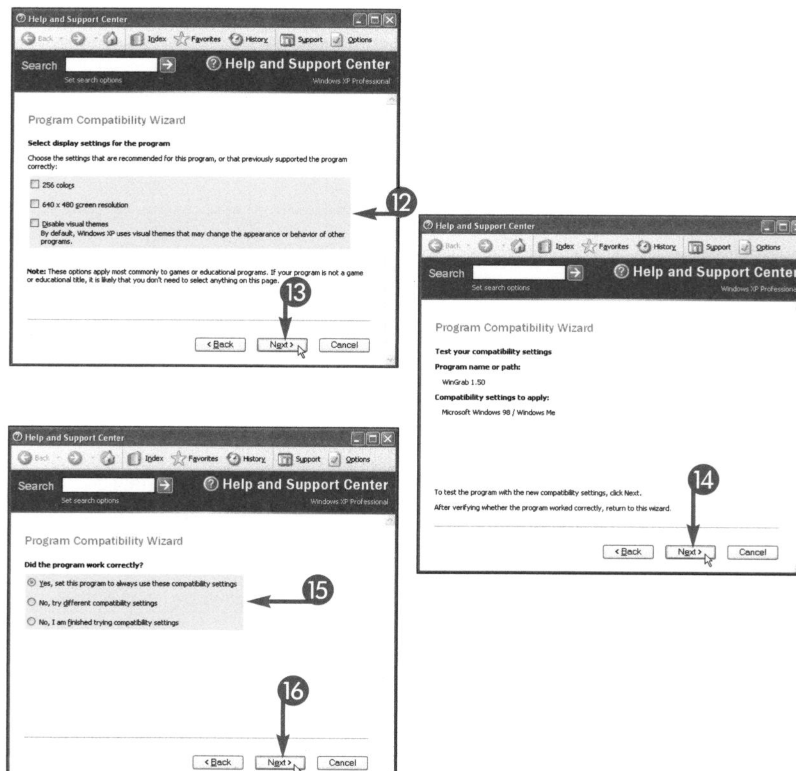

- Use these options to choose whether to send your custom configuration to Microsoft.

17 Click No.

18 Click Next.

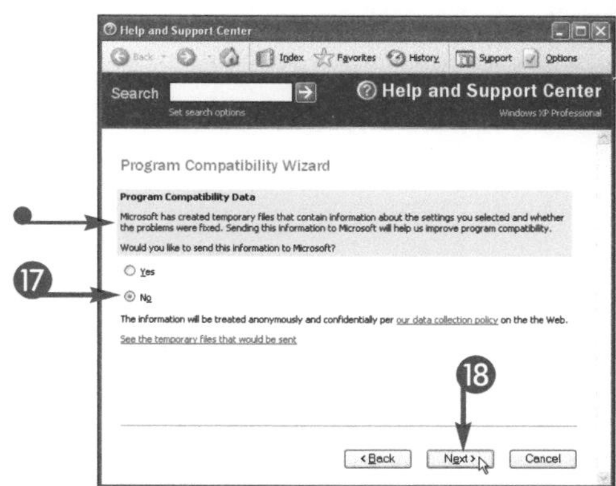

19 Click Finish.

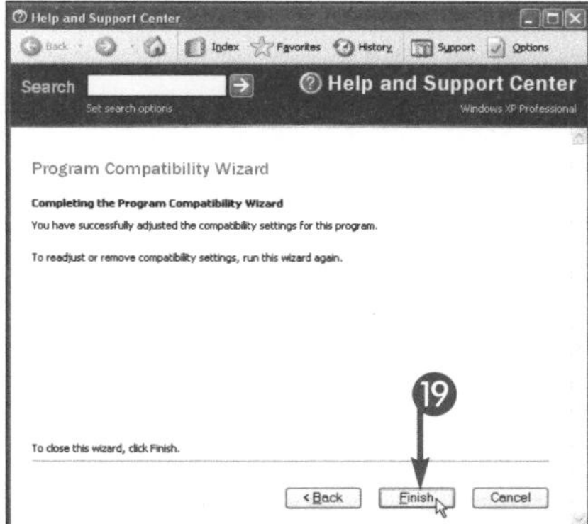

I have configured everything, but my MS-DOS application runs too fast. Can I slow it down?

▼ Very old MS-DOS applications relied on the CPU clock speed to determine how fast the application ran. Even if you configure the environment correctly, there is no easy way with Windows XP to slow down the emulation environment. Your best bet is to download a third-party "slowdown" applet that you can run prior to launching your older application. This can provide some relief for impossibly fast applications. However, this is not guaranteed, and the environment may not be stable, so use slowdown applications at your own risk.

I do not want to spend my time playing with settings. Is there an easier way to create a compatible environment?

▼ Microsoft offers an advanced set of applications, intended for system administrators, called the Application Compatibility Toolkit. Its core application is the Compatibility Administrator, which contains a number of fixes and settings for many applications. They are settings that have worked in other environments and may work in yours. You can download the toolkit at http://msdn.microsoft.com/library/default.asp?url=/downloads/list/appcomp.asp.

4 Using the Windows XP Interface

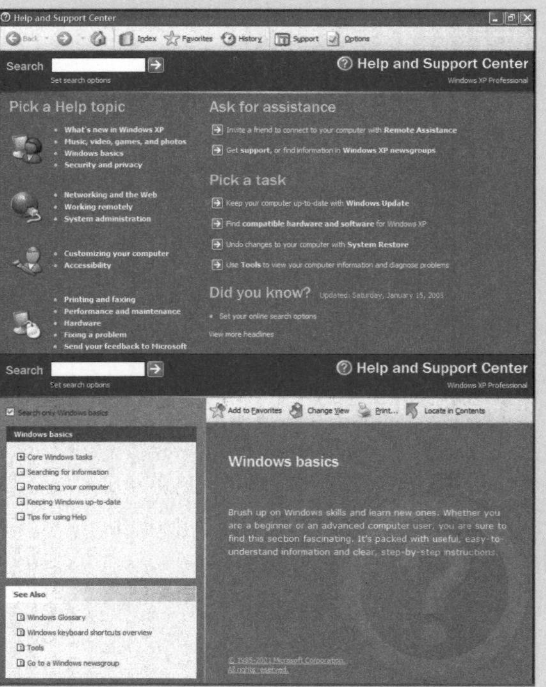

5 Customizing the Desktop

List of valid modes
640 by 480, 256 Colors, 60 Hertz

6 Managing Users

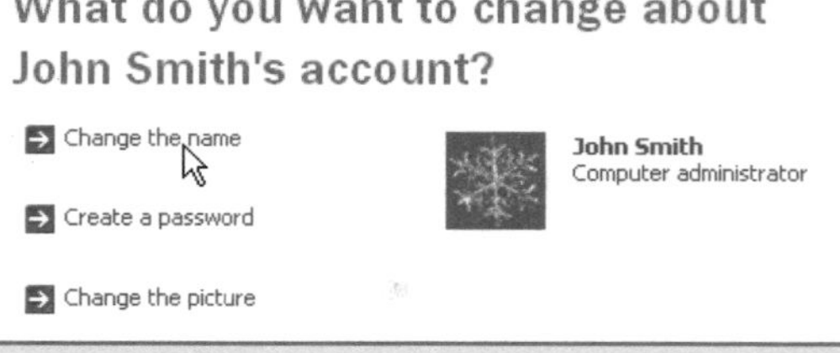

PART II

MANAGING THE DESKTOP ENVIRONMENT

7 Managing Files and Folders

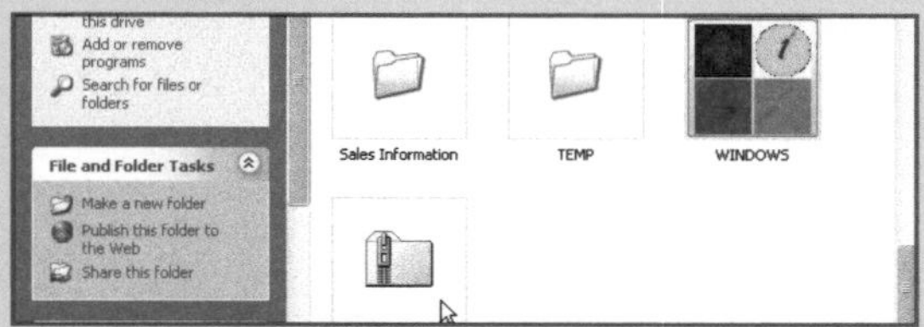

8 Managing Security

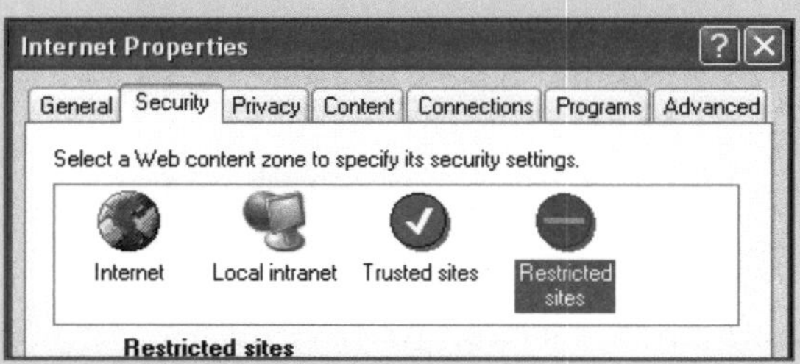

9 Mastering Multimedia with XP

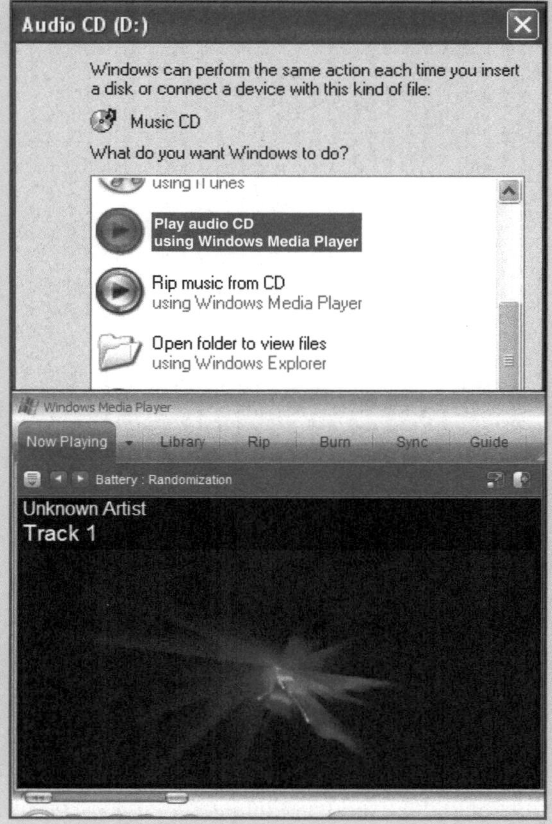

Get to Know the Windows XP Desktop

You can save time by spending a few moments familiarizing yourself with the Windows XP desktop. If you have used an earlier version, you will see mostly similarities and a few differences. When you first log on to Windows XP, a pop-up window appears asking if you want to take a tour. If you do not want to view the Windows XP Tour the first time you log on, you can always view it later.

The screen below shows the Windows XP desktop with its default settings. The Windows XP desktop is designed to be highly customizable to suit your individual needs. Consequently, your PC's desktop may have a different background picture (or no picture), or it may have additional icons. You can learn about some of the additional icons and features available, as well as how to customize your desktop, in Chapter 5.

A Double-click the Internet Explorer icon to browse the Web.

B Click Start to launch programs, change settings, or get help.

C The taskbar displays open files and allows you to switch between them.

D Click here to display hidden icons.

E Move your mouse over the clock to display the day and date.

F Drag files to the Recycle Bin to delete them or retrieve them later.

Get to Know the Windows XP Start Menu

By clicking the Start button, you can display the Windows XP Start menu. From the Start menu you can launch programs, change settings, access Help, open your documents, view your pictures, and play your music or videos. The Start menu is also where you find the commands to log off, shut down, and restart your computer. The screen below shows a sample Start menu. Yours may be slightly different.

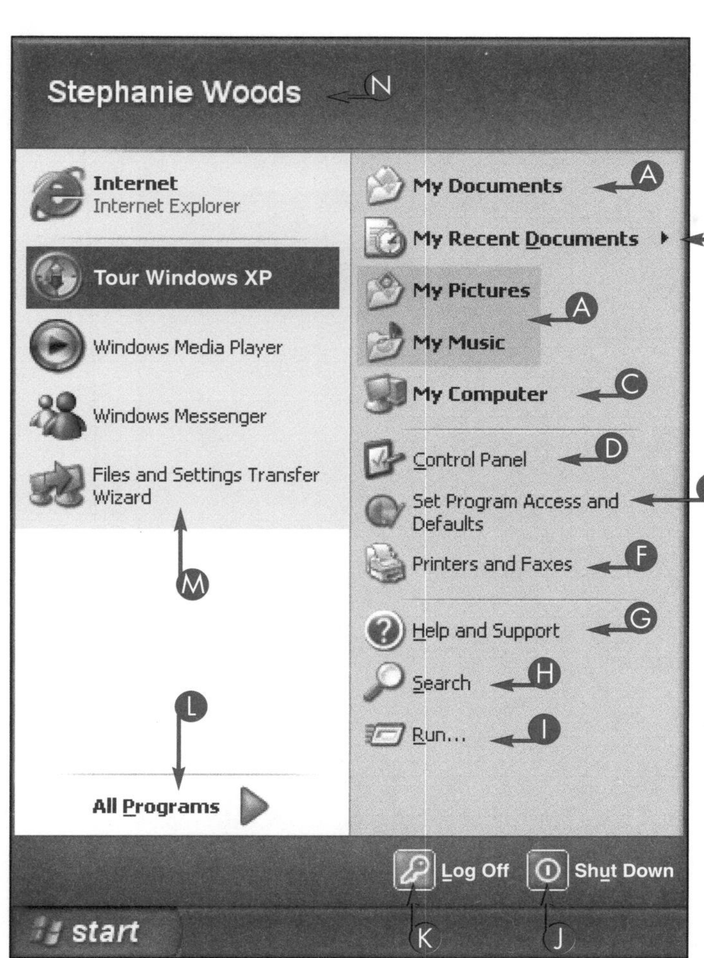

A Open folders containing your documents, pictures, and music.

B Choose from a list of the documents with which you most recently worked.

C Access the files, folders, and settings of your PC.

D Adjust the settings on your PC.

E Set default programs associated with specific tasks.

F Select or manage output devices such as printers and faxes.

G Get help or technical support.

H Search for files, folders, or other computers on a network.

I Run a program.

J Shut down your computer (in Windows XP Home, this button is labeled Turn Off Computer).

K Log off as current user.

L A complete list of installed programs.

M Commonly and most recently used programs.

N Name (and graphic in Windows XP Home) of the user currently logged in at this PC.

Find Help on a Topic

You can get help on a given topic from the Start menu. The Start menu has a Help and Support option that takes you to the Help and Support Center. This is a centralized location for help, technical support, and training for Windows XP. Many computer manufacturers customize the Help and Support Center for their products. Consequently, you may see additional manufacturer support information or a slightly different organization of the Help and Support Center information. The Help and Support Center allows you to look for a Help topic from a list of categories, to search for a topic using a text search, to get online support or Remote Assistance, or to perform some common tasks with help as you go.

From the Help and Support Center, you can go back and forth between topics you have recently viewed. If you cannot find what you are looking for in the list of topics, you can use the Search or Index features to find what you need. If you are curious, you can also use the Did You Know section to fill in gaps in your knowledge about Windows XP. These topics are updated and change frequently.

Find Help on a Topic

1. Click Help and Support from the Start menu.

   The Help and Support Center appears.

2. Click Windows basics from the Pick a Help topic column.

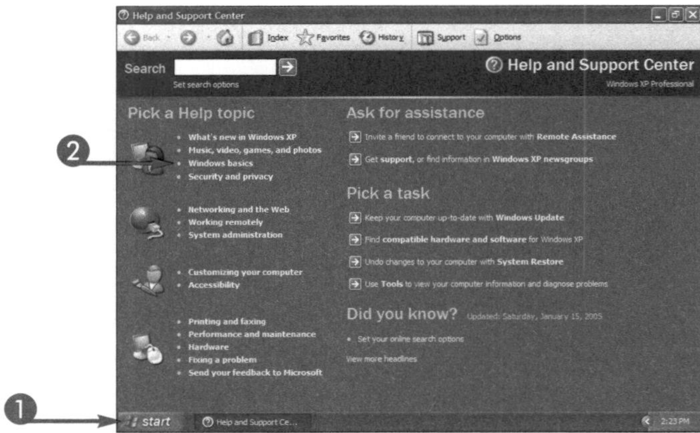

The Windows basics screen appears.

3. Click Tips for using Help.

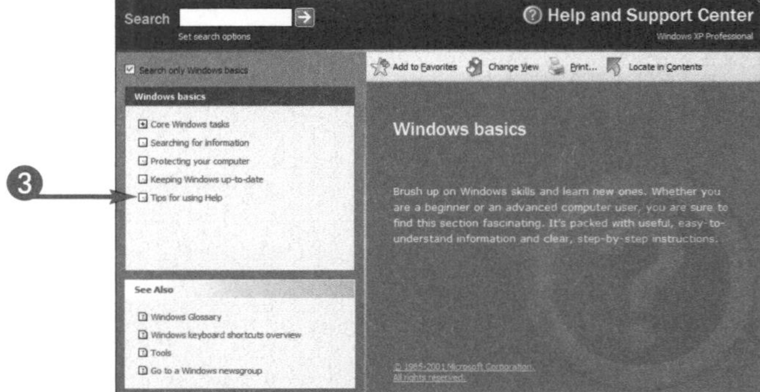

A list of Tips for using Help is displayed in the right column.

4 Click a task in the Pick a task section.

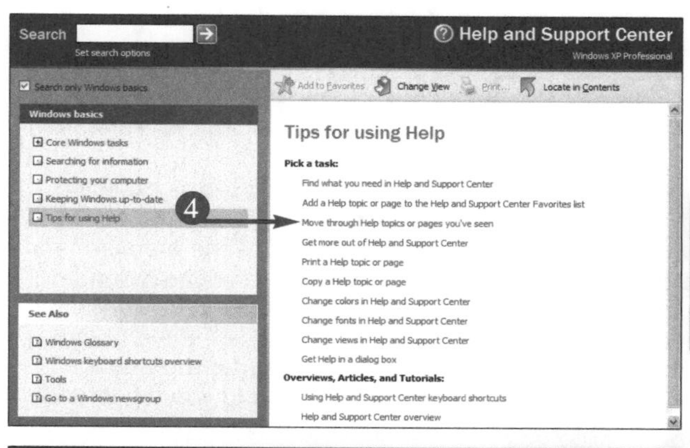

The Help topic for that task is displayed.

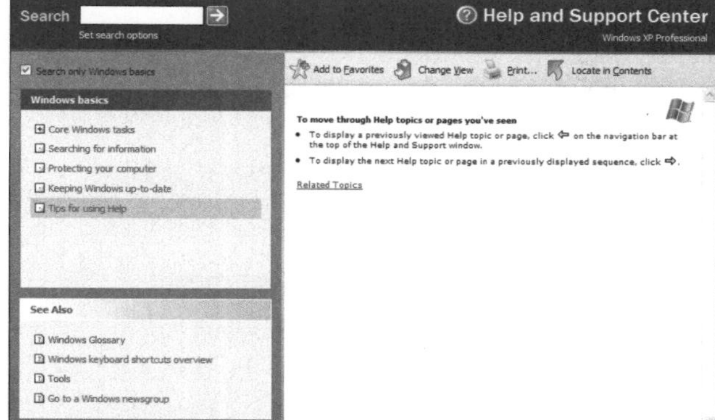

What if I cannot find the topic I need in the list displayed?

▼ You can type any word or phrase in the Search box and press Enter to search through the Help topics, or you can click the Index icon (▣) and then begin typing a word or phrase to quickly find a topic in the Help index.

How can I make the Help screen smaller so I can see what I am working on at the same time?

▼ Click the Change View icon (▣) to reduce the Help screen to just the Help instructions. Click Change View again to display the full Help and Support window.

What if I frequently need to refer to a Help topic? Is there a way I can get back to it quickly?

▼ If you know you will have frequent need to refer back to a topic, click the Add to Favorites icon (▣) when you are viewing the topic. You can then select it later from your short list of Help topic Favorites by clicking the Favorites icon (▣) and then selecting your topic.

If you have not added the topic to your Favorites list, you can still get back to it by clicking the History icon (▣). The History screen displays a list of the Help topics you have viewed in the past. You can then select the Help topic from the list.

Fix a Problem with Troubleshooters

If your computer is not operating quite as expected, you can use the Windows XP set of tools called *troubleshooters* to get to the root of the problem pragmatically by ruling out likely problems one-by-one. Much like a good auto mechanic or computer technician, Windows XP troubleshooters work to locate the problem by process of elimination, asking you along the way if your problem has been solved, and giving you the chance to try the next item or skip and try something else.

Sometimes troubleshooters can perform the necessary diagnostic procedures on your computer via software and inform you directly how to resolve the problem. Other times the troubleshooter requires your feedback in the form of selecting one of several possible answers to a question. Depending on the nature and severity of the problem, you may want to have a pen and paper ready to write down specific technical information, especially if you are not able to use a printer. Also, it is a good idea to have your Windows XP disks and any hardware installation disks at the ready.

Fix a Problem with Troubleshooters

1. Click Help and Support from the Start menu.
2. From the Help and Support Center, select Fixing a problem from the Pick a Help topic column.

   The Fixing a problem screen appears.
3. Click Troubleshooting problems from the left column.

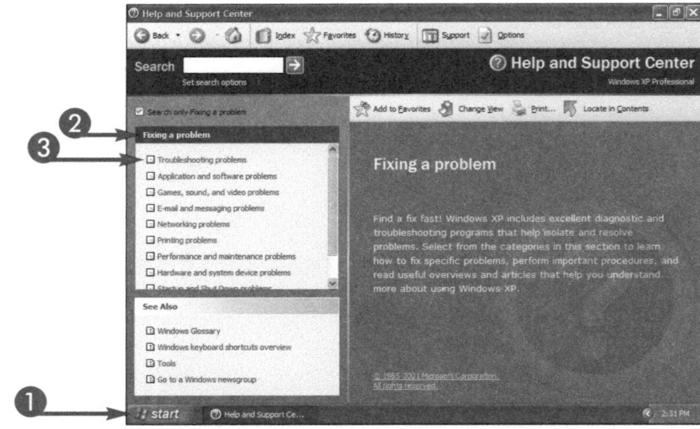

The Troubleshooting problems screen appears.

Scroll down the right column until you see the List of troubleshooters entry.

Note: *The List of troubleshooters entry may be in a different place in your list of entries from the one shown here.*

4. Click List of troubleshooters.

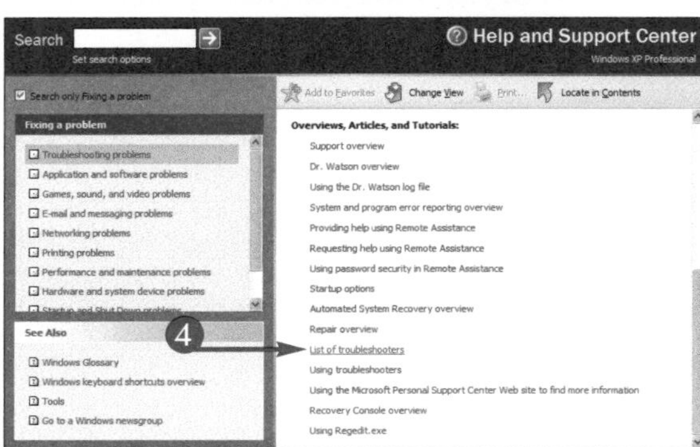

The list of troubleshooters is displayed.

5 Click the name of the troubleshooter in the left column of the table to start the troubleshooter.

Note: *You may need to write down settings or instructions during the course of a troubleshooting session. The troubleshooter lets you know if this is necessary.*

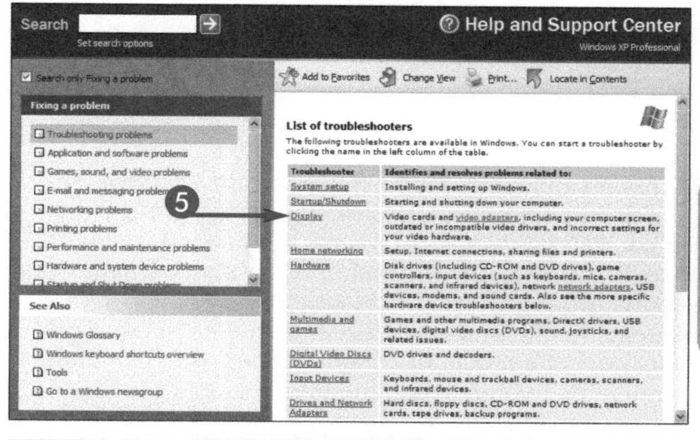

The troubleshooter poses a question about the nature of your problem and presents you with a set of possible answers.

6 Click the answer that best fits.

7 Click Next.

Continue to follow the guided questions and procedures of the troubleshooter until your problem is resolved.

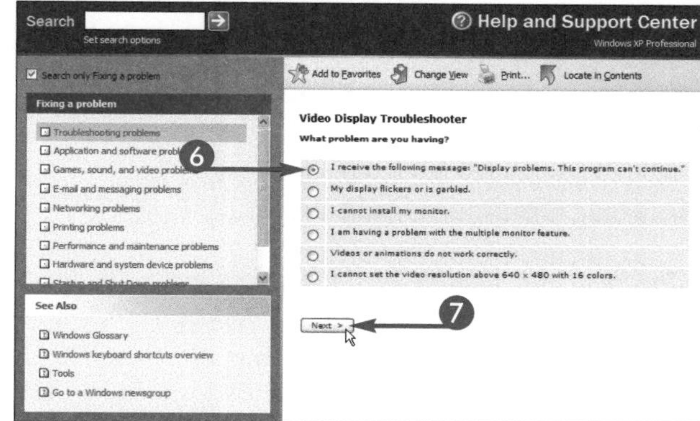

I do not know exactly what the problem is, so I do not know which troubleshooter to pick. Where do I start?

▼ Click Fixing a problem in the left column on the Help and Support Center screen and then choose the category in the left column that best fits your problem.

The troubleshooter says I have an outdated driver for my hardware device. What do I do?

▼ Most hardware manufacturers have free, downloadable updates to their drivers to support the latest Microsoft system updates. Check the manufacturer's technical support page on the Web to see if such an update is available.

What if my problems require me to restart Windows XP during a troubleshooting session?

▼ If possible, launch the troubleshooter from a second computer and answer the questions for the first one. If you only have access to a single computer, the troubleshooter tells you to print out or write down where you are in the troubleshooter before it requires you to restart. When Windows XP is restarted, retrace your steps to get to where you left off in the troubleshooter.

Get Support Online from Microsoft

If you cannot find help you need from Windows XP alone and you have a working Internet connection, you can get help from Microsoft's online support. Microsoft provides such extensive online support that it can be overwhelming. This also means the information you need may be deeply buried. It is a good idea to familiarize yourself with the organization and various tools of online support so that you can find the information efficiently when you need it.

You can get your online support in whichever way best suits your needs and preferences. You can read how-to articles that have been grouped in categories or ask direct questions to a technical support professional through Microsoft Online Assisted Support. You can get help via e-mail, chat, telephone, or Remote Assistance, where the technician takes control of your desktop and works through the solution with you as if they were there. (Articles and downloads are free, as are most types of upgrade and installation support. You may be charged for some types of additional online and telephone support, but you are notified in advance in such cases.) You can also discuss your problem with other Windows XP users in newsgroups moderated by Microsoft.

Get Support Online from Microsoft

1. Click Help and Support from the Start menu.
2. From the Help and Support Center, click the Get support link, or find information in Windows XP newsgroups under Ask for assistance.
   - You can also reach Support by clicking the Support icon.

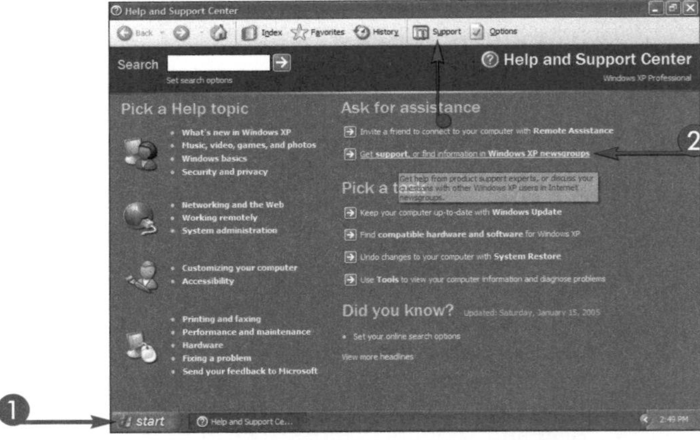

The Welcome to Support screen appears.

3. Click Get help from Microsoft under Support.
   - To ask a friend for online support, click Ask a friend to help.

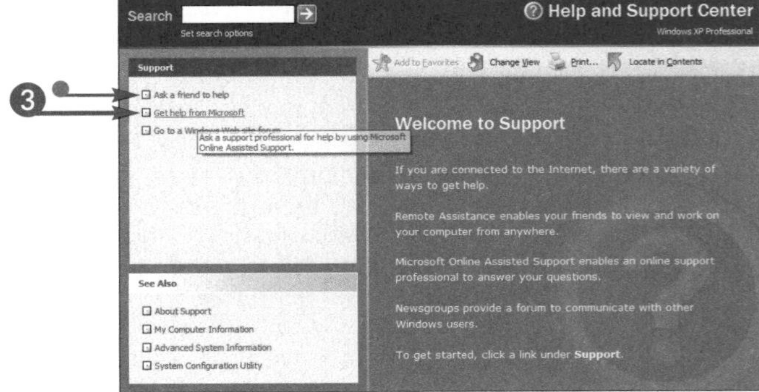

The Microsoft Help and Support home page appears.

4. Click here and select your location from the dropdown list.
5. Click here to continue.

Note: *If you have already used online help before, this step does not appear and you can move on to the next screen.*

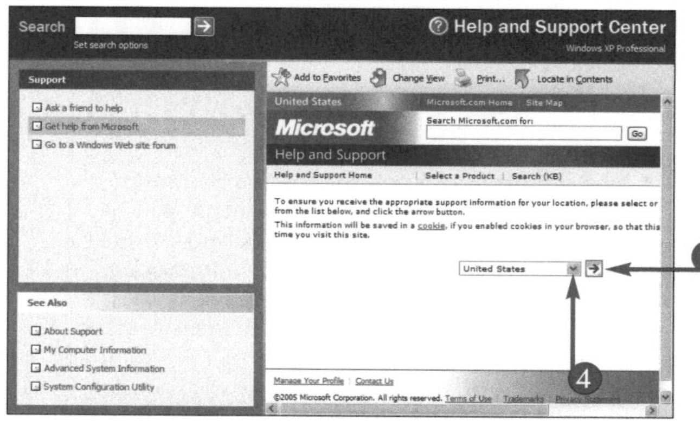

The next screen displays a list of Microsoft products for which support is offered.

This screen contains a large amount of information. Maximize the window by clicking the Maximize button to see as much of it at one time as possible.

6. Click Select a Product.

If I have a friend or colleague who I know can help me with my problem, can they help me online?

▼ Yes, if your friend or colleague uses Windows XP Professional and you are both connected to the Internet, you can take advantage of Remote Assistance to use online chat, have him view your screen, or (with your permission) take over your desktop. Firewalls and protected corporate networks can sometimes make this feature require some additional work on your part. See the instructions for the Remote Assistance feature for more details.

What if I have questions related to Windows XP Service Pack 2?

▼ Windows XP Service Pack 2 has its own dedicated area for support. Microsoft has free e-mail and telephone support for issues caused by SP2. To access this support, click Select a Product as you did in Step 6 and then click Microsoft Windows XP Service Pack 2.

continued

Get Support Online from Microsoft *(Continued)*

When you have reached Microsoft's Help and Support home page, you can select any product and find support for it. Checking online support is also the best way to get the latest information about updates and service packs. Periodically check the Help and Support home page at Microsoft to keep yourself up-to-date on Windows XP.

The Help and Support home page for Windows XP also has a Solutions Center, with how-to articles on the most commonly requested and latest topics, as well as the latest downloads, including security updates. (The best way to make sure you have the most current security updates is to have Automatic Updates turned on using the Security Center. See Chapter 8 for more details.) The Help and Support home page also has links to related newsgroups, where you can discuss issues with other users in a moderated forum.

If the help you need is more specialized, you can also access the Microsoft Support Knowledge Base from the Help and Support home page. This topic is covered in depth in the next section, "Search the Microsoft Support Knowledge Base."

Get Support Online from Microsoft *(continued)*

A list of Microsoft products appears, grouped by category.

7 Scroll down to the Windows category and click the Microsoft Windows XP link.

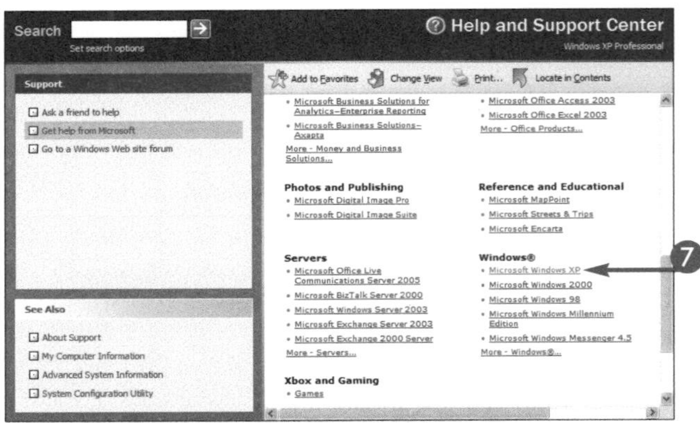

The Windows XP support page appears. The top left portion of the page is a section with the latest news about Windows XP.

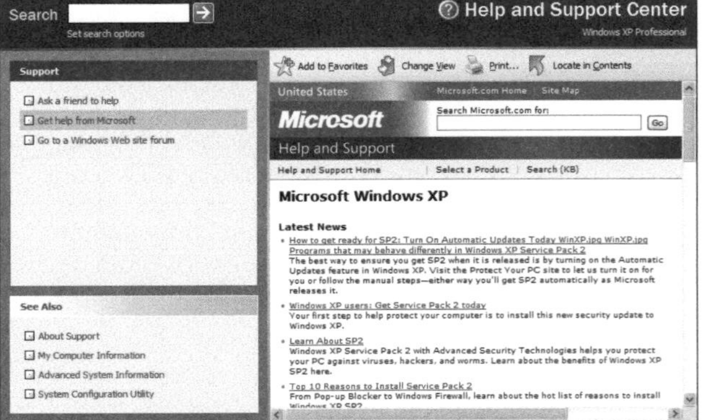

Scroll down to display the Solutions Center section of the page. The Solutions Center has how-to articles grouped in categories, as well as links to the latest downloads along with information about each one.

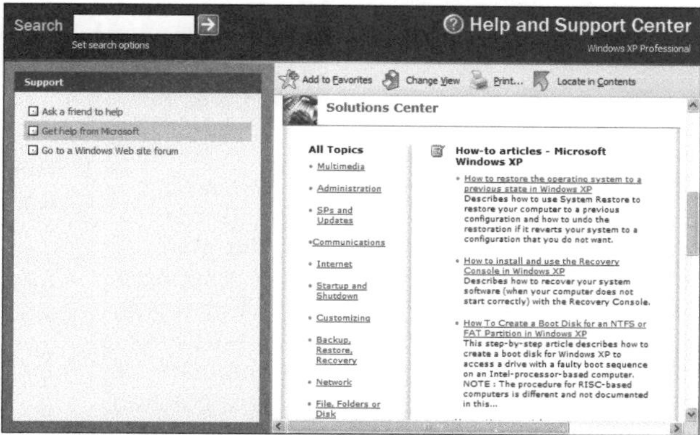

Scroll to the top of the window.

Scroll to the right of the window. Several Support features appear in the right column.

- Search Microsoft's online support database.
- Access interactive support from Microsoft.
- Go to related Microsoft Web sites.

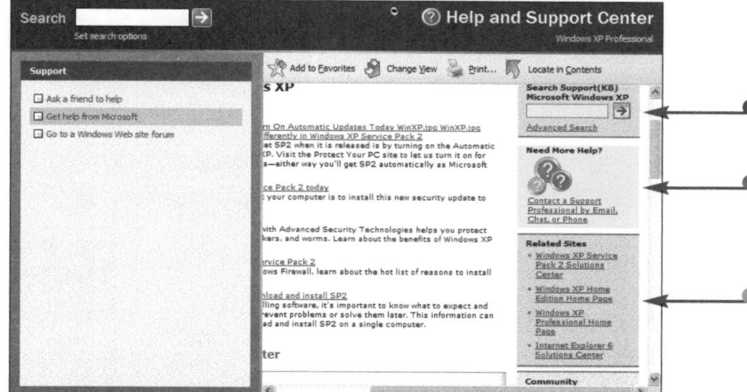

Can I view more support information on the screen all at once instead of scrolling around?

Yes. Click the Options icon (☐) and then click Change Help and Support Center options. Reduce the font size by selecting the Small or Medium option under the Font size used for Help content heading (○ changes to ◉). You can also move your cursor over the border between the left and right panes of the Help and Support Center until the pointer changes from a Select pointer (↖) to a Horizontal Resize pointer (⟷), and then drag the mouse to the left to reduce the size of the left pane and increase the size of the right pane.

How do I view a how-to article?

Scroll to the Solutions Center and then click the topic category from the All Topics column. A list of how-to articles appears for that category, with each article title followed by a brief description of its contents. Click the link to view the table of contents of the article. You can either click a heading in the contents or scroll down and read the article all the way through. Each article has an Article ID number, a date of Last Review, and a Revision number, so that you can see how recently it was created.

Search the Microsoft Support Knowledge Base

If the help you need is more specialized, you can get help efficiently for your problem by searching the Microsoft Support Knowledge Base (KB). This is an extensive, indexed, frequently updated database of support articles from Microsoft. When you have a problem that you suspect is less common (such as issues with your particular hardware or software configuration), this is a good place to start to try to find a solution. KB articles often have practical workarounds as temporary solutions to help customers before updates and fixes are available. They also have detailed instructions for helping to recover from hardware failures and data loss. You can access the Microsoft Support Knowledge Base from the Help and Support home page.

The Advanced Search feature has several useful options to help you refine your search in an intelligent and efficient way. You can efficiently limit the scope of the search to just one product, such as Windows XP (or Windows XP Service Pack 2). If you select a product, you then have the option to perform a Filtered Search (to look for only information about your selected product) or a Weighted Search (weighted towards your product, but also searching other related topics).

Search the Microsoft Support Knowledge Base

1. From the Help and Support Center, click Get support, or find information in Windows XP newsgroups under Ask for assistance.
2. Click Get help from Microsoft under Support.
3. Click Search (KB).

The Advanced Search screen for Search the Support Knowledge Base (KB) appears.

- You can go to a simplified search screen by clicking Basic Search.

4. Click Specify a product or version in the Search Product field.
5. Select a product (such as Microsoft Windows XP) from the product list.

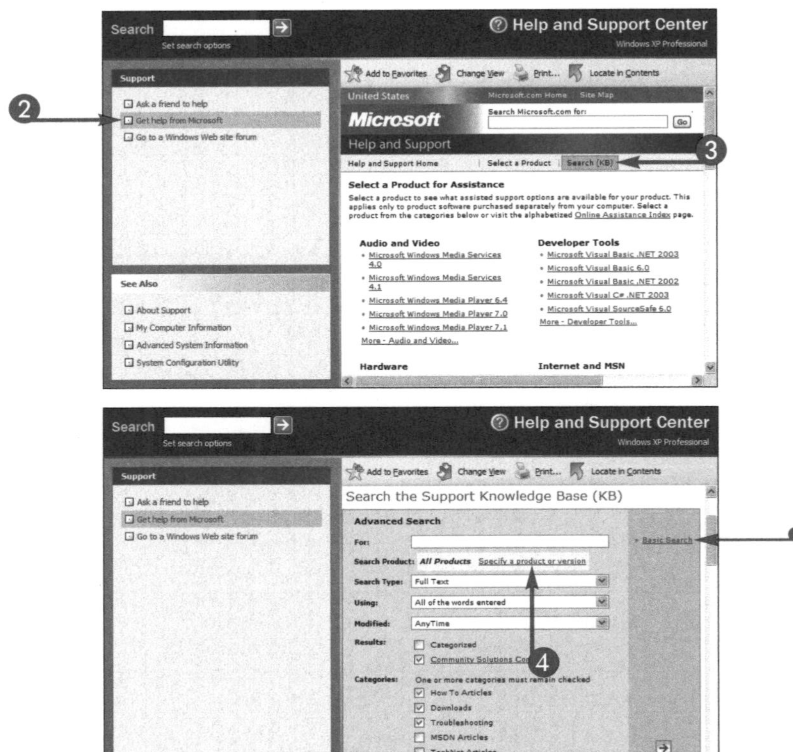

- The product you selected appears.

6 Select Filtered Search to search only articles that mention the product you selected in Step 5.

7 Select Full Text for most searches.

8 Select All of the words entered to search on all of the text you type in Step 10.

9 Use this field if you want to filter your search based on how recently the article was added or modified.

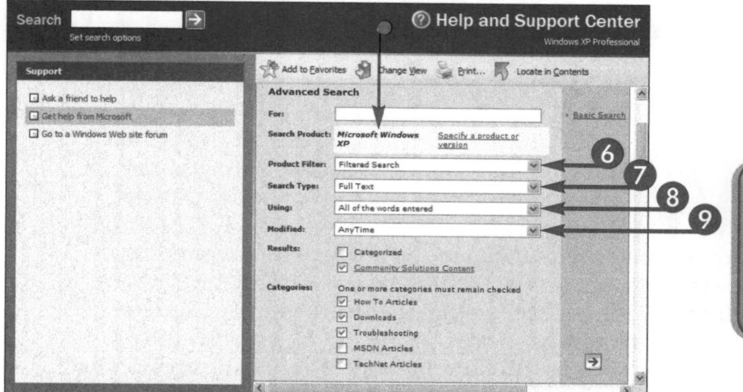

10 Type in key words you want to search for in the KB.

11 Click here to start your search.

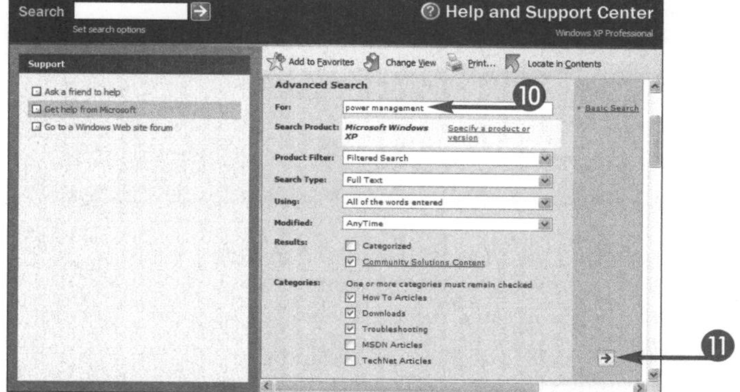

PART II

How do I find a particular KB article quickly if I already know the article ID number?

▼ Select Article ID from the Search Type dropdown list and type the article ID number (six digits) in the For field. Click [→] to search.

I want to narrow my search to just printer problems with SP2. How do I do that?

▼ Type **SP2 AND printer problem** in the For field. Select Boolean (text contains AND/OR) in the Using dropdown list. Click [→] to search.

continued

Search the Microsoft Support Knowledge Base *(Continued)*

When you have launched your search, you can select articles from the Search Results. Articles are displayed with the closest match first. Scroll through the articles, reading the article title and summary to ascertain whether it is what you are looking for. The article's ID is listed in parentheses after the title. Click the title (underlined and in blue at the top of the article) to view the article. Do not worry about losing your place if this turns out not to be the article you need; you can simply click Back (◉) to return to the Search Results page.

When you view the KB article, there is a section at the beginning of each article called On this Page with links that help you navigate to the part of the article that interests you. If the article addresses a specific problem, there are headings such as Symptoms, Cause, and Resolution (or Status if there is as yet no resolution). If the article is purely informational (not problem solving), it has Summary and More Information. To print an article, click Print (🖨).

Search the Microsoft Support Knowledge Base *(continued)*

Note: *You can click Back (◉) if you are not happy with the results and want to refine your search.*

Scroll through the list of articles to find the one you think best suits your needs.

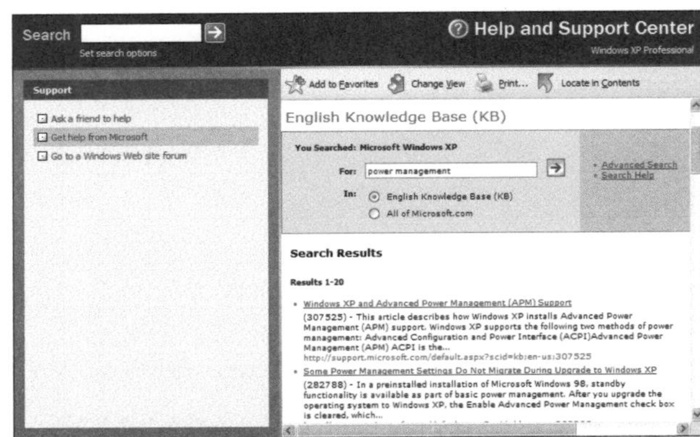

⓬ Click the title to view the article.

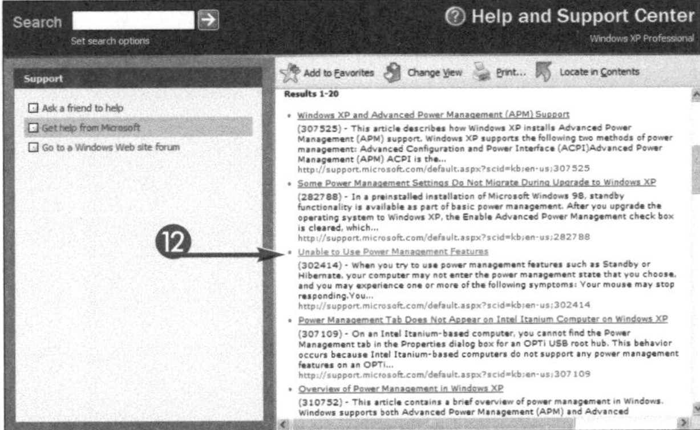

13 Click a link in the On this Page section to quickly navigate through the article.

- The preference number is used by Microsoft and IT support technicians. You can also check to see how recent the information is, or to see if there has been an update or correction to the article.

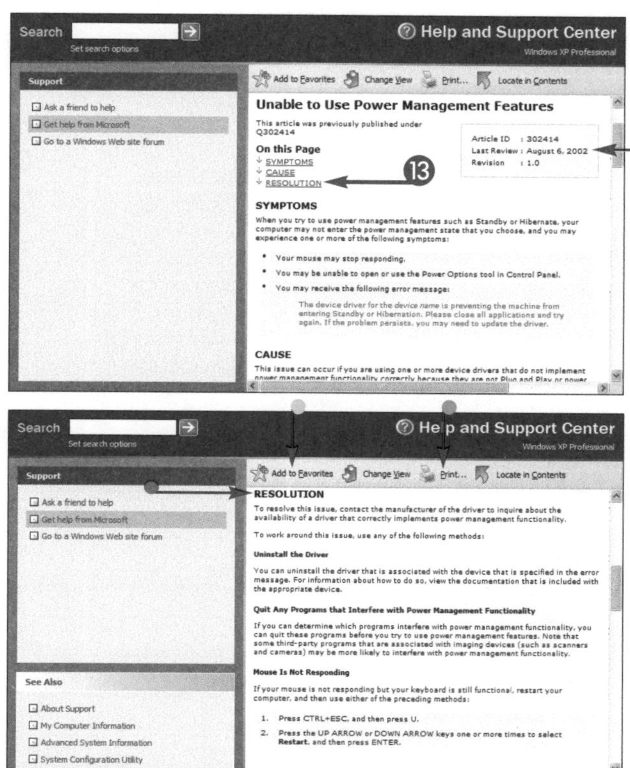

- The link you clicked in Step 13 takes you to the appropriate section of the article.
- You can click here to print the article.
- You can click to add this KB article to your support Favorites list.

What if I want to send this information to someone in e-mail?

Scroll to the right column of the page and find the Page Tools section. Click E-mail this page.

What if I found too few or no KB articles to choose from?

You can click the Back button ( ) and refine your search. To broaden your search, make sure Weighted Search is selected as the Product Filter option. Take out any words that are not relevant.

What if I did not find what I needed in the KB article?

Scroll to the right and select from one of the additional help categories: Need More Help? (for direct interactive help), Related Sites, Community Newsgroups, or Additional Resources.

Adjust Mouse Controls

You can adjust your mouse settings to meet your needs and to fit your work style in Windows XP: You can switch the functions of the left and right mouse buttons (for those who are left handed), adjust the speed of double-clicking to match your personal comfort level, and turn on ClickLock (which lets you drag something without holding down the left mouse button — this can be especially handy if you are trying to perform this operation with a touchpad on a laptop computer).

You can also adjust the mouse pointer. You can adjust the speed of the pointer, enhance its precision, and use the Snap To feature to have the pointer automatically move to the default button in a dialog box. You can also change settings related to the pointer's visibility: You can display pointer trails that leave a trace of the path the pointer has traveled across the desktop so that it is easier to follow (especially useful on large monitors working with graphics or large spreadsheets), make the pointer appear or disappear while you are typing, and show the pointer location when you press the Ctrl key.

Adjust Mouse Controls

1. From the Control Panel, click Printers and Other Hardware.

Note: *You can reach the Control Panel by clicking Start on the desktop and then clicking Control Panel.*

- If your Control Panel appears different and shows Switch to Category View here instead of Classic View, click Switch to Category View to follow these steps.

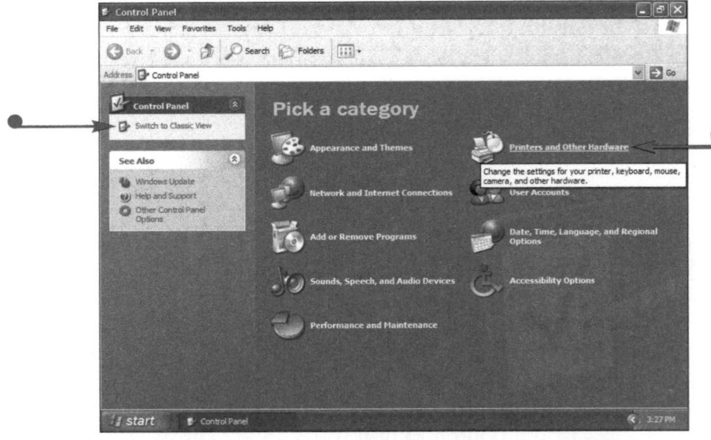

2. Click Mouse.

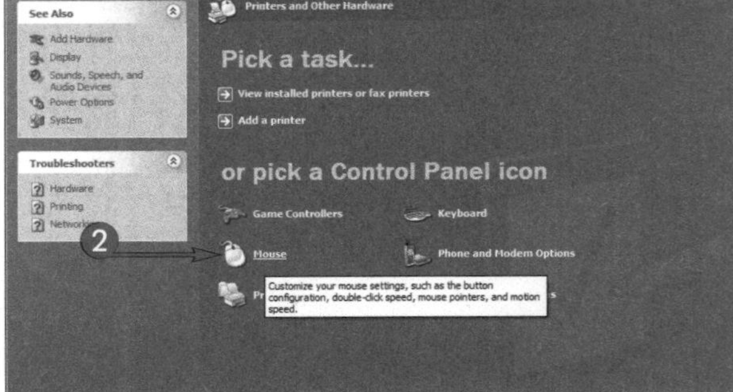

The Mouse Properties dialog box appears.

Note: *If you have a touchpad, you may see an extra tab in this dialog box. See "Disable (or Enable) Touchpads" for more.*

3 Click here to swap the order of the mouse buttons if you are left handed.

4 Drag the slider and then double-click the folder icon to adjust the double-clicking speed.

5 Click here to enable ClickLock.

- Click the Wheel tab to adjust the speed of your mouse wheel.

6 Click the Pointer Options tab.

The Pointer Options screen appears.

7 Adjust the speed of the pointer relative to mouse movements here.

8 Click here to enable the Snap To feature.

9 Click here to display pointer trails. You can adjust the speed of the pointer trails with the slider control.

10 Click here to show the location of the pointer when you press the Ctrl key.

11 Click OK to save your changes.

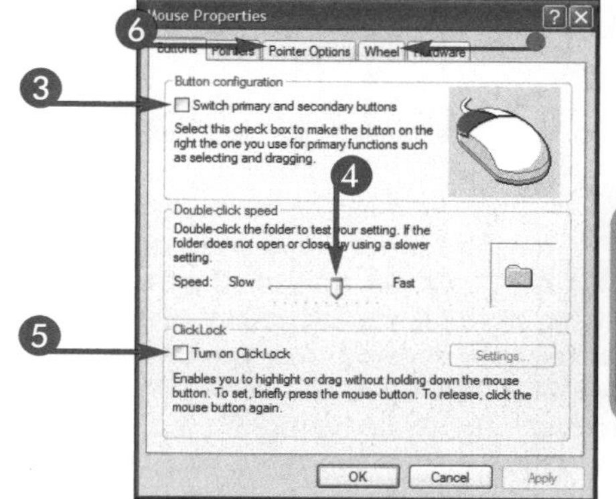

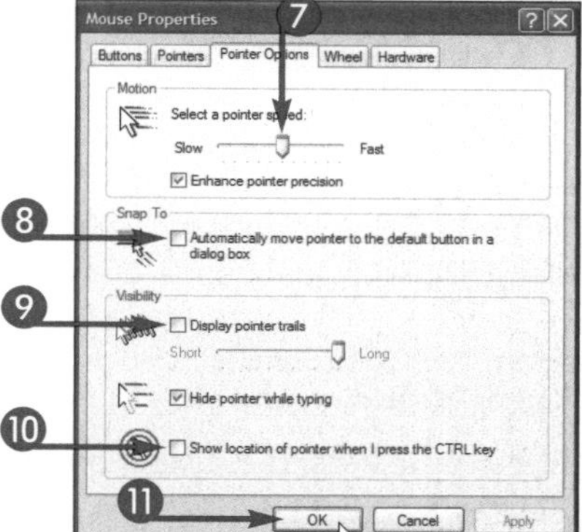

I have trouble finding the pointer on the screen. How can I make it more visible when it is not moving?

▼ Pointers can be hard to see, especially on large monitors. From the Pointer Options tab of the Mouse Properties dialog box, click the Show location of pointer when I press the Ctrl key option (☐ changes to ☑). With this option enabled, an animated feature zeroes in on your pointer when you press the Ctrl key.

My mouse often does not react when I double-click it. How do I get the mouse to recognize my double-click?

▼ Everyone double-clicks at a different speed. Fortunately, this setting can be easily adjusted. From the Buttons tab of the Mouse Properties dialog box, move the slider to a slower or faster setting depending on your needs. Then click the sample folder (📁) to the right of the slider to see if it opens when you double-click. Keep adjusting the slider until the rate is just the way you like it.

Disable (or Enable) Touchpads

If you have a laptop computer with a touchpad, you may find times when you want to disable the touchpad. Because touchpads are positioned directly in front of the keyboard, many users find that they are inadvertently moving their pointer or clicking buttons without intending to by accidentally hitting their wrist on the touchpad while typing. If you have a mouse attached to your computer, or choose to use only keyboard commands, you can disable the touchpad in Windows XP from the Control Panel.

Because touchpads vary from manufacturer to manufacturer, your screen may look slightly different from the one shown in this book. Some touchpads also have a physical on/off button located near the touchpad. Consult your laptop computer's manual if you are not sure about whether there is a physical on/off button.

Disable (or Enable) Touchpads

1. From the Control Panel, click Printers and Other Hardware, and then Mouse.

   The Mouse Properties dialog box appears.

Note: *For the laptop computer used in this example there is an additional tab, Advanced Features. Yours may have a different name.*

2. Click the Advanced Features tab.

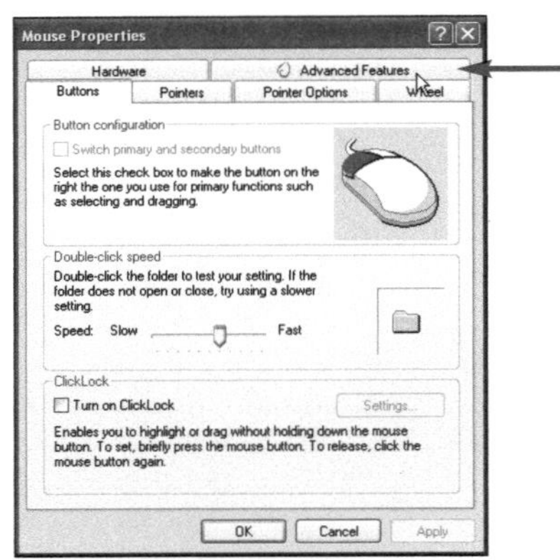

   The Advanced Features settings appear.

3. Click Disable to deactivate the touchpad (or Enable to activate it).

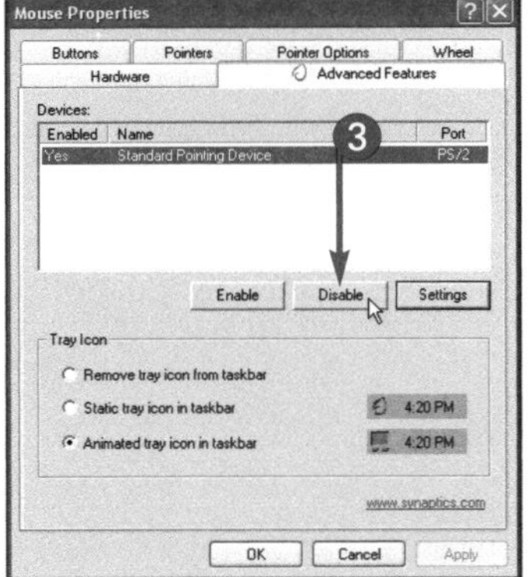

If you clicked Disable, you may be warned that you are disabling your touchpad.

4 Click OK.

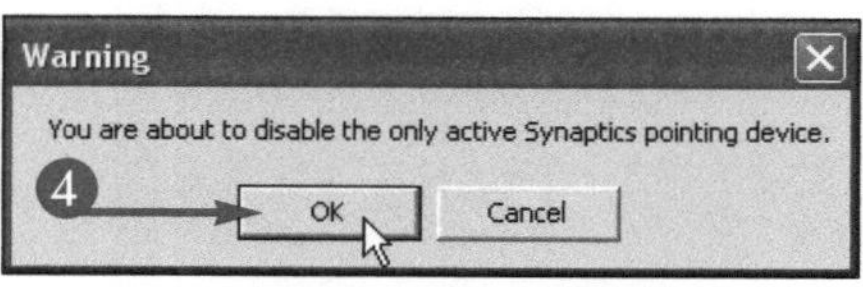

The touchpad is now disabled.

5 Click OK to close the dialog box.

Or, if you have no other pointing device attached to your computer, use the Tab key to select OK and press Enter.

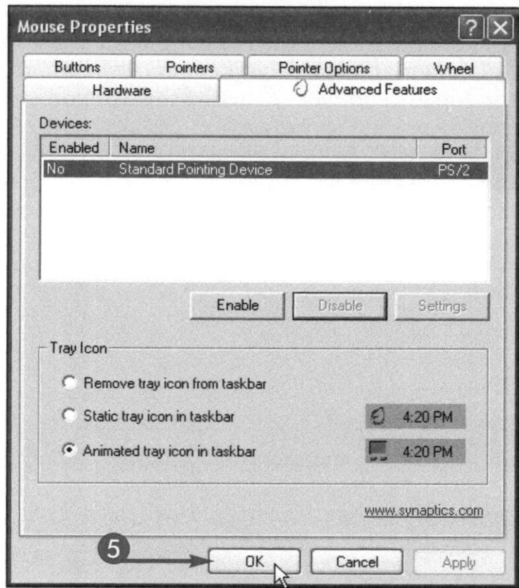

What if I do not have another pointing device installed? How do I enable my touchpad without a mouse attached to my laptop?

- Press the Windows key on your keyboard to access the Start menu. Next, use the up-arrow key to select Control Panel and press Enter. Use the Tab and arrow keys to move the pointer until Printers and Other Hardware is selected and press Enter. Use the Tab and arrow keys to select Mouse and press Enter. The Mouse Properties dialog box appears. Use the Tab key to move to the tabs section of the dialog box and then use the arrow keys to select the appropriate tab (Advanced Features on the laptop used for this example). Use the Tab key until Enable is highlighted and press Enter. You now have access to your touchpad again.

I switch my touchpad on and off frequently. Is there a quicker way to do this?

- That depends on your laptop. Many laptops have a physical button located near the touchpad that you can press to turn it on and off. Others have a tray icon option for the Windows XP taskbar that allows you to quickly access the touchpad settings by clicking the touchpad icon on the taskbar and then selecting Properties or some similarly named menu option. This takes you directly to the appropriate tab in the Mouse Properties dialog box where you can enable or disable the touchpad whenever you need to.

Save Time with the Right Mouse Button

You can save time in your work with Windows XP simply by taking advantage of the secondary mouse button. This is usually the right mouse button (unless you have switched the position of the two buttons — see the earlier section "Adjust Mouse Controls" for more details). By right-clicking (if you have switched the buttons, substitute left-click in all of these instructions), you access the short list of most likely operations in any given context in Windows XP. Make a habit of right-clicking any icons or desktop areas to see whether the task you want to perform is in the list that pops up when you right-click.

Right-clicking the desktop brings up options to arrange the icons, create a new file, paste a file or shortcut, or change the Display properties. Right-clicking the toolbar allows you to change settings related to the toolbar, right-clicking the Recycle Bin gives you a quick way to empty or open the Recycle Bin, and so on. Take a moment to right-click the various desktop elements; you will see many timesaving shortcuts. (Do not worry about experimenting with right-clicking — it always brings up a menu; it never executes a command.)

Save Time with the Right Mouse Button

Note: *This is just one example of how using the right mouse button can save time. You could also accomplish this task via the Control Panel, but it would take more steps.*

1. Right-click an unoccupied area of the desktop.

   A menu appears with several frequently used options.

   - Move your mouse pointer over Arrange Icons By.

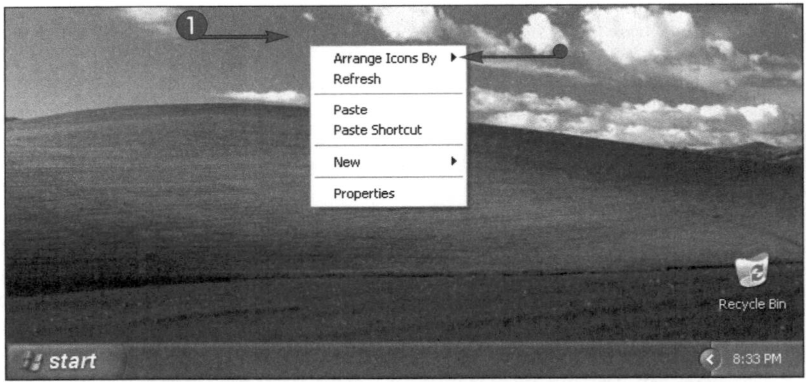

A submenu appears with tasks relating to ordering icons on your desktop.

- Move the mouse pointer so that New is selected.

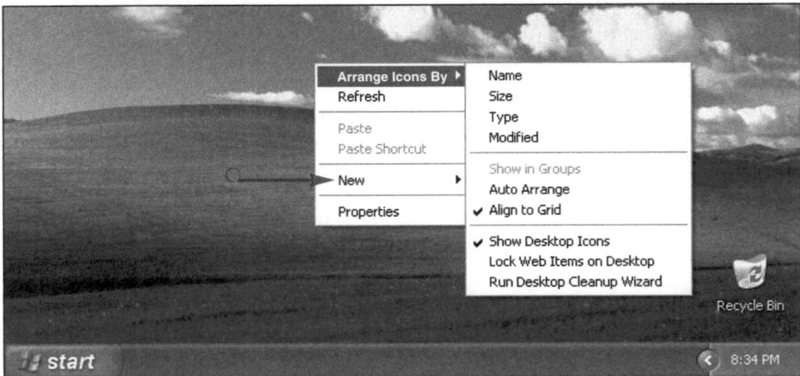

A submenu appears with a choice of applications from which you may create a new file, as well as options to create a new folder or shortcut.

2. Scroll down the menu and click Properties.

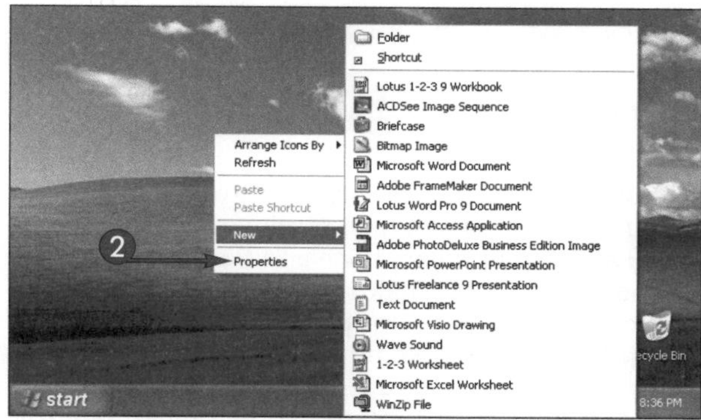

The Display Properties dialog box appears.

3. Click here and then select a theme.

- A preview of what your desktop would look like if you changed it to look like an earlier Windows version, for example, appears in the Sample window.

4. Click OK to save your theme change.

Note: *You have now changed your theme in just four steps, where changing it via the Control Panel would have taken seven steps.*

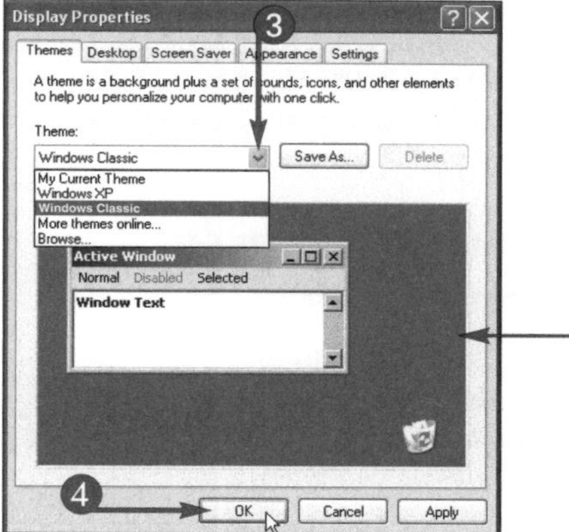

Is there a quick way to change my Internet settings?

▼ Yes. Right-click the Internet Explorer icon on the desktop and click Properties from the menu that appears to change your Internet settings.

Is there a quick way to change my date and time settings?

▼ Yes. Right-click the time in the lower-right corner of the taskbar and click Adjust Date/Time from the menu that appears.

If I have a lot of application windows open, is there a quick way to minimize them all and show me just the desktop?

▼ Yes. Right-click the taskbar and click Show the Desktop. All of your open windows are minimized to buttons on the taskbar, and your desktop is clear.

Make Use of Speech Recognition

If you have speech recognition software installed on your computer and a high-quality microphone, you can adjust your microphone and train your speech recognition software in Windows XP. Starting with Office XP, Microsoft began shipping speech recognition capabilities such as voice commands and dictation with its Office product suite. (Text to speech is covered in the section "Make Use of Text to Speech.") You may also have specialized speech recognition software. If your computer has Office XP (or later) or other speech-recognition software, use the related tools in the Windows XP Control Panel to make the best use of speech recognition capabilities. After you have set up speech recognition, you can also use it with Windows XP accessories such as Notepad.

For speech recognition to function reliably, it is critical that you have a quiet work environment and a good (preferably headset) microphone, that you take the time to adjust your microphone sound levels, and that you train the speech engine to recognize your personal speech profile. While dictation may never be perfect, using voice commands can work surprisingly well if you take the time to adjust the settings and train your computer to understand you.

Make Use of Speech Recognition

Note: *Before you get started, make sure that your work environment is quiet and that your microphone is attached, and make sure your sound is on (not muted).*

1. Click Sounds, Speech, and Audio Devices from the Control Panel.

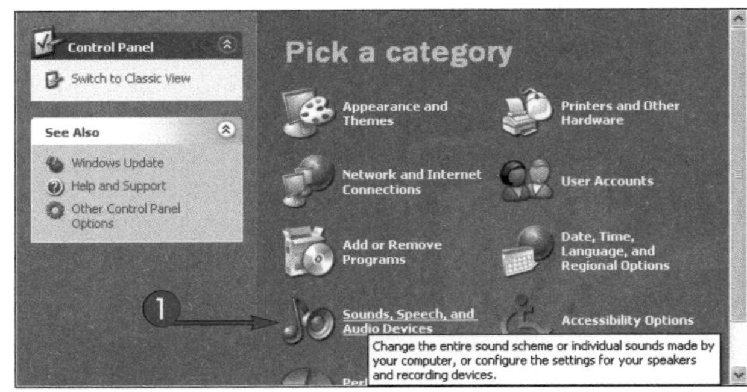

2. Click Speech.

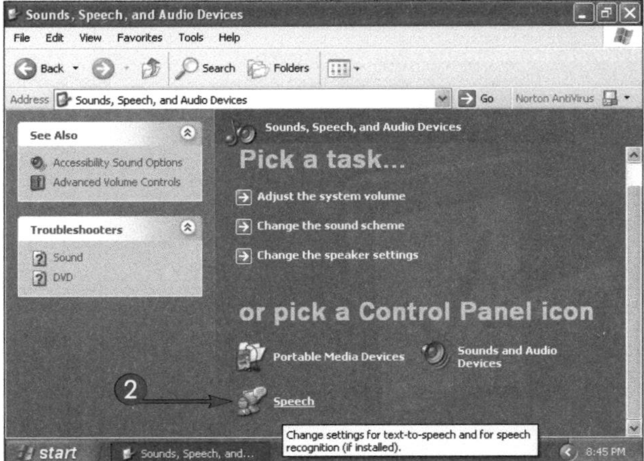

3. In the Speech Properties dialog box, click here and select a language.
4. Click here and select a profile if more than one person uses the computer.
5. Click Settings to adjust settings such as speed versus accuracy.
6. Click Train Profile to improve speech recognition with samples of your voice.
7. Click Audio Input to select an input channel if you have more than one, or to adjust recording volume manually.
8. Click Configure Microphone.

The Microphone Wizard begins. Follow the step-by-step instructions in the wizard to have Windows XP adjust your microphone for optimal performance by sampling your voice.

9. Click Next to advance to the next page within the wizard.

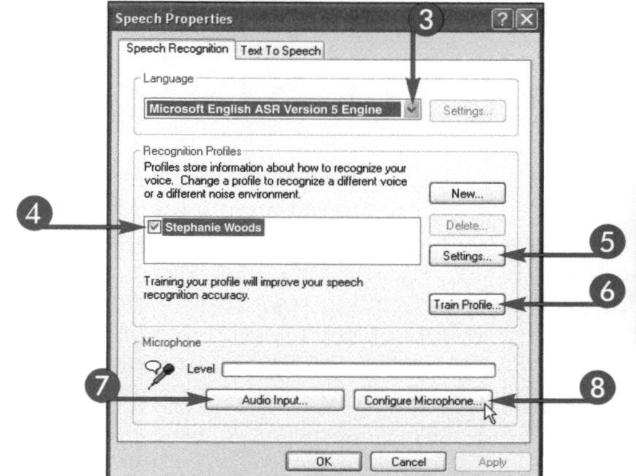

Microphone Wizard - Welcome
Welcome to the Microphone Wizard!
This wizard helps you test your microphone for use with speech recognition.
Before you begin, make sure that your microphone and speakers are properly connected to your computer. Refer to your microphone and speaker instructions for more information.
If you are using a headset microphone, adjust the headset microphone as shown. Position the microphone so that it is about an inch from the side of your mouth and so that you are not breathing directly into it.
To continue, click Next.
< Back
Next >
Cancel

How do I get the best performance out of my speech recognition?

- Train your profile by reading the samples provided. Each takes some time (about 10 to 15 minutes), although you may pause during any training session and take a break. The more samples the software has to work with, the greater the accuracy of the speech recognition software.

  Try to speak clearly and at an even volume level. Make sure that you are at the right distance from your microphone. The Microphone Wizard and profile training screens give other tips as you go along. When you are using voice commands or dictation, you also get text balloon cues such as "What was that?" or "Too loud" to help you along the way.

How can I improve the accuracy of the dictation?

- If you are noticing that the dictation is keeping up with your speed of talking but frequently making incorrect word choices (such as "the felt second" instead of "the Phelps account"), go to the Speech Recognition tab of the Speech Properties dialog box and click Settings. In the Accuracy vs. Recognition Response Time section, move the slider closer to High/Slow and away from Low/Fast.

Make Use of Text to Speech

If you have text to speech software installed on your computer, you can select a computerized voice and adjust your speaker volume and talk speed settings in Windows XP. Starting with Office XP, Microsoft began shipping text to speech and speech recognition capabilities with its Office product suite. (Speech recognition is covered in the section "Make Use of Speech Recognition.") You may also have specialized text to speech software. If your computer has Office XP (or later) or other text to speech software, use the related tools in the Windows XP Control Panel to adjust text to speech capabilities.

For optimal text to speech, make sure you have a good set of headphones or external speakers and a sound environment that allows you to hear the computerized voice clearly. From the Text To Speech tab in the Speech Properties dialog box, you can select a preferred voice (the number of voices varies based on what speech-enabled software is installed on your computer), usually allowing you to choose between a male and female voice. Computerized text to speech works quite well for certain applications, such as reading documents and e-mail.

Make Use of Text to Speech

Note: *Before you get started, make sure that your work environment is quiet, your headphones or speakers are attached, and your sound is on (not muted).*

1. Click Sounds, Speech, and Audio Devices from the Control Panel.

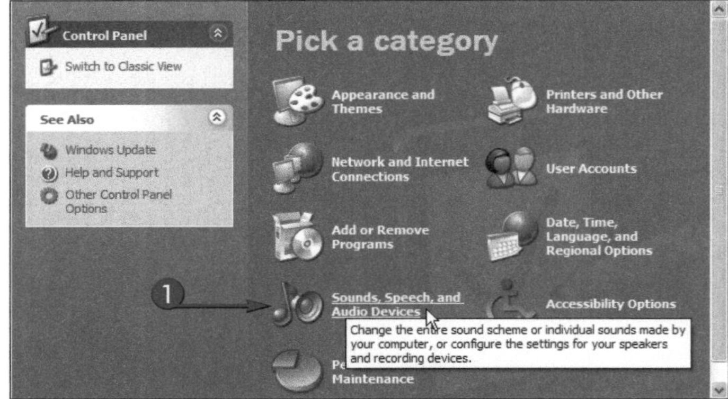

2. Click Speech.

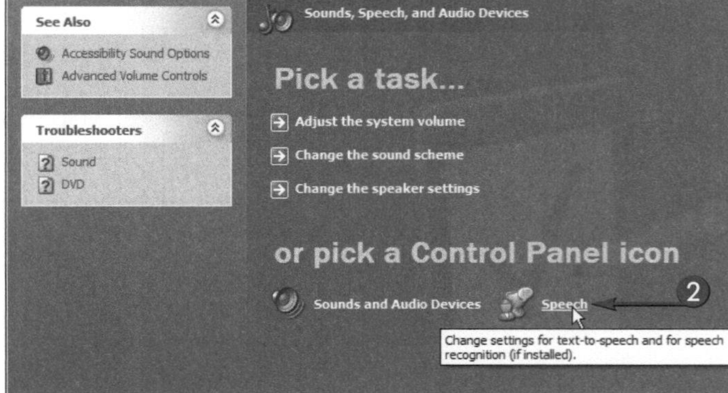

3 Click the Text To Speech tab (if not already selected).

4 Click here and select a voice in the Voice selection list.

5 Click Preview Voice to hear a sample of the voice you chose.

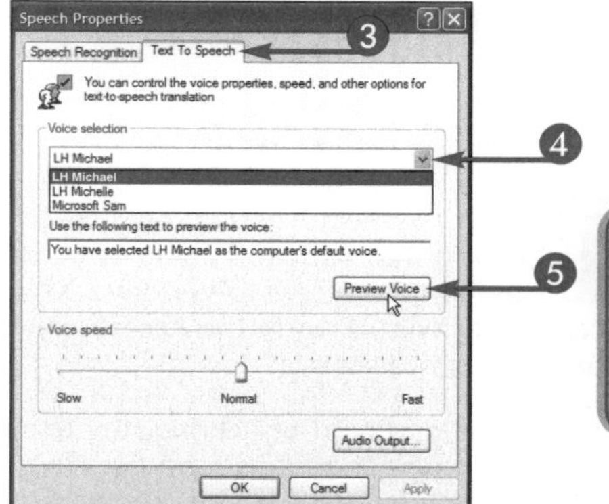

The computerized voice you selected says the sample sentence, highlighting each word as it is said.

6 Move the slider to quicken or slow the speed of speech. (You can click Preview Voice again to hear the effect.)

- Click Audio Output to change audio output devices or adjust volume.

7 Click OK to save the voice sample.

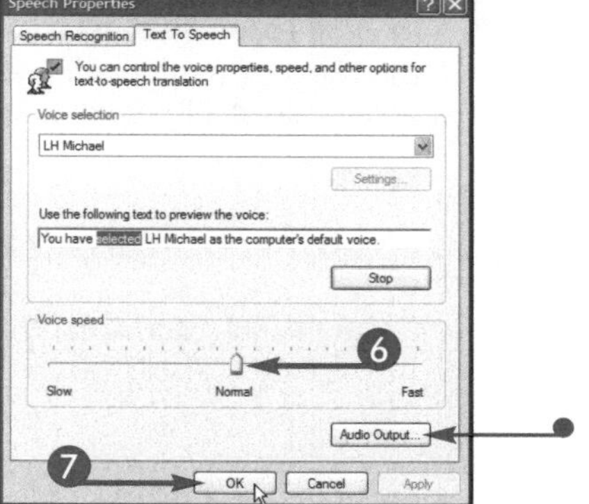

I am having difficulty understanding the computerized voice. What can I do?

Here are several things you can try: On the Text To Speech tab of the Speech Properties dialog box of the Control Panel, try moving the slider to slow the voice speed. Click Audio Output to adjust the volume to a higher level. Switch from external computer speakers to headphones.

When I try to use text to speech in Microsoft Word, I get prompted to adjust my microphone. Why is this necessary?

With some software, you may need to set up Speech Recognition first before you can get text to speech to work. This is because the speech capabilities are integrated together (in Microsoft Office for example). See the section "Make Use of Speech Recognition" to see how to enable this capability.

Activate Accessibility Features

If you or someone you know is deaf, hard-of-hearing, blind, or has impaired vision or limited mobility, you can improve access to Windows XP using the Accessibility Wizard to set the Accessibility Options, reached from the Control Panel.

For the deaf and hard-of-hearing, the ShowSounds feature directs programs that use sound cues to give visual cues such as displayed text or icons. SoundSentry gives visual warnings with blinking and flashing to take the place of sounds intended to get your attention.

For the blind, the Narrator (currently only supported in the English version of Windows XP) reads aloud text elements on the screen in Windows, Notepad, Wordpad, and Internet Explorer. For the sight-impaired, the Magnifier is provided to enlarge the active area of the screen, and options exist to increase the size of screen fonts and provide higher contrast display.

For those with impaired mobility, FilterKeys, MouseKeys, On-Screen Keyboard, SerialKeys, and StickyKeys allow for easier user input.

These features were designed to provide basic accessibility to the largest amount of users. Those with special needs can visit www.microsoft.com/enable for more tools and information.

Activate Accessibility Features

1. From the Control Panel, click Accessibility Options.

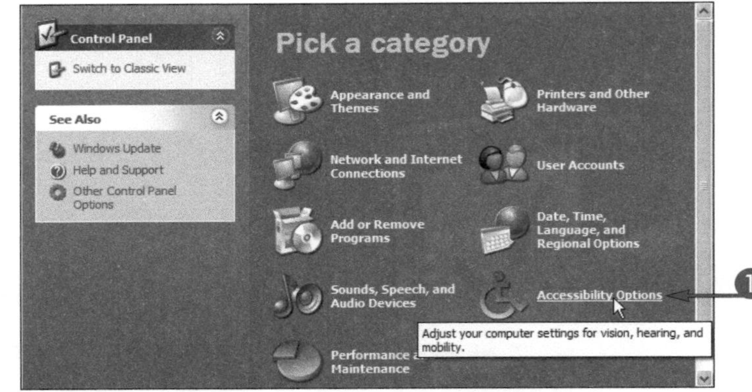

- Click Magnifier to greatly enlarge the currently active area of the screen as if under a magnifying glass.
- Click On-Screen Keyboard to use the mouse on-screen to point to keys as an alternative to typing on the computer's physical keyboard.

2. Click the Configure Windows option to run the Accessibility Wizard to set up Windows XP to meet your accessibility needs.

- Click Accessibility Options to set options in a dialog box (best for those who have already made initial settings).

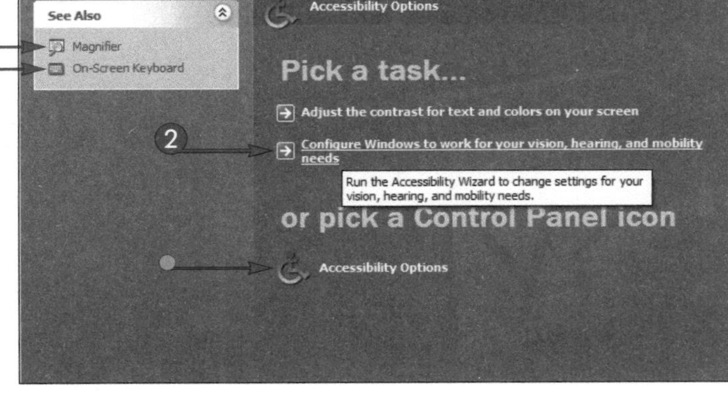

The Accessibility Wizard welcome screen appears.

3 Click Next to start the wizard.

The Accessibility Wizard begins. Follow the instructions and answer the questions to let Windows XP guide you through the setup of those accessibility options that are right for you.

Note: *Some users may need assistance in this initial setup phase.*

4 Click Next to proceed through the wizard's steps.

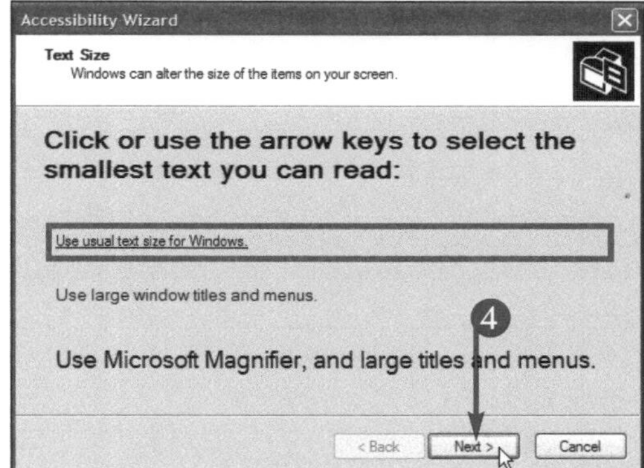

I just want to have visual alerts when there is a system sound. How do I do that?

- From the Control Panel, click Accessibility Options, and then click Accessibility Options again on the next screen. A dialog box appears. Click the Sound tab and click Use SoundSentry (☐ changes to ☑). You can then choose the visual warning and click OK.

Where can I go for more help with accessibility?

- These features were designed to provide basic accessibility to the largest amount of users. Those with special needs can visit www.microsoft.com/enable for more tools and information.

Launch Programs with the Run Command

You can use the Run command to quickly launch a program by typing in the name of the executable file. This feature is particularly convenient if you are running a system administrative or diagnostic tool and do not want to go through several levels of menus to get to the program you need.

Some users who make frequent use of batch files such as network administrators and programmers, or those familiar with Unix and MS-DOS who still prefer a command-line interface for some tasks, will find this feature helpful.

It is not necessary to know the exact filename of the executable to use this feature, however. The Browse button allows you to explore folders graphically as well. The dropdown list also keeps track of the last few entries you have made while using this feature. If you are performing a task often, find your previous entry in the list to save time. The example below shows how to quickly bring up the MS-DOS style command line.

Launch Programs with the Run Command

1. Click Start.
2. Click Run.

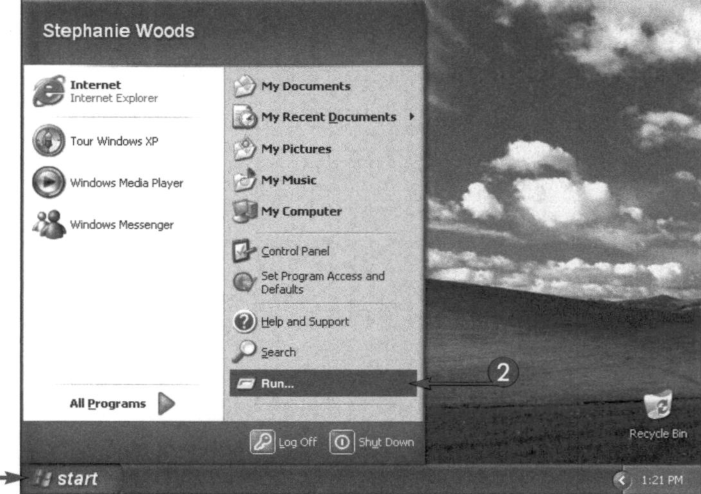

The Run dialog box appears.

3. Type **cmd** in the Open field.
   - Click here to select from a list of previous entries.
4. Click OK.
   - Click Browse to explore folders to find the program or file you want to launch.

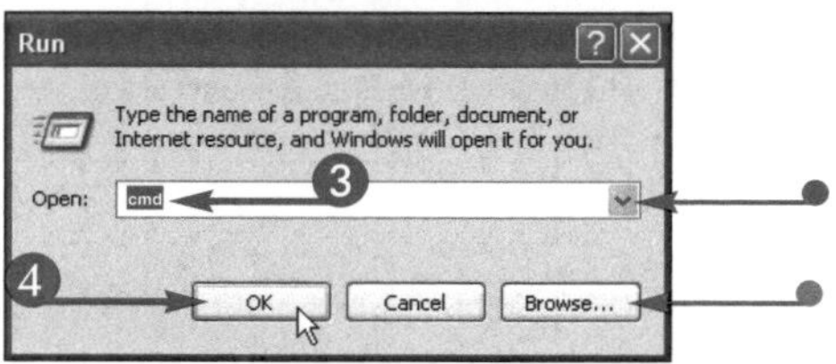

The program launches. In this example, the Windows XP command prompt appears.

5 Type **exit**.

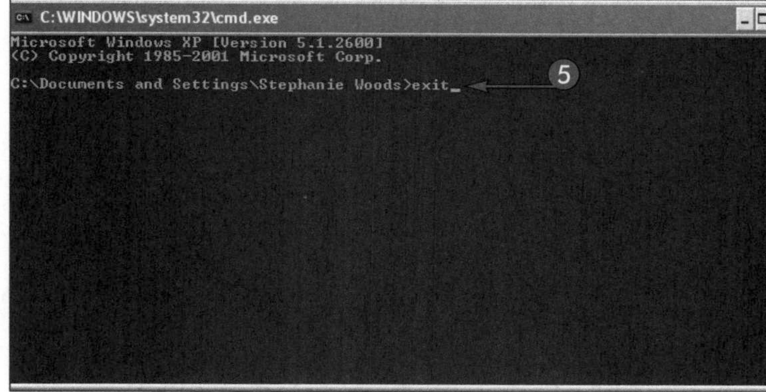

6 Press Enter to close the command prompt.

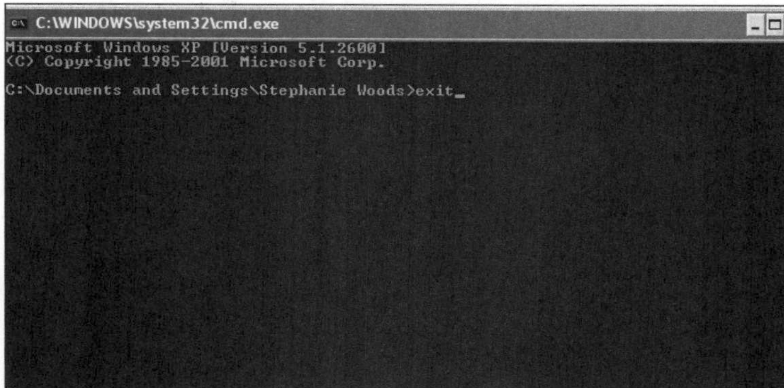

How do I launch a program from somewhere other than my hard drive?

▼ Type the assigned drive letter, followed by a colon and a backslash (:\). For example, to run a program called setup.exe located on a CD-ROM in the CD-ROM drive E, type **e:\setup.exe** in the Open field of the Run command and then click OK.

Can I get to a Web site this way?

▼ Yes. Type the Internet address (URL) in the Open field. For example, to reach the Microsoft home page, type **www.microsoft.com** in the Open field and then click OK.

Change Display Settings

You can adjust your display settings according to your needs in Windows XP. If you have a large monitor, you may have chosen it so that you could view lots of detailed information. If so, you may want a different set of settings than if you chose a large monitor because you wanted everything to be larger and more readable on-screen. The PC's video adapter sends signals to draw the images on your display. The tiny dots that make up the images on your screen are referred to as *pixels.* By selecting the size of these pixels, you can adjust the relative size and sharpness of the images on your screen.

You can also select the number of colors Windows XP displays on your screen. For example, you may want to ensure that you have the most accurate color representation when working with photos, or you may want to choose to display fewer colors in order to gain speed or to play a game designed to use fewer colors. You can make these adjustments from the Settings tab of the Display Properties dialog box.

Change Display Settings

1. Right-click the desktop.

   A menu appears.

2. Click Properties.

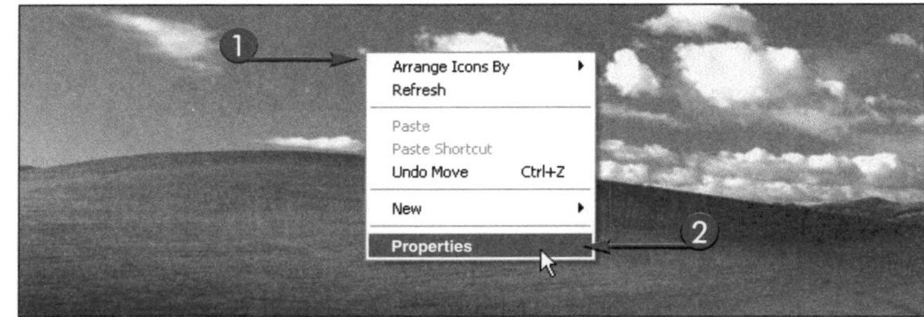

The Display Properties dialog box appears.

3. Click the Settings tab.

   - Display shows which display screen is attached and which video adapter is installed.
   - Click Troubleshoot to have Windows XP help you through a display problem.
   - Click Advanced to make other display adjustments.

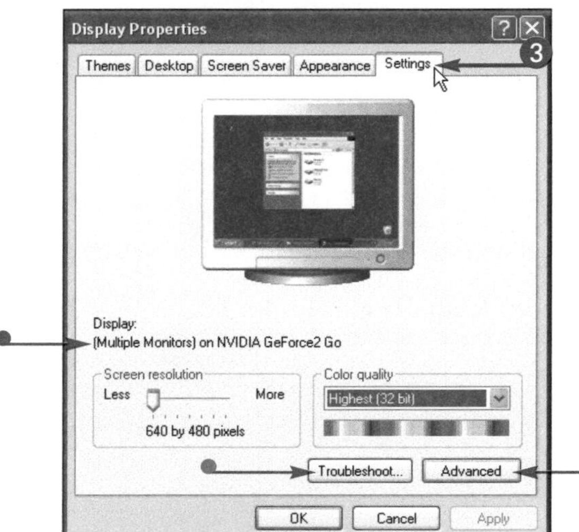

4 Drag the Screen resolution slider from Less towards More.

Screen resolution controls the dimensions of the pixels that are used to draw your display screen.

- In the preview window, you can see the relative size of the desktop elements change.

5 Click here and select another quality, such as Medium (16 bit).

6 Click Apply.

Your screen redraws again with the new settings.

7 Click OK to save your new screen settings.

Note: *To change back to your original settings, change the screen resolution and color quality back to your previous settings and click OK.*

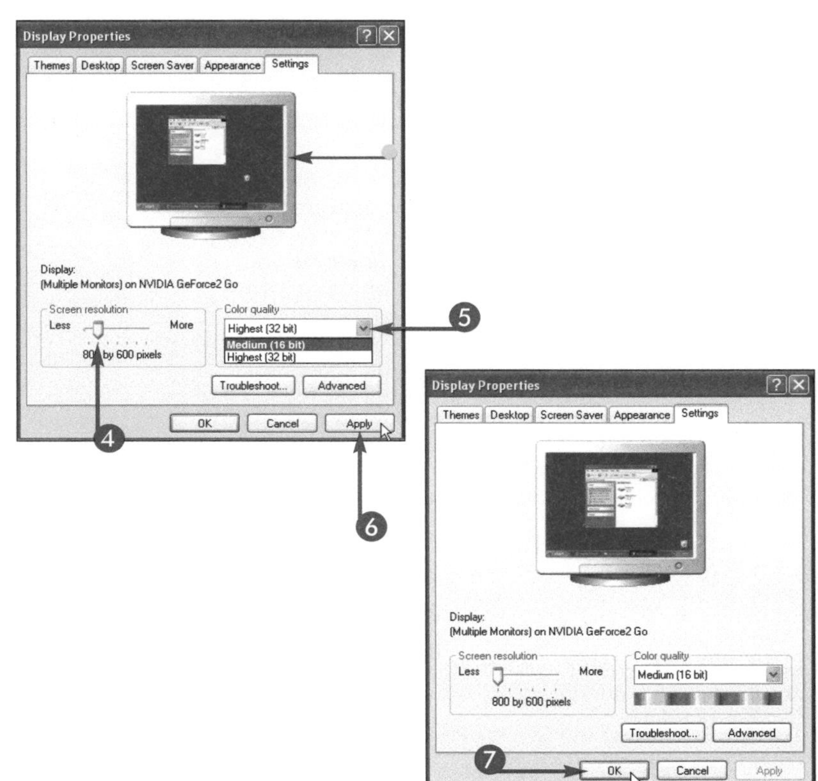

I increased my screen resolution but now I cannot see Start or the taskbar. How do I get them back?

▼ Windows XP allows you to set a higher screen resolution, even if your monitor cannot physically display a screen of those dimensions. A frame within a larger, "virtual" display is what you are actually seeing. To move this frame to the part of the "virtual" display you want to see (such as the taskbar), drag your mouse pointer to the corresponding edge of the display: It scrolls until you see the part of the display that you need.

If you do not like this effect, simply adjust your screen resolution to a setting that entirely fits on your display.

My display is only showing a few colors and the display is of poor resolution. How can I correct this problem?

▼ In the Settings tab of the Display Properties dialog box, make sure that your screen resolution is 800×600 pixels or higher. Next, click the Color quality dropdown list and then click the last selection available; it is always the highest color quality available to display with your video adapter (graphics card) and monitor. If this does not fix the problem or if the highest available color quality is very low (8 bit), you may have a problem with your video adapter or monitor. Click Troubleshoot and follow the procedures to diagnose the problem and find a solution.

Change to 640×480 256-Color Mode

The Settings tab of the Display Properties dialog box allows you to make the most basic adjustments to screen resolution and color quality. There are many other settings you can access from here to fine-tune your display. You can troubleshoot display problems by clicking Troubleshoot, or make other adjustments by clicking Advanced.

Many older applications, especially games, require that you have your screen resolution set to 640×480 and your color quality set to 256-color mode. If you attempt to make these changes to your settings, you find that they are not available to you in the controls.

You can still make these changes by clicking Advanced. This brings up a dialog box corresponding to your display, with several tabs: General, Adapter, Monitor, and Color Management, with fine-tuning adjustments. If your video adapter has additional controls (such as the ability to work with more than one monitor at a time, or switch between two monitors), there may be additional custom tabs to the dialog box. From the Adapter tab, you can access more color and resolution modes by clicking List All Modes.

Change to 640×480 256-Color Mode

1. Right-click the desktop, click Properties, and then click Settings.

   The Settings tab of the Display Properties dialog box appears.

2. Click Advanced to bring up more options.

   The properties dialog box that corresponds to your video monitor and adapter appears.

3. Click Adapter.
   - Click Monitor to select a monitor or make adjustments.
   - Click Troubleshoot to make hardware acceleration adjustments recommended by the Troubleshooter.
   - Click Color Management to select a color profile for your model of monitor.

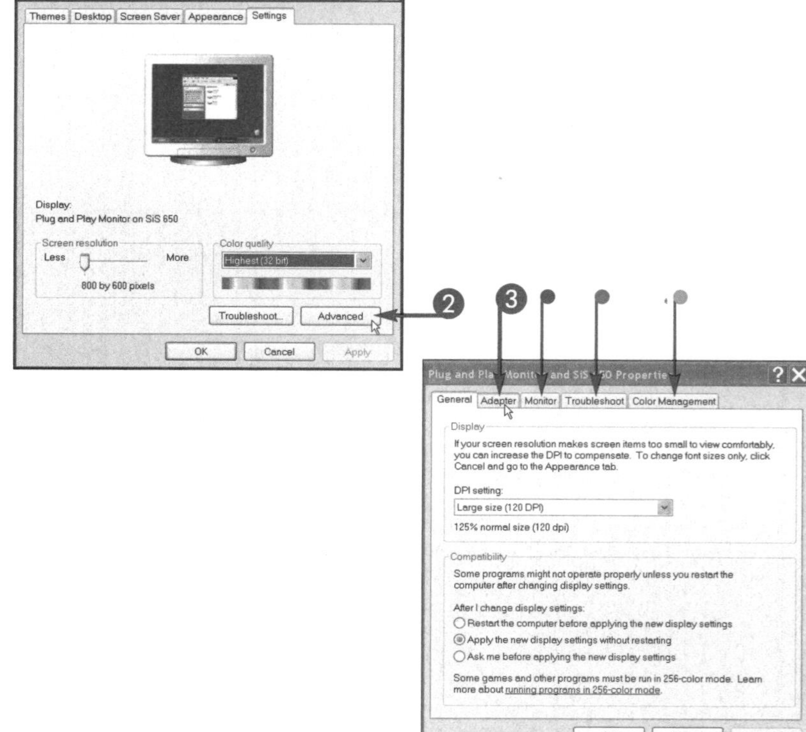

The Adapter tab appears.

4 Click List All Modes to bring up a longer list of possible display modes.

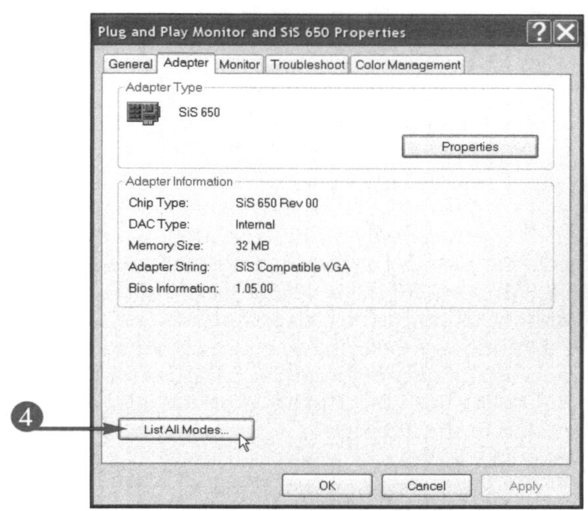

5 Click 640 by 480, 256 Colors, 60 Hertz from the dropdown list.

Note: *If your monitor is set to a refresh rate other than 60 Hertz, scroll through the list and select the setting that contains 640 by 480, 256 Colors but corresponds to your monitor's refresh rate.*

6 Click OK to close the List All Modes dialog box.

7 Click OK to close your monitor's properties dialog box.

8 Click OK to close the Display Properties dialog box.

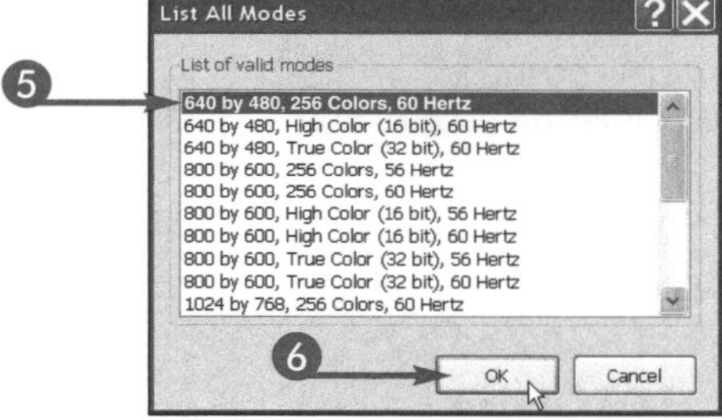

Is there a way to have Windows XP switch to the 256-color whenever I use a certain program and then return to my higher quality mode automatically when done?

▼ If the program that requires 256-color mode is installed on your local hard drive, the answer is yes. From the Start menu, click All Programs and then right-click the program in question and select Properties from the menu that appears. Next, in the properties dialog box, click the Compability tab. From there you click Run in 256 colors (☐ changes to ☑).

Is there a way to do this with 640×480 resolution as well?

▼ Yes. Again, this only works if the program is installed on your local hard drive. If it is, from the Start menu, click All Programs and then right-click the program in question and select Properties from the menu that appears. Next, in the properties dialog box, click the Compability tab. This time, click Run in 640×480 screen resolution (☐ changes to ☑).

Choose Windows Themes

Windows *themes* are a collection of graphic elements and sounds that allow you to customize your desktop around a central subject. You can also change settings and create your own theme. Windows XP has a default theme and a Windows 98 or Windows 2000 theme called Windows Classic. If you have a Windows XP Plus pack, you received additional themes. You can learn about Plus packs by selecting More themes online from the Themes dropdown list while connected to the Internet.

You can select a theme, change icons, sounds, and so on, and then click Save As and give your theme a new name. In this way you can have several themes (one for work and one for play) and name them accordingly. You can view themes in the sample window and then switch back to your current theme by clicking My Current Theme, or back to the default Windows XP theme. If, after sampling different themes, you decide to change yours, when you click OK your desktop fades to gray and Windows XP displays a Please Wait pop-up window for several seconds. This is normal; Windows XP is making changes and redrawing your screen.

Choose Windows Themes

1. Right-click the desktop.

   A menu appears.

2. Click Properties.

The Themes tab of the Display Properties dialog box appears.

- If you want to be able to save your current theme and revert to it later, be sure to click Save As and give your current theme a name so that you can quickly return to it later.

3. Click here and select a theme in the Theme dropdown list (Windows Classic in this example).

- Click Delete to delete a selected theme.

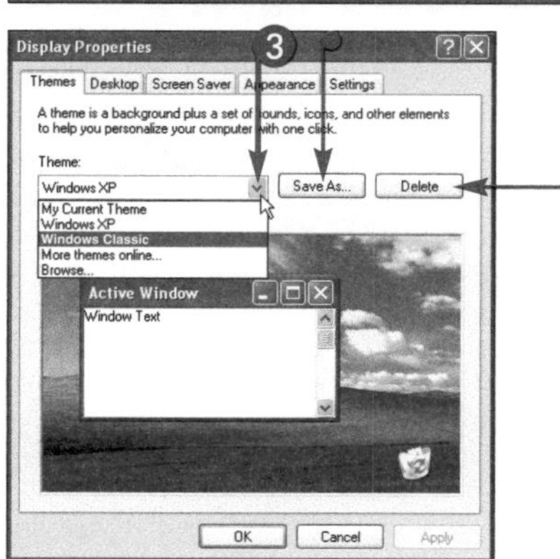

- The selected theme appears in the Sample window.

4 Click OK to change the theme and close the dialog box.

- Click Apply to change the theme but keep the Themes tab of the Display Properties dialog box open.

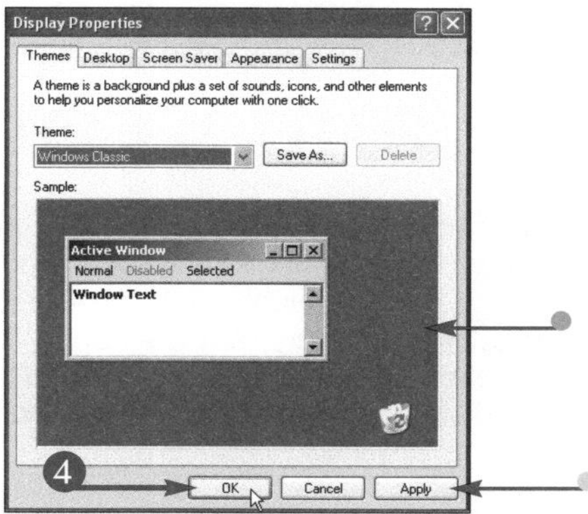

The new theme is now installed.

5 Click Start to view the changes in appearance of the new theme to the Start menu.

6 Press Esc to exit the Start menu.

Note: *To return to your previous theme, follow the same steps and choose your previous theme from the list.*

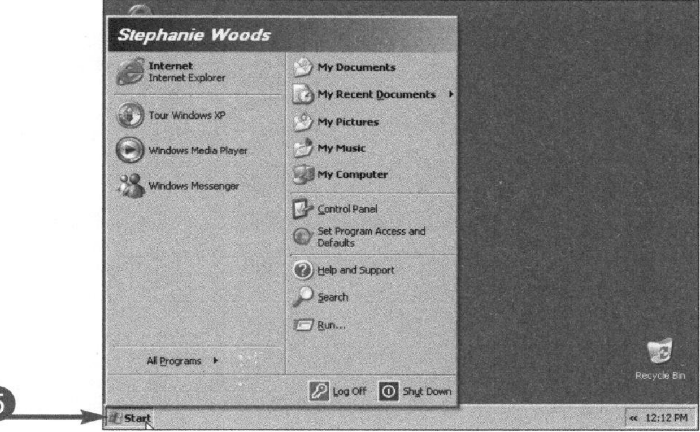

Do I have to keep all the same icons and other settings of the theme I select?

▼ No. You can make any modifications to individual desktop settings that you want. The theme then appears in the Theme dropdown list with the theme name followed by *(Modified)*, indicating that you have made changes to the theme.

Do the changes I make affect other users of this PC?

▼ No, each user can have their own theme selection. When you log on as a new user, that new user's theme appears in Windows XP.

Switch to Large Windows Fonts and Icons

You can use larger fonts and enlarge the icons in Windows XP. This is especially useful if you are using a large monitor with a high screen resolution. You may be able to fit everything onto the display, but the text and icons appear relatively small and difficult to read in such a situation. Changing these settings is also useful if your eyesight requires larger text and icons to work with Windows XP comfortably.

Making these changes is most readily accomplished through the Appearance tab of the Display Properties dialog box. From here you can make changes not only to the size of the fonts, but you can also change the style of windows and buttons (choosing between Windows XP or Windows Classic), and choose the Windows XP color scheme. Clicking Effects takes you to a dialog box that controls the size of icons. It also allows you to control how menus appear on the screen, how font edges are smoothed (Standard or ClearType), whether to show a window's contents while dragging it, and whether to hide or display underlined letters for keyboard navigation.

Switch to Large Windows Fonts and Icons

1. Right-click the desktop and click Properties from the menu that appears to bring up the Display Properties dialog box.
2. Click Appearance.

   The Appearance tab appears.

   - Click here to choose between Windows XP and Classic window and button styles.
   - Click here to select a color scheme: Blue (default), Olive Green, or Silver.
3. Click here and select Large Fonts.

   The preview window changes to show what windows will look like with larger fonts.
4. Click Effects.

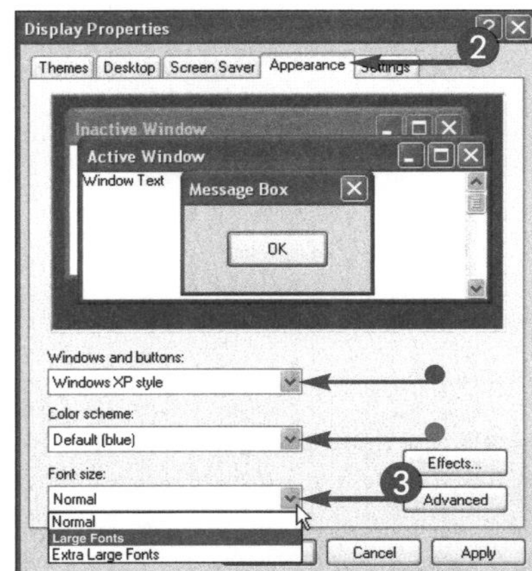

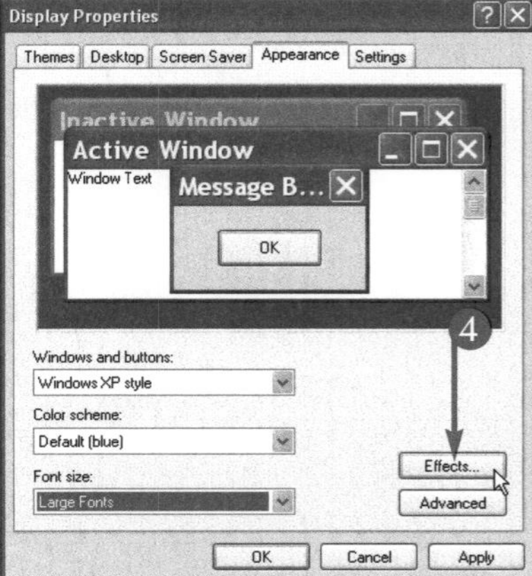

The Effects dialog box appears.

- Click here to choose between a Fade or a Scroll effect.

5 Click here to use large icons on your desktop.

6 Click OK to close the Effects dialog box.

7 Click OK to close the Display Properties dialog box.

- The desktop now displays larger icons and text. Note the increased font size of "start".

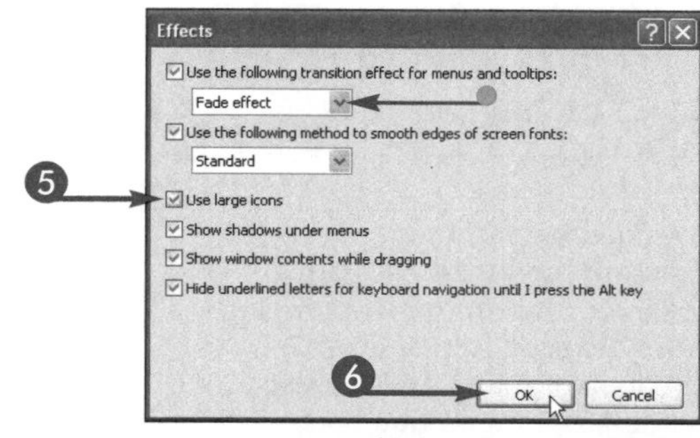

Can I make the fonts display even larger?

▼ Yes. In the Font size dropdown list, you can choose between Normal (the default size), Large Fonts, and Extra Large Fonts. Bear in mind that using extra large fonts often means that only part of a list of menu options appears on the screen, and you may need to scroll down to view all the options in a menu in such a case.

It feels like scrolling or fading menus slows down my work. Can I turn off the menu transition effects?

▼ Yes. Click Effects on the Appearance tab of the Display Properties dialog box. Next, clear the Use the following transition effect for menus and tooltips option (☑ changes to ☐). No transition effect will be used when displaying menus, and your PC will display menus more rapidly.

Change the Look of Windows and Menus

You can make custom refinements to the appearance of windows and menus by clicking Advanced on the Appearance tab of the Display Properties dialog box. From the Advanced Appearance dialog box, you can change the look of many desktop user interface elements, such as the desktop, menu title bars, text, and buttons, with changes in font, color, and size. Windows XP attempts to standardize some of these attributes, so some are only customizable with Windows Classic menus.

You can select the item on the desktop whose appearance you want to modify either by selecting it from the Item dropdown list or by clicking the corresponding item on the preview window in the Advanced Appearance dialog box. If you select a nontext item, you can choose a different size and/or color (or two colors if applicable). If the item contains text, such as the Active Title Bar, you can also choose the font, font size, and any font attributes (bold or italic). If you decide to change the font, experiment with several to find one that appears readable to you on-screen; fonts that are pleasing to the eye on paper are sometimes hard to read on-screen.

Change the Look of Windows and Menus

1. Right-click the desktop and click Properties from the menu that appears to bring up the Display Properties dialog box.
2. Click Appearance.

   The Appearance tab appears.
3. Click here and select Windows Classic style from the dropdown list.

Note: *Some changes only work with Windows Classic style, so this style will be selected for this example.*

4. Click Advanced.

   The Advanced Appearance dialog box appears.

   - The preview window shows how changes you make will affect the appearance of Windows.

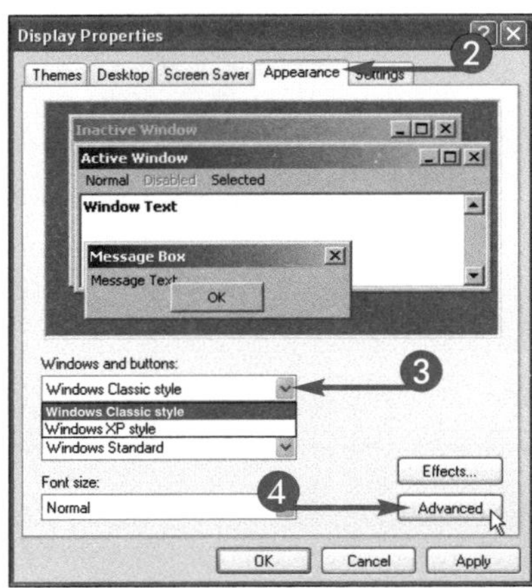

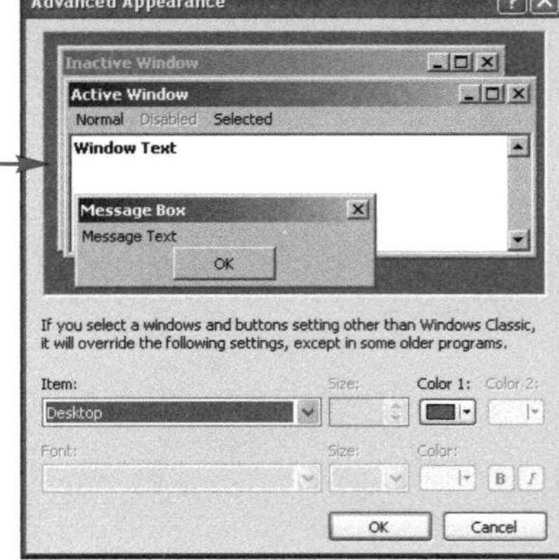

5 Click Active Window in the preview window to select the Active Title Bar.

- Active Title Bar appears in the Item dropdown list.
- The font for the selected item appears in the Font dropdown list.

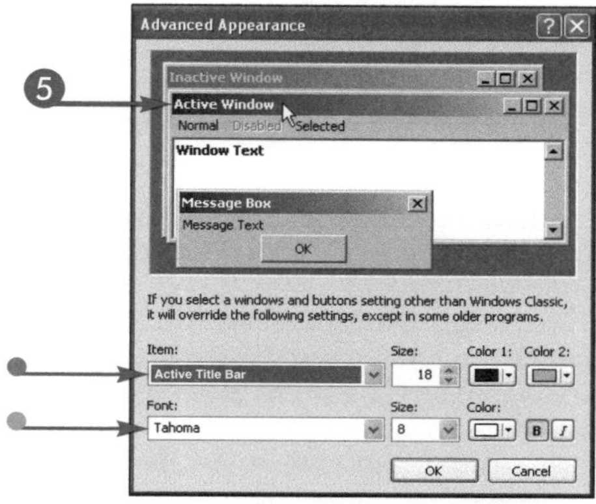

6 Click a font attribute.

- The text in the preview windows is italicized in this example.

7 Click the Color 1 down arrow to bring up a color palette.

8 Click a new color.

The new color appears in the left side of the menu bar.

9 Click OK to close the Advanced Appearance dialog box.

10 Click OK to close the Display Properties dialog box.

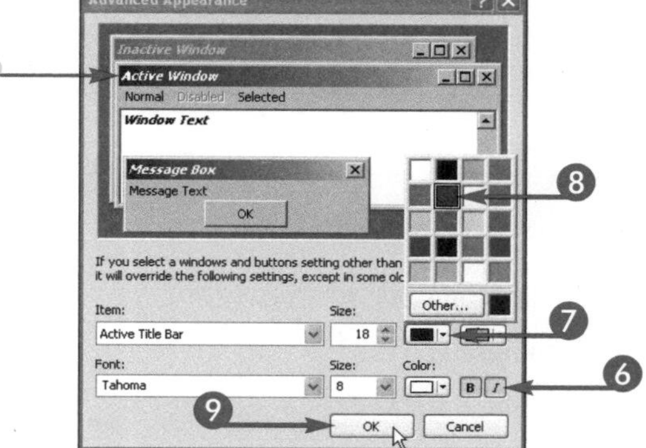

I made a number of changes; is there a way I can save these settings?

▼ Yes. After you have saved your settings by clicking OK to close the Display Properties dialog box, open the dialog box again and, at the Themes tab, select My Current Theme from the Theme dropdown list. Click Save As and assign your current settings a name, and then click OK. (For more details on themes, see the section "Choose Windows Themes," earlier in this chapter.)

I changed the color of the menu bars and I changed the font, but when I saved the changes, only the font changed. What happened?

▼ Unless you changed windows and buttons to Windows Classic style on the Appearance tab of the Display Properties dialog box before clicking Advanced, only some of your changes will be made (even though they appear on the preview window). You can either choose from one of the three color schemes of Windows XP style or change to Windows Classic style to have your color changes take effect.

Clean Up the Desktop

You can take advantage of a handy Windows XP feature, the Desktop Cleanup Wizard, to help you clean up your desktop when it becomes too cluttered with old or unused shortcuts. This feature is especially useful if you have many programs, because most commercial software creates a shortcut on your desktop automatically during installation. You may also have a work style that entails creating shortcuts to frequently accessed files, folders, or Web sites that become less needed as time goes by.

The Desktop Cleanup Wizard consolidates all of the shortcuts (without deleting them) into a desktop folder called Unused Desktop Shortcuts. Along the way, it first lists all the shortcuts, allows you to decide which ones to remove, and has you confirm your choice before the wizard finally moves all the unused shortcuts to the Unused Desktop Shortcuts folder on your desktop. Remember that shortcuts are not the programs themselves, just handy ways to access them. You are not deleting any programs by doing this cleanup, and you can still use the shortcuts from within the Unused Desktop Shortcuts folder.

Clean Up the Desktop

1. Right-click the desktop.

   A menu appears.

2. Click Arrange Icons By.
3. Click Run Desktop Cleanup Wizard.

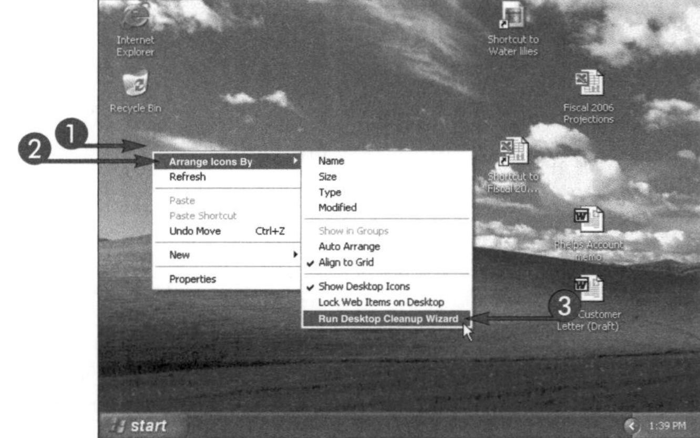

The Desktop Cleanup Wizard appears.

4. Click Next.

The Desktop Cleanup Wizard searches your desktop and lists all your shortcuts, along with the date the shortcut was last used.

Note: *If you have never used a shortcut, it is selected as a candidate for cleanup. Conversely, if you have recently used a shortcut, the wizard assumes you want to keep it and it is not selected.*

5. Click the check box if you do not want the shortcut to be removed (☐), or click the check box if you do want the shortcut to be removed (☑).
6. Click Next.

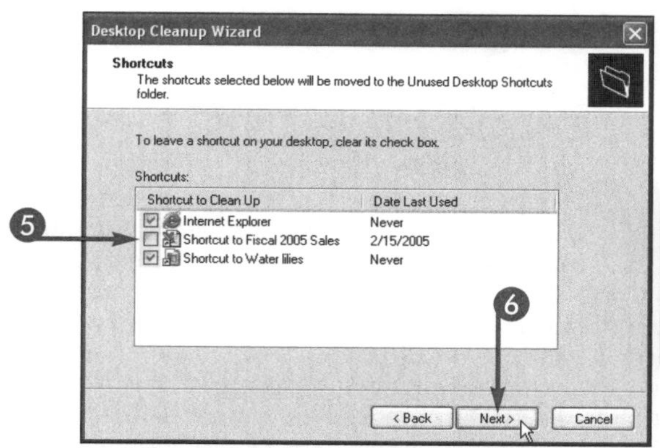

- The Desktop Cleanup Wizard displays a list of shortcuts that it will move to the Unused Desktop Shortcuts folder on your desktop, based on your selections.
- If you want to make changes to the list displayed, click Back and repeat Steps 5 and 6 until you are satisfied with the list.

7. Click Finish to perform the cleanup.

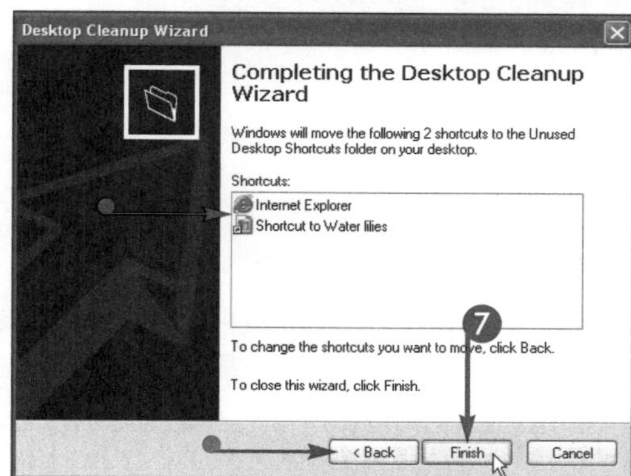

Can I move the Unused Desktop Shortcuts folder from my desktop to clean up further?

▼ Yes. The Unused Desktop Shortcuts folder is an ordinary file folder. To move it off your desktop, right-click the folder and select Cut. Open a destination folder (such as My Documents) and click Edit, and then Paste to paste the Unused Desktop Shortcuts folder into the new destination folder.

Is there any reason why I should not delete the Unused Desktop Shortcuts folder?

▼ That depends. Doing so does not delete any original files or programs, so if you are confident you will not have trouble finding these files, folders, programs, or Web sites again, simply drag the Unused Desktop Shortcuts folder to the Recycle Bin. Another Unused Desktop Shortcuts folder will be created the next time you use the Desktop Cleanup Wizard.

Select a Screen Saver

You can choose from a number of screen savers in Windows XP that replace your current desktop display when it is not in use. The screen saver can be a slide show viewer, a marquee for your company, an interesting graphic animation, or simply a blank screen. There is a preview to allow you to view each screen saver. You can also set the number of minutes that must pass without a keystroke or mouse movement before the screen saver starts. If you have Windows XP Professional or if you have chosen to use a password with Windows XP Home, you also have the option of protecting your computer with a password when the screen saver is activated.

You can make changes and select screen savers on the Screen Saver tab of the Display Properties dialog box. If you have a Windows XP Plus pack or other additional screen savers, they are also accessible from that location. If you have Windows XP Home and have set it to use a Welcome screen instead of a user logon, you will not see the option to resume on password protect, but instead will see an option to display a Welcome screen on resume.

Select a Screen Saver

1. Right-click the desktop and click Properties from the menu that appears to bring up the Display Properties dialog box.
2. Click Screen Saver.

   The Screen Saver tab appears.
3. Click here and select a screen saver from the dropdown list (3D Text in this example, or (None) to display a blank screen).

Note: *Not all screen savers have additional settings. This example does.*

- Type a number (1 to 9999) here to select the number of minutes Windows XP waits with no user input before launching the screen saver.
- Click here to require a password when resuming.
- Click here for a full screen preview of the screen saver.
- Click here to adjust power settings related to having your monitor idle.

4. Click Settings.

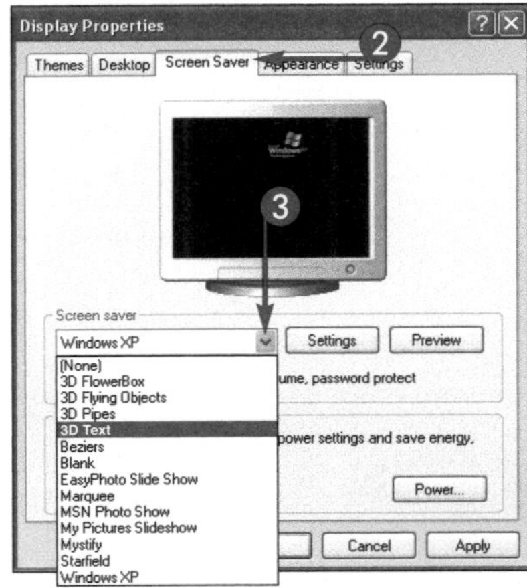

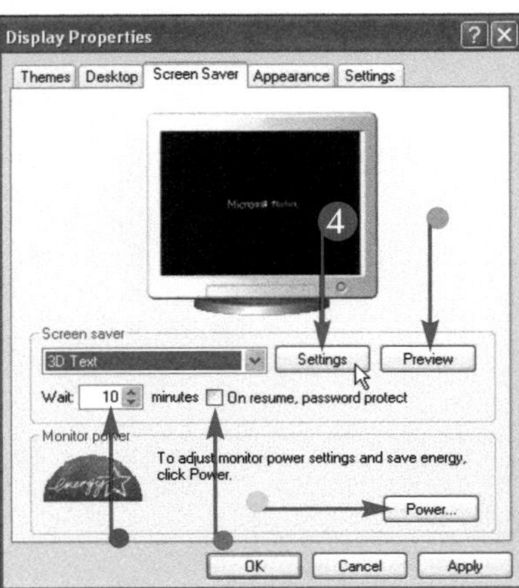

The settings screen for the selected screen saver appears (3D Text in this example).

5 Type your text (Master Visually in this example) here.

6 Click OK.

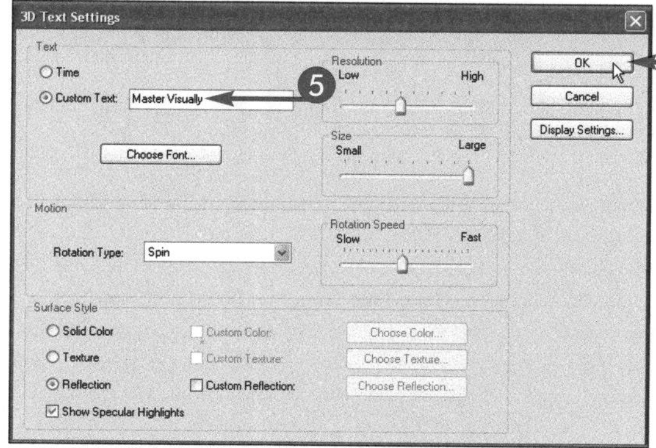

The Screen Saver tab of the Display Properties box appears again. Click Preview to see the full screen preview shown here. Moving your mouse or pressing any key takes you back to the Screen Saver tab where you can click OK to confirm the selection or Cancel to exit without saving your changes.

How do I show my photos in a slide show?

▼ Select My Pictures Slideshow from the Screen saver dropdown list in the Display Properties dialog box. Click Settings to make changes to how often the pictures are swapped, transition effects, and so on. The Settings screen is where you can select the folder from which Windows XP pulls the pictures. By default this is My Pictures.

I have selected a screen saver, but it displays for a few minutes, and then my monitor goes blank. What is happening?

▼ It is likely that you have your screen saver set to display after a certain number of minutes, and your PC's power management features are also set to turn off your monitor after a certain number of minutes to conserve power. Try clicking Power on the Screen Saver tab and making adjustments according to your preferences.

Change Items on the Start Menu

You can choose which items display on the Start menu in Windows XP. If you make no changes, Windows XP uses its own guidelines and rules to learn which programs you use the most often, and adapts to your work habits to some extent. However, you probably know right at the outset which items you want to have readily available, and which items are more of a distraction.

To customize the Start menu, you can right-click the Start menu and select Properties. This brings up the Start Menu tab of the Taskbar and Start Menu Properties dialog box.

At this point you can choose between Windows XP and Classic start menu styles and then click Customize. This section assumes XP style. The General tab of the Customize Start Menu dialog box gives you some basic settings. You can change icon size (large for readability or small to fit more on the menu) and the number of programs to list that you have most recently used (click Clear List to clear this list). You can also choose whether to permanently display a browser or e-mail program, and if so, which one.

Change Items on the Start Menu

1. Right-click the Start menu.

   A menu appears.

2. Click Properties.

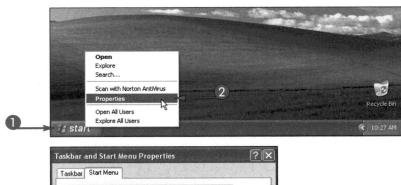

   The Start Menu tab of the Taskbar and Start Menu Properties dialog box appears.

   - Click to revert to Windows Classic style start menu and customization.

3. Click Customize.

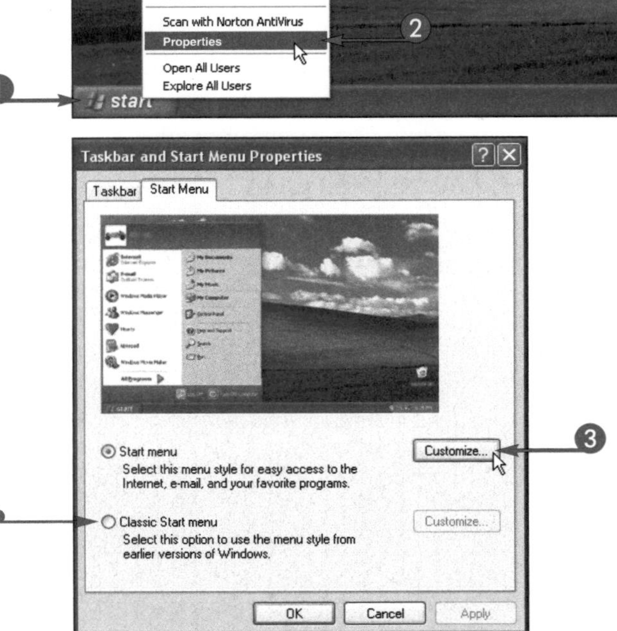

The General tab of the Customize Start Menu dialog box appears.

4 Click an icon size.

5 Type the number of programs to show on the Start menu.

6 Click to remove the check and not show Internet or E-mail on your Start menu.

7 Click OK to close the Customize Start Menu dialog box.

8 Click OK to close the properties dialog box.

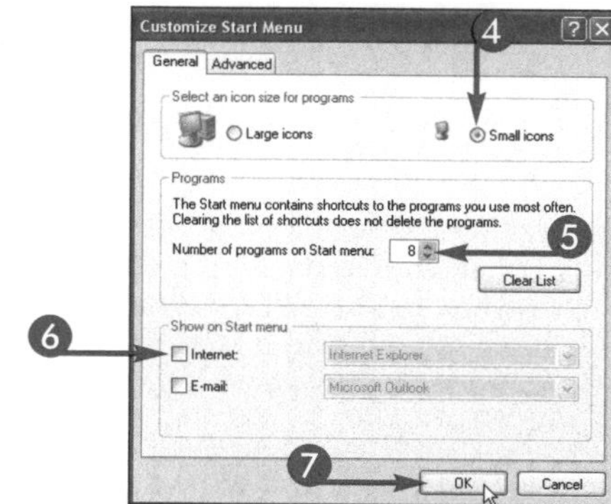

9 Click Start to show the changes.

- The Internet browser no longer appears on the permanent list.
- Items now display small icons.
- Up to eight items last used are now displayed (your screen may show fewer if you have used less than eight programs).

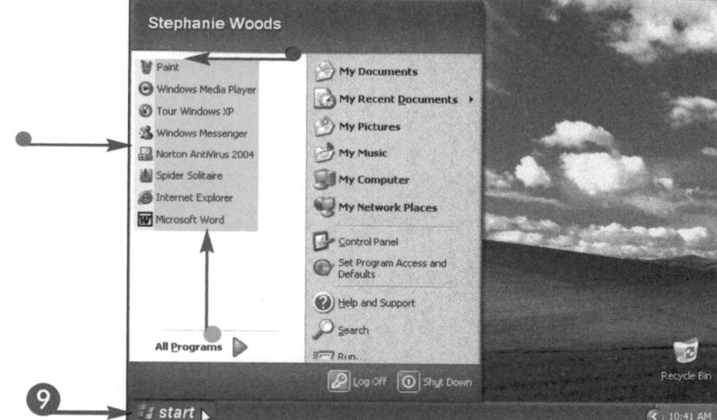

I want to keep a particular program on my permanent list, but it is not my e-mail or Internet program. How can I do this?

▼ From the Start menu, find the program you want to have on your permanent list (it can be on the temporary list of most recent programs or in the set of menus found when you click All Programs) and right-click the program. In the menu that appears, click Pin to Start menu. You can remove it at any time by right-clicking the program's icon again and clicking Unpin from Start menu.

Can I remove one item from my recently used programs list without clearing the entire list?

▼ Yes. Right-click the item's icon and click Remove from This List from the menu that appears. This only removes the program from the list and does not uninstall or delete the program from your PC.

continued

Change Items on the Start Menu *(Continued)*

You can make many other changes to your Start menu, such as the behavior of items on the Start menu and choosing what items from Windows XP you want to display in the right column of the Start menu. You can access these settings from the Advanced tab of the Customize Start Menu dialog box.

The Start menu settings allow you to choose whether you want to have submenus open when you pause over them with your mouse and whether you want to be notified about newly installed programs. The next section of the Advanced tab, Start menu items, allows you to decide which items to display, and if they are displayed, whether they are displayed as a link (bringing up a Web page or dialog box containing further links, icons, and buttons) or a menu (with corresponding submenus). This part of the Advanced tab has many individual items with check boxes and radio buttons, so it is necessary to use the scroll bar to view all of the settings. Recent documents allows you to choose whether to keep track of your most recent documents, and if you do, allows you to clear the list if you so choose.

Change Items on the Start Menu *(continued)*

10. Follow Steps 1 to 3 from the first part of this section to bring up the Customize Start Menu dialog box.
11. Click Advanced.

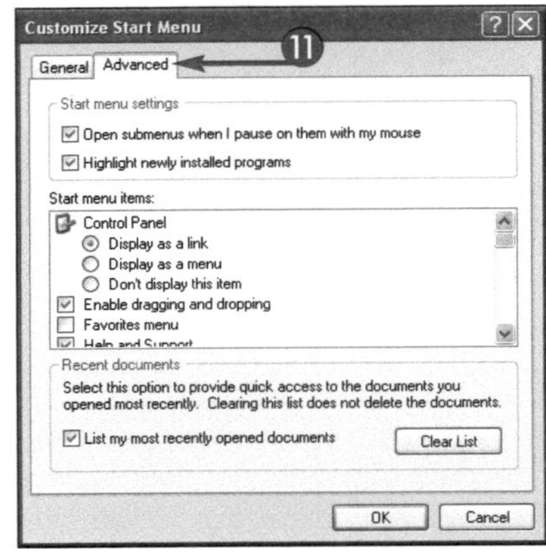

Scroll down the Start menu items until you reach System Administrator Tools.

12. Click Display on the All Programs menu and the Start menu.
13. Click OK to close the Customize Start Menu dialog box.
14. Click OK to close the properties dialog box.

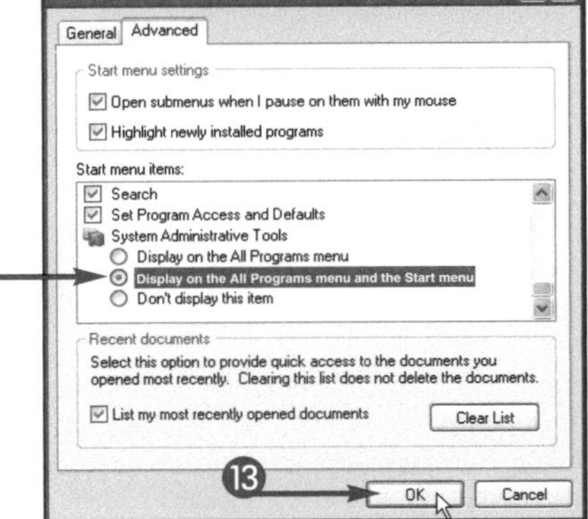

15 Click Start.

Administrative Tools now displays.

16 Click Administrative Tools.

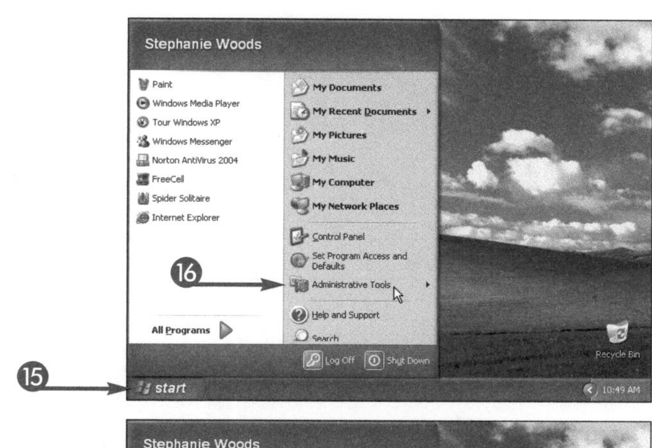

A list of administrative tools is now displayed.

17 Click Start again to close the menu.

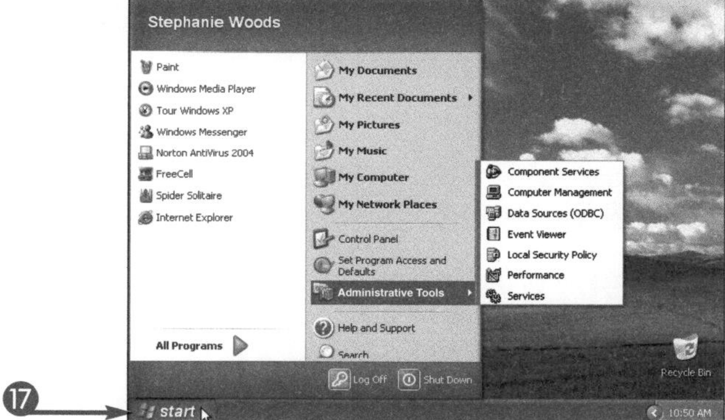

I have a lot of programs; is there a way to change the Start menu so that All Programs does not completely fill my desktop?

▼ Yes. From the Advanced tab of the Customize Start Menu dialog box, scroll through Start menu items until you find Scroll Programs. Check this option (☐ changes to ☑) and click OK. When you next click All Programs on the Start menu, a single column menu appears with arrows at the top and bottom. To see something at the top of the list, move your mouse to the arrow at the top and scroll until you find what you need. The bottom of the list functions much the same way.

Can I view printers from my Start menu?

▼ Yes. From the Advanced tab of the Customize Start Menu dialog box, scroll through Start menu items until you find Printers and Faxes. Check this option (☐ changes to ☑) and click OK. When you next click the Start menu, you see a Printers and Faxes icon ( ) in the right column. Clicking this icon takes you to a window that allows you to select and work with printers, faxes, and other output devices.

Hide or Show Notifications on the Taskbar

You can control how and when icons for notifications are displayed on the taskbar in Windows XP. You may find that the number of helper applications running on your PC that display on the taskbar is very large. Antivirus software, printer software, sound software, and any software designed to work with specialized hardware tend to have icons for notifications that appear on the taskbar. For this reason, Windows XP has a feature that allows you to hide icons for all of these applications while they are inactive (this is the default setting), or to individually set them to always show, always hide, or hide when inactive.

You can change these individual settings by right-clicking the taskbar, clicking Properties, and clicking Customize in the properties dialog box. Each notification is listed by Name (as it appears when you pause with your mouse over the icon) and Behavior (whether it is set to hide when inactive, always hide, or always show). By clicking the Behavior setting next to the notification you want to change, you can select one of the other two remaining settings from a dropdown list. You can choose behavior for past items, too, for when they occur again in the future.

Hide or Show Notifications on the Taskbar

1. Right-click the taskbar.

   A menu appears.

2. Click Properties.

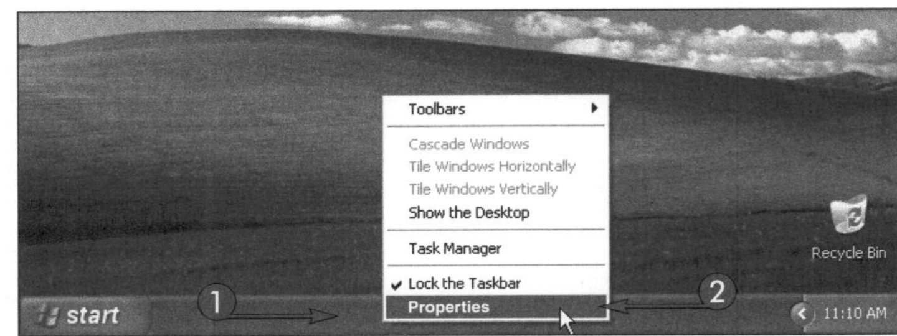

   The Taskbar tab of the Taskbar and Start Menu Properties dialog box appears.

3. Click Customize.

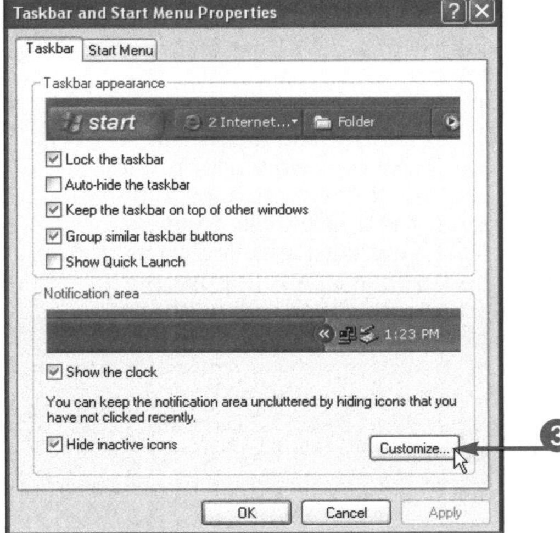

The Customize Notifications dialog box appears.

4 Click the setting in the Behavior list for a notification (Always show for Volume in this example).

- Click to restore notifications to their default settings.

5 Click OK to close the Customize Notifications dialog box.

6 Click OK to close the properties dialog box.

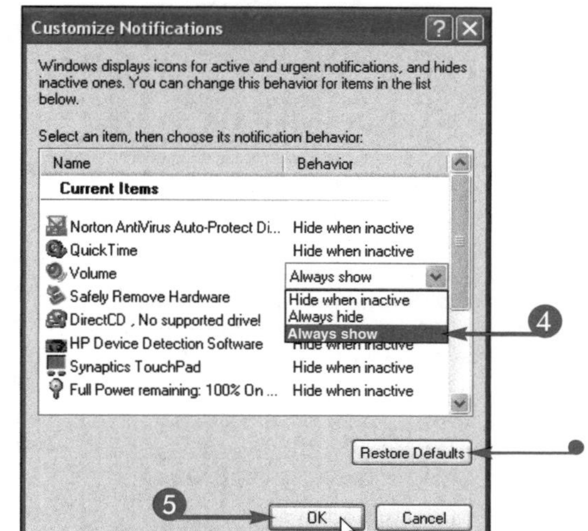

- The icon for Volume is now displayed (even when not in use).

I can bring up the Customize Notifications dialog box, but it does not allow me to make changes to the settings. Why not?

▼ You must have administrator privileges for your PC to make changes to these settings. If you would like to make changes to notifications, log on as network administrator (if possible) or contact your network administrator.

How can I quickly view the hidden icons?

▼ Click the show hidden icons button (◀) to display any icons for hidden but currently running items. Click the hide button (▶) to hide them again.

Enable and Add Items to Quick Launch

You can use the Quick Launch feature to launch your most frequently used items with a single click on the taskbar. To do this, you must enable the Quick Launch toolbar. When you have enabled it, a set of icons appears just to the right of Start. You can add items to the Quick Launch toolbar by dragging them from the start menu. You can also change the order in which they appear by simply dragging them to the left or right. If your taskbar is locked, only three items appear on the taskbar. If you choose to have more than three with the taskbar locked, you must first click ▪ to see the remaining Quick Launch items.

You can add not only programs, but also individual folders, files, Web links, or other Windows XP desktop items (such as the Control Panel or My Computer). To remove an item, drag it to the Recycle Bin. This only removes it from the Quick Launch toolbar; it does not delete the item from your PC.

To enable the Quick Launch toolbar, right-click the taskbar and click Toolbars. From the Toolbars submenu, click Quick Launch so that a check mark (☑) appears next to Quick Launch.

Enable and Add Items to Quick Launch

1. Right-click the taskbar.
2. Click Toolbars.
3. Click Quick Launch.

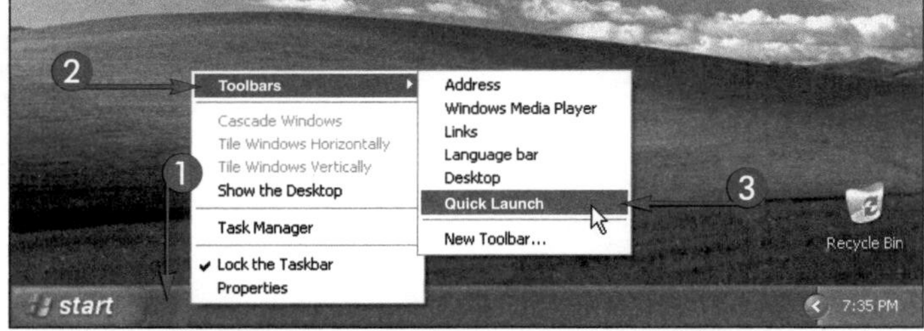

- The Quick Launch icons now appear to the right of Start.

4. Click Start.
5. Drag the item (Spider Solitaire in this example) from the Start menu to the Quick Launch section of the taskbar.

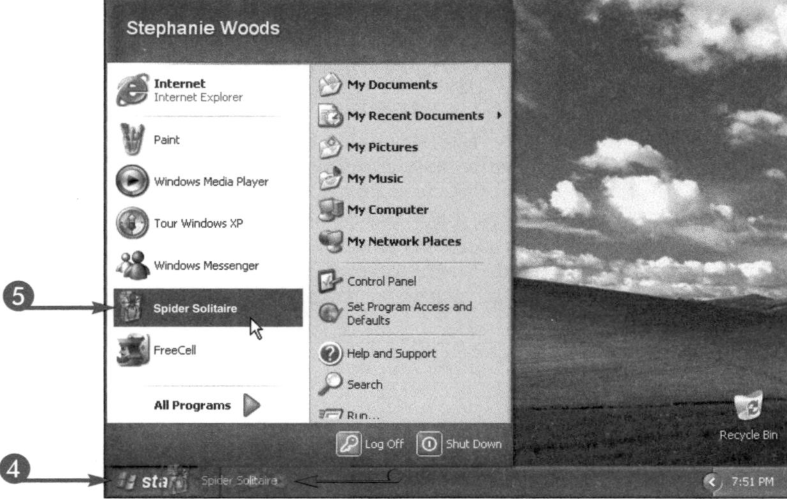

The item's icon now appears in the Quick Launch section of the taskbar.

- Pause with the mouse pointer over the icon to see the name of the item (and sometimes additional information). Click to launch the item.

6 Click here to see additional Quick Launch items.

- A list of one or more additional Quick Launch items is displayed.

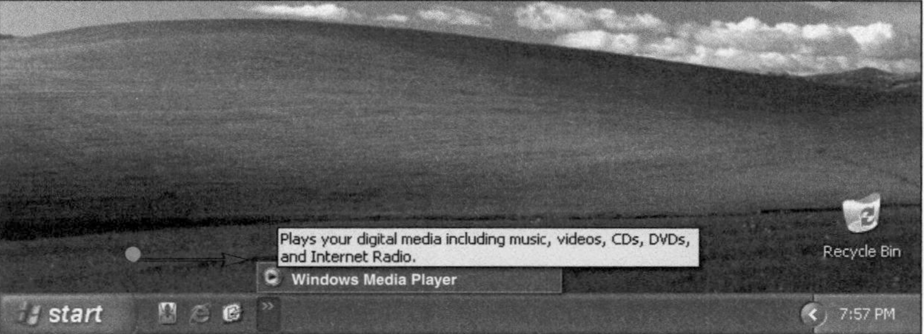

Is there a way to minimize all my open applications so that I see a clear desktop with one click?

▼ Yes. If you have enabled Quick Launch, one of the default items, Show Desktop ( ) performs this function. Just click this icon once and all of your open applications are minimized as buttons on the taskbar and the desktop is clear.

Can I change the icon or description for the item in Quick Launch?

▼ Yes, in most cases. Right-click the icon on the Quick Launch section of the taskbar, and then click Properties. To add or change the description, edit or add something to the Comments field. To change the icon, click Change Icon and browse visually through a list of Microsoft stock icons or select one of your own.

Create Your Own Toolbar

If you want to have ready access to a folder that you use all the time, but you want to keep your desktop clear, you can create your own toolbar that takes you to a shortcut, file, Web address, or folder, and you can also create a folder that groups together any collection of items (such as shortcuts, files, Web links) that are accessible by one click on the taskbar. You can also use this feature for an entire drive or storage device if you so choose.

To create a new toolbar, right-click the taskbar, click New Toolbar, and select a folder, file, or other item from the list or type a Web address. You can also create a new folder here by clicking New Folder. (If you click New Folder, be sure to select New Folder and rename it accordingly or it will remain New Folder.) When you are finished, click OK and the name of your new toolbar appears at the right side of the taskbar near the notification and clock area. Click ■ to the immediate right of your toolbar name to launch the toolbar.

Create Your Own Toolbar

1. Right-click the taskbar.

   A menu appears.

2. Click Toolbars.
3. Click New Toolbar.

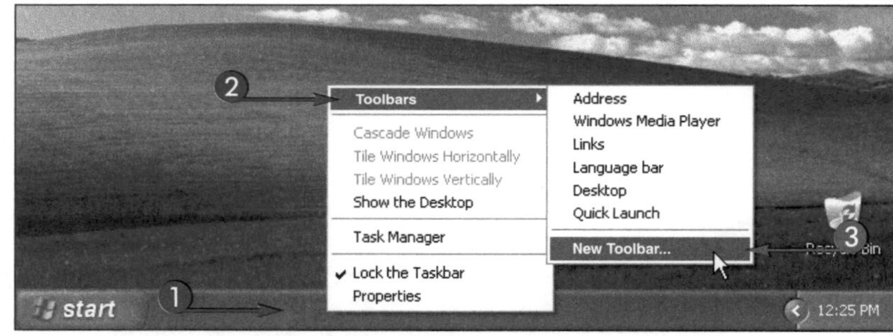

The New Toolbar dialog box appears.

4. Select a folder. For this example, click My Computer.

Note: *If you type an Internet address, you must use the complete address (you may not omit http://).*

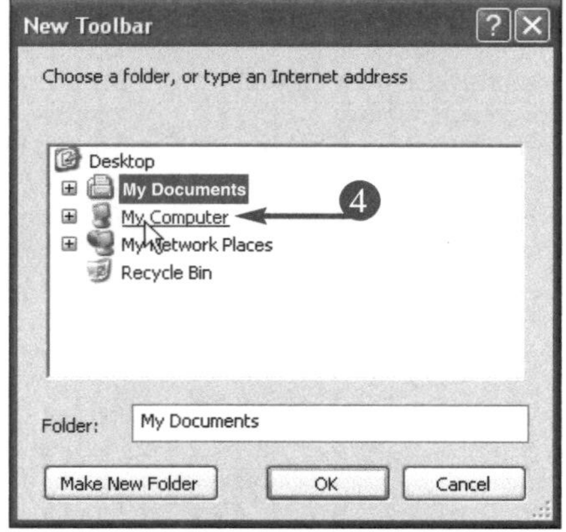

5 Click Control Panel.

6 Click OK.

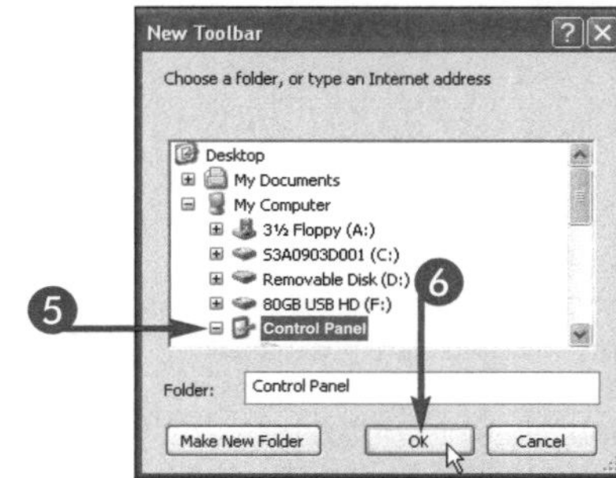

- The new toolbar (Control Panel in this example) appears on the taskbar.

7 Click ■ to launch the toolbar menu.

8 Click ■ again to close the toolbar menu.

Note: *If you typed an Internet address of a Web page instead of a folder or desktop item, you will not see ■. You must right-click the toolbar name and select Open in Window to go to that address.*

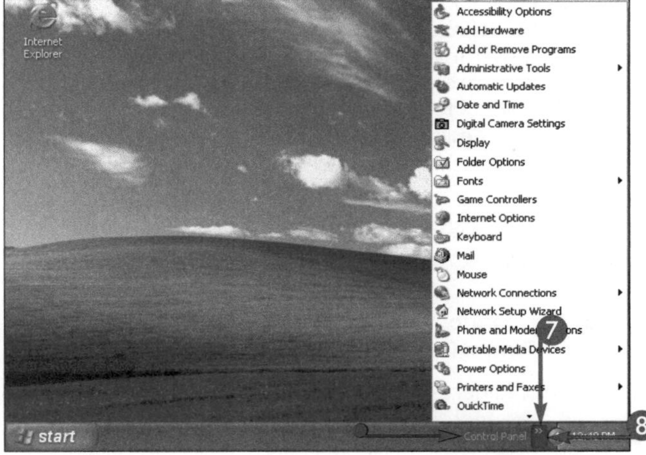

How do I remove a toolbar?

▼ Right-click the taskbar and click Toolbars. Any toolbars that are currently displayed have a check mark (☑) next to them. Click the toolbar you want to remove. If it is a predefined toolbar such as Quick Launch or Language Bar, it remains on the list but does not have a check mark and does not appear on the taskbar. If the toolbar is one you created, it is removed from the menu and you need to create it again later if you change your mind.

Can I open my custom toolbar as a window instead of a menu?

▼ Yes. To open as a menu, click or right-click ■. To open as a window, right-click the name of the custom toolbar instead, and then click Open Folder to open in a standard Windows XP folder window.

Add a User Account

You can add user accounts to Windows XP to allow multiple users to share the same computer. By default, Windows XP creates a default administrator for your computer. Unless you specify one during setup, a password is not created for the computer. This computer boots straight into Windows. Because you should always password-protect your computer, you can create a password for the default administrator user, or, better yet, create a second user for your computer. You also can create additional users in case others need to use your computer. Each user can have different environmental setups, including different desktop icons, individualized wallpaper settings, unique printer setups, and so on.

The easiest way to create additional users is through the User Accounts program in the Control Panel. With User Accounts, you can add a user account, modify accounts, and even delete accounts.

User accounts can be set as Limited or Administrator. Limited allows users to use programs and make a few system changes (such as wallpaper and themes changes). Administrators have full authority over Windows, including adding and removing programs.

Add a User Account

1. Display the Control Panel by clicking Start and then Control Panel.

   The Control Panel appears.

2. Click User Accounts.

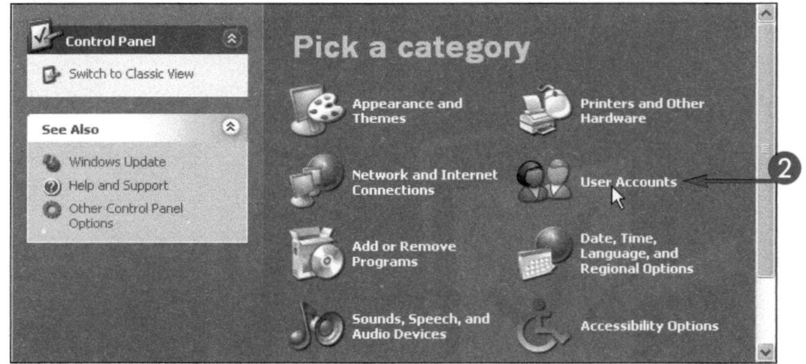

   The User Accounts window appears.

3. Click Create a new account.

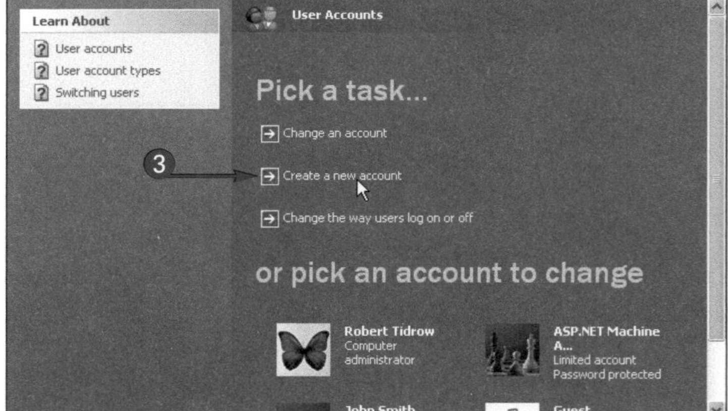

4. Type a name for the new user account.
5. Click Next.

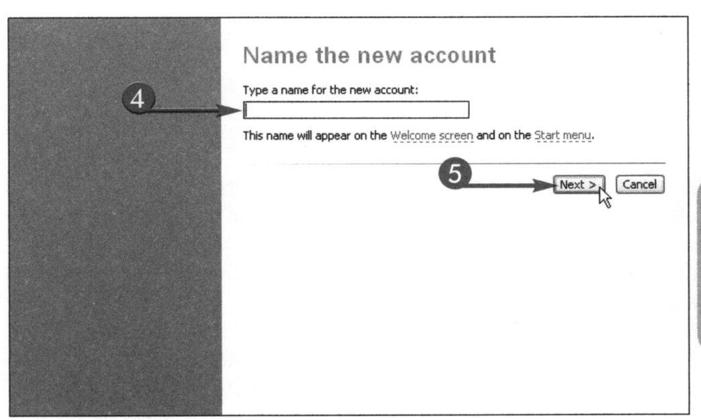

6. Choose whether you want the account to be an administrator or a limited user.
7. Click Create Account.

   Windows creates a new user account and the User Account window appears. See the next section for more about the User Account window.

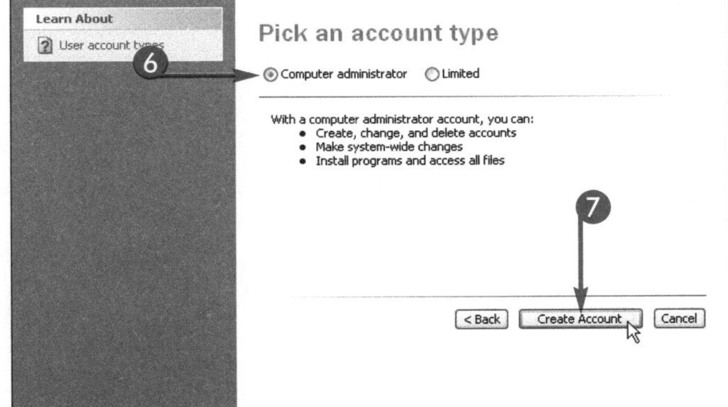

Can user accounts be made from a server?

- When connecting to a Windows domain controller, such as to a Windows 2003 network, the domain controller stores authorized domain user accounts. When you log on to the domain, you use a user name and password for the domain, which in turn authorizes you to work in the Windows XP computer.

Can more than one user account be an administrator?

- You should have only one administrator account per computer. However, you can assign additional users as administrators if you feel that they are responsible enough to make system-wide changes, such as install programs and access all files (including system and hidden files).

Can nonadministrators make user accounts?

- Windows does not allow Limited Users to create new user accounts. This way only those deemed adminstrator can make critical system changes. For example, if any user could create new user accounts, a malicious user (even one from the Internet) could create an administrator account and then have access to all your files and settings.

Modify User Accounts

You can modify user accounts with the User Accounts feature. One modification is to add a password for the user. Other modifications you can make include changing the user account name, changing the Welcome screen picture associated with the user account, modifying the account type, and deleting the account. The changes you make using the User Accounts feature are changes that affect the user account and account type, not how Windows is set up or behaves.

Other settings for each user account are saved while the user works inside Windows. For example, when a user logs in and makes changes to the Windows wallpaper, that wallpaper setting is saved for that user. Similarly, each user can set up a collection of desktop icons and shortcuts to suit their work habits. When the user logs out and logs back in later, those same icons are available for that user.

Modify User Accounts

Access user accounts

1. Click Start.
2. Click Control Panel.

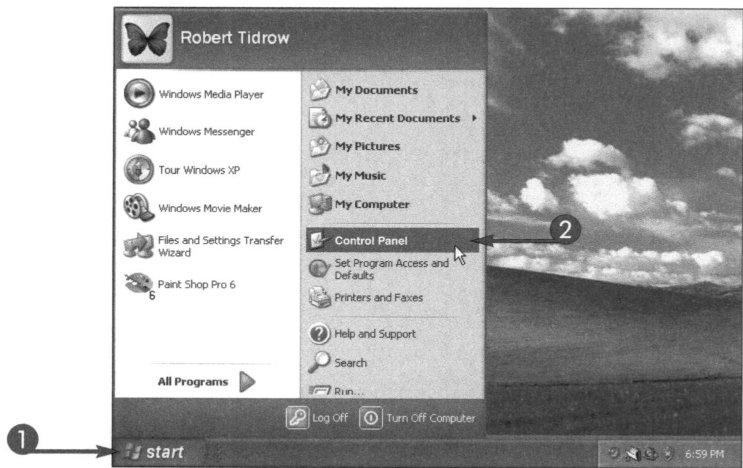

The Control Panel appears.

3. Click User Accounts.

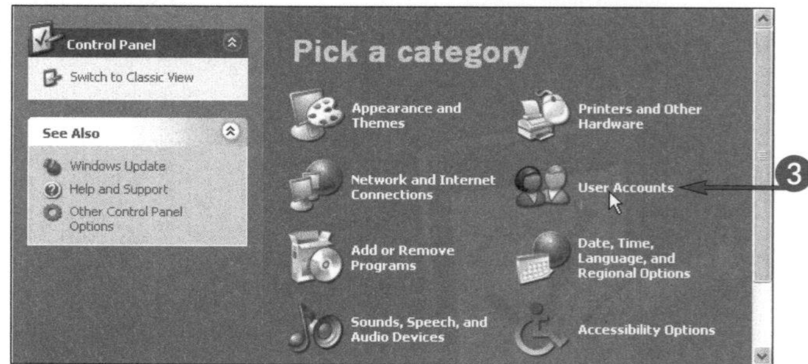

The User Accounts window appears.

4 Click Change an account.

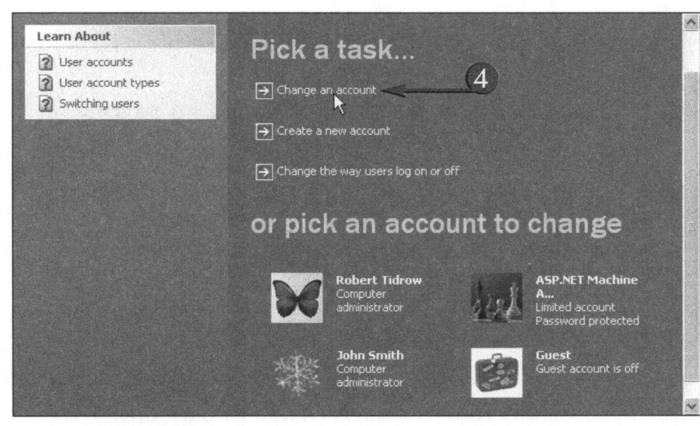

The next screen, asking you which account you want to change, appears.

5 Click the account to change.

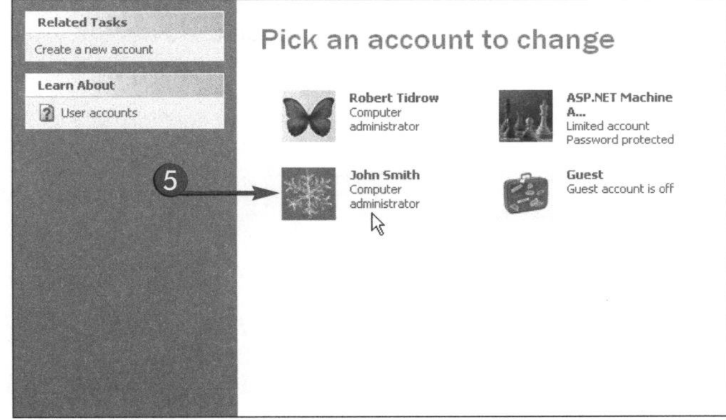

Why does Windows show a Guest account?

- The Guest account is automatically created when Windows is installed. Users not set up on your computer can log on using the Guest account. This account includes only the basic authorizations, such as starting Windows and using programs available to all users. Password-protected files, Windows settings, and protected folders are not accessible to Guest accounts.

Is the Guest account enabled?

- By default, Windows does not enable the Guest account. You must select it in the User Accounts window and then click Turn on the Guest Account. Later, you can go back and turn off the account if you want to disable it. Microsoft recommends that you leave the Guest account disabled unless you change its default password. This way unauthorized users cannot access your computer using the default Guest account user name and password.

How do you switch from one user to another?

- The current user must log off for another user to use the computer. Click Start and then Log Off. Click the user account name, type a password (if required), and press Enter.

continued

Modify User Accounts *(Continued)*

You can change the name of an account. Changing the name is handy if you have a user who no longer needs to use your computer, but you want to keep all the settings associated with that user. Or, the original user may leave: In that case, another user can use the same setup. Simply change the user account name to the new person.

Password-protecting your Windows machine is a good practice to thwart others from accessing or destroying your files. In fact, some companies require that all users have passwords to access company computers. When you create a password, use passwords that are difficult to guess (do not use last names, common nicknames, or children's names) and that are at least six characters in length. Some companies require passwords to include a combination of letters and numbers.

The picture associated with a user account can be changed to one that closely matches the personality of the user. For example, a person who likes sports can choose a soccer ball, motocross racer, martial arts person, or skateboarder. If one of the default pictures does not work, choose a different one using the Browse for more pictures link.

Modify User Accounts *(continued)*

Change the account name

The next screen, asking you what you want to change about the account, appears.

6 Click Change the name.

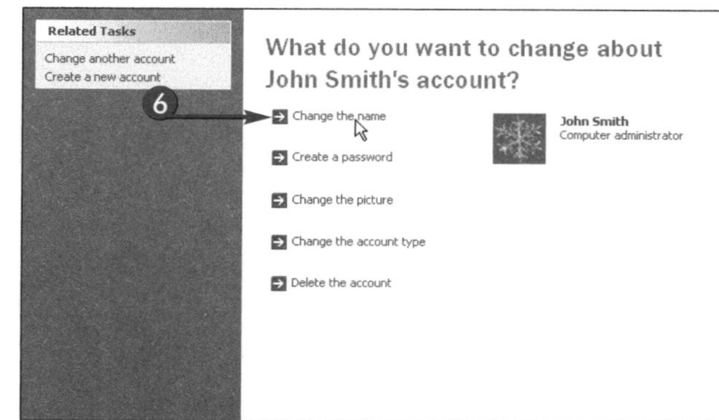

The next screen, asking you for a new name for the account, appears.

7 Type a new name for the account.

8 Click Change Name.

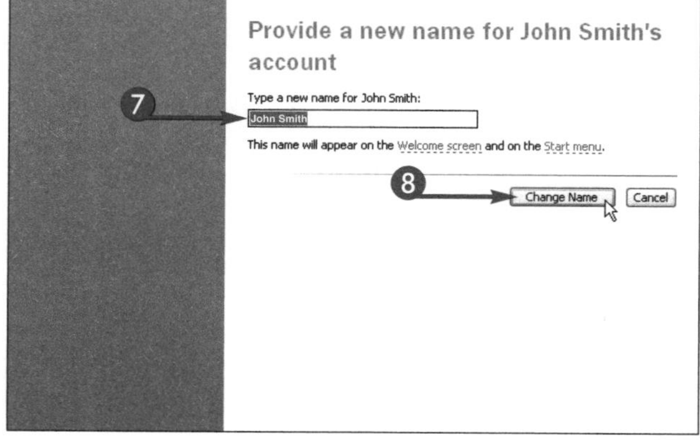

The next screen, asking you for a password for the account, appears.

9 Type a new password.

10 Confirm the new password.

11 Type a password hint.

12 Click Create Password.

Windows saves the new account name and password.

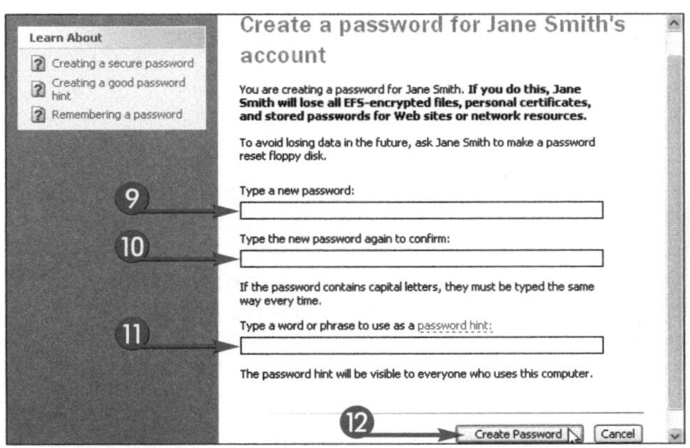

Change the account picture

13 Repeat Steps 1 to 5 from the previous pages to return to the screen that asks you what you want to change about the account.

14 Click Change the picture.

The next screen, asking you to pick a new picture, appears.

15 Click a picture.

16 Click Change Picture.

Windows saves the new account picture.

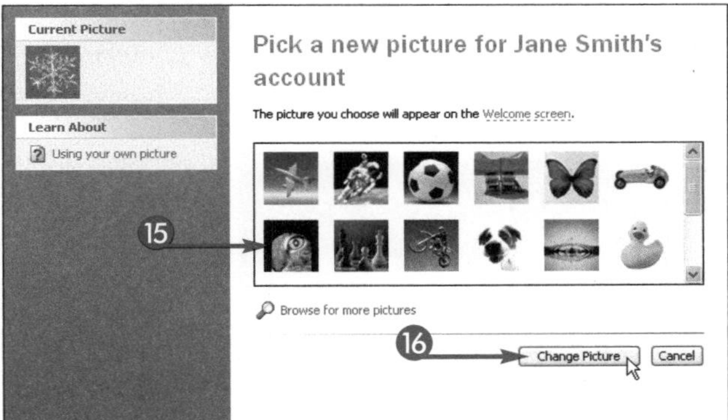

How can I change the way users log on?

Windows includes two ways to log on. The default is to use the Welcome screen, which lists all the users set up on the current computer. Each user is shown with a name and a picture. The other way to log on is the classic Windows logon prompt that requires users to type an account name into a dialog box.

To change how users log on, click Start, Control Panel, and then User Accounts. Click the Change the way users log on or off option. If the Offline Files feature is enabled, a screen appears telling you that you cannot use the Fast User Switching feature. (See the section "Configure Fast User Switching" for more about this feature.) Click Cancel. To change to the classic Windows logon prompt, click the Use the Welcome screen option (☐ changes to ☑). Click Apply Options.

When I delete a user, are the user's files removed as well?

Files stored in a user's My Documents folder can be saved or deleted when you delete an account. You must specify which you want to do. If you want to maintain those files, click Keep Files and a folder named after the user will be created. Click Delete Files to delete files in the My Documents folder. Some files, such as Internet favorites, desktop settings, and e-mail messages cannot be saved.

Change Group Membership

Windows lets you join users to groups using Local Users and Groups. Local Users and Groups is a Windows XP Professional security feature that lets you assign users to groups that have specific rights and permissions granted to them. For example, a user can be part of the administrator group that grants that user full rights to the Windows environment.

On the other hand, a user can be added as a member of the Users group (called *limited* in the User Accounts window). This group prevents users from changing system settings, installing programs, and adding new printers.

Administrators and limited types of users are available when you set up a user. Additional built-in groups available only through Local Users and Groups include Backup Operators, Power Users, Remote Desktop Users, and Network Configuration Operators. You also can create your own groups and add users to them.

To work with Local Users and Groups, use the Computer Management program.

Change Group Membership

1. Click Start.
2. Click Control Panel.

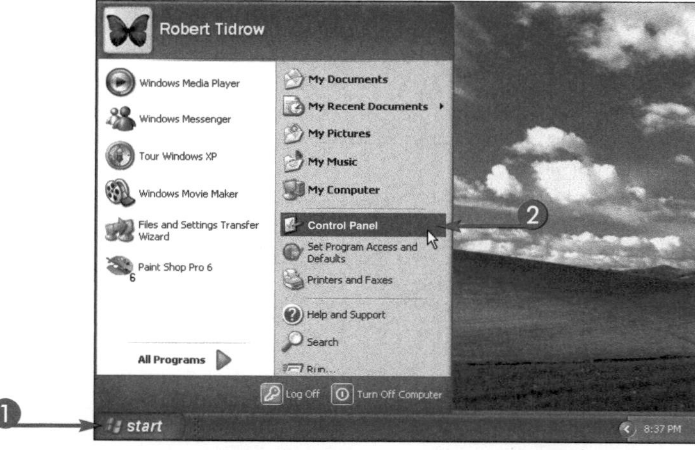

The Control Panel appears.

3. Click Performance and Maintenance.

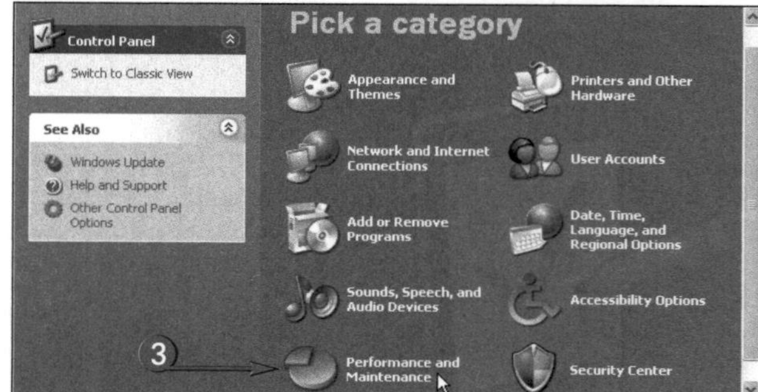

The Performance and Maintenance window appears.

4 Click Administrative Tools.

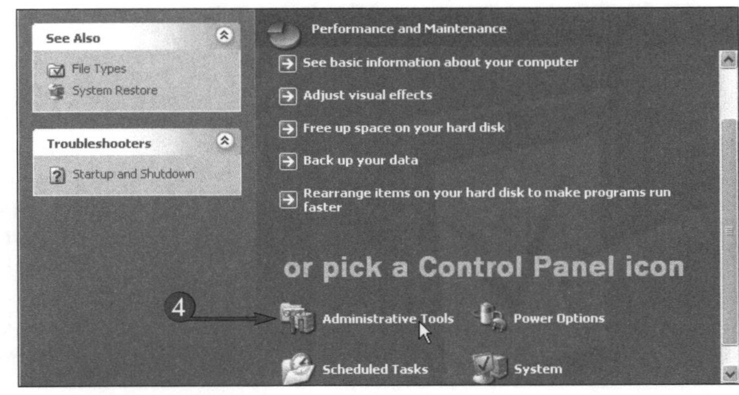

The Administrative Tools window appears.

5 Click Computer Management.

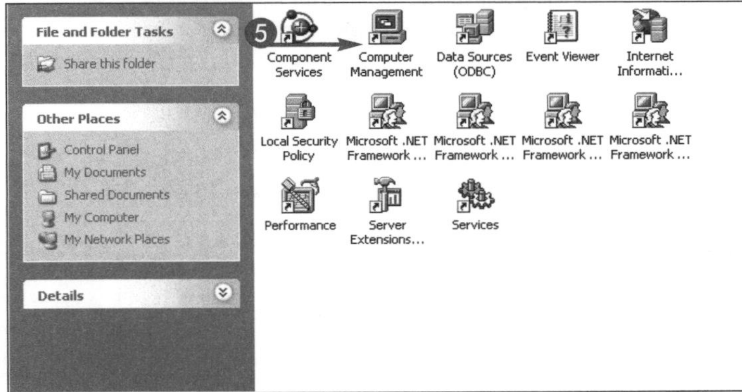

Do I have to use the Local Users and Groups feature?

- You do not have to assign a user to a group beyond what you set up when you created the user. You should, however, consider using Local Users and Groups if you need to enforce tighter security on your group of users.

I belong to a domain at work. Should I be changing my Local Users and Groups settings?

- Anytime you change something locally, remember that it could change how your computer works on the network. That said, check with your network administrator before changing your Local Users and Groups settings.

I am using Windows XP Home Edition. Why can I not see the Local Users and Groups information?

- Local Users and Groups is not available on Windows XP Home Edition. Because Local Users and Groups security features are considered to be mainly business related (rather than in a home environment), only Windows XP Professional, Windows 2000 Professional, and member servers in a domain include it.

continued

Change Group Membership *(Continued)*

One reason to become familiar with Local Users and Groups is to make your system as secure as possible. Most computers have only one person who uses it. If this is your case, consider making a second user so you do not run your system as an administrator. Anytime you run as an administrator, you open yourself up to possible security risks encountered on the Internet or even your local area network.

Instead, you can set yourself up as a member of the Power Users group. After you create a user using the User Accounts program, change your membership from administrator or limited to a power user. This group allows you to perform many Windows tasks, including installing programs, adding or deleting printers, and activating many of the Control Panel items.

When you need to do administrative tasks, such as change policy settings, access all files on the system, and perform Windows setup tasks, log out and log back in as an administrator.

Change Group Membership *(continued)*

The Computer Management window appears.

6 Click here to see all System Tools folders.

7 Click here to see all Local Users and Groups folders.

8 Click Users.

9 Double-click a user name.

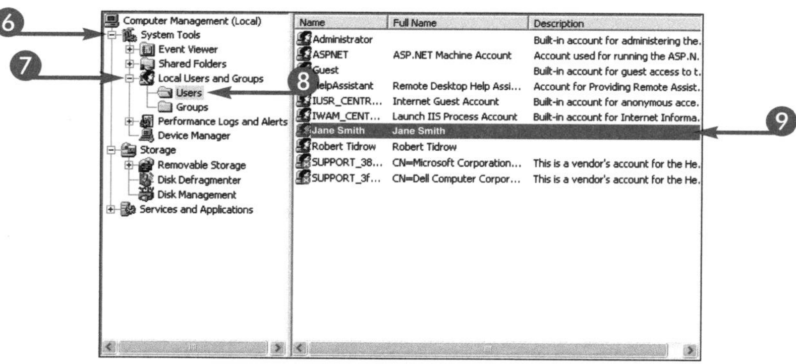

A properties dialog box appears.

10 Click the Member Of tab.

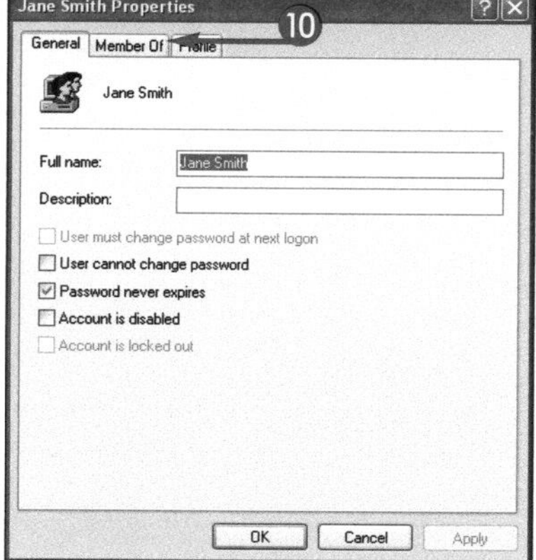

- This area displays groups to which the user belongs.

⓫ Click Add.

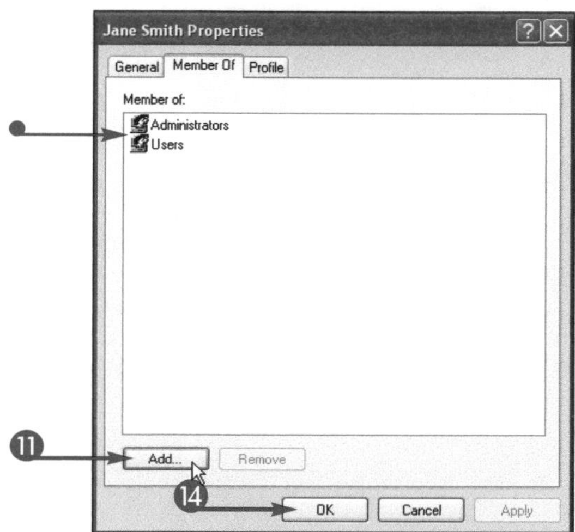

The Select Groups dialog box appears.

⓬ Type the name of a group here.

For this example, Power Users is the group.

⓭ Click OK to close the Select Groups dialog box.

⓮ Click OK to confirm your changes in the properties dialog box.

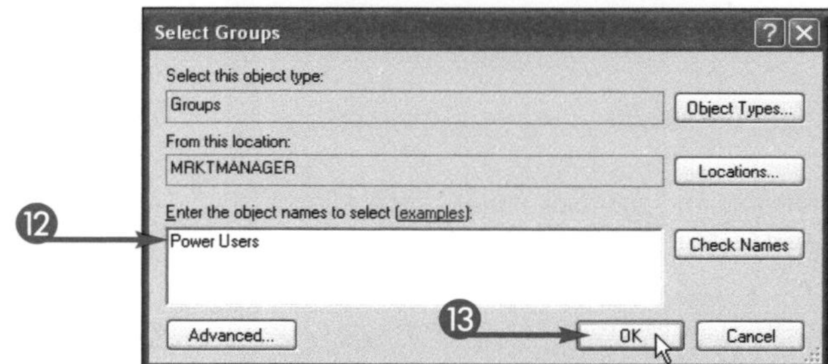

How do I create a group?

▼ Groups are created using Local Users and Groups in the Computer Management window. Repeat Steps 1 to 8 to display Local Users and Groups. Click the Groups folder instead of Users (as you do in Step 9). Then, choose New Group from the Action menu. Add a group name, description, and members to the New Group dialog box. Click Create.

Can I belong to more than one group?

▼ Yes. For example, you can add yourself to Power Users and Backup Operators groups if you plan on administering backups and restores from your computer. In fact, if you are the administrator of a group of computers, you should place yourself in as many groups as possible. This way you can have all the necessary priveleges for each group even if you do not log on as adminstrator on a particular computer. For example, assume you are the system adminstrator for a marketing department. In most cases you would use the Adminstrator user name to log on to servers, not workstations (Windows XP computers). Instead, you would use your "everyday" user name (jsmith, for example) when you needed to log on or access a user's computer.

Create a Password Reset Disk

With the Password Reset Disk, you can create a new password that lets you access your computer. Windows XP is a very secure operating system. If you forget your logon password, you cannot bypass the setup screen to access your files. For this reason, Windows lets you create a Password Reset Disk that enables you to recover your Windows settings if you forget your password.

There are two primary considerations to keep in mind about the Password Reset Disk. First, this is a preventative task. You must do it within Windows; that is, you cannot wait until after you forget your password and can no longer access Windows. So perform this task now so that you will have the disk ready if you ever need it.

Second, the disk can let anyone reset your password and have access to your user account. For this reason, make the disk and then keep it in a secure location.

Create a Password Reset Disk

1. Display the Control Panel by clicking Start and then Control Panel.

   The Control Panel appears.

2. Click User Accounts.
3. In the User Accounts window, click your user name.

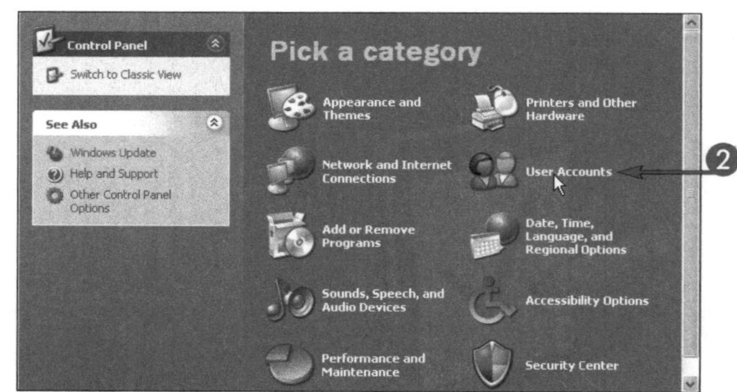

The next screen, asking you what you want to change about the account, appears.

4. Click Prevent a forgotten password.

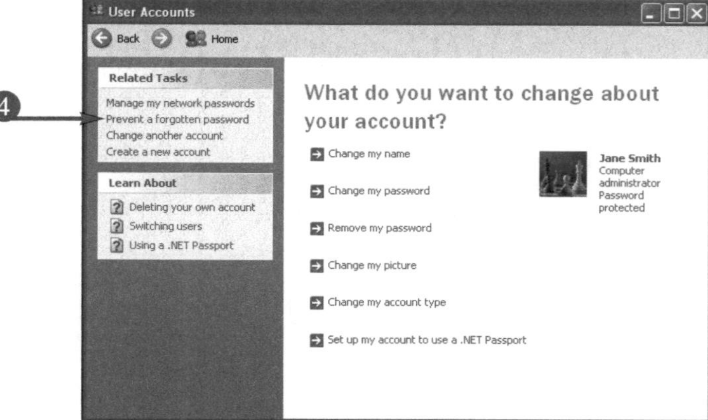

The Forgotten Password Wizard appears.

5 Click Next.

6 The Create a Password Reset Disk screen appears, telling you to insert a blank floppy disk into drive A.

7 Click Next.

8 In the next screen, type your password and click Next.

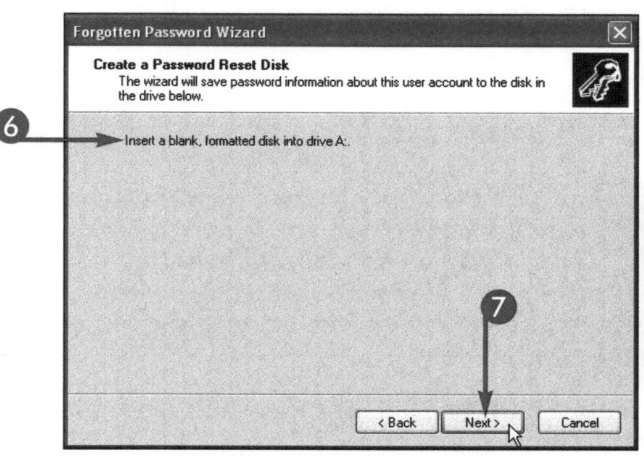

9 The wizard creates your disk. When complete, click Next.

10 Click Finish in the last screen.

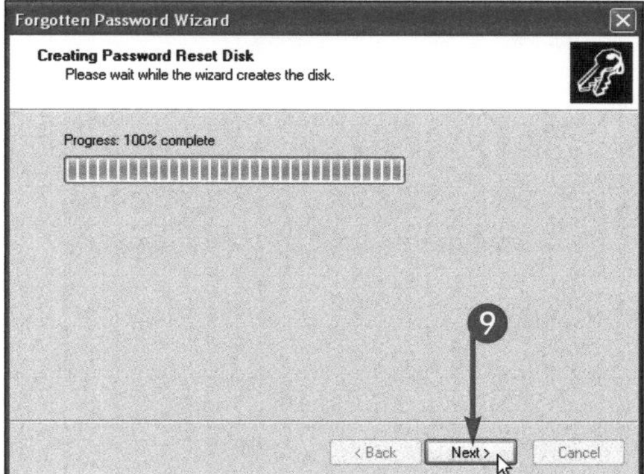

What is on the Password Reset Disk?

- There is only one file on this disk. It is called userkey.psw and is an encrypted version of your password. Be sure to keep this disk in a safe place so other people cannot use it to break into your computer. Some organizations, in fact, require the Password Reset Disk to be stored in the company safe, accessible only by system administrators or executives.

How do I use the Password Reset disk?

- At the Welcome screen, click your user name, type a password, and then press Enter. If your password is wrong, a message appears asking if you forgot your password. Click the option to use your Password Reset Disk. Click Next, and then make sure your Password Reset Disk is inserted in drive A. Click Next. Type a new password, type it again, and type a password hint. Click Next and then Finish. Your new password is created. Now you can type the new password at the Welcome screen to access Windows.

Can I create a Password Reset Disk for another user?

- No. You must be logged on as the user for which you are creating the Password Reset Disk.

Configure Fast User Switching

Fast User Switching enables you to switch users without logging out. This feature is handy if you want to log on as a different user, but not stop all the programs you are using. You simply switch out of the user account in which you are working and log on with another user account.

To set up Fast User Switching, you must be a computer administrator on a workgroup computer or stand-alone computer. When you have Fast User Switching enabled, you cannot turn it off if multiple users are logged on to your computer. This way you do not lose any settings for the user account from which you have switched.

Even though Fast User Switching is handy for many occasions, you will find that shutting down your applications and logging out will greatly speed up your computer for the next person logging on.

Configure Fast User Switching

1. Click Start.
2. Click Control Panel.

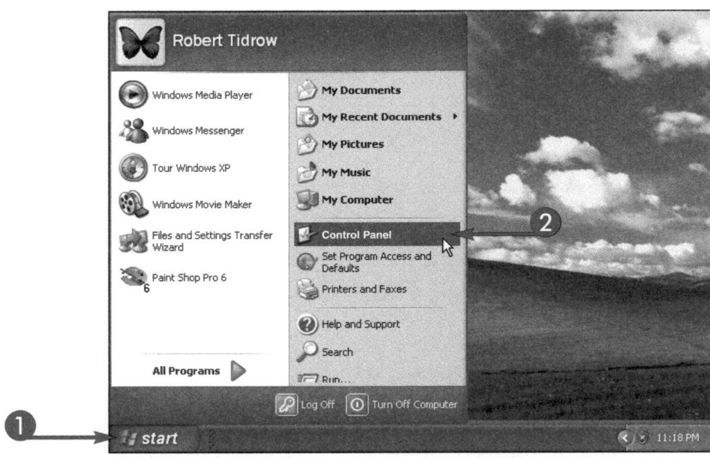

The Control Panel appears.

3. Click User Accounts.

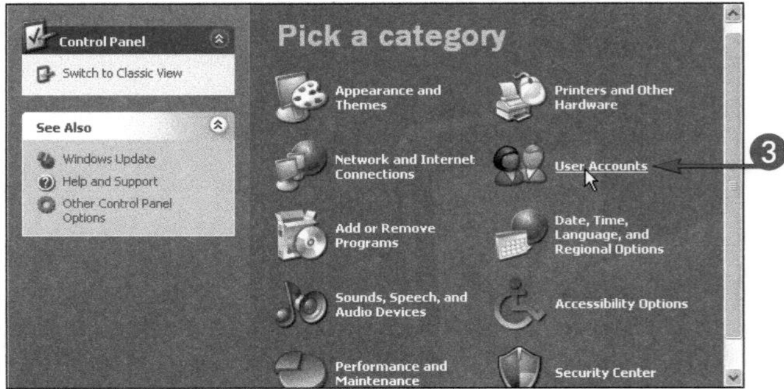

The User Accounts window appears.

4 Click Change the way users log on or off.

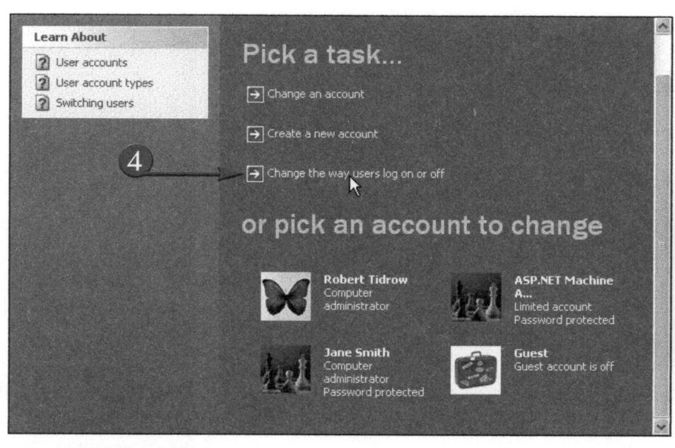

5 Click Use Fast User Switching.

6 Click Apply Options.

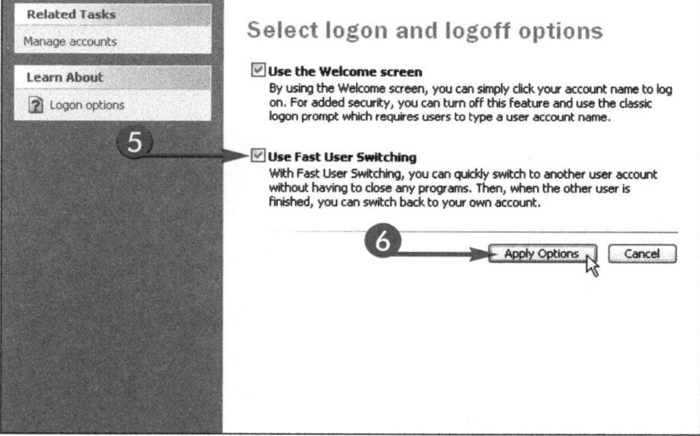

When I go to set Fast User Switching, I get a message that it will not work because of offline file access. What is this?

- Offline file access lets you store shared files on your computer so you can work on them when you are not connected to a network. Usually this is more popular for mobile users who are sometimes disconnected from a local area network. Shared files can be synchronized between the mobile computer and the network server.

We have a network domain at work. Can Fast User Switching work here?

- No. Fast User Switching works only on stand-alone computers or on a workgroup. It will not work if your computer is a member of a domain.

I am not an administrator for my computer. Can I set up Fast User Switching?

- You must have administrator privileges to configure Fast User Switching on your computer. Ask your computer administrator to set up this feature, or ask her to make you an administrator of the computer. You then can set up Fast User Switching.

Launch the Run As Command

The Run As command lets you start programs as a different user than you currently are logged on as. For example, you may be logged on as a Limited user, but you need to run a program that is configured only for administrators. The Run As command lets you log on as the administrator and run that program.

The Run As command lets you stay logged on as the current user and run the command without the hassle of shutting down all your applications, logging on as administrator (or any other user for that matter), and then running the desired program. An example of a program that you may want to run as administrator is the Group Policy editor. Limited users are not authorized for access to the group policy settings.

The Run As command should be treated seriously if you are an administrator. Keep in mind that if you use the Run As command on a user's computer and encounter a virus, you could destroy all the accounts on the computer, including the Administrator account. This could render Windows and your data useless until you clean up the virus.

Launch the Run As Command

1. Log on as a Limited user.
2. Click Start.
3. Click All Programs.
4. Click Accessories.
5. Click Windows Explorer.

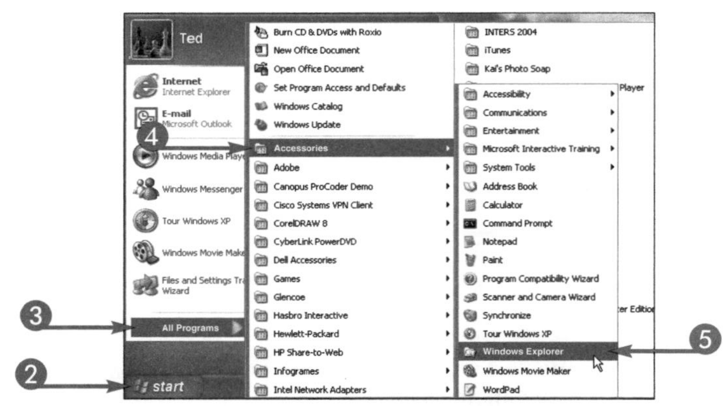

- Windows Explorer opens. Locate the program file you want to open as a different user.

6. Right-click the program name.

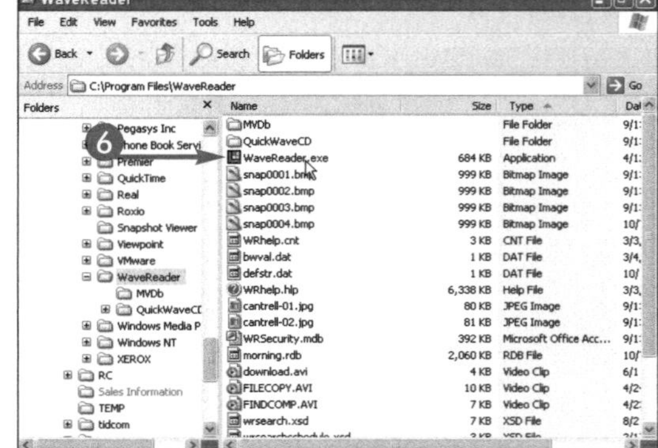

7 Click Run as from the menu that appears.

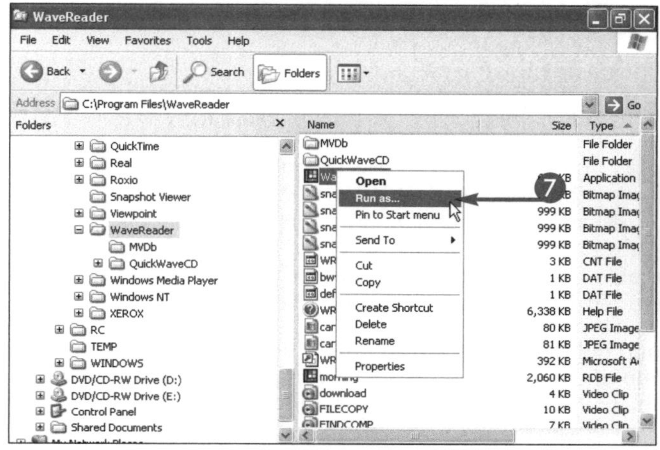

The Run As dialog box appears.

8 Click the option to specify a user.

9 Click here and select a user from the User name dropdown list.

10 Type the user's password in the Password box.

11 Click OK to run the program.

I do not know the administrator password. How can I run a program as that user?

▼ To use the Run As command, you must know the password for the user you want to run as.

When I use the Run As command to run a program under a different user, the program does not run. Why not?

▼ More than likely the user you selected from the User name dropdown list in the Run As dialog box did not have sufficient rights to run the program. Check Local Users and Groups (see the section "Change Group Membership") to see in which groups the user belongs. If the privileges are too restrictive, you may need to change the user to a different group, such as to the Power User group.

I do not see the Run As command when I right-click a file. Is there another way to start it?

▼ The Run As command is installed by default now with Windows XP SP2. If you are having difficulty using it, be sure you are right-clicking an executable file and not a non-executable file. For example, the Run As command is not available if you right-click a document file (.doc). It is, however, available when you right-click a program file (.exe).

Edit Group Policies

A group policy is a collection of settings that controls a user's Windows environment. System and computer administrators can use group policies to enable or disable access to various items available to a user. For example, a group policy can be set up to restrict users from accessing the Start menu.

Group policies can be applied to a single computer, a group of computers, or to all the computers on a Windows domain. Policies can be set for the entire computer, for local users, or both. One policy that a computer may have enabled is to disallow printers to be published. This means that a shared printer cannot be shown in the Active Directory of a Windows domain. By doing this, a network administrator can restrict other users on the network from "seeing" this printer and printing to it.

A policy that can be user-specific, for example, is one that removes access to the Microsoft Windows Update site. Administrators can disable access to this site so that a user cannot download update software to his computer.

Edit Group Policies

1. Click Start.
2. Click Run.

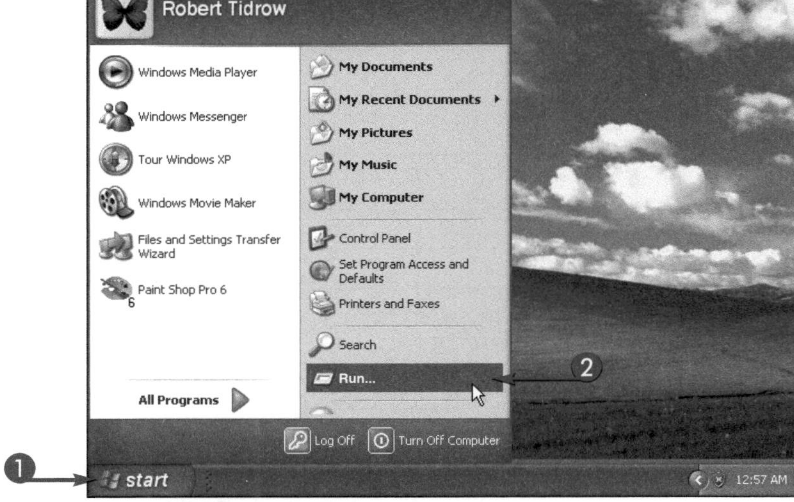

The Run dialog box appears.

3. Type **gpedit.msc** in the Open box.
4. Click OK.

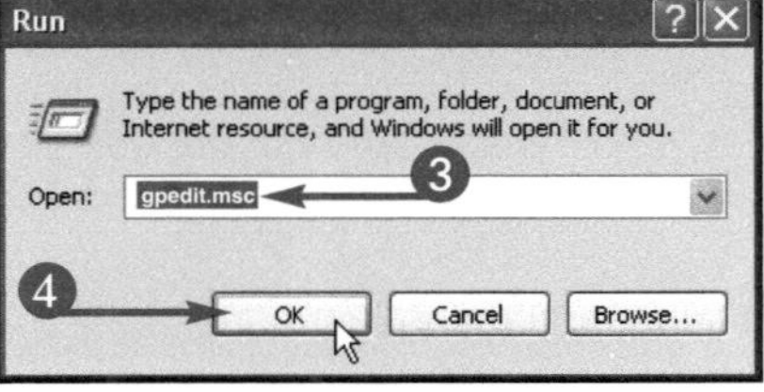

The Group Policy editor appears.

- This area displays computer and user folders. To modify a setting, click the plus sign next to a folder and then click a folder.

5. Click Administrative Templates.
6. Click Printers.
   - This area displays subfolders and specific policy settings.
7. To edit a setting, double-click it.

A properties dialog box for the setting appears.

8. Click Enabled.
9. Click Apply.
10. Click OK.

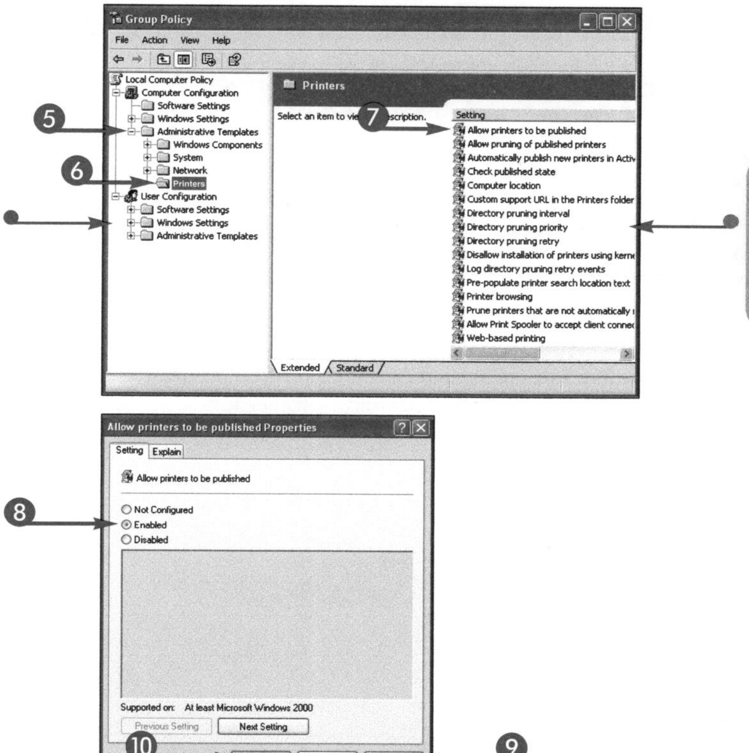

Why are group policies even available? They seem rather confusing to me.

▼ The main reason is that many power users and administrators want a way to configure advanced environmental settings without using the Windows Registry (the main Windows database). With the Group Policy editor, administrators can create templates that can then be applied to multiple computers in an enterprise, workgroup, or domain.

Do I need to use group policies?

▼ No, but if you are part of a domain, you may be using them right now without knowing it. Your system administrator may have created a group policy template that your computer applied to your system when you logged on to the network.

How can I find out more about the policies available in Windows XP SP2?

▼ There are a few resources on the Internet, including Microsoft.com, that provide documentation on the thousands of policies available. One way to learn which settings are available, however, is to open up the Group Policy editor and scan through the collection of policies you have available. Most policies include a short description.

Configure Roaming Group Policies

One of the most useful ways to deploy group policies is for roaming users. These are users who must log on to several different computers in an organization. With roaming policies, that user's Windows environment can be copied to any computer they log on to, regardless of the location within the company.

To use roaming group policies, an organization must have a Windows domain and use Active Directory. The roaming policy (sometimes referred to as roaming profiles in previous Windows versions) is stored on the network server and then downloaded to the machine a user logs on to. Any changes a user makes to Windows settings are then saved to both the local copy and the network copy. This ensures that the profile is always the most current one for that user.

Mobile group policies can be used to assign user logon requirements, restrict folder access, or redirect a local folder to a network drive. A user's My Documents or My Pictures folder can be redirected.

Configure Roaming Group Policies

1. Right-click My Computer.
2. Click Manage.

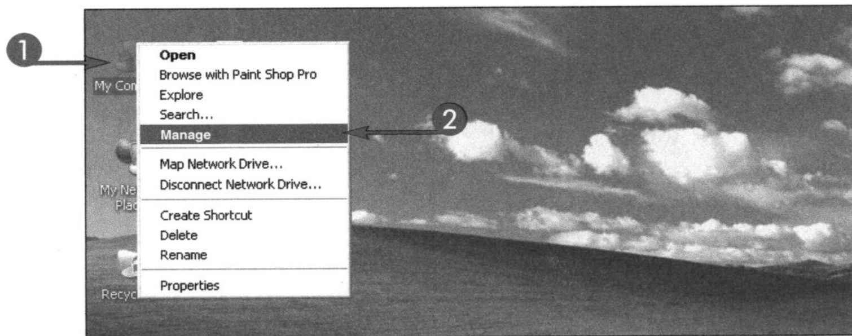

The Computer Management window appears.

3. Click here to see the Local Users and Groups folders.
4. Double-click Local Users and Groups.
5. Click Users.
6. In the right pane, double-click the user you want to configure.

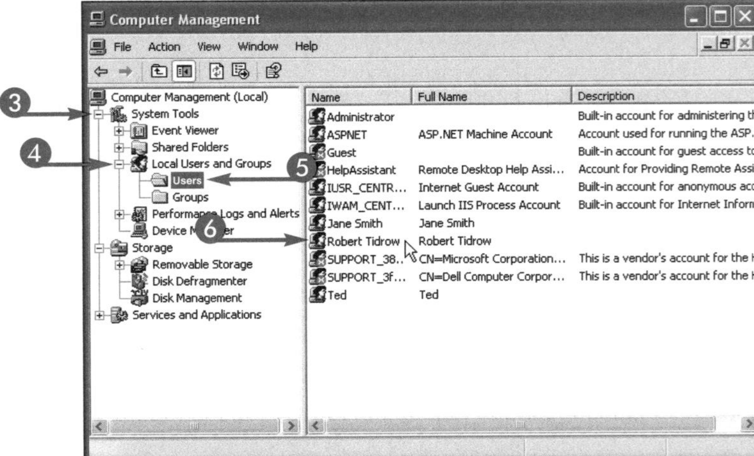

The properties dialog box for that user appears.

7 Click the Profile tab.

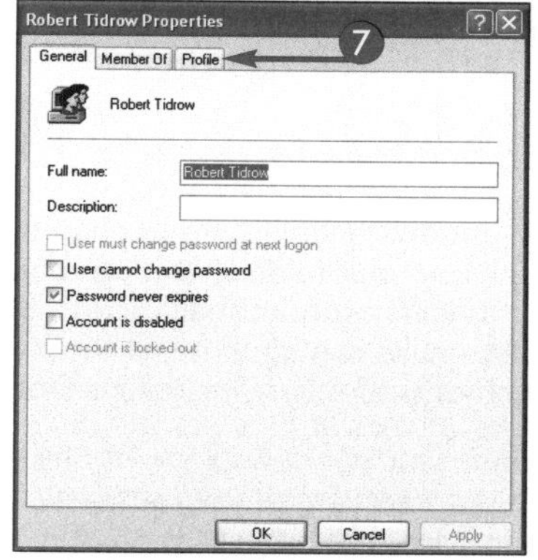

8 Type the network path where the profile is stored. For example, the path may look like *servername**folder*\profile.

9 If the home folder for this user is on the network, click Connect.

10 Click here and then select the network drive.

11 Type the path to the home folder.

12 Click OK.

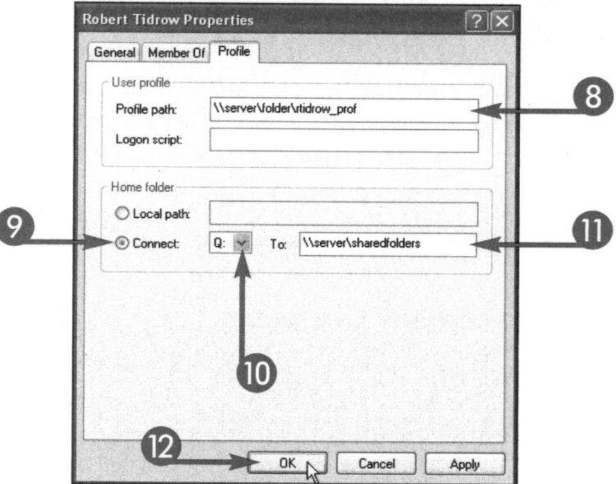

Can roaming group policies be used for mobile users?

▼ Yes. In fact, this is one way companies can help mobile users get up and running quicker each time they visit the office. With mobile group policies, you can set up scripts, redirections, and software settings that laptop users can download each time they access the company network. A script is a file that has specific instructions that computers will execute during startup. For example, a script can tell a computer to look for updated software and how to install that software.

Sometimes a roaming profile is not available. How can I use a local one?

▼ Open the Control Panel and click Performance and Maintenance. Click System to open the System Properties dialog box. Click the Advanced tab, and then click Settings under User Profiles. Select a profile to change, click Change Type, and then click Local profile from the Change Profile Type dialog box. Click OK and OK again. Click OK to close the System Properties dialog box.

Change Folder Views

Windows enables you to change the way you view your folders. You can choose to view folders as thumbnails, icons, tiles, or lists. Changes you make can apply to all the folders, some of the folders (such as subfolders), or the current folder.

To keep important Windows systems files and hidden files from view, you can hide them from view. You also can remove from view the file extension of files that Windows knows how to open. This keeps users from accidentally changing file extensions.

Windows lets you see full filename pathnames in the address bar and title bar. If you do not want to see this information, you have the option to turn off those views.

Another option for your folders is to have Windows display a pop-up description of each folder item. You can see these by moving your mouse over an item and pausing it there for a few seconds.

Windows also lets you change how you share folders on a network. If you choose simple file sharing, you can set up shared folders so everyone in your workgroup can access your folders. To set up folder permissions to limit which users and groups can access your folders, however, you can disable simple file sharing.

Change Folder Views

1. Double-click My Computer.

The My Computer window appears.

2. Click Tools.
3. Click Folder Options.

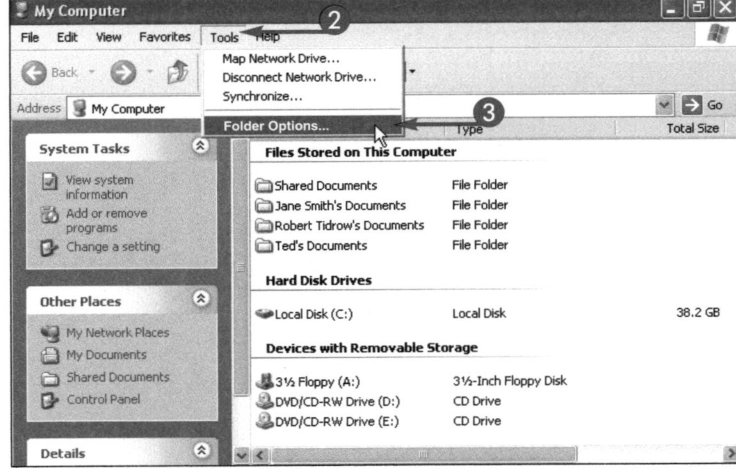

The Folder Options dialog box appears.

4 Click the View tab.

- This option has Windows search networks for printers and shared folders.
- These options display or hide hidden files and folders.

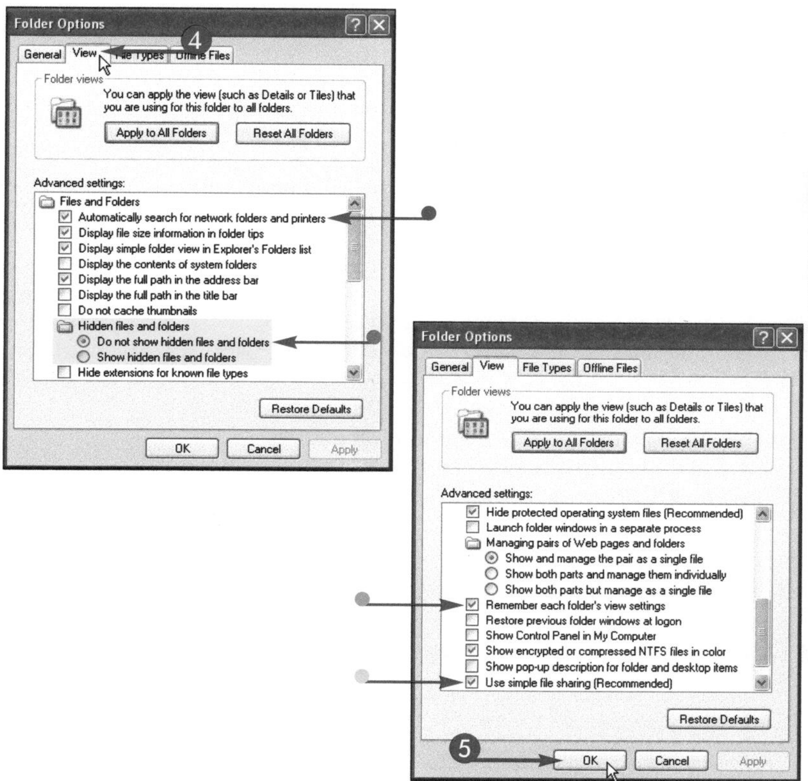

- This option tells Windows to remember how your folder view is configured. It opens the same way the next time.
- This option uses simple file sharing instead of sharing in which you can specify permissions and users.

5 Click OK to save any changes.

What is a file extension?

▼ Windows uses file extensions (those three characters after the period of a filename) to associate that file with installed applications. For example, Microsoft Excel worksheet files use an .xls extension. When you click or double-click any file with an .xls extension, Windows knows which application to start — Excel — in order for you to view the selected file.

Why would I want to cache thumbnail views?

▼ By caching thumbnail view files, Windows can display thumbnail views much faster the next time you view a folder in thumbnail view. The downside is that your system memory is depleted a little with each cache file created.

What happens if I change a file extension to a file?

▼ When working in a file management program (My Computer or Windows Explorer), be sure to change the file extension back to its proper extension. You can do this by answering No when prompted during a name change procedure that changing a filename can make the file unstable. If, however, you make the change, click Edit and then click Undo to return the filename back to its original name. One exception to this is if you change a file extension on the desktop. The Edit menu and Undo command are not available. You would need to right-click the filename, choose Rename from the menu that appears, and then rename the file with the original filename extension. Press Enter to complete the renaming procedure.

Customize Folder Details

When you view folders and files in My Computer or Windows Explorer, the information that displays for each item is called the details. With Windows XP, you can see a whole host of details, including name, type of file, modification date, and so on.

These details are shown in columns that you can click to sort folders and files. For example, if you want to sort files by type, click the Type column heading. Or, to see files sorted by size, click the Size column heading.

The detail columns that display depend on the folder template that is used to describe how a folder displays its contents. Folders set up as pictures, for example, display columns relating to photographs, such as Date Picture Taken and Dimensions. Music Album folders, on the other hand, show Artist, Album Title, Year, Track Number, and Duration.

Windows lets you change which column headings are showing. You may, for example, want to see the author of a particular document. In Microsoft Excel, you can choose File and then Properties to see summary information about a workbook's author.

Customize Folder Details

1. Open the folder whose folder detail you want to change.
2. Click here and choose a view.

   This example changes the view to Details, letting you view folder detail columns.

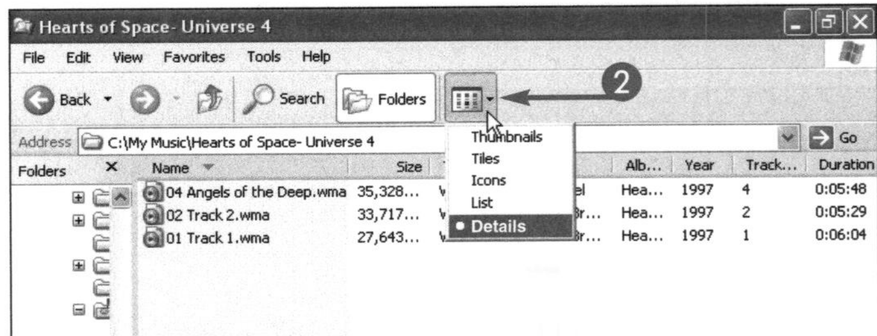

3. Right-click a column.

   A list of column headings appears. Those selected include a check mark (☑) next to them.

4. Click a heading name to add it to your list of column headings.
5. To see additional column headings, click More.

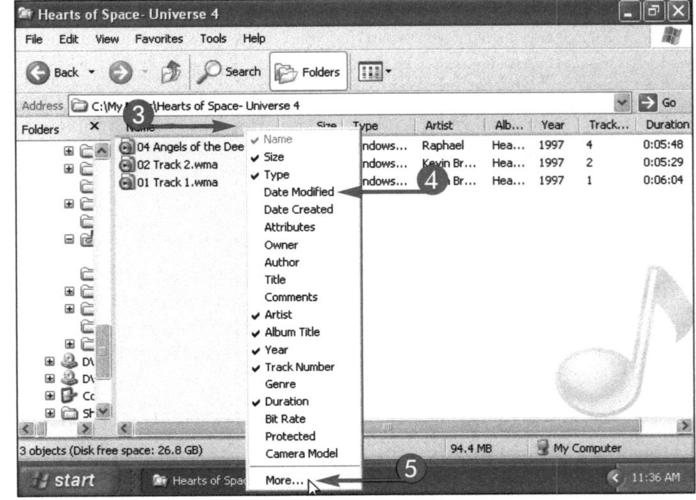

The Choose Details dialog box appears, letting you select several different column headings, such as Pages, Copyright, Genre, and so on.

- To rearrange the columns, select a column and click Move Up or Move Down.

6 Click OK to confirm your changes.

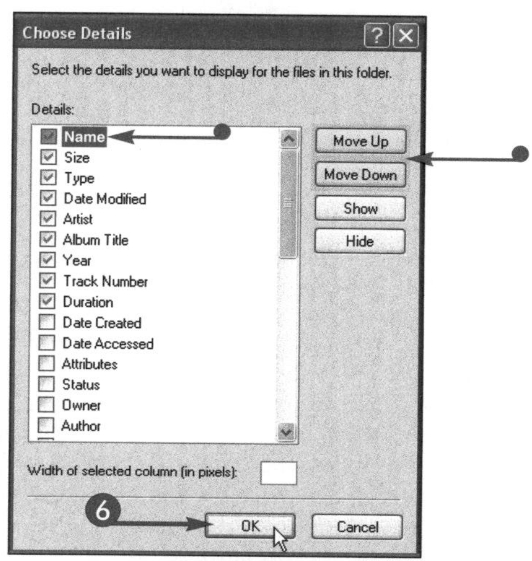

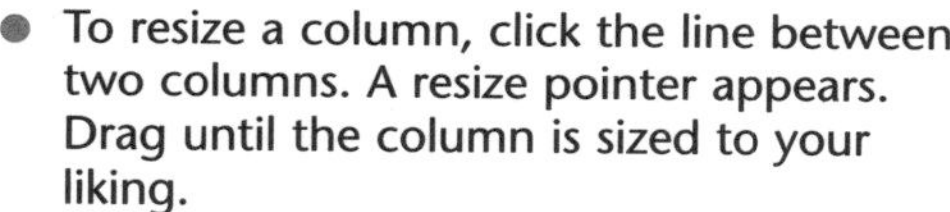

- To resize a column, click the line between two columns. A resize pointer appears. Drag until the column is sized to your liking.

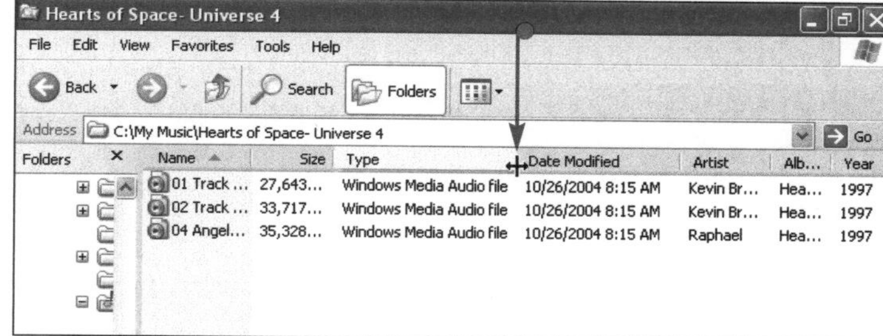

How do I sort folders and files in a column?

▼ To sort using a column as the sort criteria (such as by Name, Size, Type, and so on), click the column name. This sorts the folders and files in alphanumeric order (for example A–Z). Click the column name again to reverse the sort (Z–A).

Can I remove or resize a column that I have added?

▼ Yes. Right-click a column and then select the column name you want to remove.

You also can display the Choose Details dialog box and clear a selection to remove the column. Or, select a column name and then click Hide. Click OK to confirm your changes.

You also can resize a column to make it larger. In the Choose Details dialog box, select the column you want to change and increase the width of the selected column (in pixels) to a larger number, such as 30. Click OK.

Can I rearrange folder detail columns?

▼ Yes. Select the column you want to move and hold down the left mouse button. Drag the column to the new location and drop. A solid black line appears as you drag the column. This line shows where the column will be moved to when you release the mouse button.

Change File Associations

A file association is information that tells Windows which program to launch when you double-click a filename. Windows knows which program to open based on the file's extension (which is the three-character name to the right of the period in a filename). All files with the same file extension are opened by the same program.

For example, files with the extension .doc are opened by Microsoft Word if you have Microsoft Office installed on your computer. However, if you do not have Microsoft Word installed, Windows WordPad opens files with a .doc extension. If you want to change this so a different program opens DOC files, such as Corel WordPerfect, you can change the file association to that program.

File associations can change without your modifying them manually. After you install a new program, the new program may automatically change a file association so it opens a file type. Sometimes programs prompt you first before changing your file associations. If so, read over the types of files changed before accepting the change.

Windows lets you open a file with a different program (if that program supports that file type) on a file-by-file basis. This is handy if you want to open a file in Notepad, for example, that is normally opened by a spreadsheet program. In Notepad you can view the raw data without any formatting applied.

Change File Associations

1. Double-click My Computer.

   The My Computer window appears.

2. Click Tools.

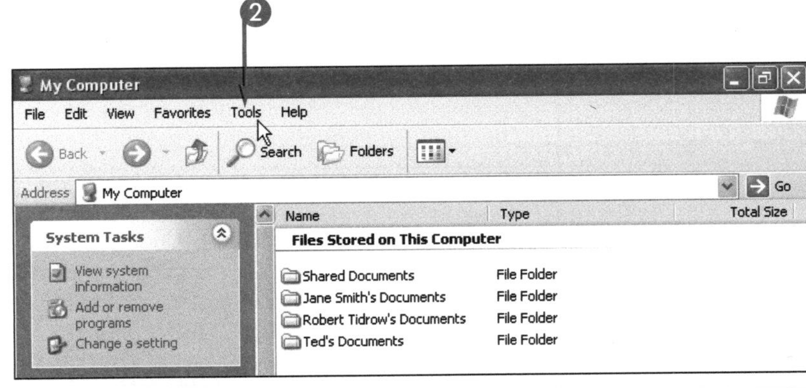

3. Click Folder Options.

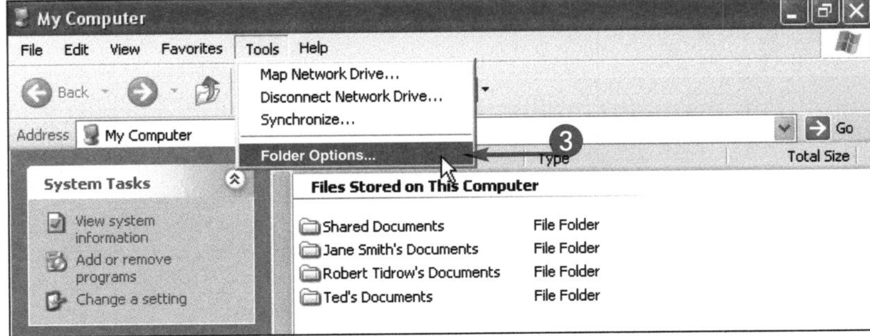

The Folder Options dialog box appears.

4 Click the File Types tab.

- This area lists the file extensions and associated file types on your computer.

5 To change a file type association, click a file type.

6 Click Change.

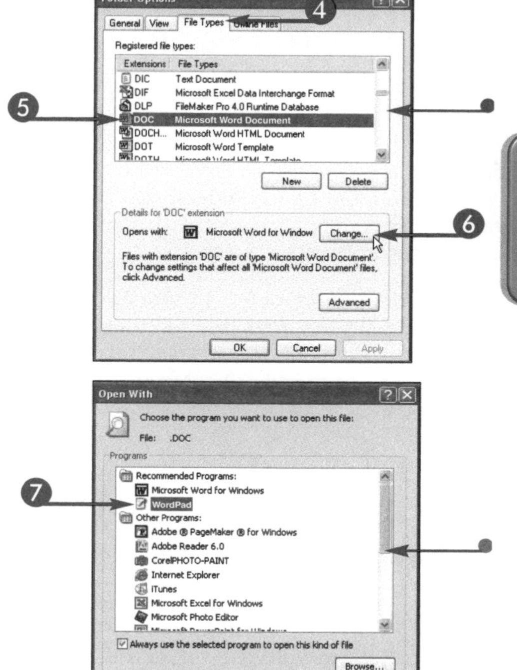

The Open With dialog box appears.

- This area displays a list of programs installed on your computer.

7 Click the program you want to associate with the file type you selected in Step 5.

8 Click OK to confirm the changes.

9 Click OK to close the Folder Options dialog box.

After I installed Netscape Navigator, all the Web pages I have saved to my hard drive are opened by Navigator. However, I want Internet Explorer to open Web pages that I double-click. Can I change this setting?

▼ To change the file association from Navigator to Internet Explorer, open My Computer and click Tools and then Folder Options. In the Folder Options dialog box, click the File Types tab and select HTM. Click Change, and in the Open With dialog box, select Netscape Navigator, and then click OK. Do the same with the HTML file type. Click OK when finished to confirm your changes.

How can I open a file in a different program than the one assigned to it?

▼ Right-click the file you want to open and then select Open With. From the Open With dialog box, select the program you want to use to open the selected file. Click OK.

When I click the File Types tab to change my file associations, why does it take so long to show registered file types?

▼ Windows needs to find all the file types registered on your computer to display them on the File Types tab. The more programs and files you have stored on your computer, the longer it takes to fill the Registered file types list. When the list is filled for the current Windows session, however, the File Types tab is filled quicker the next time you use it.

Add Files and Folders to the Start Menu

When you access the Windows Start menu, you are viewing a special Windows folder that contains files, folders, and links to your programs. There are also links to special Windows system folders and commands.

You can add files and folders to the Start menu if you are not satisfied with the ones that are there. For example, you may want to add a link to Netscape Navigator at the top of the Start menu to quickly start Navigator each time. Or you can add a link to a folder or file directly to the Start menu to find what you need quickly.

When you install most programs, Windows automatically creates a shortcut to the program folder and other important program files. If the program does not create a shortcut during the install process, you can add one yourself later.

The Start menu on Windows XP is much more sophisticated than the one on previous versions of Windows. For example, you have the option of highlighting newly installed programs, listing most recently used programs, displaying the Control Panel applets as links or as a menu item, or showing or hiding the Favorites menu.

Add Files and Folders to the Start Menu

1. Right-click Start.
2. Click Properties from the menu that appears.

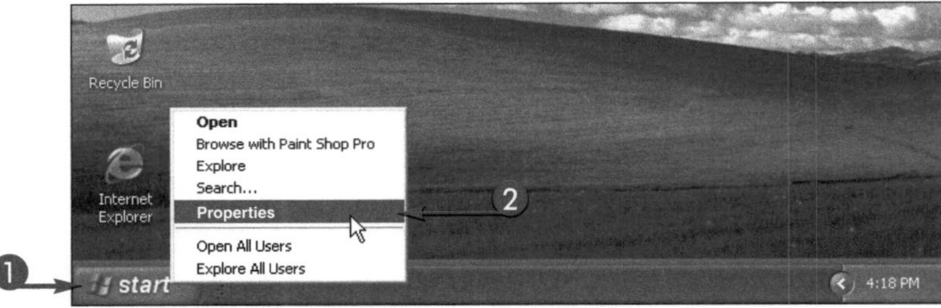

The Taskbar and Start Menu Properties dialog box appears.

3. Click Customize.

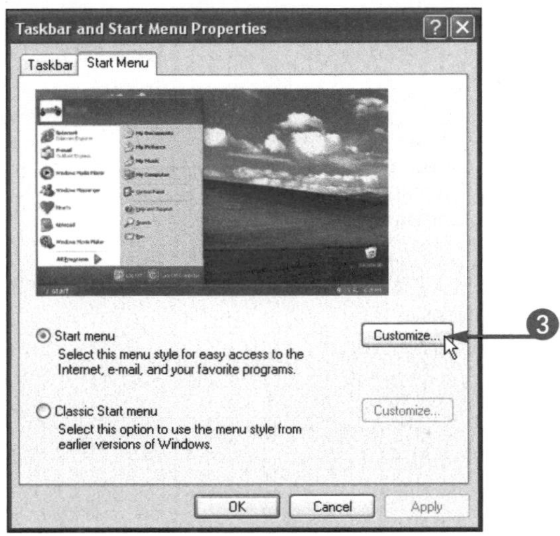

The Customize Start Menu dialog box appears.

4 Click the Advanced tab.

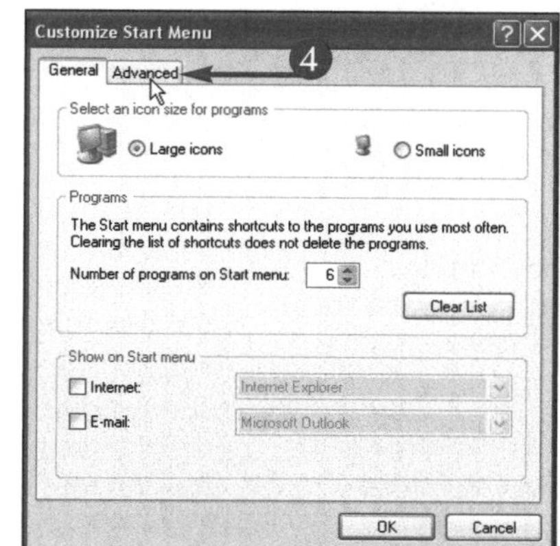

- This area shows a list of items you can add to the Start menu. To add one, click it in the list.

5 Click OK to confirm your changes.

6 Click OK to close the Taskbar and Start Menu Properties dialog box.

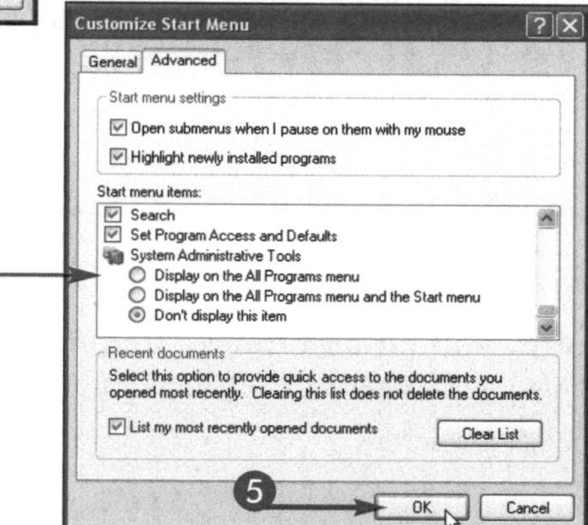

Is there a quick way to add items to and remove items from the Start menu?

▼ It depends on if you have drag-and-drop enabled on the Start menu. If so, all you have to do is drag the item to the Start menu and drop the item there. The item appears at the top of the Start menu.

To remove an item, open the Start menu and right-click the item you want to remove. A menu appears. Click Remove from This List if the item is in the left column of the Start menu. If the item is in the All Programs lists, select Delete and click Yes.

I dragged-and-dropped an item to the Start menu. Can I put it someplace else besides the top of the menu?

▼ Yes. Drag the item to the location you want it to appear and drop. You cannot place the item on the right side of the Start menu, such as where the Control Panel and Run command options are. You can place an item only on the left side of the Start menu, or on the All Programs section.

How do I rename a folder or file I added to the Start menu?

▼ Click Start to display the Start menu. Right-click the file or folder you want to modify and choose Rename. Type a new name and click OK.

Customize Folder Properties

Each folder has properties that you can customize. These properties include what type of folder template to use, a folder picture to help you know what type of file is stored in the folder, and what icon is used to illustrate the folder.

With a folder template, you can apply certain features to a folder based on the type of files you store in the folder. When you view the contents of the folder, the type of details Windows displays is based on the template you selected. For example, if a folder contains music files from an album, a template named Music Album exists. Viewing Music Album folders shows Artist name, Album title, Year of the recording, Track number, and Duration of each track.

Folders can be represented by pictures. Folder pictures help you quickly identify the contents of folders when you view them in thumbnail view. By default, Windows uses the first four images in the folder as the folder picture. You can, however, change this picture to one more representative of the folder.

Customize Folder Properties

Customize a folder template

1. Right-click the folder whose template you want to change.
2. Click Properties.

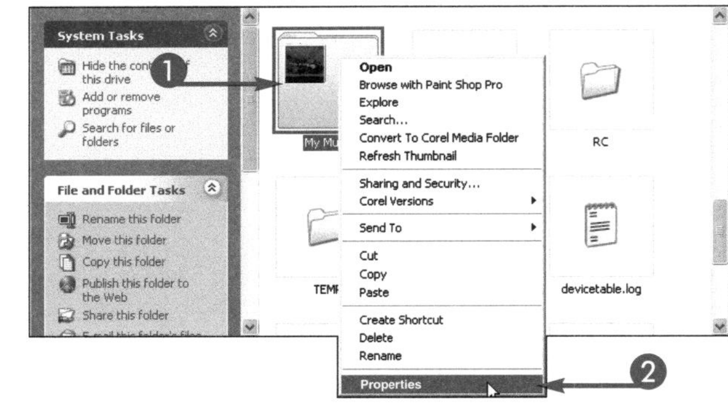

The properties dialog box appears.

3. Click the Customize tab.

- This area displays the names of the folder templates.

4. To change the folder template, click here and select the template name.

Customize a folder picture

- This area displays the folder picture assigned to the selected folder.

5. To change the folder picture, click Choose Picture.

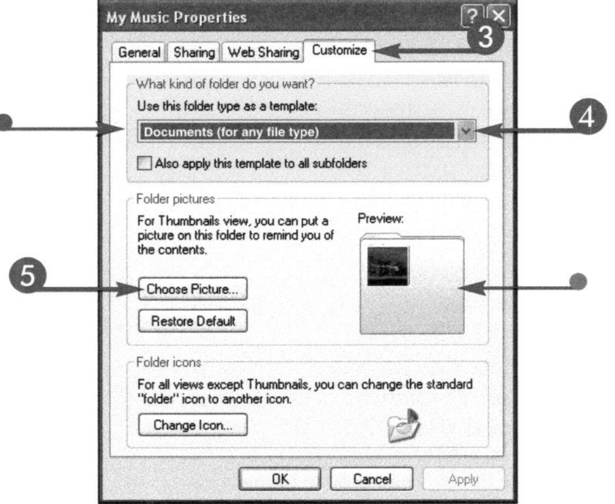

The Browse dialog box appears.

6. Click a picture you want to use as the folder picture.
7. Click Open to confirm your change.

Customize a folder icon

8. To change the icon, click Change Icon in the properties dialog box.

   The Change Icon dialog box appears.
9. Click an icon
10. Click OK.
11. Click OK in the properties dialog box to confirm your changes.

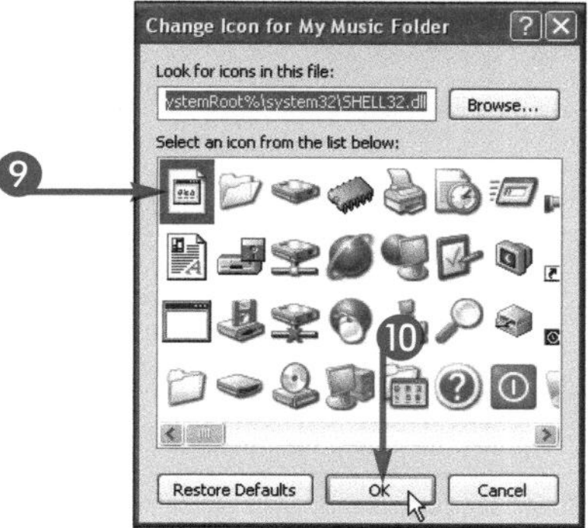

Do I have to use a folder template for all my folders?

▼ No. By default Windows uses the Documents (for any file type) folder for your folders. The folder templates are just another way to customize your Windows environment to your needs.

When you create a folder and save files to it, Windows attempts to "guess" the type of contents of a folder and apply the closest template choice to that folder. Windows uses file types and file extensions to guess the contents.

Can I have subfolders use the same folder template as their root folder?

▼ Yes. When you apply a template to a folder, you also have the option of applying it to the folder's subfolders. Do this only if the subfolders contain the same type of folders as the main folder. Right-click a folder, click Properties, and then click the Customize tab. Choose the option to also apply this template to all subfolders (☐ changes to ☑). Click OK.

When I click Choose Picture, I do not see any pictures. How can I find them?

▼ You may need to navigate to other folders to find a picture you want to use for your folder. To do this, click the My Computer icon on the left pane of the Browse dialog box and navigate to a folder that contains pictures.

Configure Simple File Sharing

Windows enables you to share files with other users when you are part of a network. The network can be a workgroup network, in which you are connected to a few other computers through a centralized hub or switch (often called peer-to-peer networking). Another type of network is a domain-based network, in which a centralized server controls directory services.

When you have a workgroup network, Windows XP uses Simple File Sharing, which limits the amount of security you can place on a shared file. Password-protection and file access restrictions are not available for this type of file sharing. For Windows XP Home Edition users, only Simple File Sharing is offered.

Windows XP Professional automatically enables simple file sharing when your computer is part of a workgroup. You should be aware of this: As soon as you share files on your system, others can see them over the network.

The easiest way to enable Windows for file sharing is to use the Network Setup Wizard. This wizard walks you through configuring your computer to be part of a workgroup.

Besides setting up Windows, you need to also make sure your computer has the correct hardware set up. This includes network cards, network cables, and a hub or switch. As you work through the Network Setup Wizard, a helpful link is available that describes all you need.

Configure Simple File Sharing

1. Double-click My Network Places.

   The My Network Places window appears.

2. Click Set up a home or small office network.

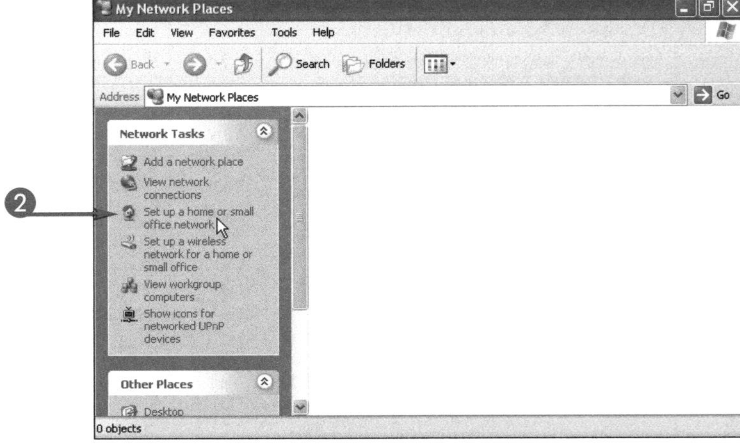

The Network Setup Wizard appears.

3. Click Next.

The next screen explains the steps of setting up the network.

- Click the checklist for creating a network link for more information.

4. Click Next.

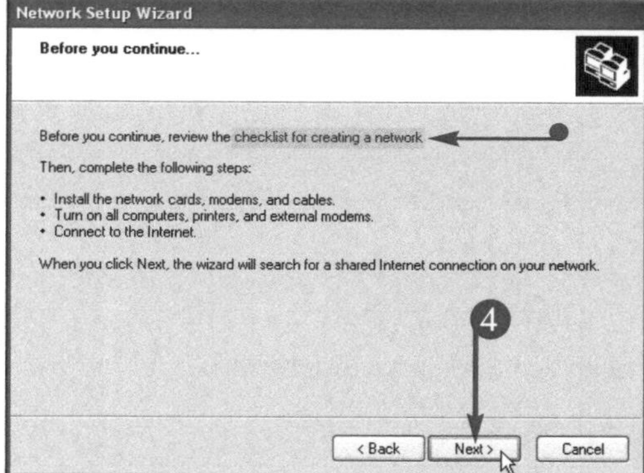

What is a workgroup?

A workgroup is a collection of computers on a network. For computers to share files and printers, they must all belong to the same workgroup. The default workgroup name is MSHOME; however, you can change this to one more suited to your working environment. For example, a workgroup in a marketing department might be named MARKETING.

Do I need to turn on file sharing on my computer?

Not necessarily. If, when you first install Windows XP, your PC is part of a workgroup, Windows automatically sets up file and printer sharing on your computer.

If you become part of a workgroup after installation, however, you can enable it manually.

Can I disable file sharing if I do not want anybody to access my files?

Yes. To do this, double-click the My Network Places icon on the desktop. On the Network Tasks pane of the My Network Places window, click the Set up a home or small office network link. Click Next four times on the Network Setup Wizard screens. Then select Turn off file and printer sharing (○ changes to ◉). Click Next until the end of the wizard and then choose Yes to shut down and restart your computer.

continued

Configure Simple File Sharing *(Continued)*

Not only can you share files, you also can share printers using the Simple File Sharing feature of Windows XP.

By sharing printers, you can reduce the number of printers required for a small office or home. Instead of requiring a separate printer for each computer, you can invest in one printer, connect it to one computer, and then share it with other computers in your workgroup.

Another way shared printers work is to set up multiple printers in a workgroup that each have different paper inserted. For example, one printer could print regular hard copies, while a second printer could be dedicated to printing on your business letterhead. This way users would not have to empty a printer bin, add letterhead, and print whenever a business correspondence was needed.

You also could invest in one nice color printer that the entire workgroup could share. Users could then send color documents, pictures, and Web pages (when color was needed on them) to this shared color printer.

Configure Simple File Sharing *(continued)*

- The next screen lets you select an Internet connection method.

5 Keep the default setting for now.

6 Click Next.

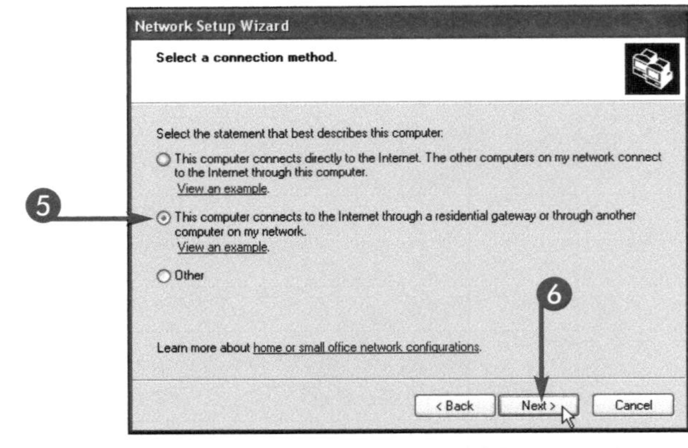

The next screen lets you give your computer a description and name.

7 Type a description in the Computer description text box.

8 Type a name for the computer in the Computer name text box. This name must be unique for the network.

9 Click Next.

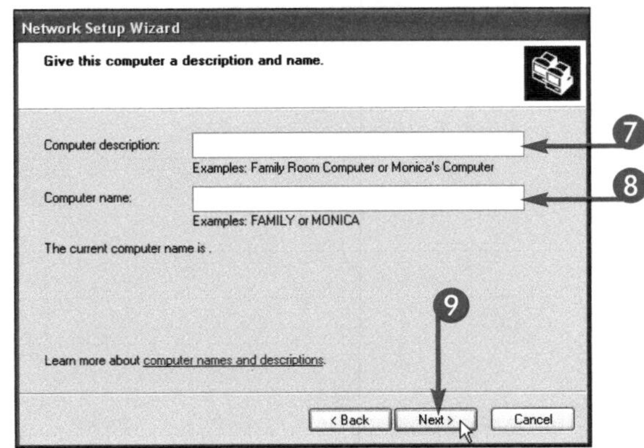

The next screen lets you name your network workgroup.

10 Type a workgroup name.

11 Click Next.

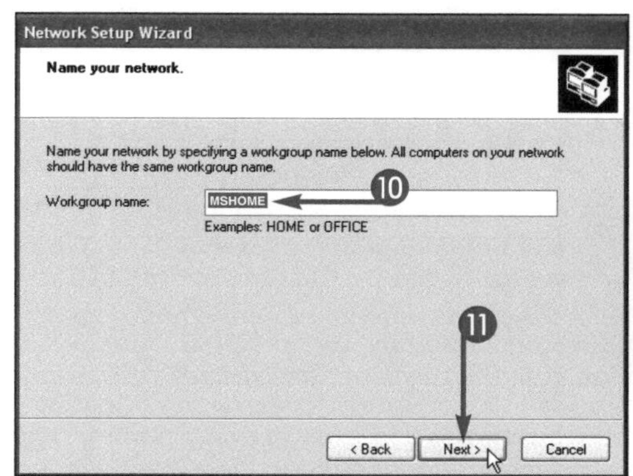

The next screen asks if you want to turn on or turn off file and printer sharing.

12 Make sure the Turn on file and printer sharing option is selected.

13 Click Next.

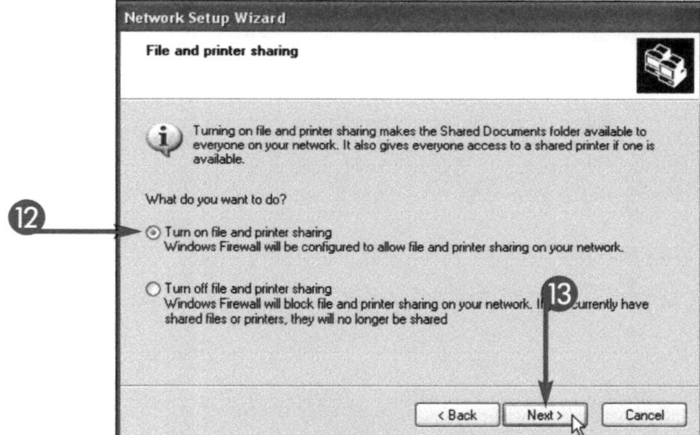

When I go to start the Network Setup Wizard, I do not see the My Network Places icon. Can you help?

▼ Yes. Right-click anyplace on the desktop (not on the taskbar, however) and select Properties. Click the Desktop tab and then click Customized Desktop. The Desktop Items dialog box appears. Select the My Network Places option under the Desktop icons area. Click OK twice to confirm your changes. The My Network Places icon appears on the desktop.

I still do not see the My Network Places icon. Is there anothere way to start the wizard?

▼ Yes. Click Start and then click Control Panel. Double-click Network and Internet Connections. This opens the Network and Internet Connections window. Click the Set up or change your home or small office network link under the Pick a task heading.

continued

Configure Simple File Sharing *(Continued)*

Part of the process of sharing resources (files, folders, and printers) across a network is to make sure that everyone else on the network can access your files. If your workgroup is made up entirely of Windows XP computers, you do not have much to worry about. Simply configure all the machines for Simple File Sharing.

In most businesses and even in many homes, however, there is a mixture of computers. Some are running Windows XP, while others are running earlier versions of Windows, including Windows 98, Windows Me, and Windows 2000.

You need to run the Network Setup Disk on computers not running Windows XP. This disk is created during the Network Setup Wizard.

After you set up simple file sharing, you can make your My Documents folders private so others cannot access them. You may want to do this if some of your My Documents subfolders contain company or private information that only you are authorized to view. You do this by right-clicking the folder, choosing Sharing, and then selecting Make this folder private so that only I have access to it. Click OK to finish.

Configure Simple File Sharing *(continued)*

This screen shows your network settings.

⓮ Click Next.

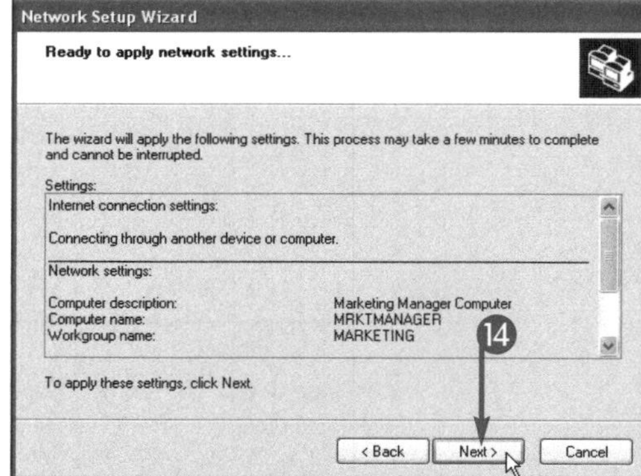

The next screen explains that you need to run Network Setup Wizard on all the computers in your workgroup.

⓯ Select Create a Network Setup Disk (for non-Windows XP computers).

⓰ Click Next.

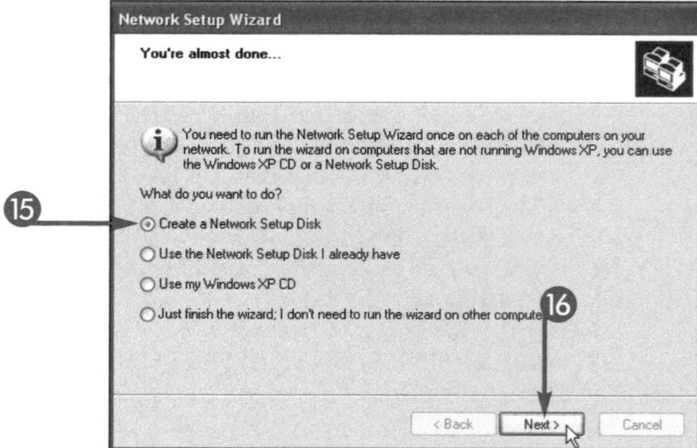

The next screen asks for a disk.

17. Insert a floppy disk into drive A: and click Next.

Windows creates a Network Setup Disk for computers running Windows 98 and Windows Me.

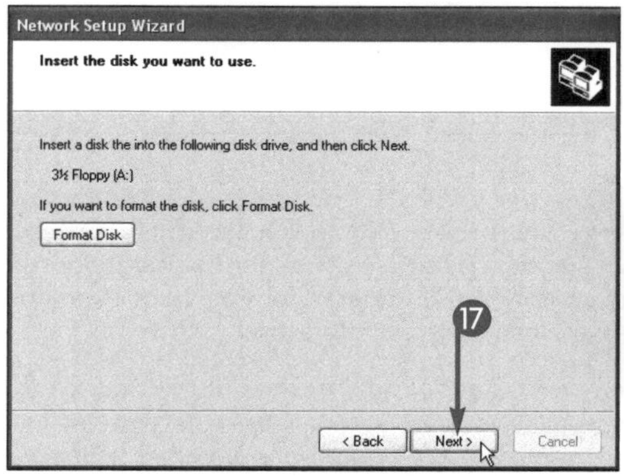

The next screen explains how to execute the Network Setup Disk on other computers.

18. Click Next.

19. Click Finish to complete the Network Setup Wizard.

20. Click Yes to shut down and restart your computer.

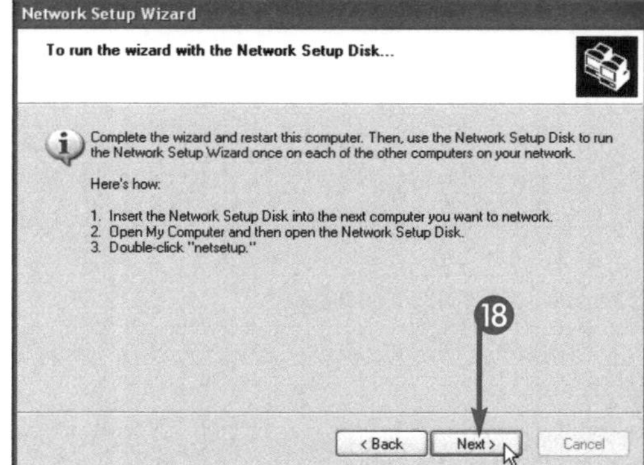

I set up Windows XP and now my Windows Me computer cannot see the new computer. Why not?

▼ You must create a Network Setup Disk for your Windows Me computers. You can create this disk when you run the Network Setup Wizard. One of the last steps in the wizard is to create this disk. Make sure that you select the Create a Network Setup Disk option (○ changes to ◉) when you come to that screen. Take that disk to the Me and 98 machines and run the NETSETUP program on those computers.

How do I find the NETSETUP program to run the Network Setup Disk?

▼ Insert the Network Setup Disk into the floppy disk drive of your Windows 98 or Windows Me computer. Double-click My Computers and then double-click 3½ Floppy Disk (A:) drive. Double-click the NETSETUP file.

Can I share files with users who have Windows 95?

▼ Windows XP is not designed to support simple file sharing with Windows 95. However, if you are part of a Windows domain (see Chapter 13 for more details), you may be able to share files between Windows XP and Windows 95 computers using Windows 2000 Active Directory Services.

Share a Folder Using Simple File Sharing

After you have your computer configured to share files using Simple File Sharing, you need to specify which folders you want to share. You should choose only those folders that you want everyone else on the network to be able to access.

There are many reasons to share folders across a network. One reason is to let others have access to a shared document on which many people need to work, such as a marketing plan or sales budget. Another reason for shared folders is to allow others to quickly copy files, such as templates, programs, videos, and pictures, from one computer to the next.

Windows enables you to share entire drives, such as your C: drive, but this is not recommended. For security reasons, you do not want to give others this kind of access to your entire drive. A user could gain control over your system and delete vital system files, introduce harmful viruses, or access confidential documents.

Instead, select subfolders that contain documents and files to which others should have access. Anytime you work on a file or document that others also must work on, save it to the shared folder. Then you are assured that the folder always includes the latest edits.

Share a Folder Using Simple File Sharing

1. Double-click My Computer.
2. Double-click the C: drive (or your root drive letter).

   The contents of the C: drive appear.

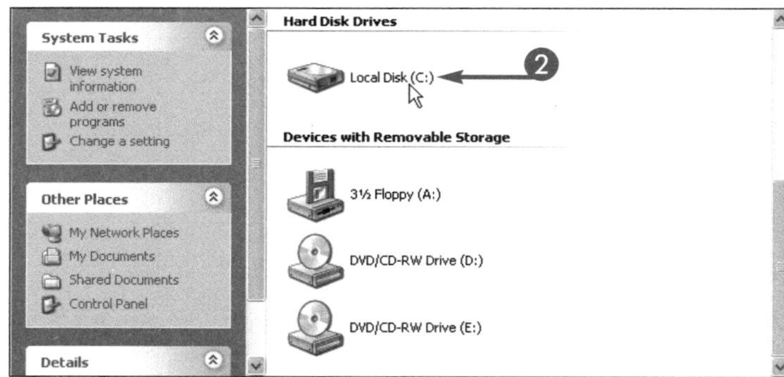

3. Right-click the folder you want to share.
4. Click Sharing and Security from the menu that appears.

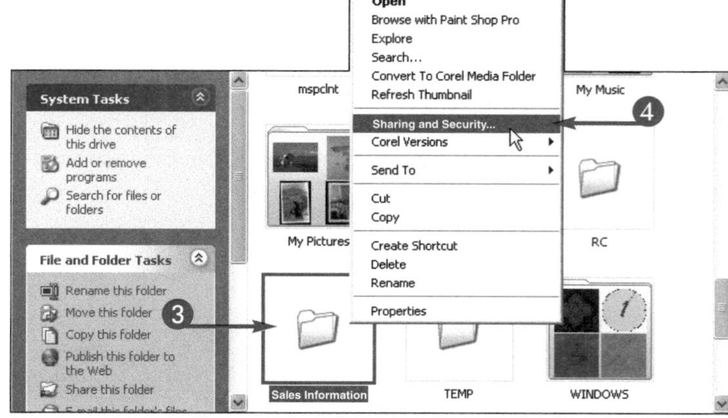

The Sharing tab of the folder's properties dialog box appears.

5 Select Share this folder on the network.

6 Type a name for the network share in the Share name text box. This is the name of the share that others see over the network. Keep it 12 characters or smaller.

7 Click the Allow network users to change my files option if you want others to modify your files.

Note: *This option lets others modify (including delete) your shared files.*

8 Click OK to confirm your changes.

- This icon indicates that a folder is shared on the computer.

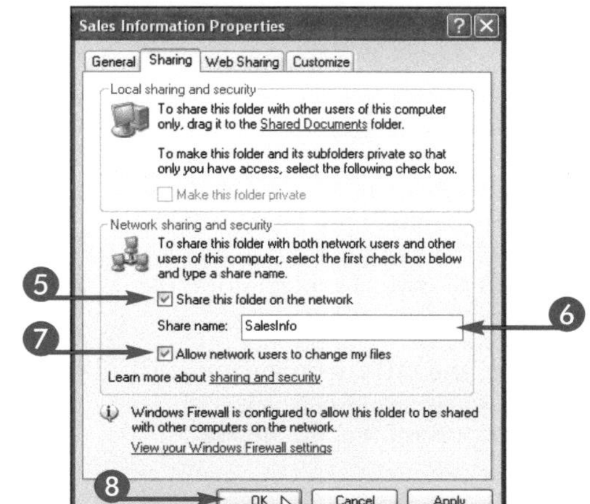

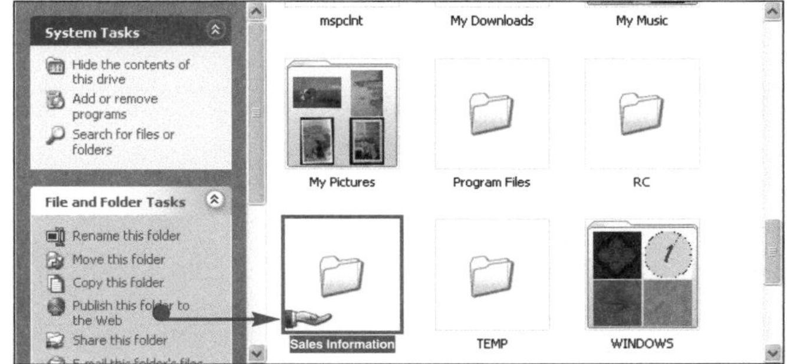

When I try to share a folder that belongs to another user on this computer, Windows does not let me. Why not?

▼ You cannot share folders that are in another user's profile. To be able to do this you must have Administrator privileges on that computer. Otherwise, the owner of that profile must set up the folder to be shared. The same is true for your profile as well. Others users, unless they are administrators, cannot share your folders on the network. If you notice that your folders are being shared and you did not set up the share, contact your administrator and find out why. The other users may have been granted privileges that they probably should not have.

A user has full access to my files. If he deletes the file, is the file sent to a Recycle Bin? If so, which one?

▼ No, the file is not sent to a Recycle Bin. As soon as the file is deleted, it is gone for good. The only way to regain the file is to copy it from another location — if you have it stored someplace else — or restore it from a backup. Windows requires that you manually set up backup services, so unless you specifically configured a backup for your sytem, you may not be able to retreive the deleted file.

Can I share the Windows folder?

▼ No. The Windows folder is one of a few folders — the other ones being the Documents and Settings and Program Files folders — that you are not allowed to share.

Configure NTFS File Sharing

Another way that Windows XP allows you to share files is using the NTFS file sharing feature. NTFS stands for Windows NT File System, a secure file system that allows users to add password-protection to file sharing.

Simple File Sharing uses part of the NTFS security permission strategy. However, to use the full features of NTFS file sharing, you need to turn off the Simple File Sharing feature.

To configure NTFS file sharing, your computer must be using the NTFS file system. Some systems still use the older Windows and MS-DOS file system called FAT16 or FAT32. You can run the NTFS CONVERT command to change your system to the NTFS system. However, you cannot change from NTFS back to FAT16 or FAT32. Most computers that have only Windows XP installed, however, are already using the NTFS system.

A feature of NTFS sharing is that you can designate user permissions. That is, you can specify which users on your network can access the shared folder.

Configure NTFS File Sharing

1. Double-click My Computer.
2. Double-click the C: drive.

   The contents of the C: drive appear.
3. Right-click the folder you want to share.
4. Click Sharing and Security from the menu that appears.

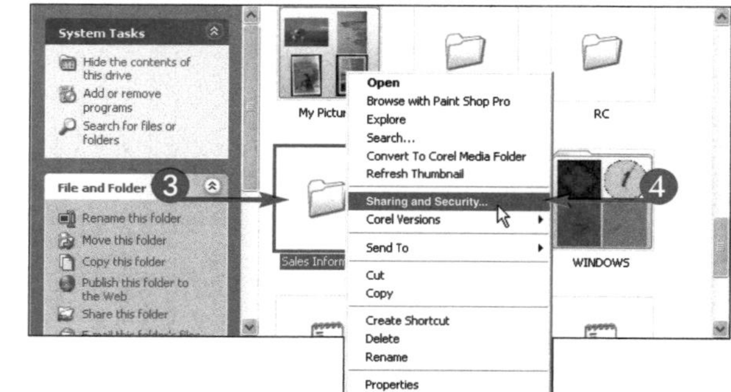

   The Sharing tab of the selected folder's properties dialog box appears.
5. Click Share this folder.
6. Type a name for the network share in the Share name text box. This is the name of the share that others see over the network. Keep it 12 characters or smaller.
7. Click an option to specify the number of simultaneous users.

   This example uses the maximum allowed.
8. Click Permissions.

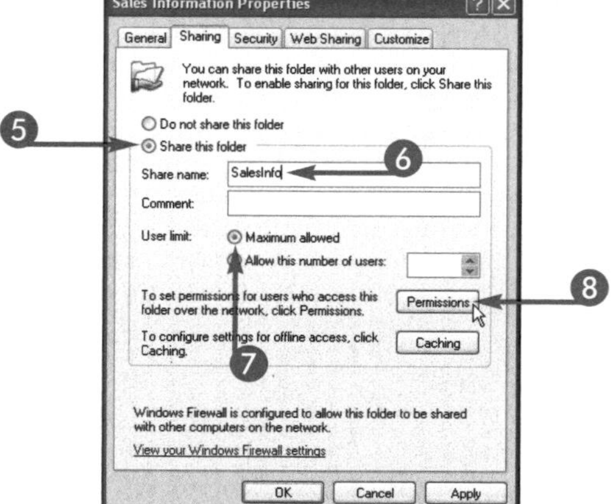

The Permissions for the folder share appears. By default, Everyone is listed.

9 To change permissions, click the Allow or Deny options for Full Control, Change, or Read.

10 To change who can access the share, click Add.

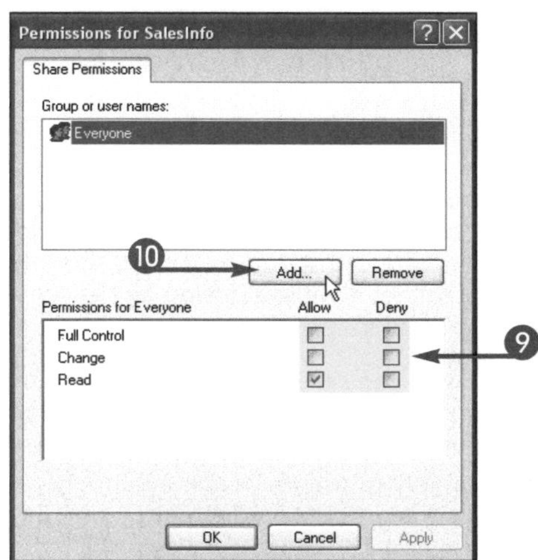

The Select Users or Groups dialog box appears.

11 Type a user or group name.

12 Click OK to close the Select Users or Groups dialog box.

13 Click OK to close the Permissions dialog box.

14 Click OK in the properties dialog box to confirm your changes.

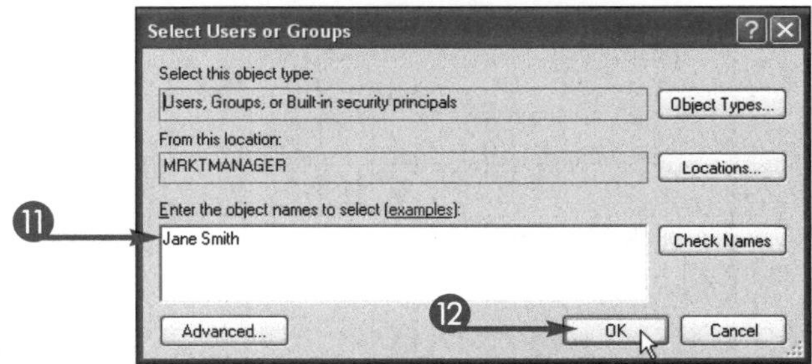

How do I know if my system is NTFS?

▼ A quick way is to open My Computer and right-click your C: drive. Choose Format and choose the General tab. The File system line shows the type of file system installed. If NTFS appears, you know your system is set up as NTFS.

Another way is to run the NTFS CONVERT command. Click Start, All Programs, Accessories, and Command Prompt. Type the following command:

convert C: /fs:ntfs

Press Enter. If Windows says Drive C: is already NTFS, then you know that your computer is set up with the NTFS system.

Are there other reasons to use NTFS file sharing?

▼ With NTFS file sharing, you can specify several sharing features. One includes limiting the number of users who can access a shared folder simultaneously. This way you can limit how many "hits" a share gets and not overwhelm the sharing computer.

Can I give different permissions for different users?

▼ Yes. When you use NTFS file sharing, you can specify if a user has Full Control rights, Change rights, or just Read rights. When you select Full Control, users can read, write, delete, and create files in the shared folder. Users with only Change rights can modify and read files, but not take complete ownership of a file. To limit users only to reading, but not changing, a file, use the Read permission.

Create Compressed Folders

Nowadays folders can get fairly large. To reduce the amount of space they consume, folders can be compressed. When you compress a folder, you shrink the contents of it without losing any information contained in the folder.

In some cases, you can save up to 90 percent of the original space consumed by the folder. For systems that have limited disk space, this is a handy tool to help save space.

When you are ready to use the folder again, you can uncompress the folder to its original size.

Another reason to compress a folder is to transfer it to other users. You can compress a folder full of files you want to send to someone over the Internet. This reduces the bandwidth needed to send the file, and in some cases, greatly speeds up delivery time.

You can also compress a folder full of files so they can fit on a removable disk, such as a Zip disk, CD, or other media. Transport the files to another computer, copy the files to that computer, and then uncompress the files to their original size.

Create Compressed Folders

1. Double-click My Computer.

   The contents of the C: drive appear.
2. Right-click the folder you want to compress.
3. Click Send To from the menu that appears.
4. Click Compressed (zipped) Folder in the menu that appears.

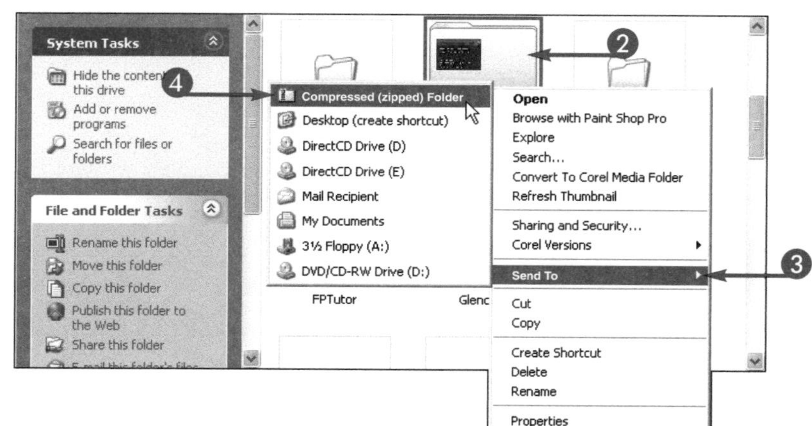

The folder automatically begins compressing. A window appears telling you the progress.

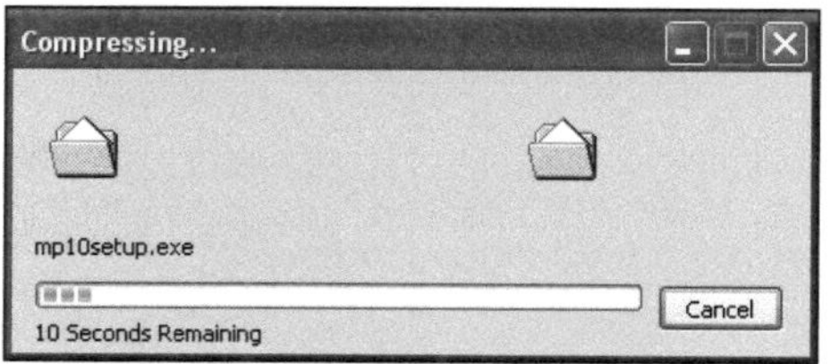

When finished compressing, Windows creates a folder using the original folder name with a .zip extension.

5 Double-click the compressed file.

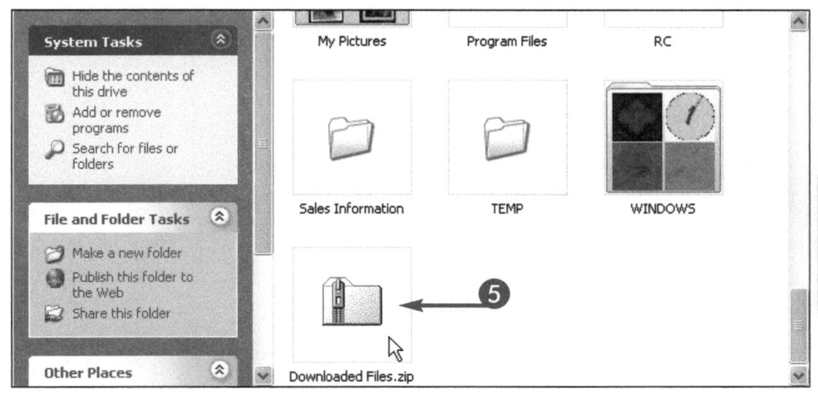

The contents of the compressed file appear.

6 To see the contents of a compressed folder, double-click it.

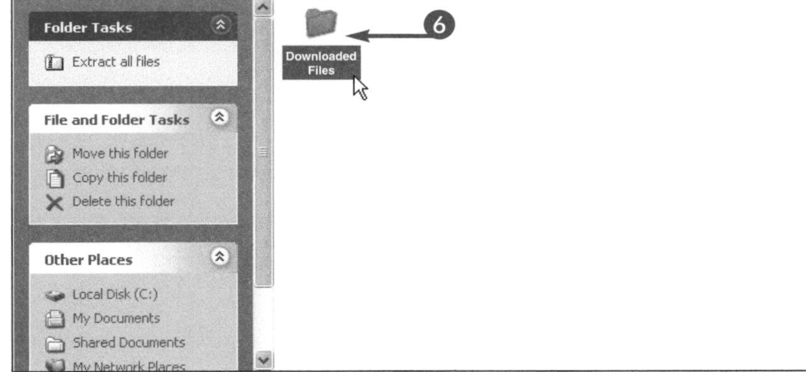

I have used the Windows XP compression tool, but I still like other compression programs. Can I use them with Windows still?

▼ Yes. Programs such as WinZip and ZipToA are very nice programs to use when you want to compress files and folders. Many times these third-party compression programs include many more features than the built-in Windows compression tools, such as uncompressing folders that are compressed using different algorithms than the one Windows uses.

I have a number of picture files saved on my computer. When I compress them, they do not get any smaller. Why not?

▼ Some picture formats, such as GIF and JPG/JPEG, are already compressed when you create them. Windows compression cannot reduce them anymore. This is true of some video and most music formats. MPEG-3, for example, is a highly compressed format for music and video. Compressing folders that include these types of files does not decrease the amount of space they take on your hard drive.

After I create a compressed folder, is there a quick way to attach it to an e-mail message?

▼ A quick way is to right-click the compressed folder, click Send To, and then click Mail Recipient. Your e-mail program launches with a new message created. The compressed folder is attached to that message.

Encrypt a Folder

Windows includes a feature that enables you to encrypt a folder and its contents. Encrypting a folder lets you add a layer of security to the folder so other users cannot modify or delete it.

Working with an encrypted folder or file is the same as working on one that is not encrypted. As long as you are the one who encrypted the folder (that is, the encryption was done while logged on under your user name), you should not have any problems using, editing, or even deleting the file.

One difference you see in My Computer is that the encrypted folder names appear in green font color instead of the default black font color.

Encrypted folders open for anyone, but their contents do not. When a user who is not the one who encrypted the folder tries to open an encrypted file, Windows displays an Access is denied screen.

When you encrypt a folder, you have the option of applying the encryption to all subfolders and files within those subfolders as well.

Encrypt a Folder

1. Double-click My Computer.

   The contents of the C: drive appear.

2. Right-click the folder you want to encrypt.
3. Click Properties from the menu that appears.

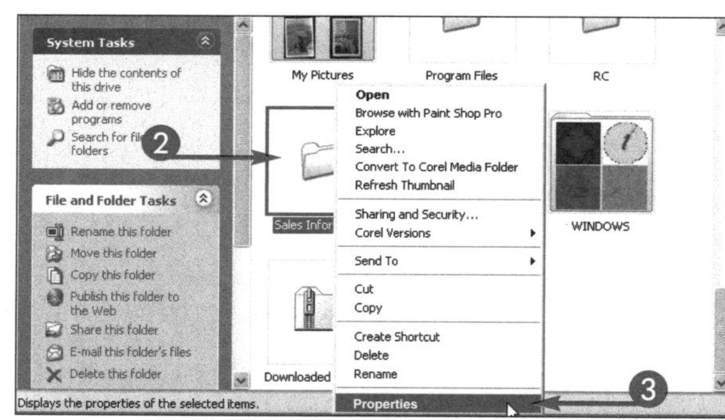

   The properties dialog box for that folder appears.

4. Click Advanced.

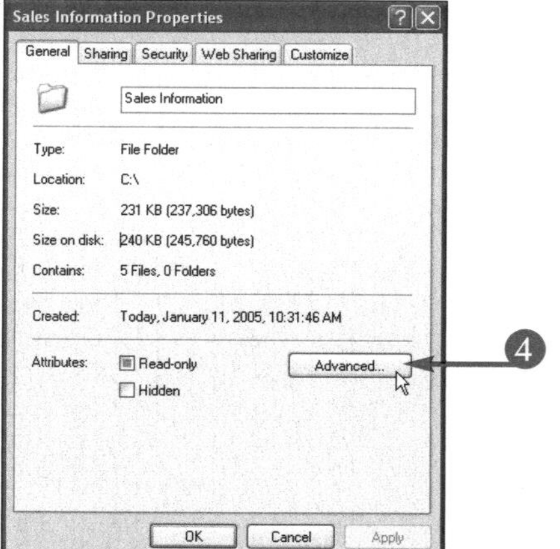

The Advanced Attributes dialog box appears.

5. Click the Encrypt contents to secure data option.
6. Click OK to close the Advanced Attributes dialog box.

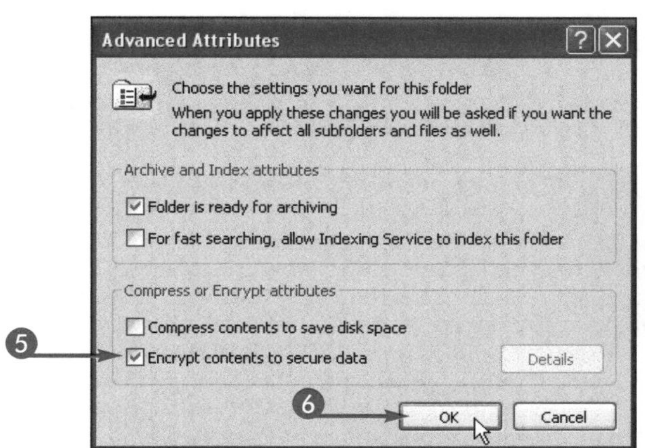

The Confirm Attribute Changes dialog box appears.

7. Click an option to encrypt the folder only, or to encrypt the folder, subfolders, and files.
8. Click OK to confirm your changes.
9. Click OK to close the properties dialog box.

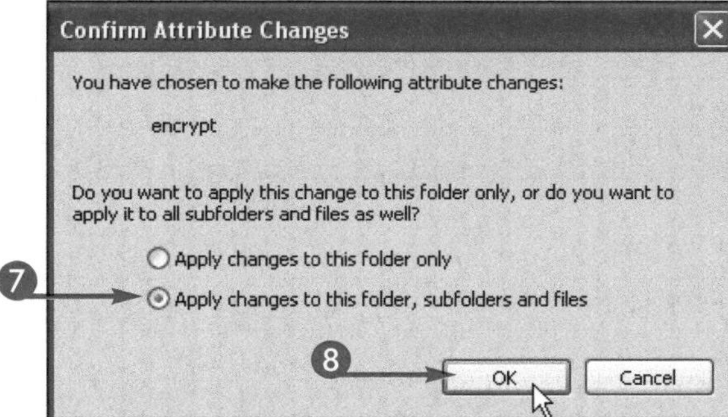

I have a folder that is compressed. I am trying to encrypt it, but Windows is not letting me. Why not?

- You should be able to encrypt a compressed folder that was compressed using Windows compressing. If the file was compressed with a different program, you may not be able to encrypt it.

There is a file on the system that does not open for me. Is there any way to turn off encryption?

- No. The only user who can disable encryption on a folder is the user who applied it in the first place. You can get around this if you are an administrator for the computer. You then have ample rights to unencrypt a file.

An encrypted folder I have on my computer was deleted by another user. I thought you could not do this unless you encrypted the folder.

- Not true. You can move or deleted an encrypted folder, even copy to a different computer, regardless of who created the encryption. The problem is that you cannot open the files within the folder unless you are the owner. The only way to ensure your files are not deleted is to use the Security tab in the properties dialog box and assign permissions and users to the folder.

Check Security at the Security Center

One of the best reasons to install Windows XP Service Pack 2 is the improved security, but the security enhancements are only effective if they are turned on and set properly. Part of guaranteeing that your computer is secure is the ability to quickly see your security-related settings. With SP2, you can monitor most of your security settings from a centralized location called the Windows Security Center. From the Security Center, you can enable and configure Windows Firewall, enable Automatic Updates, monitor antivirus software, verify that it is working, and make changes to your security settings for your firewall and Internet options.

The Security Center is easily accessible from the Control Panel. The Security Center has a shield icon that displays in the notification area of the taskbar when security-related notices appear. You can determine the nature of the security setting or issue by the color of the shield: Green means secured, yellow means that something warrants your attention, and red indicates a security breach or unprotected data. Because antivirus software is not part of Windows XP, Security Center only checks to verify that the antivirus software is working.

Check Security at the Security Center

1. Click Start.
2. Click Control Panel.

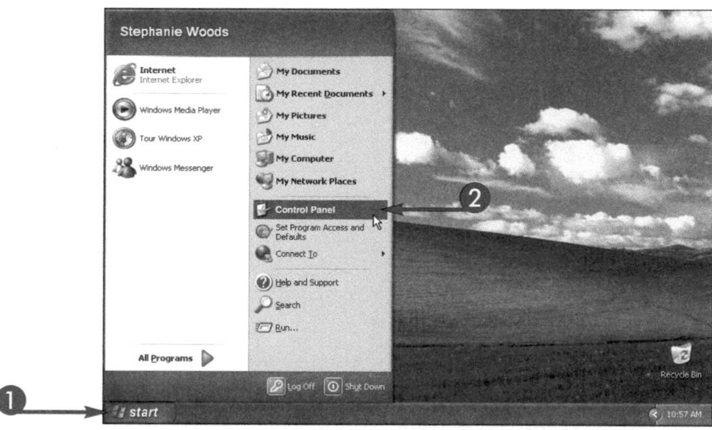

The Control Panel appears.

3. Click Security Center.

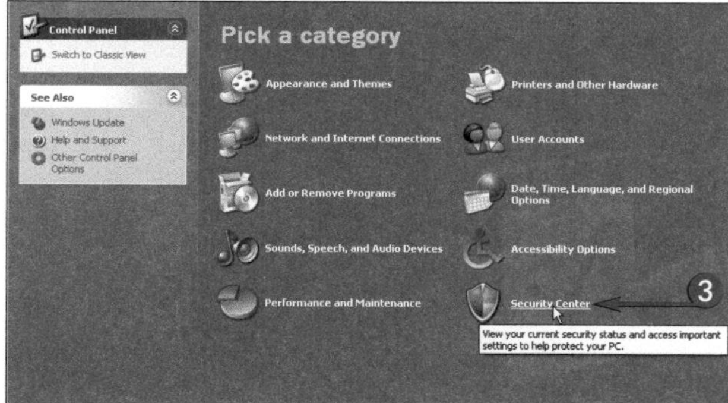

The Windows Security Center appears, indicating whether the three security essentials are turned on.

4 Click here to display more information about one of the security essentials.

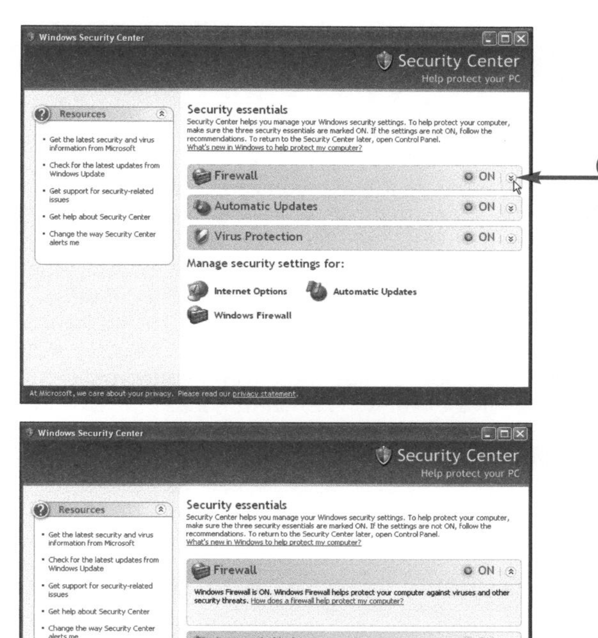

A dropdown box appears with brief explanatory text and a link to more detailed information.

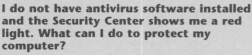

I do not have antivirus software installed and the Security Center shows me a red light. What can I do to protect my computer?

- Assuming you have a working Internet connection, you can download antivirus software from a trusted location and install it. Microsoft does not produce antivirus software per se, but does offer links from www.microsoft.com/security/partners/antivirus.asp to trusted partners who provide such software, often with a free trial period from 90 days to a year. Once installed, make sure that you keep your antivirus software up-to-date, installing any updates from the software publisher. Also, make sure to get software that has real-time scanning of files as they arrive on your computer, and make sure that feature is turned on.

Does antivirus software protect me from spyware?

- No. Spyware (software that monitors your Internet browsing and collects information without your knowledge) can be detected by antispyware software, however. At the time of this writing, Microsoft offers a beta version of its own antispyware software and links to several trusted antispyware software vendors at www.microsoft.com/athome/security/spyware/default.mspx.

Manage Windows Firewall

With Windows XP SP2, you can control access to your computer from your network and the Internet using Windows Firewall. Windows Firewall monitors incoming network and Internet traffic and protects your PC from unauthorized access via the Internet. If you are in a corporate environment, your IT department may use a different firewall, in which case Windows Firewall is turned off. In a home computing environment, you should always have Windows Firewall turned on unless you use another firewall, such as one that may be provided with antivirus software.

The default setting with SP2 is to have Windows Firewall turned on for maximum protection. However, there are situations in which you want to allow a trusted source to have access to your machine, such as interactive technical support or interactive gaming. For this reason, Windows Firewall allows exceptions for those situations, in which you can elect to allow access to a specific program or service. Conversely, there are some situations in which security breaches are especially likely, such as browsing the Web in an airport over a wireless Internet connection. For such cases, there is an option that allows no exceptions to the Windows Firewall settings.

Manage Windows Firewall

1. From the Windows Security Center, click Windows Firewall.

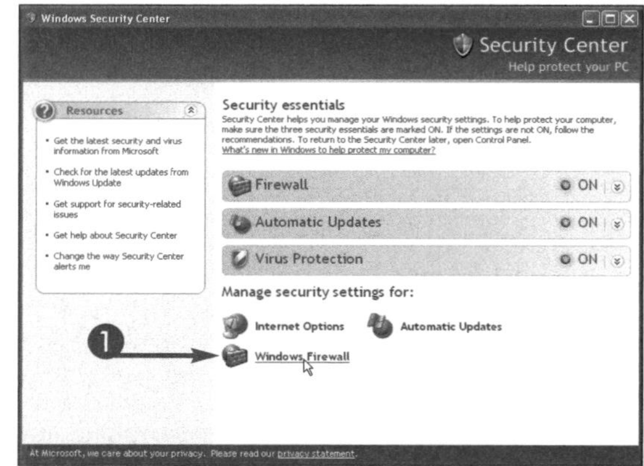

The Windows Firewall dialog box appears.

- Click here (☐ changes to ☑) to allow *no* exceptions, such as when using a public WiFi hot spot to access the Internet.
- Click here (○ changes to ◉) to turn off Windows Firewall. Only use this option when you have an alternative firewall in place.

2. Click the Exceptions tab.

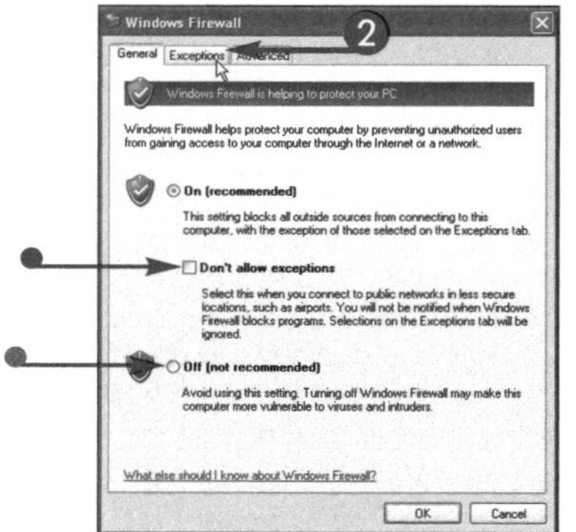

The Exceptions tab of the Windows Firewall dialog box appears.

3 Click one of the exceptions listed to remove it from the exceptions list (☑ changes to ☐). You can change it back whenever you want.

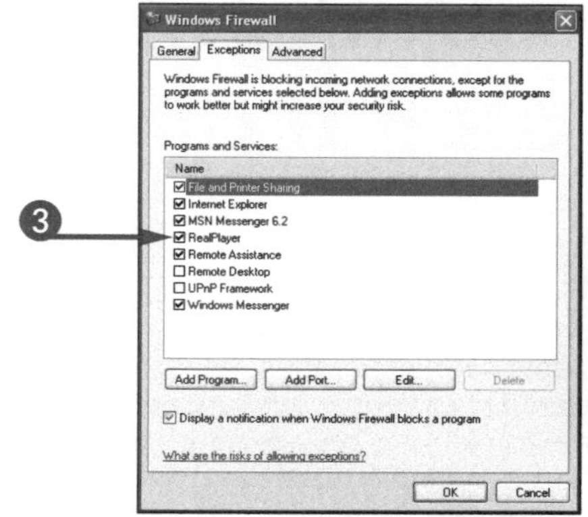

4 Click OK.

5 Click Close (☒) to close the Windows Security Center.

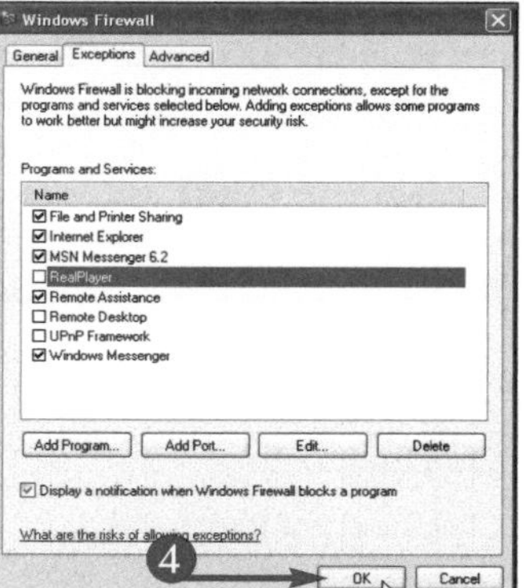

The Security Center shows Windows Firewall is turned off, but when I check the security status with my antivirus software, it says my firewall is turned on. What is happening?

▼ The Security Center in Windows XP SP2 only reports whether Windows Firewall is running; it does not check on the status of any other firewall, such as one provided with antivirus software. If you are using such a firewall, use the antivirus software to check on your firewall status.

Is there any risk in allowing an exception so that a program or service may get through the firewall?

▼ Yes. Every time you allow an exception you increase your security risk to some degree. With each exception you must weigh whether the program or service is sufficiently trustworthy. It is a good security practice to periodically review the exceptions and remove any that you no longer need.

Manage and Monitor Antivirus Software

With Windows Security Center in Windows XP SP2, you can quickly check to see whether your PC has any virus protection. While Microsoft addresses security breaches with periodic updates (see Chapter 3 for information on automatic updates), it does not produce antivirus software per se. What Microsoft has done instead is to provide information about why you should have antivirus software and how it works, and links to where you can obtain such software from trusted sources. In addition, Windows Security Center integrates with most antivirus software so that if you have antivirus software installed, Windows Security Center can report to you whether it is turned on and up-to-date.

In the Security Center, if you have up-to-date antivirus software running on your PC, the Virus Protection section should show a green light. If antivirus software is not present, turned off, or undetected (some antivirus software is not integrated with the Security Center and will not be detected), a red bar and red light appear, along with a Recommendations button that directs you to how you can fix the problem.

Manage and Monitor Antivirus Software

Check antivirus software

1. Click Start.
2. Click Control Panel.

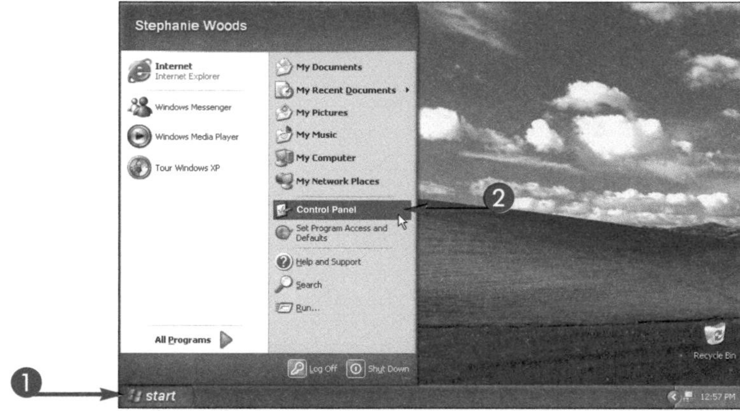

The Control Panel appears.

3. Click Security Center.

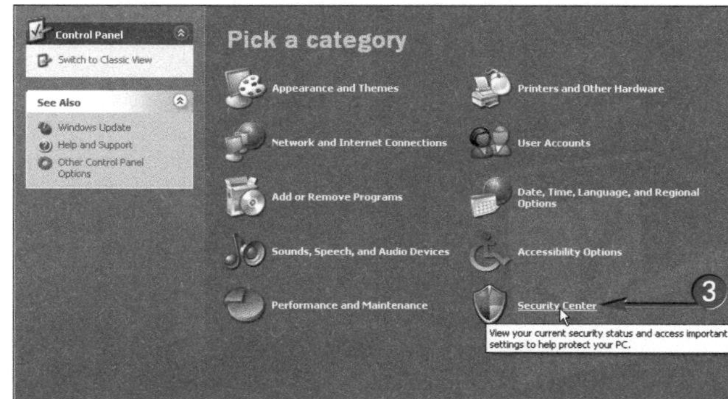

The Windows Security Center appears.

4 Click here to display more information about Virus Protection.

Note: *In this example, Norton AntiVirus reports that it has an up-to-date virus definition list and that virus scanning is currently turned on.*

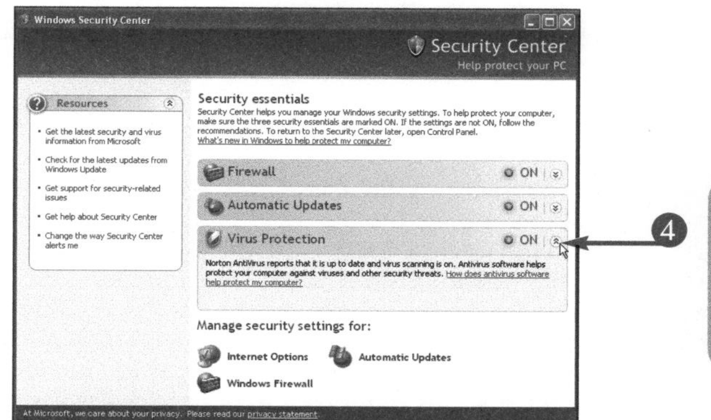

Note: *Here is how your screen might look if you had antivirus software but had turned it off.*

- Virus Protection bar and light display red, and OFF is displayed.
- The antivirus software has reported that it has been turned off.
- Click Recommendations to find out how to remedy the situation.
- A red × appears through the antivirus software in this example, indicating that it has been disabled. (Some programs use a red warning shield or other symbol to indicate this status.)

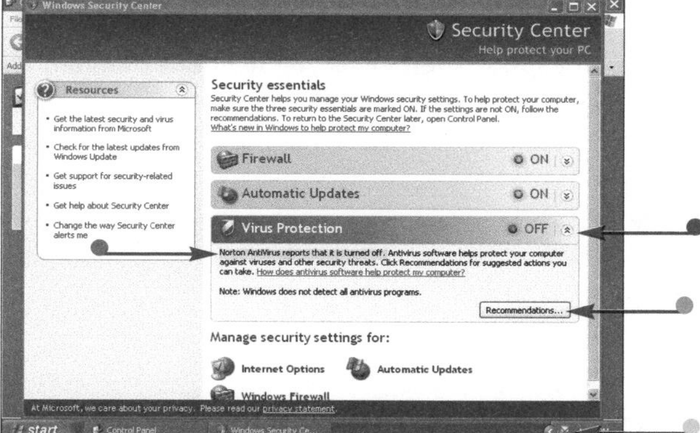

How do I find out more about antivirus software?

Click [expand] in the Virus Protection area of the Windows Security Center, and then click the How does antivirus software help protect my computer link. You can also check out the other informational links in the left pane of the Windows Security Center.

I have installed antivirus software and scanned my system for viruses, but the Security Center says that Virus Protection is turned off and the light is red. What should I do?

This probably means that you have at some time performed a scan for viruses, but do not have the antivirus software's real-time scanning turned on (the feature that checks all files as they arrive on your computer). If you do not have real-time scanning turned on, you should enable that feature in your antivirus software.

continued

Manage and Monitor Antivirus Software *(Continued)*

Norton AntiVirus 2004 from Symantec is used in this example, but many other programs are available. See the section "Check Security at the Security Center," earlier in this chapter, for information on how to find antivirus software. With Norton AntiVirus 2004 (as well as most other antivirus products), an icon displays in the notification area of the taskbar showing the status of virus protection. To access the software, right-click the icon and select Open from the menu that appears.

After you have launched the antivirus application, you can perform several tasks. These differ slightly from program to program, but conceptually three key operations are installing virus definition updates (new viruses are continually being developed, so antivirus software providers need to send your program frequent updates of what to look for), scanning of existing files, and then dealing with any infected files the software might find (by quarantine, deletion, repair, and so on). Make sure that the automatic virus definition update feature (in this example, the feature is called Live Update) is turned on, and that you schedule regular system scans of all the files currently on your PC. This example shows you how to launch Norton AntiVirus 2004 and scan your system for viruses.

Manage and Monitor Antivirus Software *(continued)*

Scan for viruses

1. Right-click the Norton AntiVirus icon.
2. Click Open Norton AntiVirus.

The Norton AntiVirus System Status window appears.

- This feature performs the real-time file scanning and is turned on.
- A full system scan was performed recently (Norton AntiVirus recommends that you do this weekly), and Virus Definitions were recently updated.
- Automatic virus updates are enabled.

3. Click Scan for Viruses.

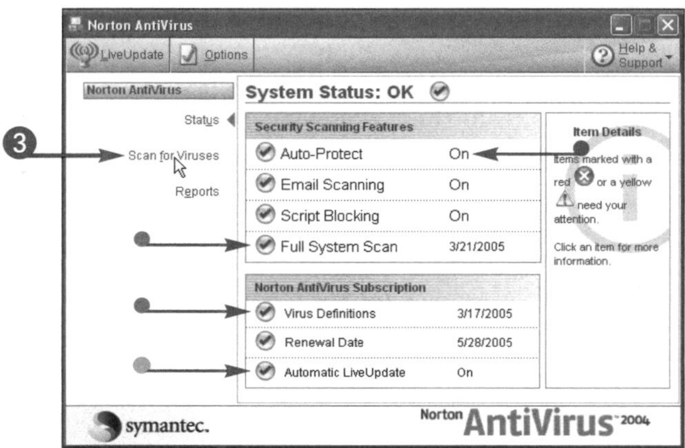

The Scan for Viruses screen appears.

4 Click here to scan your computer for viruses.

- Click here to use the Task Scheduler to have a regular virus scan performed weekly at a time when you are not using your computer.

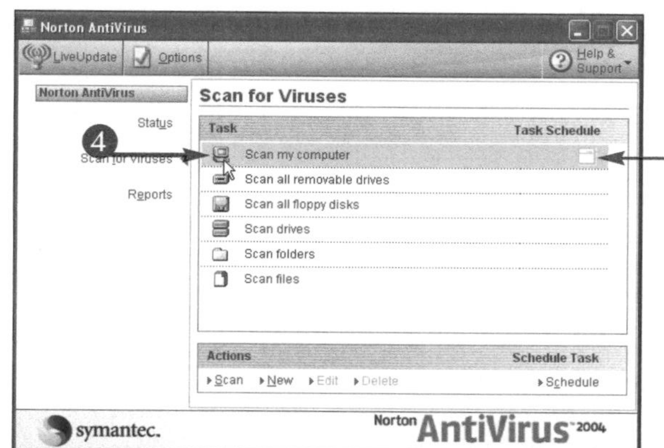

Norton AntiVirus scans your entire system for viruses.

Note: *A system scan can take quite some time, depending on the size and number of files and speed of your disk drives. If you want to pause or stop the scan, click Pause or Stop Scan at the bottom of the Scan Progress window.*

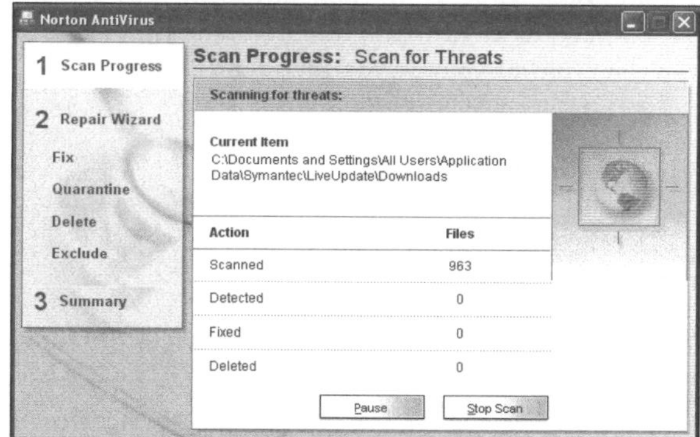

I have heard about a new virus that is spreading. What can I do to protect my PC from it?

▼ First, go to the Control Panel to make sure that you have your Virus Protection and Automatic Updates turned on. If you are not using Automatic Updates, click the Get the latest security and virus information from Microsoft link and follow the instructions. Next, use the online update feature of your antivirus software (with Norton AntiVirus, used in this example, this feature is called LiveUpdate) to download the latest virus information. Make sure that the automated update feature of your antivirus software is enabled so that you can receive any new definitions about new variants of the virus and so on. Perform a full system scan to ensure that you have not already received the virus. For information about viruses coming in e-mail, see the sections later in this chapter.

I do not remember when I last scanned my computer for viruses. How do I find that out?

▼ Antivirus software keeps track of virus scanning history. In the Norton AntiVirus software used in this example, this is called the Activity Log. To view the report of recent activity, click Reports and then click View Reports in the Activity Log section. You see a report of each activity and which user initiated the activity (if your PC has more than one user).

PART II

Add a Logon Warning

If you are running Windows XP Professional and have administrator privileges, you can add a logon warning or message whenever a user logs on to the system. Many corporate networks have a legal notice expressively notifying anyone who attempts to log on to their network that only those authorized to log on may do so. To add such a warning, you can launch the Security Settings snap-in to the Microsoft Management Console (MMC). Access to MMC snap-ins is not displayed on the All Programs menu by default. From the Customize Start Menu dialog box, you can elect to show System Administrative Tools on the All Programs menu and the Start menu.

The Administrative Tools menu contains a list of MMC snap-ins such as Component Services, Computer Management, Data Sources (ODBC), Event Viewer, Local Security Policy, Performance, and Services. To make changes to security, such as adding a logon warning, select Local Security Policy. Note that you can make adjustments to *local* security policy here. It is beyond the scope of this book to discuss network-wide security policies and their enforcement. Local Security Settings contain the Security Options section of Local Policies.

Add a Logon Warning

1. Right-click Start and click Properties from the menu that appears.

   The Taskbar and Start Menu Properties dialog box appears.

2. Click Customize.

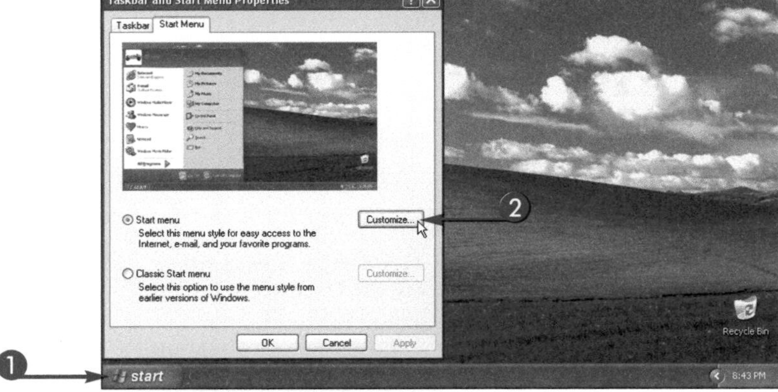

The Customize Start Menu dialog box appears.

3. Click the Advanced tab.

   Scroll to the bottom of the Start menu items list box.

4. Click Display on the All Programs menu and the Start menu.
5. Click OK to close the Customize Start Menu dialog box.
6. Click OK to close the properties dialog box.

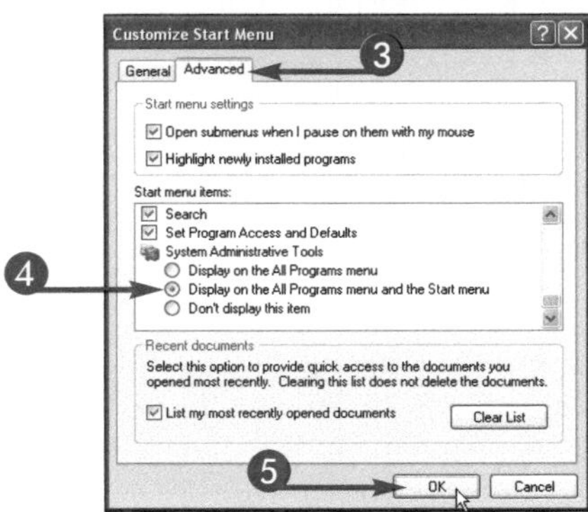

7 Click Start.

8 Click Administrative Tools.

9 Click Local Security Policy.

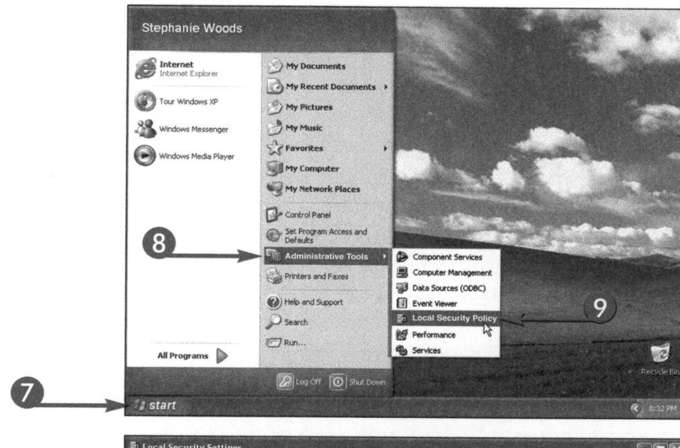

The Local Security Settings MMC snap-in appears.

10 Click the plus sign to expand Local Policies.

11 Click Security Options.

Scroll through the Policy list in the right pane.

12 Click Interactive logon: Message text for users attempting to log on.

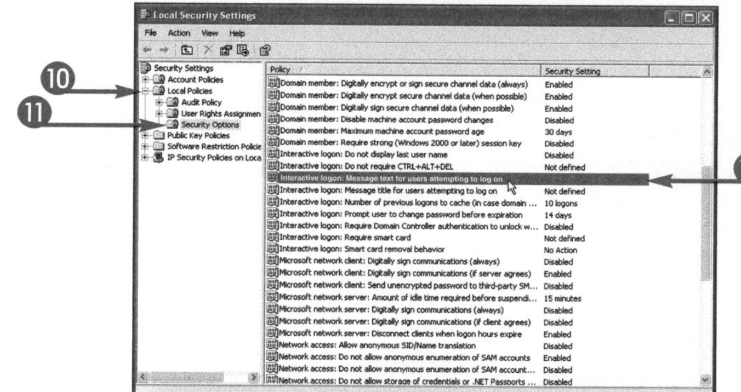

When I click Local Security Policy, it takes me directly to Security Options. Why is this different from the steps listed above?

▼ MMC snap-ins keep track of how they were last used. For example, if you have been working with the security options, and then close the snap-in, when you next open it, the security options are expanded. Likewise, if you have not yet used an option, it may be minimized; you can expand it by clicking the plus sign to access that option.

My computer already has a logon message. Can I remove or change the message that my network administrator has included?

▼ If you are working in a corporate network environment, such messages tend to be for the entire department or network and are not subject to modification by individual users. If your network does not use a logon message, you may still be able to add one locally (just for your computer). However, if there is already a network- or department-wide message, you cannot change or remove this message without the help of a network administrator.

continued

Add Logon Warning *(Continued)*

Assuming you have local administrator privileges, you can make changes to the interactive logon security policies for your local system from the Local Security Settings MMC snap-in. To add a warning message that comes up in a window at logon time, click Interactive logon: Message text for users attempting to log on. You can then type a message regarding the authorized use of the system (or other appropriate logon notice). In order for the warning message or notice to pop up at logon, it is also necessary to add a message title. You can do this by clicking Interactive logon: Message title for users attempting to log on. Type a brief message title (such as **Warning** or **Legal Notice**) in the text box. This appears in the title bar of the logon's warning message box.

The next time a user logs on to the system, immediately prior to the logon screen for user name and password, the user sees your text message box with the message title you have assigned against a blank screen. In order to proceed to the logon screen, the user must click OK or press Enter to acknowledge reading the message.

Add Logon Warning *(continued)*

After clicking Interactive logon: Message text for users attempting to log on, the corresponding dialog box appears.

13. Type **Unauthorized use of this computer is strictly prohibited.** in the text box (or your own text message).
14. Click OK.

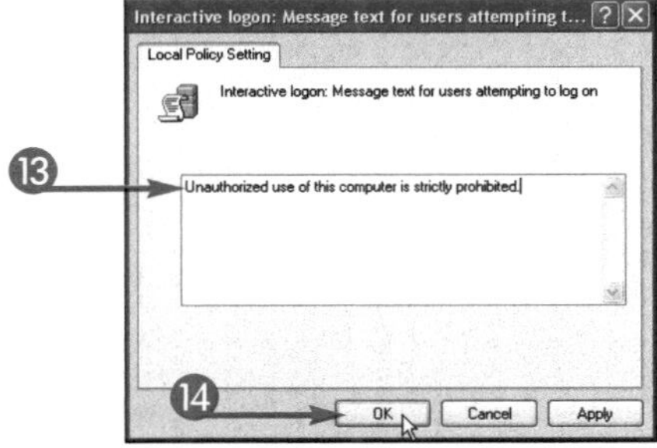

15. Click Interactive logon: Message title for users attempting to log on.

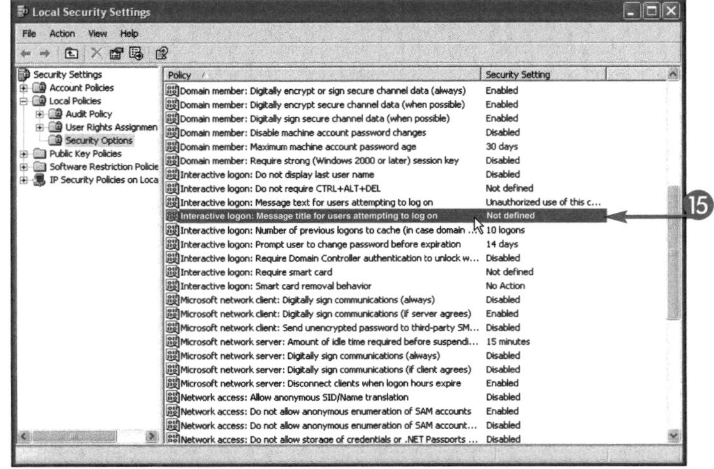

The corresponding dialog box appears.

16 Type **Legal Notice** (or your own brief message title) in the text box.

17 Click OK to close the dialog box.

18 Click ☒ to close the Local Security Settings snap-in.

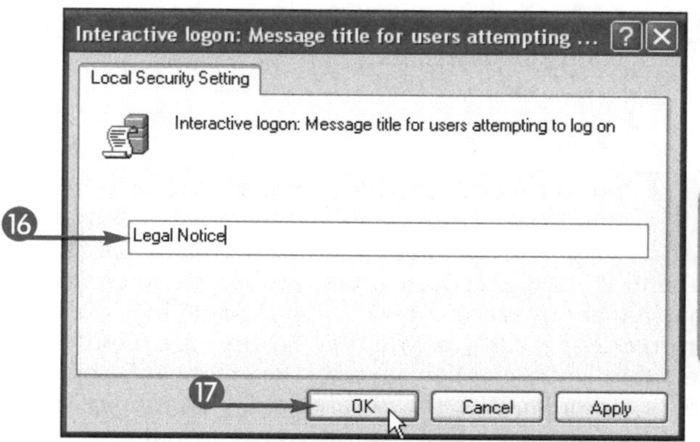

When a user next attempts to log on, he sees the message title and text you entered.

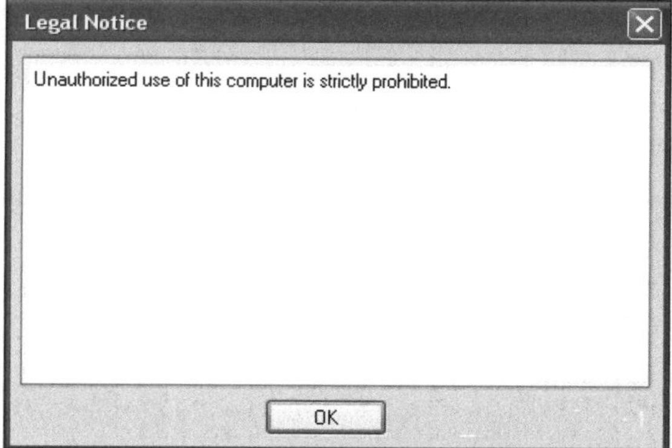

Can a user avoid seeing this message when attempting to log on?

▼ No. The only user action possible is to view the screen and click OK or press Enter, other than Ctrl+Alt+Del or a hardware power-down or reset. If such a reset occurs, it simply brings the user back to this screen.

Can I modify the message title and text or remove it later?

▼ Yes. You can change the message title and text at any time, provided you have the necessary privileges. To remove the logon message, simply delete the message title and text from the Local Security Settings snap-in.

Install and Manage Digital Certificates

You can view and manage digital certificates in Windows XP SP2 by adding the MMC Certificates snap-in. Certificates are a way to guarantee the authenticity of digital data so that you can be sure that what you are receiving is really what it is and that the person or entity really is who they say they are. Certificates use public key encryption to verify the identity of a person, service, program, Web site or other entity electronically. The Certificate Authority (CA) is a trusted entity that issues and verifies these certificates. The CA issues a public key for a person or other entity, and that person or entity retains the corresponding private key. In this way, certificates can safely be broadly distributed because they must be verified by the CA with a private key before being authorized.

To add the Certificates snap-in, you can run MMC and add Certificates. This snap-in has several functions. You can manage certificates for your user account, a service, or a computer. However, you must add a separate instance of the Certificates snap-in for each of these tasks; for example, MMC does not allow you to switch between managing the certificates for your user account and managing the certificates for your PC.

Install and Manage Digital Certificates

1. Click Start.
2. Click Run.

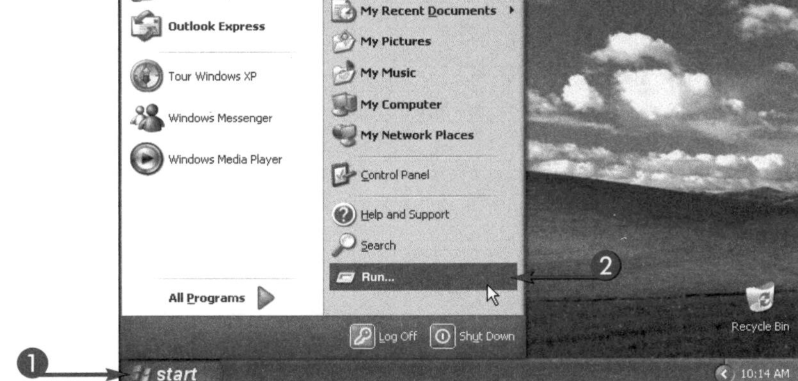

3. Type **mmc.exe**.
4. Click OK.

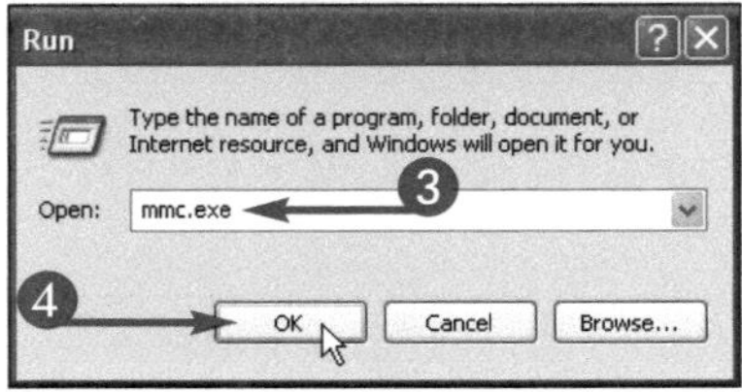

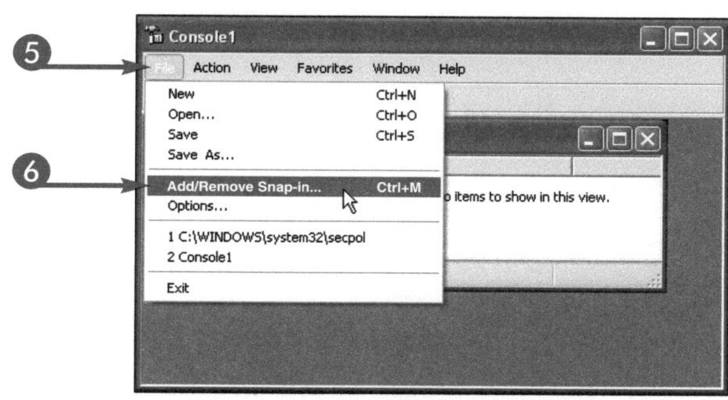

An MMC console window appears.

5 Click File.

6 Click Add/Remove Snap-in.

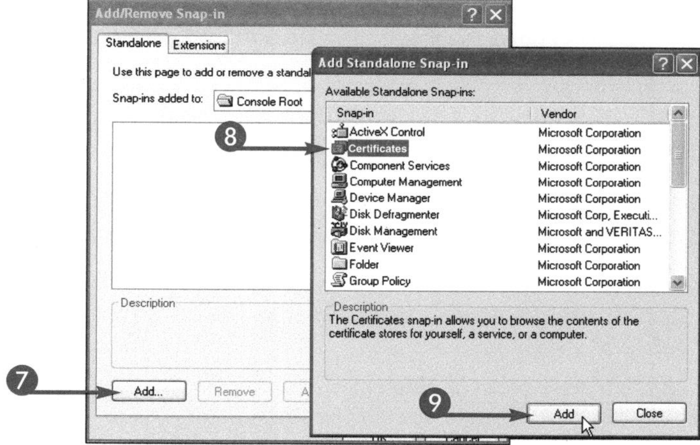

The Add/Remove Snap-in dialog box appears.

7 Click Add.

The Add Standalone Snap-in dialog box appears.

8 Click Certificates.

9 Click Add.

How do I obtain a personal digital certificate?

▼ If you have the need for a personal digital certificate (for such things as verifying the authenticity of e-mail), you can obtain one from one of several certificate authorities via the Web. One way is to click Get a Digital ID on the Security tab of the Options dialog box from the Tools menu in Microsoft Outlook. This takes you to a Microsoft Web page with a list of partners who provide digital IDs (personal digital certificates), along with customer ratings for each of these partners.

Is it necessary to install and use the Certificates MMC snap-in to have or use digital certificates?

▼ No. This snap-in simply allows you to monitor and manage your certificates. It is not required that you install the snap-in to use digital certificates.

continued

Install and Manage Digital Certificates *(Continued)*

Some of the most common uses for public key certificates are secure Web sites, which use the https protocol, and software program code. You can also use personal digital certificates to verify authenticity in sensitive e-mail correspondence, provided each person has an e-mail application (such as Outlook or Outlook Express) that supports certificates.

When you have added the Certificates snap-in to the MMC console, you can click it to view the various categories of certificates: Personal, Trusted Root Certification Authorities, Enterprise Trust, Intermediate Certification Authorities, Active Directory User Object, Trusted Publishers, Untrusted Certificates, Third-Party Root Certificate Authorities, and Trusted People. The most relevant to individual PC users are the Personal category (containing your own certificates for e-mail and EFS) and Trusted Persons (containing certificates for verified e-mail correspondents). When the MMC Certificates snap-in is installed and saved, you can return to manage these certificates by running MMC, opening up the corresponding snap-in, and by typing **mmc.exe /s [/path/filename.msc]** in the Run command's text box, and clicking OK. You can review existing certificates, copy personal certificates to a file (if for example, you need to move to another PC), or delete certificates.

Install and Manage Digital Certificates *(continued)*

After clicking Add in the Add Standalone Snap-in dialog box, the Certificates snap-in dialog box appears.

10. Click the type of account to manage certificates for (My user account in this example).
11. Click Finish.

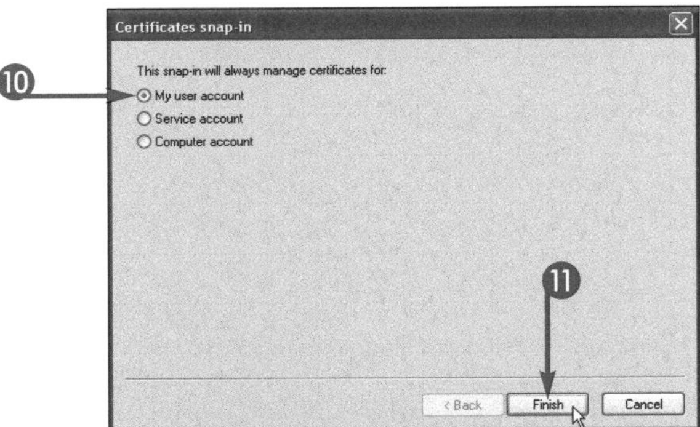

- The Certificates snap-in now appears in the Standalone snap-in list.

12. Click Close.
13. Click OK.

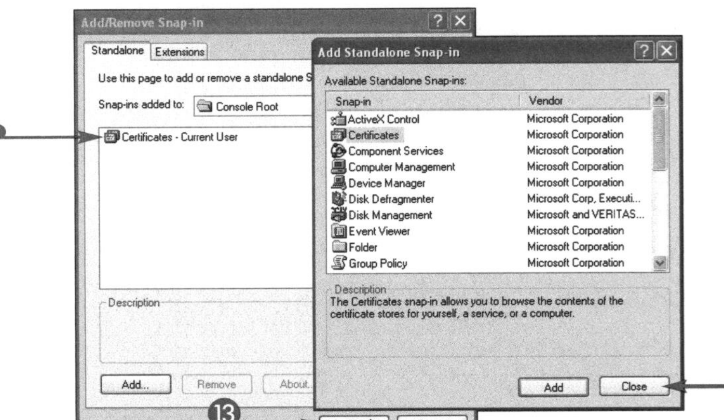

⑭ Click Certificates - Current User to display a list of certificate categories in the right pane of the MMC console.

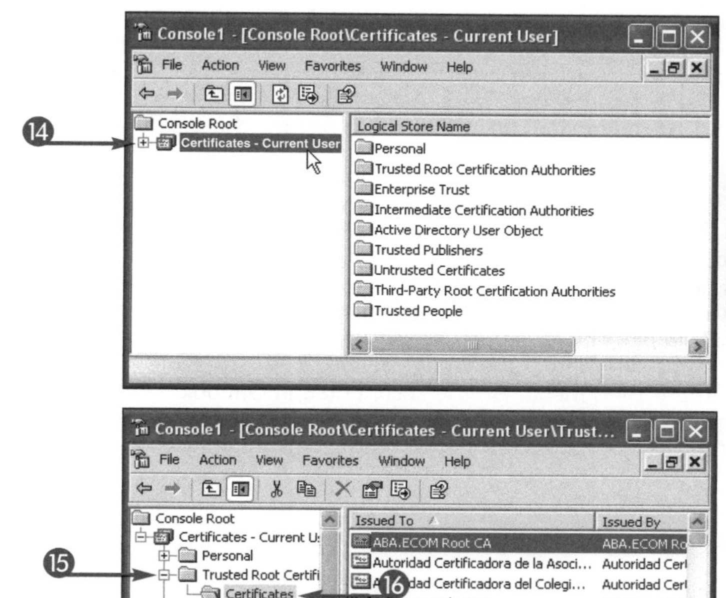

⑮ Double-click a certificate category folder (Trusted Root Certification Authorities in this example).

⑯ Double-click Certificates to view and manage certificates in this category.

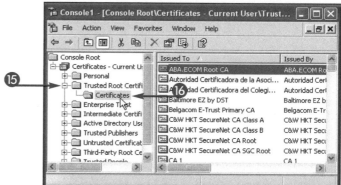

What if I want to save this snap-in view and work with it again?

▼ When you exit MMC, you are prompted to save this file. Choose a name (such as Certificates) and save the file. That way, if you want to reopen the snap-in, you can either use the Run command and specify the filename (using the .msc extension) or you can simply type **mmc.exe** from the Run command and then click File and then Open to select the file from a list.

How do I move my personal certificate from one computer to another?

▼ From the Certificates snap-in, locate the certificate in the Certificates folder of the Personal certificate category and double-click the certificate. Next click the Details tab and then click Copy to file. This takes you to the Certificate Export Wizard, which walks you through the steps of exporting a certificate.

Secure Outlook and Outlook Express

You can keep your Outlook and Outlook Express e-mail more secure by setting the security options. Because Outlook and Outlook Express have similar security options interfaces, the material is covered in one section for both, using screens mostly from Outlook Express 6 (from Windows XP SP2). To access the security features in Outlook or Outlook Express, launch the program and select the Security tab from the Options dialog box, accessible from the Tools menu. On the Security tab in Outlook Express, the first set of options has to do with Virus Protection (Security Zones in Outlook). When you receive HTML messages, you need protection from malicious scripts and other code. You can also elect to block images (in Outlook Express). This is useful because sometimes malicious code can be hidden in image file formats.

Another level of security that can be added is to obtain a digital ID (or certificate). With a digital certificate, you can send your e-mail in an encrypted format and the recipient can verify that it has arrived unaltered. After you have put an address with a certificate in your Contacts list, that certificate is stored and you can communicate securely over e-mail.

Secure Outlook and Outlook Express

1. After launching Outlook Express (or Outlook), click Tools.
2. Click Options.

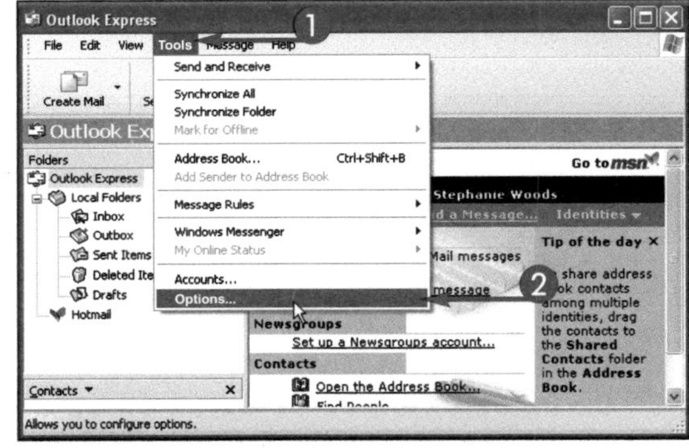

The Outlook Express Security tab

The Options dialog box appears.

3. Click the Security tab.

Note: *To see the corresponding tab for Outlook, see the next page.*

4. Select Restricted sites zone for more security.
5. Make sure these options are selected for more security.

- Click here to manage a Digital ID.
- Click here to be taken to a list of trusted digital certificate vendors from whom you can obtain a personal digital certificate.

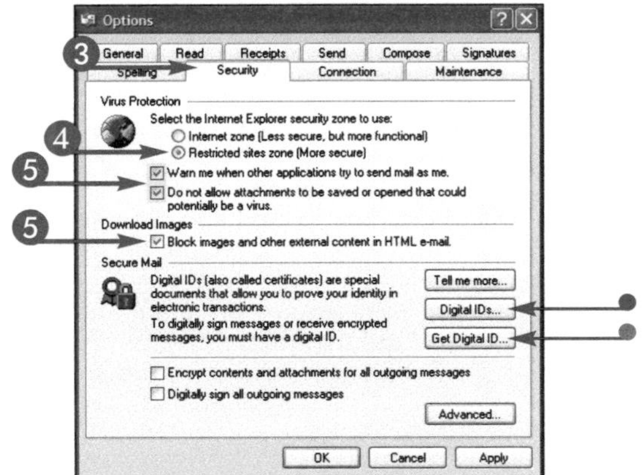

6 If you have a digital ID (certificate) and want to encrypt your outgoing e-mail, click here.

7 If you have a digital ID (certificate), click here to digitally sign your outgoing mail as authentic.

8 Click OK to save your changes.

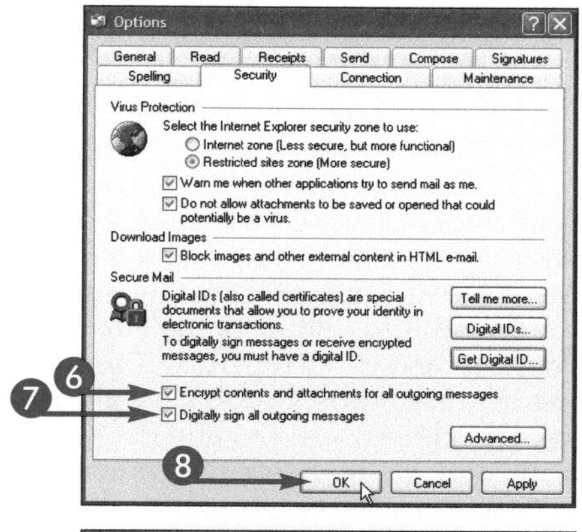

The Outlook Security tab

1 Repeat Steps 1 to 3 to access the Security tab.

2 If you have a digital ID (certificate) and want to encrypt your outgoing e-mail, click here.

3 If you have a digital ID (certificate), click here to digitally sign your outgoing mail as authentic.

4 Click here and select Restricted sites for more security.

- Click here to import or export a Digital ID.
- Click here to be taken to a list of trusted digital certificate vendors from whom you can obtain a personal digital certificate.

5 Click OK to save your changes.

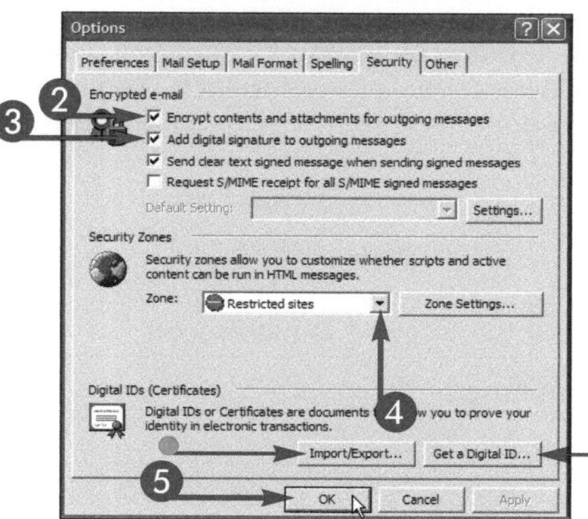

Are there any other ways I can help keep e-mail more secure?

▼ Yes. Here are some principles to follow:

- Use antivirus software that integrates with Outlook.
- Use junk e-mail and spam filters when possible.
- Delete any suspicious e-mail with attachments (even if it claims to be from someone you know).
- Use a secured e-mail application (preferably not an open Web browser–based system).
- Avoid or limit use of wireless networking in unsecured public hot spots for e-mail.
- Use a digital ID and encrypt your messages for sensitive e-mail.

How can I keep up-to-date on the latest e-mail virus threats?

▼ You can click Windows Security Center on the Control Panel and then click Get the latest security and virus information from Microsoft, or use your Web browser to go to www.microsoft.com/security. Your virus protection software company will also have information at its Web site.

Secure Internet Explorer

You can ensure that you have a more secure Web browsing experience if you take some time to review Internet Explorer's security settings. The easiest way to do this is to right-click the Internet Explorer icon on the desktop and click Properties. This brings up the Internet Properties dialog box. (If you have already launched Internet Explorer, you can also get to this dialog box by clicking Tools and then Internet Options.) Several tabs on this dialog box relate to security.

The Security tab on the Internet Properties dialog box allows you to view the setting for each Web content zone. The four categories are Internet (for all sites not put into other zones), Local intranet, Trusted sites, and Restricted sites. The *Internet* zone has a medium level of security so that you have relative safety but maintain functionality. The *Local intranet* zone has your local network and intranet sites, assumes the trust level is high, and allows maximum functionality. The *Trusted sites* zone contains sites other than your local intranet that have a high trust level and therefore allow maximum functionality. The *Restricted sites* zone contains sites that may have higher risk, such as external mail and file servers.

Secure Internet Explorer

1. Right-click the Internet Explorer icon.
2. Click Properties.

The Internet Properties dialog box appears.

3. Click the Security tab.
   - Indicates the Web content zone selected.
   - Click the slider to adjust the security level for this zone.
   - Click to make changes to individual settings.
4. Click Restricted sites.

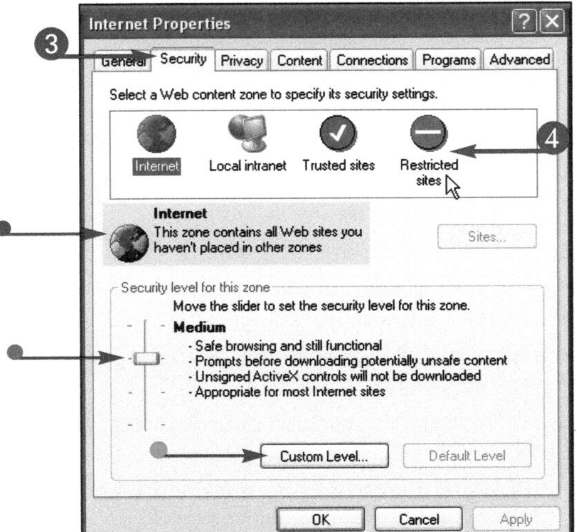

- The settings for the Restricted sites Web content zone are now displayed.

5 Click Sites to add a site to this zone.

The Restricted sites dialog box appears.

6 Type the address of the Web site you want to add to this zone (**http://www.irs.gov** in this example).

7 Click Add.

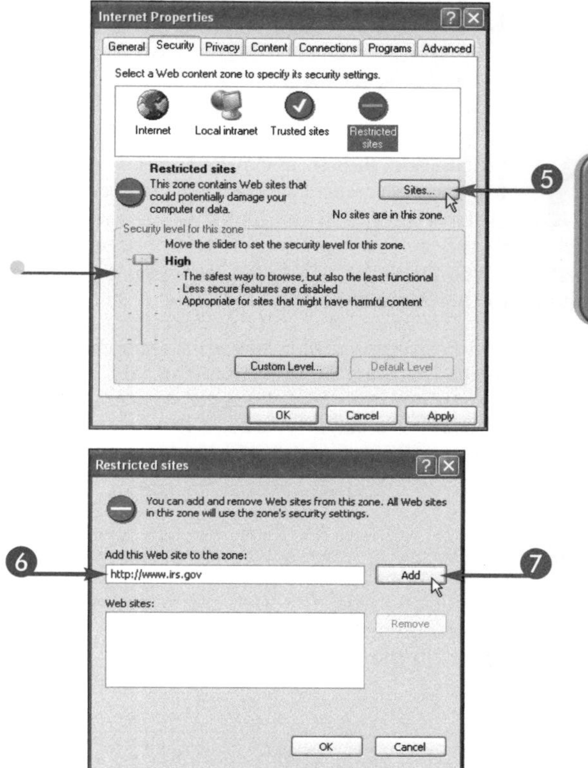

I want to be notified every time an attempt is made to download an ActiveX control to my computer for the Internet Web content zone. How do I do this?

▼ Click the Internet zone, and then click Custom Level. In the ActiveX controls and plug-ins section, find Automatic prompting for ActiveX controls, and click Enable (○ changes to ◉). Click OK. If you were using the default level (Medium), it now appears as Custom Level.

How can I get maximum functionality for a specific trusted Web site?

▼ The easiest way to do this is to add the site to your Trusted sites Web content zone. To do so, click Trusted sites. Next, click Sites and type the address of the Web site that you trust. Make sure that the Require server verification (https:) for all sites in this zone option is selected (☐ changes to ☑), otherwise you will be using minimum security with an open protocol — an unsafe procedure.

continued

Secure Internet Explorer *(Continued)*

You can add sites to and remove sites from each of the security zones by selecting the zone and clicking Sites. You can also make changes to individual security settings for each security zone by clicking Custom Level. By clicking Default Level, you can restore any settings to their default values.

The Internet Properties dialog box also has additional security-related settings on the Advanced tab; these are grouped together in the Security section of the Settings list. Although privacy is a security issue, it is a category unto itself as well, and therefore has its own Privacy tab on the Internet Properties dialog box. Web sites often use *cookies* to store information on your computer for later retrieval. While cookies only contain information that you provide, you may not want to restrict such information. From the Privacy tab, you can use a slider to set the privacy level from Accept All Cookies (least privacy) through Medium (default level) to Block All Cookies (most privacy). Blocking all cookies considerably reduces functionality on some sites (such as travel reservations), so you should consider the setting that best fits your needs.

Secure Internet Explorer *(continued)*

- After clicking Add, the Web site added to the Restricted sites Web content zone appears in the Web sites window.

8 Click OK.

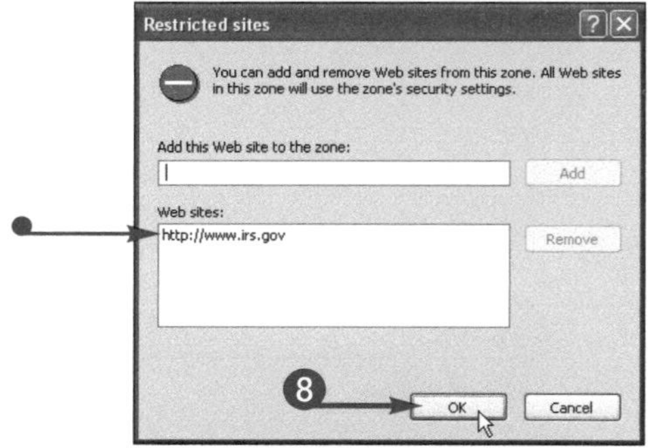

9 Click the Advanced tab.

Drag the scroll bar of the Settings window downward until you see the Security settings.

- Click here to restore *all* advanced settings defaults (not just security).

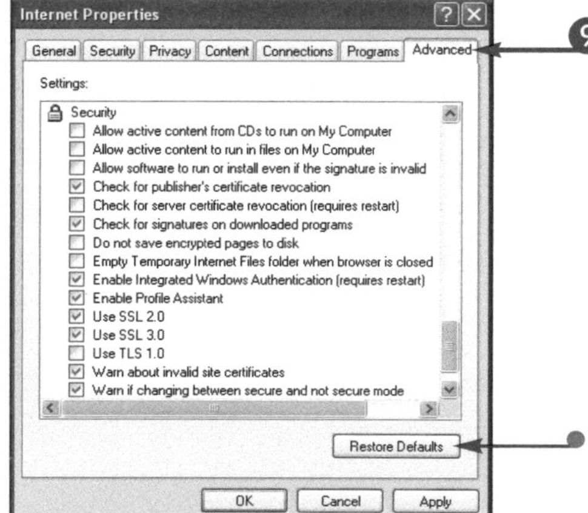

⑩ Click here to delete temporary Internet files every time you close your browser.

⑪ Click the Privacy tab.

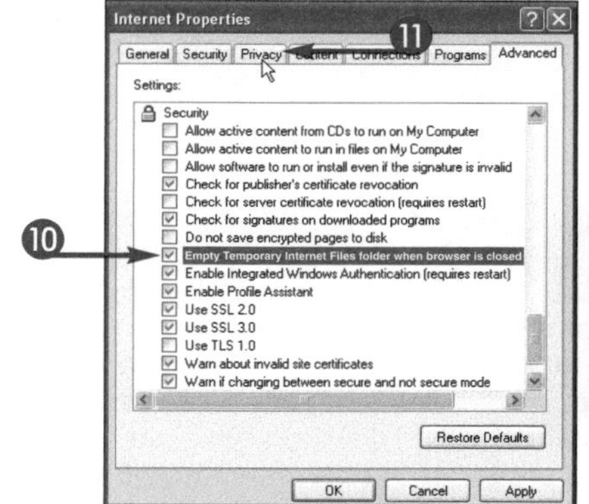

The Privacy tab of the Internet Properties dialog box appears.

- Dragging this slider adjusts the privacy level by determining whether to accept certain cookies.
- Click Sites to expressly block or allow cookies from a specific Web site, regardless of overall privacy settings.

⑫ Click OK to accept changes.

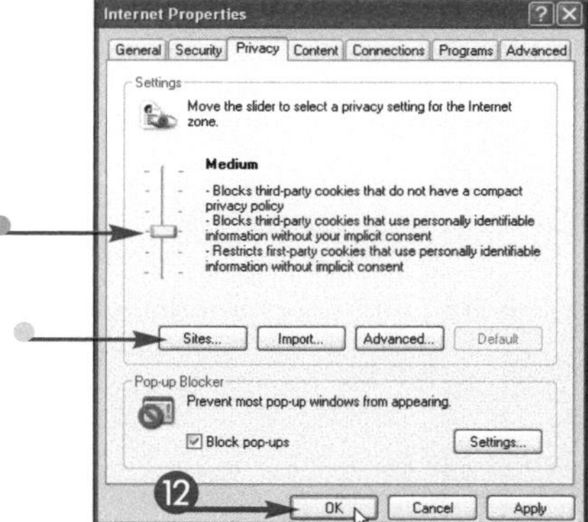

Is there anything else I should do to secure Internet Explorer?

▼ Make sure that Automatic Updates are turned on in the Security Center, or frequently click the Tools menu in Internet Explorer and click Windows Update. This takes you to a Microsoft update site and checks for critical updates (these usually have to do with security).

How can I maintain a high privacy level but allow cookies from one site that I trust?

▼ From the Privacy tab of the Internet Properties dialog box, move the slider upward (from Medium to High, for example), and then click Sites. This brings up the Per Site Privacy Actions dialog box. Enter the name of your trusted site and click Allow.

Install .NET Passport

You can use Windows Messenger instant messaging and access many Web sites safely by installing a .NET Passport. .NET Passport is a Microsoft service that attempts to do away with the problem of keeping track of multiple user names and passwords for numerous Web sites by creating a broadly available service. When you have obtained a .NET Passport, you can use your e-mail address and password to sign in to any .NET Passport-enabled site. By assigning the .NET Passport to your Windows XP user account, you further simplify your logon procedures to many sites.

Windows XP SP2 provides a wizard to walk you through the steps necessary to obtain a .NET Passport. To access the wizard, launch Windows Messenger from the Start menu and click to sign in. The .NET Passport Wizard begins. It first asks you whether you already have an e-mail account or if you want to open an MSN Hotmail account (the basic account is available at no cost). This example assumes you as yet have no account. Next, the wizard opens a browser window with a registration form for you to enter some basic information about yourself, such as your name, language, country, and so on.

Install .NET Passport

1. Click Start and select Windows Messenger.
2. Click to sign in.

The .NET Passport Wizard launches.

3. Click Next.

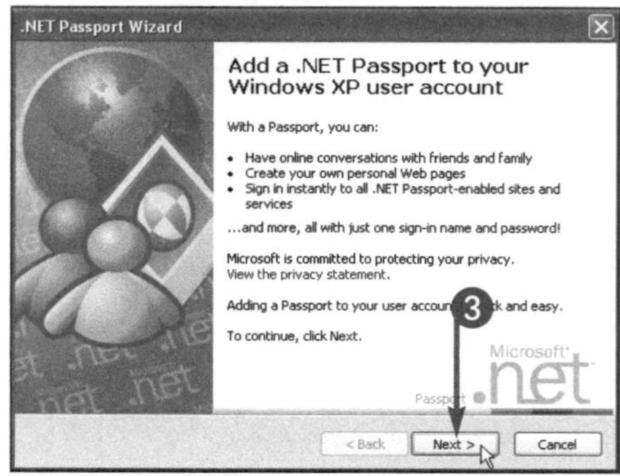

- Click here to use an existing e-mail address. (This example assumes you are creating a new one.)

4 Click to open a new MSN Hotmail account.

5 Click Next.

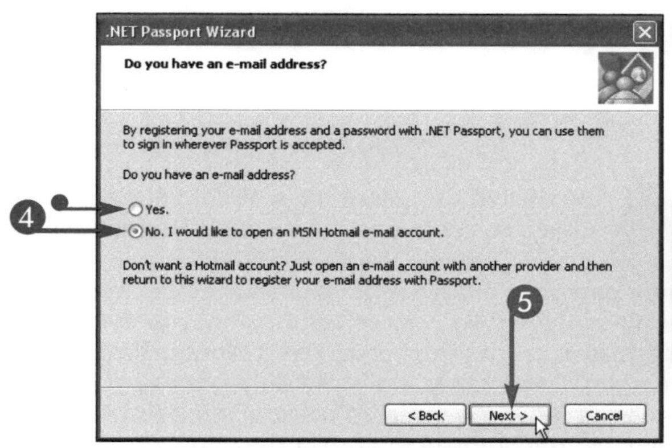

PART II

The Register with Hotmail and .NET Passport screen appears.

6 Click Next.

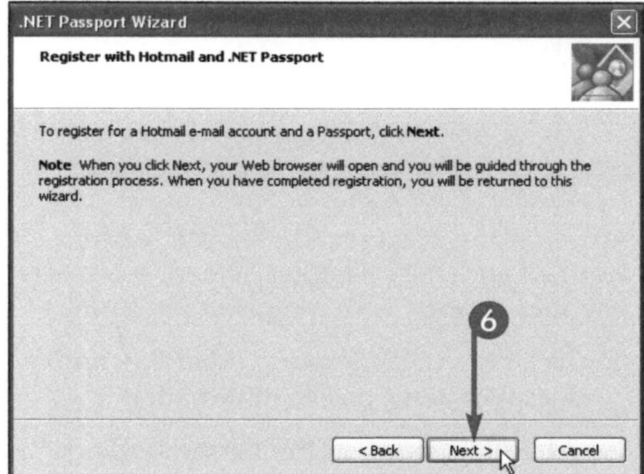

If I choose to assign my .NET Passport to an existing e-mail address, does it have to be a Microsoft one?

▼ No. You just need a valid Internet e-mail address and a password that conforms with the .NET Passport requirements.

Can I have more than one .NET Passport?

▼ Yes. You can, for example have one for your work and one for your personal needs, as long as you have a separate e-mail address for each one.

continued

Install .NET Passport *(Continued)*

After filling out information about yourself, you are asked to come up with an MSN Hotmail account name (such as Stephanie576410 in this example), and a password of at least six characters. Assuming no one has already reserved your account name, you are assigned an e-mail account (Stephanie576410@hotmail.com in this example). If you made a mistake during the registration process or left out a required piece of information, you are redirected to complete or correct the information before proceeding.

Next you are asked if you want to assign the .NET Passport to your Windows user account. If for some reason you do not want to associate the .NET Passport with your account (such as keeping personal information separate from business), just make sure that you clear the check box. The last step is to click Finish to close the .NET Passport Wizard. From here you can sign in to Windows Messenger. Any time you see .NET Passport's Sign In, click it, type your e-mail address and password, and you are signed in to the Web site or service.

Install .NET Passport *(continued)*

After clicking Next on the Register with Hotmail and .NET Passport screen, a browser window appears with a registration form.

- Click here to understand what Passport does with your profile information.

7 Type in information in the corresponding fields on the registration form, or select it from dropdown lists when appropriate.

Note: *At the end of the form you will be asked to agree to the terms of .NET Passport and Hotmail.*

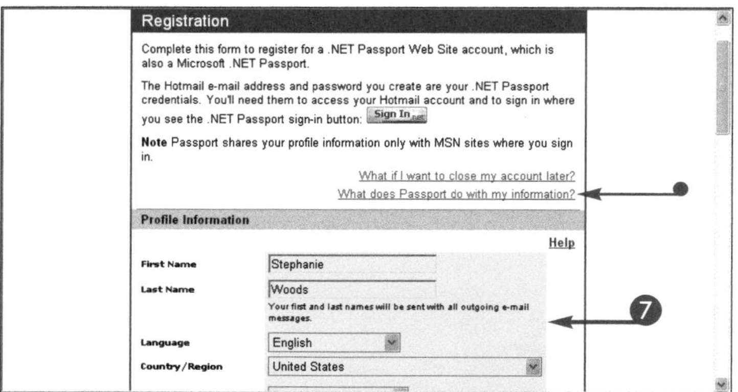

- Your newly assigned e-mail address appears (stephanie576410@hotmail.com in this example).

8 Click Continue.

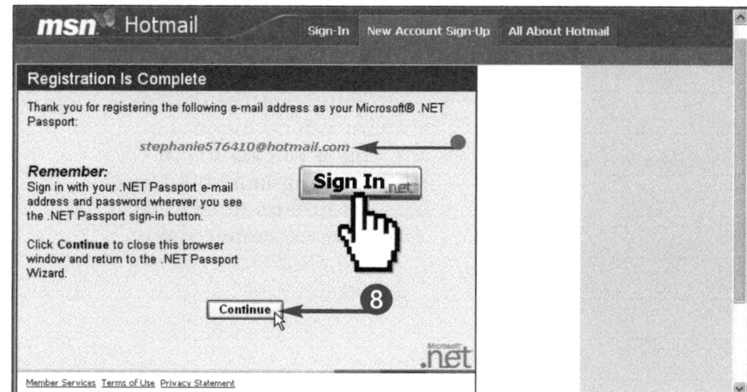

- Click here to clear the check box if you do *not* want to associate your .NET Passport with your Windows user account.

9 Click Next.

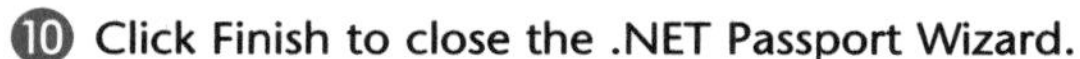

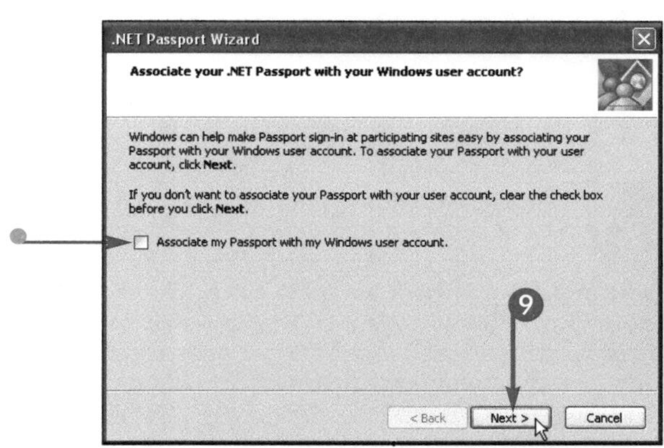

10 Click Finish to close the .NET Passport Wizard.

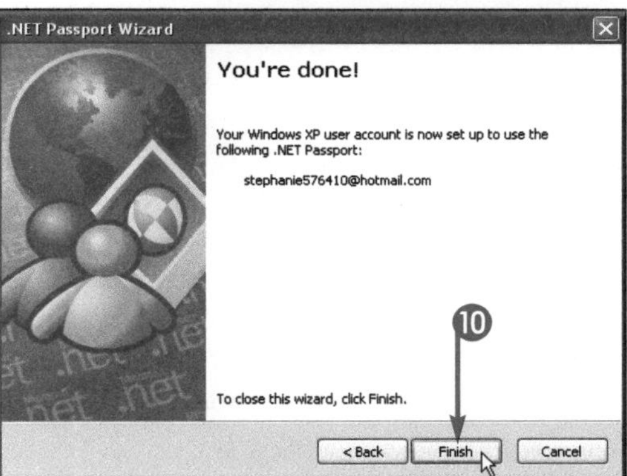

Can I close my .NET Passport account at a later time?

- Yes. If you have used an MSN Hotmail account, that account will no longer be available if you do so. To close your account, launch Internet Explorer and go to the Web site http://memberservices.passport.net/ and click Close my .NET Passport account.

Can I change my .NET Passport password?

- Yes. Launch Internet Explorer and go to the Web site http://memberservices.passport.net/ to and click Change my password.

Work with Windows Media Player 10

Windows XP SP2 includes Windows Media Player 10, a program that enables you to play audio and video on your computer. Media Player makes it easy to play back an audio CD or file. By default, Windows is configured to launch Media Player any time you insert an audio CD (such as a CD from your favorite rock group). Likewise, when you click an audio file supported by Media Player (such as WAV or MPG), Media Player launches and plays the file.

Media Player also can be used to play video on your computer. You can use it to play digital video files and DVDs. With Media Player 10, you can insert a DVD into your DVD drive and watch a movie. Video clips, thousands (or millions perhaps) of which are available on the Internet, can be downloaded and played on Media Player. You also can create your own home movies using a digital video camera and video capture software, and then play back the video files using Media Player.

The first time you run Media Player, you are lead through a series of setup steps. Click the default choices for Media Player to be set up on your computer. You can customize Media Player later if you need to change its behavior. By default, Media Player is your video and audio playback software.

Work with Windows Media Player 10

1. To play an audio CD, insert the CD-ROM in the CD tray.

   The Audio CD dialog box appears.

2. Click the option to play audio CD using Windows Media Player.

   - Click this option to have Windows perform this action every time you insert an audio CD.

3. Click OK.

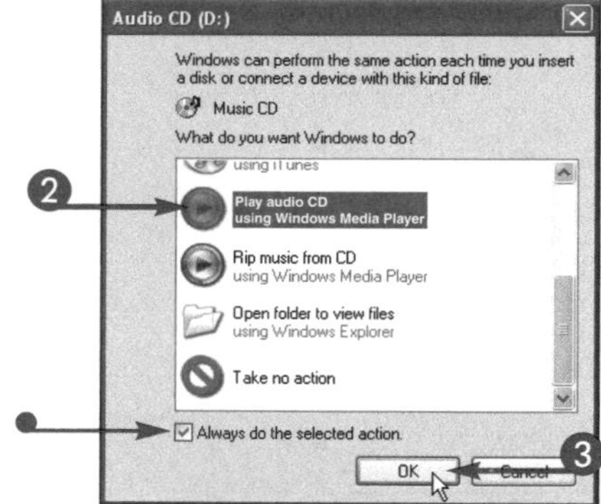

The Media Player window appears, with the Now Playing tab displayed.

The first track on the CD begins playing.

4. To pause the track, click the Pause button.
5. To stop the track, click the Stop button.
6. To move to the next track, click the Next button. Or, double-click the name of the track in the playlist.
7. To mute the sound, click the Mute button.

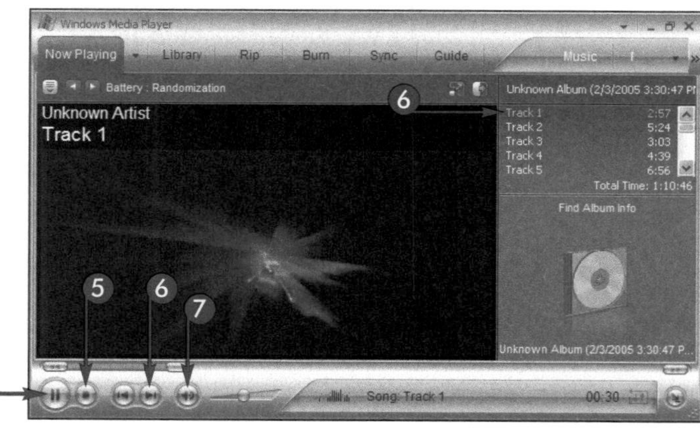

8 Click the Play button to continue playing after you have paused or stopped the track.

9 To move to different parts of a track, slide the Seek slider to the left or right. Or, click the Fast Forward or Rewind button.

10 Graphic visualizations can play as your audio file plays. To change a visualization, right-click the visualization area.

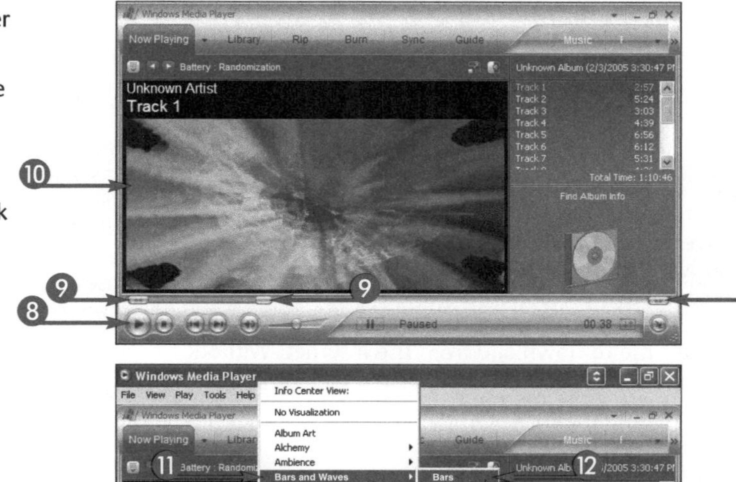

A menu of visualization categories appears.

11 Click a category.

12 Click a visualization name.

The new visualization plays.

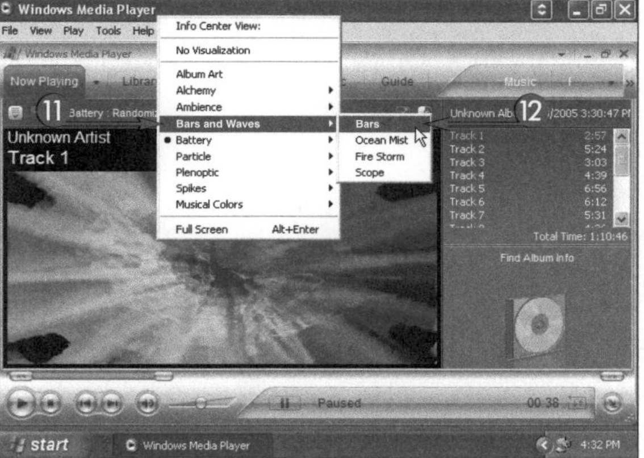

I have Media Player installed, but another program opens when I insert a CD. What can I do to change this?

▼ You must change the file association with your audio file formats. An easy way to do this is to start Media Player, and click Tools, Options, and then the File Types tab in the Options dialog box. In the File Types dropdown list, click Select All to make Media Player the default player for audio and video files. Click OK to confirm your changes. The main Media Player window appears. Now when you insert an audio CD, Media Player is the program that launches to playback your songs.

Are there updates available for Media Player? If so, how do I get them?

▼ Microsoft routinely announces updates to Media Player. As of this writing, the latest version of Media Player was 10.00.00.3646. To check for Media Player updates, you must have an Internet connection. Next, start Media Player and click Help. From the Help menu, click Check for Player Updates. Media Player checks your version against the latest one on the Microsoft Web site. If your version is the most current, a message appears letting you know this. Click OK to confim and to return to the Media Player window. If your version is not the most current, a wizard appears to download the Media Player update.

Install and Remove Codecs for Media Player 10

Windows Media Player makes it easy to install codecs for playing audio and video files. *Codecs* are encoded programming code that instructs Media Player how to decompress an audio or video file when you want to play it back. Codec is short for COmpressor/DEcompressor. Audio and video files are compressed so they take up less room on your computer and take less time to download from the Internet. Without a codec on your computer, Media Player does not know how to decompress a type of file.

When you install Media Player, some codecs are automatically installed. As newer compression formats are introduced, however, new codecs are written. Some codecs are free, while others cost money. Media Player is set up to download codecs automatically when you attempt to play back a video that uses a codec not already on your computer. You must be connected to the Internet for this to occur.

Media Player also lets you remove codecs. You may want to remove codecs if they expire (due to licensing concerns) or if they are too outdated for your media clips to play back properly.

Install and Remove Codecs for Media Player 10

Install a codec

1. To enable Media Player to automatically download and install codecs, start Media Player.

   The Media Player window appears.

2. Click Tools and then Options.

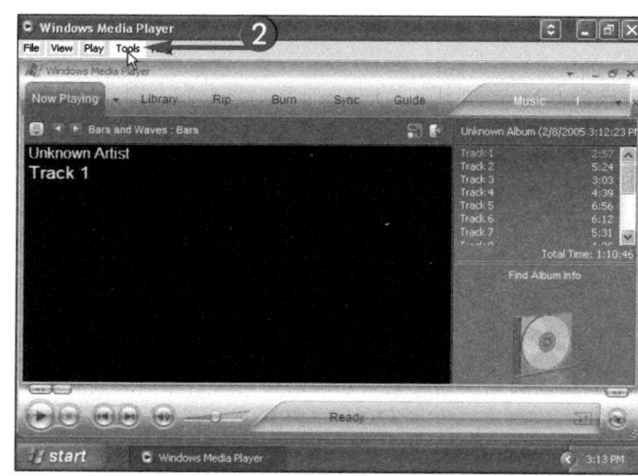

   The Options dialog box appears.

3. Click the Player tab.
4. Click the option to download codecs automatically.
5. Click OK.

   When you open a file that requires a codec not currently on your computer, Media Player automatically searches for the right one to download and install.

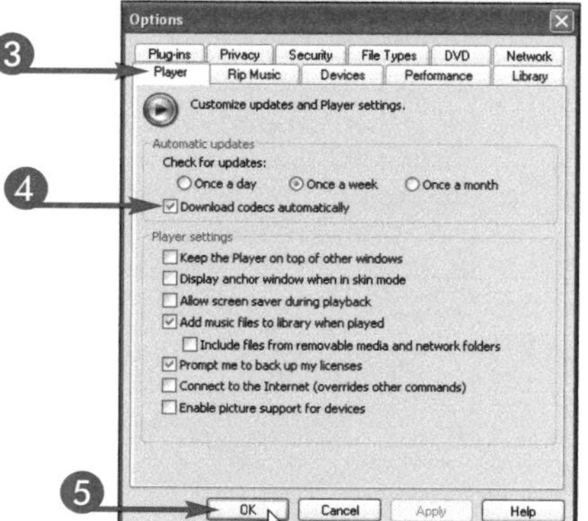

Remove a codec

1. To remove a codec, open the Control Panel.
2. Click the Sounds, Speech, and Audio Devices icon.
3. In the Sounds, Speech, and Audio Devices dialog box, click the Sounds and Audio Devices icon.
4. In the Sounds and Audio Devices Properties dialog box, click the Hardware tab.

   In the Devices list are names of multimedia related-hardware devices, as well as names of video and audio codecs installed.
5. To remove an audio codec, click Audio Codecs.
6. Click Properties.
7. In the Audio Codecs Properties dialog box, click the Properties tab.
8. Click the codec to delete, such as Microsoft GSM 6.10 Audio CODEC in this example.
9. Click Remove.

   The Remove dialog box appears warning that the system may not work properly if this codec is removed.
10. Click Yes to continue with the deletion.
11. Click OK.
12. Click OK to close the Sounds and Audio Devices Properties dialog box.

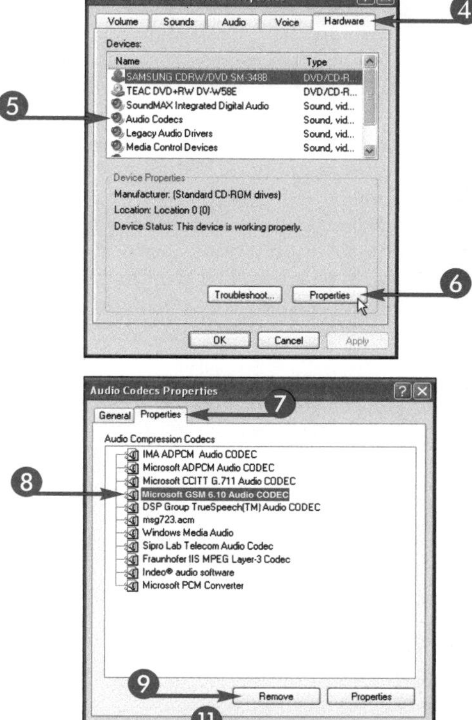

Sometimes when I try to play back an AVI video file, I get an error saying it cannot find the DivX codec. What is this and can I get it on the Internet?

▼ The DivX codec is one of the oldest codecs around. Originally it was designed to compress and play back DVD files on regular CDs. Now, however, it is a high performance compression codec that is used for video files, including WMV, MPEG-4, and AVI files. With DivX, video producers can shrink an entire DVD-sized movie to fit on a CD without losing too much of the quality.

To download DivX, visit DivX.Com at http://go.divx.com. You can download DivX (which is free and has some features disabled), DivX Pro, or Dr. DivX. The latter two are used to create your own DivX video files and currently cost around $20 and $30, respectively, to acquire.

I have a codec but Media Player says it is not installed. Do codecs ever have updates?

▼ Yes, some codecs are being updated constantly. A codec may be updated with new user features, have better compression algorithms included, or be ported to other operating systems. When Media Player tells you that it cannot locate a specific codec and you know it is on your system, be sure the option for allowing Media Player to download new codecs is enabled.

Rip Music with Windows Media Player 10

Media Player makes it very easy to rip music from your audio CDs. When you rip music, you copy the music from the CD to the computer, saving each song (called a track) into a file. You can then play back the ripped music as an album, create playlists by combining individual tracks from various albums into your own "album," or copy music to another device.

When you begin ripping music, you select the tracks you want to rip. To rip the whole album, you select all the tracks. To rip only selected tracks, select them in the Rip tab of Media Player. When you start ripping, Media Player shows you the progress of the ripping process. While you are ripping a CD, you can even listen to it.

When you rip music and you are connected to the Internet, Media Player automatically downloads information about the album. For example, Media Player downloads the track title, artist name, music genre information, and other information. Although many CDs have this information available on the Internet, some do not. If the information is not available, Media Player displays labels such as Unknown Artist, Track 1, Track 2, and so on.

Rip Music with Windows Media Player

1. Insert an audio CD into your CD-ROM drive.

   Windows displays the Audio CD dialog box.

2. Click the option to rip music from CD using Windows Media Player.
3. Click OK.
   - You can click the option to always do the selected action if you want Media Player to automatically start and rip your audio CDs from now on. However, you may not want to choose this if you plan to simply play back CDs using Media Player in the future.

   The Rip Options dialog box appears. Here you can read about Media Player's audio formats, which optimize file size and audio quality.

4. To keep your current settings, click the option to keep your current format settings.
5. Click OK.

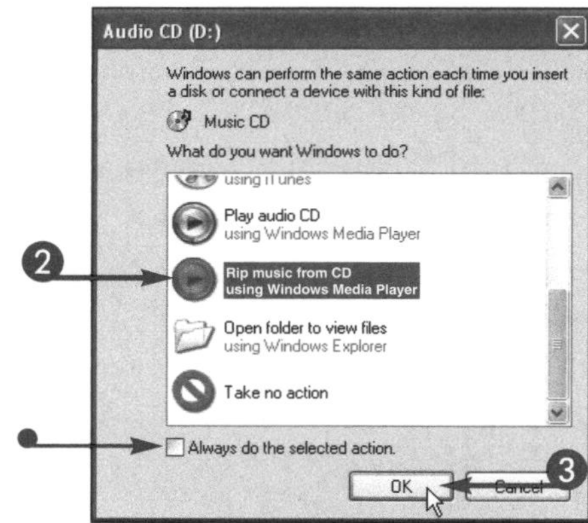

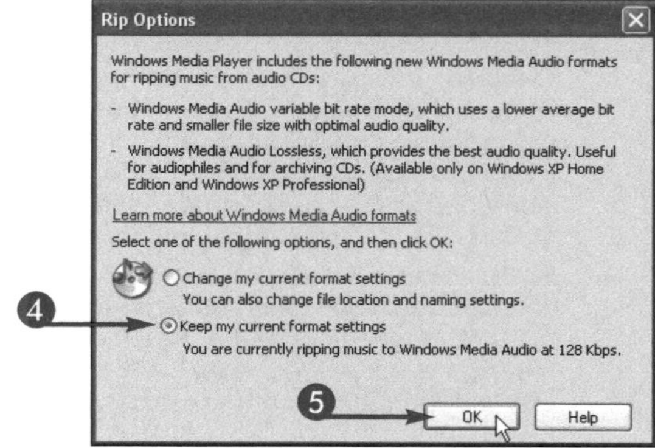

The Windows Media Player window displays with the Rip tab open.

Media Player automatically begins ripping the CD.

If you are connected to the Internet, Media Player also downloads artist, track, and license information about the album.

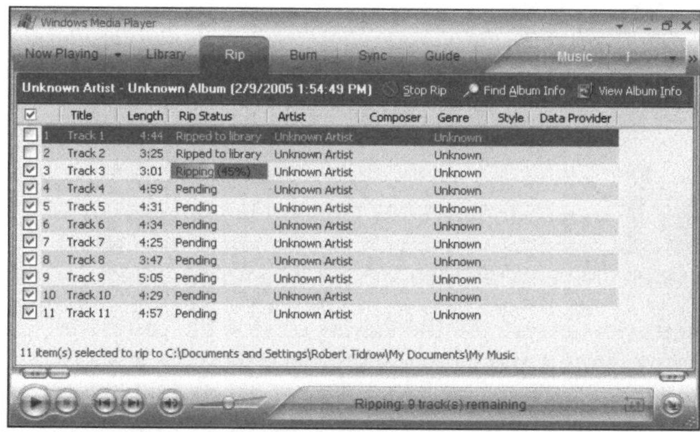

When the CD is finished ripping, the Media Player window appears as shown here. You can play back tracks, record to another media device, create playing lists, or close Media Player.

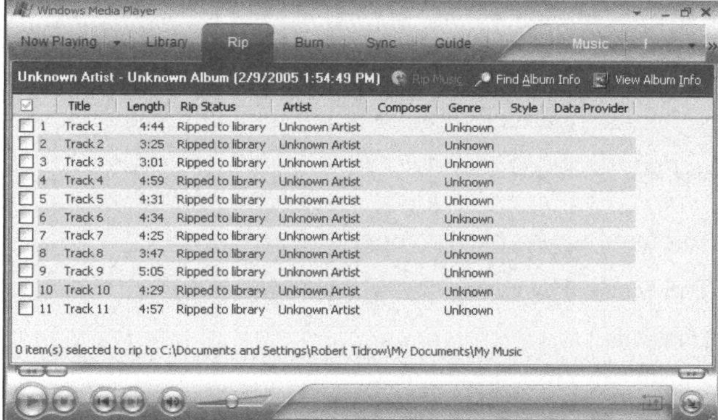

Some of the CDs I try to rip have a copy protection item selected. What is this and how can I play back the tracks?

▼ CDs that have the Copy protect music check box enabled are protected files. You must obtain a license (called license migration) to play back the tracks. The license includes information about restrictions on the file. This information depends on the creator of the license, but can include restrictions on copying the music to other computers. The license you download while ripping a track is associated with the computer on which you download the license. This license can only be played on the computer where you create the license file.

I understand that I should back up my Media Player licenses. How can I do this?

▼ Microsoft does recommend that you back up your Media Player licenses periodically, especially when you plan upgrades to Media Player or to your system. You then can restore the licenses if your working set gets corrupted for some reason. To make a backup, click Tools and then License Management. The Manage Licenses dialog box appears. Click Back Up Now to back up Media Player licenses. When the backup completes, the Transfer complete dialog box appears. Click OK to close the dialog box and to return to the Media Player window.

Create Playlists

Media Player enables you to create playlists, which are customized lists of files that you want to listen to or watch. A playlist can be one song, one video file, a list of video files, or a complete album.

You can view playlists in the Playlist pane while you have the Now Playing and Library tabs selected. Items in a playlist can be played back in order, repeated, shuffled, and sorted. When you shuffle a playlist, Media Player automatically plays files back in random order.

After a playlist is created, you can add files to it. Files can be added to playlists using Media Player or by selecting files from Windows Explorer or My Computer. The playlist can be modified (by adding files to it, renaming files, or removing files), resorted, or removed.

Create Playlists

1. To create a new playlist, open Media Player.

   The Media Player window appears.

2. Click File.
3. Click New Now Playing List.

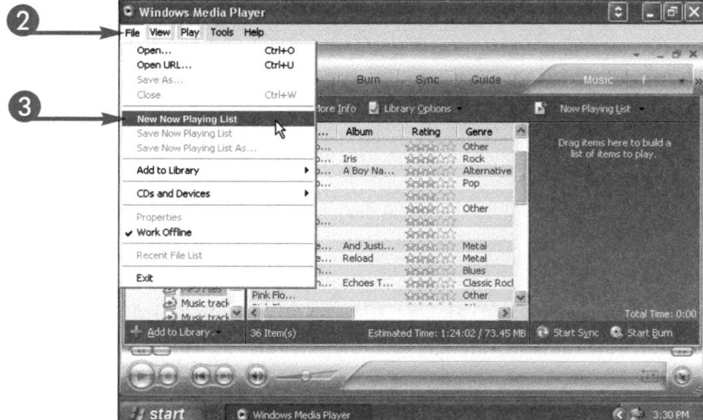

The Library tab appears with the Now Playing List showing.

4. Click the Now Playing List down arrow.

   A menu of choices appears.

5. Click New List.
6. Click Playlist.

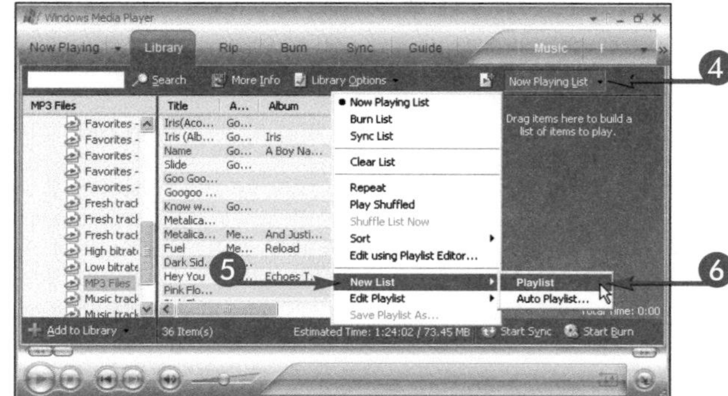

- The Playlist pane instructs you to drag items to it to build your list.

7. In the Contents or Details pane of the Library tab, select a track.
8. Drag the track to the Now Playing List pane.

   The file is added to the Now Playing List.
9. Continue adding files to the new playing list.
10. Click the Now Playing List down arrow.
11. Click Save Playlist As from the menu that appears.

    The Save As dialog box appears.
12. Type a filename.
13. Click Save.

- The new playlist is saved to your computer. To play it, choose the playlist name after clicking My Playlists in the Contents pane.

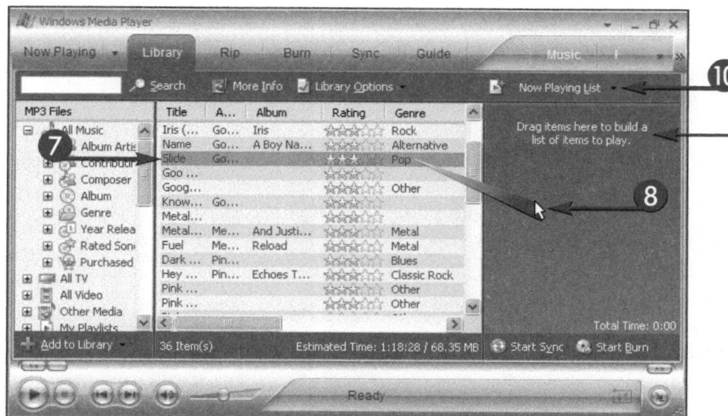

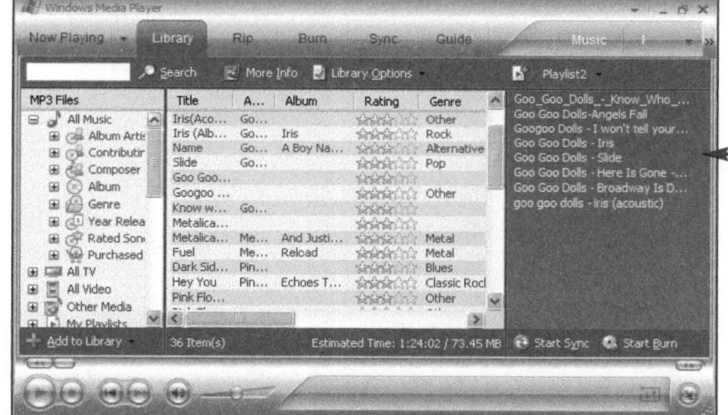

What are auto playlists?

▼ Auto playlists are playlists that Media Player creates automatically based on certain criteria. To see auto playlists, open Media Player and click the Now Playing tab. Click the down arrow next to the Now Playing tab and select Auto Playlists from the menu that appears. Auto playlists display, including Favorites – 4 and 5 star rated, Favorites – Listen to on Weekends, Fresh Tracks, and Music tracks I dislike. These lists are automatically updated each time you open them in Media Player.

How do I create an auto playlist?

▼ To create an auto playlist, choose File and then New Now Playing List. The Library tab appears. Click the Now Playing Lists down arrow and choose New List from the menu that appears. Choose Auto Playlist to open the New Auto Playlist dialog box. Type a name in the Auto Playlist name box. Click the green plus signs to choose various criteria for the auto playlist. For example, from the first list, select File Type. Click the Contains link and select an option, such as Is. Next choose the click to set link to show a list of file type choices (such as MP3, WAV, and WMA). Click a type you want in your auto playlist. Continue adding criteria as needed to create your list. Click OK when ready to save your list. Media Player adds the new auto playlist to the list of auto playlists.

Burn CDs

Media Player makes it easy to burn audio tracks and digital data files to CD. When you burn a CD, you copy files from your computer to a recordable CD. You must have a CD-R or CD-RW device installed on your computer to burn CDs.

Files saved in WMA, MP3, and WAV format can be burned to CD. Audio CDs you create can be played back on most computers, as well as car, home, and portable CD players that support CD-Rs and CD-RWs.

To set up a list of items to burn, you can create a burn list that is just used for one-time burning. Or you can select a playlist you have created and burn those tracks to CD. Media Player keeps track of the amount of space available on the CD so you can see if your burn list can fit on one CD. Disks can hold about 72–80 minutes of audio, or about 600MB of data.

Media Player enables you to modify burn settings if you want to increase the quality level of your recordings. If you do this, however, the file size for each track increases, so fewer songs can fit on a CD.

Burn CDs

1. To burn a CD, open Media Player.
2. Click the Burn tab.

   The Burn tab appears. The left pane is the Items to Burn pane. The right pane is the Items on Device pane.
3. Insert a blank CD-R or CD-RW into your CD-R/RW drive.

   If the CD Drive dialog box appears, click Cancel.

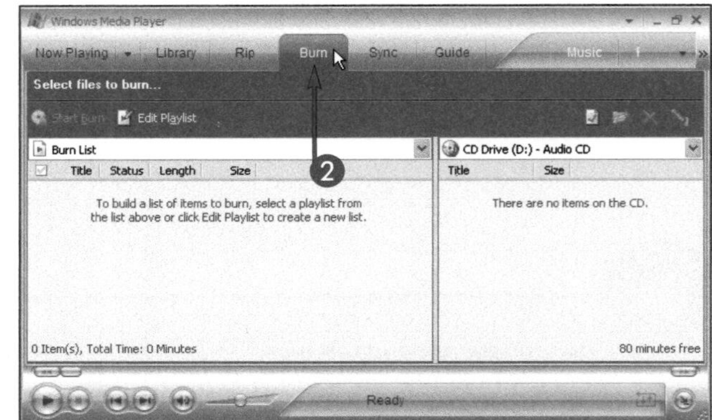

4. Right-click items from playlists or the Library tab that you want to burn.
5. From the menu that appears, click Add to.
6. Click Burn List to add the item to the burn list.
7. Continue adding items to the burn list.

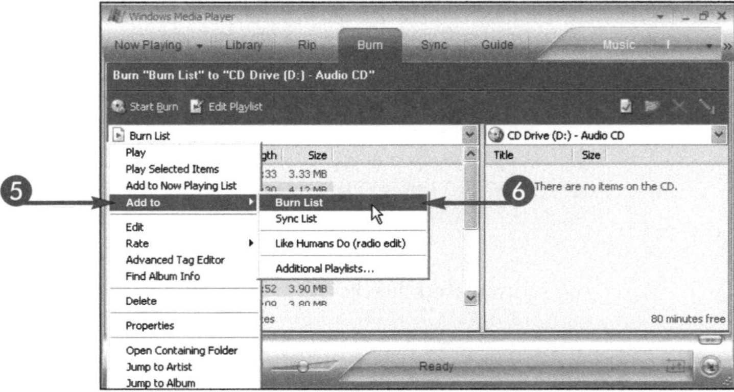

- The items you add to your burn list appear here.
- The amount of time for your currently selected burn list shows here.

Note: *An average CD holds approximately 80 minutes or 600MB of data.*

8 Select all the items you want to burn.

9 Click Start Burn.

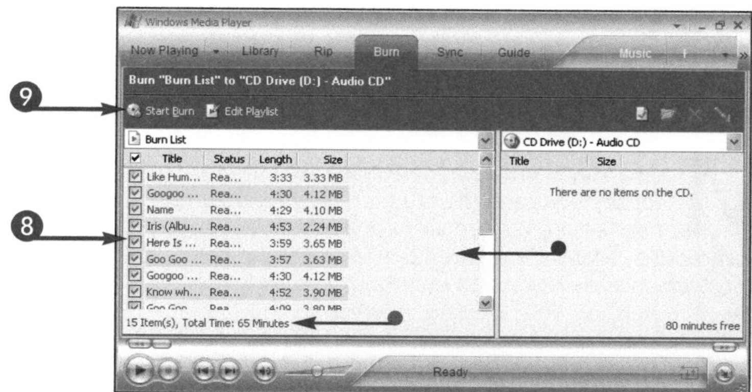

Media Player begins burning your list to the blank CD.

First it converts the file to the format you choose to save to your disk (such as MP3). It then burns the item to disk.

When finished, your CD ejects from the CD-ROM drive and is ready to be played on other devices.

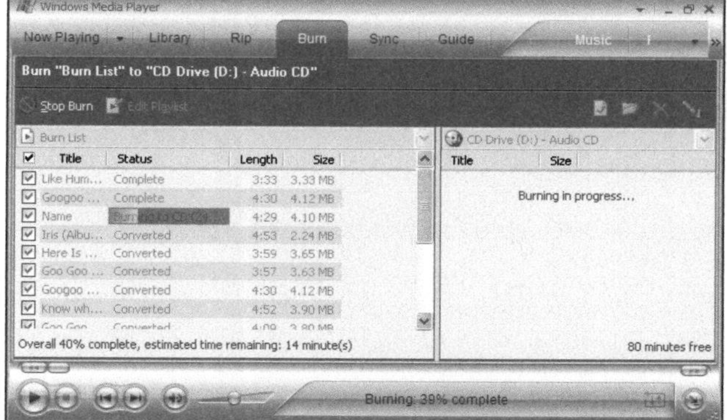

How can I make the highest possible digital data CDs?

▼ You use the Quality tab of the CD drive properties. To see these settings, click the Burn tab in Media Player and then click the Display properties and settings button (▣). The CD Drive Properties dialog box appears. Click the Quality tab and choose the Select quality level option. This activates the quality level slider, which you can move to the right to increase burn quality settings. When you do this, however, the amount of space required for the recording is increased, leaving less space for audio tracks. Click OK to confirm your changes. The Media Player window appears.

When I rip music, Windows Media Player saves it in WMA format. However, I want to burn CDs in MP3 format. How can I change this in Media Player?

▼ To change from the default WMA (Windows Media Audio) to MP3, choose Tools and then Options from Media Player. Click the Rip Music tab and click the Format dropdown list. This displays a list of formats that Media Player can rip. Click OK to save your settings. The audio files you rip now are saved in MP3 format.

Play DVDs

Media Player enables you to play back DVDs. This means you can rent or purchase your favorite movie on DVD and sit back and enjoy it on your computer. Many users who have to travel use their DVD players in their laptops to entertain themselves on planes, in hotels, or while waiting in airports.

Media Player includes controls similar to the controls you find on stand-alone DVD players. These controls enable you to skip to specific titles and chapters, play movies in slow motion, access special features, switch audio settings, and change languages.

Play DVDs

1. To play a DVD, insert a DVD into the DVD or CD/DVD drive.

   The DVD Video dialog box appears.

2. Click the option to play DVD Video using Windows Media Player.
3. Click OK.

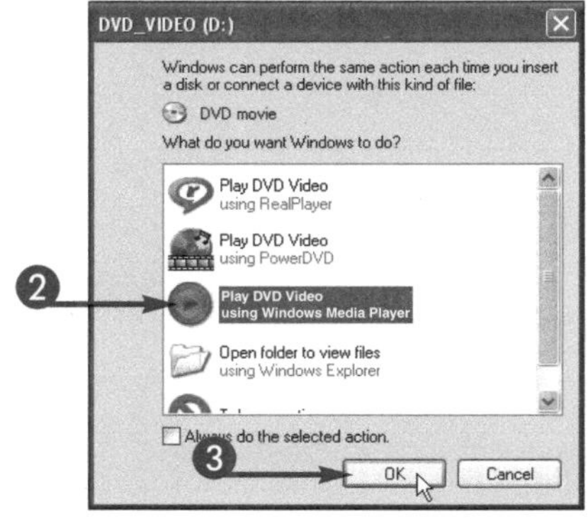

The Media Player starts playing the DVD.

Note: *Usually the first thing that plays is the DVD menu. Here you can choose to play the movie, look at any special features, choose subtitles, or click other choices that the particular movie gives you. In the Show Media Information pane, you also can click Find DVD Info to locate more information about your DVD from the Internet.*

4. Click the choice that lets you play the movie. Or click the Play button on Media Player.

The Now Playing pane begins the movie.

5 Use the controls at the bottom of the Now Playing pane to control the movie playback.

- Click Previous to go to the previous chapter.
- Click Next to go to the next chapter.
- Click Mute to turn the sound off.
- Click here to adjust the volume.

6 Click Pause to pause the DVD.

7 Click Play to resume playing.

8 To change to a different chapter on the DVD, double-click a chapter in the Playlist pane.

Media Player jumps to the part of the movie associated with that chapter name.

9 To stop a movie, click Stop.

The DVD stops and returns to the beginning of the movie.

The DVD menu appears. You can select another menu option, such as view bonus material if included.

I have seen some users in my office that play DVDs, but they have extra information about some of the movies that I do not have. How can I get this information?

▼ DVDs usually contain additional information that you can download from the Internet. Before you insert your DVD the next time, make sure your computer is connected to the Internet. Next insert the DVD. Click the Find DVD Info link on the Media Player Information pane. Media Player looks on the Internet for information associated with your DVD and downloads it to your computer.

Where can I get decoders to play DVDs in Media Player?

▼ DVD decoders can be found on the Internet at several different sites. Like codecs, DVD decoders come in a variety of choices and prices. Some are free, while others require you to pay for them. To locate them, do a Google search on **DVD decoders**. Another place to start is the Microsoft page called Plug Ins for Windows Media Player at www.microsoft.com/windows/windowsmedia/mp10/getmore/plugins.aspx#DVDDecoder.

Is there any way to resize the movie in Media Player?

▼ Yes, you can change it from normal size to full screen mode. To do this, start the movie and click the View Full Screen button (). This changes Media Player so the Now Playing window consumes the entire display. To change back to normal size, press the Esc key on the keyboard.

Synchronize with Portable Devices

Windows Media Player enables you to synchronize digital music files with media devices, such as MP3 players. MP3 players are portable devices (like the previously ubiquitous Sony Walkman cassette and CD players) that store and play back digital music files.

You can use Media Player to rip, store, organize, and then copy music to your media device. You use the Sync tab in Media Player to copy, or synchronize, items to the media device. When items are synchronized, you can disconnect the media device and listen to the music.

The type of tasks you can do with the media devices depends on the media player. Some devices let you view track names, length of track, name of artist, and other information. Other devices may also include features that let you organize and sort tracks, delete individual tracks, and even download small pictures associated with the artist or album.

When you are ready to remove items from the media device, you can delete them from within Media Player or use a file management tool (My Computer or Windows Explorer) to complete the task.

Media Player includes an automatic synchronization feature that enables Media Player to automatically synchronize files with your media device when connected to the computer. Media Player tries to fit your entire library on the device if it fits. Otherwise, it copies files that you specify as most important, such as items rated as 5-star music.

Synchronize with Portable Devices

1. Start Windows Media Player.

   The Media Player window appears.

2. Connect the media device to your computer.

   The Device Setup window appears.

3. Select the option to synchronize your device automatically.
4. Select the option to customize the playlists that will be synchronized.
5. Click Next.

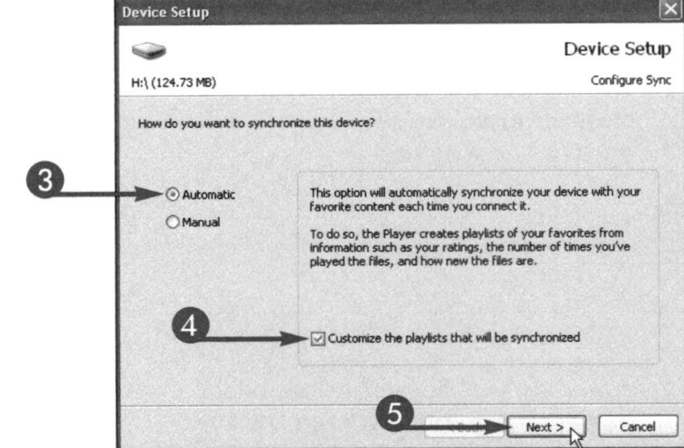

   The Custom Sync Settings screen of the Device Setup window appears.

6. Select the playlists you want to sync automatically.
7. Click Finish.

   Media Player begins to synchronize the selected playlists.

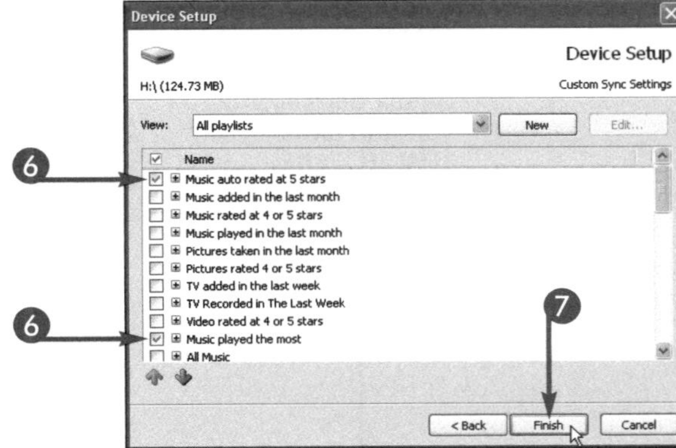

8 To synchronize manually, which you can do even after your automatic synchronization occurs, click the Library tab.

The Library tab appears.

9 Click the Now Playing List down arrow.

10 Click Sync List from the menu that appears.

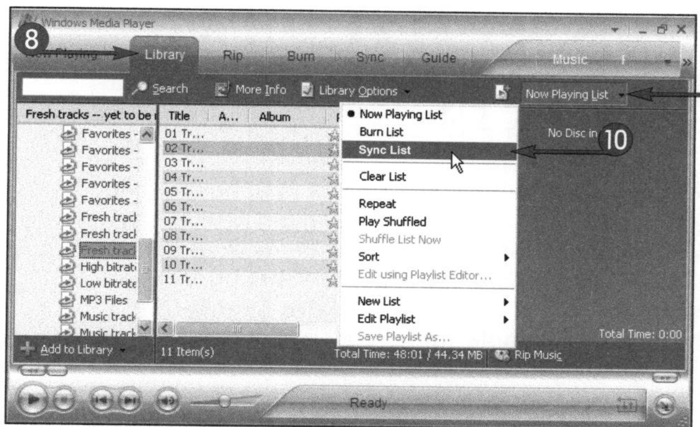

The Sync List appears.

11 Click and drag items from the Contents list to the Sync list.

12 Click Start Sync when you are ready to synchronize the device.

Media Player copies the items shown in the playlist to the media device. When finished, it displays a label that says Synchronizing 100 percent complete in the Details pane.

13 Disconnect the media device to listen to the stored music.

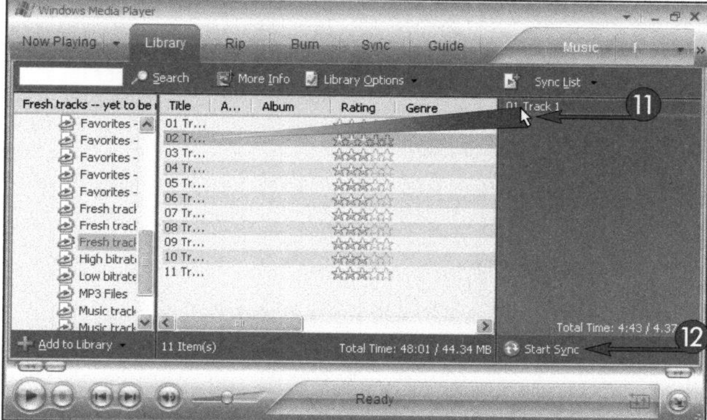

I have a portable device that does not hold enough songs. What can I do?

▼ Some devices enable you to expand their built-in memory by inserting flash memory cards. Flash memory is similar to a computer's random access memory (RAM), but has the capability of storing information for long periods of time. Media devices that can be expanded let you add flash memory cards in the 65MB, 128MB, 256MB, 512MB, or 1GB range. You have to look at the specifications that came with your media device to see if it allows for expansion memory, the type of memory card you have to use (such as SD, xD, Smart Media, and so on), and the maximum size card it can hold.

When I insert my memory card, the media device says it needs formatted. How can I do this?

▼ Media devices are essentially devices that hold computer files (like a hard drive or Zip drive), but have the added bonus of including music playback capabilities. So to format a media device expansion card, open My Computer or Windows Explorer and locate the listing for the media device. It appears as a drive name, such as Drive H. Right-click the device name and choose Format. The Format Disk dialog box appears. Click Start to format the drive. After the format finishes, you can then use Media Player to copy music to the media device.

Work with Scanners

Microsoft Windows XP makes it easy to install and use digital scanners. Until digital cameras became affordable and easy to work with, scanners were the primary device for transferring photographs and other printed documents to your computer. Scanners enable you to convert hard copy documents, photographs, and other printed material into digital files. When these files are on your computer, you can view them, edit them, transfer them to other computers, e-mail them to other people, or store them for future reference.

When you connect a scanner to your computer, Windows XP manages it using the Scanners and Cameras tool. After you install and set up your scanner, you can use the Scanner and Camera Installation Wizard to scan and view documents on your computer.

Windows also includes two programs that let you perform rudimentary editing and viewing of scanned images. With the Windows Picture and Fax Viewer, you can view, rotate, zoom in on, save to a different format, or delete photo files. The other program is called Paint and is a drawing tool that lets you view and modify picture files. You can resize images, save them to different formats, cut selections from an image, or even add text boxes and shapes to a picture.

Work with Scanners

1. Connect the scanner to your computer.

   The Scanner and Camera Installation Wizard appears.

2. Click Next.

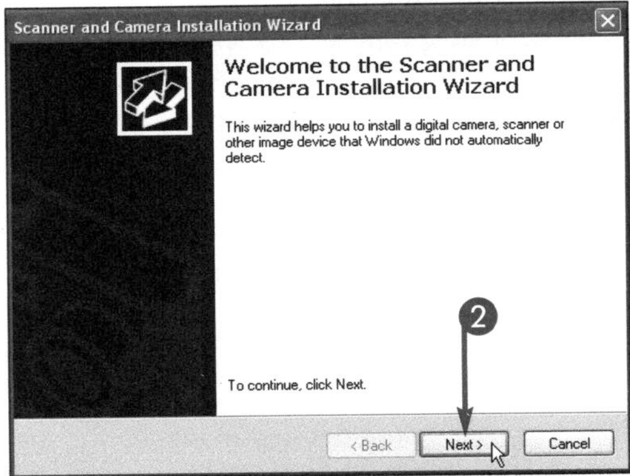

The next screen asks you which scanner or camera you want to install.

- If your device is not listed here, click Have Disk to install your scanner using the scanner's install disk.

3. Select a manufacturer.
4. Select a model.
5. Click Next.

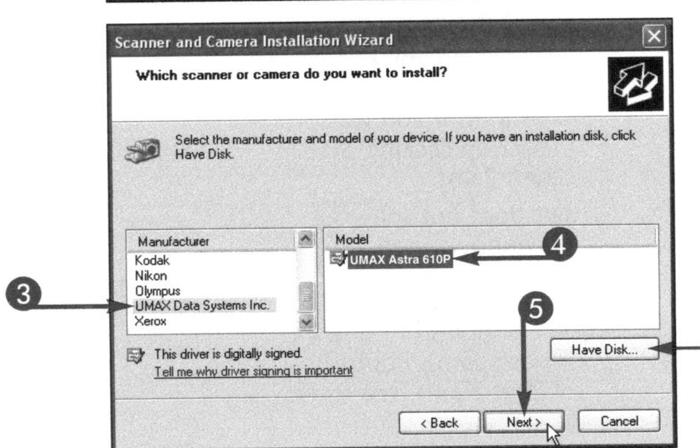

The Connect your device to your computer screen appears.

6 Select the port to which your scanner is connected to.

Note: *Many scanners support connections to parallel ports, USB ports, and SCSI ports. Refer to your scanner's documentation to find out which port your scanner supports.*

7 Click Next.

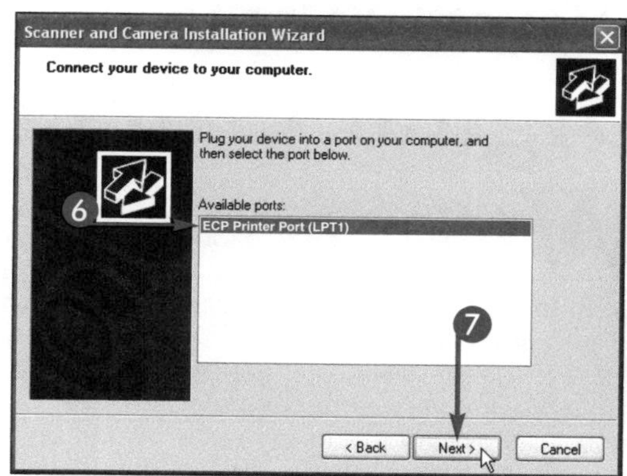

The next screen asks you the name of your device.

- You can type a name to identify your scanner. In most cases, users leave the default name, as shown here.

8 Click Next.

9 Click Finish in the final screen of the wizard.

After Windows installs your scanner, you may be prompted to shut down and restart your computer. If so, click Yes to restart your computer.

After Windows restarts, you can use the Scanner and Camera Installation Wizard to scan images to your computer.

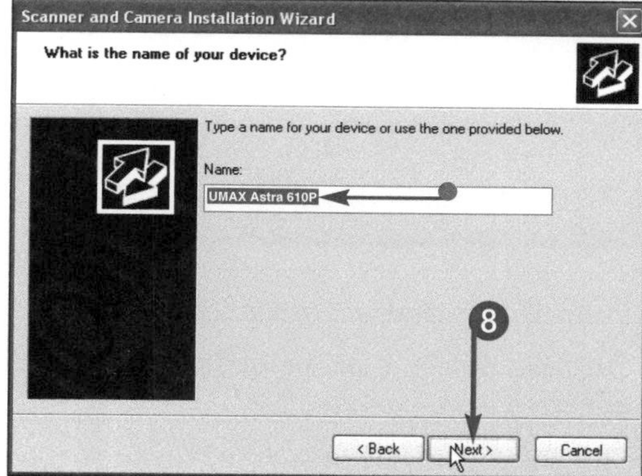

PART II

My scanner is working fine, but I want to make some changes on the scanned picture. How can I do this with Windows Picture and Fax Viewer?

▼ You cannot do any editing of your pictures in Windows Picture and Fax Viewer. You only can view pictures in it. If you want to modify a picture, open it in Paint by clicking Start, All Progams, Accessories, and then Paint.

If Paint does not suit your needs, which is true of most Windows users (even those who do not plan on producing professional quality pictures), you should consider purchasing picture-editing software. Some examples of these include PaintShop Pro (www.jasc.com), Photoshop (www.adobe.com), and Corel PhotoPaint (www.corel.com).

What formats can I save picture files to in Paint?

▼ Paint enables you to save pictures in BMP, JPG, GIF, TIFF, and PNG format. To do this, open Paint and then open the image you want to convert. Click File and click Save As. The Save As dialog box appears. Click the Save as type dropdown list and select the file format in which you want to save the picture. The two most prevalent picture formats on the Web are JPG and GIF. These two formats are easily inserted into most e-mail programs, and can be viewed by all major Web browsers (Internet Explorer, Netscape, Mozilla Firefox, and Opera). Click Save to save the file.

Work with a Digital Camera

Windows XP makes it easy to connect digital cameras to your computer and download pictures to it. In most cases, you just have to plug in the camera, using a USB cable, to the computer's USB port and Windows walks you through setting up the camera and then downloading pictures. When you have set up the camera on your computer, the next time you connect the camera to the computer, Windows automatically recognizes the camera. This enables you to start downloading pictures immediately.

You use the Scanner and Camera Installation Wizard to set up the digital camera. This wizard walks you through installing the camera to work with Windows. In some cases, you can simply connect the camera to the computer and Windows automatically locates the correct hardware drivers and files for your camera. In other cases, you may be prompted to insert an installation CD or disk to complete the setup.

After you connect your camera, you then can download — or copy — pictures from your camera to your computer. When the pictures are safely stored on the computer, you can delete them from your camera, providing free space to snap more pictures. Also, with the pictures on your computer, you can edit them, rename them, print them, store them, or delete them.

Work with a Digital Camera

1. Connect the camera to your computer.

   The Scanner and Camera Installation Wizard appears.

2. Click Next.

The next screen asks you which scanner or camera you want to install.

- If your device is not listed here, you can click Have Disk to install your camera using the camera's install disk.

3. Select a manufacturer.
4. Select a model.
5. Click Next.

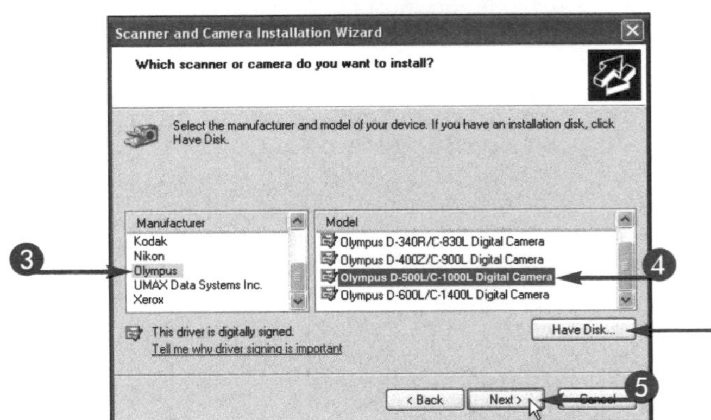

The Connect your device to your computer screen appears.

6 Select the port to which your camera is connected or select the automatic port detection option.

Note: *Many cameras support connections to USB or serial (COM) ports. Refer to your camera's documentation to find out which port your camera supports.*

7 Click Next.

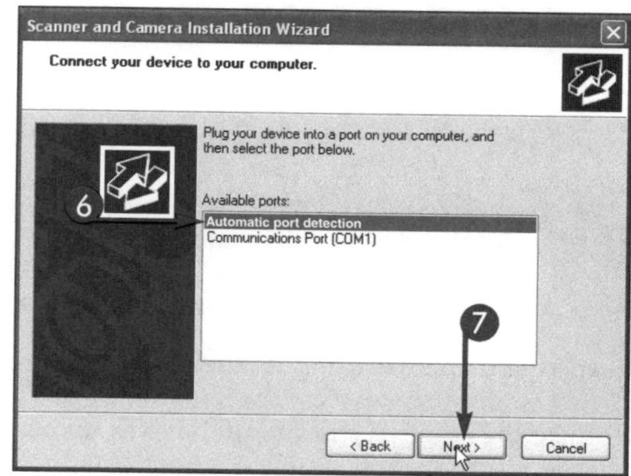

The next screen asks you for the name of your device.

- You can type a name to identify your camera. In most cases, users leave the default name, as shown here.

8 Click Next.

9 Click Finish in the final screen of the wizard.

After Windows installs your camera, you may be prompted to shut down and restart your computer. If so, click Yes to restart your computer.

After Windows restarts, you can use the Scanner and Camera Installation Wizard to download pictures from your camera to your computer.

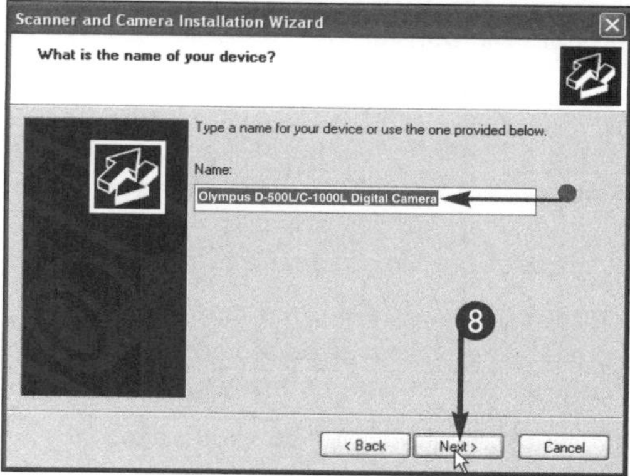

My digital camera uses an xD memory card. Can I remove it from my camera and upload pictures to my computer?

▼ Yes, but you must have a device called a card reader that allows you to do this. The card reader usually has slots that support multiple sizes of flash memory cards, such as SD, xD, and so on. You connect the card reader to your computer, insert the flash memory card, and then download pictures to your computer. Card readers are handy because they offer one device that can read several different cards. Plus they use their own power source (or the power source of the USB connection), allowing you to save your camera's batteries.

I have several pictures on my computer, but do not know how to organize them. How do I create a photo album on my computer?

▼ Windows includes some basic tools for viewing pictures, such as the Windows Picture and Fax Viewer and Microsoft Paint. However, these tools do not offer organizational or thumbnail viewing features. For these types of tasks, you can use My Computer (or Windows Explorer). Double-click My Computer and then double-click the My Pictures folder. Under File and Folder Tasks, click the Make a new folder link. Type a name for the folder and press Enter. Right-click the new folder and choose Properties from the menu that appears. The Properties dialog box for the folder opens. Click the Customize tab and select Photo Album from the Use this folder type as a template dropdown list. Click OK. Move your photos into this folder and open the folder. The photos appear in Filmstrip view, allowing you to scroll through the album one picture at a time.

Work with a Digital Video Camera

Windows XP enables you to view and save video from a digital video camera. Windows makes it easy to connect and set up your digital video camera, and then record video clips to your computer.

The video you capture using a digital video camera can be recorded straight to your computer. That is, unlike analog video (like VHS tapes), you do not have to convert it and then save it to disk. You simply connect your video camera to the computer, such as via a USB or Firewire port, and then begin the transfer.

Windows XP is a nice platform for creating digital video files and editing those files. Windows XP SP2 includes free movie editing software called Windows Movie Maker 2. With Movie Maker you can capture video from an external video device, such as a VCR, digital video camera, analog video camera, or a Webcam. As you copy video to Movie Maker, Movie Maker creates segments of the video so you can manipulate those segments into your own custom movie. To learn more about using Movie Maker, see the following section, "Work with Windows Movie Maker 2."

Work with a Digital Video Camera

1. Connect your video camera to the computer.

   This example assumes that you are using a digital video camera connected to the Firewire port of your computer.

2. Turn on the video camera so it is set to playback mode.

   The Digital Video Device dialog box appears.

3. Click the option to record video using Windows Movie Maker.
4. Click OK.

   Windows Movie Maker appears, with the Video Capture Wizard screen open.

5. Type a name for the new video.
6. Specify a location for the video clip.
7. Click Next.

   The Video Setting screen appears.

8. Click the option for the best quality for playback on your computer.
9. Click Next.

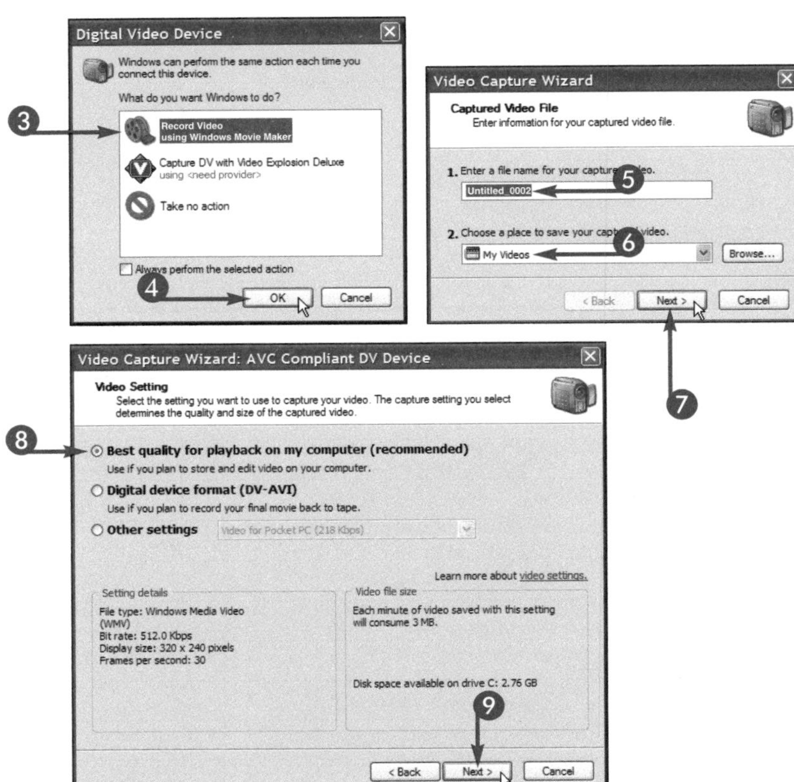

The Capture Method screen appears.

⑩ For this example, click the option to capture the entire tape automatically.

⑪ Click Next.

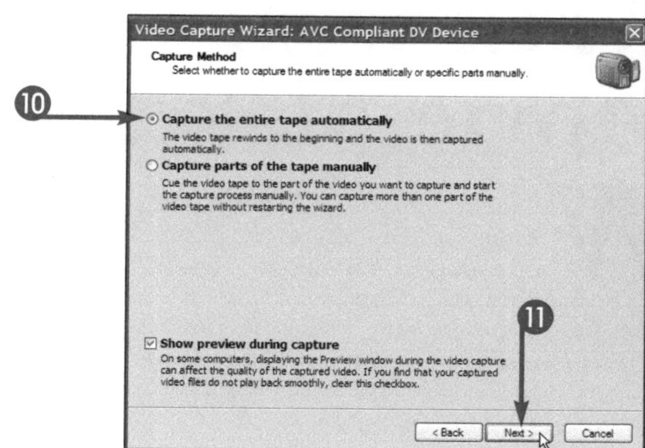

The DV Capture in Progress screen appears.

Movie Maker rewinds your video tape back to the beginning of the tape. When finished, it starts capturing the video from the tape.

⑫ Click Finish to close the wizard.

After it is captured, you can work with the video clips in Movie Maker. Read the next section, "Work with Windows Movie Maker 2," to learn how to perform basic editing tasks in Movie Maker.

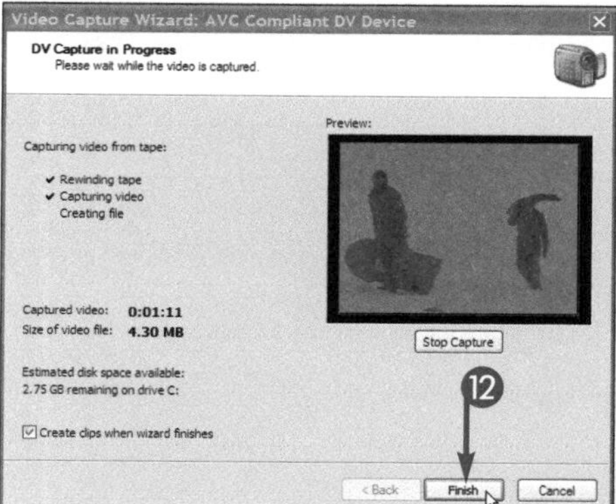

My video camera does not have a DVi port. How can I download my clips to my computer?

▼ To copy video content from a video device, you must have a way to download the video to your computer. With a digital video (DV) camera, this is usually accomplished by using an IEEE 1394 cable connected between the camera and the computer. IEEE 1394 is also referred to as Firewire. Webcam content, which is live content, is copied to your computer via the Webcam connection. This connection is usually via a USB port. For older video analog content, including VHS, Beta, and 8MM, you have to have a hardware device that allows you to connect your camera to the computer. One such product is the AVerMedia DVD EZMaker Pro USB2.0 device.

Can I use other software for capturing and editing video?

▼ Yes, Movie Maker 2 is just one of many video editing programs available. Movie Maker 2 is free and actually has some very nice features for creating and editing video. If you need more sophisticated features, such as editing pixels in the movie clips, overlays, and other professional quality options, consider products like Pinnacle Systems' Studio (www.pinnaclesys.com) or Nova Development's Video Explosion Deluxe (www.novadevelopments.com).

Work with Windows Movie Maker 2

Windows Movie Maker 2 is a free program available from Microsoft. It enables you to view, edit, and save digital movies on your computer. You can capture video from your video camera, import videos from other sources, import pictures into a movie, and add sound files to a movie. When you create a movie, you can add special effects to the movie, as well as create transitions between scenes.

Windows Movie Maker also enables you to add titles and credits to your movies. This enables you to create movies customized for your family, business, or church without burdening you with costly creation fees from professionals.

Another handy feature of Movie Maker is the AutoMovie tool. This tool takes a clip or set of clips and creates a movie quickly using editing styles you choose. It also incorporates music into the movie. The AutoMovie tool is not something you would want to use every time you create movies, but it is a good tool if you are in a hurry to create a movie based on a collection of clips. It is also a good way to see how different Movie Maker enhancements can be used with your clips.

Work with Windows Movie Maker 2

1. Start Windows Movie Maker.

   The Movie Maker window appears.

2. Capture clips from a digital video camera.

Note: *The previous section shows how to capture video into Movie Maker.*

3. Click and drag a clip from the Collection area to the storyboard.

   The clip appears on the storyboard.

4. Continue adding clips to the storyboard to create your movie.

5. To add an effect to the movie, click a link in the Edit Movie area.

   For this example, click the link to make titles or credits.

   The next screen asks where you want to add a title.

6. Click the link to add a title at the beginning of the movie.

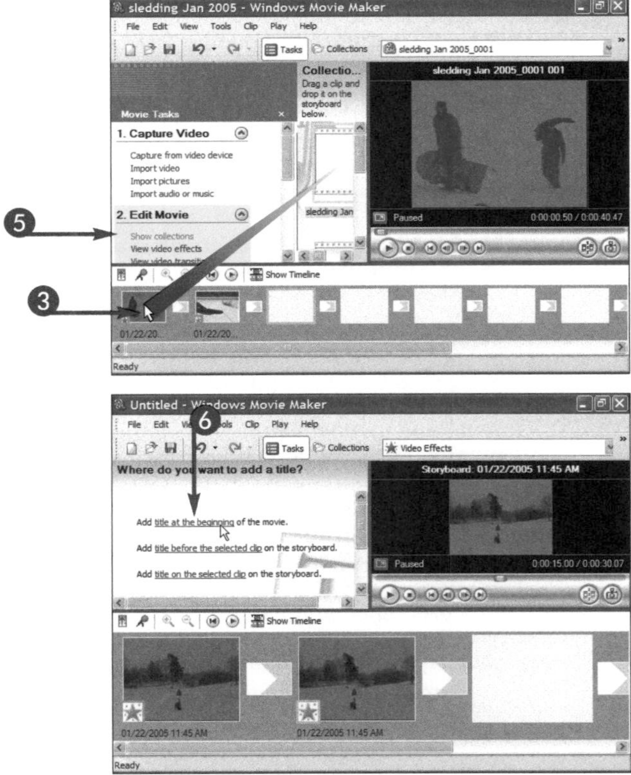

The Enter Text for Title window appears.

7 Type a title for the movie.

8 Click this link to add your title to the movie.

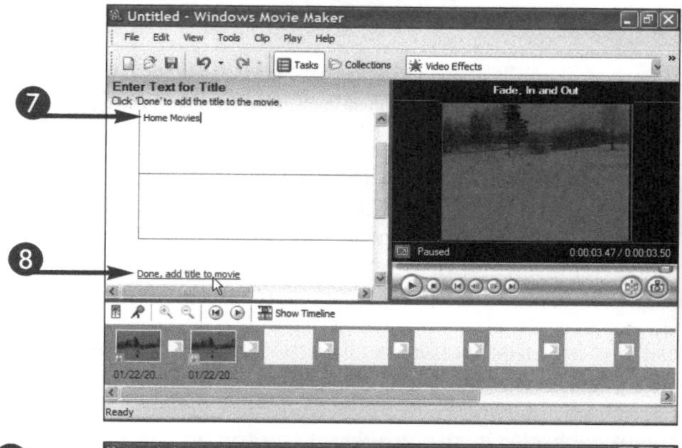

- The title is added to the storyboard.

9 To add a transition between clips, click the link to view video transitions in the Edit Movie area.

The Video Transitions window appears.

10 Click and drag a transition to the storyboard, such as the Diagonal, Down Right transition.

- The transition appears on the storyboard between two clips.

11 To save your movie, click File and then Save Movie File.

MASTER IT

I have looked all over for Movie Maker on my computer. What if I do not have it installed? How can I get it?

▼ Movie Maker 2 is available with Windows XP SP2. However, you can download a copy of it from www.microsoft.com/windowsxp/moviemaker. There are additional transitions and visual effects available for Movie Maker included with the Microsoft Plus! Digital Media Edition software. To learn more about that package, visit www.microsoft.com/windows/plus/dme/dmehome.asp.

When Movie Maker is capturing my video, I have the option of creating clips. Why would I want to do this?

▼ Clips are small segments of your video. With clips, you can find parts of your video much easier and quicker than looking over one large copy of the video. In addition, clips allow you to move parts of the movie around, perhaps creating a different feel for the finished movie. For example, a clip that was taken at the beginning of the day can be moved to the middle or end of the movie if it better illustrates a point in the movie.

If I choose to create an AutoMovie, how long does Movie Maker take to complete the movie?

▼ The length of time it takes depends on how long your clips are. Generally, however, AutoMovie takes about one-third the total time of your clips to complete the movie.

continued

Work with Windows Movie Maker 2 *(Continued)*

When you create movies with Windows Movie Maker, you can add transitions and special effects to your movies. These types of enhancements give your movies a more finished, somewhat professional look.

Transitions are used between clips to help ease viewers into the next scene. Some of the transitions include Keyhole, Fan, Pixelate, Rectangle, Shatter, and Wipe. Because you can view each clip in the Preview Monitor on the Movie Maker window, you can experiment with each transition until you find the one you want.

Video effects are like special effects you can add to your clips. For example, if you want a clip to look like an old-fashioned clip, use the Film Age, Oldest effect. This adds a layer of dust and other particles to your clip, making it appear older than it is. You can use more than one video effect on a clip. For example, you can use the Speed Up, Double and the Grainy effects on one clip to make it appear like an old speeded up film strip.

Work with Windows Movie Maker 2 *(continued)*

The Movie Location screen appears. This screen gives you choices on where you can save your movie, such as to the hard drive, to a CD-R, e-mail, Web site, or a digital video camera.

12 To save to your hard drive, click My computer.

13 Click Next.

The Saved Movie File screen appears.

14 Type a name for your movie.

15 Type a location, or use the default, as shown.

16 Click Next.

The Movie Setting screen appears. By default, only one selection is here if you choose to save to your hard drive in Step 15.

- You can see additional quality settings by clicking Show more choices.

17 Click Next to accept the default quality setting.

The Saving Movie screen appears as Movie Player saves your movie.

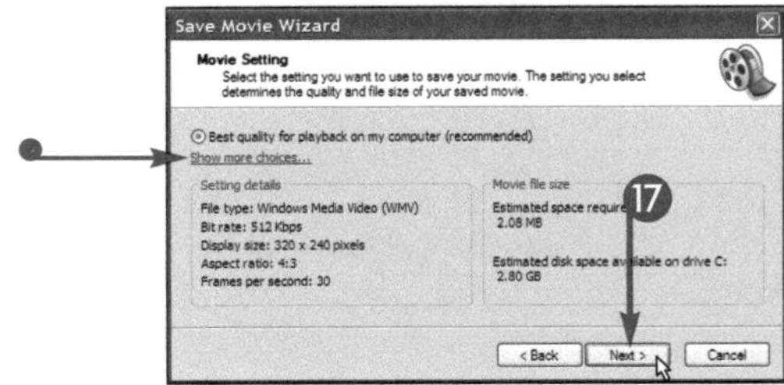

After your movie is saved, the Completing the Save Movie Wizard screen appears.

18 Click Play movie when I click Finish to see your new movie.

19 Click Finish.

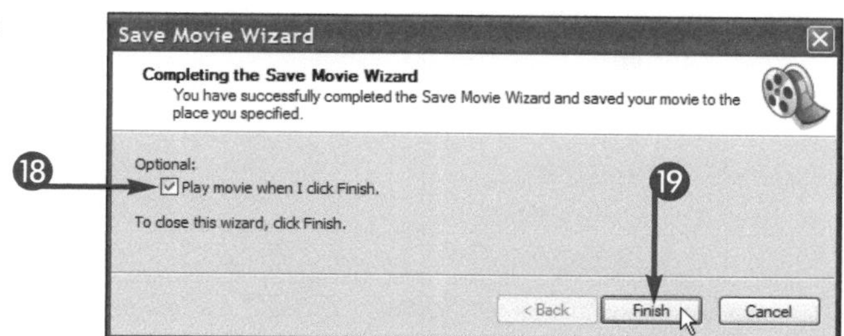

Media Player appears and starts playing back your movie.

PART II

If I am working on a movie and not finished with it yet, how can I save it?

▼ To save an unfinished movie so you can return to it later and edit it, you must save it as a Movie Maker Project. A project keeps the movie as separate clips and lets you continue adding effects, transitions, or titles to it. To save a movie as a project, click File and then click Save Project As. The Save Project As dialog box appears. Type a name in the File name box. Movie Maker gives the file a .mswmm (Windows Movie Maker Projects) file extension. Click Save. This saves the movie as a project. If you later come back and want to edit this project, click File and then Open to open the project file.

I hear voices and other noise on the clips that I have added to Movie Maker. How can I see the audio information for the clip?

▼ The audio that is on a video clip is part of that clip. You cannot isolate that audio unless you use a different editing program (such as Nova Development's Video Explosion Deluxe). Movie Maker does not have separate tracks for audio and video inside a clip. However, you can overlay audio, such as from a separate audio clip or audio CD, by clicking the Show Timeline button (▤). This shows the Video, Audio, and Title Overlay tracks of the movie you are making. You can then mute the sound that is part of a video clip by choosing Clip, Audio, and then Mute.

10 Networking and the Internet

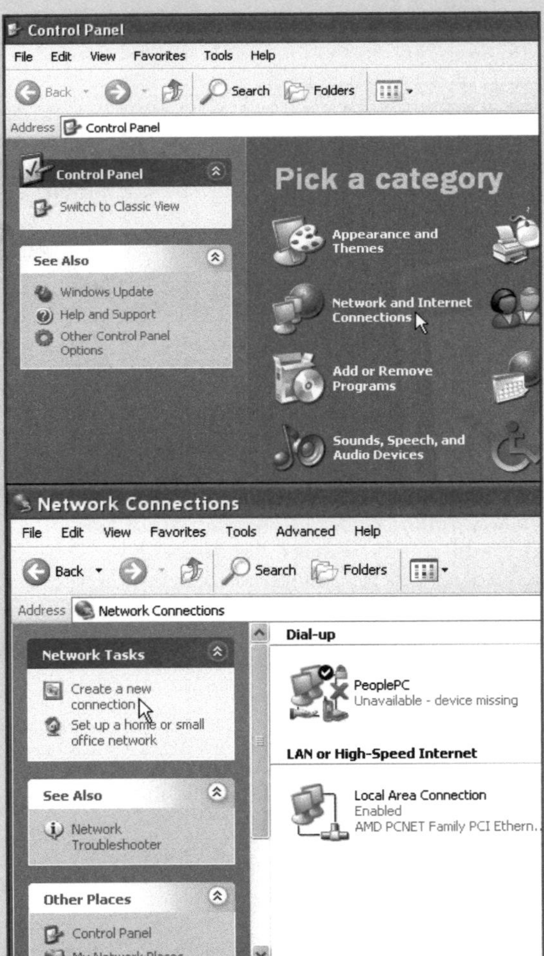

11 Working with Network Services

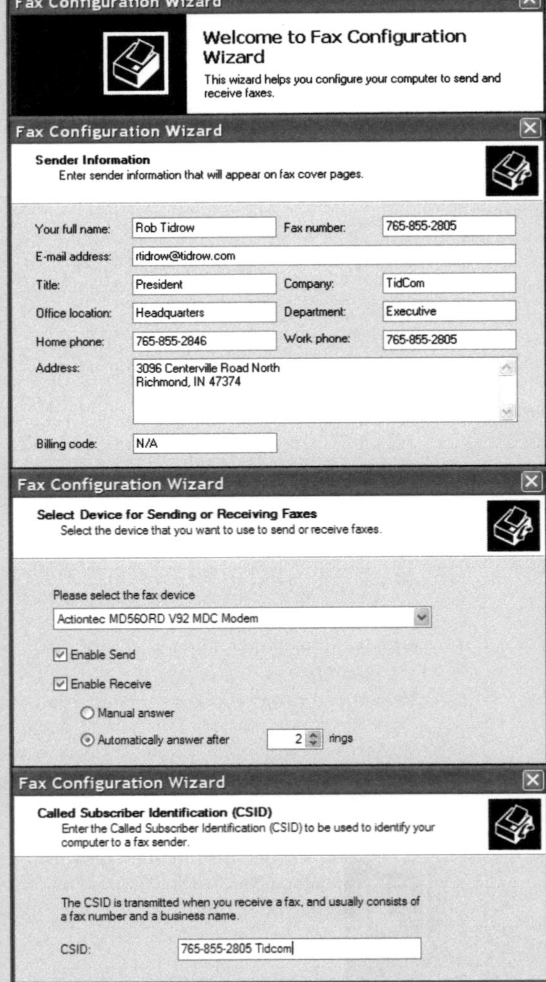

PART III
NETWORKING WITH WINDOWS XP

12 Working with IIS Components

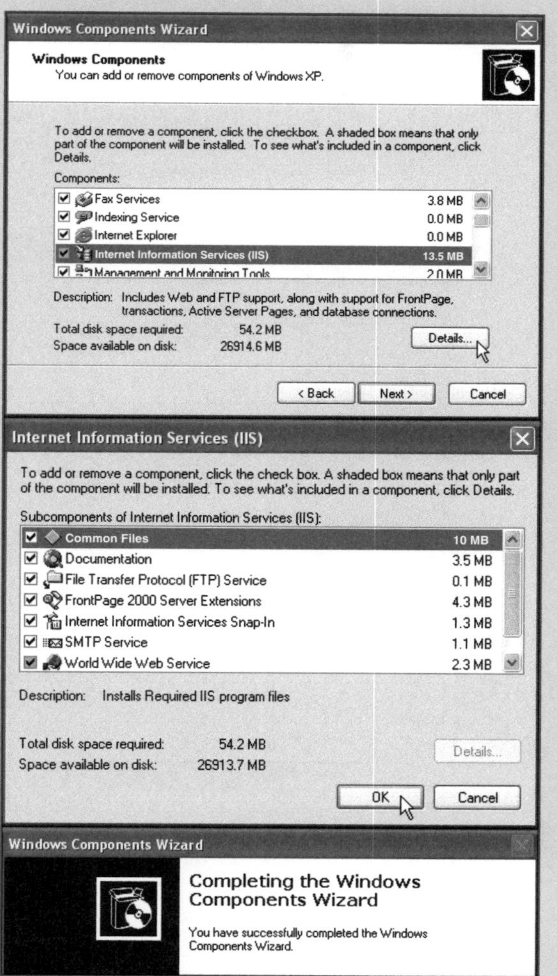

13 Integrating with Active Directory

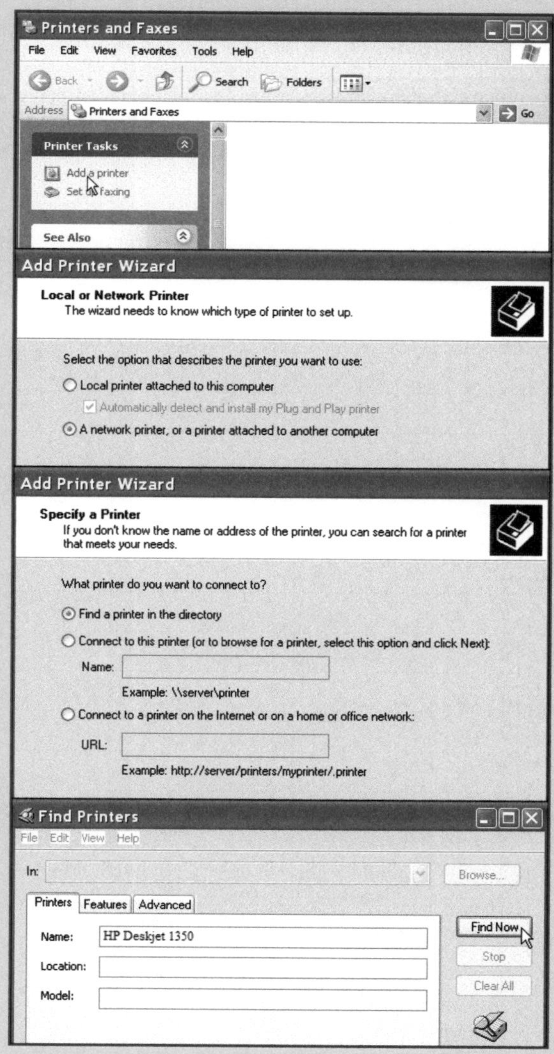

Configure LAN Connections

Windows XP makes configuring your computer for network connections much easier than the same task was in previous Windows editions. With Windows XP, you can configure your computer to work on local area networks (LANs), be part of wide area networks (WANs), and connect to the Internet using broadband connections. In this section, you learn how to set up Windows XP to be part of a local area network.

Setting up a network requires hardware and software components. For hardware, your computer must have an installed network interface card (NIC). A NIC has an opening in which a network cable is attached. The network cable, another required piece of hardware, is what connects your computer to another computer on the network. Although you can get cables that connect two computers directly together, usually a third piece of hardware is used: a switch. A switch is a device in which network cables from two or more computers are connected, and that directs network traffic to each computer on the network. Finally, you need at least one other computer connected to your switch to complete your network.

The software you need for a network includes network protocols, network services, and a network operating system. All of these software requirements are built in to Windows.

Configure LAN Connections

1. From the Start menu, choose All Programs, Accessories, and then Communications.
2. Choose Network Setup Wizard.

   The Network Setup Wizard window appears.
3. Click Next.

   The second Network Setup Wizard screen appears.
4. Click Next.

5. In the next screen that appears, select the Internet connection option that best fits your network configuration.

   This example uses a computer that connects directly to the Internet.
6. Click Next.

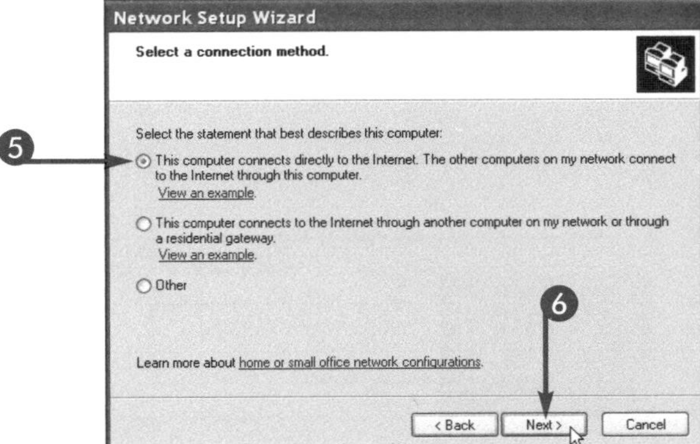

The Select your Internet connection screen appears.

7 Select your Internet connection from the list of connections.

8 Click Next.

The Select your private network connections screen appears.

9 Select your private network connection from the list of connections.

Note: *Usually the private network is called Local Area Network and then the name of your network adapter.*

10 Click Next.

The Give this computer a description and name screen appears.

11 Type a description of your computer.

12 Type your computer's name.

13 Click Next.

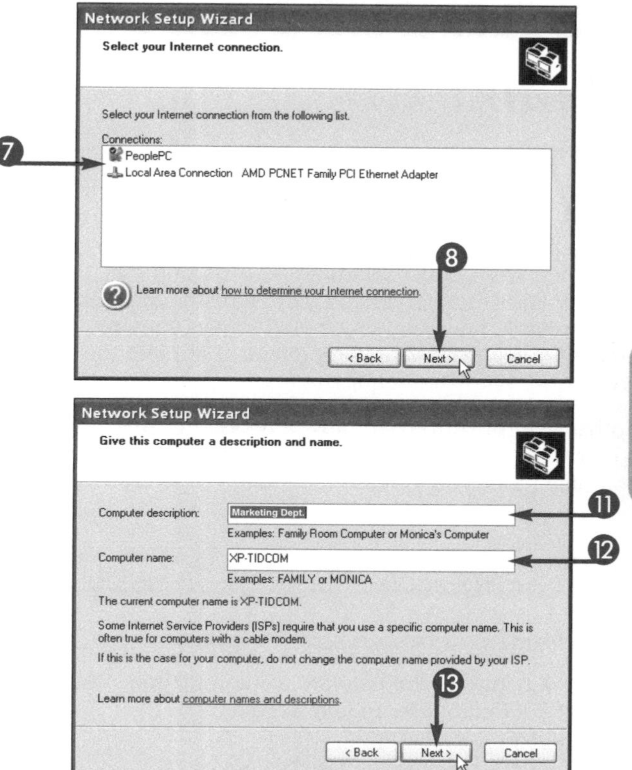

Can I set up a network even if I do not have a network server?

- Yes. Windows XP enables you to connect two or more Windows XP computers together even if you do not have a server. A server, however, is useful because it allows you to share large quantities of files, allows centralized backups and maintenance, and provides other network services.

How many computers make up a network?

- Networks can be small (two) or very large (millions in the case of the Internet). Your company may have a network that includes computers that allow for sharing of files, printers, scanners, and other resources.

  Some networks are layered: One large network encompasses many smaller networks. A large company may have individual networks for marketing, sales, design, accounting, and so on. Each smaller network has specialized needs. Design may need access to high-quality printers. Marketing may need access to some sales data but not to everything that sales does. To complete the network, a large corporate-wide network (Wide Area Network, or WAN) connects all these networks together for corporate requirements, such as Internet access and e-mail.

continued

Configure LAN Connections

(Continued)

Windows XP makes it fairly painless to set up and configure your LAN connections. This is true if you have all networking devices working and installed properly. It seems that the biggest problem with configuring LANs under Windows XP is getting that hardware layer established correctly. To eliminate most of the guesswork, however, you should always consider purchasing new hardware components that meet the Windows XP hardware requirements.

Another item of concern for any network is to make sure you have the workgroup named correctly. You can use about any name within reason, although organizations that have multiple types of Windows installed should use shorter names, under 14 characters. Sometimes organizations like to create workgroup names that correspond to the employees' responsibilities in the organization (for example, SALES or MARKETING), or the team to which employees belong (PROJECT for example).

When you set up your workgroup name, you may want to use a name different from the name of a computer on the network. A computer named MARKETING that is part of the MARKETING workgroup may create some confusion later, particularly when users are setting up file and printer shares.

Configure LAN Connections *(continued)*

The Name your network screen appears.

14. Type a name for the network workgroup you want your computer to join, such as MSHOME.

Note: *All computers on your network should have the same workgroup name specified.*

15. Click Next.

- The File and printer sharing screen appears. Here you can specify if you want to set up file and printer sharing on your network. Do this only if you want others to be able to access shared files and printers on your computer.

16. Click Next.

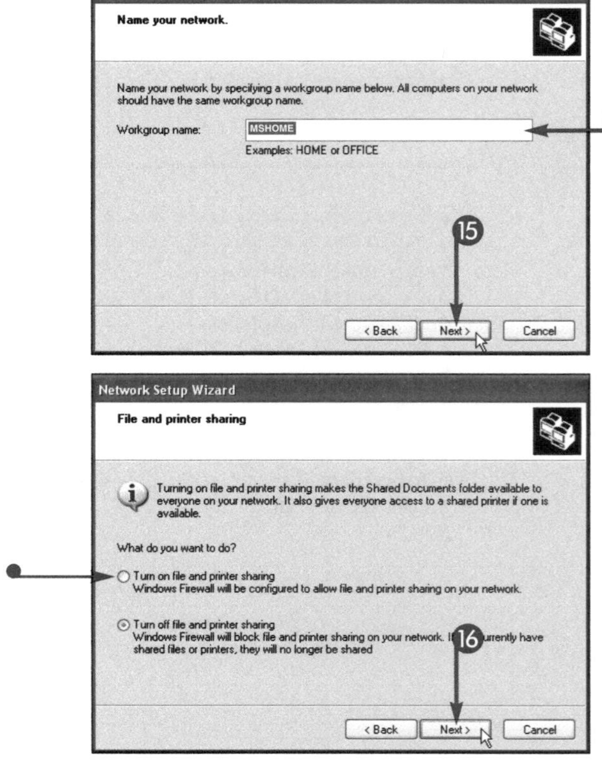

The Ready to apply network settings screen appears.

17 Click Next.

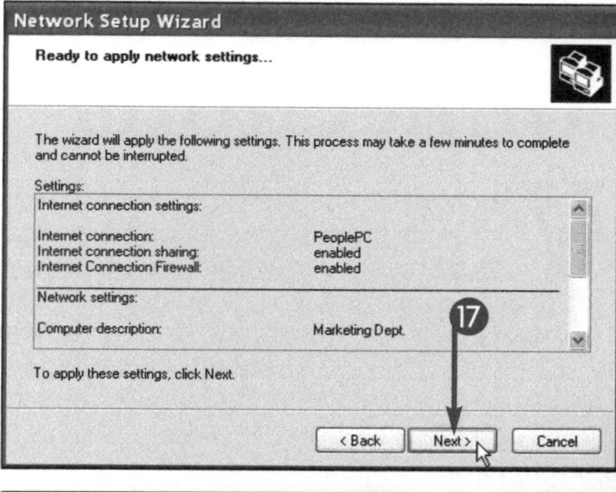

Windows configures your computer with the network settings you specify.

The You're almost done screen appears.

- Select the option to create a setup disk if you have non-Windows XP computers on your network.

18 Select the option to finish the wizard.

19 Click Next.

20 In the next screen, click Finish.

21 Click Yes to shut down and restart Windows.

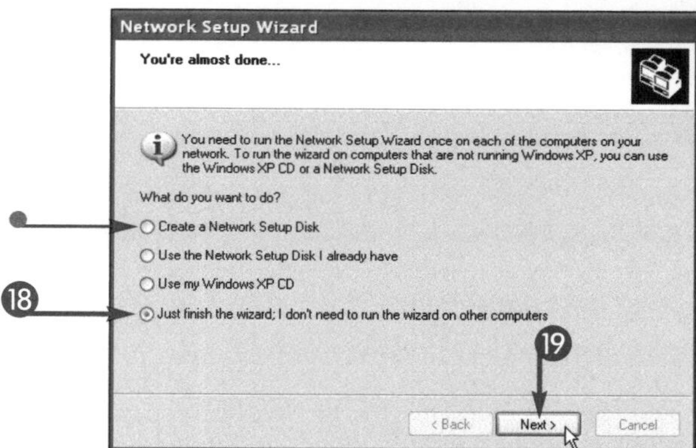

MASTER IT

Can I run Active Directory from my copy of Windows XP Professional?

▼ No. Windows XP Professional is not designed to be a domain controller (DC) on a Windows network. You must have Microsoft Windows 2000 Server or Microsoft Windows Server 2003 to run Active Directory. You can, however, use some tools to manage server resources from your Windows XP Professional computer. For example, you can use the Computer Management, Services, and Event Viewer tools from the Control Panel's Administrative Tools folder to view and manage server processes and disks.

When I look at the properties for my network connections, I have several different protocols, including TCP/IP, IPX, and NWLink NetBIOS. I thought all I needed was TCP/IP to get on the Internet. Do I need these others?

▼ Maybe. The protocol installed on your computer corresponds to protocols found on other computers on the network. If you connect strictly to a Windows 2000 Server that uses DNS (Domain Name System), TCP/IP is probably the only protocol you need. However, if you connect to a Windows 2000 Server and a Novell NetWare server, you may need other protocols, such as NwLink NetBIOS or IPX/SPX. If in doubt, do not remove a protocol until you contact your system administrator. Sometimes a protocol is in place for reasons that are not obvious to end-users. For example, a system administrator may use a protocol you are not familiar with so as to allow him to manage your computer from a remote location.

Configure Broadband Connections

Windows XP enables you to set up access to the Internet using a broadband connection. Broadband connections are those that are rated at high speeds, usually cable, DSL (digital subscriber line), or T1 connections. For most home or small businesses, cable or DSL are the most affordable broadband solutions. T1 connections are dedicated digital telephone lines that can cost as much as $1,000 per month, leaving them for medium to large companies, public libraries, schools, and the government.

Before you begin setting up a broadband connection, contact a local Internet service provider (ISP) and obtain a broadband account. Many times you also must have the ISP arrange for additional hardware to be provided to you, including a router (sometimes referred to as a cable modem), cable or telephone wiring, and sometimes connection software.

You need to set up any required hardware for your broadband connection before you can follow the steps in this task. Because hardware devices differ in their features and configurations, you must consult the hardware manuals for setup information. These steps assume you already have the hardware installed and connected to your computer.

Configure Broadband Connections

1. Open the Control Panel.
2. Click Network and Internet Connections.

   The Network and Internet Connections window appears.
3. Click Network Connections.

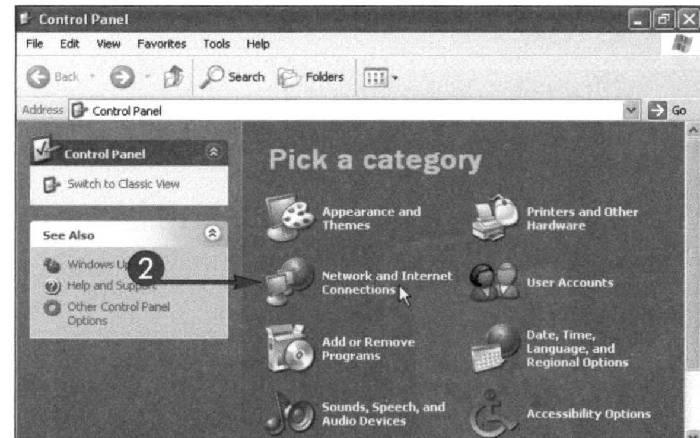

   The Network Connections window appears.
4. Click Create a new connection.

   The New Connection Wizard window appears.
5. Click Next.

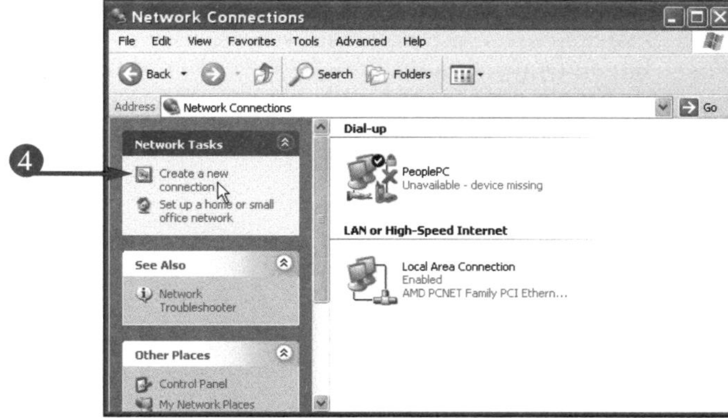

The Network Connection Type screen appears.

6. Select the network connection option that best fits your configuration.

   This example uses the option to connect to the Internet.

7. Click Next.

The Getting Ready screen appears.

8. Select the Internet connection that reflects your configuration.

   This example uses the option to set up the connection manually.

9. Click Next.

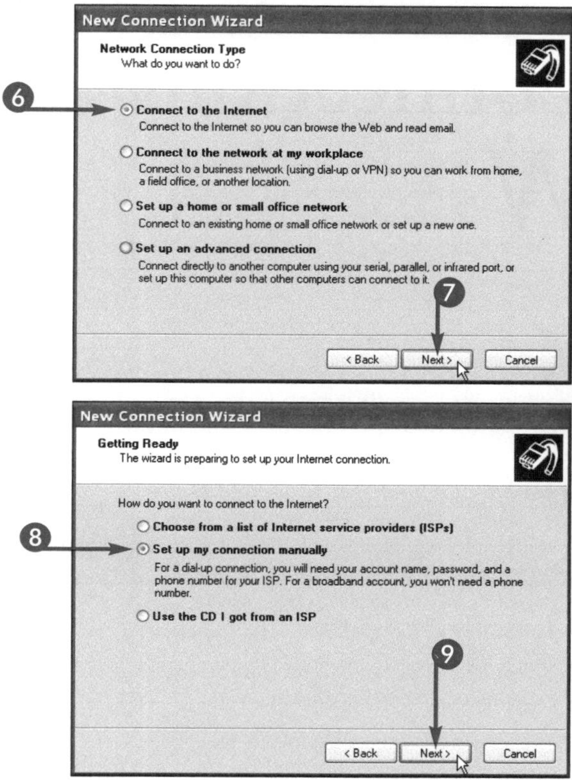

PART III

If my ISP gives me a setup CD, why do I have to use these instructions?

- You do not have to use the instructions shown here. In fact, use the instructions provided by your ISP. Those instructions are usually customized specifically for your ISP and, in some cases, specifically for your computer. In addition to the customized ISP instructions, there are instructions provided by the companies that manufacture the cable modems required to access many broadband connections. Again, refer to the instructions provided with the cable modem; they may be customized for that particular cable modem device. The instructions provided in this section should be used by those readers who do not have specific instructions from their ISP or their hardware manufacturer.

I cannot get Windows to connect to my broadband ISP. What should I do?

- The best thing to do is to contact your ISP. They can walk you through troubleshooting steps that may uncover problems you have with your connection or setup. Many times the problem is with the TCP/IP settings of your computer. To see those settings, open the Control Panel, click Network and Internet Connections, click Network Connections, and then right-click your Internet connection. Choose Properties, click Internet Protocol (TCP/IP), click Properties, and then examine the TCP/IP settings. Make sure these match what your ISP has given you.

continued

Configure Broadband Connections *(Continued)*

Windows XP enables you to access Internet resources over a fast broadband connection. The speeds with which you can access the Internet vary depending on the service in your area. Generally, however, speeds for cable modems (cable lines connected to routers) are determined by the underlying cabling hardware used by the Internet service provider (ISP).

The average speed for broadband is around 3Mbps (Megabits per second), which is thousands of times faster than a dial-up modem. Recently some service providers have announced broadband speeds of over 10Mbps, with one ISP offering 15Mbps.

Broadband speeds are listed as two speeds — a download speed and an upload speed. Usually the download speed is much faster than the upload. A number like 10Mbps/1Mbps means that the download speed is 10Mbps, while the upload speed is only 1Mbps (which is still extremely fast compared to dial-up speeds). Dial-up modem speeds are measured in kilobits per second (kilo is thousands, whereas mega is millions). A fast modem speed is 56Kbps, many thousands of times slower than most broadband connections.

Configure Broadband Connections *(continued)*

The Internet Connection screen appears.

⑩ Select the Internet connection option that best fits your configuration.

This example uses the option to connect using a broadband connection that requires a user name and password.

- If your broadband connection is one that is always on, select the option that reflects that

⑪ Click Next.

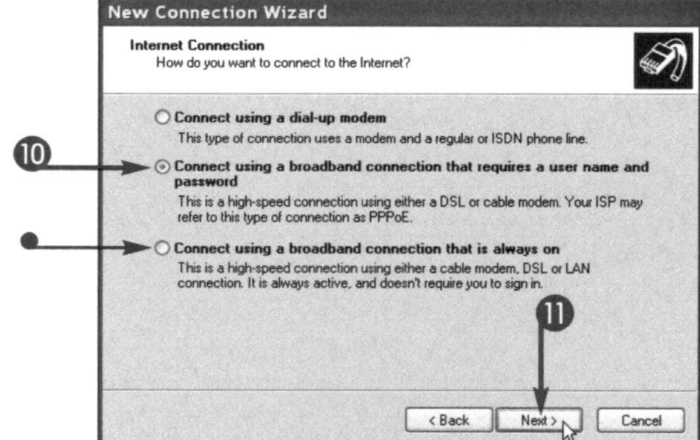

The Connection Name screen appears.

Note: *If you have multiple network and Internet connections, be sure to make the name descriptive enough to distinguish it from other connections.*

⑫ Type your ISP's name.

⑬ Click Next.

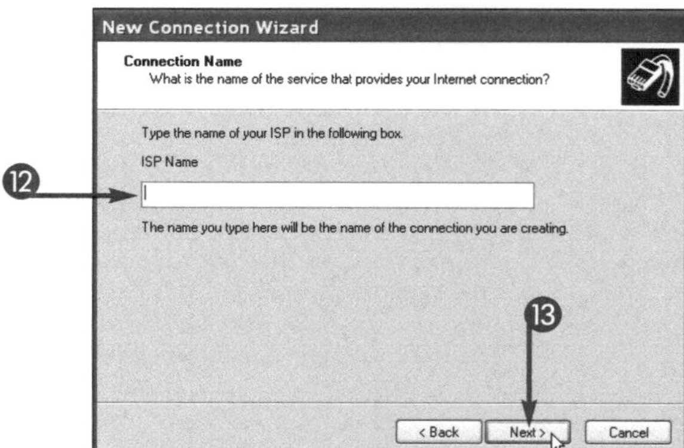

The Internet Account Information screen appears.

14 Type your ISP account name and password.

15 Click Next.

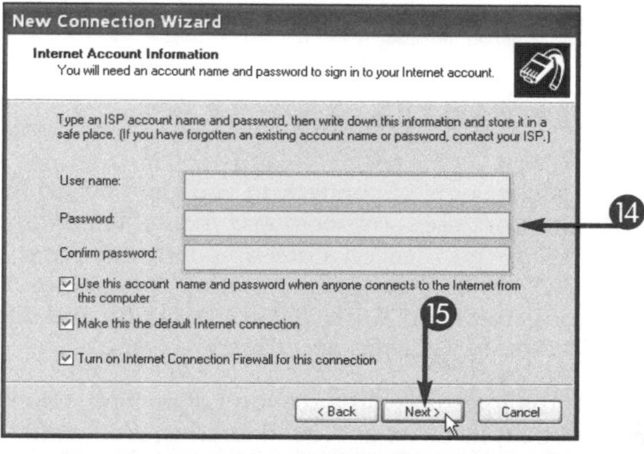

The Completing the New Connection Wizard screen appears.

- Select this option to add a shortcut for this connection to your desktop.

16 Click Finish.

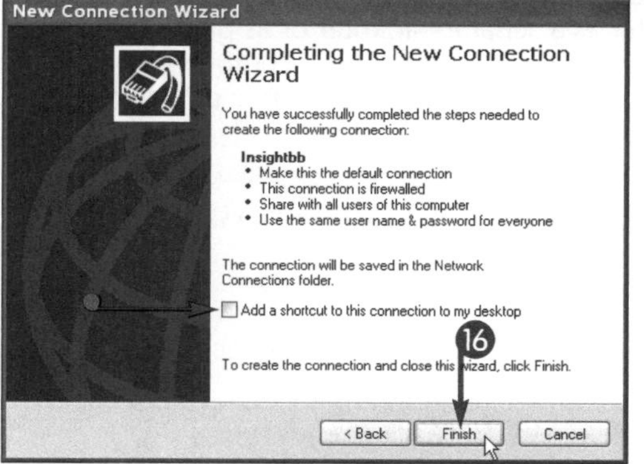

What if I do not have a broadband connection? Can I connect to the Internet using a modem?

▼ Yes. Windows XP enables you to configure and connect your modem to a dial-up Internet connection. Dial-up connections are substatinally slower than broadband connections. However, dial-up connections are more widely available, especially to those users in rural areas.

My broadband connection works, but is slow. How can I speed up my connection?

▼ First contact your broadband network provider and ask them to run a system test on your cable line. The amount of traffic that can flow over broadband cable — called bandwidth — is reduced when new customers come online in your area. If too many customers are using the same cable, the cable company may need to install amplifiers or other hardware to increase the speed of your connection.

If your cable provider tests your connection and all is well, find the extraneous programs running while Windows is running. These programs are called spyware, malware, or adware. Download Adaware Personal (www.lavasoftusa.com) and Spybot Search and Repair (www.safer-networking.org/en/download); run these programs weekly to find and delele malicious software that can slow down Internet connections.

Configure Dial-Up Connections

Another type of connection you can have to the Internet uses a modem and regular telephone wire. This is called a dial-up connection, and Windows XP makes it very easy to set up these types of connections. You need a user name, password, and dial-up number to set up a dial-up account.

To access the Internet with a dial-up connection, you must have a modem installed and configured to work with Windows XP. Usually modems are installed inside your computer as a separate adapter or as part of your computer's motherboard. If your computer does not have an internal modem, you can purchase one and install it inside your computer. Another option is to purchase an external modem that connects to your serial port (also called a COM port). These devices do not require you to open your computer case for installation.

When setting up a new dial-up account, consider the method of payment. For most national ISPs, such as AOL, MSN, NetZero, and PeoplePC, a credit card is required to sign up a new account. Each month the ISP bills your credit card. Some local ISPs, such as those in your town or a nearby town, can set up an account for you and then bill you each month via invoice. You can then pay for the account using a credit card, check, or another method.

Configure Dial-Up Connections

1. Open the Control Panel.
2. Click Network and Internet Connections.
3. In the Network and Internet Connections window, click Network Connections.

   The Network Connections window appears.
4. Click Create a new connection.

   The New Connection Wizard window appears.
5. Click Next.

The Network Connection Type screen appears.

6. Select the network connection option that best fits your configuration.

   This example uses the option to connect to the Internet.
7. Click Next.

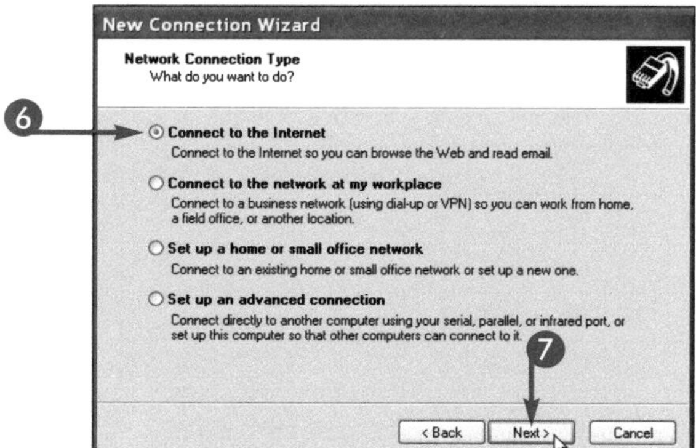

The Getting Ready screen appears.

8. Select the Internet connection that reflects your configuration.

   This example uses the option to set up a connection manually.

9. Click Next.

The Internet Connection screen appears.

10. Select the Internet connection option that best fits your configuration.

    This example uses the option to connect using a dial-up modem.

11. Click Next.

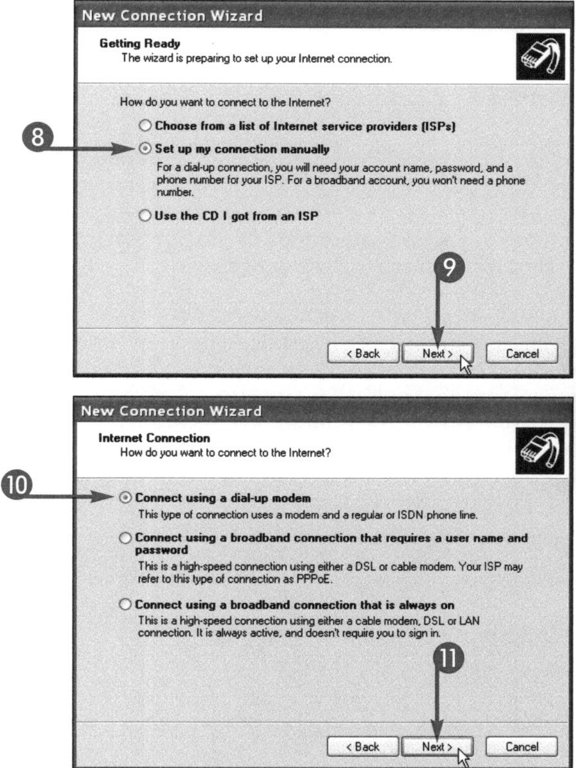

PART III

My ISP requires me to contact them over the Internet before setting up my account. How can I do this without first setting up Windows for an Internet connection?

▼ Make sure your modem works and then dial into the ISP setup modem. These are special modem accounts used by ISPs, such as PeoplePC, AOL, and MSN, that let you set up and configure new accounts. After your account is set up, you download setup software that you then run to complete your initial setup. After this happens, the ISP disconnects you from the first modem and then allows you to dial up and reconnect using your new account. In most cases, the first modem you dial is a toll-free number; subsequent connections use local phone numbers.

Can I set up an Internet connection using Windows XP even if I do not have an account yet?

▼ Yes. When you use the New Connection Wizard, you can connect to a site provided by Microsoft that enables you to pick an ISP that services your area. To use this feature, start the New Connection Wizard, click Next, select the Connect to the Internet option (○ changes to ◉), click Next, and then select the Choose from a list of Internet service providers (ISPs) option (○ changes to ◉). Click Next and follow the on-screen instructions. You need to have your modem set up and working before you can access these online services.

continued

Configure Dial-Up Connections

(Continued)

Windows XP enables you to configure modems to use standard phone lines for communications. Dial-up modem connection speeds are measured in kilobits (thousands of bits) per second. Standard modem speeds are 56Kbps.

The actual speed with which you connect to the Internet (or other online service) varies depending on several factors. One factor that greatly affects your modem speed connection is line noise. This is the amount of *white noise* that is found in your telephone line — those crackles and other noises you can hear on your phone line. Line noise can reduce modem communication speed by interfering with the data transmission. Lots of line noise can even cause your connection to your ISP to be lost, requiring you to re-dial your ISP.

Another factor that affects modem speed is how some software settings are configured on the modem. Some modems include compression technology that enables data to be compressed into smaller chunks to decrease transmission time. When the data is received by a modem on the receiving side (or other network device like a network interface card), the data is uncompressed back to its original size. Some modem software lets you enable or disable software compression.

Configure Dial-Up Connections *(continued)*

The Connection Name screen appears.

12 Type the name of your ISP here.

13 Click Next.

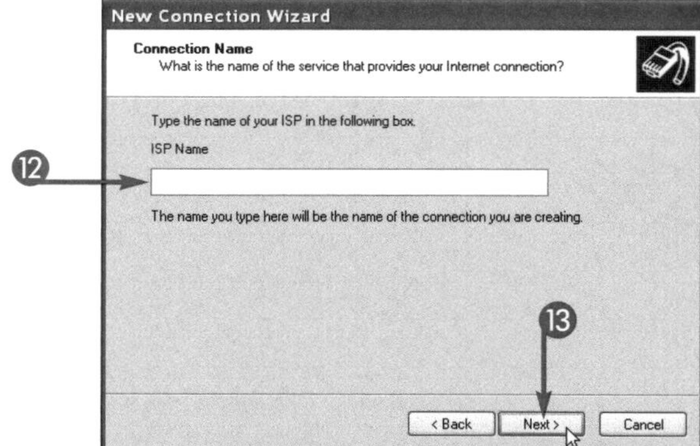

The Phone Number to Dial screen appears.

14 Type the ISP phone number.

Note: *The phone number you type is one that is provided by the ISP that allows you to connect to the Internet. Usually this is a local number, but in some cases it is long distance, requiring you to enter 1 plus the area code before the ISP number.*

15 Click Next.

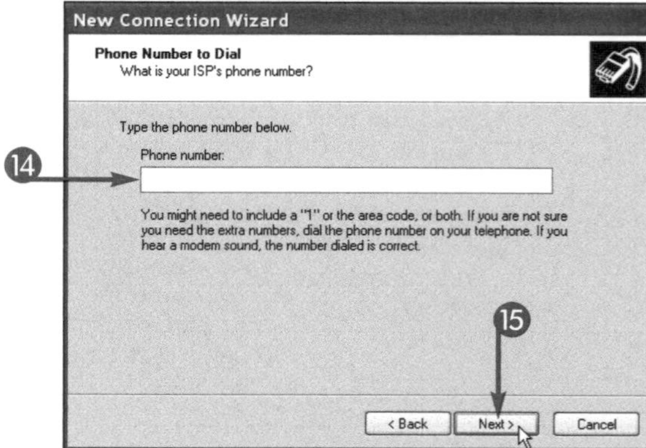

The Internet Account Information screen appears.

16 Type your ISP account name and password (enter the password again to confirm it).

17 Click Next.

The Completing the New Connection Wizard screen appears.

- Select this option to add a shortcut for this connection to your desktop.

18 Click Finish.

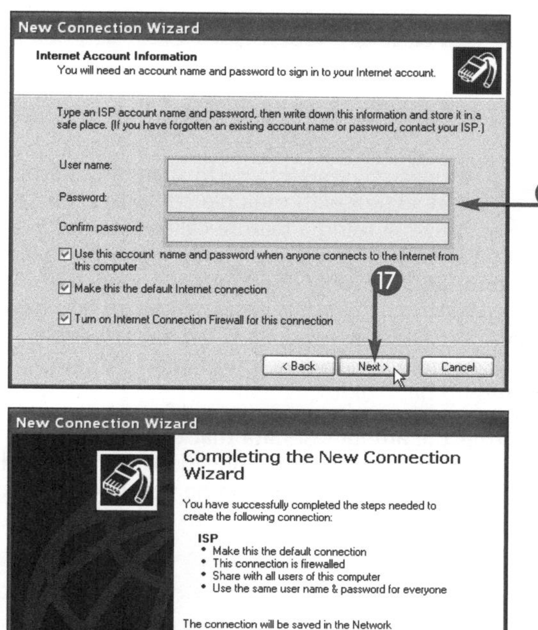

I connected a regular telephone to my modem line and I hear a lot of noise. What can I do to eliminate the noise?

▼ First you must contact your local telephone provider. Ask them to run a line test, which usually requires a field technician to visit your home or office and run tests on the line. Some line tests can be conducted from the main office, but may not pick up all noise on your individual line. Usually line noise is a result of older copper lines being used instead of newer fiber optic or state-of-the-art copper lines. If your area is experiencing population growth, line noise also can be the result of additional customers being placed on your line. When line noise is recognized, the telephone service technician needs to fix the problem or new telephone wire needs to be installed in your area.

Can I have more than one modem installed on my computer?

▼ Yes, but each needs to have its own COM port. If you have one modem set up as COM1, your second modem should use COM3, leaving COM2 and COM4 unused. You may want to have multiple modems if you use a wireless device (such as a cellphone) and a regular land-line modem from the same computer. You cannot have both modems in use at the same time, but you may want the option of a wireless modem when you do not have access to a telephone jack.

Configure Internet Connection Sharing

Windows XP enables you to share an Internet connection with multiple computers on your network using a feature called Internet Connection Sharing (ICS). ICS is handy when you have several computers but only one Internet connection. Internet connection sharing is best used when you have a broadband or faster connection. This allows multiple computers to be downloading information without compromising bandwidth.

Bandwidth is the amount of data that can be uploaded and downloaded from an Internet connection. The higher the bandwidth, the more data that can be "pushed" through a connection at one time. As you share an Internet connection with more computers on your network, the bandwidth for each computer decreases, thereby slowing down each connection.

To set up Internet Connection Sharing, your computer must be part of a local area network. When ICS is set up, the computer on which ICS is configured is given a static IP address (Internet Protocol address) of 192.168.0.1. Other computers in the network are then given addresses in the same range, such as 192.168.0.2, 192.168.0.3, and so on.

Configure Internet Connection Sharing

1. Set up two network connections, one to your local area network and one to the Internet, as discussed in the preceding sections.
2. Open the Network Connections window from the Control Panel.
3. Click the network connection you want to share.

   The Network Tasks pane changes to show options available for the selected connection.
4. Click Change settings of this connection.

   The properties dialog box for the connection appears.
5. Click the Advanced tab.

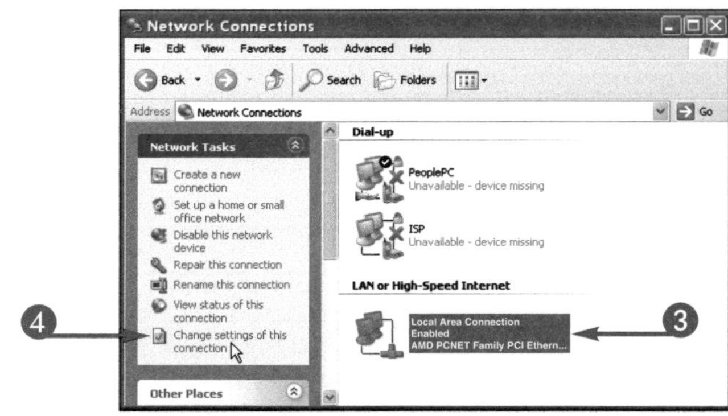

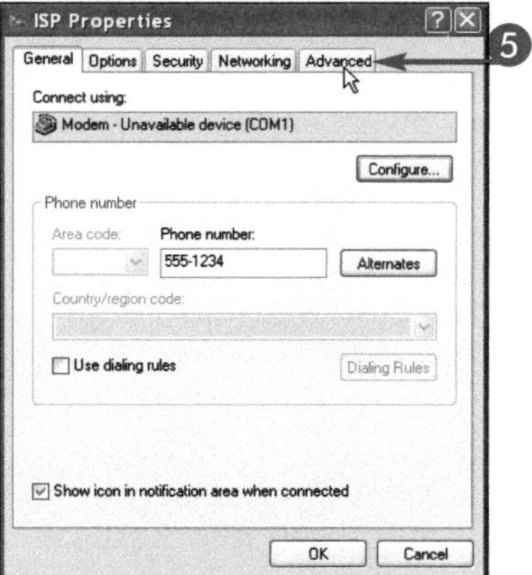

6 Select the option to allow other network users to connect through your computer's Internet connection.

- Select this option to allow your connection to dial automatically when another computer on the network attempts to access external resources.
- Select this option to allow other network users to enable or disable the shared Internet connection.

7 Click Settings.

In the Advanced Settings dialog box, you can set other options that users can modify, such as DHCP, FTP server, and other settings.

8 Click OK to close the Advanced Settings dialog box.

9 Click OK in the properties dialog box to save your settings.

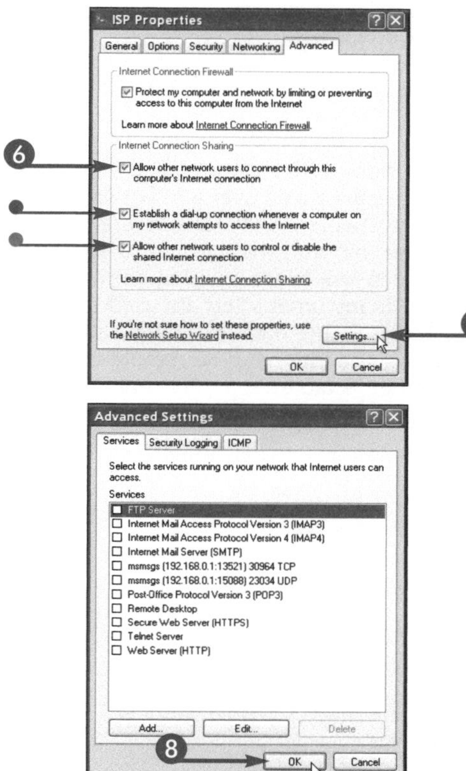

My ISP said I can have only one computer connected to my Internet account at the same time. Can I work around this with Internet Connection Sharing?

▼ You can try, but using your Internet account in this manner may not be a good idea. If your ISP requires separate accounts for individual computers, contact them and inquire about a package deal they may offer for bulk connections. Some ISPs give you discounts if you have a number of computers you want to get onto the Internet.

I have two networks set up in my company. Is there a way to share an Internet connection with both networks?

▼ Yes. You can use Internet Connection Sharing to set up a network bridge, which enables you to connect two or more networks together to share one Internet connection. This type of sharing is especially helpful if you have a wired and wireless network set up in your house, company, or workgroup.

My network administrator says that my IP address has changed since adding ICS to my computer. Why is this important for her to know?

▼ This is important if your computer needs to be configured with a different IP address or needs to have a dynamic address. If so, let your network administrator know that to set up ICS, your computer must have the 192.168.0.1 address. She should then be able to set up the local domain server so your computer is recognized using the 192.168.0.1 address.

Manage IPSec

Windows XP includes IPSec as a way to help secure traffic over a VPN (Virtual Private Network). A VPN is a secure network configuration that uses the Internet to allow you to connect to another network or server using a private, secure connection. Many times VPNs are used to allow remote users to access secure data on a corporate network by traveling over the Internet. The remote computer connects to the Internet, establishes a VPN connection to the corporate computer, and then navigates on the corporate network as if the user were using a computer inside the corporation.

IPSec provides a secure "language" for VPN connections to occur. With Windows XP, you can perform some management tasks as a user. To manage IPSec, you can use the Microsoft Management Console (MMC). You can then install MMC snap-ins to control the IPSec features.

Manage IPSec

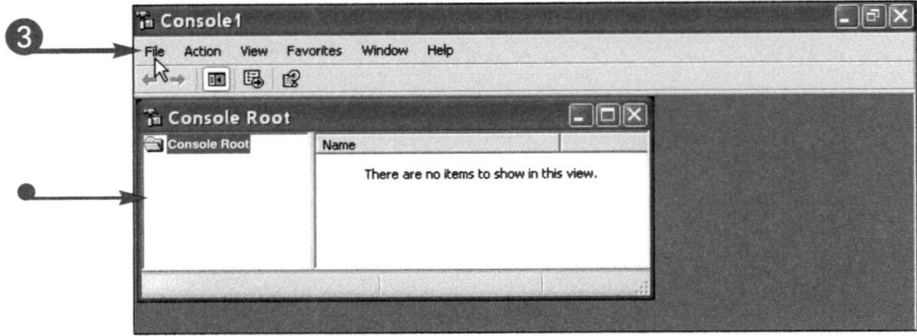

1. From the Start menu, click Run.

   The Run dialog box appears.

2. Type MMC and then click OK.

   - A blank MMC Console window appears.

3. Click File and then Add/Remove Snap-in.

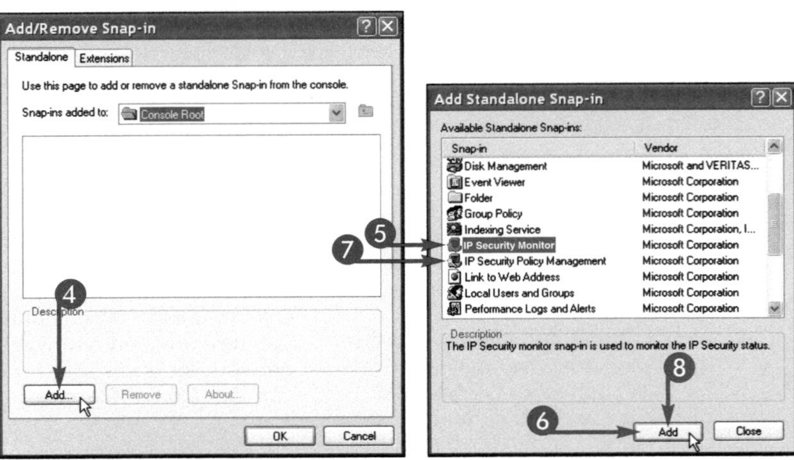

   The Add/Remove Snap-in dialog box appears.

4. Click Add.

   The Add Standalone Snap-in dialog box appears. You can load these snap-ins into the blank MMC Console window.

5. Click IP Security Monitor.
6. Click Add.

   The IP Security Monitor item is added to the Add/Remove Snap-in dialog box. The Add Standalone Snap-in dialog box remains open.

7. Click IP Security Policy Management.
8. Click Add.

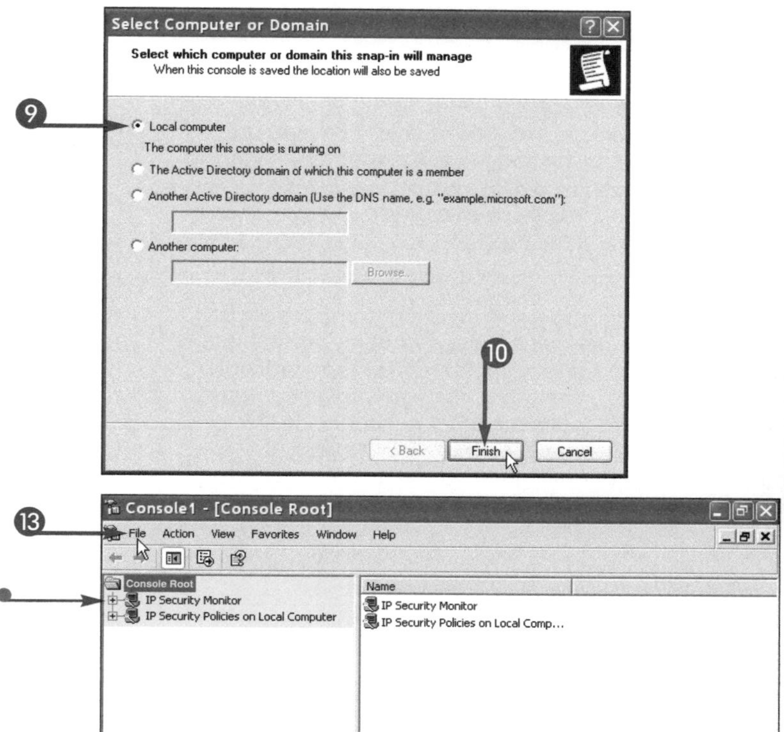

9. In the Select Computer or Domain screen, select the local computer option.
10. Click Finish.

    The IP Security Policy Management item is added to the Add/Remove Snap-in dialog box.
11. Click ☒ or Close to close the Add Standalone Snap-in dialog box.

    The Add/Remove Snap-in dialog box shows the newly added IPSec items in the snap-ins list.
12. Click OK.
    - The MMC Console window appears, with the IPSec items showing.
13. Click File and then Save. Name the console and then click Save.

    Windows saves the MMC console so you can return to it later without reinstalling the IPSec snap-ins.

Note: *Some of the management tasks you can do include set up a new IP Security Policy, manage client IPSec policies, and view server IPSec security settings.*

Do I need to use IPSec to access basic Internet resources?

▼ No. IPSec is a feature that can be used as an additional layer of security for VPN connection. If you do not have a VPN connection, you do not have to worry about IPSec.

My college allows VPN connections for laptop users. How can I set up my laptop to access their VPN?

▼ Because each VPN configuration can be different, there is not one way to set up a laptop for a VPN. However, here are general steps to connect to a VPN: Open the New Connection Wizard from the Network Connections window. Click Next, click the option to connect to the network at your workplace (○ changes to ◉), click Next, and then click Virtual Private Network connection (○ changes to ◉). Click Next and enter the company name. Click Next and select a dialing option (○ changes to ◉). Click Next, enter the host name for the VPN (get this from your college), click Next, and, if you have multiple users configured for your computer, select which users can connect to this server. Click Next and then Finish.

Configure Wireless Networking

Windows XP enables you to set up your computer on a wireless network. Wireless networks use infrared technology to link computers, handheld devices (such as personal digital assistants, or PDAs), wireless printing devices, and mobile phones. With wireless networks, you do not need the standard cables to connect your devices together.

Wireless networking makes it convenient for those users who travel a great deal with laptops or other devices. Many hotels and airports, some restaurants (you have probably heard of cybercafés), and a few cities are providing access to wireless networks to enable users to connect to the Internet when away from the office. This is handy if you need to check your e-mail, browse a Web site, or connect to your office via a VPN.

To use the wireless networking features of Windows XP, your computer must be equipped with a wireless network interface adapter (NIC). This can be either an internal one that is housed inside your computer, or an external NIC that is connected to your computer from the outside. Usually these use one of the USB (Universal Serial Bus) ports. The wireless network also must have a wireless hub or router that connects your computer to the network or Internet.

The following steps assume you have a wireless networking card installed and working. Also, it assumes you have a network connection to a hot spot.

Configure Wireless Networking

1. Display the Control Panel.
2. Click Network and Internet Connections.

   The Network and Internet Connections window appears.
3. Click Wireless Network Setup Wizard.

   The Network Tasks pane appears.
4. Click View Available Wireless Networks.

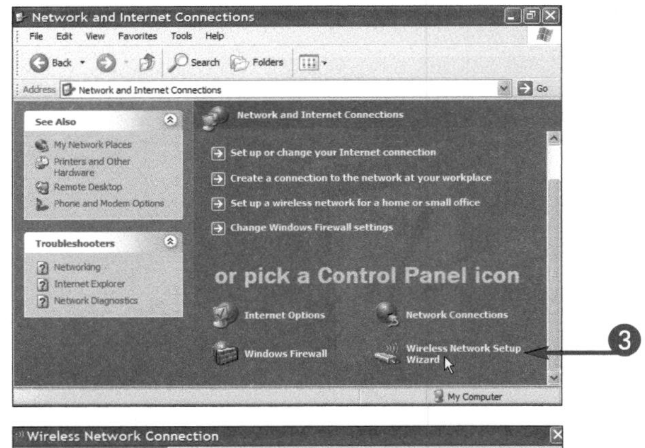

   The Choose a wireless network window appears. This window lists all wireless networks currently available to you.
5. Select the network to which you want to connect.
6. Click Connect.

   If the network is unsecured, a message appears warning you of possible security breaches.
7. Click Connect Anyway.

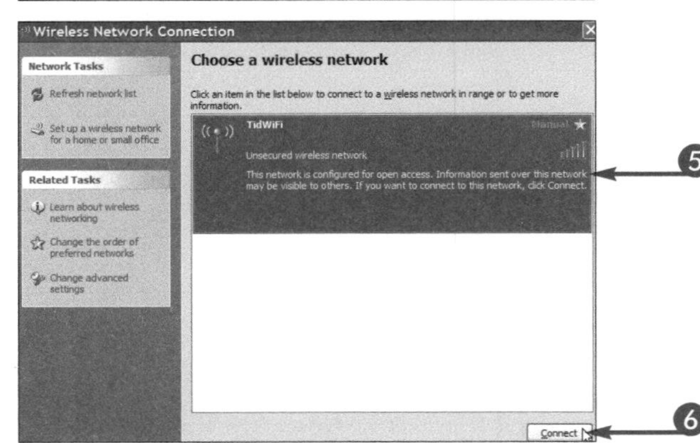

The Wireless Network Connection Window shows progress of connecting to the network.

- When connected, the Connected label appears in the window.

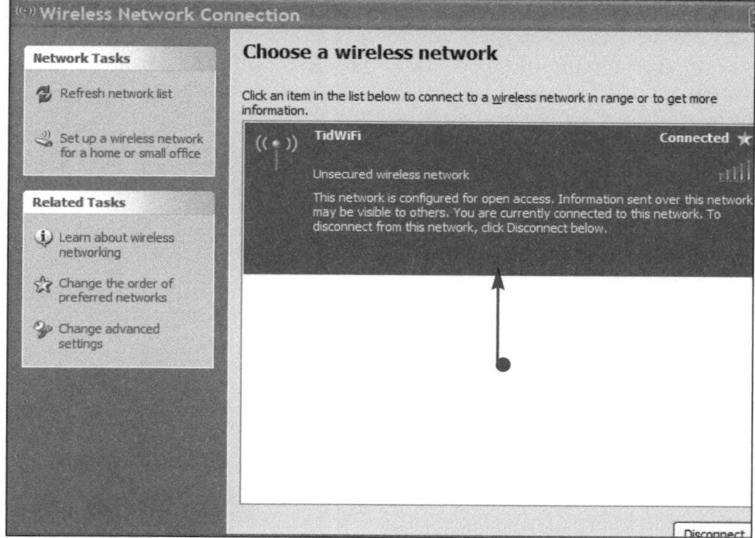

I have heard of several different wireless terms, such as WiFi and hot spots. What are these?

▼ WiFi is short for the term wireless fidelity. This term is used when referring to wireless networking specifications known as the 802.11 networks, including 802.11a, 802.11b, and 802.11g. To connect to a WiFi network, a computer must be able to locate WiFi hot spots. These are wireless access points that are offered by companies, organizations, and local governments that allow consumers or workers to connect to the wireless network.

How can I find hot spots?

▼ One place to begin looking for them is from the Hotspots Directory on the Web at www.jiwire.com/search-hotspot-locations.htm. Also, if a restaurant, hotel, or airport has wireless networking available, it usually posts information about these hot spots on doors, signs, menus, and brochures. Finally, you can call and ask a place of business if it offers wireless hot spots. If it does, you can ask the rate per hour for connecting to the hot spot.

Also, if you have Windows set up to receive wireless communications, when you enter a hot spot zone, Windows can display a message that you are in a hot spot area. This is handy if you are in an airport, restaurant, or café and need to find a seat that is in a hot spot.

Modify Internet Explorer's Behavior

Internet Explorer (IE) includes several options that enable you to modify its behavior. One common change is to set up the Pop-up Blocker to prevent pop-up ads from opening while you navigate the Web. Pop-up ads are those annoying windows that automatically appear on your screen when you visit many Web sites. Most pop-ups are advertisements for the Web site you are visiting or for related sites. When you click on these pop-ups, Internet Explorer links to a Web site associated with the pop-up.

Windows XP includes many different features you can change in IE. The task that follows shows just a few of them. A number of resources and online help show you additional changes that can be made. One place to start searching for these changes is with the Windows Help and Support Center. To open this feature, click Start to open the Start menu and then click Help and Support. You can enter a keyword to search for IE customizations and then click the Start searching button (→) next to the Search text box to begin your search.

Modify Internet Explorer's Behavior

1. Start Internet Explorer.

   The Internet Explorer window appears.

2. Click Tools.
3. Click Internet Options.

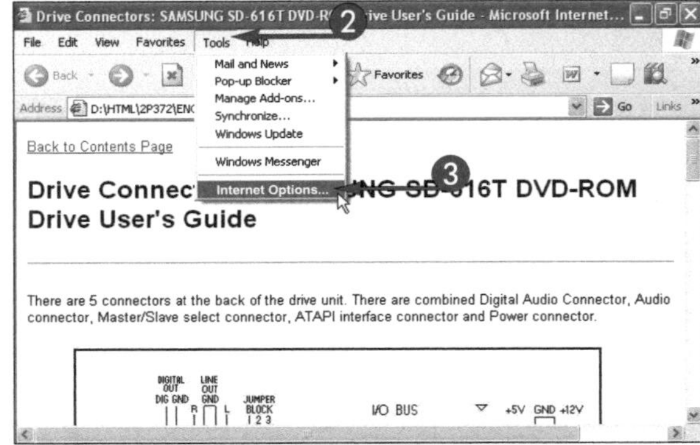

The Internet Options window appears. Here you can choose to modify a number of IE settings.

- Click the General tab to set home page, cache, and History options.

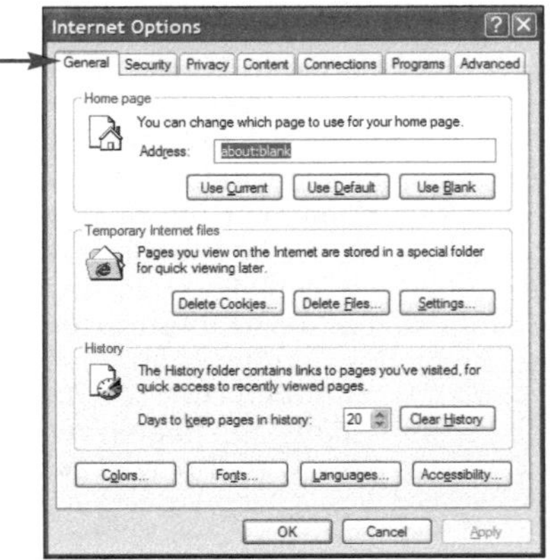

- Click the Security tab to set security settings for Internet and local intranet connections.

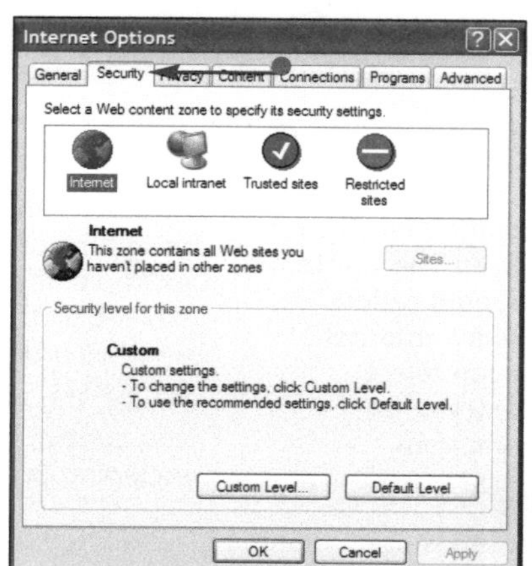

- Click the Privacy tab to set options for controlling how strict IE should be when downloading and running scripts and cookies.
- Click here to set the Pop-up Blocker.

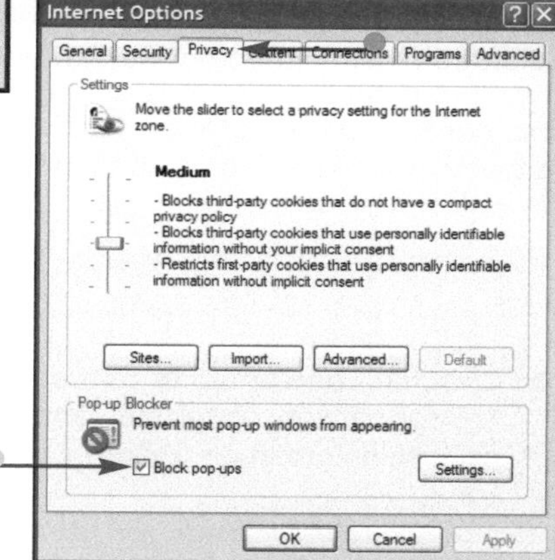

When I have the Pop-up Blocker turned on, some Web sites do not display or do not display their entire content. How can I work around this?

The Pop-up Blocker is designed to stop sites that display pop-up windows when you connect to the site. Usually these *pop-ups* contain advertisements, unwelcome information, or graphics that some users do not want to view. Unfortunately, the Pop-up Blocker cannot distinguish between these unwelcomed pop-ups and windows that some sites display to show legitimate information. To view this content, click the Pop-up Blocker toolbar and select Temporarily Allow Pop-ups. If you want IE to remember this site in the future, select the option to always allow pop-ups from this site (☐ changes to ☑) and then click Yes. After you select one of these options, the page is redisplayed and the pop-up window(s) is displayed as well.

Is there a way to control the add-ons that are installed to work with IE?

Yes. With Windows XP SP2, IE now includes a long-awaited Add-Ons Manager. This utility shows a list of all the add-ons installed on your computer that work with IE. The manager enables you to enable or disable each add-on. For ActiveX controls, such as Macromedia Flash, you can click Update to allow IE to check for and download any available updates to the control. To access the Add-On Manager, start IE, click Tools, and then Manage Add-Ons. The Manage Add-Ons window appears.

continued

Modify Internet Explorer's Behavior *(Continued)*

Internet Explorer 6 enables you to change several features and tools built into the browser. The Content tab, for example, is used for several identification purposes. One is to allow you to control which Internet content is allowed on your computer. You can select categories (language, nudity, sex, and violence) that disallow Web pages fitting these descriptions from displaying on your screen.

The AutoComplete option on the Content tab is used when you want Internet Explorer to retain personal information (name, e-mail address, mailing address, and so on) you have typed in online forms to be used to fill out future forms with similar data.

Another behavioral change is to modify the types of helper programs used to open and edit unsupported content. For example, if you encounter a DOC file on the Web, you can have IE open the DOC file in Microsoft Word, WordPad, or another program that supports DOC files.

Finally, the Advanced tab includes many options that let you control how Internet Explorer displays content, including JavaScript applications and multimedia files.

Modify Internet Explorer's Behavior *(continued)*

- Click the Content tab to set Content Advisor, security certificates, and personal information options.

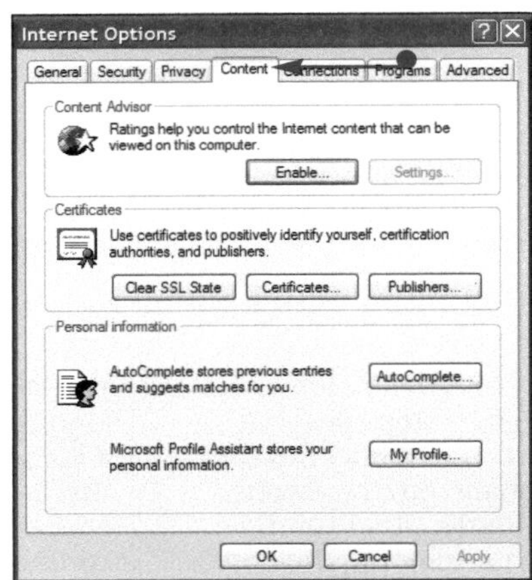

- Click the Connections tab to set network and Internet connections.

- Click the Programs tab to set which programs and add-ons IE uses for extended Web page content.

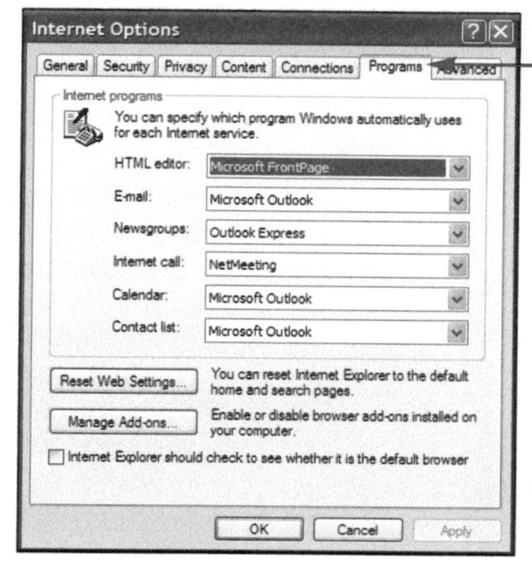

- Click the Advanced tab to set advanced IE options here. Some of the options include turning on or off Java support, setting printing options, and enabling multimedia support.

4 Click OK to save your settings.

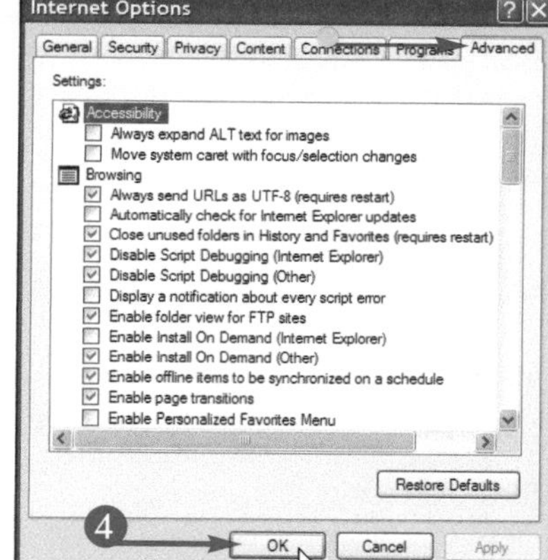

I set the Ratings tab to filter all sites that have sex on them. However, some sites still get through. Why does Internet Explorer allow these sites to display?

▼ The Ratings tab relies on the ICRA rating service (originally RSACi) to block inappropriate material. The ICRA (Internet Content Rating Association) is a standard on the Internet to which some, but not all, Web sites adhere. If a site does not code using the RSACi standard, and there are many that do not, Internet Explorer's Ratings categories do not apply. See www.icra.org/about for more information about this rating service.

How can I set up a profile that Internet Explorer uses?

▼ To do this, use the Windows Address Book. Choose Tools, Internet Options, Content, and then My Profile. Click OK. In the properties dialog box, fill out Name, Home, Business, Personal, Other, NetMeeting (if applicable), and Digital Ids (if applicable). Click OK to close the properties dialog box. The Content tab reappears. To see your profile information, click My Profile. The properties dialog box appears with your information displayed. Click OK to close this dialog box. If you want to view the profile in the Address Book, open the Windows Start menu, click All Programs, Accessories, and then Address Book. The Address Book opens with your new contact listing in the right-hand pane.

Read Newsgroups with Outlook Express

Windows XP includes Microsoft Outlook Express, which is an e-mail and newsgroup tool. One of the most widely used areas of the Internet is a feature called Usenet newsgroups. Usenet newsgroups are electronic bulletin boards that allow users to post messages for others to read and respond to. You can use Outlook Express to participate in newsgroup activities.

The Internet offers thousands of newsgroups. Newsgroups are categorized into areas of interest or subjects. Newsgroups are available for users who want to discuss different tastes in music, sports, hobbies, computer topics, and similar discussions.

To participate in newsgroups, users must have access to them from their Internet service provider (ISP). Some larger ISPs have discontinued offering support for newsgroups, but many still enable users to access them. When you set up Outlook Express for newsgroups, you instruct it to connect to a news server (information provided by your ISP), download a list of the newsgroups available, and then subscribe to the newsgroup. After you subscribe to a newsgroup (you can subscribe to as many as you like), you can download message headers that are similar to e-mail message headers. You then can download and read entire messages by downloading the body of the message.

Read Newsgroups with Outlook Express

1. Start Microsoft Outlook Express.

   The main Outlook Express window appears.

2. Click Tools and then Account.

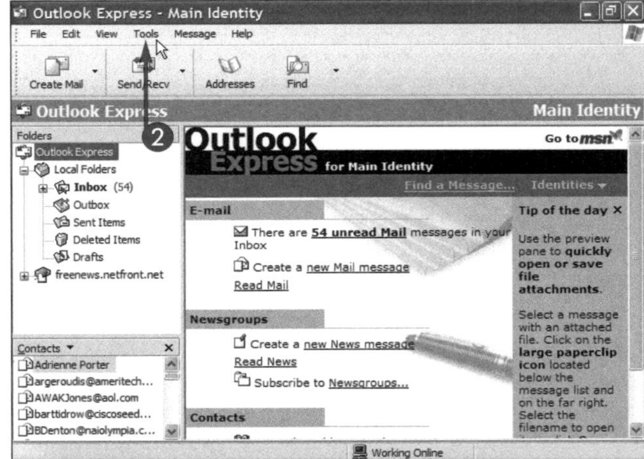

The Internet Accounts window appears.

3. Click Add.
4. In the small menu that appears, click News.

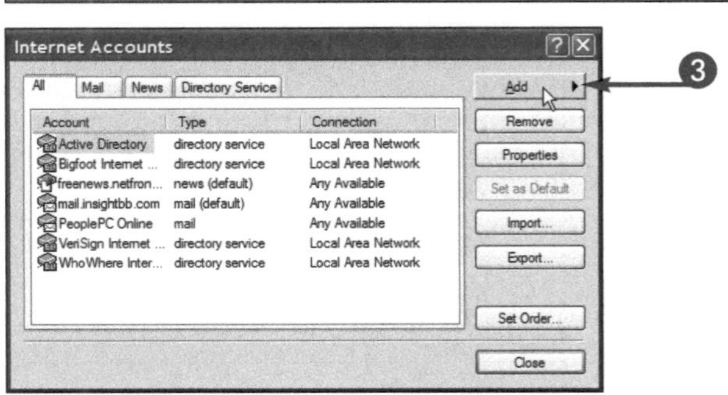

The Your Name screen of the Internet Connection Wizard window appears. This starts a new wizard that walks you through setting up a news server account.

5 Type your name or a name that you want to use for others to know who is posting a message.

Note: *You do not have to use your real name here. In fact, many users do not, especially children.*

6 Click Next.

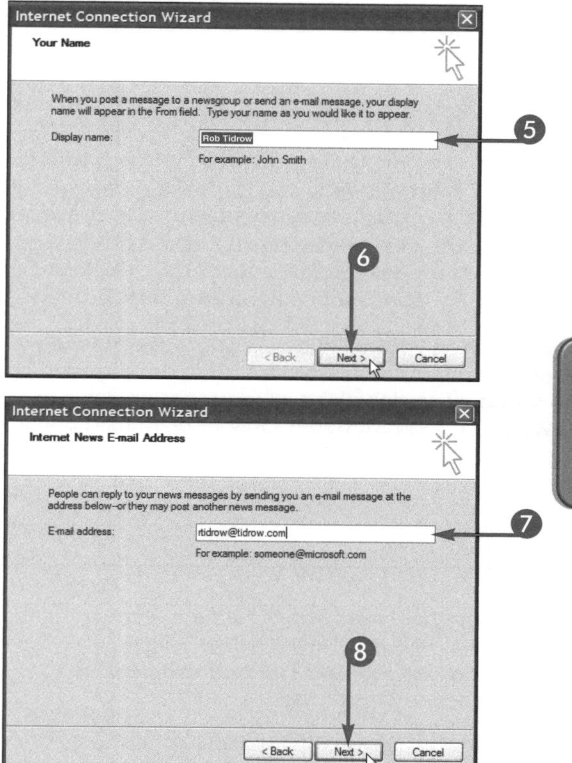

The Internet News E-mail Address screen appears.

7 Type your e-mail address.

The e-mail address is used so other participants who read messages posted by you can send you e-mail messages directly.

8 Click Next.

My ISP does not offer newsgroups. How can I get them?

▼ Some ISPs do not have access to newsgroups through their own services. If this is the case for your ISP, you can find news servers on the Internet by searching for them on the Web at Yahoo.com or Google.com. When you locate a server, you can use that information to set up Outlook Express to access those servers and download messages. Some of these news servers are free, while others have a fee to access them.

Sometimes messages have paperclips beside them to indicate they have attachments. However, I cannot read or see the files after I download them. Can you help?

▼ Sometimes messages include binary files — such as picture files — that Outlook Express can display as part of the message body. If Outlook Express cannot display the binary file as part of the body, you can save the file to your computer and then display the file in another program. For example, some messages include sound files that Outlook Express cannot play back. To use these files on your computer, download the message and save the attachment to your computer, such as to the My Music folder. Open the My Music folder and double-click the file to play it back in Windows Media Player or a similar application.

continued

Read Newsgroups with Outlook Express *(Continued)*

Microsoft Outlook Express, which is available as part of Windows XP, is used to let you participate in online newsgroup communities. When you use Outlook Express for accessing newsgroups, you can use the synchronize tool to have Outlook Express automatically download content from selected newsgroups.

This feature is controlled by clicking Settings when viewing your subscribed-to newsgroups. Click Settings and choose All Messages to download all messages available in the newsgroup, New Messages Only to download only those messages that are new since you last visited the newsgroup, or Headers Only. The latter option downloads just the message header information and not the message itself. If, after reading the header, you want to download the entire message, you can do so by double-clicking the header information.

After you read a message, you can post a reply to the message by clicking Reply. This opens a reply window with the original message displayed. You can type your response at the top of the window and then click Send. Others reading the newsgroup can now read and respond to your message.

Read Newsgroups with Outlook Express *(continued)*

The Internet News Server Name screen appears. This is the news server name provided by your ISP. The example used here is freenews.netfront.net.

9 Click here if you need a user name and password to log on to your news server.

Note: *These items are provided by your ISP.*

10 Click Next.

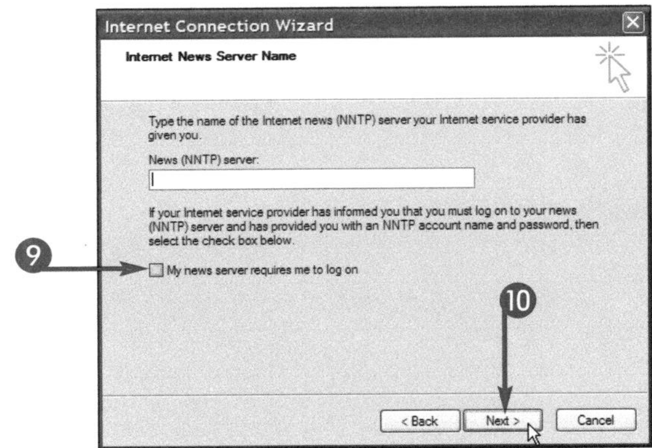

The Internet News Server Logon screen appears.

11 Type your name.

12 Type your password.

13 Click Next.

The Congratulations screen appears.

14 Click Finish.

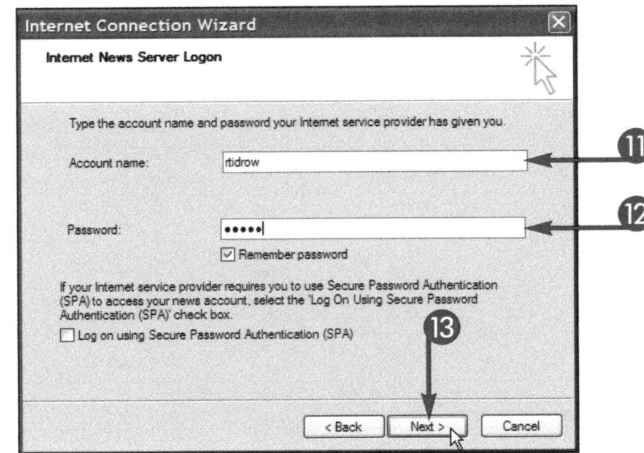

- Outlook Express adds the news server account to the All and News tabs of the Internet Accounts window.

15 Click Close.

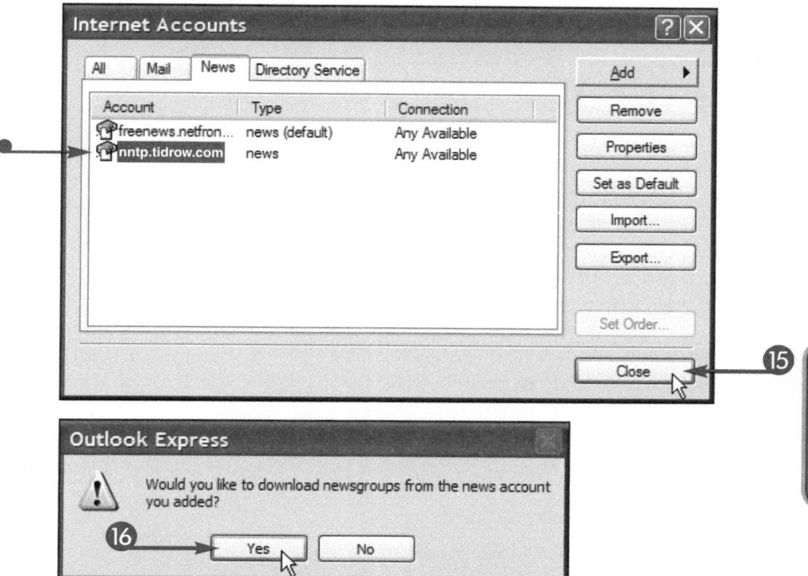

The Outlook Express dialog box appears asking if you want to download newsgroups from the news server.

16 Click Yes.

Outlook Express connects to the news server and downloads, a list of newsgroups available from the news server.

Caution: This list can be very large (over 30,000 entries, for example) and can take a long time on a slow dial-up connection.

When the list downloads, you can subscribe to a newsgroup and read messages from it.

I do not use Outlook Express for e-mail or newsgroups. Can I remove it from my computer?

According to Microsoft, Outlook Express is an integral part of Windows XP and so it cannot be removed without altering the Windows subsystem. You can, however, remove access to Outlook Express from the Windows Start menu. To do this, display the Control Panel and double-click the Add or Remove Programs icon. Click Add/Remove Windows Components. In the Components list, click the Outlook Express option to clear the check box next to it. The Windows Component Wizard appears. Click Next. Windows removes access to the Outlook Express icon from the Start menu. Click Finish to close the Windows Components Wizard.

Are there any newsgroups that allow me to participate without using Outlook Express?

Yes, you can use Internet Explorer to access some newsgroups. In fact, Microsoft has available hundreds of newsgroups that are easily accessible using Internet Explorer. To find these groups, start Internet Explorer and visit www.microsoft.com/communities/newsgroups/default.mspx. Here you can choose from several categories — such as ApplicationCenter, Office, and Windows Storage Center — and find specific newsgroups relating to these categories. As an example, click the Windows XP link to see newsgroups called Windows XP General, Windows XP Tablet PC Edition, and so on. Click these categories to read newsgroup messages relating to them.

Share and Manage Printers

Windows XP enables you to share printers across a network. If you do not have a printer directly connected to your computer, you can use a printer that is connected to another computer on your network. You can do this provided the printer is shared on the computer to which it is attached.

The installation process for setting up a shared printer is much the same as setting up a local printer. The main difference is you have to know the name of the printer to which you are connecting, or at least know the type of printer you want to set up. You can then usually find the printer in the network directory.

In this task, however, you are shown how to use Windows XP to set up a printer to be shared and then how to manage it. To set up a shared printer, you need to install the printer as you would a local printer. Then, during the installation process, you can decide to set it up as shared.

Share and Manage Printers

1. Click Start and then Control Panel. Double-click Printers and Faxes.

***Note:** You can also click the Printers and Faxes icon on your Start menu.*

The Printers and Faxes window appears.

2. On the Printer Tasks pane, click Add a printer.

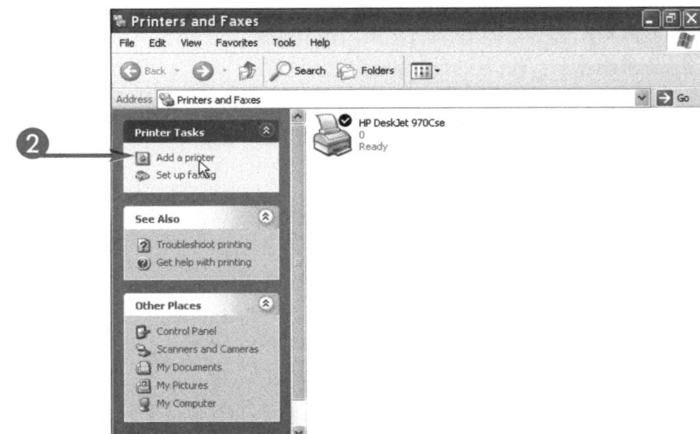

The Add Printer Wizard appears.

3. Click Next.

The Local or Network Printer screen appears.

4 Select the local printer option.

5 Click Next.

- Click this option to have Windows locate any plug and play devices.

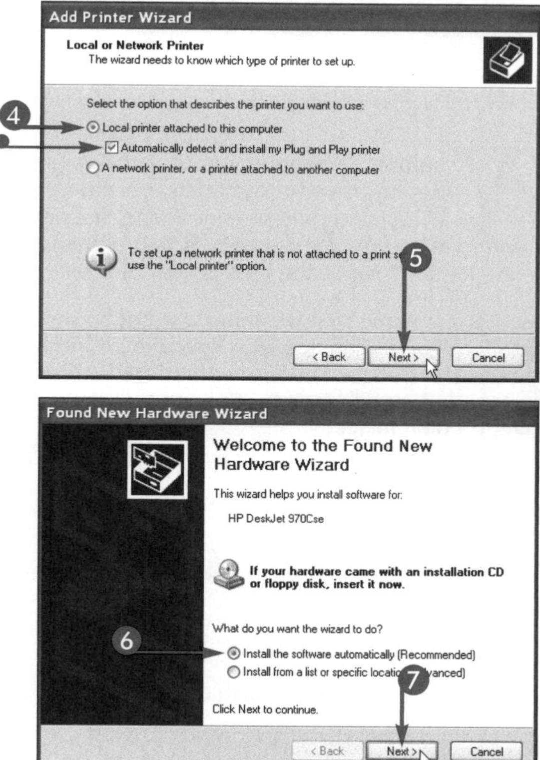

Windows searches for your printer.

When the printer is found, the Found New Hardware Wizard displays options for installing the printer software.

Note: *See the tip on the next page to find out what to do if your printer is not automatically found.*

6 Click the recommended option to install the software automatically.

7 Click Next.

PART III

In my office we each have our own printer. Why should we share them?

▼ You may decide to share a printer if you have the only color laser printer in your general office area. Or, you may have a printer set up that is designated as the only one that prints office letterhead. Finally, knowing how to share printers is invaluable if one of those printers quits working during a critical time of your work. Instead of moving files to a different computer to print them, simply change the print destination to one of the shared ones and print. You will be the hero (or heroine) of the office.

My printer is already set up as a local one. Can I set it up as a shared one now?

▼ Yes. To do this, open the Printers folder and right-click the icon of the printer you want to share. Choose Sharing from the menu that appears. The Sharing Tab of the printer's properties dialog box appears. Click Share this printer. Type a share name in the Share name field. Make this name descriptive enough so other users know the printer is set up to your computer. You can name a color laser printer connected to the budget computer Budget Color Laser, for example.

continued

Share and Manage Printers

(Continued)

Windows XP enables you to name your printer during the printer sharing procedure. The name you pick should be one that is descriptive to you and to others on the network. A name that is generic, such as "Printer," is not the best one to use.

Instead, use a name that describes the printer and describes its location. For example, a high-speed color inkjet printer may be connected to a computer in the Advertising department. A good name for this printer would be Ad_Dept_Color_Inkjet.

Windows enables you to manage print jobs that are sent to a printer you share. Some printers provide their own management software that is installed as part of the printer installation routine.

If your printer does not provide management software, or if the management software is limited in what it can perform, you can use the Windows XP management features. Windows XP uses the printer window to display print jobs, the size of print jobs, the status of the job, and the owner. To display the printer window, double-click your printer icon in the Printers and Faxes window of the Control Panel.

Share and Manage Printers *(continued)*

Windows searches for the best printer driver for your printer.

Windows displays the available printer drivers.

8 Click the printer driver that matches your printer name.

Note: *You may need to look at the printer or printer documentation for the exact name of the printer model. For example, the HP DeskJet 970Cse is not the same as the HP Deskjet 970Cxi. Be sure you pick the driver for your printer model.*

9 Click Next.

Windows copies the driver files and sets up your new printer. When finished, the Completing the Found New Hardware Wizard screen appears.

10 Click Finish.

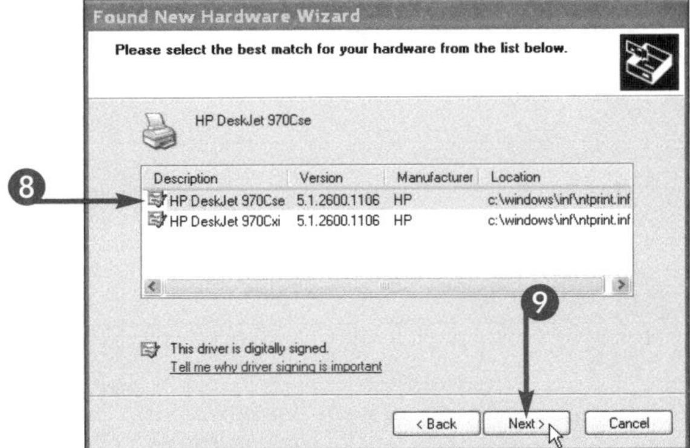

The New Printer Detection screen appears.

⑪ Click Yes to send a test page to the printer.

The Completing the Add Printer Wizard screen appears.

⑫ Click Finish.

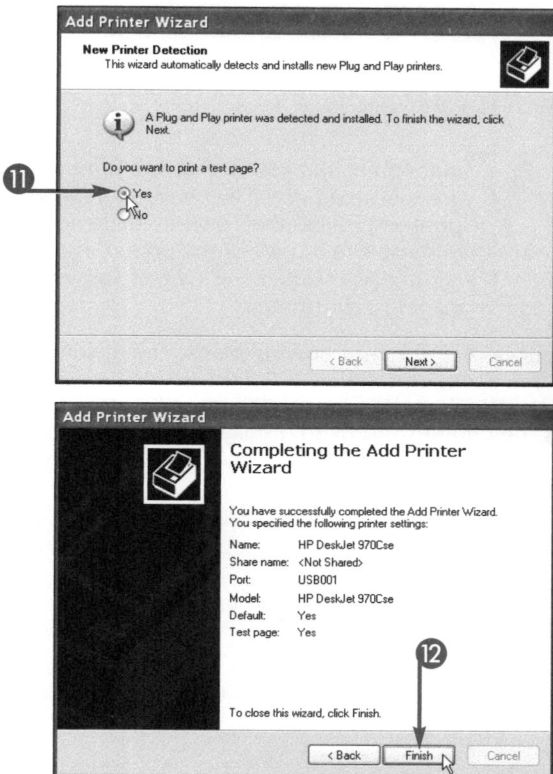

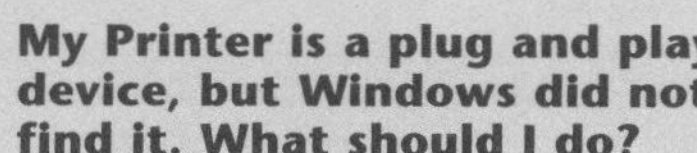

My Printer is a plug and play device, but Windows did not find it. What should I do?

▼ If the device is plug and play, Windows usually finds it unless a problem occurs in the printer, Windows printer services, or the cabling. During the installation, if the printer is not found, a dialog box appears telling you that the printer cannnot be located. Install the printer manually.

How do I install a printer manually?

▼ When Windows cannot locate your printer, a window tells you that it cannot be found. Click Next to install the printer manually. On the Select a printer port screen, select the port to which the printer is connected. If the printer is connected to a USB port and a USB port is not available from the list of ports, select LPT1 and continue. Click Next. The Install Printer Software screen appears. Select the manufacturer and printer model. Click Next. The Name Your Printer screen appears. Name the printer and click Next.

The Printer Sharing screen appears. Click Share name and enter a name for others to locate your printer. Click Next. The Location and Command screen appears. Fill out the Location and Comment fields, describing the location of your printer and other information you want to provide. Click Next. The Print Test Page screen appears. Click Yes and click Next. Click Finish when the Completing the Found New Hardware Wizard screen appears.

continued

Share and Manage Printers

(Continued)

Windows enables you to manage print jobs that are sent to a printer you have shared. Some printers provide their own management software that is installed as part of the printer installation routine. If your printer includes this type of software, use it to begin managing your printer.

If your printer does not provide management software, or the management software is limited in what it can perform, use the Windows XP management features. Windows XP uses the printer window to display print jobs, size of print jobs, status of the job, and owner. To display the printer window, double-click your printer icon in the Printers and Faxes window.

One of the most common management tasks is to cancel a print job. To do this, open the printer window and right-click the print job you want to cancel and click Cancel. Or, you can click the print job, Document, and then Cancel. The Printers window appears, asking if you are sure you want to cancel the print job. Click Yes.

Share and Manage Printers *(continued)*

A dialog box appears telling you that the test job is being sent.

13 Click OK.

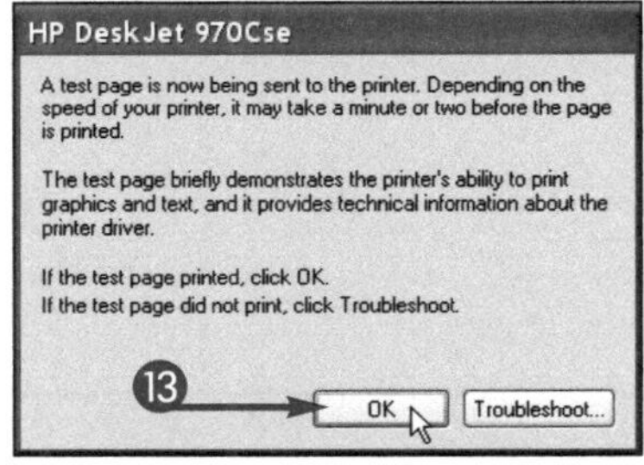

The new printer appears in the Printers and Faxes window.

14 Right-click the printer icon.

15 Click Properties from the menu that appears.

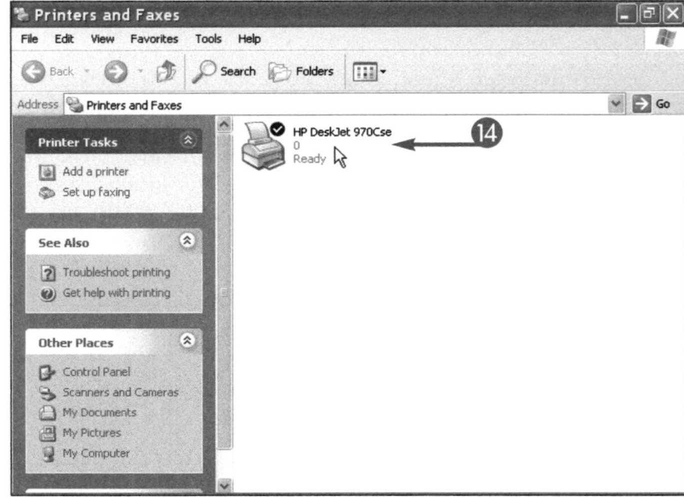

The printer properties dialog box appears.

16 Click the Sharing tab.

Here you can enable printer sharing, provide a name for the printer, and install additional drivers if necessary.

17 Click Share this printer.

18 Type a name for the printer.

19 Click OK.

If prompted that the name is too long for MS-DOS workstations, click Yes to continue.

The Printers and Faxes window appears. The printer icon now shows a hand cradling the printer, indicating that the printer is being shared.

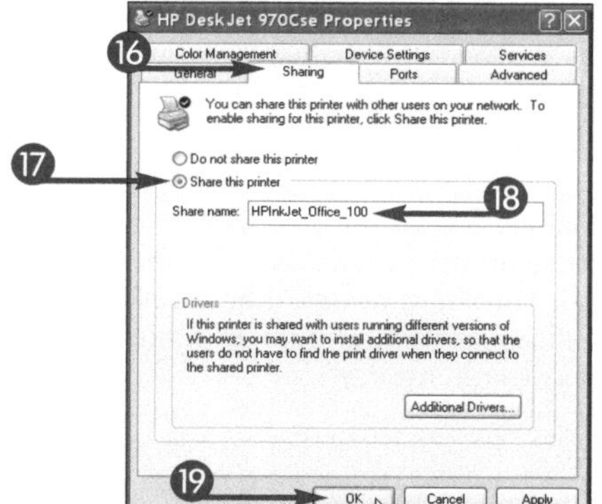

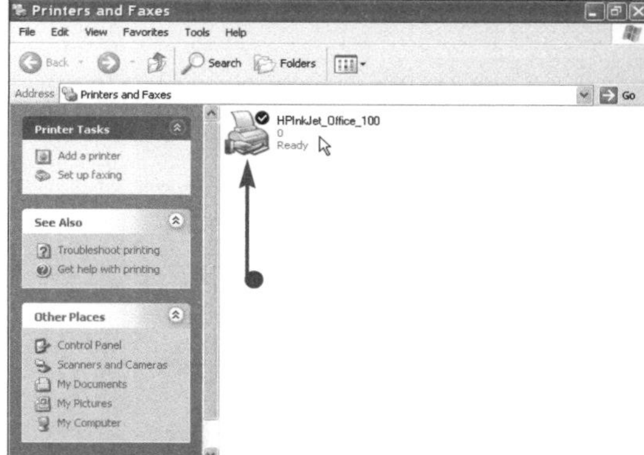

After I set up the printer, why should I finish by sending a test job? I would think the printer would work fine now.

▼ The printer test is a great way of confirming that your printer is set up and working the way that it should be. If you take the time to test the printer now and find that the printer is not working correctly, you will not be surprised (or aggravated) later when you need to send a document to the printer.

I understand what software is, but can you tell me what a printer driver is?

▼ Yes. It is a program designed to allow the printer to work with your computer and with Windows XP. Windows has what is called a printing subsystem that is designed to recognize some general printers. However, most printers have more features than the standard generic printer handled by Windows. Manufacturers write printer drivers to take advantage of these features, as well as make it easier for users to use their printers. In short, if you do not have the correct printer driver for your printer and version of Windows (XP SP2 in this case), your printer will probably not work correctly. In some cases, however, you can fake your printer into working as another type of printer — emulate that other printer. One example is the HP LaserJet printer family. Many times you can make your laser printer work by installing LaserJet drivers provided by Windows XP.

Configure and Send Faxes

Windows enables you to set up support for a fax modem to send and receive faxes. A fax modem is a hardware device that enables your computer to act like a fax machine. The fax modem can be an internal modem or external modem.

Internal modems are ones that are installed inside your computer as an expansion board or are a built-in component of the motherboard. External modems connect to your computer via a serial or USB port. Both types require that Windows be configured to recognize the modems. Most fax modems include setup CDs that help you set up and configure the hardware part of the modem.

After you install the fax modem, you must set up Windows XP SP2 Fax, a service that enables Windows to handle incoming faxes, send outgoing faxes, display your faxes, and store the faxes. By default, Fax is not installed when you install Windows. You can run the Add or Remove Programs applet from the Control Panel to install it.

Configure and Send Faxes

1. Open the Control Panel.
2. Double-click Add or Remove Programs.

   The Add or Remove Programs window appears.
3. Click Add/Remove Windows Components.

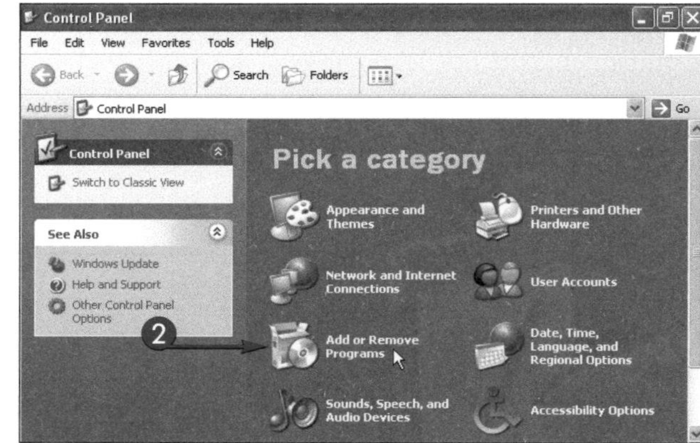

   The Windows Components Wizard appears.
4. Select Fax Services.
5. Click Next.

   The Configuring Components screen appears.

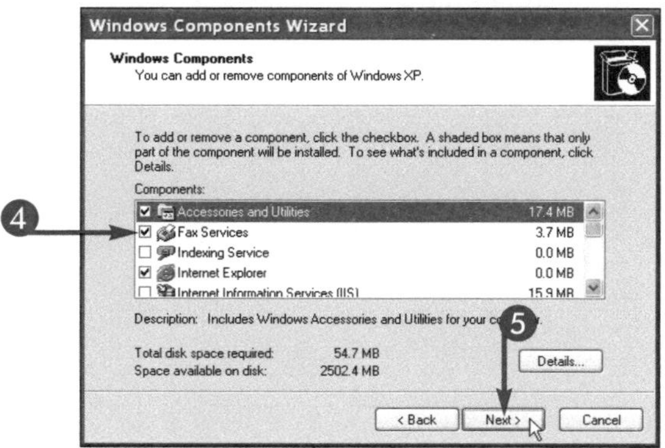

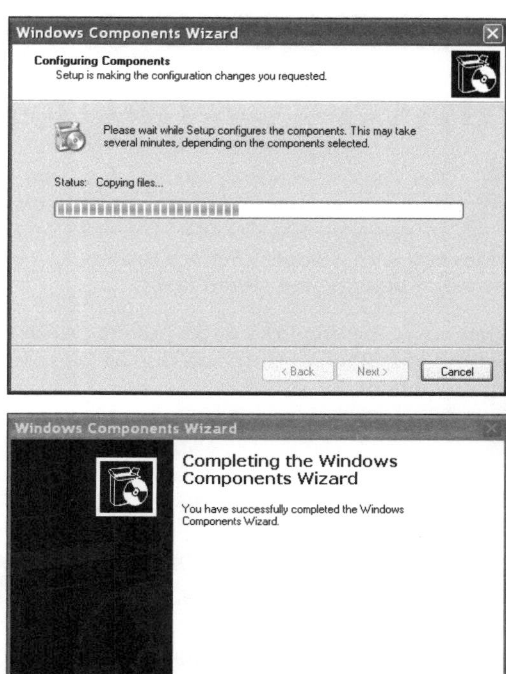

Here you can see the progress of the Fax Service setup.

The Completing the Windows Components Wizard screen appears.

6. Click Finish.
7. Click ☒ to close the Add or Remove Programs window.
8. Click ☒ to close the Control Panel window.

I have a fax machine at work. Why would I need a fax modem?

▼ You may not. If you send a lot of faxes, fax machines are the easiest and most efficient ways to send faxes. This is especially true if you send a lot of faxes of signed documents or hard copy forms. If you just have a fax modem, you need to scan the document into Windows and then fax the document from there. Another reason to have a fax machine is that you can share that machine with others in the office or department. Sharing the services of a fax modem is not as easy, because other users would need to use your computer to send a fax.

What are reasons to have a fax modem?

▼ Fax modems are very convenient for users who send a lot of unsigned documents to other fax machines. You can create a document in Word, for example, and then simply fax it to another person while still within Word. You do not have to print out the document first and then fax it. Another benefit of a fax modem is that you can receive faxes from other fax modems or fax machines and then store that document as a file. This is handy if you want to then e-mail that document to another user, eliminating the need to scan the document before sending it.

continued

Configure and Send Faxes *(Continued)*

After you get Windows Fax installed, you can send and receive faxes. Windows enables you to do this by using the Fax Console. The Fax Console provides you with a single interface to view and manage incoming, outgoing, and stored faxes.

Windows uses the Windows Address Book (WAB) as its default Address Book to store and display fax numbers. If you have Outlook XP or Outlook Express installed, then Fax uses the Outlook Address Book (OAB) instead. Address Books enable you to store and retrieve contact information, including a contact's fax number. When you set up a new fax message, you just need to retrieve the recipient's fax number and other information from your Address Book.

After you add Fax as a new service, you must configure Fax to work with your fax modem to send and receive faxes. The following steps show you how.

Configure and Send Faxes *(continued)*

9. Click Start, All Programs, Accessories, and then Communications.
10. Click Fax and then Fax Console.

    The Fax Configuration Wizard window appears.
11. Click Next.

The Sender Information screen appears. Here you can fill out information about you and your company. This information will appear on the fax cover pages you send.

12. Fill out the Sender Information screen.

Note: *You should fill out at least your full name and Fax number here.*

13. Click Next.

    The Completing the Fax Configuration Wizard screen appears.
14. Click Next.

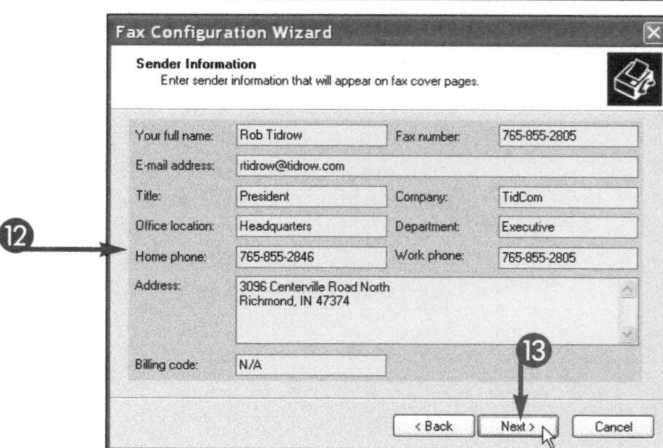

The Select Device for Sending or Receiving Faxes screen appears.

15 Click here and select your fax modem device.

- By default, the Enable Send option is selected.

16 Select the Enable Receive option to receive faxes.

17 Click Next.

The Transmitting Subscriber Identification (TSID) screen appears. The TSID identifies the faxes you send out.

18 Type your fax number and company name.

The Called Subscriber Identification (CSID) screen appears. The CSID identifies your fax/modem to the machine sending you a fax.

19 Click Next.

The Called Subscriber Identification (CSID) screen appears.

20 Type your fax number and company name.

21 Click Next.

The Routing Options screen appears.

22 Click Store a copy in a folder and specify a folder, such as My Computer, in which to store the incoming faxes.

23 Click Next.

The Completing the Fax Configuration Wizard screen appears.

24 Click Finish.

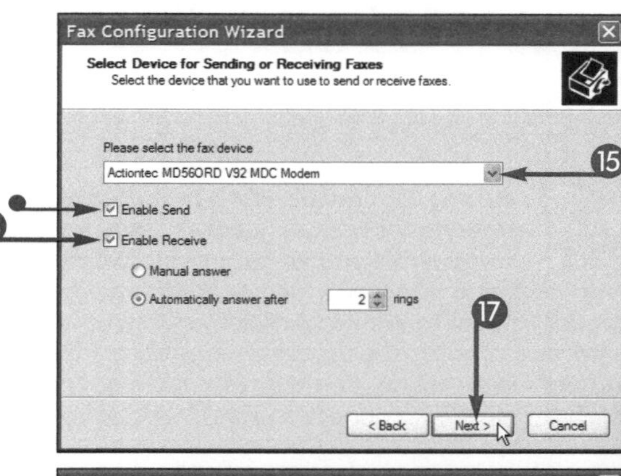

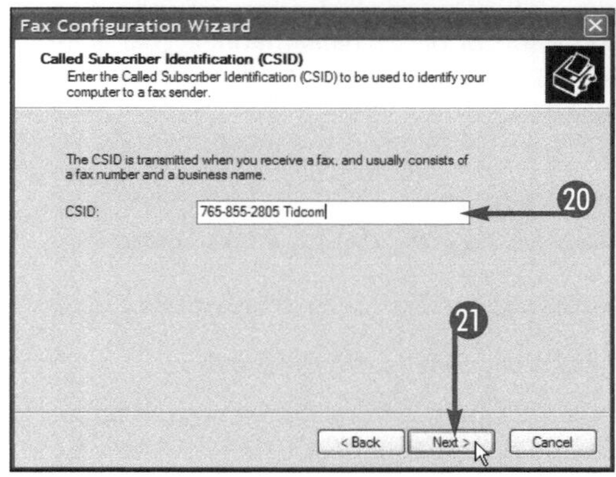

MASTER IT

I have a fax modem installed on my computer. Can I use it to connect to the Internet?

▼ Yes, but you cannot be online and send or receive faxes at the same time. (There are Internet services that allow faxing via the Internet, but these services use Internet technology to send and receive your faxes and do not use your fax modem to do the faxing.) To send and receive a fax, you need to disconnect from the Internet, just as if you are making a phone call with the telephone line.

When I first used Windows XP, it called Fax by a different name. What was that and why the name change?

▼ Windows XP SP1 used Fax Service as the full name of the fax support. When you install Windows XP SP2, the name is now changed to simply Fax. Why Microsoft decided to change the name no one knows. Just be glad Fax is part of Windows still. There was a time (when Windows 98 was released) that the fax feature was removed, causing many users to write Microsoft asking (demanding!) them to reinstate Fax.

Microsoft Word and other word processors have fax cover sheet templates. Can I use these with Fax?

▼ Yes, and in fact using those kinds of templates make creating and sending your faxes easier. To see an example of a fax cover sheet template (if you have Microsoft Word XP), open Word and click File. Then click New. The New Document pane appears. Click General Templates. The Templates window appears. Click Letters & Faxes. This shows fax templates and the Fax Wizard. The Fax Wizard is handy for walking you through setting up a new fax document.

Troubleshoot Network Errors

Windows XP provides tools that enable you to troubleshoot network errors. You can solve some errors you encounter by tweaking something inside Windows, such as adding a different network protocol to Windows. Other problems are a result of hardware problems. One common problem users have is with network cabling. Sometimes a cable goes bad, causing the network connection not to operate properly.

As you encounter network errors, you should approach them in some sort of hierarchical manner. That is, do not assume that the problem is always an advanced problem that requires you to examine the deepest reaches of the Windows Registry to solve. Instead look at the most obvious problems first.

The following is an overview of the steps you might take in locating a network problem with your computer:

- Make sure the network cable is plugged in.
- Make sure the network adapter card light is turned on.
- Make sure the switch or hub is plugged in and the network cables are connected.
- Make sure the network server is turned on (you may need to ask your network administrator about this).
- Shut down and restart Windows.
- Examine your network settings, as described in the following task steps.

Troubleshoot Network Errors

Troubleshoot the local area network connection

1 Right-click My Network Places.

2 Click Properties from the menu that appears.

The Network Connections window appears, displaying the network connections installed on your computer.

Note: *Your connection may be named something else.*

3 Right-click the connection with which you are experiencing problems.

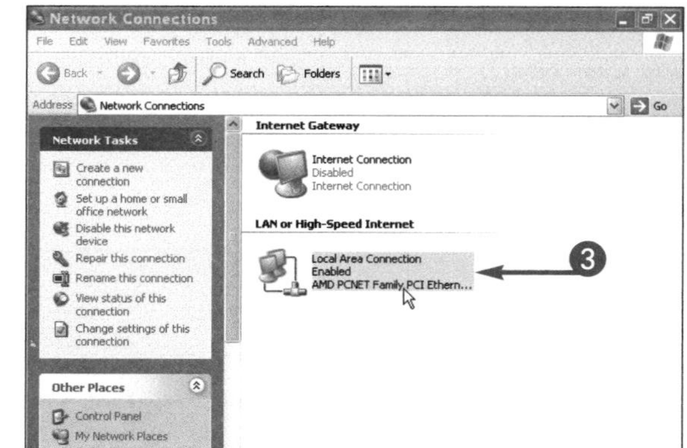

4 Click Properties from the menu that appears.

The Local Area Connection Properties dialog box appears.

- Make sure this is the correct network adapter for your computer.
- If not, click Configure and set up a new adapter.
- The network items list should have at least one network client (usually Client for Microsoft Networks) and a protocol (usually Internet Protocol [TCP/IP] for Internet connections).

5 If a required item is not listed, click Install.

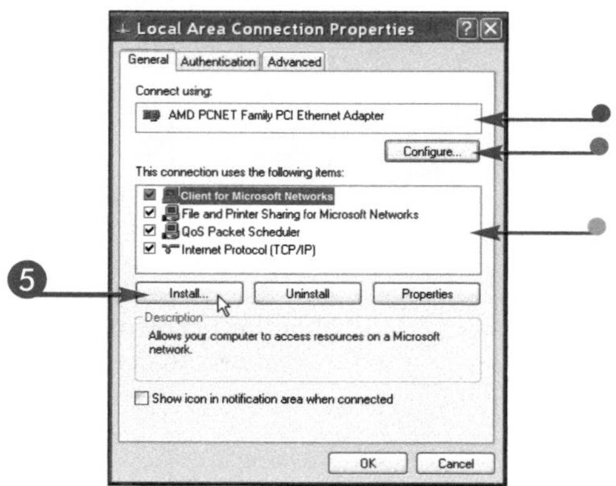

The Select Network Component Type dialog box appears.

This example covers how to install another protocol on the network.

Note: *Sometimes you can add IPX/SPX/NetBIOS to help you connect to other workgroup computers.*

6 Click Protocol

7 Click Add.

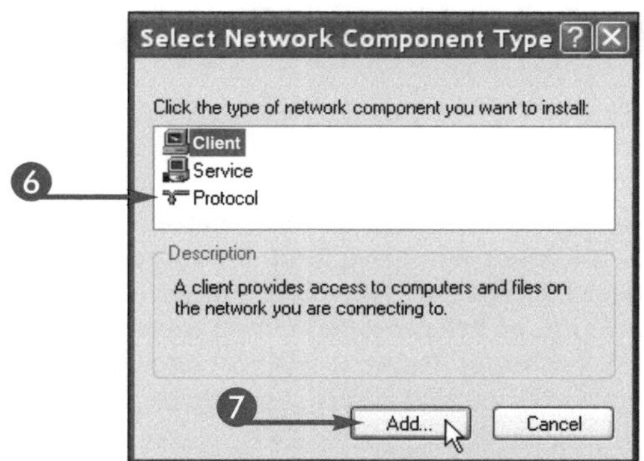

The Select Network Protocol dialog box appears.

8 Click NWLink IPX/SPX/NetBIOS Compatible Transport Protocol.

This protocol is good if you have other operating systems on the network, such as Windows 98, Windows Me, and Novell NetWare.

9 Click OK.

The protocols are installed and listed on the General tab of the network properties dialog box, showing that they are ready to be used to help connect your computer to the network.

10 Click ☒ to close the Local Area Connection Properties dialog box.

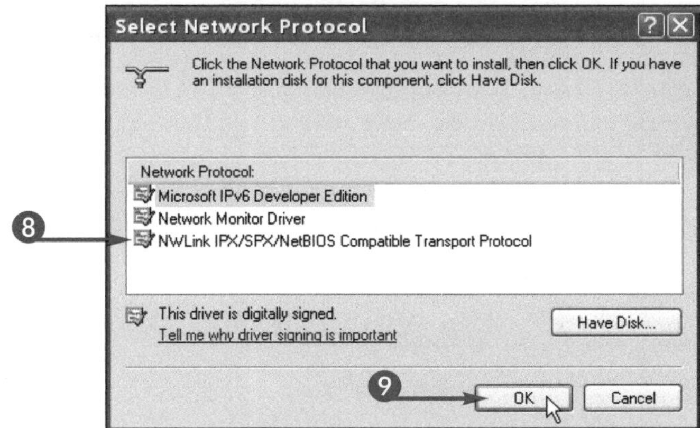

PART III

My network is not working correctly. Are there some other problems I should be looking at?

▼ Another problem could be that a virus has attacked your computer, the network servers, or both. To look for viruses, you must have an antivirus program installed on your computer. The most common ones include Symantec AntiVirus (formerly known as Norton AntiVirus), MacAfee Virus Scan, and Trend MicroScan (Trend was recently purchased by Microsoft). Run an antivirus program on your computer to scan for any viruses. If found, delete the file that contains the virus. Shut down and restart your computer.

Another problem is that your network adapter is malfunctioning. There are some hardware tests you can perform on these cards, but sometimes the easiest way to determine if a card is bad is to swap it out with another one. If the network problem goes away, then the adapater was probably the problem. Consult your computer's manual for steps on changing your network adapter.

I recently began getting pop-up messages on my screen. Could these be causing my network problems?

▼ They might be. Some spyware programs have been known to cause network problems. Two that come to mind are New.Net and Alexa. These programs are notorious for changing network settings, including IP address settings, firewire protection settings, and proxy configurations. Spyware tools such as Adaware, Spybot Search and Destroy, and Spy Sweeper find and terminate these and other spyware programs. These tools are available as downloads from the Internet.

continued

Troubleshoot Network Errors *(Continued)*

A number of different types of errors can cause problems with Windows networking. If you have all the correct protocols installed for your network, examine the configuration of the protocol named Internet Protocol (TCP/IP). Click Internet Protocol (TCP/IP) and then click Properties from the General tab of the Local Area Connection Properties dialog box.

On the Internet Protocol (TCP/IP) Properties dialog box, the Obtain an IP address automatically and Obtain DNS server address automatically options should be selected. These are the default settings for networks using DHCP and WINS, which are common for networks running Windows 2000 Server and Windows Server 2003. If you are not sure if these options should be selected, ask your network administrator.

One of the most useful tools for troubleshooting network errors is the Event Viewer. This tool is provided with Windows and gives you a glimpse of the activities and events that are happening within Windows. When something happens in Windows (which can be several times every second), Windows logs the event. Although you probably do not want or even need to see every event, you can isolate just the bad events (called Warnings and Errors) that occur.

Troubleshoot Network Errors *(continued)*

Troubleshoot with the Event Viewer

1. Display the Control Panel.
2. Click Performance and Maintenance.

   The Pick a task window appears.
3. Click Administrative tools.

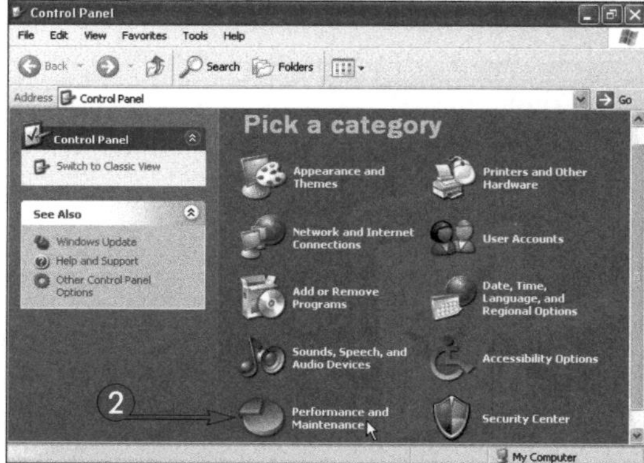

The Administrative Tools window appears.

4. Double-click Event Viewer.

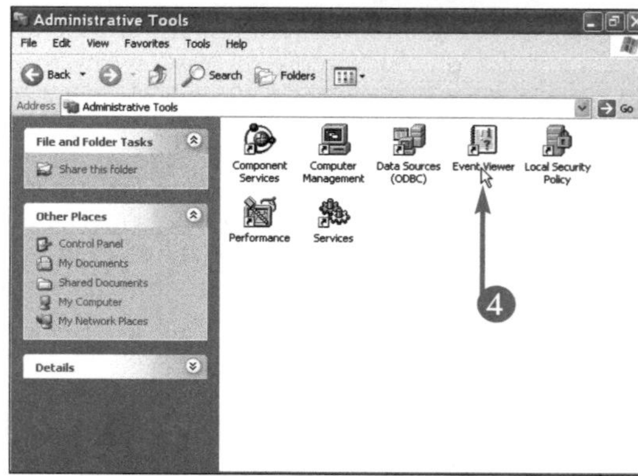

The Event Viewer window appears.

- Application shows events related to Windows programs such as Dr. Watson, Fax, and third-party programs.
- Security shows events related to security policies running under Windows.

5 Click System. System shows information related to Windows system events.

- The right pane displays System events. Event Viewer has five types of events: Information, Success audit, Warning, Failed audit, and Error.

6 Double-click an event that appears next to an Error.

The Event Properties dialog box appears.

- Here you can see details about the event, including when it occurred, the event ID, computer name, and a description of the event. If a link appears in the description, click it for more information.

7 Click OK.

Continue opening events in the Event Viewer to read about them.

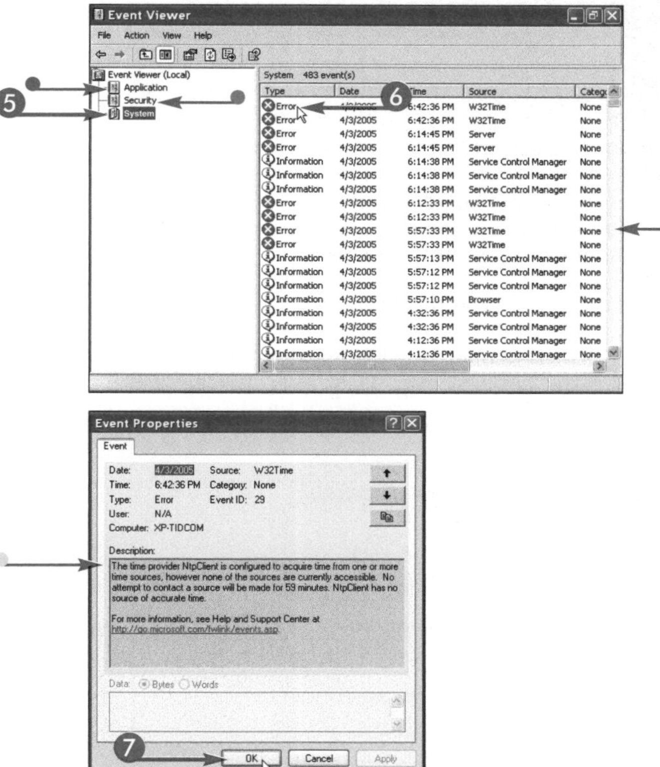

I have seen the network administrator use Event Viewer to help solve problems on the local area network. Why would I want to use Event Viewer on my own computer? It looks too intimidating for me.

▼ Event Viewer does not provide any options or tools that allow you to change settings or program behavior. Instead, Event Viewer simply shows you what has happened. This information is critical for helping you diagnose what a problem is. In some cases, the Event Viewer, in tandem with Microsoft.com, can provide you with information on how to solve the problem. Again, however, you cannot make the change from within Event Viewer. To learn more about Event Viewer, see the task steps on the following pages.

Event Viewer is nice, but it does not always give me information on the error. Can I download or purchase other network error tools?

▼ Yes, there are dozens of these types of programs available. Some are designed to run locally (that is, on your computer), while others must be installed and run from a network server. The first kind is what you want. These programs are usually designated for "client" or "host" computers. Generally, the way they work is to analyze the network from a client computer, not from a server. The software cannot analyze the inner workings of the network server. This is okay, because you need to find local problems, not worry about the server. You can leave that to the network administrator. To find this type of software, go to Google.com or another search engine and type **Windows XP Network Utilities**.

Configure Remote Desktop

Windows XP includes a feature called Remote Desktop. It enables you to remotely control your computer from another location. This is handy if you want to access your home computer from the office, such as to obtain files you forget at home. Conversely, you can set up Remote Desktop on your work computer so you can access it from home.

To use Remote Desktop, you must have the following:

- Windows XP Professional installed on the computer you plan to operate remotely. This computer is known as the host.
- A remote computer running Windows XP or another version of Windows, including Windows XP SP1, Windows 95, 98, 98 SE, or Me running the Remote Desktop Connection client software. This computer is known as the client.
- An Internet connection. Although a broadband Internet connection can improve performance, a low-bandwidth Internet connection still allows you to remotely control your remote computer.

Configure Remote Desktop

1. Right-click My Computer and click Properties.
2. In the System Properties dialog box, click the Remote tab.
3. Click the option to allow users to connect remotely to your computer.
4. In the Remote Sessions dialog box, click OK, and click OK again in the properties dialog box.

   Your computer is now set up for Remote Desktop sessions.
5. From another computer, click Start, All Programs, Accessories, Communications, and then Remote Desktop Connection.
6. In the Remote Desktop Connection window, type the name of the computer to which you want to connect.
7. Click Connect.

   Remote Desktop Connection connects to the remote desktop and prompts you for a user name and password.
8. Type a user name and password for the remote computer, and press Enter to log on.

Note: *If you are connecting to a remote user over the Internet, you must also type the IP address of the remote computer.*

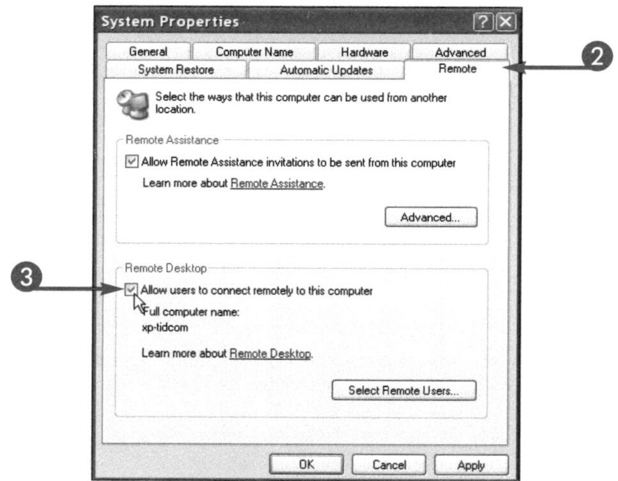

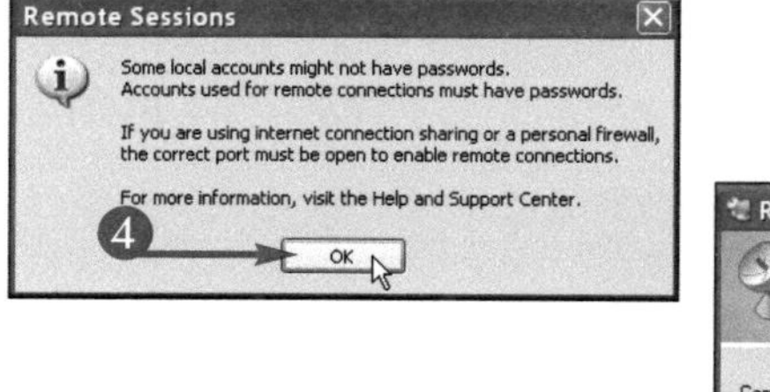

- A view of the remote desktop appears. At the top of the window are controls to minimize, maximize, or close the remote window.

Note: *If you also had the remote computer nearby, you would see that that computer goes into lockdown mode. You cannot have a remote session and local session at the same time.*

9 Click here to minimize the remote desktop.

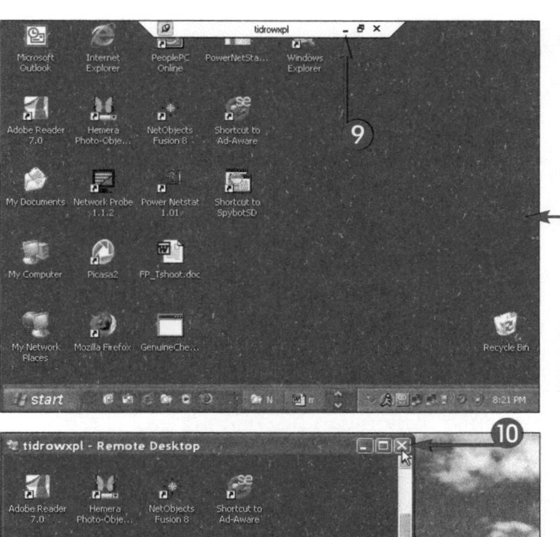

- You can now see the local computer's desktop behind the remote desktop.

Navigate around on the remote computer as needed.

10 When finished with the remote session, click here to close the remote desktop window.

The remote session closes.

11 Click Close in the Remote Desktop Connection window.

What is the Remote Desktop Connection client software and where can I get it?

The Remote Desktop Connection client software is software that enables other versions of Windows (previous releases to Windows XP) to be client computers during the Remote Desktop session. The software is on the Windows XP installation CD. Or you can obtain a copy from the Microsoft.com Download Web site (www.microsoft.com/downloads). Type **Remote Desktop Connection** and click Go. Click the Remote Desktop Connection Software link. The Windows XP Remote Desktop Connection software page appears. Click Download to download the client software. The file you need to download is called MSRDPCLI.EXE and is about 3.5MB in size. After the download, run the MSRDPCLI.EXE file to install the client software. This software enables older Windows computers to remotely connect to a computer running Windows XP Professional with Remote Desktop enabled.

I tried accessing my work computer from home but cannot do it. What should I try next?

Sometimes network administrators do not allow Remote Desktop to work across their network. The main reason is security. If your company has a firewall installed, the port for Windows Remote Desktop and similar remote access software has probably been blocked. You can ask your network administrator if running Remote Desktop on your computer at work is authorized. In some businesses it is not.

Configure Remote Assistance

Windows XP enables you to use Remote Assistance, which is a tool that lets others access your computer and provide assistance to it. Conversely, if you are an experienced user or one who feels comfortable helping others fix their own computers, Remote Assistance can help you be a fix-it star.

Remote Assistance uses Windows Messenger to enable two computers to connect with one another. The two computers must be running a version of Windows XP — either XP Professional or XP Home Edition.

A Remote Assistance session can be made one of three ways. You can start Windows Messenger and send an invitation to the other user. Secondly, you can send a Help and Support e-mail message to the other user: The message includes a link to help the recipient start the Remote Assistance session. Finally, you can fill out a form and save it as a file, which is then e-mailed to a recipient.

To use Remote Assistance, you must have the following:

- One computer running Windows XP that receives assistance.
- One computer running Windows XP that provides assistance.
- Both computers connected to a network or to the Internet.
- Both computers must have Windows Messenger installed.

Configure Remote Assistance

1. Click the Windows Messenger icon ( ) on the taskbar.

   The Windows Messenger window appears.

2. Click here to sign in to the Windows Messenger network.

   The Windows Messenger window appears, showing you as logged on.

3. Select the contact to whom you want to send an invitation.

   The person you send the invitation to must be currently online.

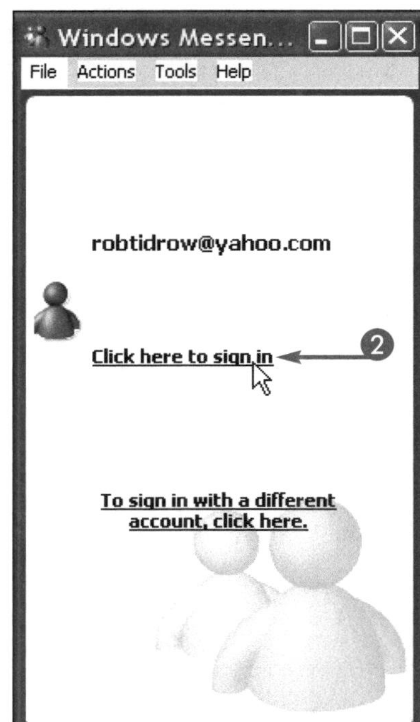

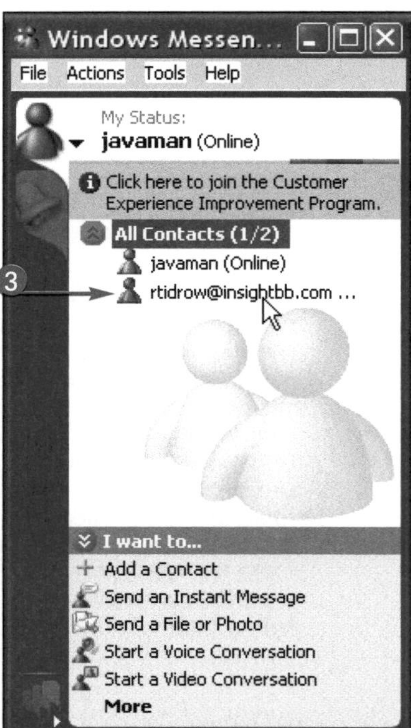

4. Click Actions.
5. Click Ask for Remote Assistance.

   Your contact receives an invitation to provide Remote Assistance. When he accepts the invitation, a password screen appears on his computer.

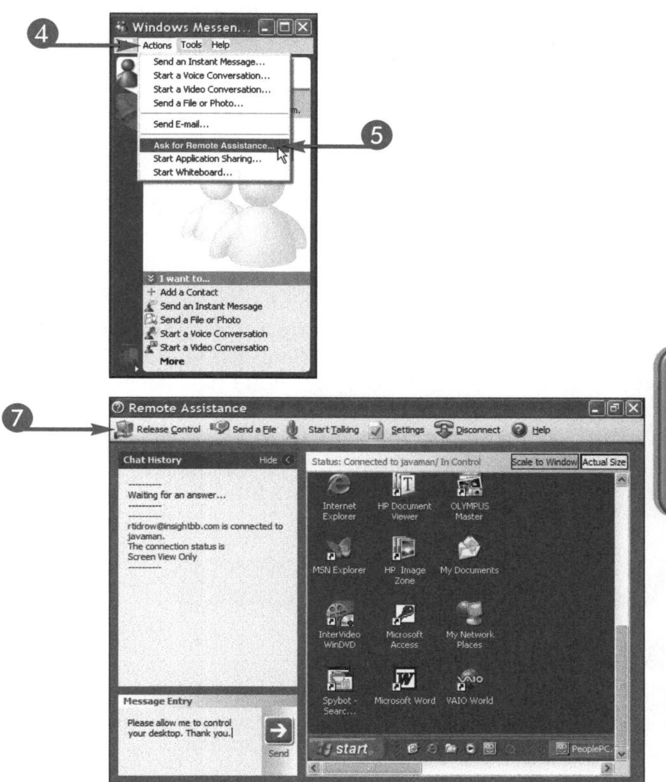

6. After your contact logs on to the Remote Assistance session, he clicks Show Chat.

   Your contact is now in charge of the session. You can take control of a session to help the person on the other end by clicking Take Control. Your contact must confirm this permission.

7. Click Release Control or press Esc to end the session.

Can I send an e-mail to someone inviting them to connect to my computer using Remote Assistance?

▼ Yes. To do this start Windows Messenger and log on. Next, click Windows Start to open the Start menu, and then click Help and Support. The Help and Support window appears. Click the Invite a friend to connect to your computer with Remote Assistance link. Click Invite someone to help you. Type an e-mail address in the text box in the or Use e-mail section. Click Invite this person. On the Provide contact information screen, type your name and a description of the problem. Click Continue. The Set the invitation to expire screen appears. Select the number of hours for the length of time you want this invitation to be in effect. (After this time, two hours, for example, the invitation and the Remote Assistance session can no longer take place.) Enter and reenter a password. You must tell the other person this password in a separate e-mail or phone call to him. Click Send Invitation.

Why should I have an expiration time for the Remote Assistance invitations?

▼ This lessens the chances that someone else besides the person you invite gains access to your computer. Although you can set a password for the invitation, you do not want to expose your computer for an indefinite amount of time in case another user figures out the password and connects to your computer.

Configure for Novell Networks

Windows XP enables you to configure client support for Novell NetWare. Novell NetWare is a separate network operating system from Windows XP and is used by many companies to provide file, printer, and application sharing.

For many years, NetWare was the most popular network operating system on the market. Microsoft Windows 2000 Server and recently Windows Server 2003 have taken over as the leaders of the network operating system market. With that said, many companies that invested in NetWare still have a combination of networks in their building — NetWare for some tasks and Windows for others.

Because of that, Windows XP provides client support so users that need to can still access the NetWare parts of the network. To get this access, you must install the Client Service for NetWare.

When you use the Client Service for NetWare, most of the logon screens are different than those you see when using the Client Service for Microsoft. Although they are different, you should be able to understand them without any problems. You need a user name and password for the NetWare server, which your network administrator can provide for you.

Configure for Novell Networks

1. Right-click My Network Places.
2. Click Properties.

   The Network Connections window appears.
3. Right-click a LAN connection.
4. Click Properties.

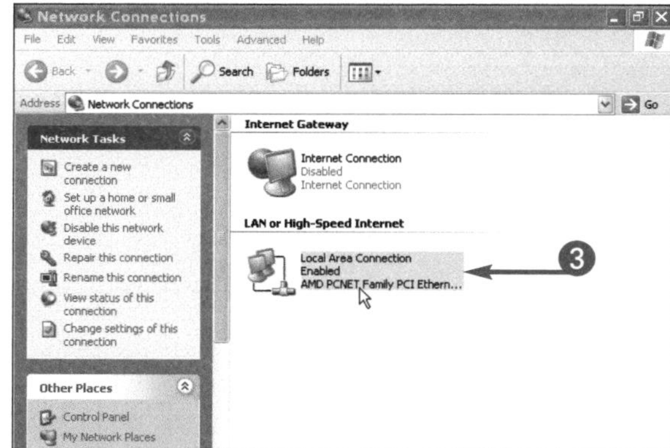

The Local Area Connection Properties dialog box appears.

5. Click Install.

   The Select Network Component Type dialog box appears.
6. Click Client.
7. Click Add.

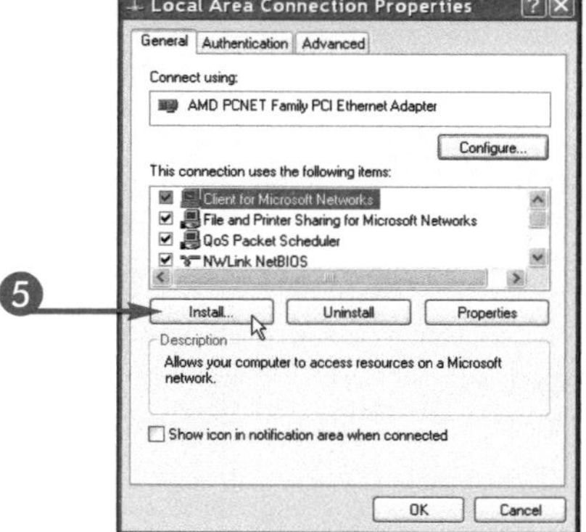

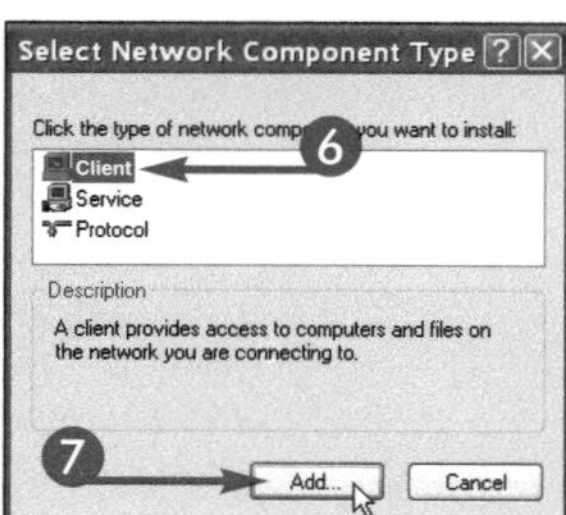

The Select Network Client dialog box appears.

8 Click Client Service for NetWare.

9 Click OK.

Windows installs the Client Service for NetWare.

The Local Network dialog box appears.

10 Click Yes.

Windows shuts down and restarts. The Welcome to Windows screen appears.

11 Press Ctrl+Alt+Del.

The Log On to Windows screen appears.

12 Type your user name and password.

13 Click OK.

The Select NetWare Logon screen appears.

14 Specify the NetWare server or tree you want to log on to. Ask your network administrator if you do not know which to select.

15 Click OK.

Windows logs you on to the NetWare server, runs any NetWare scripts assigned to your computer, and completes the Windows desktop boot process.

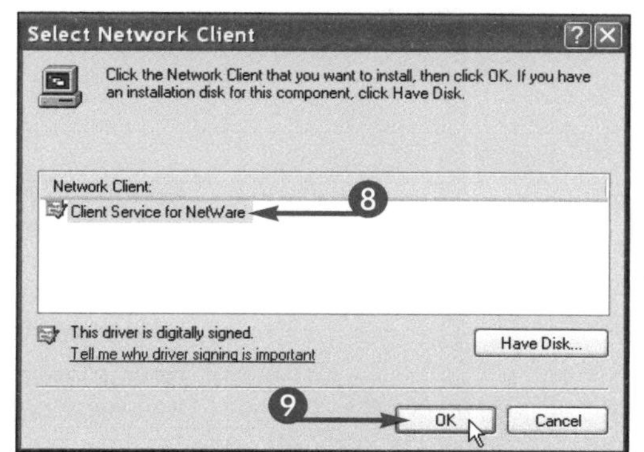

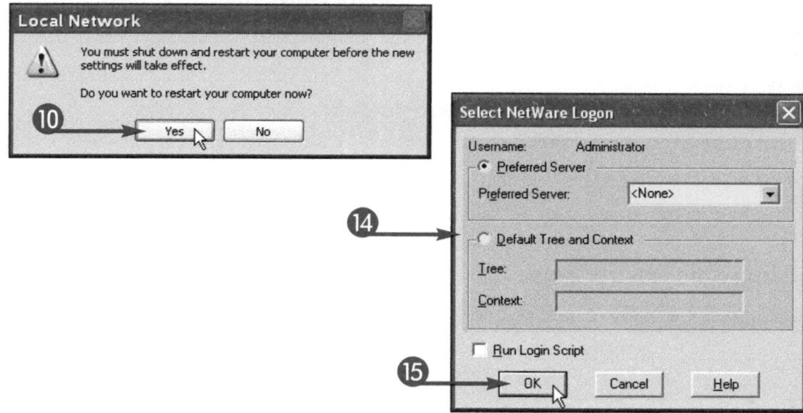

PART III

I have to connect to a Novell NetWare for logon authorization and other tasks. Is there a more advanced client software I can use?

▼ Yes. Novell provides an updated client called the Novell Client for Windows XP. This client should be used instead of the Client Service for NetWare if you need to connect to NDS servers. You should also use Novell Client for Windows XP if you want to browse authorized NetWare directories, transfer files, print documents, and use advanced NetWare services.

To obtain the Novell Client for Windows XP, go to http://download.novell.com/Download?buildid=2ss2JIYshRc~ and click Download. The file, clnt491e.exe, is over 24MB, so download only if you have a fast Internet connection.

I used to enter NetWare commands from within Windows 3.1 and 98. Are these still available with Windows XP?

▼ Windows XP does have support for some NetWare commands. The following list shows these commands:

- For Slist in NetWare, use `Net view /network:nw` or `Net view/n:nw`.
- For Attach, Login, or Logout, use `Net use`.
- For Map, use `Net use`.
- For Map root, use `Net use \\servername\share\`.
- For Capture, use `Net use`.

Install Services for Unix

Windows XP enables you to install the Print Services for Unix service. This way if your network server is running both Windows 2000/2003 and Unix printer services, you can connect to these servers and print.

You may remember that when you set up the Novell NetWare service in the previous section that there were no other options available, including no option for Unix. That is because the Print Services for Unix service is not installed yet from the Windows XP CD. The following task shows how to install it from the CD.

As you set up the Unix service under Windows, you do not see a choice specifically for the Unix print services. Instead you must first choose the Other Network Files and Print Services options, which provides the ability to install the Unix print services.

Unix printers are usually prevalent in large organizations that have been on a network for many years. This is because Unix was the original small computer operating system (since the 1960s, in fact) and is still used by many older companies as a legacy infrastructure.

Install Services for Unix

1. Display the Control Panel.
2. Double-click Add or Remove Programs.

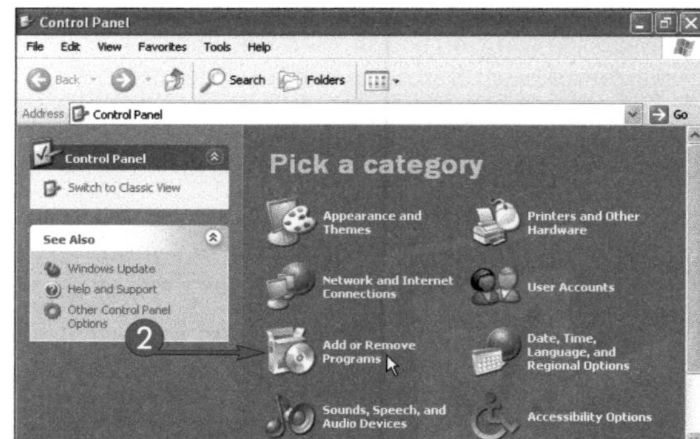

The Add or Remove Programs window appears.

3. Click Add/Remove Windows Components.

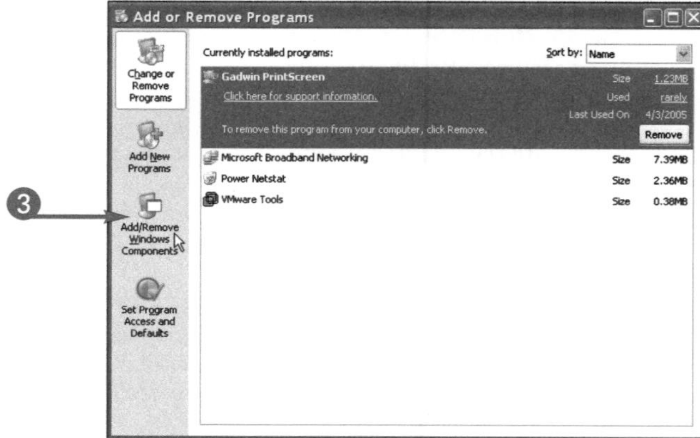

The Windows Components Wizard appears. Here you can select to install Windows components that are still on the Windows CD.

4. Select Other Network File and Print Services.
5. Click Next.

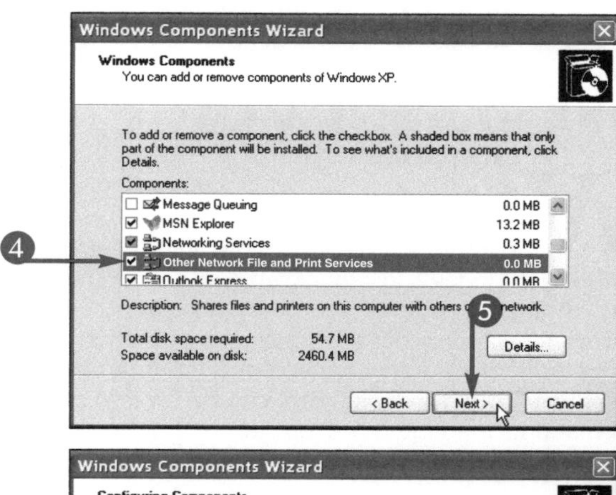

The Configuring Components screen appears. You may be prompted for your Windows XP CD during this phase. If so, insert it into your CD drive.

When finished, the Completing the Windows Components Wizard screen appears.

6. Click Finish.
7. Click ☒ to close the Add or Remove Programs window.

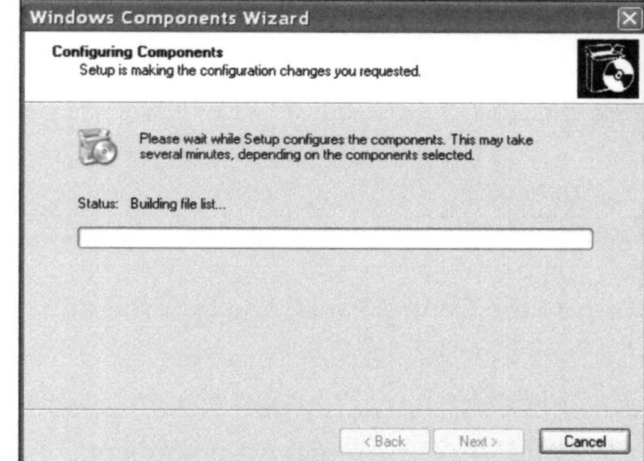

What is Unix?

- Unix is one of the oldest operating systems for micro- and mini-computers. Unix was first introduced in the 1960s and has been an important operating system since. Unix is primarily used as a networking server for large installations, for Web servers, and for client machines requiring highly stable environments (such as research departments). If you use the Internet, you have encountered Unix many times without even knowing it. Most Web sites use Unix to house Web content, execute form data, and perform other important Web activities.

Are there other utilities that allow me to work with Unix or versions of Unix?

- Yes. There are many programs and scripts available that you can install on Windows XP that let you interact with Unix. One thing to keep in mind is that Unix has many types, such as Linux. When you go looking for tools to work with Unix, know the type you have so you can obtain the correct versions of the Unix software. For example, you can obtain a tool called GRUB that enables you to have bootable versions of both Linux and Windows XP on the same computer. To find more information about the options available to you, go to Google and type **Windows XP AND Unix**. You can find thousands of links for more information.

Install and Configure Web Server

With Internet Information Service (IIS), you can set up and maintain a Web server on your computer. The Web server can be used to publish Web pages and other Web content on the Internet, to an intranet, or both. If you have an account with an Internet service provider (ISP), you can publish information on the Internet so users connected to the Internet can access your content. An intranet can be used to publish information for an internal Web site, such as for a small office or home.

To manage IIS, you use the Microsoft Management Console (MMC) snap-in, or run the Internet Information Services program from the Control Panel. With the MMC, you have the option of displaying and working with multiple snap-ins from one window. This makes it handy for managing several services at the same time.

Before you even begin to set up IIS, you should make sure that you have a working network for your organization. All the computers that access your IIS Web site must be connected to this network. If you plan on connecting your Web site to the Internet, make sure your machine is connected to the Internet. You should consider hosting your own Web site if your office or home has access to the Internet using a high-speed connection (such as cable) or a DSL connection.

Install and Configure Web Server

1. Display the Control Panel, and click the Add or Remove Programs icon.

   The Add or Remove Programs window appears.

2. Click Add/Remove Windows Components.

   The Windows Components Wizard appears.

3. Select Internet Information Services (IIS).

4. Click Details.

   The Internet Information Services (IIS) dialog box appears.

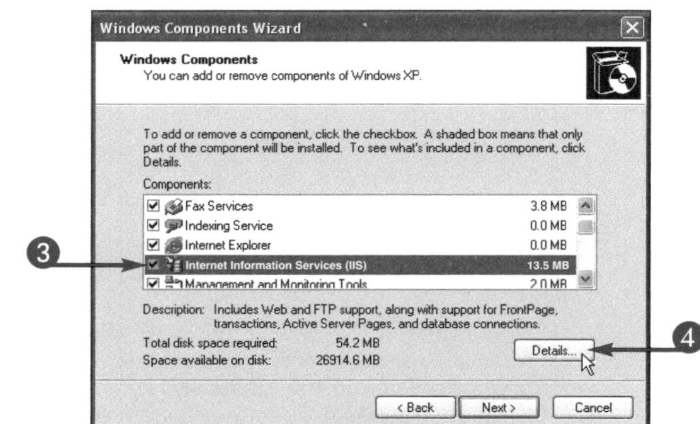

5. Select the components you want to install with IIS. For most installations, you can select all options and then remove any later that you do not use.

6. Click OK to close the Internet Information Services (IIS) dialog box.

7. Click Next in the wizard to continue with the installation.

   The Configuring Components screen appears, showing you the progress of the installation. When finished, the final wizard screen appears.

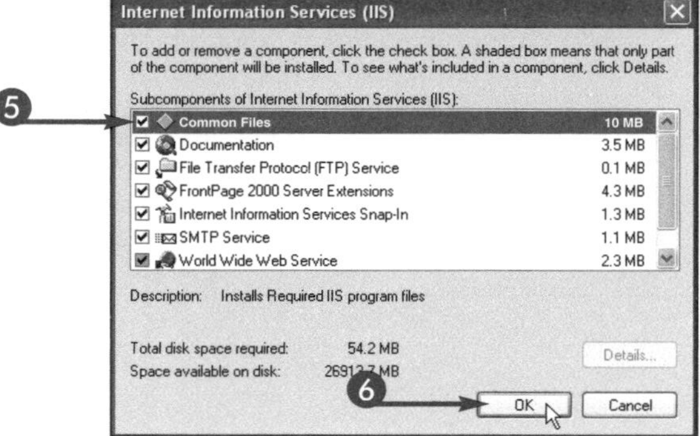

8 Click Finish to close the wizard.

9 Click ☒ to close the Add or Remove Programs window.

10 In the Control Panel, click the Performance and Maintenance icon.

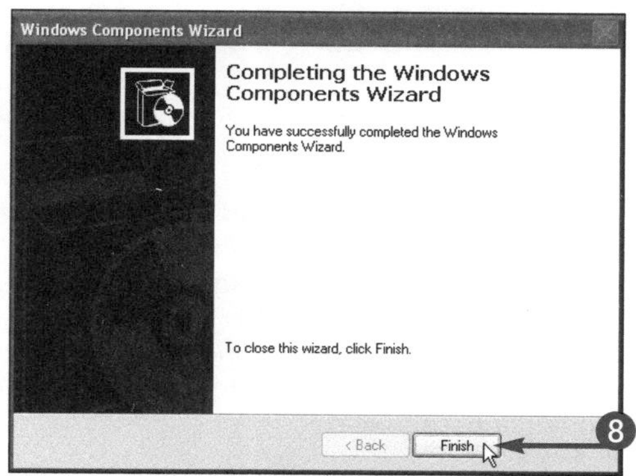

The Performance and Maintenance window appears.

11 Click Administrative Tools.

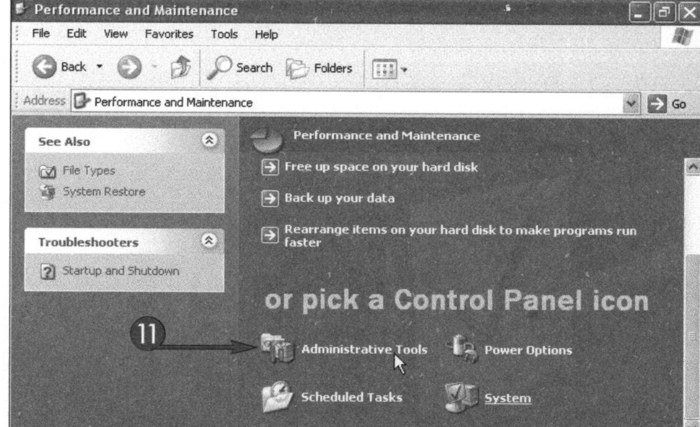

What is a Web server?

▼ A Web server is software that enables you to publish information on the Internet. A Web server can also refer to the physical computer on which Web server software resides.

Can I run a Web server for my office only?

▼ Yes, this is called an *intranet* and has some advantages over running IIS for Internet connections. First, you can assign yourself an internal IP address (such as using the 10.xx.xx.xx IP address scheme). Second, because the site is private, you probably will not be overwhelmed by too many users trying to access your site. Third, if you keep your site away from the Internet, you do not have to invest in a firewall to keep out unwanted intruders.

How can I run a Web server on a dial-up connection?

▼ You cannot. You must have a connection that is on 24 hours a day, seven days a week. With most dial-up connections, this is not possible. In fact, many ISPs shut off your connection every few hours to thrwart users from setting up private Web servers. Another reason you must have a 24/7 Internet connection is so that you can have a fixed (or static) IP address that your ISP gives you. An IP (Internet Protocol) address is a unique identifying number that is given to your computer so other computers (via the DNS system) can find your Web site.

continued

Install and Configure Web Server *(Continued)*

You can publish Web pages, files, and other content to your IIS Web server. Standard Web pages are created in hypertext markup language and saved as HTML or HTM files. You can use a number of different programs to create HTML files, including Windows Notepad, Microsoft Word, Microsoft FrontPage, Adobe GoLive, and Macromedia Dreamweaver.

HTML is not a programming language like Visual Basic, Java, or C++. Rather it is a scripting language that includes instructions to Web browsers on how information should be shown. For example, if you want a line of text to be boldface, you add an instruction at the beginning of the line to turn on boldface, and then add another instruction at the end of the line that turns off boldface.

Web browsers, like Microsoft Internet Explorer and Netscape Navigator, interpret the HTML code and display information as scripted in the HTML file. Although these two Web browsers are the most popular, other Web browsers are available, including Mosaic, Mozilla FireFox, and Opera. All Web browsers display basic HTML code. When extended coding and features are part of a Web site (such as Java and style sheets), however, not all Web browsers work. The most common browser is Internet Explorer.

Install and Configure Web Server *(continued)*

The Administrative Tools window appears.

12 Double-click Internet Information Services.

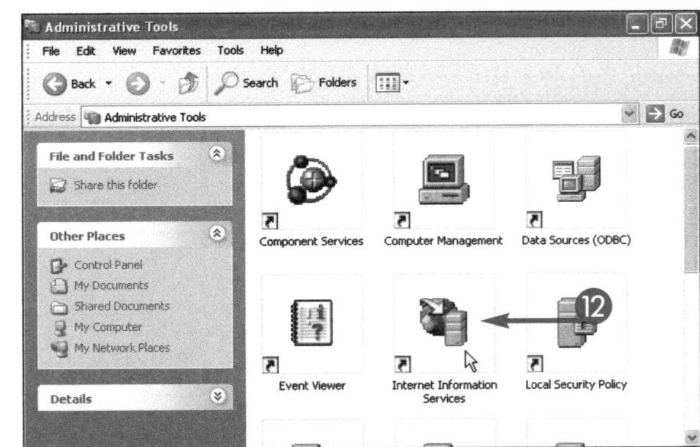

The Internet Information Services window appears.

13 Click the plus sign to expand the list of components in the left pane until Default Web Site is visible.

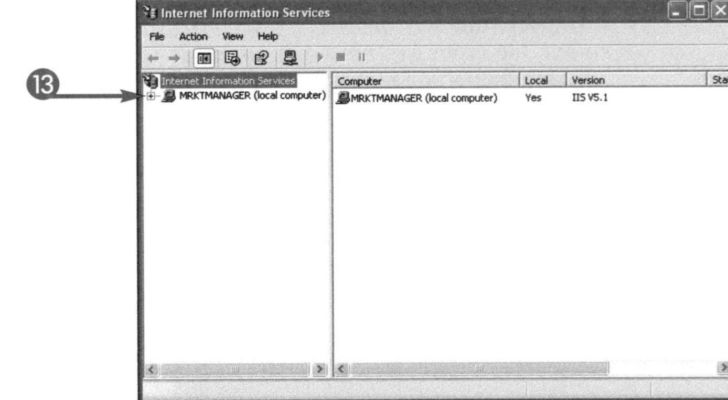

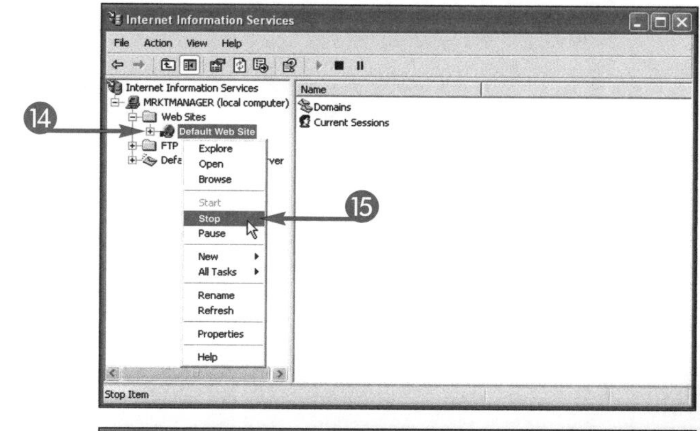

14 Right-click Default Web Site.

15 Click Stop from the menu that appears.

IIS is automatically started when it is installed. You need to stop the Web site, because the default settings can be hacked by another user.

The word Stopped appears next to the name to indicate that it is turned off.

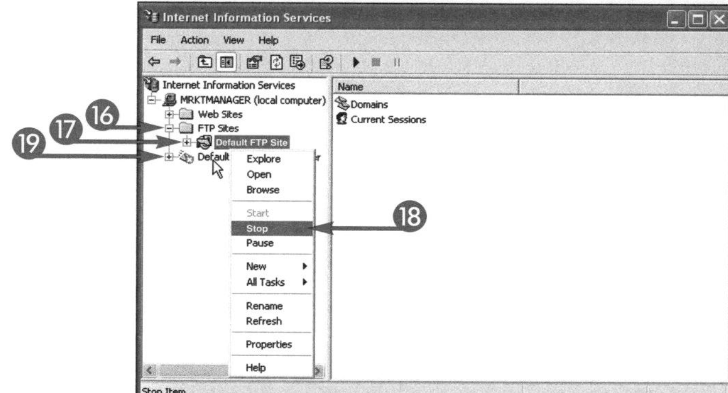

16 Click the plus sign to expand the FTP Sites listing until Default FTP Site is visible.

17 Right-click Default FTP Site.

18 Click Stop from the menu that appears.

This stops the FTP site service for now.

The word Stopped appears next to the FTP site name to indicate that it is turned off.

19 Right-click the SMTP Virtual Server and click Stop to stop its service.

changes to to indicate that it is turned off.

When I create a Web page in Notepad, Notepad will only save the page as a TXT file. How can I change this to HTM or HTML?

▼ The way to do this is to make sure you can see and edit filename extensions. Open My Computer and choose Tools and then Folder Options. In the Folder Options dialog box, click the View tab and deselect the option to hide extensions for known file types (☑ changes to ☐). Click OK. Now you can change filename extensions on all filenames. Create your Web page in Notepad and choose File and then Save. Name your file and click Save. Your file is in TXT format but you can change it. Open My Computer and locate the Web page file. Right-click the file and choose Rename from the menu that appears. DeleteTXT from the filename and add HTM or HTML (it does not matter which extension you use for Web pages). Press Enter and click Yes to complete the name change.

Are there any free HTML editors that I can try?

▼ Yes, there are several that you can download and use for free or try for a specific period of time before you must decide to purchase the product or remove it. One popular and full-featured editor is Serif Web Plus, available at www.freeserifsoftware.com/Software/WebPlus/download.asp. Another place to look for free and trial editors is the Tudogs shareware Web site (www.tudogs.com). You must sign up by using an e-mail address.

continued

Install and Configure Web Server *(Continued)*

You can learn how to create HTML pages by looking at the HTML code of other pages. To do this, when you open a Web page in Internet Explorer, click the View menu and choose Source. This shows the HTML code in a Notepad window.

At first, the code may look a little strange to you. But if you take the time to examine it you should find that it is fairly straightforward in its design. For example, code that appears as part of the Web page falls under the heading named `<html>`.

Anything that is within the < and > are called tags in HTML language. So the first tag in a Web page is the `<html>` tag. If you look at the bottom of the source document, you find a tag that looks like this: `</html>`. Notice the `/`. This means that the tag is an end tag.

Every tag (with a few exceptions) in HTML has an ending tag. So if you want to make a table in your Web page, you add the tag `<table>` to start the table, add your rows and cells using the correct HTML tags, and then end the table with `</table>`.

Install and Configure Web Server *(continued)*

20. Right-click Default Web Site.
21. Click Properties from the menu that appears.

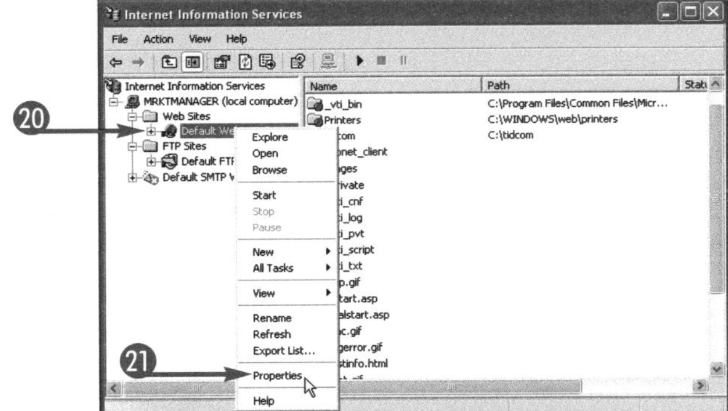

The Default Web Site (Stopped) Properties dialog box appears. You can configure and view settings of your Web site here.

22. Type the name of your Web site.
23. Click here and select the IP address for your Web site.
24. Type the port you want to use for your Web site.

Note: *In most cases, port 80 is what is used. If you are behind a proxy server, you may need to change the port setting set up to the port to which the proxy server always has access.*

25. Click OK to confirm your changes.

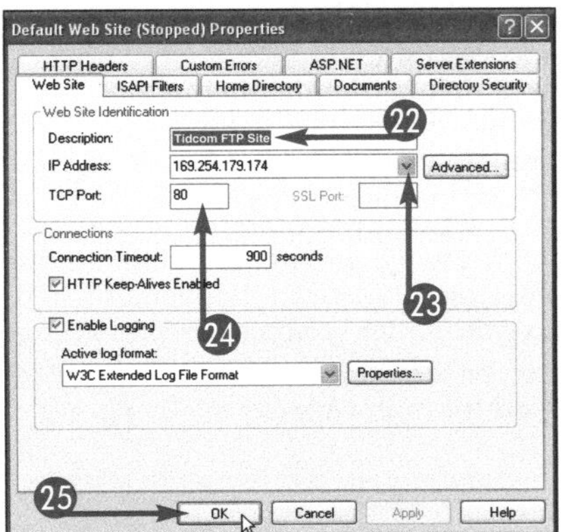

- In the Internet Information Services window, the name of your Web site appears, instead of Default Web Site.

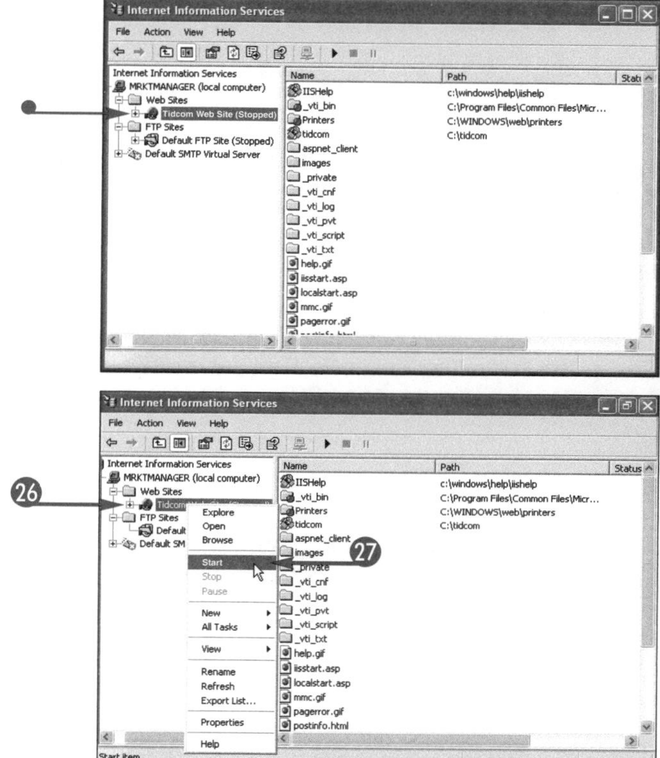

26 Right-click your Web site.

27 Click Start from the menu that appears to restart your Web site.

IIS starts your Web site so you can test it.

I have IIS 5.1 installed and working. However, after so many users connect, no additional ones can get on. Why is this?

▼ IIS 5.1 is not designed for large demand Web sites. In fact, you can have only ten simultaneous connections to the site. If you are running a large Web site and need more connections, you must upgrade your operating system to a network operating system (such as Windows 2003 Server) and use IIS or another Web server software that is designed for high-capacity sites.

How can I find out more about HTML and Web page authoring?

▼ The first place you should start is a site on the Web called W3C (www.w3c.org), or the World Wide Web Consortium. This organization is responsible for approving and expanding HTML and other specifications of the Web. There are also a number of excellent books on the market that can help you understand HTML authoring.

I have read about security problems of hosting your own Web site. What can I do to make sure my IIS site is secure?

▼ As soon as you get IIS set up, there are two directories on your computer you should delete. Open My Computer and delete the directories c:\inetpub\iissamples and c:\windows\help\iishelp. These directories contain sample script files that are vulnerable to hacking attacks.

Install and Configure an FTP Server

With an FTP server, you can allow users to transfer binary files to your Web site. FTP stands for File Transfer Protocol. It is has been one of the most stable and popular Internet protocols since the Internet was created in the late 1960s.

To configure and manage an FTP server, you use the Internet Information Services (IIS) window. You can set identification features of the FTP server, set connection setting defaults, configure site operators, create an FTP site banner message, and set up other features. In this section you learn how to set up the FTP server to get it running.

Once set up, users can transfer files to your FTP server. To transfer files using FTP, you can use Internet Explorer or the built-in FTP Command Prompt tool. For most users, using Internet Explorer is easier because it provides a graphical user interface during the FTP exchange. The FTP Command Prompt tool requires users to type commands to initiate transfers.

Install and Configure an FTP Server

1. Open the Internet Information Server window from the Administrative Tools window of the Control Panel.
2. Click the plus sign to expand the FTP Sites folder.
3. Right-click Default FTP Site and click Properties from the menu that appears.

   The Default FTP Site (Stopped) Properties dialog box appears.
4. Type a name for the FTP site.
5. Click here and select the IP address for your FTP server.
6. Click OK to confirm your changes.

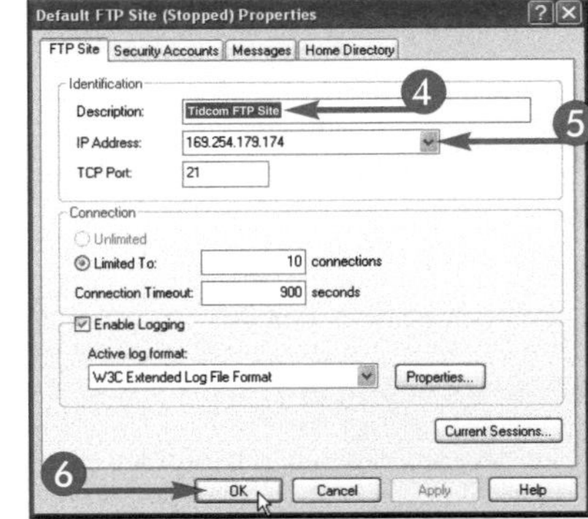

   In the Internet Information Services window, the name of your FTP site now appears, instead of Default FTP Site.
7. Right-click your FTP site.
8. Click All Tasks.
9. Click Permissions Wizard.

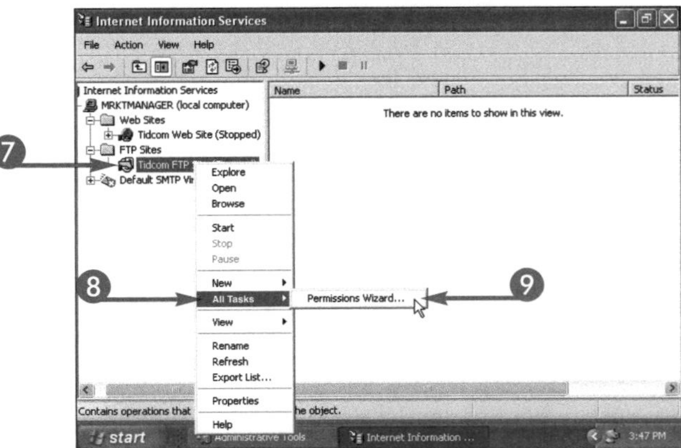

The Permissions Wizard appears.

10 Click Next.

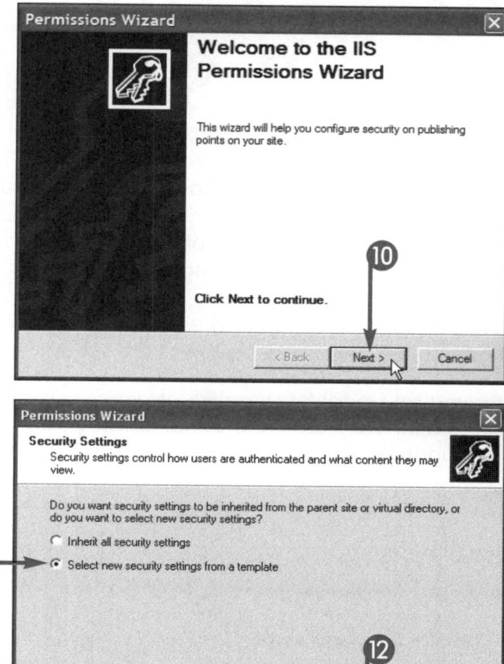

The Security Settings screen appears.

Here you can configure security settings. In some cases, security settings are not set up on a computer, so best practice is to select new security settings now.

11 Click the option to select new security settings from a template.

12 Click Next.

I want to test my FTP server, but am not sure what to do. What are some commands that I can use?

▼ Because FTP has its roots in the Unix operating system, the commands for FTP can be a little intimidating to learn for some users. To start the FTP tool, click Start, All Programs, and then Accessories. Click Command Prompt to start a DOS window. Type **FTP** and press Enter. The command to start a session is **Open** and then the name of the site. To end a session, type **Close**. To see a complete list of commands you can use with FTP, type **?** and press Enter.

What kind of security concerns should I be aware of when hosting an FTP server on my computer?

▼ Just having an FTP server installed on your Web server can open you up to getting dangerous files, including viruses that can damage or delete vital files. You should never allow anonymous users to access your FTP site. Instead, allow only specific users, such as co-workers, technical support people, and other trusted users. You also should run an antivirus program on your computer at all times. This way files are scanned as they are being uploaded to your computer.

continued

Install and Configure an FTP Server *(Continued)*

Windows XP enables you to set up an FTP server on your computer to allow others — usually users from the Internet — to access your computer to transfer files. One of the most important aspects of setting up and running an FTP server is security. Because others will be accessing your computer via FTP, you should pay special attention to who accesses your computer and how folder and file permissions are set up.

When you set up folder permissions, you tell Windows which folders users can have access to. In addition, you can configure which users have access to which folders. For example, you may want outside sales people accessing a folder called SALES-DATA. Other users, such as team managers, may be given access to the SALES-DATA and PROJECT folders.

By setting up file permissions, you tell Windows what types of actions users can take on files. File permissions include read-only, read and write, and full. Read-only permission allows users to download files from the FTP site. Read and write permission allows users to download and upload files to the FTP site. With full permission, users can download, upload, and delete files on the FTP site.

Install and Configure an FTP Server *(continued)*

The Site Scenario screen appears.

13 Select Public FTP Site.

- A description of this type of site appears in the Description window.

14 Click Next.

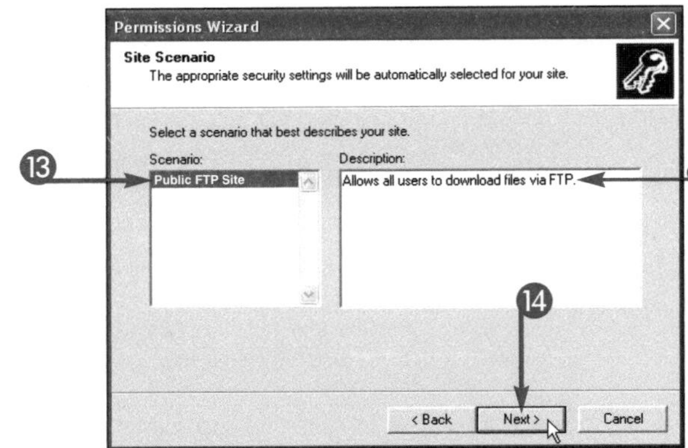

The Windows Directory and File Permissions screen appears.

15 Click the option to replace all directory and file permissions.

16 Click Next.

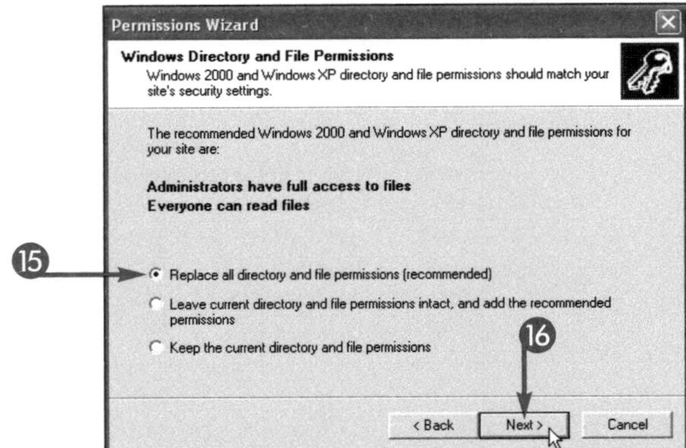

The Security Summary screen appears, listing the security options you chose.

⑰ Click Next.

The final wizard screen appears.

⑱ Click Finish to apply your file and folder permission changes.

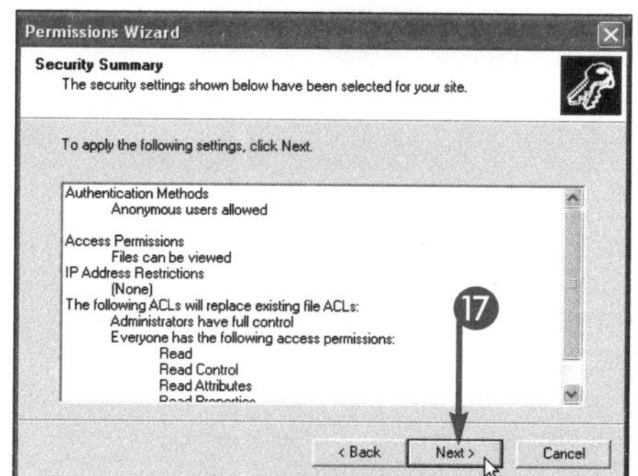

⑲ In the Internet Information Services window, right-click your FTP site.

⑳ Click Start from the menu that appears.

Your FTP site starts.

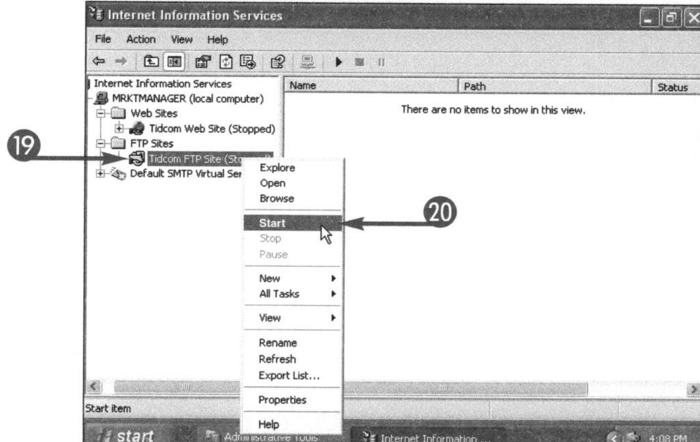

I have IIS installed and started on my computer. How can I test that it is running, including on my FTP server?

▼ An easy and quick way is to use the Ping command from another computer. From the other computer, open a Command Prompt window. Type **PING** and the name of your FTP server. Press Enter. The PING command connects to your FTP server and displays a message that it was successful and shows the connection speed to the FTP server. If the PING command cannot find your FTP server, it displays a message that the host (your FTP site name) could not be found.

I have permissions set up for some folders on my FTP site. How do I copy files to those folders?

▼ When your computer acts as both your working computer (the one on which you do your daily work) and your FTP server, you can simply copy files from other folders into the folders set up for the FTP site. To do this, use My Computer or Windows Explorer. For example, start Windows Explorer by clicking Start, All Programs, Accessories, and then Windows Explorer. Expand the My Computer icon and find the disk (such as C:\) that has the files you want to copy. Expand the folder in which the files you want to copy reside and then copy them to the FTP server folder.

Install and Configure SMTP Virtual Server

IIS 5.1 enables you to set up an SMTP virtual server. SMTP stands for Simple Mail Transport Protocol. SMTP is an Internet protocol that lets users send messages from one computer to another on a network. This allows you to send messages within an organization or across the world using the Internet.

With the SMTP virtual server on your computer, you can host your own e-mail server. As soon as you set up an SMTP virtual server on your computer and start receiving messages, you need an e-mail server (such as Microsoft Exchange Server) to help you deliver and route messages to end-users' e-mail programs (such as Microsoft Outlook or Outlook Express).

Many of the options available on the SMTP virtual server go beyond the scope of this introduction. To fully understand how to configure and run the SMTP virtual server, consult online documentation or a separate book on SMTP.

Install and Configure SMTP Virtual Server

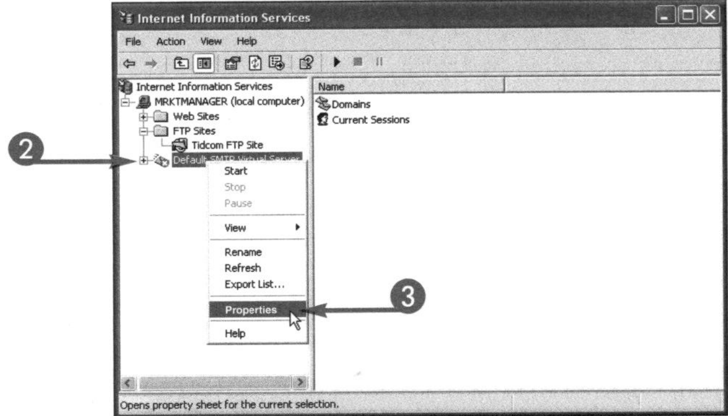

1. Open the Internet Information Services window from the Administrative Tools window of the Control Panel.
2. Right-click Default SMTP Virtual Server
3. Click Properties from the menu that appears.

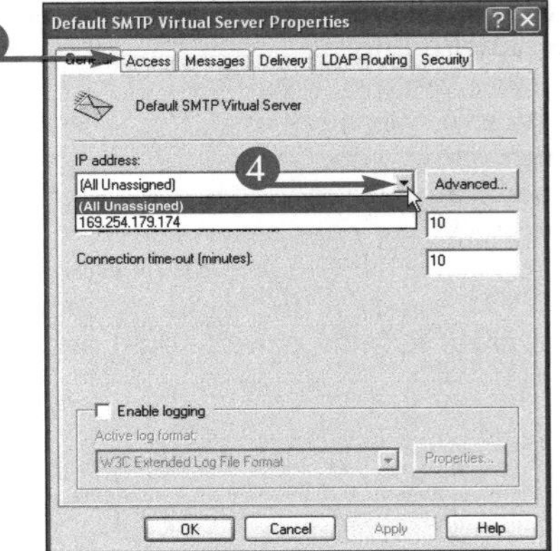

The Default SMTP Virtual Server Properties dialog box appears. This is where you configure and manage your SMTP virtual server.

4. Click here and select the IP address for your SMTP virtual server.
5. Click the Access tab.

6. To select those computers that can relay mail through this SMTP virtual server, click Relay.

   The Relay Restrictions dialog box appears.

7. Click Add.

   The Computer dialog box appears.

8. Type the IP address of the computer.

9. Click OK.

   The Computers area of the Relay Restrictions dialog box now includes the computer you added in Step 8.

10. Click OK to close the Relay Restrictions dialog box.

11. Click OK to close the properties dialog box.

12. In the Internet Information Services window, right-click the Default SMTP Virtual Server item and then click Start.

    This starts the SMTP virtual server, allowing e-mail to be sent and received by IIS.

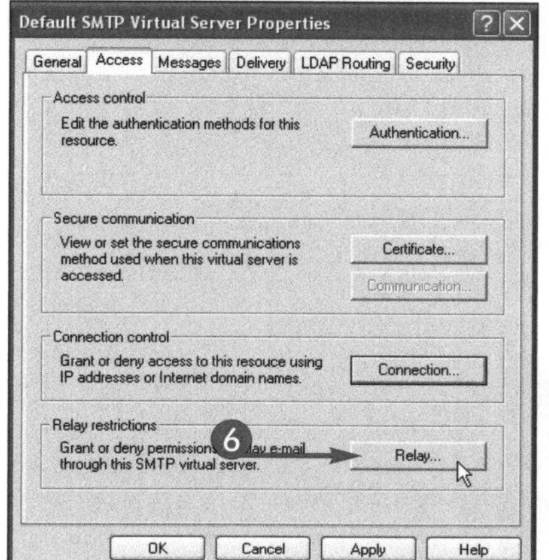

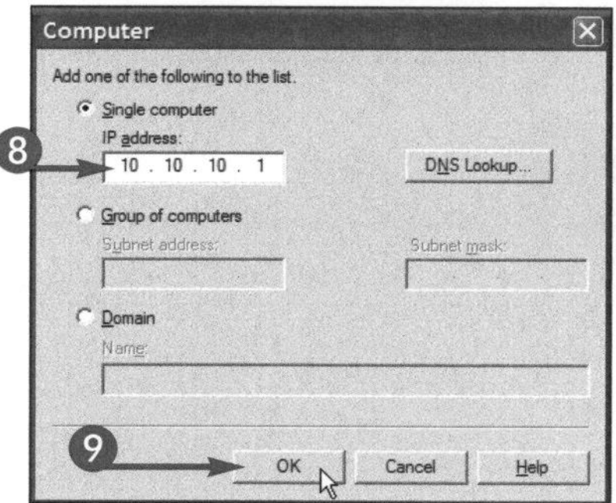

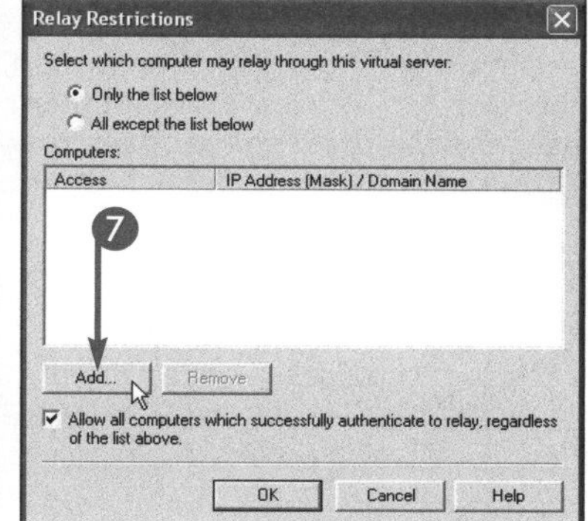

PART III

Do I have to install the SMTP virtual server on the same computer that runs my Web server?

▼ No. In fact, most organizations separate the two servers so as not to overwhelm one computer. Also, because users send and receive messages to your domain name, your SMTP virtual server may be vulnerable to outside attack.

Is there a way to prevent spam from entering my SMTP virtual server?

▼ You cannot stop all spam. However, you can reduce the number of unwanted messages your company gets. Click the Messages tab in the SMTP Virtual Server Properties dialog box and change the option that limits number of recipients per message to a small number, such as 10. This way messages sent to your domain that have a large *bulk* address list (several hundreds or thousands of e-mail addresses) are denied entrance to your site.

A co-worker is trying to send me a large file via e-mail. The message keeps getting returned to him. Why is this happening?

▼ It is possible that the size of the entire message, including the attached file, surpasses the session size setting. On the Messages tab, you can see that the maximum session size is set to 10,240KB, which is 10MB. You may be tempted to increase this setting to enable large file transfers via e-mail. However, you can bog down your e-mail system by doing this. For large file transfers, consider FTP.

Install and Configure Remote Desktop Web Connection

One of the oldest Internet technologies is Telnet. With Telnet, users can connect to and take control of a remote computer. Windows XP Professional includes an optional component with IIS called Remote Desktop Web Connection.

With Remote Desktop Web Connection, you can run remote desktop sessions from another computer. To do this, you use the Internet Explorer Web browser. To use Remote Desktop Web Connection effectively, many companies create client-side applications that work with other applications that are running on a Windows Terminal Server client.

When Remote Desktop Web Connection is installed, a new folder is added to the default Web site folder in the Internet Information Services window. This folder is named tsweb and includes the default.htm file that includes ActiveX controls for selecting the computer you want to connect to remotely.

Install and Configure Remote Desktop Web Connection

1. Display the Control Panel, and click the Add or Remove Programs icon.

   The Add or Remove Programs window appears.

2. Click Add/Remove Windows Components.

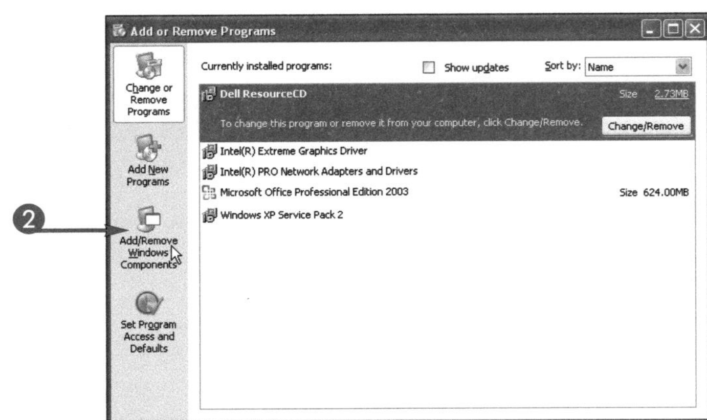

The Windows Components Wizard appears.

3. Click Internet Information Services (IIS).
4. Click Details.

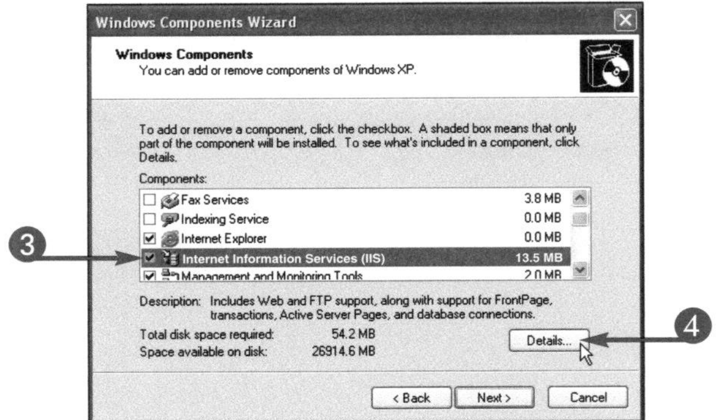

The Internet Information Services (IIS) dialog box appears.

5. Click World Wide Web Service.
6. Click Details.

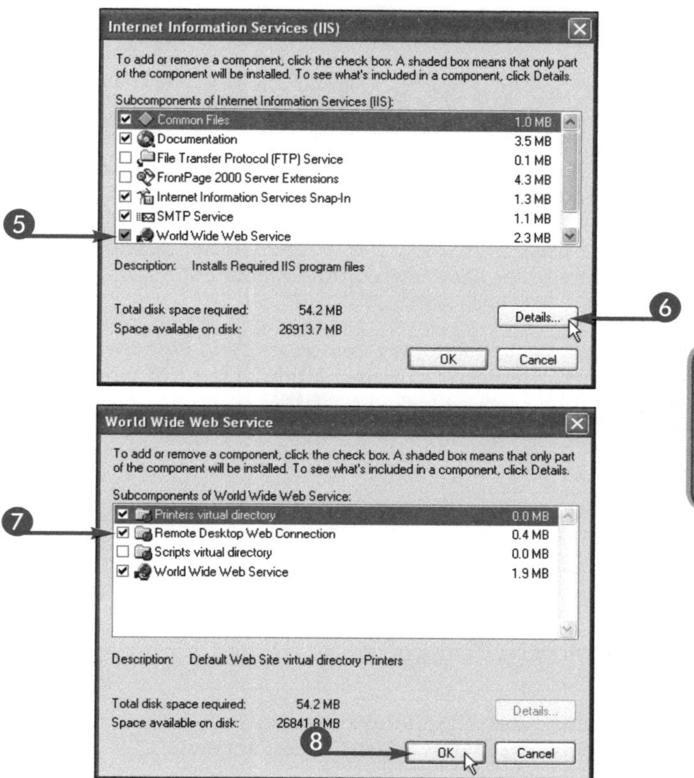

The World Wide Web Service dialog box appears.

7. Click Remote Desktop Web Connection.
8. Click OK to close the World Wide Web Service dialog box.
9. Click OK to close the Internet Information Services (IIS) dialog box.

When I installed IIS, the Remote Desktop Web Connection was not an option to install. Where can I find it?

▼ The Remote Desktop Web Connection install option is almost hidden in the Windows Components Wizard. This task walks you through installing it.

What do my client machines have to do to run Remote Desktop Web Connection?

▼ Computers that connect using Remote Desktop Web Connection must have Internet Explorer 6 or above installed and have ActiveX running. To connect to the Remote Desktop Web Connection server, type **http://*computername*/tsweb/default.htm**, in which *computername* is the name of the computer (or domain name) of the Web server. When a connection is first made, a window appears prompting you to install the Remote Desktop ActiveX Control. Click Install to automatically install these controls from your Web server.

continued

Install and Configure Remote Desktop Web Connection *(Continued)*

Windows XP enables you to connect to remote computers using Remote Desktop Web Connection. Remote Desktop Web Connection can take the place of many of the remote control stand-alone programs that have been on the market for years, including PC Anywhere and GoToMyPC.

When you connect to a remote computer using Remote Desktop Web Connection, the user sitting in front of the remote computer will be locked out of his computer. Only one user — a remote user or a local user — can use the computer at the same time. At any time during the remote session, however, the local user can log back into Windows to turn off the remote control session.

Working with a Remote Desktop Web Connection session can be slower than working in a non-remote session. For example, when you double-click an icon on the remote desktop, you may notice a delay between the time you double-click and the time the icon reacts (such as to start a program). This is due to the connection speed between your computer and the remote computer.

Install and Configure Remote Desktop Web Connection *(continued)*

10. In the Windows Components Wizard, click Next.
11. Click Finish when the Completing the Windows Components Wizard screen appears.
12. Open the Internet Information Services window.

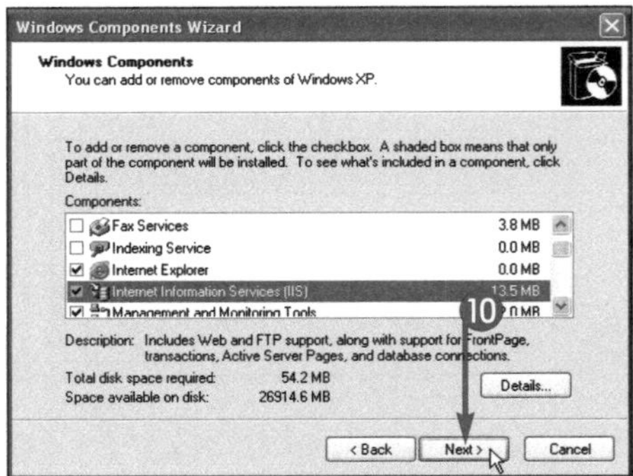

13. Click the plus sign to expand the Web Sites folder.
14. Click the plus sign to expand your Web site folder.
15. Right-click the tsweb folder.
16. Click Properties from the menu that appears.

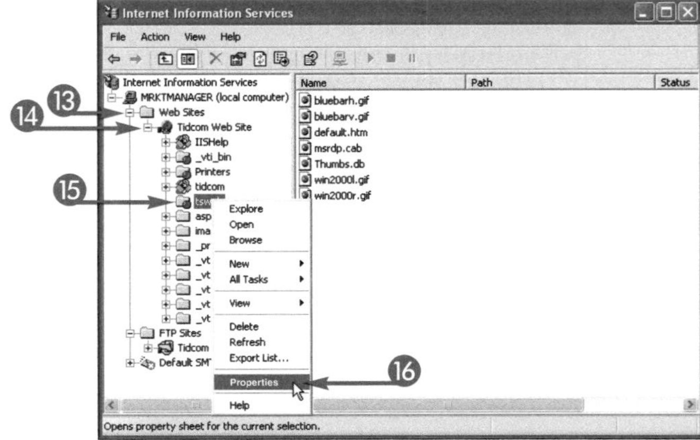

The tsweb Properties dialog box appears. This dialog box includes tabs for configuring and managing Remote Desktop Web Connection. For this example, you check to make sure anonymous access is configured.

17 Click the Directory Security tab.

18 Click Edit.

The Authentication Methods dialog box appears.

19 Click the Anonymous access option.

20 Click OK to confirm your changes.

21 Click OK to close the properties dialog box.

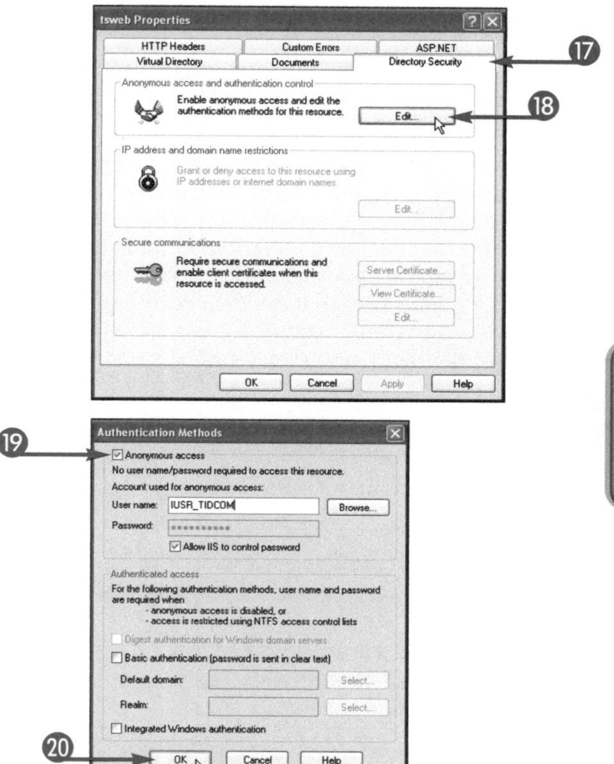

How can I connect to another computer using Remote Desktop Web Connection?

▼ Double-click the Internet Explorer icon on the desktop. In the Address box, type **http://*name-of-computer*/tsweb**. For the *name-of-computer* value, type the name of the computer to which you want to connect. For example, if the remote computer name is MRKTING, you would type this as the full address: **http://mrkting/tsweb**. Click the Go button. The first time you connect with a remote desktop, you may need to install the Remote Desktop ActiveX Control. Click Install to install the control. After the install, the Microsoft Windows Remote Desktop Web Connection Web page appears. Type the remote computer name in the Server box and then select a screen size from the Size dropdown list. Click Connect. The Log On to Windows dialog box appears. Type a valid user name and password in the User name and Password boxes. You may need to ask the owner of the remote computer for this information. Click OK.

Is the Remote Desktop ActiveX Control safe to install?

▼ This software is provided by Microsoft and allows your computer to connect to another one using the Remote Desktop Web Connection tool. It is safe to install on your computer.

Work with FrontPage Server Extensions

You can install and run FrontPage Server Extensions with your Internet Information Services server. FrontPage Server Extensions is a set of programs that extend the capabilities of IIS (and a number of other Web servers) to support advanced Microsoft FrontPage Webs (which are Web sites that are created using Microsoft FrontPage). Some of these extended Webs include hit counters, form handling, and direct Web site editing.

The FrontPage Server Extensions enable users that have Microsoft FrontPage installed on their computers to create enhanced Web sites to publish to their Web sites. The FrontPage Server Extensions enable administrators to configure security for your site, change folders into subwebs (which make it easy to create and manage your Web Site content), and keep track of site usage with counters.

FrontPage Server Extensions are administered from within the IIS interface or from a Microsoft Management Console (MMC) window. The extensions can be managed using commands available on the New and All Tasks menus (right-click your Web site name in IIS), or from the Server Extensions tab on the Web Site Properties dialog box.

Work with FrontPage Server Extensions

1. Open the Internet Information Services window from the Administrative Tools window of the Control Panel.
2. Click the plus sign to expand the Web Sites folder.
3. To enable users to access content using FrontPage, enable authoring by right-clicking your Web site folder.
4. Click Properties from the menu that appears.

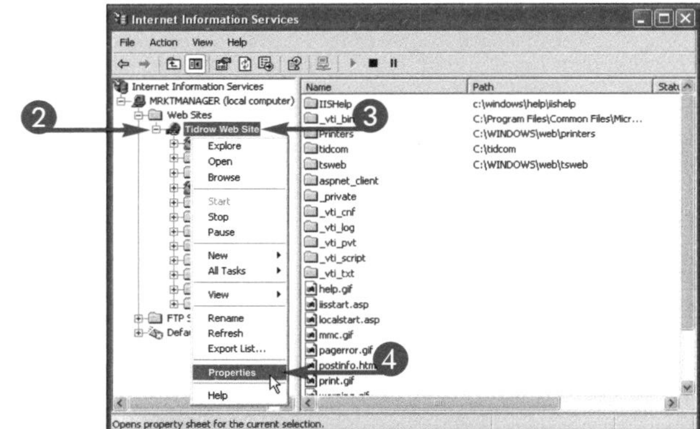

The properties dialog box for your Web site appears.

5. Click the Server Extensions tab.
6. Click the option to enable authoring.
7. Click OK to confirm your changes.

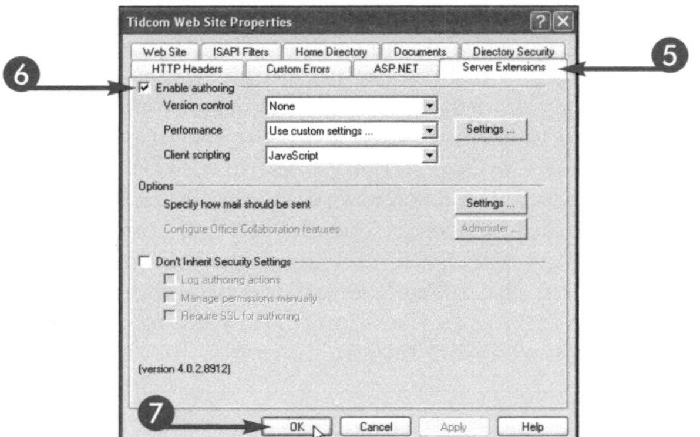

8 To create a subweb using FrontPage Server Extensions, right-click your Web site name in the Internet Information Services window.

9 Click New from the menu that appears.

10 Click Server Extensions Web.

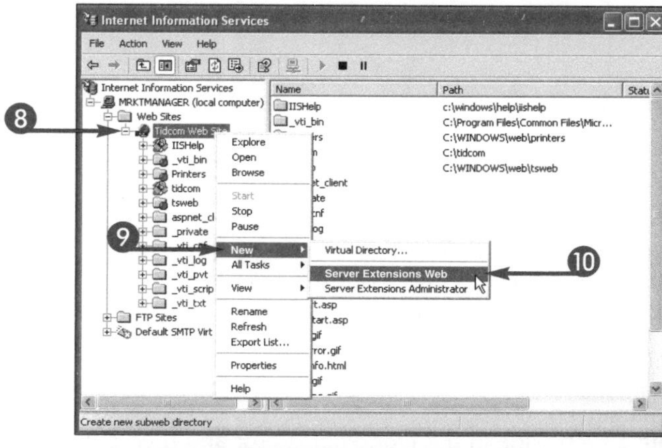

The New Subweb Wizard appears.

11 Click Next.

Is FrontPage included with Windows XP?

No. Microsoft FrontPage is a separate, stand-alone program. You must purchase it through a retailer or contact Microsoft directly to order a copy of it. You can find out more information about FrontPage on the Web at www.microsoft.com/frontpage.

Do I need FrontPage to run FrontPage Server Extensions?

No, but it does not hurt to have it on the server. Many times the server does not include Microsoft FrontPage, just the FrontPage Server Extensions. Client computers usually have FrontPage installed so users can create and edit Web pages. The content is then published to the Web server that includes the FrontPage Server Extensions.

continued

Work with FrontPage Server Extensions *(Continued)*

Windows XP enables you to administer FrontPage Server Extensions. Many of the aspects of FrontPage Server Extensions are transparent to the user; that is, you do not see these extensions doing anything. Instead they help Microsoft FrontPage interact with the Internet Information Server (IIS).

FrontPage Server Extensions have three main tasks. One is to work with Microsoft FrontPage during the authoring and file-management stage of a Web page. FrontPage users can create a Web page in the FrontPage editor and then copy the page to the IIS server from FrontPage.

Second, the FrontPage Server Extensions allow you to administer your site from one location, keeping track of who has submitted files to the Web site (if you have multiple authors for a site).

Third, the FrontPage Server extensions allow WebBots — automated Web site "robots" — to work on your computer. One example of a WebBot is a search WebBot. This type of software navigates through the Internet, going from server to server, looking for information about a search topic. Many times search WebBots run at night looking for and storing information for future searches.

Work with FrontPage Server Extensions *(continued)*

The Subweb Name screen appears.

12. Type the name of the subweb in the Directory Name and Title fields.
13. Click Next.

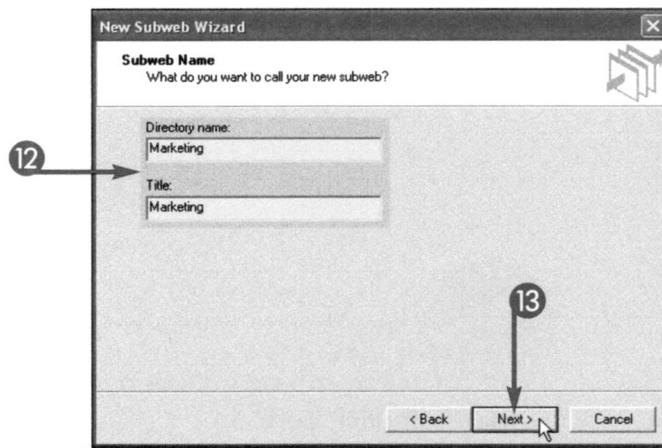

The Access Control screen appears. Here you can specify a new administrator for your subweb, or keep the same one, as in this example.

14. Click the option to specify the same administrator as the parent Web site.
15. Click Next.

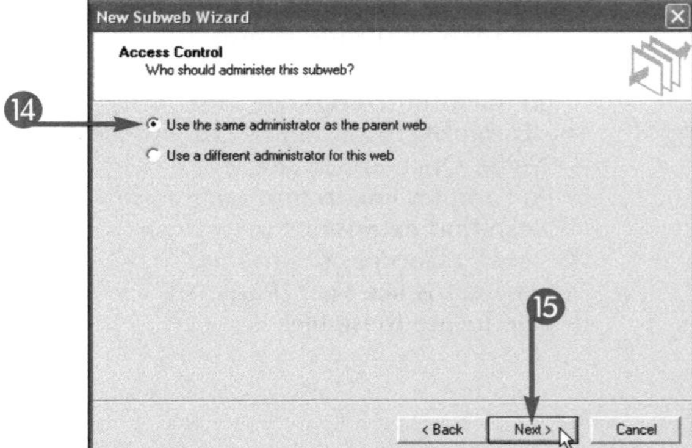

The Completing the New Subweb Wizard screen appears.

⑯ Click Finish to create the new subweb.

The new subweb is created. However, you may not see your Web site listing in the Internet Information Services window.

⑰ To see your new subweb, press the F5 key or click Action and then Refresh.

- Your new subweb appears.

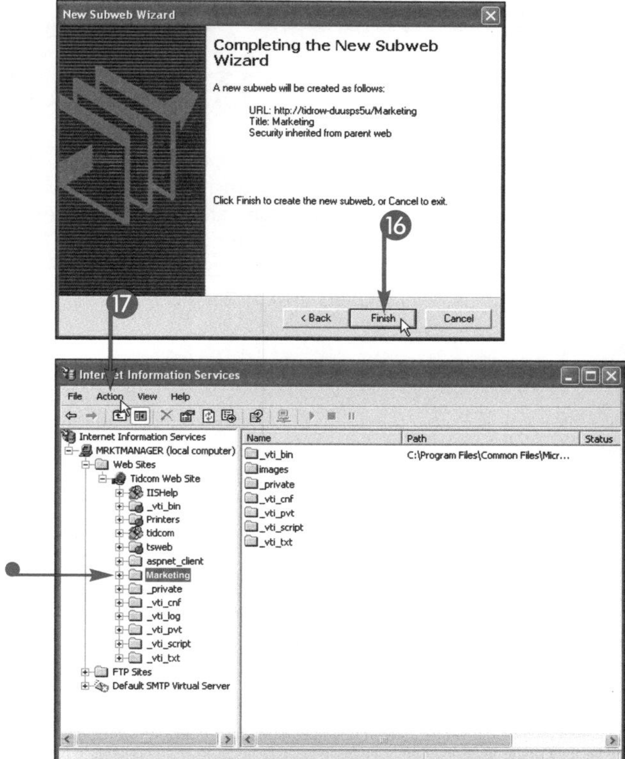

Are there additional FrontPage Server Extensions that I can install on my server?

▼ Yes. Microsoft offers additional FrontPage Server Extensions that you can download from the Microsoft.com Web site. You can also get information about the extensions from the FrontPage Server Extensions Resource Kit at http://msdn.microsoft.com/office/understanding/frontpage. This is the Microsoft Office Developer Center Web site. Once at this site, click the FrontPage Code Samples link to find server extensions. You also can find extensions by searching the Web using Google, Yahoo, or other search sites. Use keywords like **FrontPage Server Extensions** to help locate these files.

If I do not use FrontPage Server Extensions, how else can I manage FrontPage content?

▼ The easiest way is to use a file-management tool such as My Computer or Windows Explorer. With file-management tools, you can open the folders that contain your Web pages and copy them to the IIS Web site location using drag-and-drop or the Copy and Paste commands. However, if you plan to manage a large Web site (one with dozens or hundreds of pages that change often), consider using FrontPage Server Extensions. They allow you to manage and keep track of the changes, deletions, and additions that are made to your Web site. With My Computer or Windows Explorer, you do not get this type of information.

Work with the IIS Snap-In with MMC

The Microsoft Management Console (MMC) is a tool that enables you to view and manage Windows XP snap-ins. Snap-ins are system utilities that help you manage your computer and server. Some snap-ins include Internet Information Services, FrontPage Server Extensions, Event Viewer, and Services.

When you first start MMC, the console window is blank. You then add snap-ins to the console until you have all the snap-ins for that MMC. To keep your MMC view the way you want it, you then save the MMC to a filename. To view and work with the MMC console, open the MMC file. Your snap-ins appear in the left pane of the MMC. Click an item in the left pane to see the particulars of it in the right pane.

Work with the IIS Snap-In with MMC

1. To set up IIS and the FrontPage Server Extensions to use within an MMC console, click Start.
2. Click Run.

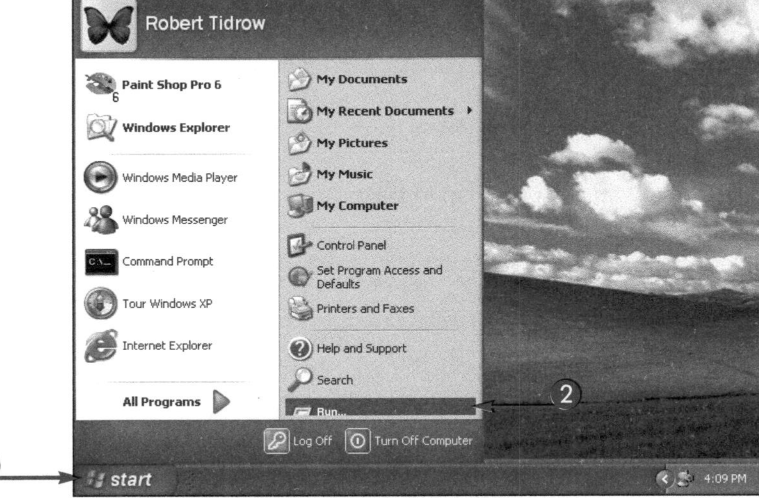

The Run dialog box appears.

3. Type **mmc**.
4. Click OK.

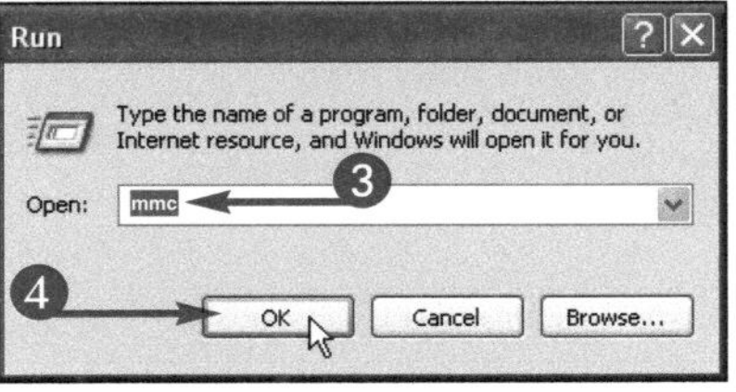

The MMC Console1 window appears. It is blank, but for this task you add snap-ins to the window and then save the console.

5 To add the IIS snap-in to the console, click File and then Add/Remove Snap-In.

The Add/Remove Snap-in dialog box appears.

6 Click Add.

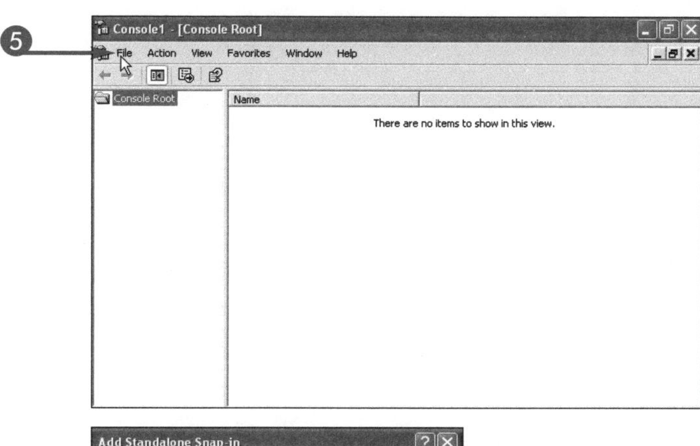

The Add Standalone Snap-in dialog box appears.

7 Select the Internet Information Services snap-in.

8 Click Add.

The Internet Information Services snap-in appears in the Add/Remove Snap-in dialog box.

9 Click Add in the Add/Remove Snap-in dialog box to add another snap-in.

10 Select the FrontPage Server Extensions snap-in.

11 Click Add.

12 Click Close when you have selected the snap-ins you want.

The Add Standalone Snap-in dialog box closes.

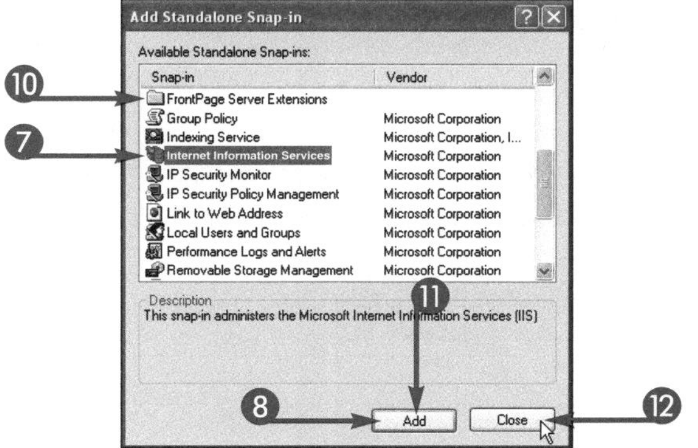

I have several snap-ins I want to manage, but do not want them all in one MMC console. Can I set up multiple MMC consoles?

▼ Yes. Configuring multiple MMC consoles lets you group similar tasks in one window. For example, you may want to include all your Internet server related snap-ins in one MMC. In another MMC console, you may have folder and hardware-related snap-ins, such as the Folder and Device Manager snap-ins.

Can I delete an MMC?

▼ Yes, but in some cases you cannot manage or view settings of a snap-in. Other snap-ins have applets available in the Control Panel or the Administrative Tools folder. For example, if you want to manage IIS, you can use a snap-in or use the Internet Information Services tool in the Administrative Tools folder. When you delete a snap-in, you do not delete settings associated with that snap-in.

continued

Work with the IIS Snap-In with MMC *(Continued)*

When you set up an MMC console, you can save the MMC file to your desktop, Quick Launch toolbar, or other location. You then can quickly open the MMC and manage the snap-ins.

You also have some access control over the MMC console. If the MMC console resides on a shared computer, you can set the MMC so that users have authoring rights, full or limited access. With authoring rights, all users can open, change, and save MMC settings to an MMC console you create. With User mode – full access, all users can access the MMC like the administrator, but cannot add or remove snap-ins.

With User mode – limited access, multiple windows, users can access only the areas of the MMC that were visible when you saved the MMC. Users can, however, open new windows. If you choose User mode – limited access, single window, the users can access only the areas of the MMC that were visible when you saved the MMC. Users cannot, however, open new windows.

Work with the IIS Snap-In with MMC *(continued)*

- The snap-ins you selected in the previous steps appear in the Add/Remove Snap-in dialog box.

⑬ Click OK.

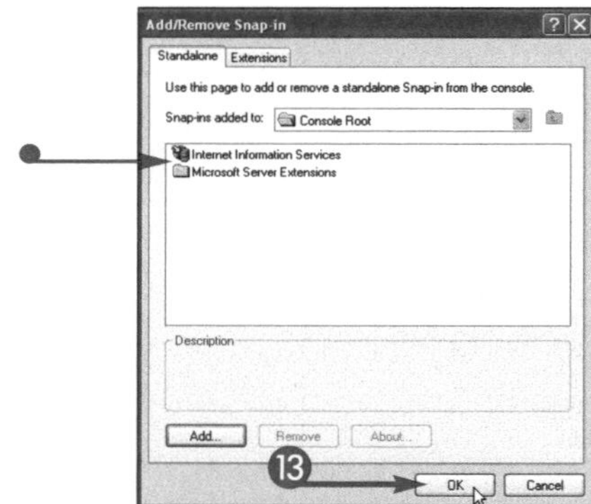

The MMC console window now includes the Internet Information Services and Microsoft Server Extensions snap-ins.

- The left pane includes the snap-in name and folders or object within the snap-in.
- The right pane includes specific items or options you can manage or modify within a snap-in.

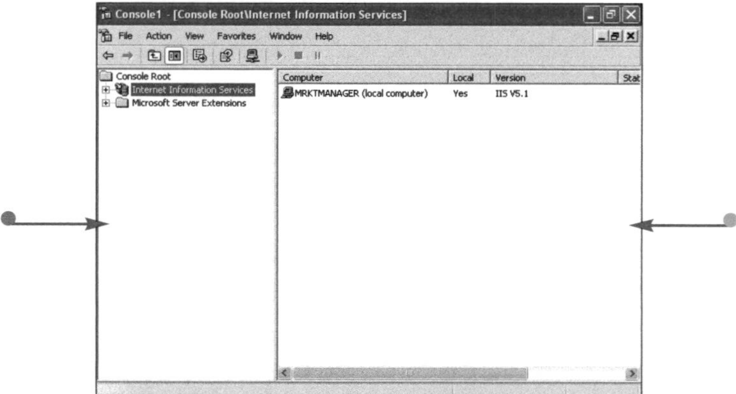

⑭ To save your MMC console, click File.

⑮ Click Save.

The Save As dialog box appears.

⑯ Type a filename.

This example names the console Console1. Windows automatically includes the MSC extension.

⑰ Click Save to save your MMC console.

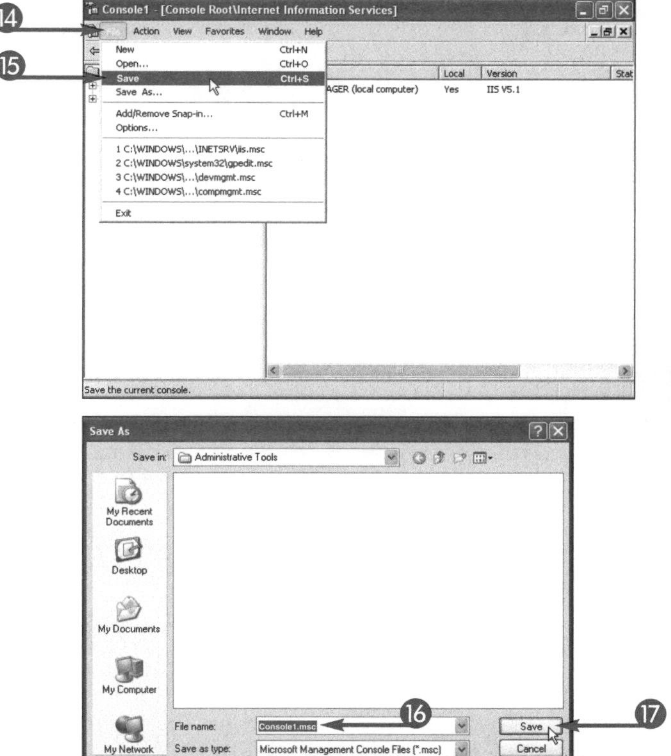

I do not want others to be able to change snap-ins to an MMC. How can I set up limited access to an MMC console I create?

▼ When you have your MMC open, click the File menu and select Options. The Options dialog box appears. Click the Console mode dropdown list and select User mode – limited access, multiple window or User mode – limited access, single window. Click OK to save your changes.

There are some snap-ins that I want to remove. How do I do that?

▼ Open the MMC console you want to modify. Select the File menu and click Add/Remove Snap-in. The Add/Remove Snap-in dialog box appears. In the Snap-ins added to list, select the snap-in you want to remove. Click Remove. The snap-in is removed. Repeat for other snap-ins you want to remove. When finished, click OK to return to the main console window. You need to save your settings, so click File and then click Save. The next time you open the MMC console, the snap-ins you removed are no longer visible.

I have a long list of items in the right pane of the MMC console. How can I get that list without manually typing the list?

▼ You can export the list as a text file. To do this, make sure the items you want to export are showing in the right pane. Click the Action menu and click Export List. The Export List dialog box appears. Type a name for the list and click Save. The exported file appears in the My Documents folder by default. You can open it using any text editor, such as Windows Notepad.

Configure XP for a Domain

Windows XP enables you to connect to a Windows domain. Domains are similar to networking workgroups but provide additional administration and networking features. In addition, when you want to connect to a domain, you must provide proper authentication — user name and password — to be allowed on the domain. Domains are established on a computer running network operating systems, such as Microsoft Windows Server 2003.

To connect to a domain, your Windows XP must have permission to do so. To get this permission, your network administrator must grant you this permission. Permissions include a user name and password that is set up in the Windows Active Directory. Active Directory is the directory service for Windows 2000 Server and Windows Server 2003. It is used to collect and store information about network objects. It is also the main way administrators manage these objects and the server itself.

Configure XP for a Domain

1. Right-click My Computer.
2. Click Properties from the menu that appears.

   The System Properties dialog box appears.
3. Click the Computer Name tab.

   The Computer Name tab appears.
4. Click Change.

   The Computer Name Changes dialog box appears. Here is where you can change your computer's name, as well as change whether it connects to a workgroup or domain.
5. Click Domain.
6. Type your domain name in the Domain text box.

Note: *The domain name can be obtained from your network administrator.*

7. Click OK.

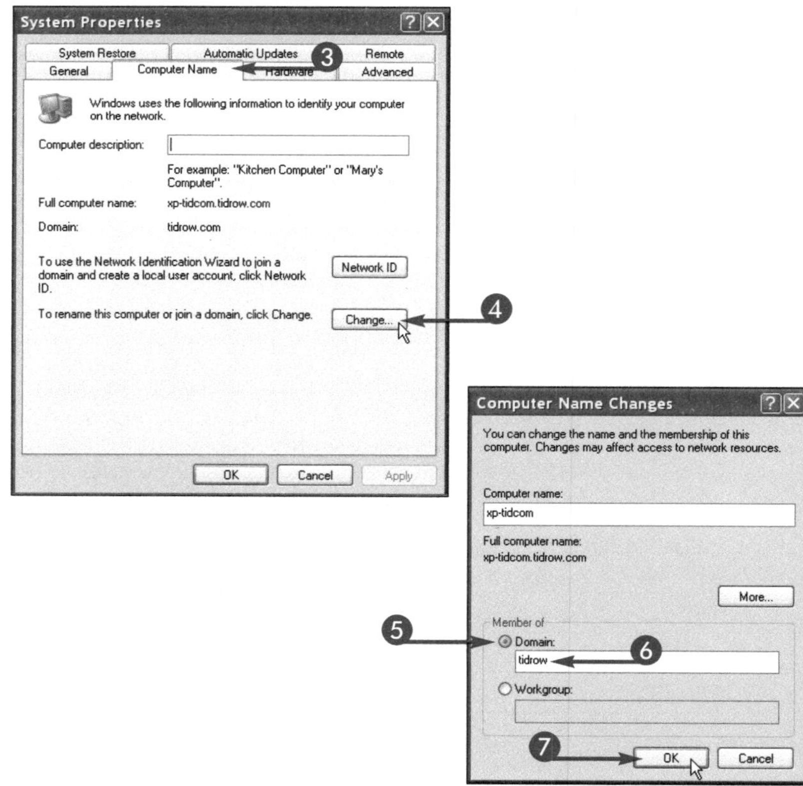

The Computer Name Changes logon appears. You must log on with your user name and password to complete the changes.

8. Type your user name.
9. Type your password.
10. Click OK.

Windows logs on to the domain to authenticate your user name and to ensure your computer has permission to connect to the domain.

11. Click OK when Windows welcomes you to your domain.
12. Click OK to close the Computer Name Changes dialog box.

A message box appears asking if you want to shut down and restart Windows.

13. Click Yes.

Windows shuts down and restarts.

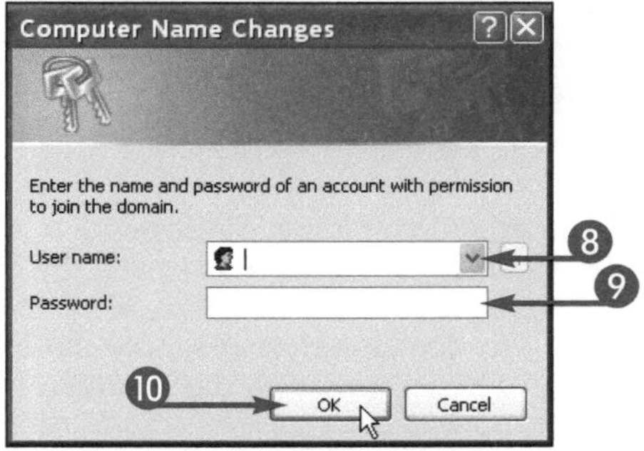

Can I manage features of a domain from within Windows XP?

▼ Yes, but you are limited to what you can do on the Windows XP client. One of the administrator duties you can perform is viewing remote Event Viewer items. This is handy if you want to see information regarding warnings and errors that occurred on the server. To use this feature, open the Control Panel and click Performance and Maintenance. Click Administrative Tools and then Event Viewer. Choose Action and then Connect To Another Computer. The Select Computer dialog box appears. Type the name of the domain server (you need to know the computer name for this server) and click OK. The Event Viewer window shows the events associated with the server.

When I attempt to connect to a domain, I receive a message saying the domain is unavailable. What should I do?

▼ This can be caused by a few things. First, make sure your computer is connected to your network. Second, make sure you type in the domain name, user name, and passwords correctly. Passwords are case-sensitive, so be sure you enter your password exactly as given to you by your network administrator. Another item to look at is the computer name. Each computer on the network must have a unique name. If your computer name is the same as another one on the domain — even if the other computer uses a different operating system — change your computer name.

Connect to a Domain

After you configure Windows XP to reside on a domain, you must connect to the domain. Upon restarting Windows (either after changing from workgroup to domain setup or simply starting your computer to begin working), the Windows logon screen appears. You must press Ctrl+Alt+Del to access the screen in which you can enter your authentication information.

One of the main reasons organizations incorporate domains into their environments is to capitalize on Windows 2000 and Windows 2003 security. Unlike previous versions of consumer-oriented Windows, Windows XP is also a secure operating system. That means if a password is required, and most domains require one, you must enter the password to gain access to the Windows desktop and programs. Previous versions, such as Windows Me and Windows 98, allowed you to bypass the logon screen by clicking Cancel or by pressing Esc. You could then access local files and programs as if you had logged on. (Networking resources still required users to log on to access information and objects, even in a simple Windows 98/Me workgroup network.)

Connect to a Domain

1. Start your computer.
2. When the Windows logon screen appears, press Ctrl+Alt+Del.

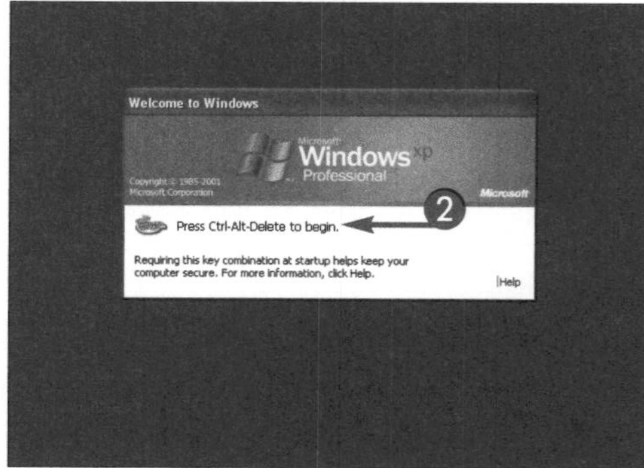

The Windows logon screen changes to show User name and Password fields.

3. Type your user name in the User name field.
4. Type your password in the Password field.
   - If you want to see the domain name, click Options.
5. Click OK.

Windows logs on to the domain and then displays the Windows desktop.

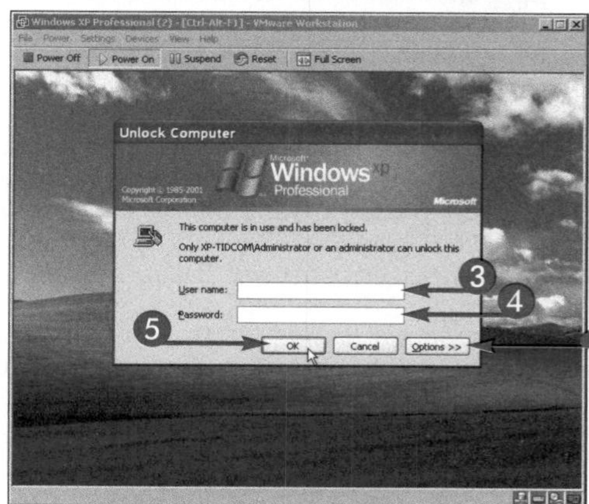

Disconnect from a Domain

Windows XP enables you to disconnect a computer from a domain. This is helpful if you move the computer to a different location that does not require domain authentication, if a domain is removed from your network, or if you perform administrative tasks that require you to be off the domain.

After you disconnect from a domain, you log on to Windows using the Welcome screen or the classic logon prompt. The latter feature requires that users enter a user name and password to start Windows.

To disconnect Windows from a domain, the user must be currently logged on to the domain using an authorized user account. After a computer is disconnected from a domain, the resources available on that domain are no longer available for that computer until the computer is reconnected to the domain.

MASTER IT

How do I know what workgroups are available on my network?

▼ Some organizations keep a hard copy list of workgroups on a bulletin board or in the system administrator's office. If you do not know a specific workgroup name when you disconnect from a domain, create a new workgroup name by typing that name in the Workgroup text box. The default Windows XP workgroup name is WORKGROUP. If in doubt, you can use that name, and you will probably locate other members of this workgroup in your organization.

Disconnect from a Domain

1. Start Windows and log on to your domain.
2. Right-click My Computer and choose Properties.
3. In the System Properties dialog box, click the Computer Name tab.
4. Click Change.
5. In the Computer Name Changes dialog box, click the Workgroup option.
6. Type the name of a workgroup.
7. Click OK.

   Windows disconnects from the domain and connects to the workgroup from Step 6.
8. Click OK when the workgroup is found.
9. Click OK to restart Windows.
10. Click OK to close the System Properties dialog box.

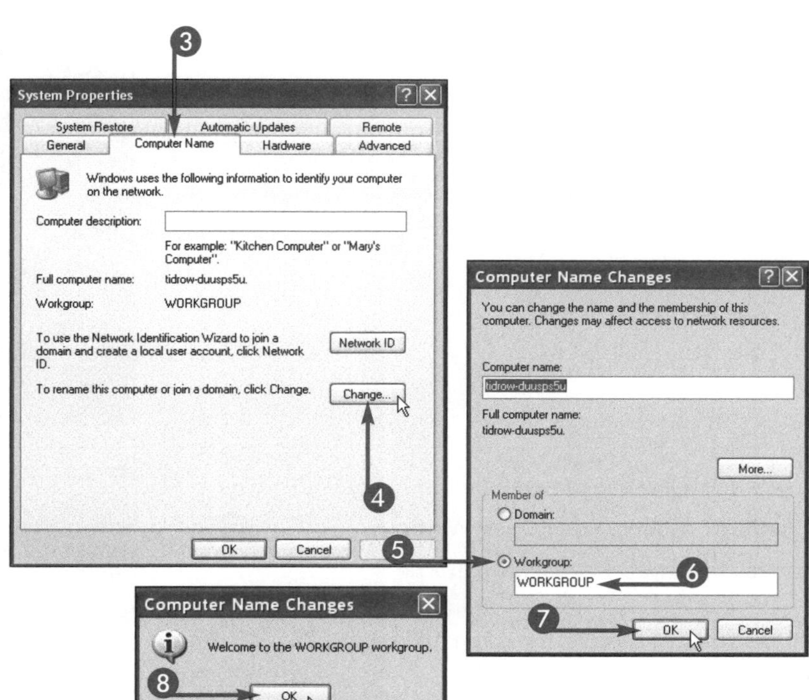

Search for Users

Windows XP SP2 enables you to search for users within your domain. This is handy if you want to find the user name for a particular person in your organization. You also may want to do a search if you are setting up new users for your organization and want to make sure the new users have unique names on the domain. In an example like that, simply search for the proposed new user names. If Windows cannot find a user name, then the new name can be used. On the other hand, if a match is made for the user name you are searching, then you know you must come up with a different user name for the new user.

By default, Windows XP does not provide a program or tool that enables you to search for users. Instead, you need to enter a command sequence to display the Find Users, Contacts, and Groups window. The command is executed from the command prompt, which many users seem a little hesitant to use. However, if you plan to search for users often, consider creating a batch file that executes the sequence automatically for you. You can then place the shortcut on the desktop for convenience.

Search for Users

1. Click Start, All Programs, and then Accessories.
2. Click Command Prompt.
   - The Command Prompt window appears.

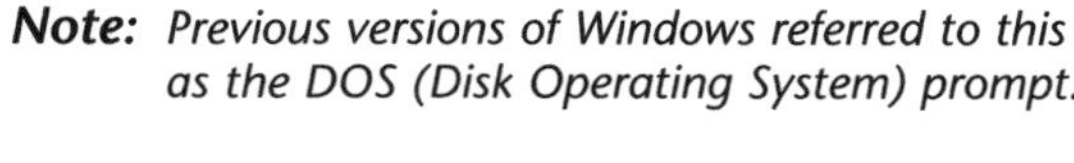

Note: *Previous versions of Windows referred to this as the DOS (Disk Operating System) prompt.*

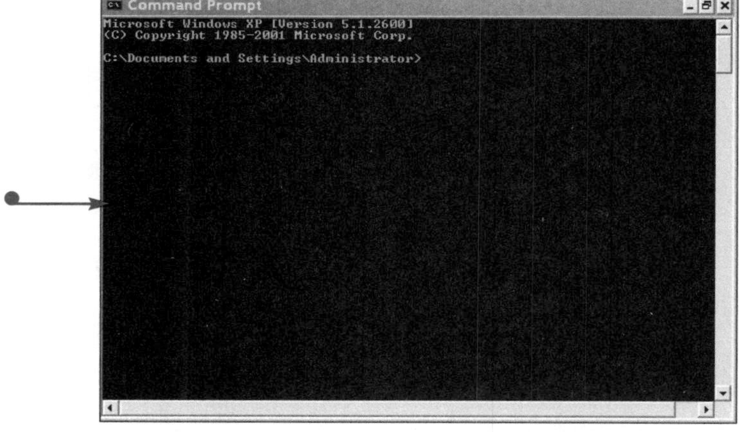

3. Type the following command:

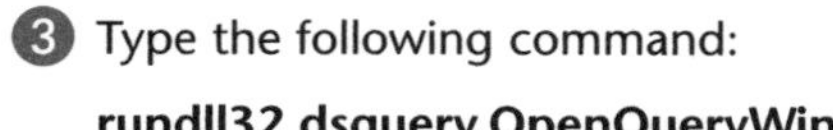

   rundll32 dsquery,OpenQueryWindow

Note: *You must type the command exactly as shown.*

4. Press Enter to execute the command.

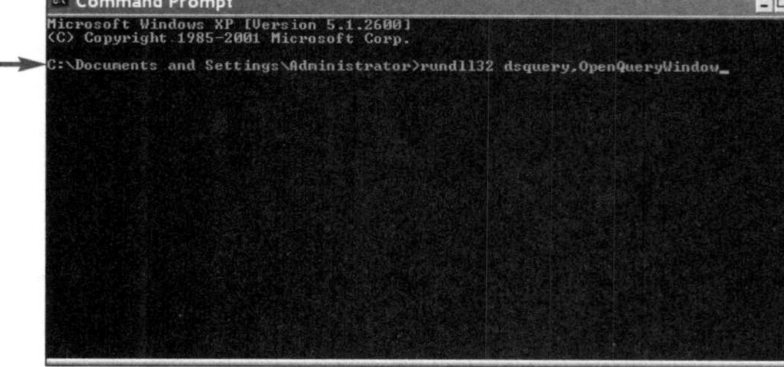

The Find Users, Contacts, and Groups window appears.

5 In the Name text box, type the name of the user you want to find.

6 Click Find Now.

If a user is found in the domain that matches the name you entered, Windows displays it in the found area of the Find Users, Contacts, and Groups window.

7 Click here to close the window.

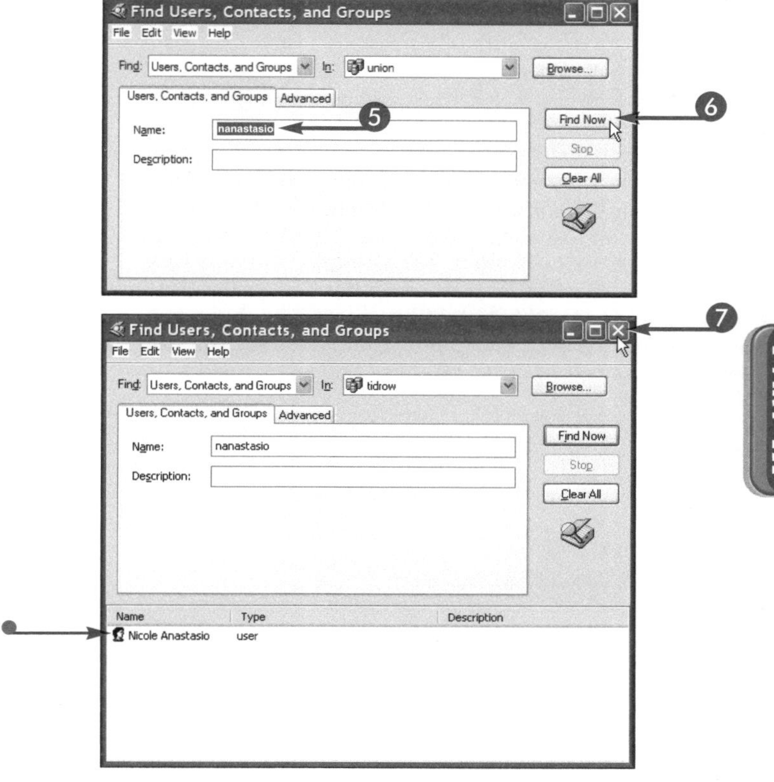

You mention creating a shortcut to a batch file. How do I do that?

▼ Right-click the Windows desktop, click New and then Text Document. Press Enter to open the new blank text document. Type **rundll32 dsquery,OpenQueryWindow** all on one line of the document. Choose File and then Exit. Click Yes when prompted to save the file. Right-click the file on the desktop and choose Rename. Type **searchuser.bat** for the new filename. You are prompted that you are changing the filename extension from .txt to .bat. Click Yes to continue. (If you do not see a filename extension, you can show these by opening My Computer, clicking Tools and then Folder Options. On the View tab, clear the option for Hide extensions for known types. Click OK.) After you create the Searchusers.bat file, click (or double-click) it to run it. The batch file allows you to launch the Find Users, Contacts, and Groups window without re-typing the long command sequence each time.

On the Advanced tab of the Find Users, Contacts, and Groups window, I see a dropdown list called Field. On the Field list is an option for Group. What is a domain group?

▼ A domain group is a collection of users, computers, and other groups. The network administrator can create groups to help manage security permissions and e-mail distribution lists. Users can be in one group or be put into many groups depending on the rights they need. For example, some users have only standard user permissions, while others may have standard permissions as well as power user permissions.

Search for Printers

Another useful feature of Windows XP that you can use in a domain is to search for shared printers. Many organizations set up shared printers so several users can use one printer. Also, shared printers allow one user to use many printers. For example, you may have a laser printer attached to your computer that only prints in black and white. Another user, who may be down the hall from you, may have a color printer that is shared. You can connect to the color printer for those times you need a color printout.

When you search for printers over a domain, Windows sends a request out over the network to return all printers who are set up as shared. Depending on the size of your network, speed of connections, the number of shared printers, and speed of your computer, this search may take several minutes to complete.

When a printer is found, you can set up the printer on your computer so you can access it for printing.

Search for Printers

1. Click Start and then click the Printers and Faxes icon.

   The Printers and Faxes window appears.

2. Click the Add a printer link in the Printer Tasks pane.

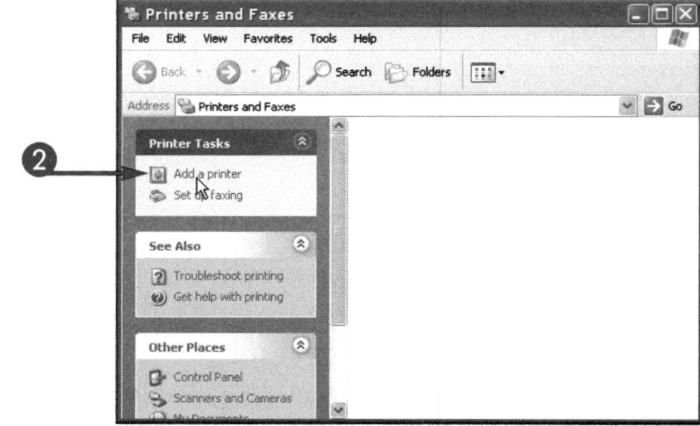

   The Add Printer Wizard appears.

3. Click Next.

   The Local or Network Printer screen appears.

4. Click the network printer option.
5. Click Next.

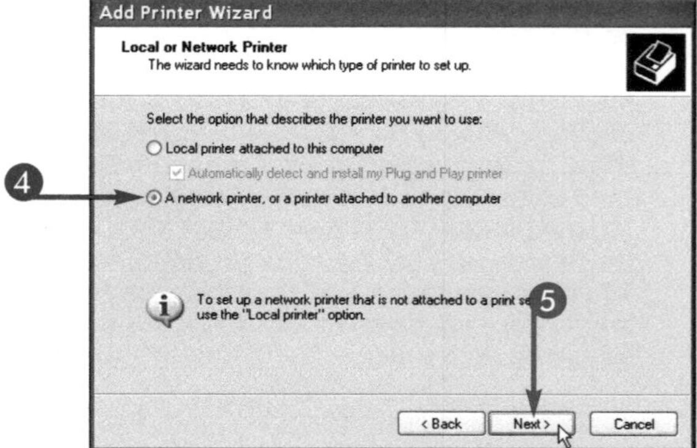

The Specify a Printer screen appears. Here you can search for a printer, specify a printer to connect to, or specify a printer using an Internet address.

6 Click the option to find a printer in the directory.

7 Click Next.

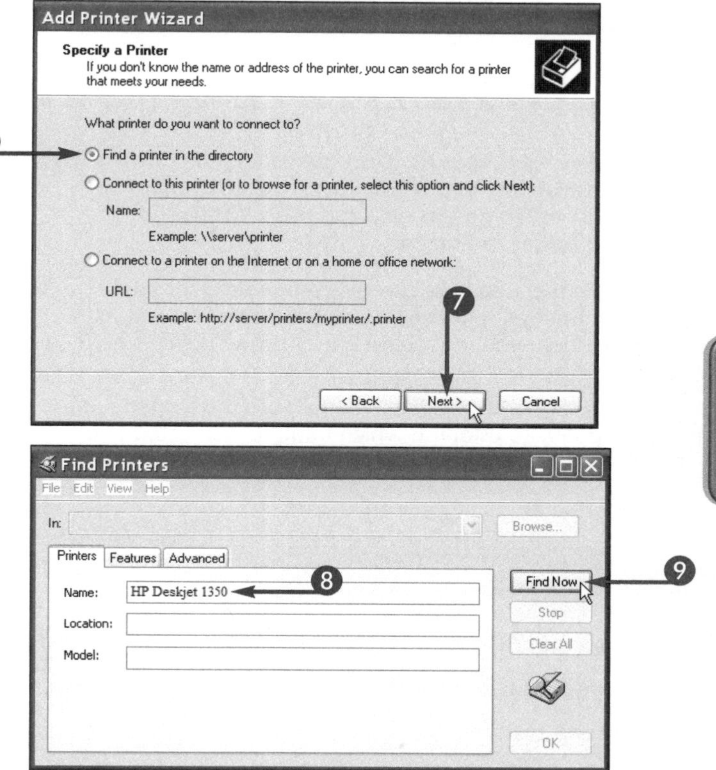

The Find Printers window appears. Here you can search for printers by name, location, or model.

8 In the Name text box, type the name of the printer.

9 Click Find Now.

Windows lists the printer if a match is made.

10 Click OK to continue setting up the printer.

Last week I set up a network printer but now I cannot print to that printer. What can I do?

▼ Here are a couple of things to do. First, make sure you are connected to the domain properly. Look for a shared file or folder, or try to access your corporate e-mail. If all these things are okay, make sure the shared printer is turned on. This may mean you need to walk around to the printer and check its power switch. Or if the printer is situated next to someone in your office, ask them if the printer is turned on. Another problem that may exist is that the printer connection needs to be reestablished on your computer. Usually this means running the Add Printer Wizard again and setting up the printer (as shown in this task). Sometimes printer connections are deleted or corrupted, requiring you to reconfigure the printer.

I know a printer is on the network, but I cannot find it using the search feature. How do I find it?

▼ To find a printer on the network requires that the printer be shared and be listed in the directory. When the printer is set up, these options are configured. If these conditions are not met, the printer will not show up in the search window. Ask your network administrator for help.

Redirect the My Documents Folder

You may want your My Documents folder to always be available to you regardless of the computer you log on to. To do this, you can use a Windows XP feature called Folder Redirection.

With Folder Redirection, you can redirect a folder (in this case My Documents) so it is on a network server. To use Folder Redirection, you must have a user group policy set up. Group policies are discussed in Chapter 6.

After a user group is established, you can use the Folder Redirection policy to establish which folder is redirected and to which location the folder is redirected. Usually the folder is redirected to the main server that the user normally accesses. For example, if you have a mobile user on your sales team who generally logs on to a server to download sales worksheets at his home office, you can locate the redirected folder on that server as well. This way Windows does not have to access multiple servers when a user logs on at the home office.

In addition, the user must be logging on to a server that is part of a domain. This means that you cannot redirect a folder when you are part of a peer-to-peer network.

Redirect the My Documents Folder

1. Click Start and then Run.

   The Run dialog box appears.

2. Type **gpedit.msc**.
3. Click OK.

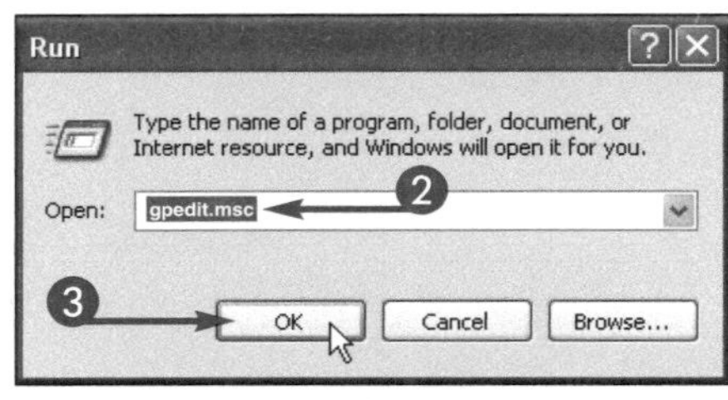

   The Group Policy editor appears.

4. Click User Configuration.

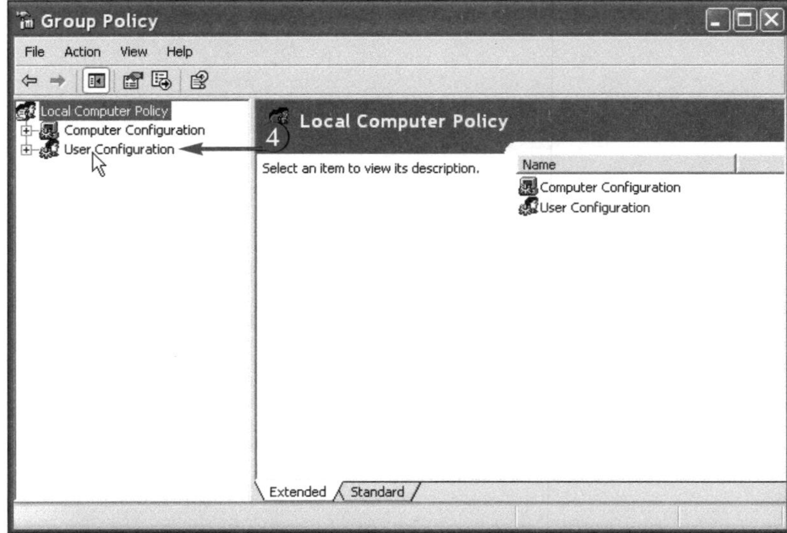

The User Configuration options expand.

5. Click Windows Settings.

   The Windows Settings options expand.

6. Right-click the folder that you want to redirect (Application Data in this example), and then click Properties.

   The folder properties dialog box appears.

7. Click the Target tab.

   The Target tab appears.

8. In the Setting area, click here and select the basic option to redirect everyone's folder to the same location.

9. In the Target folder location area, click here and select the option to redirect to the local user profile location.

10. Click OK to confirm your changes.

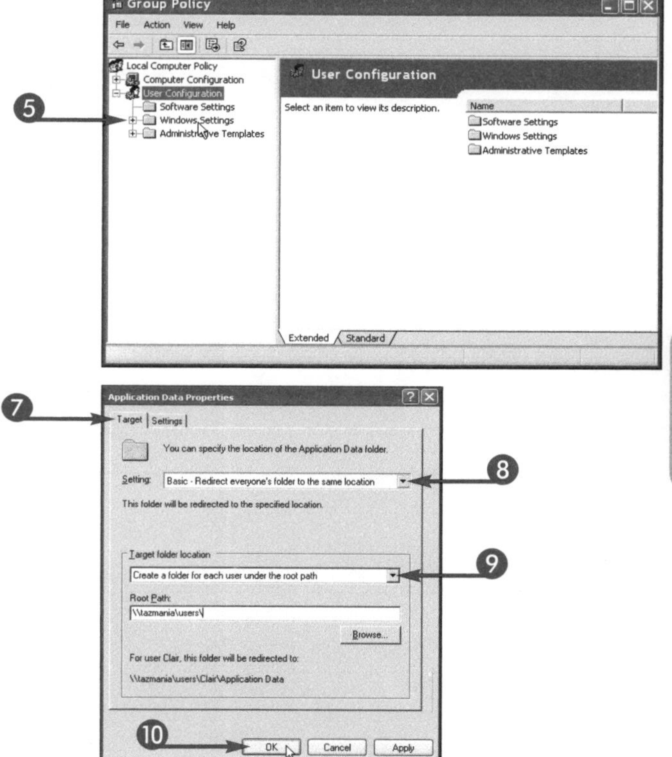

As the system administrator, I have to set up each of the redirected folders. Each user has several folders I want to redirect. Can I do them in a batch?

▼ Unfortunately, Windows requires that you set up each redirected folder separately. You also must redirect each user's folders separately. This can take some time, so do not plan on doing them all in one morning if you have dozens of users, each requiring several folders to be redirected.

I plan to use roaming profiles and redirected folders on my network. What kind of performance issues do I have to consider?

▼ Good question. Roaming profiles can consume a great deal of resources (real memory and processor cycles). The main reason for this is that anything stored by the users onto their computers — files, environment changes like desktop changes, and so on — are saved to the network server. Each time the user logs on, those files must be downloaded to the local computer. For this reason, consider establishing limits to the amount of information that a user can save to his My Documents folder (such as 30MB). This way the user must pare down his saved files when he reaches that threshold. Also, let your users know about this limitation, so they are not surprised by it when the limit is reached. Finally, tell users not to store large files, such as video files, on their desktops. This way the larger files are not sent back and forth from the server each time the user logs on.

14 Working with Windows Internals

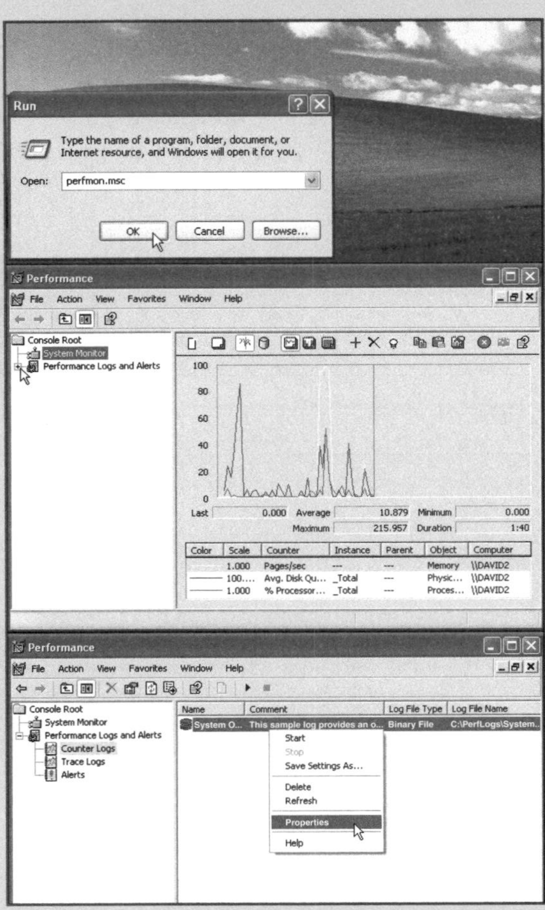

15 Working with Hard Drives

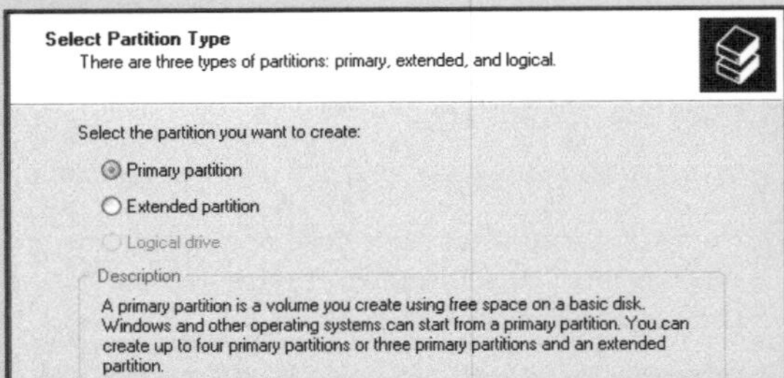

16 Managing Portable Computers

PART IV

MANAGING THE HARDWARE ENVIRONMENT

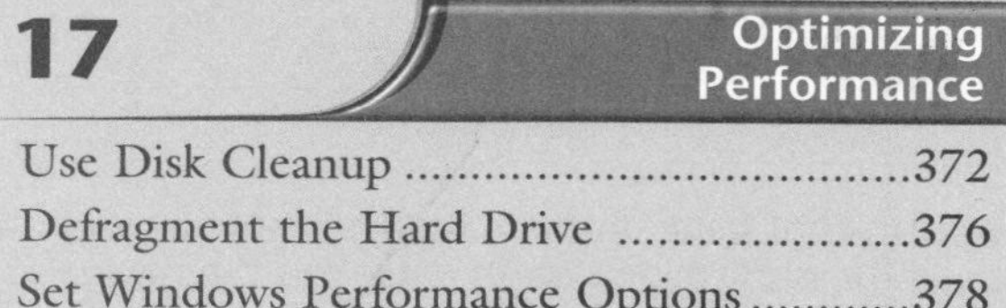

17 Optimizing Performance

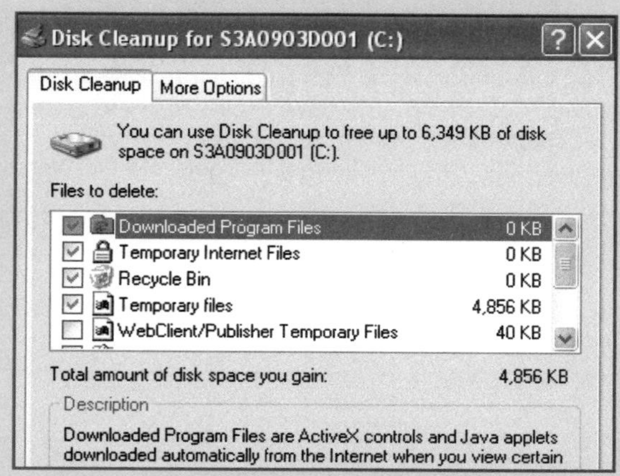

18 Troubleshooting Windows XP

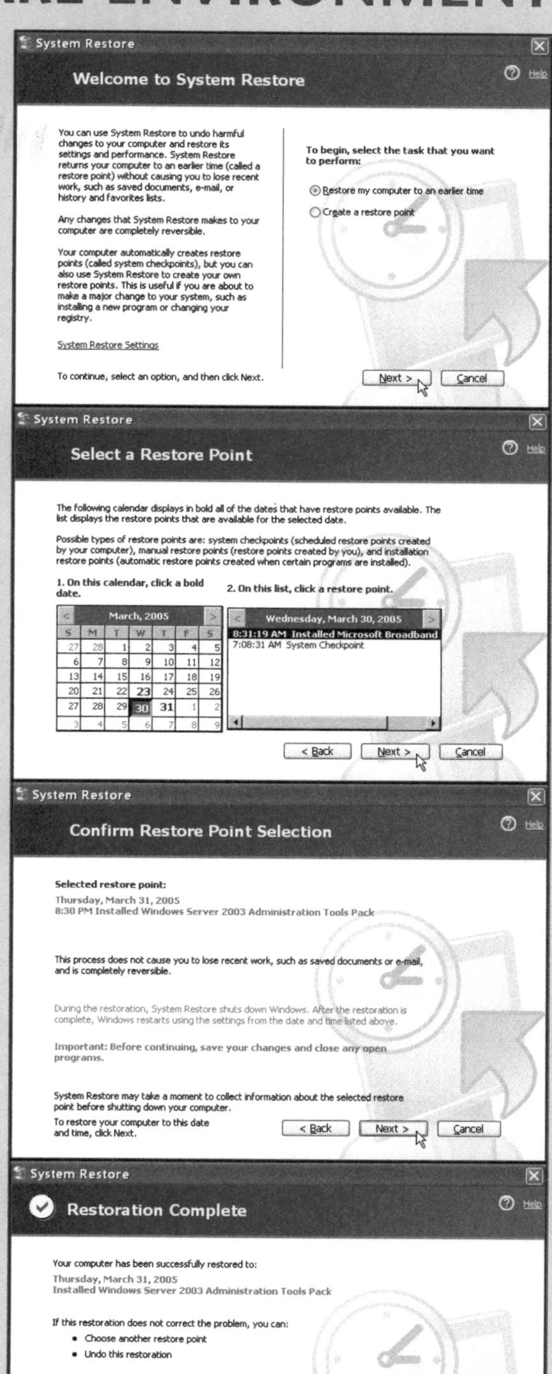

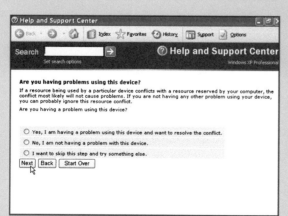

Display System Information

You can readily view information about your PC using the System Information tool. You can launch the tool either from the Run command by typing **msinfo32.exe** or by navigating from the Start menu through All Programs, Accessories, and then System Tools. (A more basic command-line tool also exists, if you prefer. It is called systeminfo.exe, and includes a subset of the information available in the System Information graphical tool.)

When you launch the System Information tool, it searches for and collects pertinent system data and then displays the System Summary information. With System Summary selected, the right pane of the System Information window displays all the most basic system data. You can navigate the tree structure in the left pane to find the information you are looking for by category, or you can use the Search feature to find all instances of a text string. From the File menu, you can export data displayed to a text file or print it. From the Tools menu, you have access to these system tools: Net Diagnostics, System Restore, File Signature Verification Utility, DirectX Diagnostic Tool, and Dr. Watson.

Display System Information

1. Click Start and then Run.
2. Type **msinfo32.exe**.
3. Click OK.

The System Information window appears.

- System Summary lists basic system information.
- Detailed additional system information is grouped by categories that can be viewed by expanding the tree (clicking the + sign) and then selecting a subcategory.
- Additional system tools such as Net Diagnostics are found on this menu.

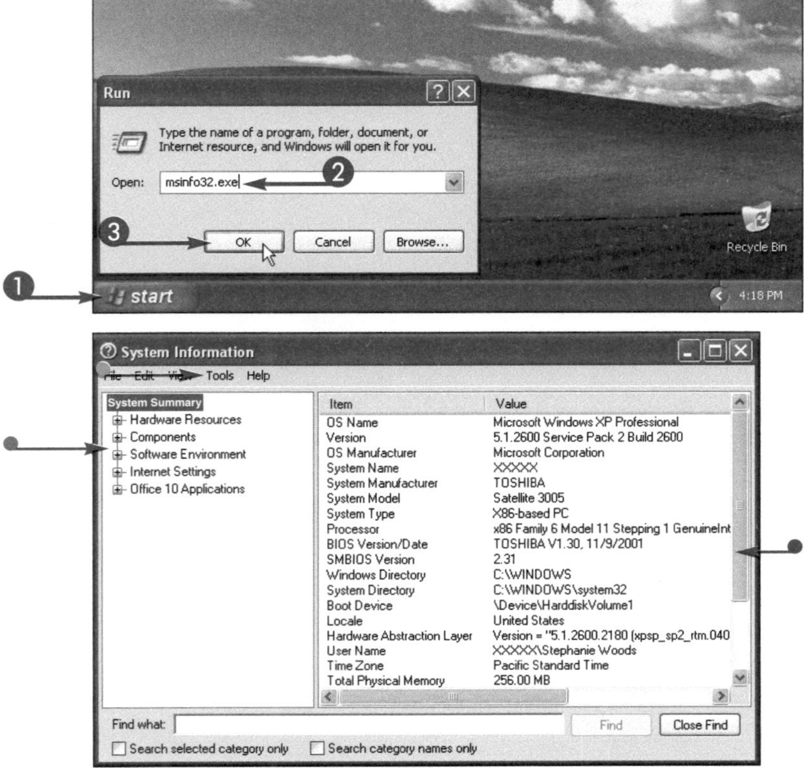

4 Type a text string here (**NTFS** in this example).

5 Click Find.

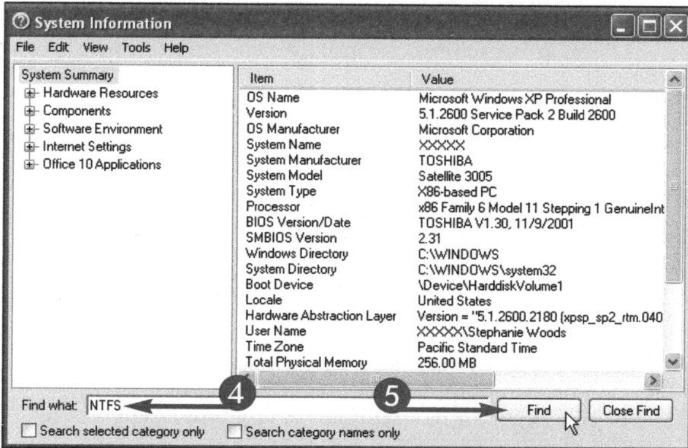

The System Information tool takes you to the first instance of NTFS.

6 Click to find the next instance of the text string you typed.

7 Click here to exit System Information.

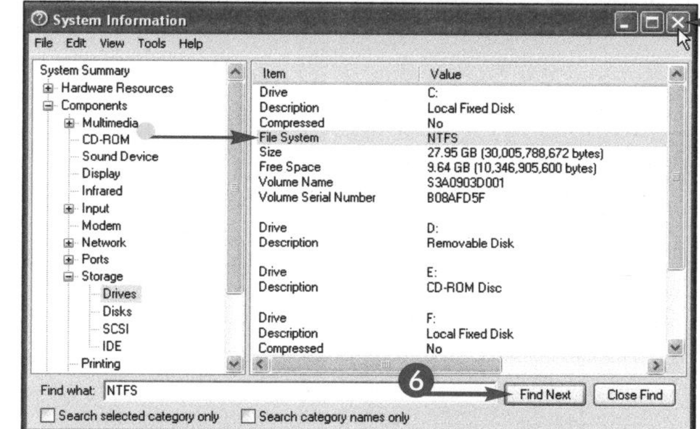

Can I find information about hardware conflicts and problems here?

▼ Yes. Click Hardware Resources in the navigation pane and then click Conflicts/Sharing to review resource conflicts. You can also click Components and then click Problem Devices. If any plug and play devices have problems, you see a list with the description of the device, a PNP Device ID, and the relevent error code.

Can I find my IP address here?

▼ Yes. In the navigation pane, click Components, Network, and then Adapter. You see your IP address, subnet mask, and other relevent information.

Manage Devices

You can manage components of your PC's hardware and logical devices with Device Manager. To access the Device Manager tool, right-click My Computer and click Manage to bring up the Computer Management window. From there you can click Device Manager to display a list of categories of devices connected to your PC, including mouse, keyboard, disk drives, network cards, display adapters, and so on. Each category has a plus sign (+) to its left; clicking + expands the tree and shows individual devices within any given category.

For each device, you can perform several operations, depending on the type of device. By right-clicking the individual device, you can scan for hardware changes, update the device's driver, uninstall the driver, or disable or enable the device. You can also click Properties to bring up a dialog box for the device in question, usually with several tabs (depending on the device). The first tab to display, the General tab, has a device status box indicating whether the device is working properly. From this tab you can disable or enable the device. Click the Driver tab to view the version and origin of the driver, and to update, roll back, or uninstall a driver.

Manage Devices

1. Click Start.
2. Right-click My Computer.
3. Click Manage.

The Computer Management window appears.

4. Click Device Manager in the left navigation pane.
   - A list of device categories is displayed in the right pane.

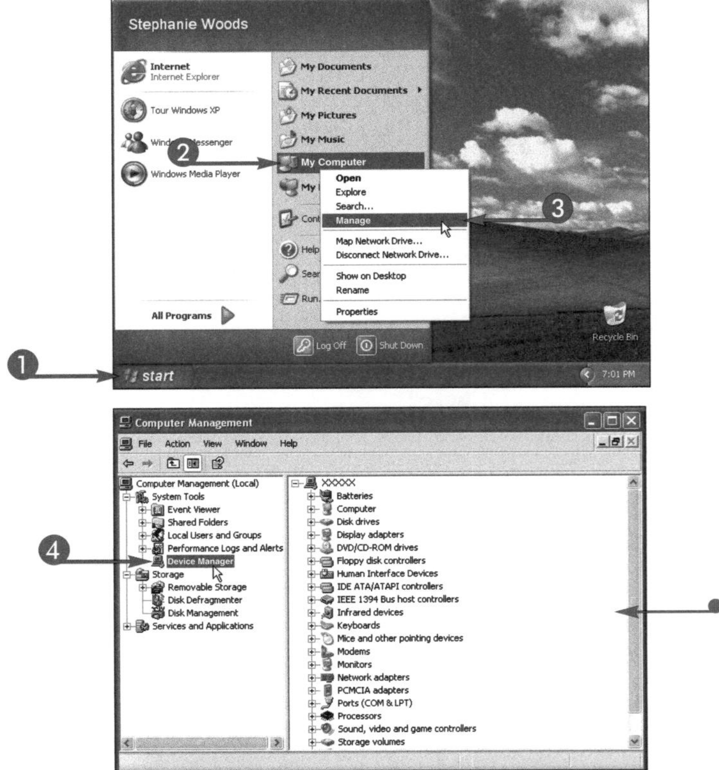

5 Click the plus sign next to a device category (Display adapters in this example) to view the individual devices in that category.

6 Right-click a device (NVIDIA GeForce2 Go in this example).

7 Click Properties.

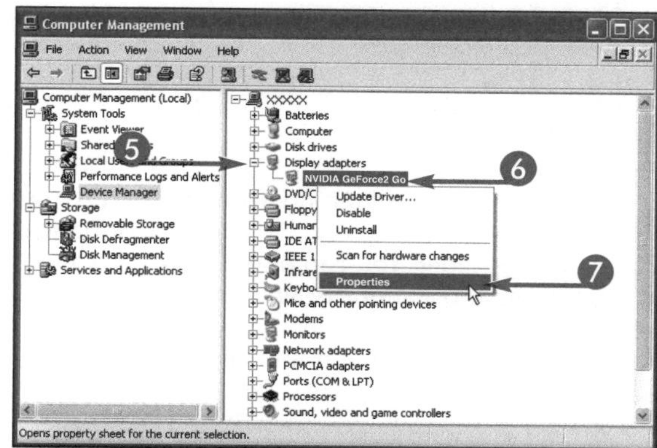

The properties dialog box for the device is displayed.

8 Click the Driver tab to view the date, version, and provider of the driver.

- Click to update the device driver to a newer version.
- Roll back to a previous version by clicking here.
- Click to Uninstall.

Note: *It is preferable to use the Add/Remove Hardware tool for this operation.*

9 Click OK to confirm your changes.

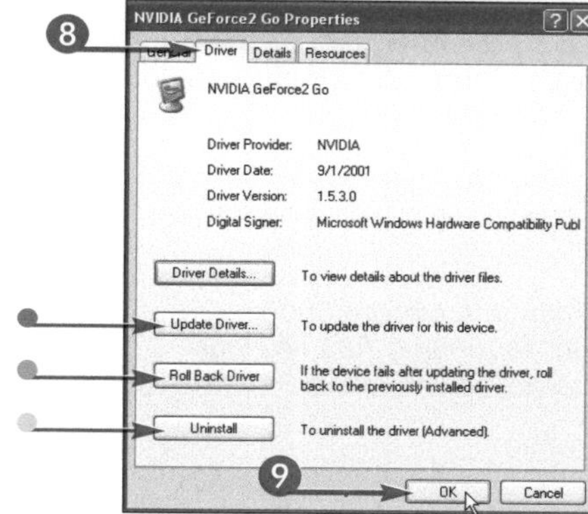

How can I tell if there is a new driver?

▼ If you click Update Driver, you have the option of checking via the Windows Update site. You must have a working Internet connection to use this feature. Often you will be directed by a support technician to download a new driver from a hardware manufacturer to fix a problem.

How do I disable a device?

▼ Right-click the device and click Disable. A red × appears over the device's icon in the display indicating that it has been disabled. To enable it again, just right-click the device's icon and click Enable. Note: Not all devices can be disabled.

Manage Tasks

You can examine running applications, processes, CPU performance, and network performance with Task Manager. You can also use Task Manager to switch between applications or end an application if it is locked up. To run Task Manager, type **taskmgr.exe** in the text box of the Run command and click OK or press Ctrl+Alt+Del once and then click Task Manager.

Task Manager has four tabs: Applications, Processes, Performance, and Networking. The Applications tab of the Task Manager allows you to see how many applications (or instances of applications) are currently running on your PC. From this tab, you can also switch between applications, or close an application. From the Processes tab, you can view the system processes that are currently running. Processes are a more detailed representation of programs that are currently executing on your computer, including those run by the system and utilities such as virus-scanning software and Task Manager itself. You can also end a process from this tab, but this can cause your system to become unstable. The Performance tab graphically represents your CPU's utilization as well as page file usage and memory details. The Networking tab measures network activity.

Manage Tasks

Note: *In this example, Paint and Notepad have been launched prior to running Task Manager to show sample applications running.*

1. Click Start and then Run.
2. Type **taskmgr.exe**.
3. Click OK.

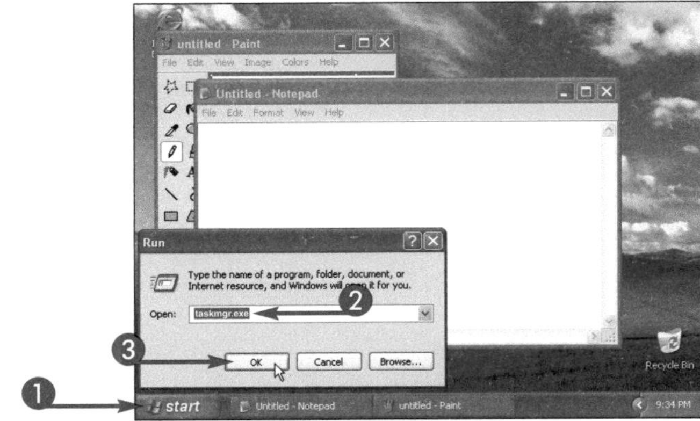

The Windows Task Manager appears, showing applications that are currently running.

- Select a task and then click End Task to end (close) the application, or click Switch To to switch to that application.
- Click New Task to bring up the Run command.

4. Click Processes.

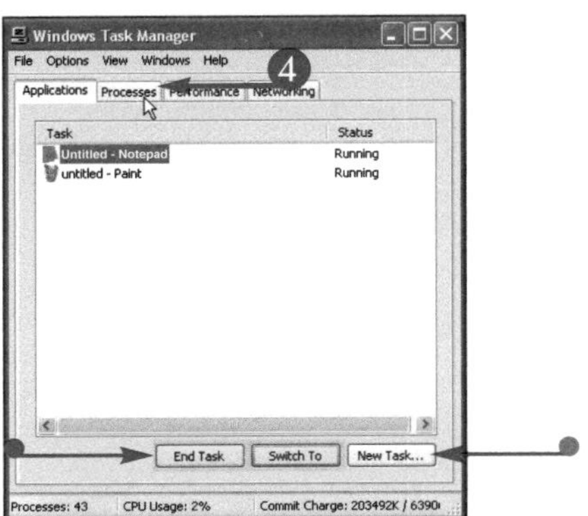

The Processes tab appears, showing the programs executing.

- Current percentage usage of CPU is shown here.
- Memory usage by process allows you to identify those processes using significant memory.

5 Click the Performance tab.

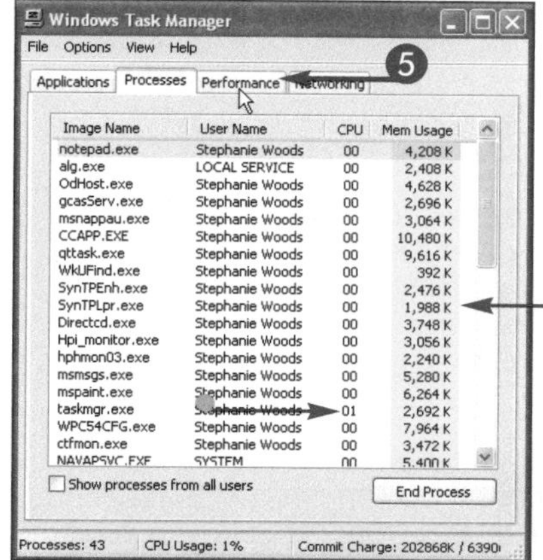

The Performance tab appears, showing graphical representation of CPU and page file usage in real time, as well as other performance measurements.

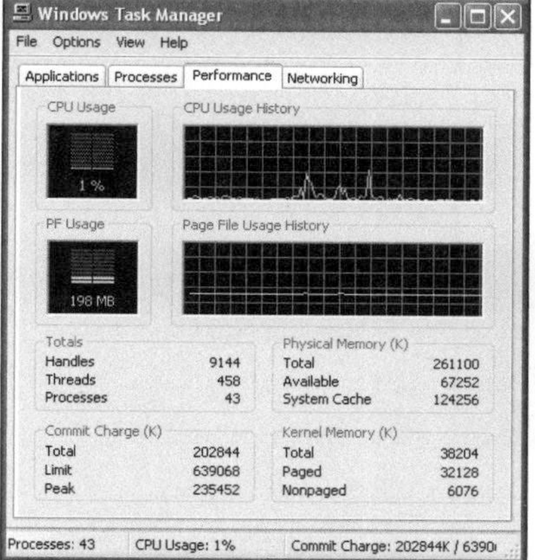

I am running an application that is not responding to my input. How can I close the application?

- Launch Task Manager. (Press Ctrl+Alt+Del if your computer is being unresponsive, and then click Task Manager.) In the Applications tab, click the application in question and then click End Task.

How can I find out whether one of my currently running applications is taking up substantial memory?

- Right-click the application in the Applications tab and click Go To Process. This takes you directly to the corresponding process in the Processes tab of the Task Manager, with the percent of CPU usage and memory usage for that process.

View Events

You can use the Event Viewer to analyze your system. Event Viewer is particularly useful for troubleshooting. It keeps three logs of events: one for the system, one for applications, and one for security. The log entries contain information about each event so that you can identify issues more easily.

To launch Event Viewer, right-click My Computer and click Manage from the menu that appears. When the Computer Management window appears, click Event Viewer from the System Tools in the navigation (left) pane. For Windows XP, Event Viewer displays Application, Security, and System logs. When you click a log, you see a list of most recent events for that category (System events in this example). There are several categories of events: Error (indicates that an error occurred), Warning (indicates a condition to watch), Information (logs a normal event), Success Audit (in the Security log, indicates a successful attempt to get through a security checkpoint), and Failure Audit (also in the Security log, indicates a failed attempt to get through security).

Each event records such information as date, time, type, user, computer, source, category, event ID, and description. Some events also contain additional data — useful to programmers and IT specialists.

View Events

1. Click Start.
2. Right-click My Computer.
3. Click Manage.

The Computer Management window appears.

4. Click Event Viewer in the left navigation pane.
   - A list of event logs is displayed in the right pane.
5. Click System.

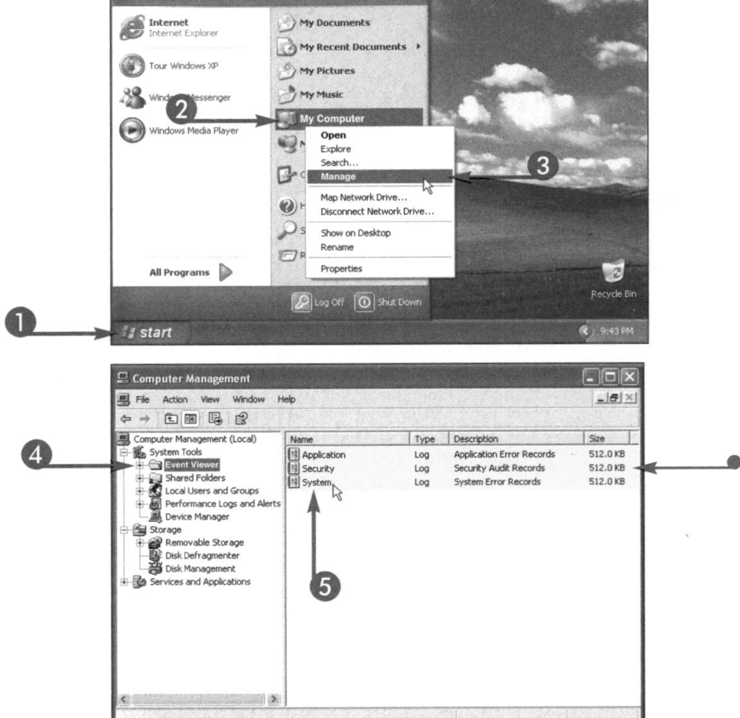

A list of System events appears in the right pane.

6 Double-click an event.

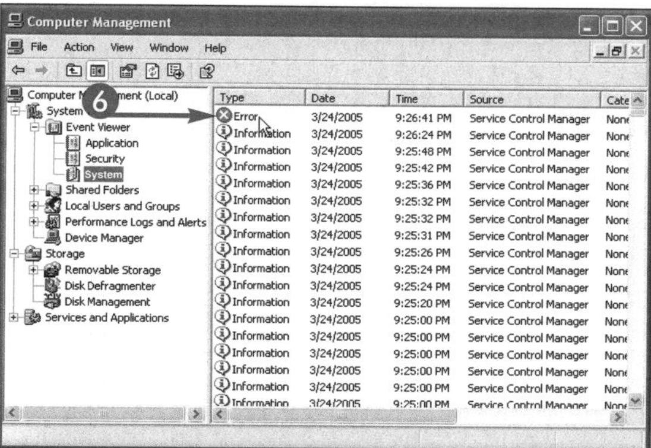

The Event Properties dialog box appears.

- Click here to move up and down the list of events in the event log.
- Click here to copy the event information displayed to the Clipboard.

7 Click OK.

8 Click to close the Computer Management window.

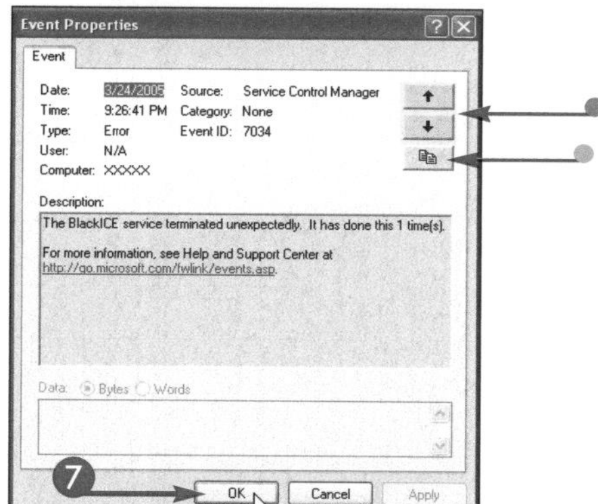

Can I find a recent error in an application to send to the tech support staff in my company?

Yes, this is usually possible if the error is recent enough. If you know the date and time of the error, you can open the Application log and look for an error at that date and time. Errors are easy to spot: They have a red icon with an ×. Open the event entry by double-clicking it. Click to copy the entry to the Clipboard, and then paste it into your e-mail to your tech support staff or paste it into a text file using Notepad.

I just wanted to view error and warning events. Can I do that?

Yes. You can filter the log entries by clicking View and then Filter from the Computer Management menus. The Filters tab of the properties dialog box for that event log appears. Clear the check boxes for all event types except Error and Warning and then click OK. Note that this filter stays on until you next check all the check boxes or click Restore Defaults on the Filters tab of the properties dialog box.

Monitor Performance

You can monitor your system performance with the System Monitor tool and Performance Logs and Alerts. If you type **perfmon.msc** from the Run command and press OK, you launch MMC with the System Monitor and Performance Logs and Alerts. The System Monitor allows you to view system performance graphically and numerically in real time. Performance Logs and Alerts provide you with a record of system performance so that you may analyze it. These tools are useful in identifying areas where your system is performing poorly so that you can address the performance bottlenecks. You can choose from various performance counters and performance objects to zero-in on a problem.

Clicking Performance Logs and Alerts in the left navigation pane brings up three elements: counter logs, tracer logs, and alerts. A counter log contains a record of performance counters. A tracer log gives you a report of specific events you have defined when they occur. Alerts report when a performance counter reaches a threshold that you define. You can set the interval at which logs are kept, you can have them cycle, or you can have them fed into a database.

Monitor Performance

1. Click Start and then Run.
2. Type **perfmon.msc**.
3. Click OK.

The Performance window of MMC appears, with the System Monitor displaying processor performance graphically in real time.

- Numeric data and a key to performance counter settings appear here.

4. Click the plus sign next to Performance Logs and Alerts.

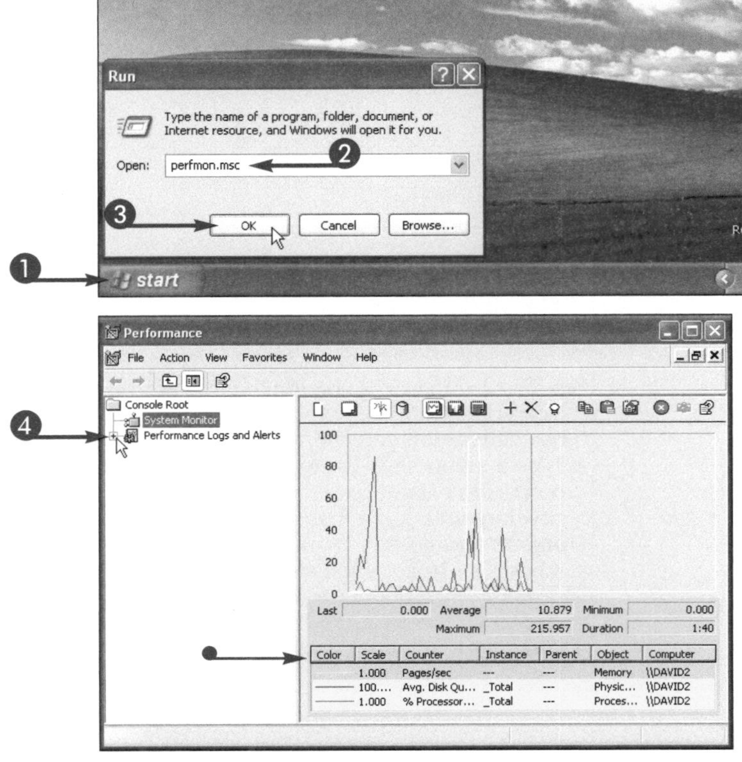

5 Click Counter Logs.

6 Right-click System Overview.

7 Click Properties.

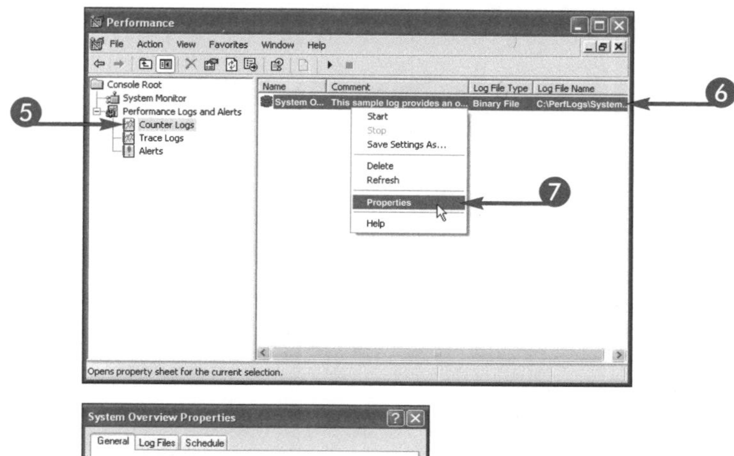

The properties dialog box for the System Overview sample counter log appears.

- Click Add Objects to add performance objects.
- Click Add Counters to add performance counters.
- Click Remove to remove the selected object or counter.

8 Choose the time interval to sample data here.

9 Click OK.

10 Click ☒ to close the Performance window of MMC.

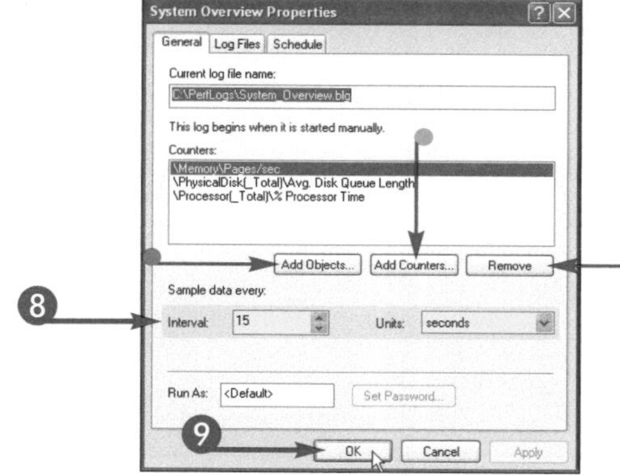

How do I create a new counter log?

▼ Right-click Counter Logs in the left navigation pane. Click New Log Settings. Type a name for the new log. When the properties dialog box appears for your new log, you can add performance objects and counters to monitor and schedule when the log should start and stop. (If you do not establish a start and stop time, the log will be a continuous loop, erasing the oldest data as it puts the new data in.)

How do I create an Alert?

▼ Right-click Alerts in the left navigation pane. Click New Alert Settings. Type a name for the new alert. Add at least one performance counter. Assign a value at which you want an alert to issue, and a limit, and click OK.

Configure and Control Services

You can configure and control services with the Services MMC snap-in. *Services* are programs that run in the background on your system locally or as part of network- or Internet-based client server applications. Depending on the type of service, you can start, stop, pause, resume, disable, or enable services from the Services snap-in. You can also configure how services behave in a given situation, or turn services on and off based on a specific hardware profile.

To launch the Services tool, type **services.msc** from the Run command and press OK. This brings up the local Services window. The Extended tab shows a description and a list of available commands for the selected service. The Standard tab does not display the description and list of commands, but shows more fields. To control a service, click its name. In the Extended tab, the description and basic commands appear. For more detailed configuration options (such as what to do when the service fails, alternate behavior with different hardware profiles, and so on), double-click the service. Use caution when manually controlling services. Read any warnings carefully and understand any program interdependencies before stopping or disabling a service.

Configure and Control Services

1. Click Start and then Run.
2. Type **services.msc**.
3. Click OK.

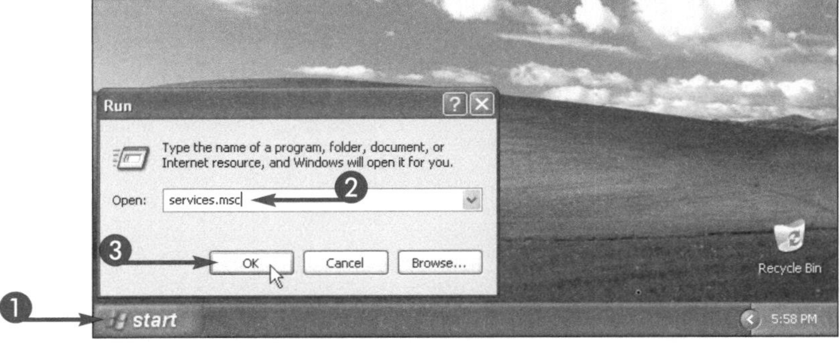

The Services window of MMC appears, showing service descriptions.

- Click the Standard tab to show more fields.

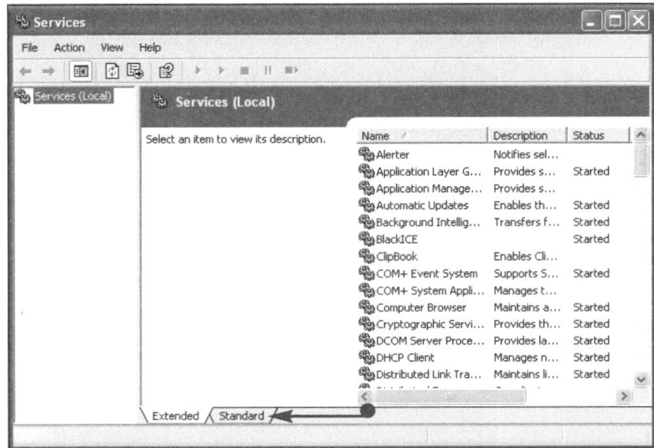

4 Click the service (Infrared Monitor in this example).

- A description of the service's function appears here.

5 Click one of the basic commands you can perform on the service (Pause in this example).

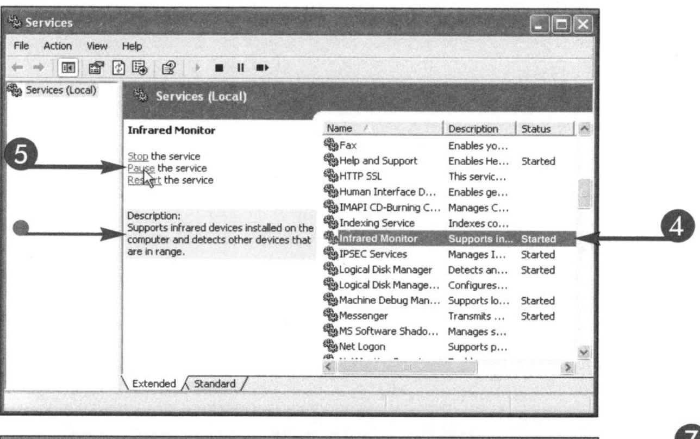

- The status changes to Paused.

6 Click Resume.

7 Click here to close the Services window.

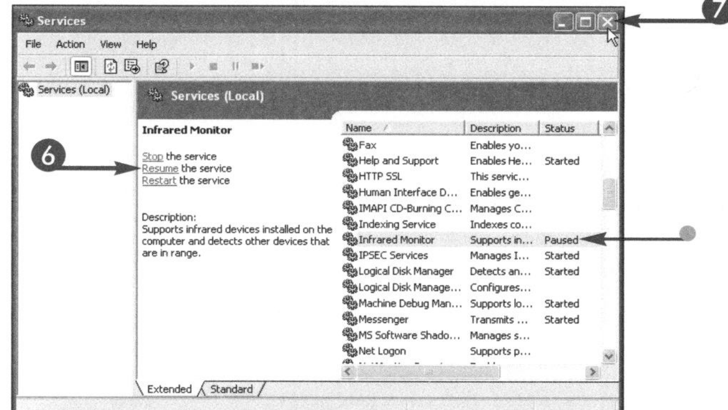

How do I disable a service for a specific hardware profile?

▼ Launch the Services snap-in. Double-click the service name from the list. The properties dialog box appears. Click the Log On tab and choose the hardware profile for which you want to disable the service. Click Disable. Click OK.

How do I change the behavior when the service fails?

▼ Launch the Services snap-in. Double-click the service name from the list. The properties dialog box appears. Click the Recovery tab. Choose an action from the dropdown list for the first, second, or subsequent failures. You can elect to take no action, attempt to restart the service, restart the computer, or run a program. If you elect to restart the computer, click Restart Computer Options for access to more parameters. If you elect to run a program in a failure situation, fill in the information in the Run Program section.

Schedule Tasks

You can schedule your PC to run tasks at a specific time in the future or at regular intervals using Scheduled Tasks on the Control Panel. The easiest way to access this tool is to click Start, select Control Panel, switch to Classic View, and then click Scheduled Tasks. (If you want more ready access to this tool, you can right-click the Scheduled Tasks icon in the Control Panel and click Create Shortcut to create a shortcut on your desktop.) The Scheduled Tasks folder appears, listing scheduled tasks and an Add Scheduled Tasks item. If you have antivirus software running or are working in an organization with IT support, you probably already have some scheduled tasks listed.

If you want to modify or reschedule an existing task, double-click the task. If you want to temporarily disable the task but do not want to get rid of it entirely, clear the Enabled option (☑ becomes ☐) on the Task tab. To reschedule a task, click the Schedule tab and modify the date and time settings accordingly. To make changes to how the scheduled task operates based on power (if you have a laptop) or idle time, click the Settings tab.

Schedule Tasks

1. Click Start and click Control Panel.

   The Control Panel appears.

2. Click Switch to Classic View from this area of the Control Panel (unless your screen already appears as it does here).

3. Double-click Scheduled Tasks.

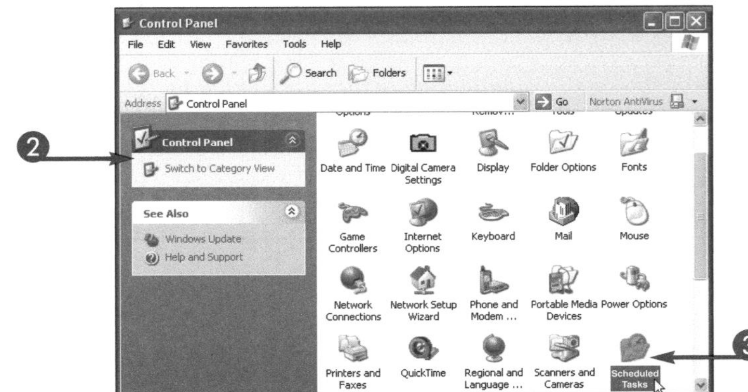

The Scheduled Tasks window appears.

- To change settings to an existing task, double-click the task.

4. Double-click Add Scheduled Task.

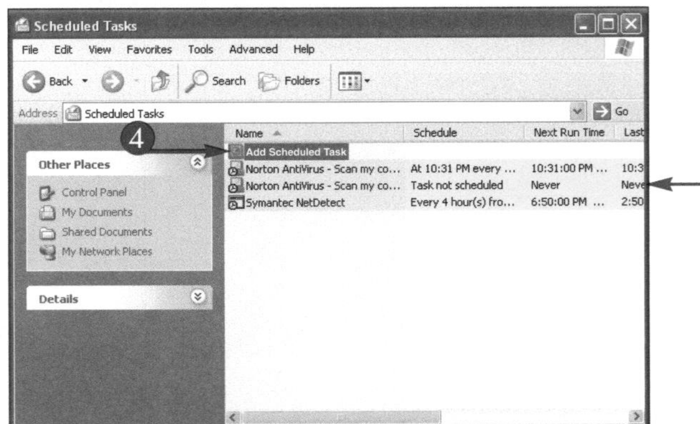

The Scheduled Task Wizard launches.

5 Click Next.

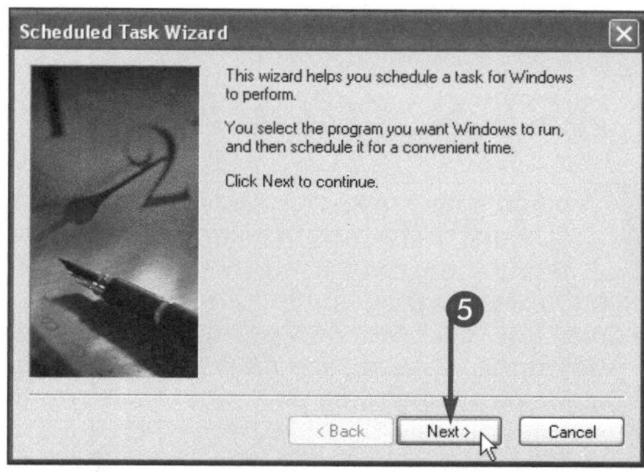

6 Click the program that you want to have perform a task for you (Disk Cleanup in this example).

7 Click Next.

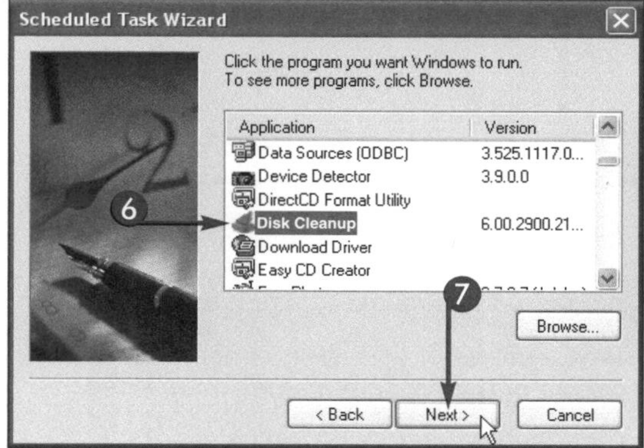

PART IV

How do I schedule an existing task to occur just once?

- Double-click the task from the list in the Scheduled Tasks folder. Click the Schedule tab in the dialog box that appears. From the Schedule Task list, click Once in the list of options, set the date and time, and click OK. In the Scheduled Tasks list, the Schedule, Next Time Run, and Last Time Run fields now all have the same date and time.

Is a task automatically removed from the list if it is not set to run again?

- No, but you can set it so that it is deleted if it is not going to run again. Double-click the task. Click the Settings tab. Click the Delete the task if it is not scheduled to run again option (☐ changes to ☑). Click OK. After the last scheduled run time, the task is removed from the list.

continued

Schedule Tasks *(Continued)*

To add a new task, click Add Scheduled Task. The Scheduled Task Wizard launches and walks you through the steps to creating a new task. First it asks you to select a program for Windows to run as a scheduled task. Click Browse if you do not see the program you want in the list. Next, you are asked to name the task and determine at what time you want to perform the task: daily, weekly, monthly, one time only, when the computer starts, or when you log on. The next screen asks you to provide the start time and date and the interval if it is a repeating task. Depending on the task (if it is specific to a given user), you may be asked to enter your user name and password in the next screen.

The final screen of the Scheduled Task Wizard confirms your task information (program, date, time, and frequency). If you want to change additional settings, click the Open advanced properties for this task when I click Finish option (☐ changes to ☑) and the wizard brings up an advanced settings properties dialog box for the task. Click Finish and the task appears in the list.

Schedule Tasks *(continued)*

After selecting the task you want to perform and clicking Next in the Scheduled Task Wizard, you are asked to name the task.

8 Type a name for your task (or accept the default of the program name you selected).

9 Click the frequency with which your task should be performed.

10 Click Next.

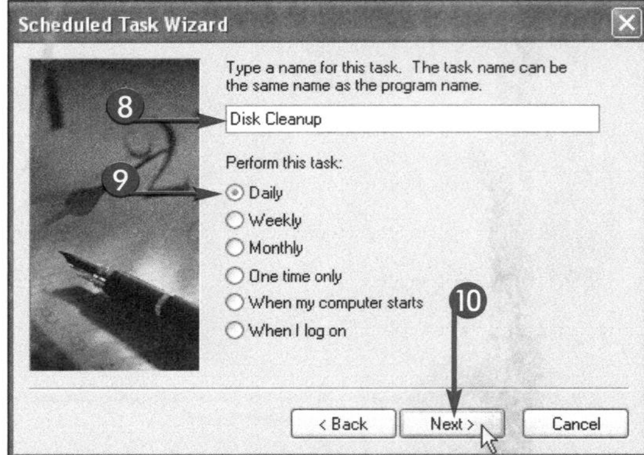

11 Type the Start time (or use the arrow keys to select a time).

12 Click to choose the frequency with which the task should be performed.

13 Type a Start date (or click ▾ to bring up a calendar and then click the date).

14 Click Next.

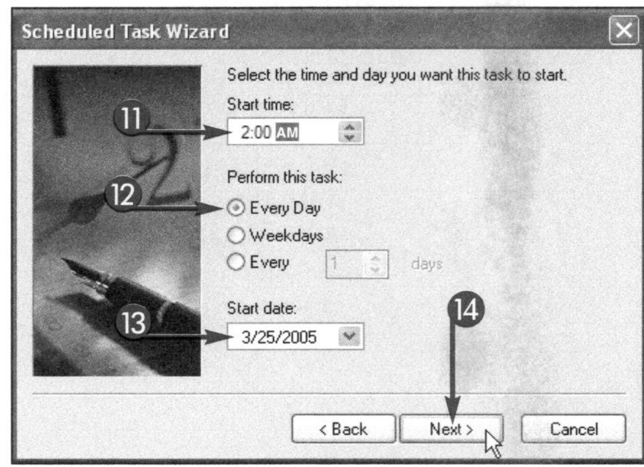

The next screen asks information about your user account.

15 Type your user name.

16 Type your password.

17 Retype your password to confirm.

18 Click Next.

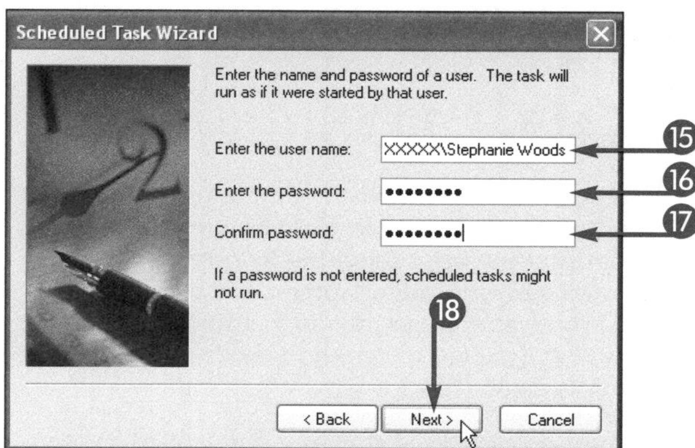

The final screen confirms successful task scheduling.

- Click here for more settings.

19 Click Finish to close the Scheduled Task Wizard.

20 Click ☒ to close the Scheduled Tasks window.

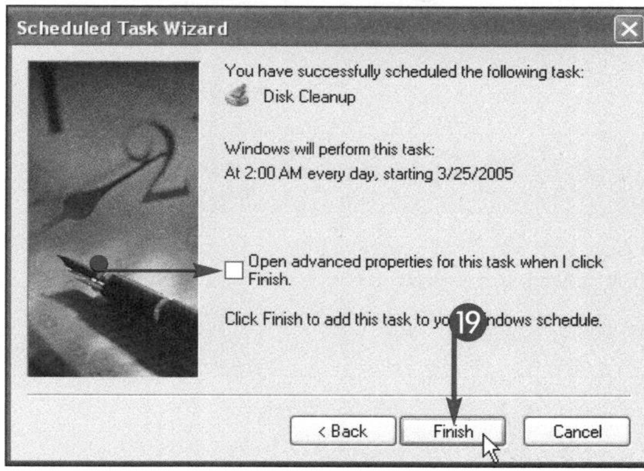

Can I make the task run even if my computer is in Sleep mode?

▼ Yes, provided your computer uses OnNow power management. Double-click the task. Click the Settings tab of the dialog box that appears. Click the Wake the computer to run this task option (☐ changes to ☑). Click OK.

Can I run a task right now rather than at the scheduled time?

▼ Yes. Right-click the task and click Run. The task launches immediately.

Diagnose Memory Problems

You can diagnose memory problems in several ways. In this section you can learn how to check the status of memory using the System Information tool discussed earlier in this chapter. You can also learn more about how to change memory settings to optimize performance in Chapter 17 and how to deal with system problems in Chapter 18.

To check system memory status, you can launch the tool either from the Run command by typing **msinfo32.exe** or by navigating from the Start menu through All Programs, Accessories, and then System Tools. Click the plus sign in the left navigation pane next to Hardware Resources and then click Memory. This lists the memory address of the hardware device, a description of the device, and the status of memory (all should show OK). If two devices show the same memory address range, there will be a resource conflict. If such a conflict occurs, you can use the Device Manager to troubleshoot the problem. Updating the device driver may also solve the problem. See the section "Manage Devices," earlier in this chapter.

Diagnose Memory Problems

1. Click Start and then Run.
2. Type **msinfo32.exe** in the text box.
3. Click OK.

The System Information window appears.

4. Click Hardware Resources.
5. Click Memory.
   - Memory addresses appear here.
   - Device names are shown here.
   - Memory status is shown here.
6. Click here to close the window.

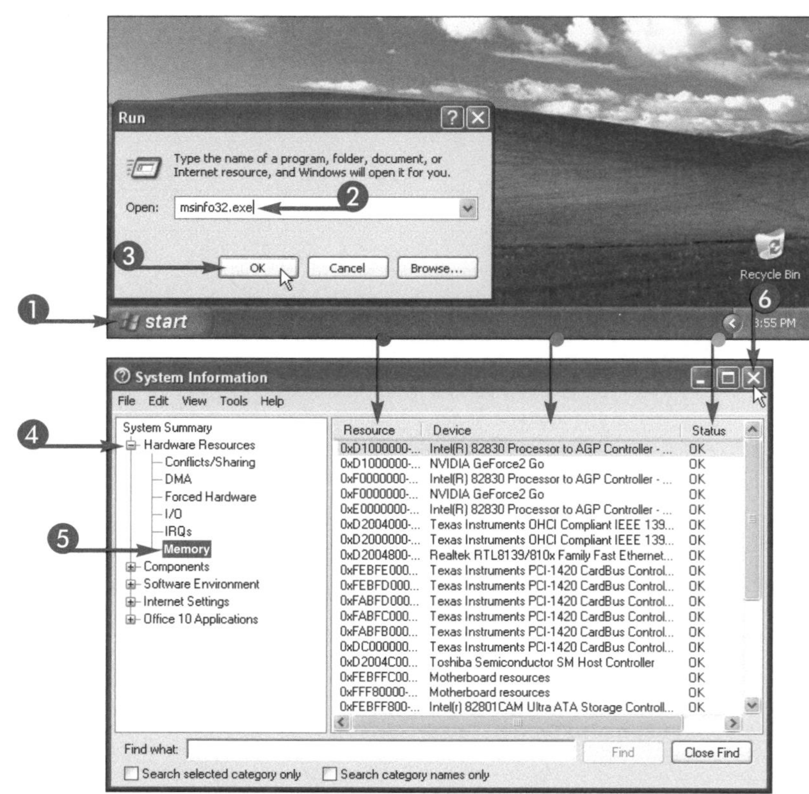

Work with the Command Prompt

You can run batch files, scripts, and command-line utilities using the command prompt. This is particularly useful for automating basic administrative and housekeeping tasks. It is also critical for some system support utilities that are only available as command-line tools. If you are familiar with and still recall the old MS-DOS command line, then this is essentially the latest version of the DOS prompt, and behaves the same way.

To launch the command line, click Start and then Run. Type **cmd.exe** in the text box and click OK. A text-based screen appears, showing you a prompt indicating the currently logged drive and directory. A blinking underscore indicates the location of the cursor. To run a command-line command, type the name of the command or program (if it is a program, do not type **.exe** or **.com**) followed by any parameters. To exit, you can type **exit** and press Enter when the command prompt next appears or click ☒ to close. You can right-click the title bar to change properties settings such as font size, color, and so on.

Work with the Command Prompt

1. Click Start and then Run.
2. Type **cmd.exe**.
3. Click OK.

- The command prompt appears in a text window with a blinking cursor.
- Right-click the title bar to change property settings such as font display size.

4. Type the command or batch filename (in this example, **dir/p** displays the first page of the directory listing for the current folder).
5. Type **exit** at the command prompt to close the command-line window. The exit command can also be used in batch files to close the command-line window.

- You can alternatively click here to exit.

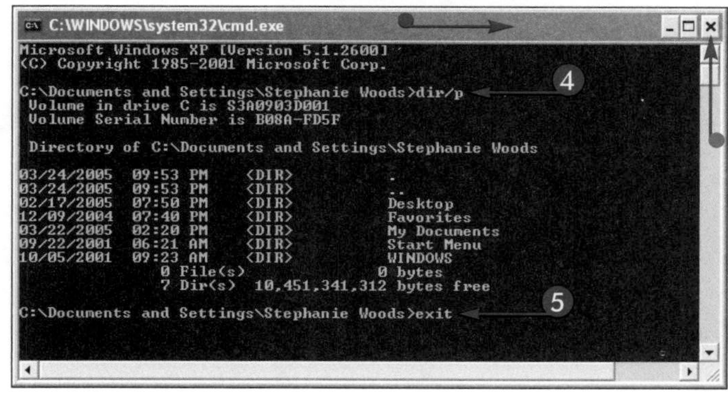

Work with the Resource Kit

You can find additional technical information and tools to help with deploying, administering, and maintaining Windows XP with Microsoft Windows XP Resource Kit. Although the focus is on deploying and supporting Windows XP in a corporate network environment, there is much useful technical information for the advanced user as well as a collection of handy tools. An online version of the Windows XP Resource Kit Documentation is available at www.microsoft.com/windows/reskits/default.asp. This page also has a link to the Windows Server 2003 Resource Kit tools. Although many of the tools are only for the server product, many are useful for working with Windows XP Professional or Home Edition.

Unfortunately, the version of the Windows XP Resource Kit Documentation that is available free online does not cover Windows XP Service Pack 2. The Resource Kit has in fact been updated by Microsoft and is available for $59.99 as a 1,523-page book and CD-ROM called *Microsoft Windows XP Resource Kit,* Third Edition. This new print edition contains information on SP2 features, configuring wireless networking, and deploying and working with Windows Firewall. Because it specifically covers SP2 features, this section shows how to install the tools and eBook based on the third edition.

Work with the Resource Kit

Note: *The following steps assume you are installing the CD-ROM for the third edition of the Windows XP Resource Kit.*

1. Insert the Windows XP Resource, Kit, Third Edition, CD-ROM into your drive, click Start, and then Run.
2. Type **e:\StartCD**, where *e* is the letter corresponding to your CD-ROM drive.
3. Click OK.

   The End User License Agreement appears.

4. After reading the license agreement, click to accept the agreement.
5. Click Next.

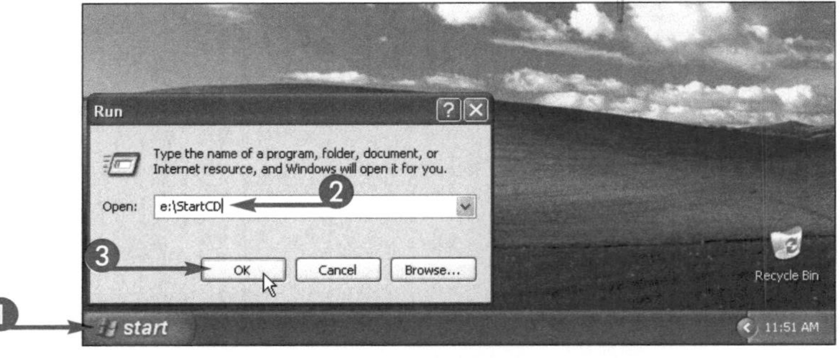

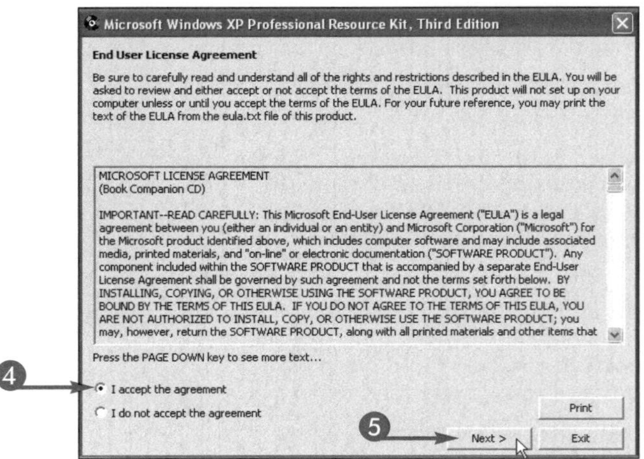

The Resource Kit screen appears.

6 Click Resource Kit Tools to begin installing the tools.

Note: *These are the Windows Server 2003 Resource Kit tools and are the same as those available online at the link listed previously.*

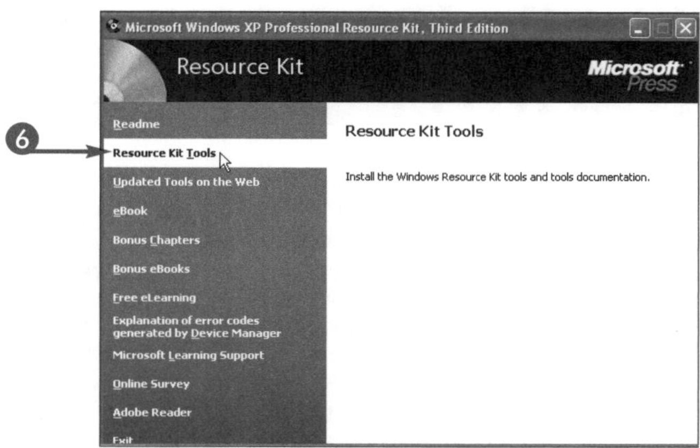

The Windows Resource Kit Tools Setup Wizard appears.

7 Click Next.

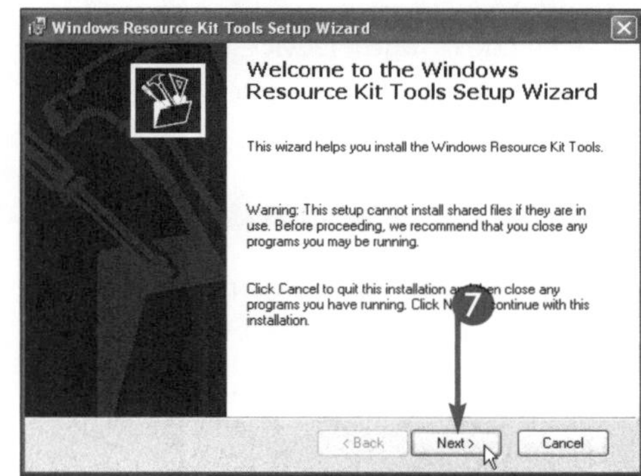

Windows Resource Kit Tools Setup Wizard
Welcome to the Windows Resource Kit Tools Setup Wizard
This wizard helps you install the Windows Resource Kit Tools.
Warning: This setup cannot install shared files if they are in use. Before proceeding, we recommend that you close any programs you may be running.
< Back
Next >
Cancel
7

PART IV

Can I get the Resource Kit tools online?

- Yes. There were no SP2-specific tools added to the Windows XP Resource Kit, Third Edition. Go to www.microsoft.com/windows/reskits/default.asp and click the Windows Server 2003 Resource Kit Tools link. This allows you to download the tools and their corresponding help file onto your computer.

Do I need Windows Server 2003 to use the tools?

- Not really. Some of the tools only make sense to use to administer server applications, but many tools are useful for an advanced user with a standalone PC running Windows XP Professional or Home Edition.

continued

Work with the Resource Kit *(Continued)*

After you insert the CD-ROM from the Resource Kit, you can install the tools and help file using the Windows Resource Kit Tools Setup Wizard. (If you do not have the *Windows XP Resource Kit,* Third Edition, you can still download the tools and corresponding help file from the link mentioned on the previous page. The installation process is much the same.) If you have obtained the third edition printed Resource Kit, you can read the eBooks, including the new information on SP2 security, Windows Firewall, and wireless networking, bonus chapters ("Configuring TCP/IP," "Common Stop Messages," "Security Event Messages," and "Device Manager Error Codes"), or bonus eBooks (*Automating and Customizing Installations of the Microsoft Windows Server 2003 Deployment Kit; Microsoft Encyclopedia of Networking,* Second Edition; *Microsoft Encyclopedia of Security;* and *Microsoft Windows Scripting Self-Paced Learning Guide*).

Reading the eBooks requires Adobe Reader or Adobe Acrobat (the files are in PDF format). You can download Adobe Reader at no cost from www.adobe.com. After agreeing to the End User License Agreement and typing your name and organization, you are asked to select a destination for the tools (they take up about 37MB of disk space).

Work with the Resource Kit *(continued)*

After launching the Windows Resource Kit Tools Setup Wizard, the End-User License Agreement appears.

8 Click to accept the agreement.

9 Click Next.

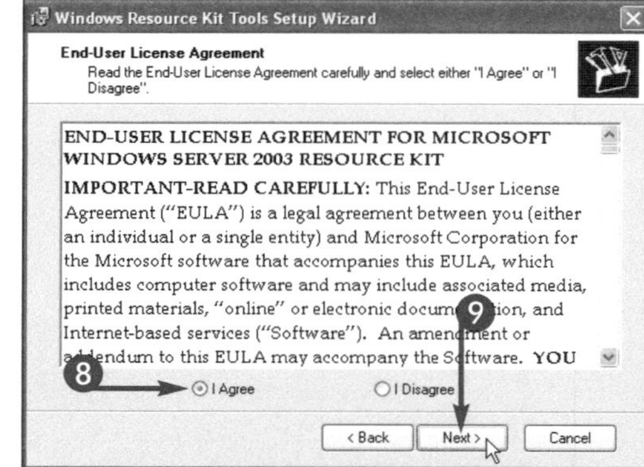

A User Information screen appears.

10 Type your name.

11 Type your organization. (You can leave these blank).

12 Click Next.

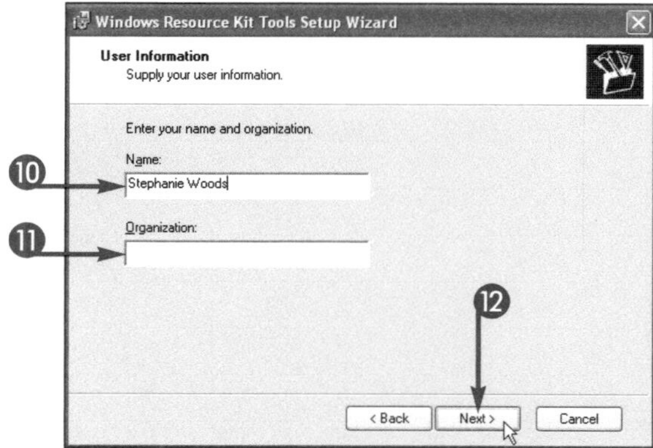

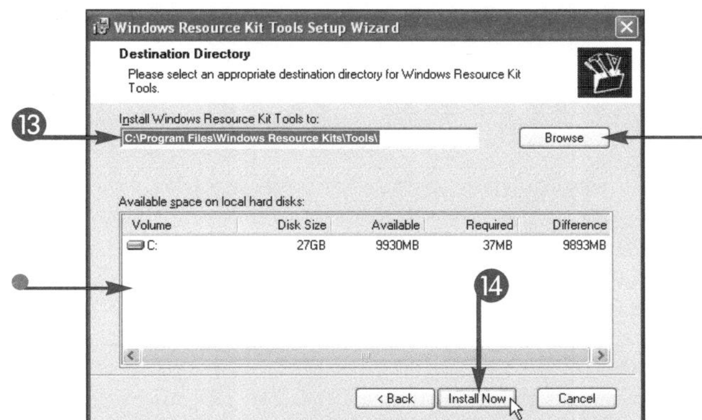

13 Indicate where to save the resource kit. You can accept the default location (C:\Program Files\Windows Resource Kits\Tools\) or type an alternate location here.

- You can also click Browse to select a location.
- This window shows available space on local hard drives.

14 Click Install Now.

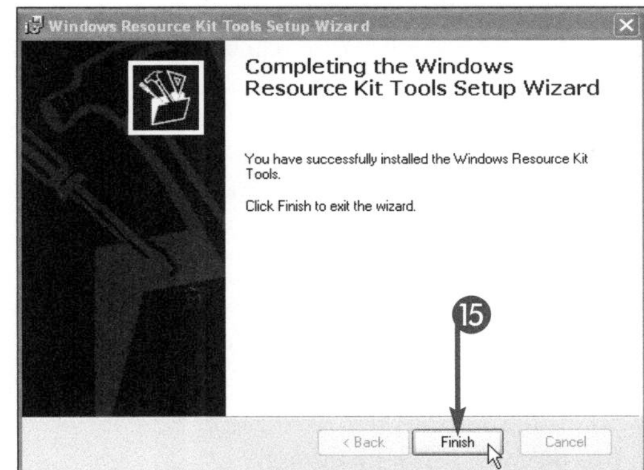

The final screen of the Resource Kit Tools Setup Wizard appears.

15 Click Finish.

16 Click ☒ to close the Resource Kit screen.

PART IV

Do the Resource Kit tools integrate with Help?

Yes. When the tools are installed, you can readily access them from the Help and Support Center. Click Start and then Help and Support. At the bottom of the left column (the Pick a Help topic column), click the Windows Deployment and Resource Kits icon. This takes you directly to the Help files for the tools.

Do the Resource Kit tools have an integrated graphical user interface?

No. Some of the tools are command-line only, and others have a graphical user interface, but each must be launched via the command line or the Run command. You can, however, treat the Resource Kit Tools Help file as a navigation tool, because it is arranged by category and alphabetically and has links to the command line from each tool's Help entry.

continued

Work with the Resource Kit *(Continued)*

When you have installed the Resource Kit tools, you can access them in several ways. If you are already familiar with the tool you want to use, simply use the command line or the Run command to launch the tool. If you need to locate a tool, or need information about the tool's parameters, usage, syntax, example uses, and so on, then your best bet is to use the Help file to access the information. You can do this in one of several ways, either by typing the location of the Help file at the Run command (the default location would be **c:\windows\help\rktools.chm**), by clicking the Windows Deployment and Resources Kits icon in the Help and Support Center as was mentioned on the previous page, or by clicking Start, All Programs, Windows Resource Kit Tools, and then Windows Resource Kit Tools Help.

When you have launched the Help file, you see on the left an introduction, a list by category, an alphabetical list, and a glossary. On the right you see a button shortcut for each letter and a list of the tools. After you have selected an entry, you may see a description, syntax, examples, and a link to the command prompt, depending on the entry.

Work with the Resource Kit *(continued)*

17. After installing the Resource Kit Tools, click Start and then Run.
18. Type **c:\windows\help\rktools.chm** (or supply an alternate path if you did not accept the default install location).
19. Click OK.

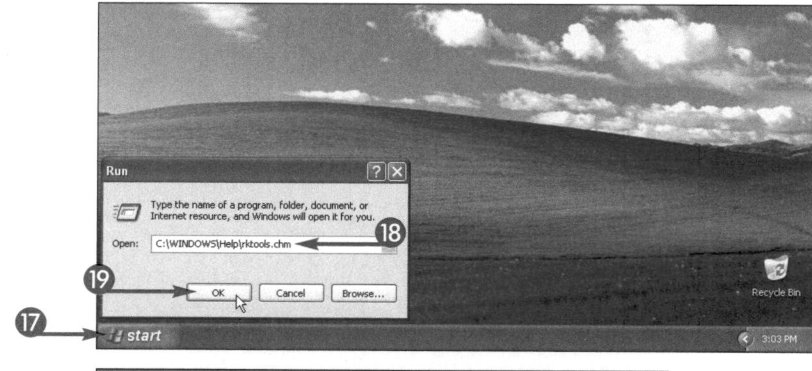

The Resource Kit Tools Help appears.

20. Click the plus sign to expand the alphabetical list of tools.

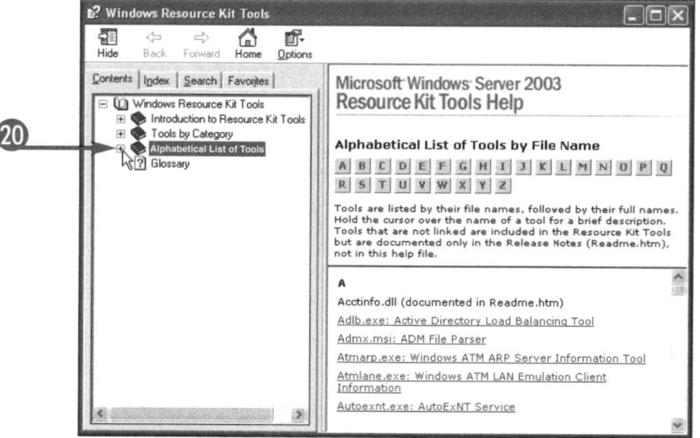

21 Click the tool you want to use (Robocopy.exe in this example).

22 Click Examples.

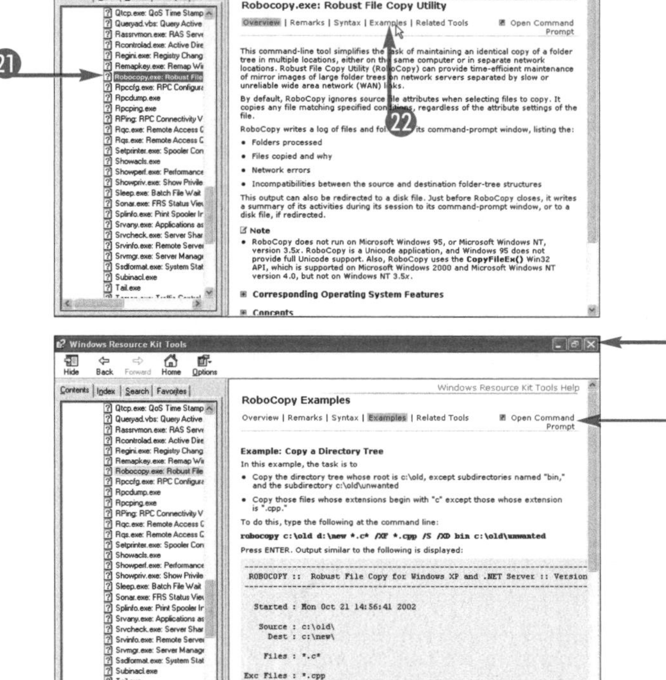

Sample syntax and output is displayed.

- Click to open the command prompt and use the tool.

23 Click here to close the Resource Kit Tools Help.

Is there any additional information about the Resource Kit tools?

▼ Yes. It is a good idea to familiarize yourself with the Windows Resource Kit Read Me file. This is an HTML file that contains additional information about tool installation, which tools have moved from the Resource Kit to become part of the operating system, documentation for a few tools not in the Help file, and other useful information. You can access this file by clicking Readme on the CD-ROM opening screen or by clicking All Programs, Windows Resource Kit Tools, and then Windows Resource Kit Tools Read Me.

Can I get Microsoft technical support for these tools?

▼ No, these tools are utilities that are provided "as-is" by Microsoft and as such are not supported. You can give Microsoft feedback about the tools, however, by sending e-mail to rkinput@microsoft.com.

continued

Work with the Resource Kit *(Continued)*

If you have the *Windows XP Resource Kit,* Third Edition, CD-ROM, you can view all the contents of the printed book as well as some bonus content online. To do so, insert the CD-ROM into your CD-ROM drive, click Start, Run, and then type **e:\StartCD** in the text box where *e* is the drive letter for your CD-ROM drive. To view the eBook, you must have Adobe Acrobat or Adobe Reader (3.0 or higher) installed. If you do not have one of these products, click Adobe Reader from the main Resource Kit screen. This takes you to Adobe's Web site, where you can download a free version of Adobe Reader. When you have Reader (or Acrobat) installed on your PC, click eBook to view the electronic version of the Resource Kit.

From Adobe Reader, you can view the Contents, navigate through the outline structure, search for a word or phrase, bookmark sections, or even have Reader read the text aloud. Although you may not print the eBook, you may copy or extract sections of text as needed.

Work with the Resource Kit *(continued)*

24 Insert the Windows XP Resource Kit Third Edition CD-ROM into your drive, click Start, and then Run.

25 Type ***e:*\StartCD**, where *e* is the letter corresponding to your CD-ROM drive.

26 Click OK.

27 Click eBook.

- Click here to get Adobe Reader software, if you do not already have it.

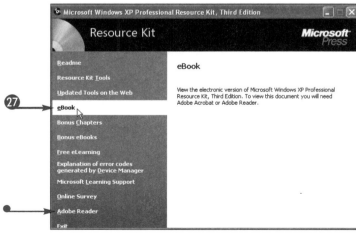

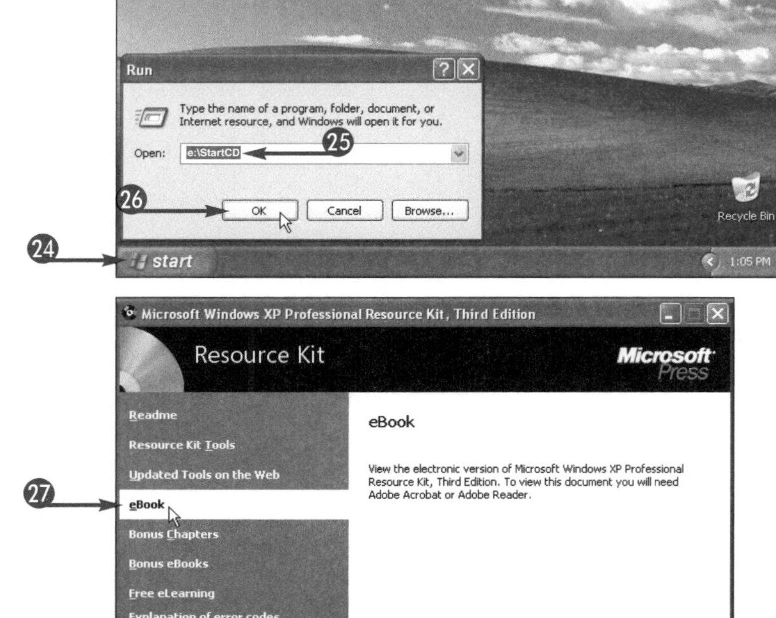

The electronic version of the Resource Kit opens.

28 Type a search topic, **Windows Firewall** in this example.

29 Click Search.

- The search results appear here. Click an entry to go to a specific instance of the search text.

30 Click here to close the electronic version of the Resource Kit.

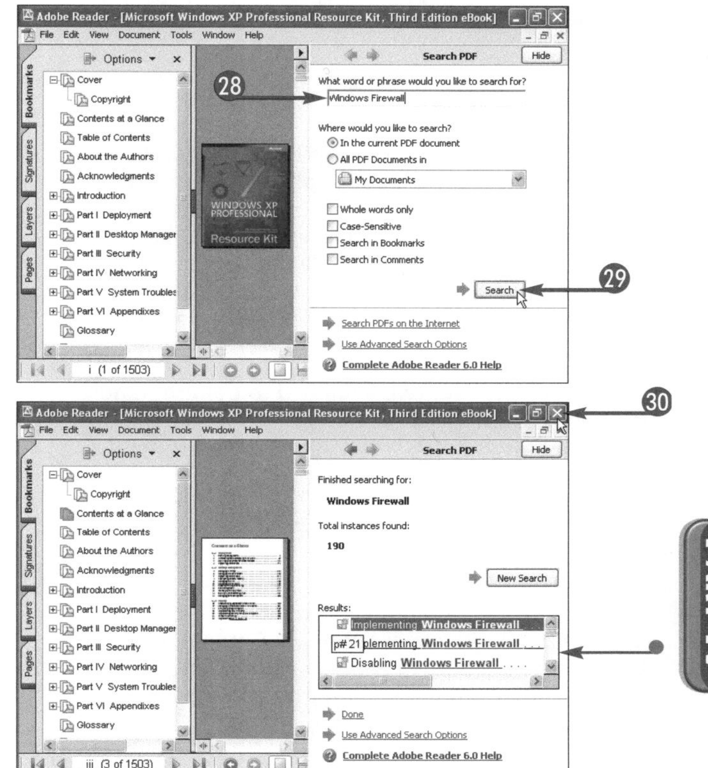

How can I find information specific to SP2 in the eBook?

Use the Search command in Reader and type the text string **Service Pack 2**. All instances of Service Pack 2 are displayed. You can also narrow your search by adding additional text to your search string.

Can I post the eBook on a network share for my colleagues to have access to it?

That depends. The End-User License Agreement for this product does not allow unlimited distribution; you are allowed one install for a desktop and one additional install to a portable computer. Check to make sure you have the correct license or license packs from Microsoft.

Improve System Performance

Windows XP includes tools to help you keep your system running at peak performance. As you use your computer, system performance degrades for various reasons. Installing new programs, uninstalling old ones, saving and deleting files, using the Internet, and other activities take a toll on your system. Other serious issues include virus and spyware problems, corruption of system files, and boot problems.

To help improve your system, you need to perform regular system maintenance. Some of the actions you can perform include freeing up disk space, defragmenting your hard drive, improving graphics performance, and running ScanDisk on the hard drive. Often these built-in utilities take care of the problem and speed up or improve system performance.

The Tools tab found on a disk's properties dialog box includes three Windows utilities: Error-checking (also known as ScanDisk), Defragmentation, and Backup. The Backup utility is not necessarily a system performance utility, but is invaluable when it comes to restoring files in the event of a system problem. See the section "Back Up and Restore Data," later in this chapter. You can set up Windows to run these tools automatically by using the Scheduled Tasks program.

Improve System Performance

Check for errors on your disk

1. To run Error Checking (also known as ScanDisk) on your computer, double-click the My Computer icon and right-click the drive you want to check. Click Properties from the menu that appears.
2. In the properties dialog box for the selected drive, click the Tools tab.
3. Click Check Now.
4. In the Check Disk window, click both check disk options.
5. Click Start to scan the selected drive.

Note: *Error Checking can take several hours to complete depending on the size of the disk, number of errors found, and speed of your computer.*

6. When finished, click OK in the properties dialog box.

Defragment your disk

7. To defragment a disk, repeat Steps 1 and 2 to display the Tools tab of the selected drive's properties dialog box.
8. Click Defragment Now.
9. In the Disk Defragmenter window, click Analyze.

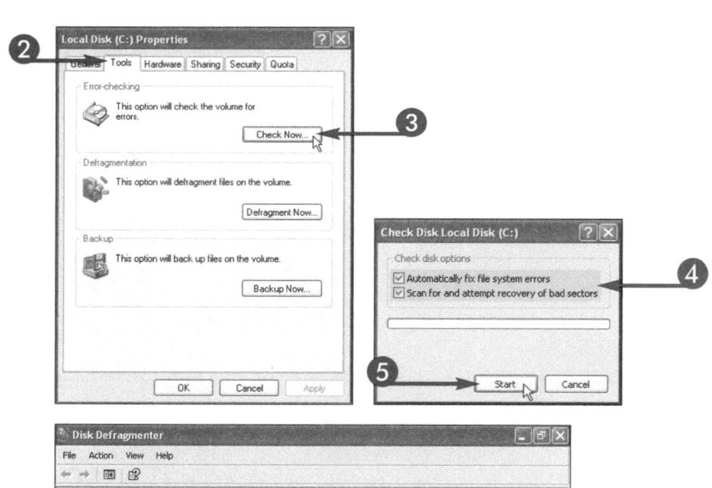

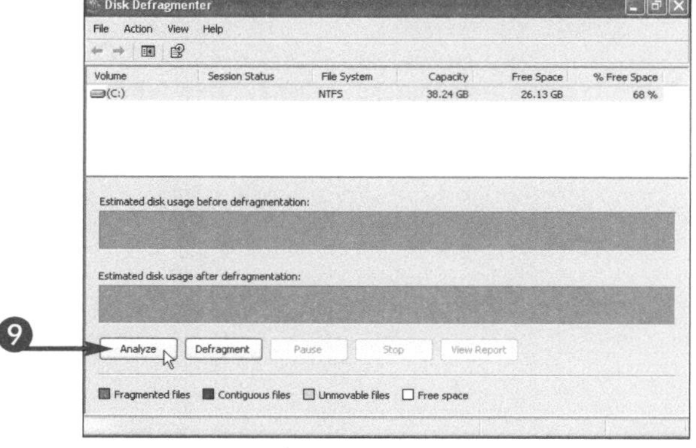

Windows analyzes the selected disk to determine if it needs defragmenting. The Disk Defragmenter window opens to report if a disk needs to be defragmented or not.

10 Click View Report to see the analysis for the selected disk.

The Analysis Report window appears.

- Windows tells you if the disk needs defragmenting, as in this example.

11 Click Defragment.

Disk Defragmenter begins the defragmentation process.

- If defragmenting is not necessary, click Close to close the Analysis Report window and then close the properties dialog box.

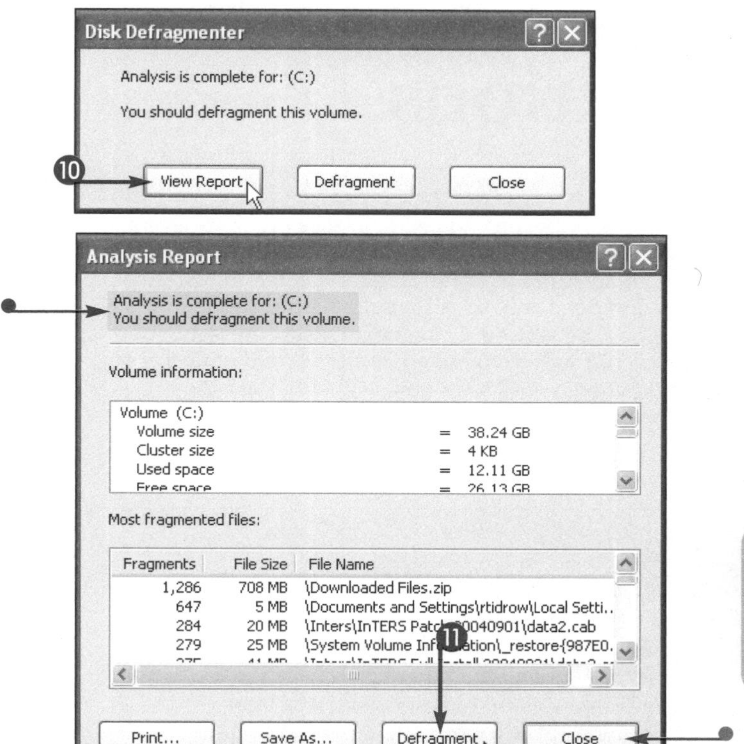

How can I see the performance of my processor?

▼ You can use the Windows System Performance Monitor. To use it, open the Control Panel, click the Performance and Maintenance icon, and then Adminstrative Tools. Double-click Performance in the Administrative Tools folder to display the Performance window. Under the Console Root folder in the left pane, click System Monitor. In the right pane at the bottom, click the % Processor Time counter. A graph appears, showing the current processor activity and peformance. If the % Processor counter is not showing, right-click the right pane and select Add Counters. Select Processor from the Performance object dropdown list. In the Select counters from list area, select % Processor Time and click Add. Click Close to confirm your changes.

Are any programs or utilities available to help me improve Windows XP system performance?

▼ Yes, several commercial products and freeware/shareware products are available to help you optimize your computer. One of the most popular commercial programs is Norton SystemWorks (formerly Norton Utilities). Do a search on www.Google.com (or other search engine) to find information about the various utilities available for download. Some of the keywords you can use in a search include **Windows XP utilities** and **Windows XP system tools**.

Create New Partitions

You can divide a disk into multiple partitions to optimize storage and performance. With partitioning, you can divide a large disk into several smaller logical disks. For example, if you have a 60GB hard drive, you could partition it into three 20GB partitions, each appearing and behaving like a separate hard drive. One partition would be labeled C, the next D, and the last E. Partitions do not have to be of equal size. One partition, say the boot partition, could have only 5GB, while another partition has the balance of the hard drive (55GB).

Partitioned drives let you organize your files and programs as you see fit. For example, you may have three partitions. Your C drive would be used for primary Windows files and system files. The D drive could be used for installing programs. Finally, the E drive could be used to store documents, graphics, and music files.

Partitioning can be done prior to installing Windows or as Windows XP is installed. If done during installation, Windows creates just one partition. However, if you perform partitioning with a DOS utility (FDISK), you can partition the disk into multiple partitions, dividing the hard drive space into several sections.

Create New Partitions

1. To create a new partition on a second installed hard drive, open the Control Panel, click Performance and Maintenance, and then click Administrative Tools.
2. Double-click Computer Management.

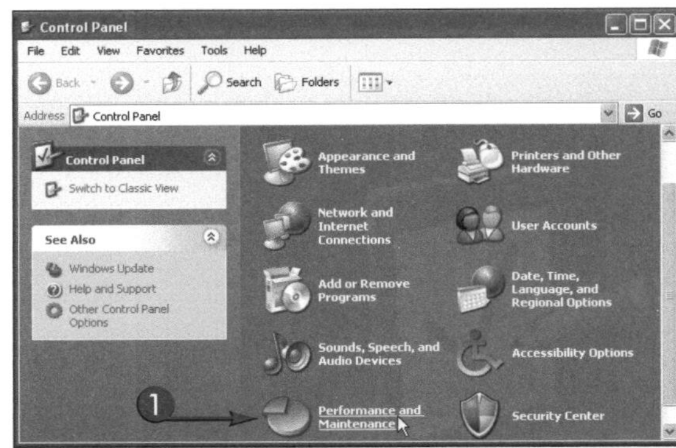

The Computer Management window opens.

3. Click the plus sign to view the Storage options.
4. Click Disk Management.

- This area shows a list of all installed disks and information about each disk appears. You can find out a disk's drive letter, its status, capacity, free space, and other important information.
- This area shows each disk in a graphical view.

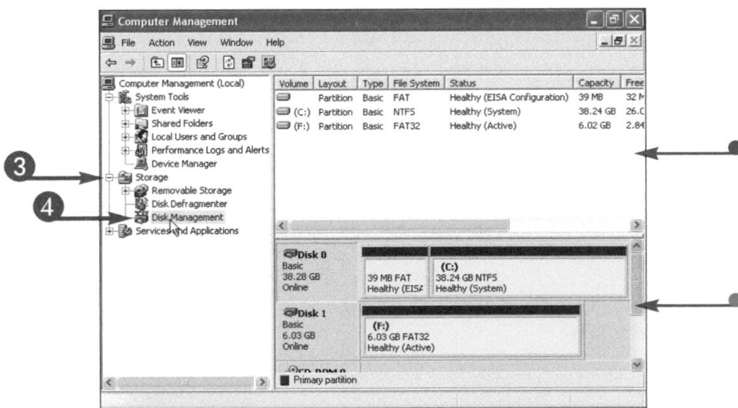

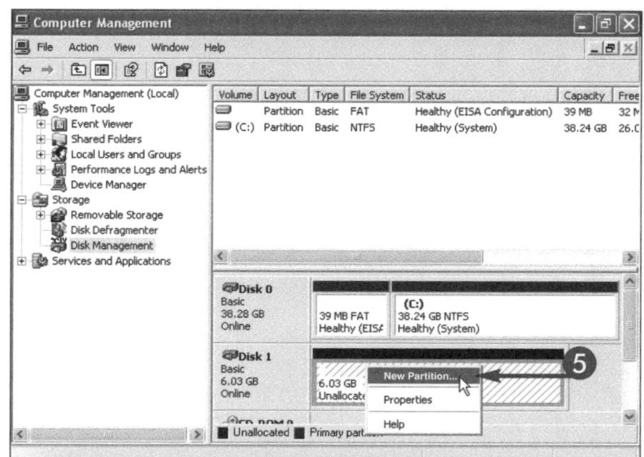

5. To partition a drive, right-click the drive and click New Partition.

   The New Partition Wizard appears. This wizard walks you through creating a partition on a basic disk.

6. Click Next.

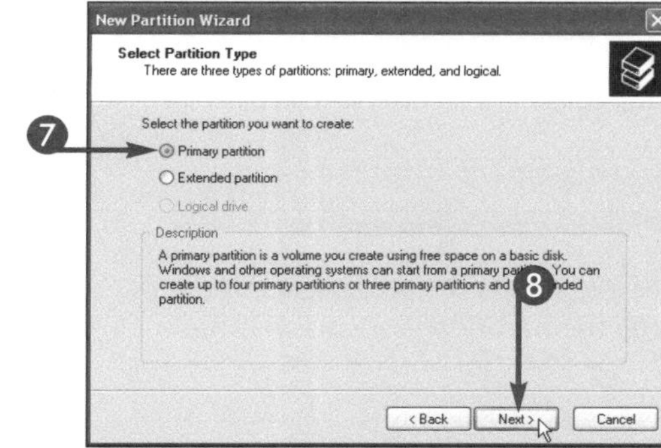

   The Select Partition Type screen appears.

7. Click Primary partition.

   For most cases, choose a primary partition if you have a second disk on your system. Choose extended partitions when you want more than four volumes on your disk.

8. Click Next.

I have Windows XP installed but want to create a partition. How do I do that with my current drive?

▼ Unfortunately, when Windows is installed, you cannot partition the drive without losing all the drive's data (including Windows itself). This is because if you have just one partition, Windows uses it as the system and boot partition. If a disk has unallocated space on it, you can partition it. Sometimes large disks come with unallocated space from vendors if you specify that you want the disk set up this way.

If you want to set up partitions on a computer and have only one disk (and the disk has one partition and no unallocated space), consider purchasing and adding a second hard drive to the system. You then can partition that drive into multiple partitions. The computer would then have your original hard drive (formatted as the primary partition and labeled as C) and a second drive with multiple partitions (such as D, E, and F).

What is a primary partition?

▼ A primary partition is a partition on the disk that Windows XP allows users to directly access. This means the user can store files and programs on the partition and then access them directly using a tool such as Windows Explorer or My Comptuer. Windows XP lets you create up to four primary partitions on a hard drive.

PART IV

continued

Create New Partitions *(Continued)*

Windows XP enables you to partition a drive into one or several partitions. Partitions help you organize data files, programs, and system files on your computer.

When you partition a drive, you can choose whether to format the partition. If the partition is set up as a FAT or FAT32 partition, you should choose to format it as an NTFS file system. Formatting it as an NTFS file system takes advantage of Windows XP advanced file system features, such as security. It is best practice to format a drive any time you create a new partition. Formatting removes all data from the drive (the data is removed when you partition a drive anyway) and cleans up any logical errors that may have formed on the disk.

Formatting also attempts to fix physical errors on the disk. However, if there are physical errors found that cannot be fixed during formatting, Windows marks those areas as unusable so new data is not stored there in the future.

When you set up a partition size, you specify the number of megabytes (MBs) each partition consumes. Some users like to create partitions of equal size. For example, on a 40MB drive that will have two partitions, each partition will be 20MB.

Create New Partitions *(continued)*

The Specify Partition Size screen appears. Here you can specify the partition size you want for the disk.

9. Type a value for the partition size.
10. Click Next.

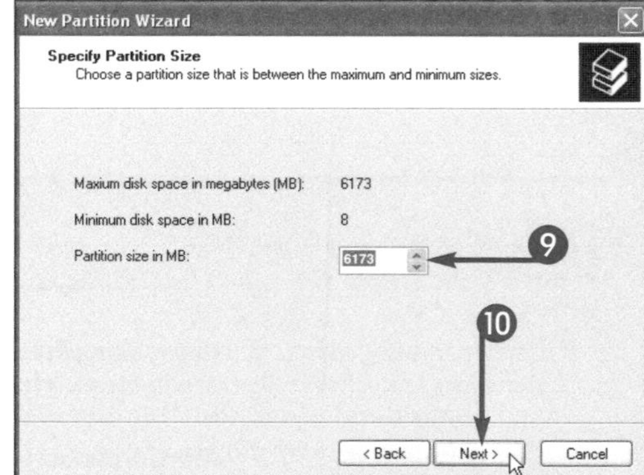

The Assign Drive Letter or Path screen appears. Here you can specify the drive letter you want to name the partitioned drive.

11. Click here and select a drive letter.
12. Click Next.

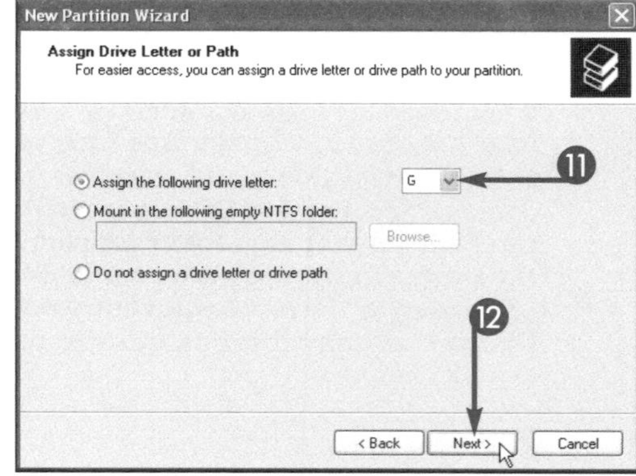

The Format Partition screen appears.

13 Click the option to format your partition with the settings you choose.

14 Click here and select NTFS.

15 Click Next.

The Completing the New Partition Wizard screen appears.

16 Click Finish to format and partition the disk.

- When finished, the information for the newly partitioned drive appears in the Computer Management window.

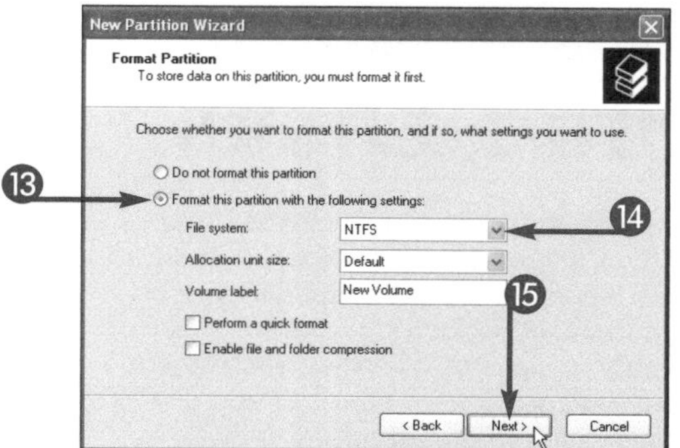

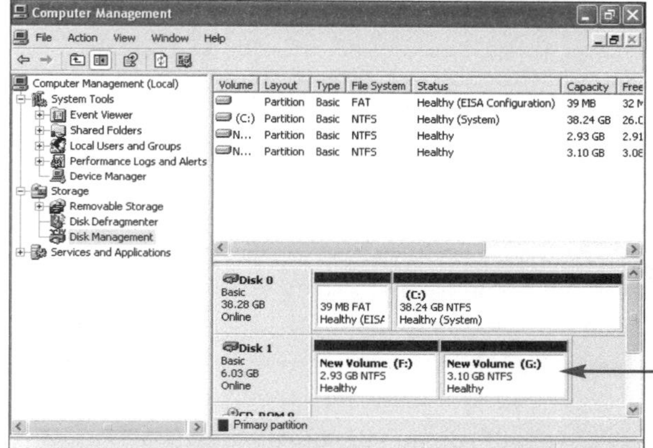

Are there any other programs that let me manage my drives, particularly setting up partitions?

Yes, there are some third-party programs that let you create and manage partitions. In fact, some of them are easier to use than the built-in tools that come with Windows. Also, some disk-partitioning software allows you to manage partitions without the risk of losing data stored on the hard drive. One such software is Acronis Disk Director Suite, which you can find more information about at www.acronis.com. Another fantastic tool for partitioning drives is Symantec's PartitionMagic, at www.partitionmagic.com/partitionmagic.

After I create partitions, can I install a second operating system on my computer?

Yes. You must have a boot manager to manage which operating system boots when you start your computer. PartitionMagic includes BootMagic to help you switch between operating systems. You also need to have the installation software for each operating system you plan to install. For example, to install Windows XP, 2003, and Linux (a Unix operating system), you must have the Windows XP CDs for Windows XP, a copy of Windows Server 2003 for that operating system, and a copy of the Linux CD for insalling Linux.

Create Dynamic Disks

Windows XP Professional allows you to set up disks in two different storage types — basic and dynamic. Basic storage is the default type of storage used by Windows XP, including Professional and Home Edition. Previous versions of Windows, such as 2000, 98, and Me, also use basic storage. A basic storage disk includes basic volumes, such as primary partitions, extended partitions, and logical drives.

With dynamic disks, Windows XP Professional (Home Edition does not support this type of storage) includes storage features normally only found in advanced operating systems, such as Windows NT Server, Windows 2000 Server, and Windows Server 2003. Dynamic disks allow you to create five different disk structures not available on basic disks. These include simple, spanned, striped, mirrored, and RAID-5.

One of the main reasons for using dynamic disks is for setting up fault-tolerance duties. Fault-tolerance is protection for your computer system against hardware problems, such as hard drive failure. When you lose your hard drive, the data on the disk is usually lost as well. For this reason, fault-tolerance is used to make redundant copies of your data. With dynamic disks, you can set up fault-tolerance through mirroring, RAID, and spanned drives.

Create Dynamic Disks

1. Display the Computer Management window.

Note: *Open the Control Panel and then click the Administrative Tools and Computer Management icons.*

2. Click the plus sign to view the Storage options.
3. Click Disk Management.
4. Right-click the drive you want to change to a dynamic disk, and click that option from the menu that appears.

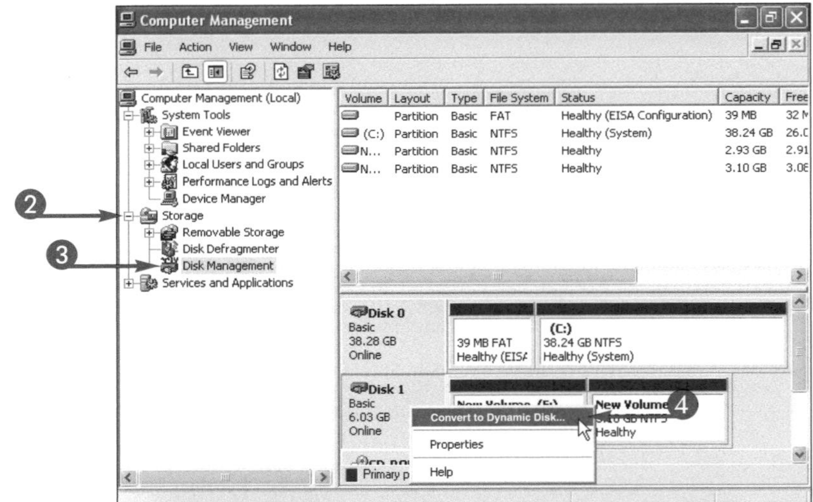

The Convert to Dynamic Disk dialog box appears. This dialog box shows a list of all the basic disks installed on your system that you can convert to dynamic disks.

Systems that have only one disk installed show only Disk 0 as the option available.

5. Select the disk you want to convert.
6. Click OK.

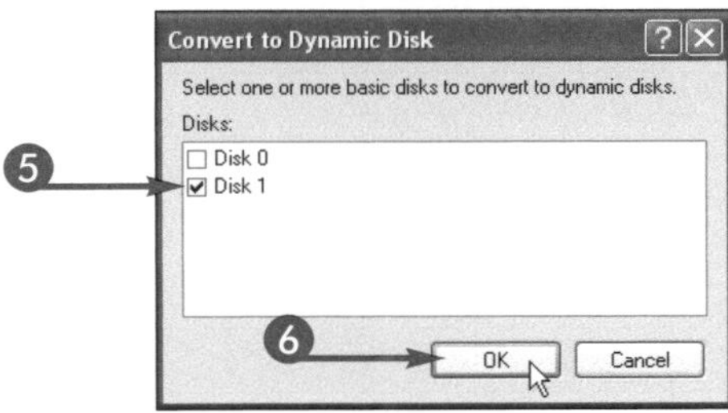

The Disks to Convert dialog box appears. This dialog box shows a list of the disks to convert and the partition information about each disk.

- To see volume information about the disks, click Details.

7 Click Convert.

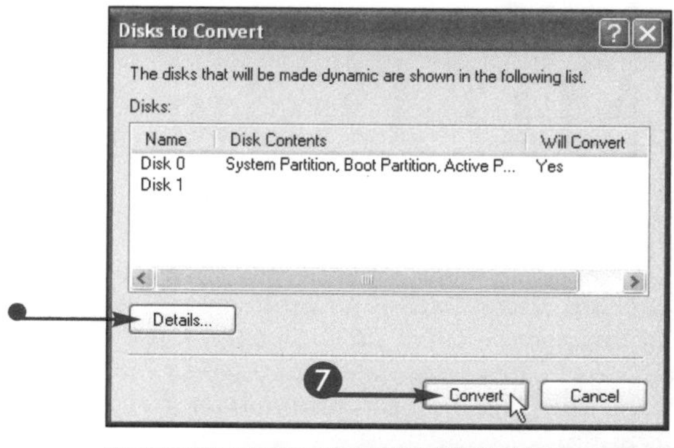

The Disk Management window appears warning you that when you convert the disk to a dynamic disk you cannot run other operating systems besides Windows XP from the volumes on the selected disks.

8 Click Yes.

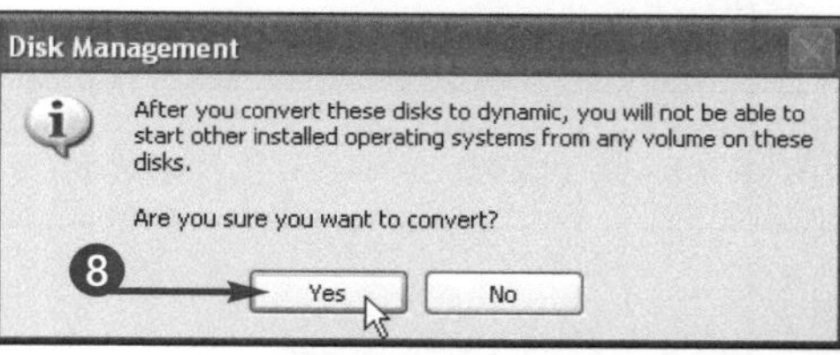

Another message appears warning you that any disks with file systems will now be dismounted, which means they will temporarily be unusable until the conversion finishes.

9 Click Yes to convert the disk to a dynamic disk.

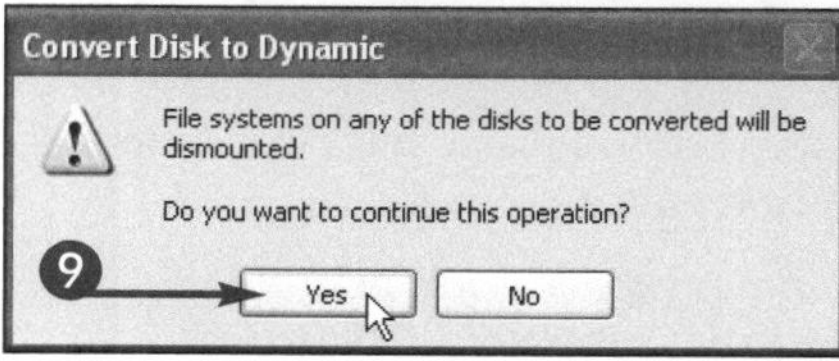

PART IV

I have several folders set up as shared objects on my disk now. Can I convert the disk to dynamic and still share those folders?

▼ Yes, but there is a catch. Only systems running Windows XP Professional, Windows 2000, and Windows Server 2003 can access those folders on the dynamic disk. Computers running Windows 95, 98, or Me, or non-Windows operating systems (Macintosh for example), cannot access those shared folders. If your company, organization, or home has a network in which shared folders are used, make sure all your systems are using XP, 2000 Server, or 2003 Server before converting to dynamic disks. Otherwise you cannot share your XP folders with the other computers.

After I have a disk configured as dynamic, can I switch it back to basic?

▼ Yes you can, but there is a caveat to this. The disk must be empty before you can switch it back to basic. This means that any disk you want to convert back to basic must a secondary drive (not the primary boot disk). Also, before converting to basic, copy all files to a backup disk or removable storage device to ensure you have all your files intact. To do this, open the Computer Management window and double-click the Disk Management object under Storage. In the bottom-right pane, right-click the disk you want convert. Choose Delete Volume for each volume on the disk. After you delete all the volumes on a disk, right-click the disk and choose Convert to Basic Disk.

Create RAID Disks

Windows XP enables you to set up fault-tolerance strategies using RAID-5 volumes. RAID-5 is a type of fault-tolerance strategy that uses three separate hard drives. RAID is an acronym for Redundant Array of Inexpensive Disks. RAID-5 volumes use striping to save data and parity information to three or more disks. If one of the disks fails, you can restore data using the other two disks.

RAID is actually an industry specification that allows system administrators, integrators, and vendors to build fault-tolerance into computer systems. If you order a system that uses RAID-5, for example, the vendor knows the specification for that RAID level. You do not have to explain the type of fault-tolerance you want for your system.

Windows XP supports RAID-1, RAID-2, and RAID-5. Of the three, RAID-5 is most fault-tolerant. When you set up RAID-5, you must have at least three disks installed and they must be set up as dynamic disks. One thing to consider when setting up RAID-5 is that the combined disk space of all three disks is not the actual capacity you can use for storage. For example, if you have three disks at 20GB apiece, the RAID-5 has a 40GB capacity, not 60GB. This is because 20GB is used for parity, which is a value used to re-create a disk after a disk failure.

Create RAID Disks

1. Open the Control Panel and click Performance and Maintenance.
2. Click Administrative Tools and then double-click Computer Management.

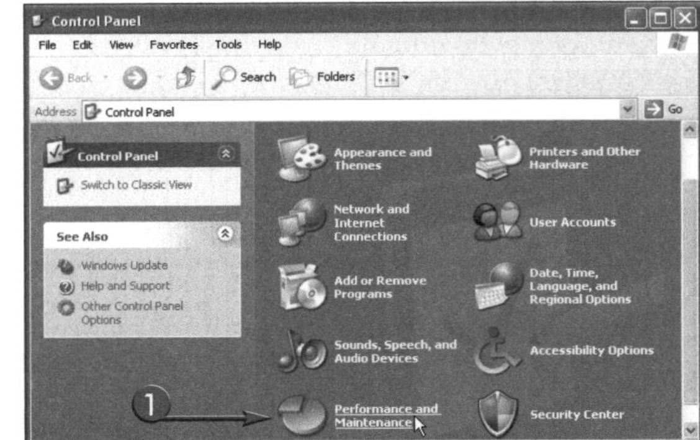

The Computer Management window appears.

3. Click the plus sign to view the Storage options.
4. Click Disk Management.
5. Right-click the dynamic disk on which you want to create the RAID-5 volume and click New Volume from the menu that appears.

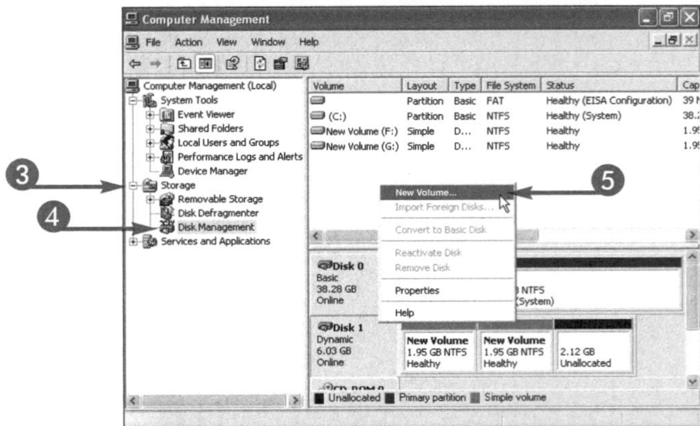

The New Volume Wizard appears.

6 Click Next.

The Select Volume Type screen appears.

7 Click the RAID-5 volume option.

8 Click Next.

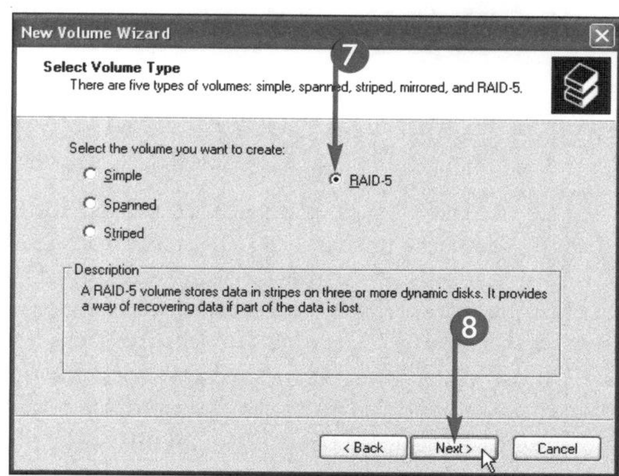

The Select Disks screen appears, showing a list of all the available RAID disks. You need at least three disks for RAID-5 to work.

9 Select the disks you want to use to create the volume.

10 Click Add.

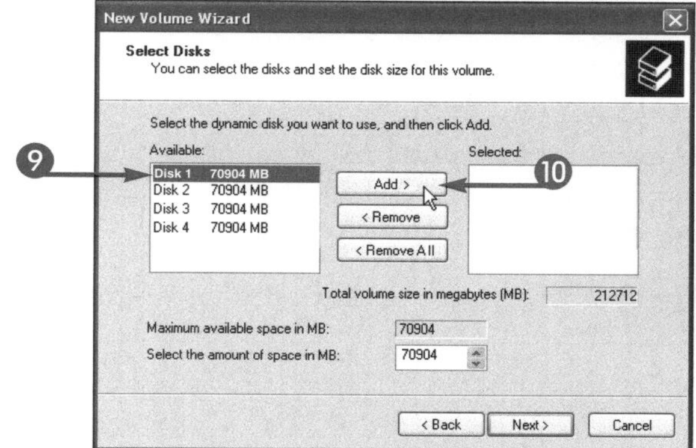

What special hardware is needed for RAID-5?

▼ You need at least three hard drives installed and a RAID controller. When you have these installed and working with your Windows setup, you usually have to restart your computer and display the computer setup information (the CMOS settings). Enable the RAID controller on your computer, set the boot order so the RAID controller boots after your floppy disk or bootable CD drive, and save your settings. For a full discussion of how to do this, consult the documentation that came with your RAID drives.

Do I need RAID disks on my computer?

▼ For most everyday computing activities, RAID is unnecessary. In fact, implementing RAID on a system can significantly increase its overall cost. Hardware specifications must include two more hard drives, a RAID controller, and usually a more powerful power supply is required for the computer. In addition to the hardware adjustments, most systems also include RAID management software that adds to the overall cost of a system. RAID is usually implemented on systems that store critical files, such as large databases, directory services data, and secure information. For an excellent tutorial on RAID, see the AC&NC Web site at www.acnc.com/04_01_00.html.

continued

Create RAID Disks *(Continued)*

Windows XP enables you to set up RAID disks for backing up data on your hard drives. When you have RAID enabled, data is automatically backed up to one or more additional disks to ensure data redundancy. Data redundancy is when you have your data stored on multiple disks. For example, you can have two disks that have exactly the same data stored on them in case the first disk is damaged. The second disk picks up the slack and restores the first disk with the saved data.

If a disk that is not the primary disk fails, you can repair it using an option found in the Computer Management window. Right-click a disk that has failed (it will have a label that says Failed Redundancy) and choose Repair Volume. Windows prompts you to choose a replacement disk and then starts the regeneration process.

As the RAID disks are regenerated, the Computer Management window displays a status of Regenerating. Let this process finish before starting any other programs or accessing any other files on your computer.

Create RAID Disks *(continued)*

- The selected dynamic disks appear here.

11. Click Next.

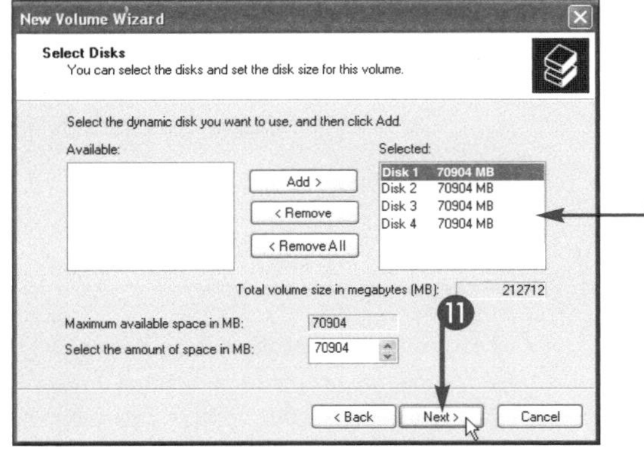

The Assign Drive Letter or Path screen appears.

12. Click here and select a drive letter for each disk.
13. Click Next.

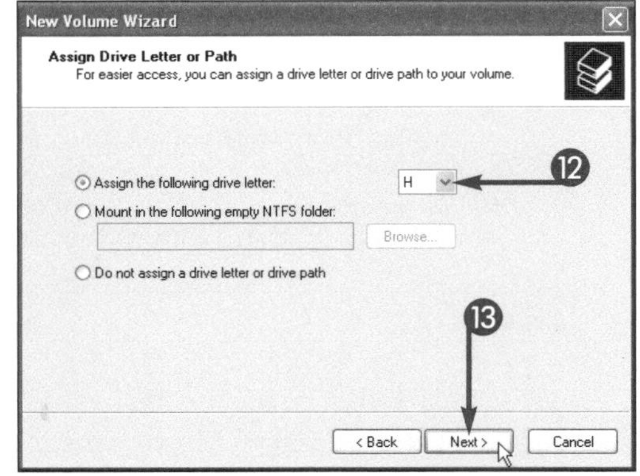

The Format Volume screen appears.

14 Click the option to format your partition with the settings you choose.

15 Click here and select NTFS.

16 Click this option to speed up the formatting of the disk.

17 Click Next.

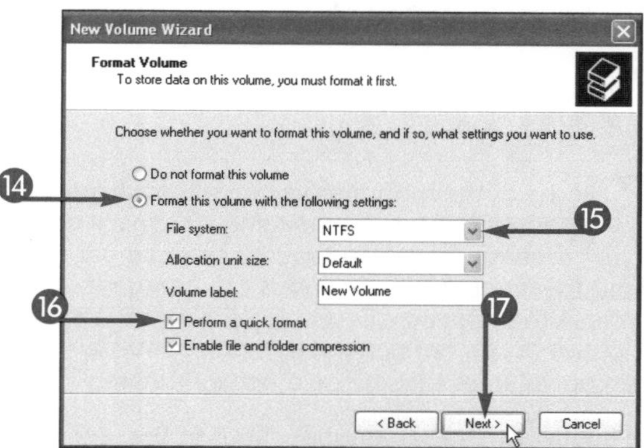

The final screen of the wizard appears.

18 Click Finish.

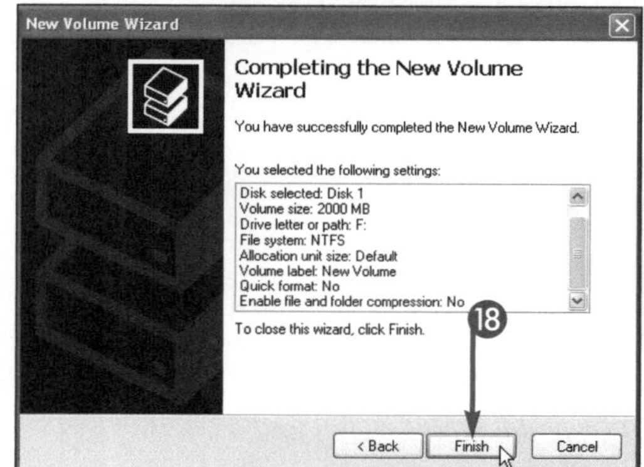

Are there other types of RAID strategies?

Yes, there are seven levels of RAID: RAID-0 to RAID-6. Each level includes different options and combinations of options of mirroring and disk striping. RAID-0, for example, is disk striping only. This is not a very good fault-tolerant level because there are no redundancies built-in, but it does provide great speed because files are saved across several disks. RAID-1 includes disk mirroring, which makes a duplication of your disk onto another disk or volume. This offers a cheap way of good fault-tolerance.

RAID seems very complicated to set up and manage to me. Are easier solutions available for ensuring my data is safe?

Yes. Other solutions include creating backup sets of your data on a daily basis. In the event of data loss, you can revert to the last backup set you created. The backup sets should be created every evening (or daytime if you work at night) when no activity is taking place on your computer. To ensure your backup set is safe, the backup should be created to a disk other than your main working disk (such as the C:\ drive). Usually this means storing the backup to a magnetic tape media. The tape can then be stored in a safe place. See the section "Back Up and Restore Data," later in this chapter, for more information.

Set Disk Quotas

One of the most important tasks for network administrators is managing disk space on their servers. With Windows XP, you can use disk quotas to limit the amount of space users can consume on a disk volume. Although you can set disk quotas on stand-alone computers (those not networked), disk quotas are generally set up on volumes that are on a network share.

Disk quotas let you set an upper limit to the amount of space users can consume. This alleviates the problem of disks running out of space when a user takes up too much space on a drive.

When you set disk quotas and a user exceeds his or her quota, you can set Windows to deny extra space or simply log the event and let the user continue to save files past the quota. When you deny users space beyond the quota, you run the risk of users losing important data. If you allow users disk space even if they exceed their quota, you can review event files periodically to see which users may need more disk space allocated.

Set Disk Quotas

1. Double-click the My Computer icon. Right-click the drive on which you want to set quotas, and click Properties from the menu that appears.
2. In the properties dialog box, click the Quota tab.
3. Click the option to enable quota management.
   - Click the option to deny space if users consume their allocated amount.
4. Click this option to set a limit on a disk.
5. Type the amount of space to set the limit to, and click ▾ to select the unit of measure for the amount. Normally the unit is a MB (megabyte) or GB (gigabyte).
6. To set a warning level so users know they have reached their disk quota, type that value here, and click ▾ to select the unit of measure for the amount.
   - To log events when users exceed quotas or when warning levels are reached, click these options.
7. Click Apply.

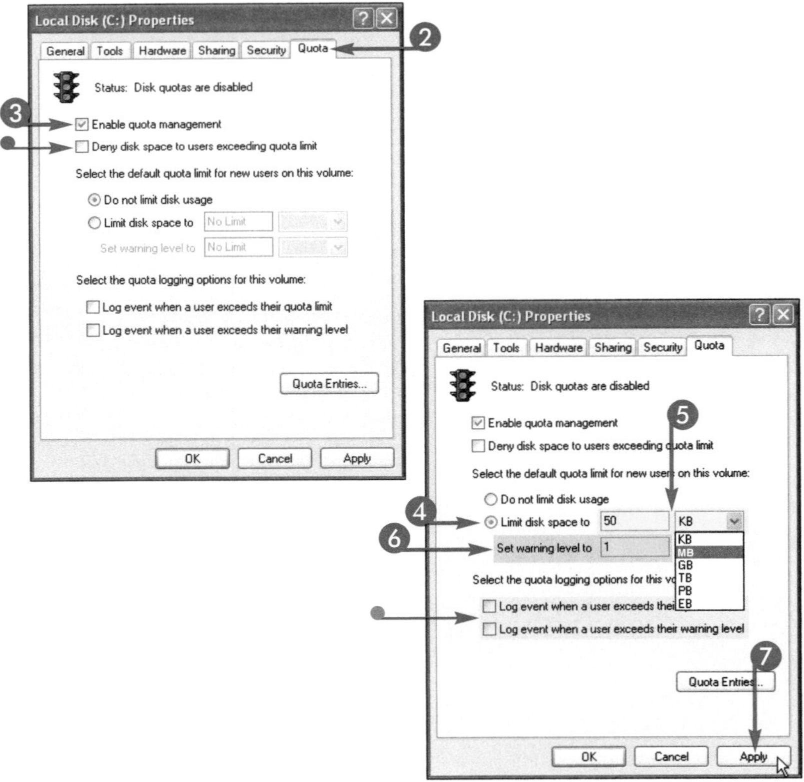

The Disk Quota dialog box appears. It tells you that Windows will take a few minutes to set up the disk usage statistics to determine storage usage per user.

8 Click OK.

9 To see the statistics, click Quota Entries in the properties dialog box.

The Quota Entries window appears. Here you can see the status of each user and how much space each user is consuming.

10 Click Quota and then Close to close this window.

11 Click OK to confirm your changes in the properties dialog box.

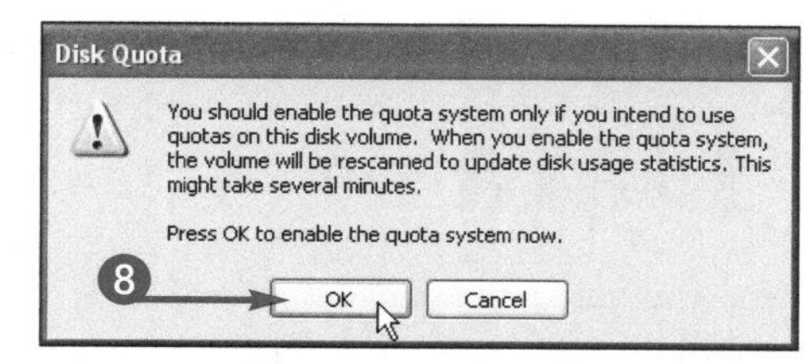

Disk Quota
You should enable the quota system only if you intend to use quotas on this disk volume. When you enable the quota system, the volume will be rescanned to update disk usage statistics. This might take several minutes.
Press OK to enable the quota system now.
8
OK
Cancel

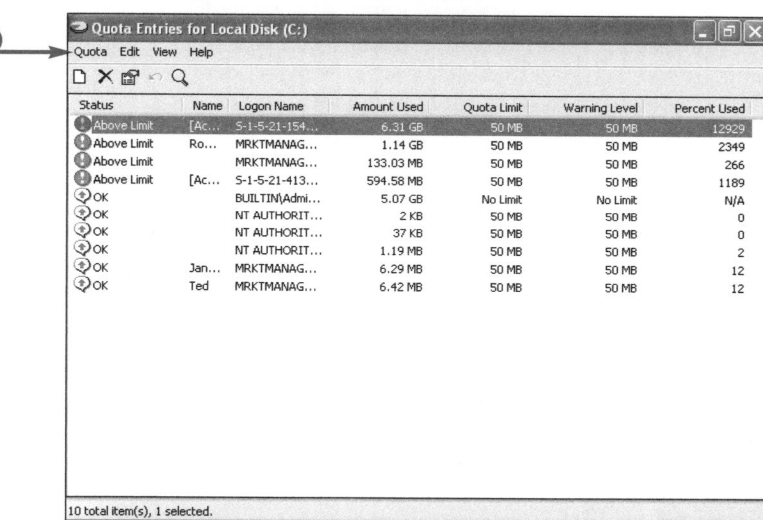

Quota Entries for Local Disk (C:)
10
Quota Edit View Help
Status | Name | Logon Name | Amount Used | Quota Limit | Warning Level | Percent Used
Above Limit [Ac... S-1-5-21-154... 6.31 GB 50 MB 50 MB 12929
Above Limit Ro... MRKTMANAG... 1.14 GB 50 MB 50 MB 2349
Above Limit MRKTMANAG... 133.03 MB 50 MB 50 MB 266
Above Limit [Ac... S-1-5-21-413... 594.58 MB 50 MB 50 MB 1189
OK BUILTIN\Admi... 5.07 GB No Limit No Limit N/A
OK NT AUTHORIT... 2 KB 50 MB 50 MB 0
OK NT AUTHORIT... 37 KB 50 MB 50 MB 0
OK NT AUTHORIT... 1.19 MB 50 MB 50 MB 2
OK Jan... MRKTMANAG... 6.29 MB 50 MB 50 MB 12
OK Ted MRKTMANAG... 6.42 MB 50 MB 50 MB 12
10 total item(s), 1 selected.

PART IV

What is a disk volume?

A disk volume is a disk area on which files can be stored. Every Windows computer has at least one disk volume. A physical disk, such as a hard drive, can be set up for one or multiple volumes. A volume can span more than one disk as well. Volumes are denoted by a letter, such as C. When you view your C drive using My Computer or Windows Explorer, you are looking at the disk volume of C. If you partition a drive into multiple volumes, you then have multiple drive letters.

How can I determine the amount of space a user needs?

One way is to ask each user what type of work he performs. Use this information to allocate enough space for his needs. For example, a user who typically creates letters and small documents does not need as much space as someone who creates and edits graphics. Another way is to allocate equal amounts of space to everyone (50MB, for example), and then check these drives periodically to ensure that space is being used. If you determine that half of that space will never be used, reallocate that space to another user.

Why have disk quotas if users can exceed them?

Quotas allow you to manage disk space more proactively even if you allow disk space for those that exceed their quota. By issuing a statement to users after you have instituted quotas and then by setting a warning level threshold, users then know that they can consume only a certain amount of space on the drives. This way you do not suddenly run out of space if one of your users decides to consume extremely large amounts of space for his or her graphics or music collection.

Back Up and Restore Data

Perhaps one of the most important jobs you can perform as a user or administrator is also one of the most overlooked jobs. This job is backing up your data. Organizations spend billions of dollars each year backing up and archiving their data in the event the data must be restored due to some kind of data loss.

You can use the Windows Backup utility to create a backup of your data. Windows can run the backup once, or run periodically to ensure data is always backed up. When you use the Backup utility to back up your data, you create backup jobs. You can have one job or several depending on your backup needs.

You may have several jobs if you want to create backup sets that include different types of data. For example, one backup job may back up only your graphics files. Another job can back up your word processing and spreadsheet files. Finally, a third job can be used to back up important system and configuration files.

When you configure your backups, you can select the type of files you want to back up. The My documents and settings option is a good choice if you use the My Documents folder to store a lot of your documents. The All information on this computer option is a great choice if you want to ensure all the data files and user settings are backed up. The downside to this last option is it consumes a great deal of backup media space.

Back Up and Restore Data

1. To create a backup job, click Start, All Programs, Accessories, and then System Tools.
2. Click Backup.

   The Backup or Restore Wizard appears.

   - For this example, use the default wizard mode.
   - Alternately, click Advanced Mode to set up backups using advanced options.
3. Click Next.

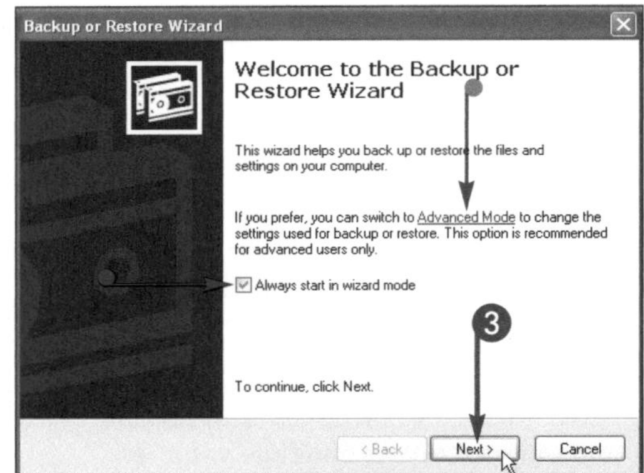

The Backup or Restore screen appears.

4. Click the option to back up files and settings.
5. Click Next.

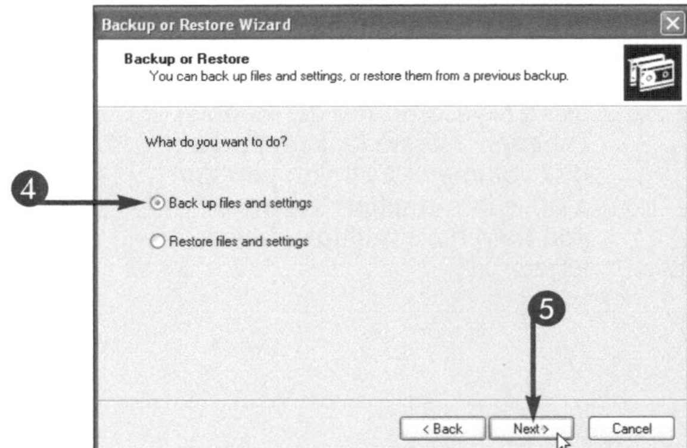

The What to Back Up screen appears.

6 Click what you want to back up.

This example uses My documents and settings.

7 Click Next.

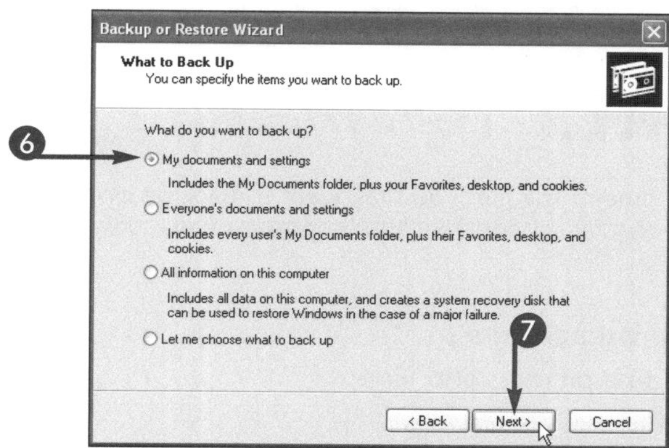

The Backup Type, Destination, and Name screen appears.

8 Click here and select a location for the backup.

- Click Browse to navigate to another location.

9 Type a name for the backup file.

10 Click Next.

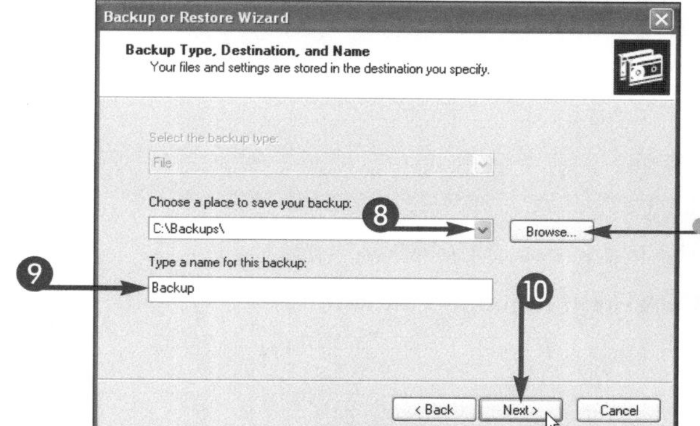

I often forget to run daily backups. Can I have Windows do it automatically for me?

▼ Yes, in fact that is the preferred choice of system administrators. Automatic backups ensure the data is backed up regardless of whether the administrator forgets or remembers that day to do the backup. Automatic backups also ensure the all the data you want backed up is actually backed up each time. You do not, for example, have to remember each day if you backed up your documents, graphics, or system files the day before. You just select the items you want backed up when you create the backup job and then Windows performs the backup each day (or time interval you specify).

I do not have any important files on my computer. Why should I back them up?

▼ Backing up is a personal choice for your own personal documents. For networks and many organizations, creating backups is a required loss-prevention and security procedure. Businesses rely on computer data for much of their daily work. The data on your computer, if in a company environment, probably belongs to the company. The company does not want to pay you to re-create loads of data each time the data is lost. You should back up any files you do not want to or cannot re-create, including databases, customer lists, accounting files, and customer correspondence.

continued

Back Up and Restore Data *(Continued)*

Some of the files you may want to back up on a regular schedule include important files, such as:

- Bank statements
- Digital pictures and videos
- Windows system files
- E-mail addresses
- E-mail messages
- Internet or network connection settings
- Music files
- Internet Explorer bookmarks
- Office templates and clip art
- Offline Web pages
- Personal financial files (Money or Quicken files, for example)

Back Up and Restore Data *(continued)*

The last screen of the wizard appears.

⑪ Click Finish to run this backup.

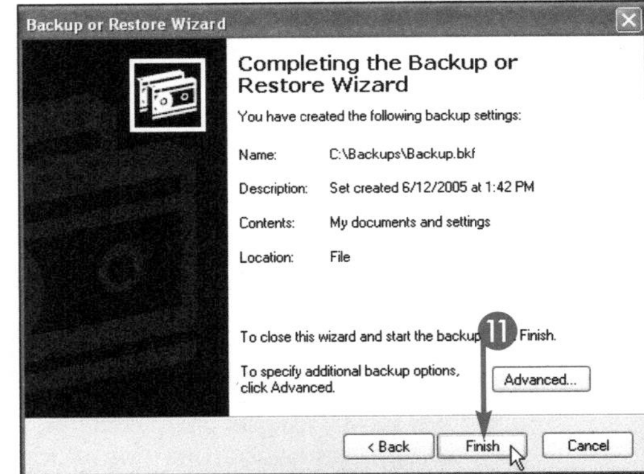

⑫ To restore the backup file, start the Backup or Restore Wizard by following Steps 1 and 2 from the previous page.

⑬ Click the Next button to show the Backup or Restore screen.

The Backup or Restore screen appears.

⑭ Click the option to restore files and settings.

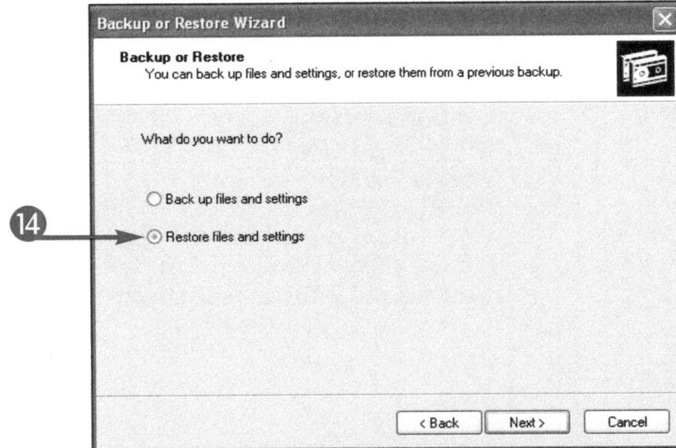

The What to Restore screen appears. This is where you select the backup file or files that you want to restore.

15 Click an item to restore.

- Click Browse to locate additional backup files.

16 Select a backup file.

17 Click Next.

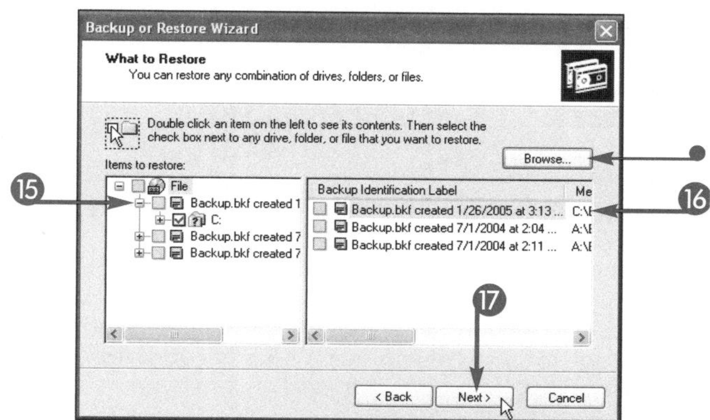

The Completing the Backup or Restore Wizard screen appears.

When you restore backup files, the default action is for the files to return to their original location, regardless of if you have more current files there now.

18 To select a different location for the restore files, click Advanced.

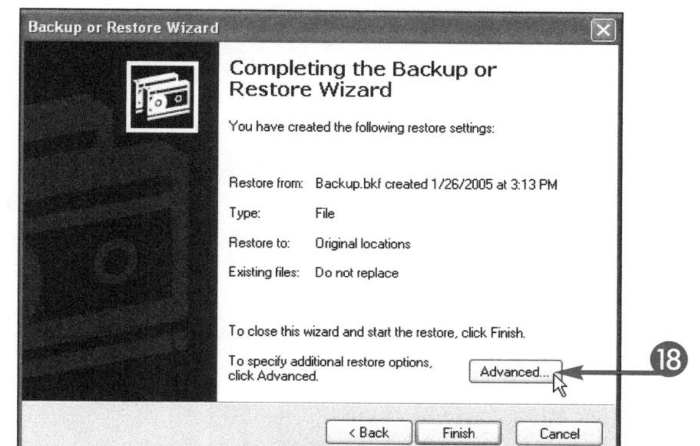

When I restore a backup file, what happens to any data that is still on my disk?

During restore, if you choose the Advanced method following Step 2 of this section, you have the choice of leaving existing files and just adding to them the ones on the restore disk, replacing existing files if they are older than the ones on the restore disk, or replace existing files. If you are looking to rebuild a computer due to a catastrophic loss or possible virus infection, the latter option is the best. However, if you want to compare files on the restore disk to ones still on your system, choose the first option.

Where should I store my backup files?

The best place to store backup files is in a place where they cannot be damaged or stolen. Many times users create daily backups to media that they store locally, such as in a locked cabinet or file box. Then, once a week another backup is made that includes all changes made during the course of the week. This backup, usually made to a file and then burned to CD-R or made directly to tape, is carried off-site and stored in a safe place. Before taking private or confidential data from your company, however, ask your system administrator or manager if privacy concerns restrict this type of activity. By having a backup off-site, you can restore the data in the event your on-site backup is destroyed or stolen.

continued

Back Up and Restore Data *(Continued)*

In the event of a disaster or data loss, you need to restore your backup files. Windows XP enables you to restore files you backed up. This is done by using Microsoft Backup and accessing the media on which you backed up your data. Backups can be saved to files, disks, removable disks (such as Zip disks), or digital tape. Another common place to store backup sets is on a network storage area, such as a disk found on your local area network.

When you run the Restore portion of Microsoft Backup, you have the option of restoring the files back to their original location or selecting a different location. If you want to restore your computer back to a previous time, such as before a virus problem or system failure, restore the backup to its original location. This copies the backup data over any data that is currently residing in the original location.

Remember that newer files may be in that original location than what has been saved to your backup set.

Back Up and Restore Data *(continued)*

The Where to Restore screen appears.

19 Click here and select a location.

This example uses the Alternate location option.

20 Type a location for the restore files to be copied to.

21 Click Next.

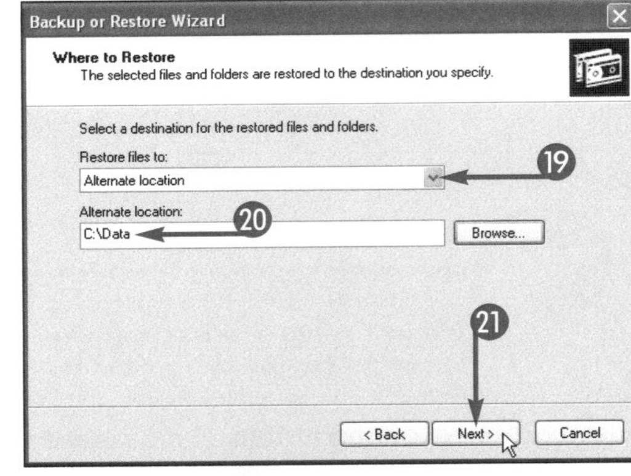

The How to Restore screen appears.

22 Select the option you want for restoring the files.

23 Click Next.

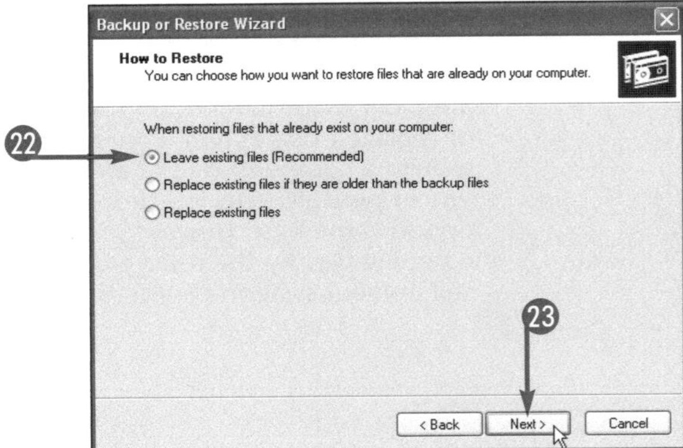

The Advanced Restore Options screen appears.

24 Click Next.

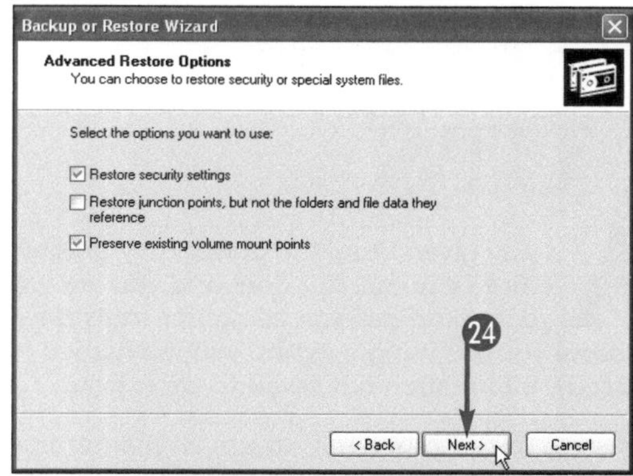

The final wizard screen appears.

25 Click Finish to start the restore process.

Why would I want to restore to a different location than the original?

- Restore to a different location if you want to keep any existing data that happens to be in the backup data original location. After the data is restored to a different location, such as to a temporary folder, you can then copy any data from the restore directory back to its original location if you want it there.

  One of the main reasons to restore to a different location is if the data in the original location has changed since your backup set was made, and you need to retain this changed data. For example, you may have a folder in which a customer relationship database is stored. You work in this database every day and your backup is created at midnight every night. That means if you restore your backup set after you started work one morning, all changes to the database you have made will be lost. Instead, restore to a different location and examine the data before copying to the original location. Of course, if the data in your original location is corrupt beyond repair, your best bet is to restore to the original location.

On one of our computers the Restore security settings option is not available during the Restore process. Why not?

- For this option to be available, the operating system must be set up as an NTFS file system, not FAT.

Configure a UPS

At any given time, the power may go out in your office or home. If it does and you are working on your computer, the computer shuts down (unless of course you are using a laptop with a charged battery installed). Information not saved to file is lost.

A solution to this problem is to use an uninterruptible power supply (known as a UPS), which can be used to provide battery power to your system for several minutes. With Windows XP, you can set up and manage UPS devices.

You can set notifications that show up in Windows when power failures have occurred, set alarms that alert you to the amount of power left in the UPS, and configure how Windows should react when the alarm occurs.

You can set Windows to shut down gracefully (that is, shut down using the Windows shut down feature) when the UPS has a few minutes of power left. This is handy if you happen to be out of the office when the power outage occurs. It also works well for network servers that should be shut down properly so shared files are not lost.

Configure a UPS

1. Open the Control Panel, and click the Performance and Maintenance icon.
2. Click Power Options.

   The Power Options Properties dialog box appears.
3. Click the UPS tab.
4. Click Select.

   The UPS Selection window appears.
5. Click here and select the manufacturer of your UPS device.
6. Click the model of your UPS device.
7. Click here and select the port to which the UPS device is connected.
8. Click Finish to close the UPS Selection window.
9. Click Configure in the properties dialog box.

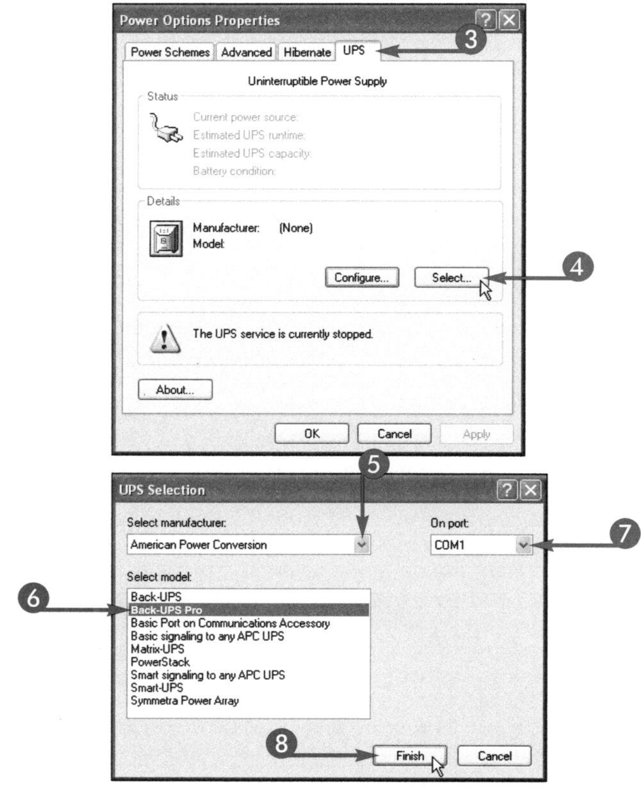

The UPS Configuration dialog box appears.

10 Click the option to enable all notifications.

11 Set the seconds for the first notification.

12 Usually you have only two to five minutes for the UPS to work after a power failure. Set the second notification within that time limit so you can shut down Windows before the UPS powers off.

13 Set the number of minutes the UPS will keep your computer running until all power is lost.

14 To have a task run when the critical alarm goes off, such as running a network logout script, click Configure.

The UPS System Shutdown Program dialog box appears.

15 Type the path to a file to run during the critical alarm phase.

16 Click OK to close the UPS System Shutdown Program dialog box.

17 Click OK to close the UPS Configuration dialog box.

18 Click OK in the properties dialog box to confirm your changes.

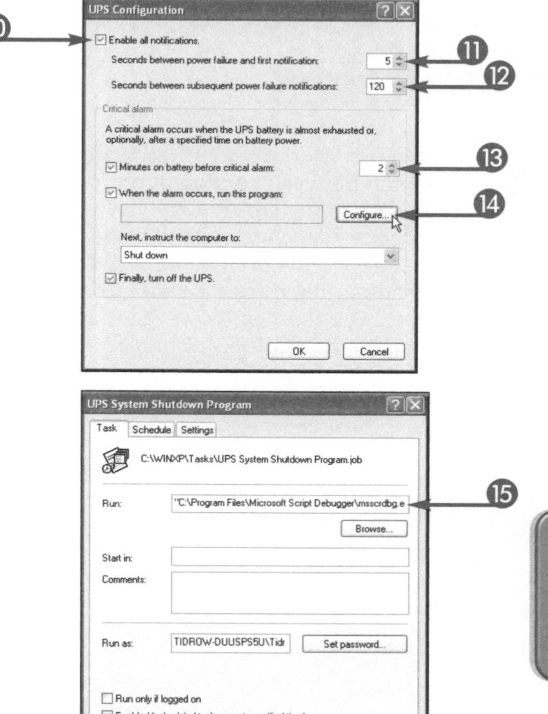

I have a UPS made by a company not listed in the UPS Selection dialog box. What should I choose?

▼ Choose Generic or refer to the documentation that came with your UPS device. Many times the UPS device comes with separate software you can use to manage the device. You are not required to use the UPS configuration settings that Windows provides. If you use Generic, you should consult the documentation for your UPS on setting the UPS signal polarity. This is an option that controls when a signal is sent to your computer during an outage — the signal is either positive or negative polarity.

Can I hook up my printer to the UPS?

▼ If you have an inkjet printer, you can connect it to the UPS in case you need to print something while the power is out. Remember, UPS devices usually only stay charged for a few minutes when running on battery only. They are intended to be used for keeping your computer running during power glitches that can bring down your computer or to help you save files and exit Windows when the power fails. UPS devices are not made for long-term usage.

Use Hardware Profiles

You can use Windows XP's Hardware Profile feature to switch between configurations on your portable computer. Many laptop users have a different monitor, a separate keyboard, a stand-alone mouse, or other devices when their PC sits on their desk in their office (often at a docking station that makes it easier to connect all this extra hardware). On the road, however, many portable PC users make do with the laptop's display screen, the touchpad instead of the mouse, and the laptop keyboard. There are also common laptop features (such as Infrared) that have little use in an office environment. (Two related settings, wireless connectivity and power management, are covered later in this chapter.)

To add another profile, access Hardware Profiles by right-clicking My Computer. Then click Properties and select the Hardware tab in the System Properties dialog box. Click Hardware Profiles. Your PC starts with at least one hardware profile, called Profile 1 by default. To add another profile so that you can switch between them, click Profile 1 and click Copy. Assign a name to your copy. Now shut down your PC. You have completed the first part of this procedure.

Use Hardware Profiles

1. Click Start.
2. Right-click My Computer.
3. Click Properties.

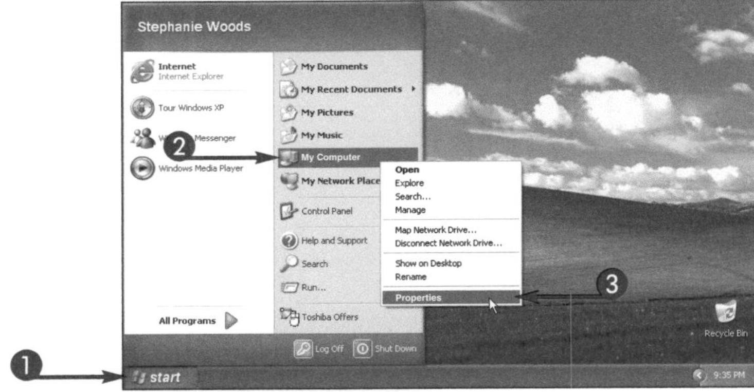

The System Properties dialog box appears.

4. Click the Hardware tab.
5. Click Hardware Profiles.

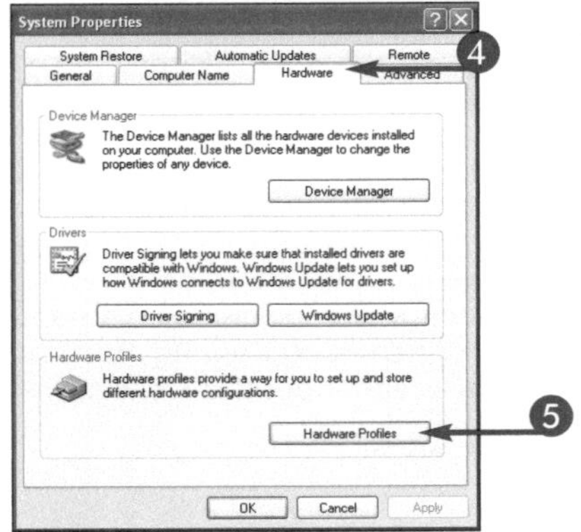

The Hardware Profiles dialog box appears.

6 Click Profile 1 (or the existing profile).

7 Click Copy.

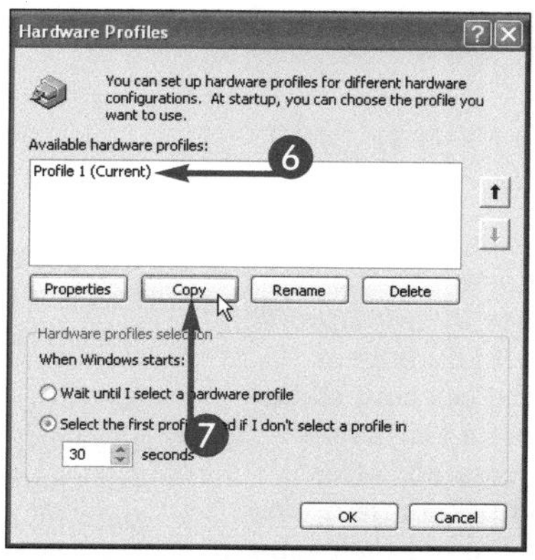

The Copy Profile dialog box appears.

8 Type a profile name.

9 Click OK.

- The new profile appears here.
- These options control how Windows performs hardware profile selection at startup.

10 Click OK.

11 Click OK to close the System Properties dialog box.

12 Click Start and then Shutdown (on XP Professional) or Turn Off Computer (on XP Home).

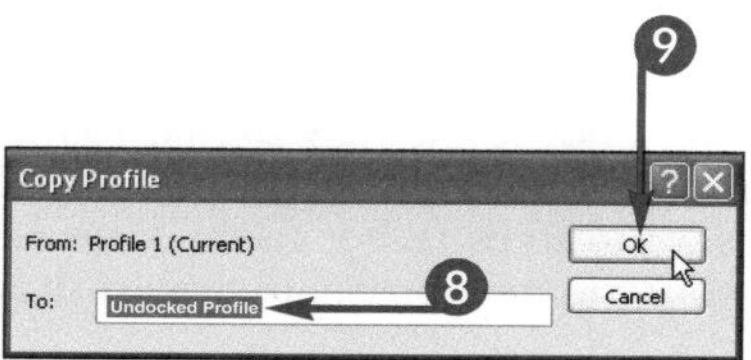

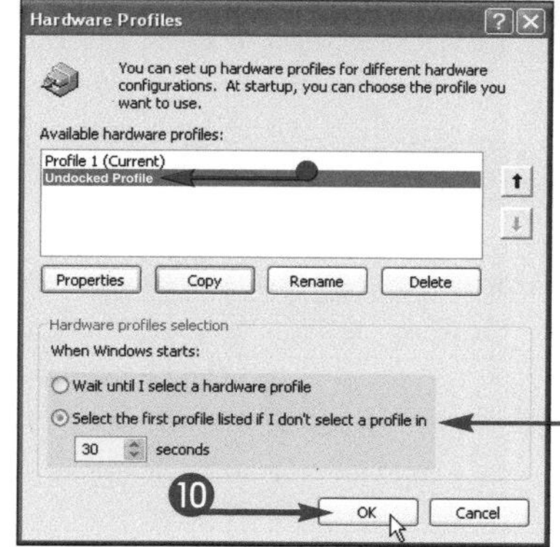

Can I use the hardware profile feature to keep track of two sets of Desktop settings as well?

No. This feature was originally developed to address laptops with docking stations and focuses only on the availability of hardware devices. To keep more than one set of desktop settings, see the section "Choose Windows Themes" in Chapter 5.

What if I have a docking station at work and one at home? Can I use this feature for both?

Yes. You can have more than one docked hardware profile and assign each a different name. The docking stations in such a situation are most likely connected to slightly different hardware. Make sure to follow the procedures in the remainder of this section to customize each one accordingly.

continued

Use Hardware Profiles *(Continued)*

After you have powered down your PC, you can connect or disconnect any hardware so that your physical hardware setup matches the new profile you have just created. Turn on your PC. If you have a docking station, remove your PC from the docking station. As Windows starts, you are asked to select a Hardware Profile. Choose the new profile you just created. After Windows has started, right-click My Computer again, and repeat the steps to get to the Hardware Profiles dialog box. Choose the new profile in the list (now showing as current).

Click Properties to bring up the properties dialog box for the current profile. Click the option (☑) to indicate that this is a portable computer. Then click OK to close the dialog box and click OK again to close Hardware Profiles.

At this point you can change hardware settings by clicking the Device Manager that applies to just this hardware profile. For example, you could enable infrared for communicating with PDAs and other laptops when you are on the road, or disable extra input devices that you are not using.

Use Hardware Profiles *(continued)*

13. Repeat Steps 1 to 5 to bring up the Hardware Profiles dialog box.
14. Click your new profile from the list.
15. Click Properties.
16. Click the option to indicate your computer is portable.
17. Click OK.
18. Click OK in the Hardware Profiles dialog box.
19. Click Device Manager.

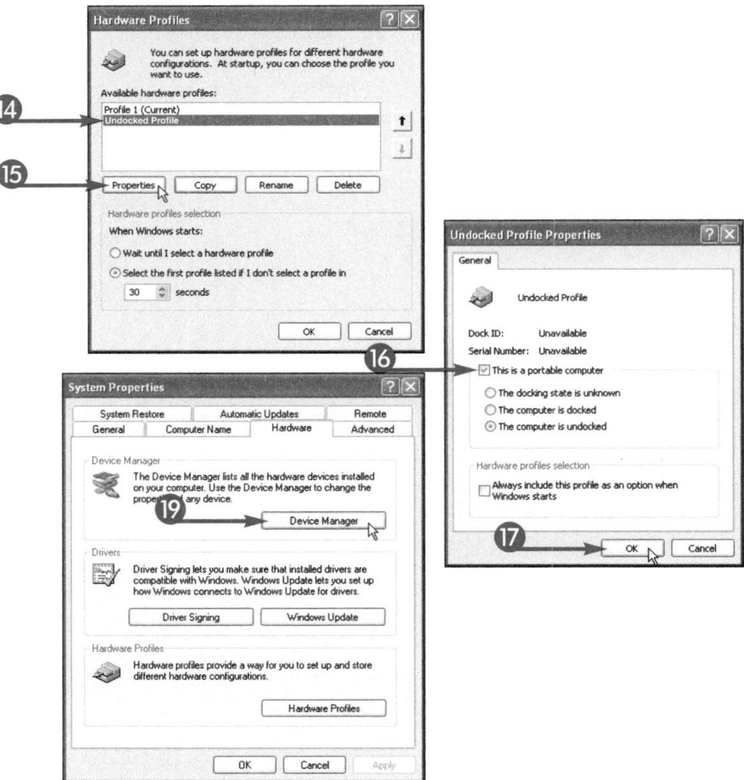

The Device Manager window appears.

⑳ Right-click a device you want to enable (an infrared port in this example).

㉑ Click Enable from the menu that appears.

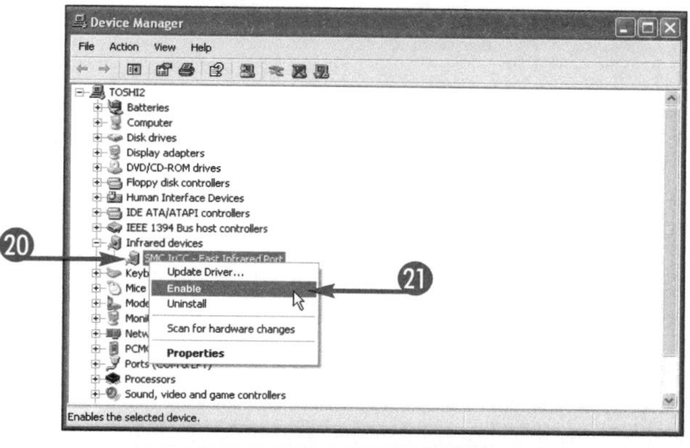

㉒ Right-click a device you want to disable in this profile (keyboard hot keys in this example).

㉓ Click Disable from the menu that appears.

㉔ Click here to close the Device Manager window.

㉕ Click OK to close the System Properties dialog box.

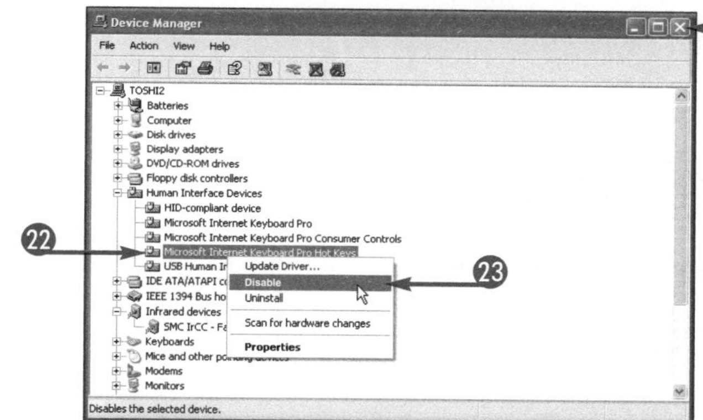

PART IV

Do I have to set up hardware profiles?

▼ That depends. If your PC and all its hardware and drivers are fully plug and play compliant, Windows can handle the different hardware changes without any manual changes on your part. If, however, you have some legacy hardware that is not plug and play compliant, or if you want to enable or disable certain hardware devices, you should take advantage of this feature.

Can I have more than two hardware profiles?

▼ Yes, if need be. Simply follow the same steps as those above. If you have more than two hardware profiles, it is a good idea to use the up and down arrows (↑ and ↓) in the Hardware Profiles list to put them in order of most frequent usage.

Work with Wireless Networks

If you have a wireless network transmitter as part of your home network, or if you are using a wireless network at work or in a public location such as an airport, convention center, or café, you can easily locate wireless networks in your area.

You must have a wireless networking adapter (either built-in or installed as an adapter card or PCMCIA card). The standard protocols for running wireless networking are IEEE 802.11*x* protocols. The most common variants that you may encounter are 802.11b (the older but broadly available protocol, running at speeds of 5.5 or 11 Mbps) and 802.11g (newer and backwardly compatible with 802.11b, running at speeds up to 54 Mbps).

If you have a wireless adapter installed in your PC but have not yet connected to your home or business wireless network, you see a wireless networking icon in the notification bar with a red × next to it (■), indicating that your wireless adapter is up and running but not connected to a network. Right-click the icon and click View Available Wireless Networks from the menu that appears to get started. Any available local wireless networks are displayed.

Work with Wireless Networks

1. Right-click the wireless networking icon.

2. Click View Available Wireless Networks from the menu that appears.

The Choose a wireless network window appears.

3. Click your wireless network from the list.
4. Click Connect.

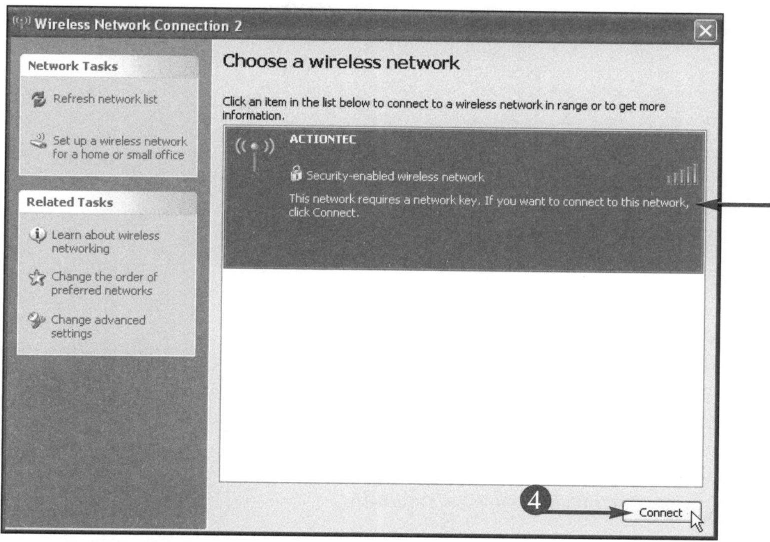

The Wireless Network Connection window appears.

Note: *This is one way to connect. Some networks require no key. In such cases, ignore Steps 5 and 6.*

5. Type your network key.
6. Retype your network key to confirm.
7. Click Connect.

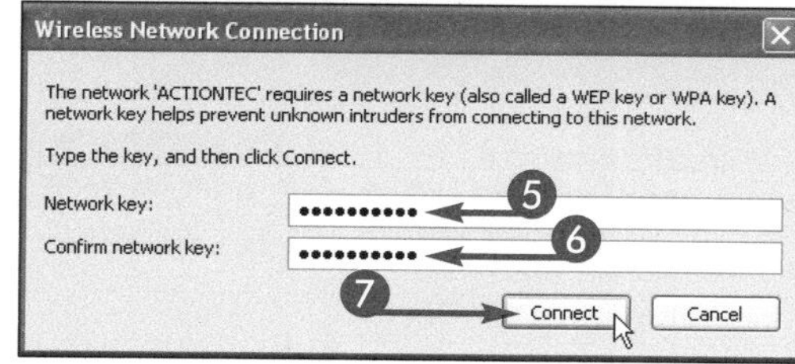

I do not see any wireless networks listed. What should I do?

▼ First, confirm that your wireless network is up and running (ideally at another computer). If it is, check to see if you are close enough to be receiving a signal (100% is optimal) by right-clicking the wireless networking icon ( ). If you are receiving a weak signal, try to move closer to the transmitter.

Apart from using a network key, are there additional ways to secure my home wireless network?

▼ Yes. You can employ WPA-based security or hide your network name (SSID), among other things. The techniques involved are beyond the scope of this book. Go to www.microsoft.com and search on the phrase **wireless networking security** for more information.

continued

Work with Wireless Networks *(Continued)*

After you have selected your local wireless network, you can click Connect. If you are using a home or business wireless network, it should be a security-enabled one. Otherwise your network is open to anyone within wireless range of a transmitter. (For more information on secure wireless networking, search on **wireless networking security** from the Help and Support Center or consult your network hardware documentation.) In most cases, you need to have the network key — usually a 64-bit or 128-bit Wired Equivalent Privacy (WEP) key — ready to access your wireless network. Enter the key (the screen displays dots instead of the characters you typed, as with a password) and confirm to access your network.

If you are trying to access a more public wireless network, be aware that this is a more risky situation in terms of security. Before accessing a public network, make sure that you have your Windows Firewall settings set for maximum protection. Right-click your wireless networking icon (■) and click Change Windows Firewall settings from the menu that appears. Make sure that Windows Firewall is on and that Don't allow exceptions is selected (☑). You then have additional protection against unauthorized access to your PC in a relatively unprotected environment.

Work with Wireless Networks *(continued)*

After connecting successfully, you are returned to the Choose a wireless network window.

- These icons indicate connection status and signal strength.

8 Click Change advanced settings.

The Wireless Network Connection 2 Properties dialog box appears.

9 Click the Wireless Networks tab.

- Click here to select the order of preferred networks.
- Clear this option if you want to use other software to configure your wireless network settings.

10 Click OK.

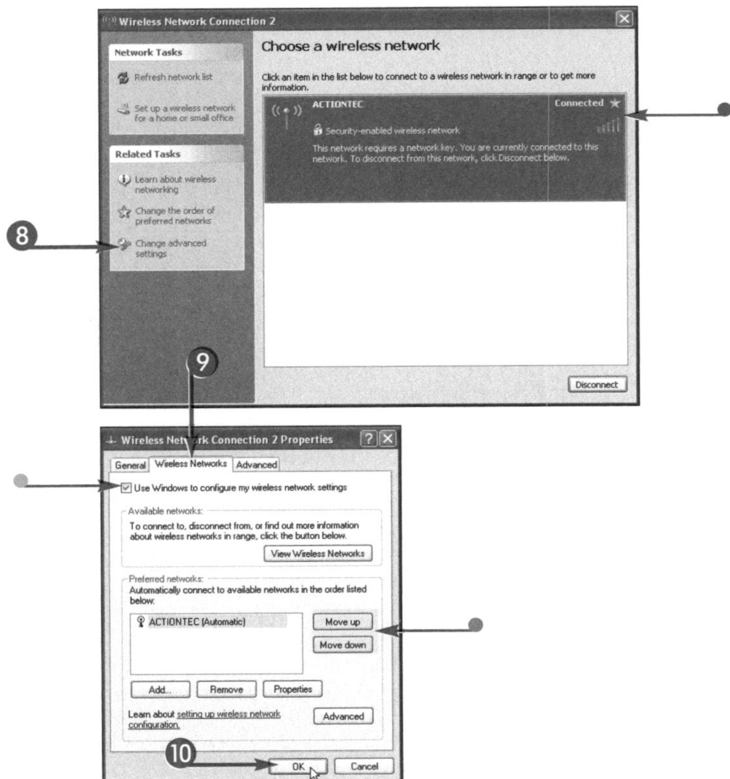

Change firewall settings for an unsecured wireless network

1. Right-click the wireless networking icon.
2. Click Change Windows Firewall settings from the menu that appears.

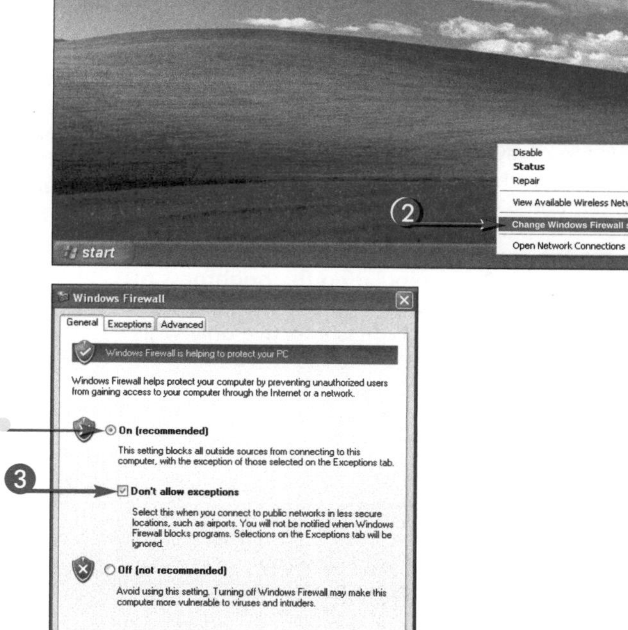

The Windows Firewall dialog box appears.

- This option indicates that Windows Firewall is on.

3. Click the option to not allow exceptions.
4. Click OK.

Just how secure is wireless networking?

▼ Using the currently and commonly available hardware with 802.11b or 802.11g and WEP, wireless networking has distinct vulnerabilities. Service Pack 2 supports the newer, more secure encryption protocol WPA (WiFi Protected Access) that works with IEEE 802.11i. At the time of this writing, however, hardware supporting this standard was not broadly available. Until this situation is remedied, you must weigh the likelihood of unauthorized access (how close is your transmitter to public access?) and the sensitivity of your data against the convenience and cost-effectiveness of a wireless solution.

My wireless adapter has separate software to access wireless networks. Which should I use?

▼ Windows XP SP2 defers to software from card manufacturers. Clear the option Use Windows to configure my wireless network settings (☑ changes to ☐) to enable third-party software.

Install and Use ClearType

You can take advantage of Microsoft's ClearType technology to make the text on your screen easier to read, especially if you are using a liquid crystal display (LCD) screen, such as those found on portable computers and flat panel monitors.

ClearType reduces the jaggedness (commonly referred to as *raster jag*) of screen fonts. By manipulating the brightness of individual subpixels in each character, ClearType makes the characters appear smoother. ClearType is effective only with color quality settings of 256 colors or higher. It works best with 24-bit or 32-bit color (High or Highest).

ClearType technology is at its most effective when used with a flat panel screen. Although it usually improves the appearance of screen fonts on traditional cathode ray tube (CRT) monitors as well, there are some situations in which ClearType makes the text appear slightly less well defined on this kind of monitor. Use the Standard method of smoothing screen fonts if you are using a CRT monitor and the text appears blurry to you.

ClearType comes already installed with Windows XP. You can activate it or determine whether it has already been activated by following these steps.

Install and Use ClearType

1. Right-click in an empty area of your desktop and click Properties from the menu that appears.

The Display Properties dialog box appears.

2. Click the Appearance tab.
   - Note the appearance of the text without ClearType.
3. Click Effects.

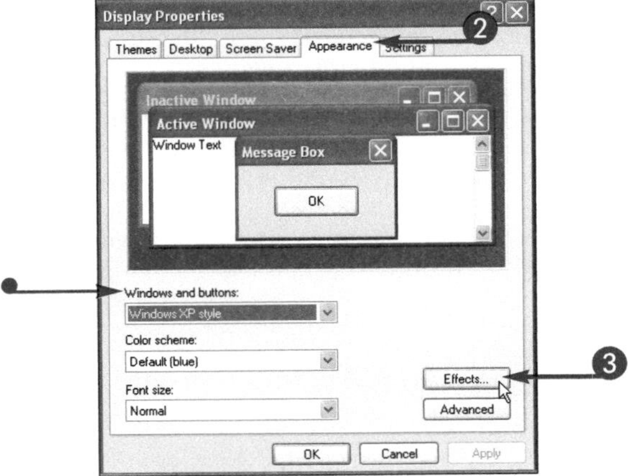

The Effects dialog box appears.

4. Click this option to choose the method to smooth text.
5. Click here and then select ClearType.
6. Click OK.
7. Click OK again to close the Display Properties dialog box.

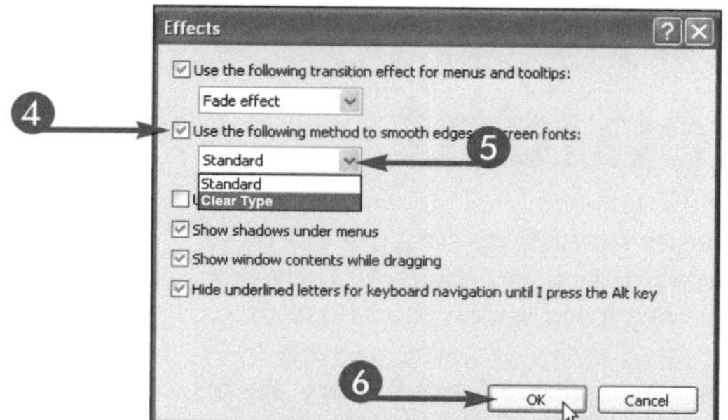

- Note the improved appearance of the text.

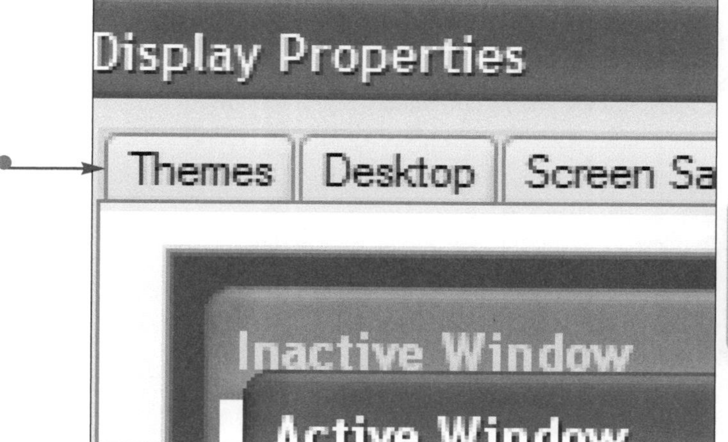

How can I make sure my display colors are set correctly for ClearType?

Right-click in any empty area of your desktop. Click Properties from the menu that appears. In the Display Properties dialog box, click the Settings tab. The Color quality settings available to you depend on your video card and monitor capabilities. The greater the number of colors, the more finely ClearType can adjust the screen fonts. Choose the highest setting shown in your dropdown list, preferably High (24-bit) or Highest (32-bit).

When I am adjusting my ClearType settings, can I compare samples side by side so I can pick which one looks best?

Yes. Microsoft has a ClearType tuner on the Web. Start Internet Explorer and go to www.microsoft.com/typography. Mouse over ClearType in the left column and a list of options appears. Click ClearType tuner. Depending on your security settings, you may be asked whether you want to install the ActiveX control for ClearType tuner. After the ClearType tuner is installed, you can follow a simple four-step process to make adjustments by comparing samples side by side on your screen.

Configure Power Management

You can configure power settings for your portable PC from the Control Panel. Windows XP provides a list of power schemes from which to choose or change individual settings and assign a name to your own custom power scheme. You can also set low-battery alarms, view the amount of power remaining in your battery or batteries, and have your battery power display in the taskbar notification area.

To configure power options, open the Control Panel and click Performance and Maintenance, and then Power Options (if you are using the Classic View, you can go directly to Power Options). The Power Options Properties dialog box appears. Select a power scheme that applies to your situation. Each scheme has separate settings for AC and battery power if you have a portable PC. The preferred settings for a portable PC are Portable/Laptop and Max Battery. These schemes turn off your monitor and hard drives sooner than schemes for desktop PCs. Max Battery turns off devices and goes into standby or hibernate mode after very little idle time. Presentation scheme leaves everything on so that your PC stays fully functional for giving a presentation. The remaining schemes are intended for desktop PCs.

Configure Power Management

1. Click Start.
2. Click Control Panel.

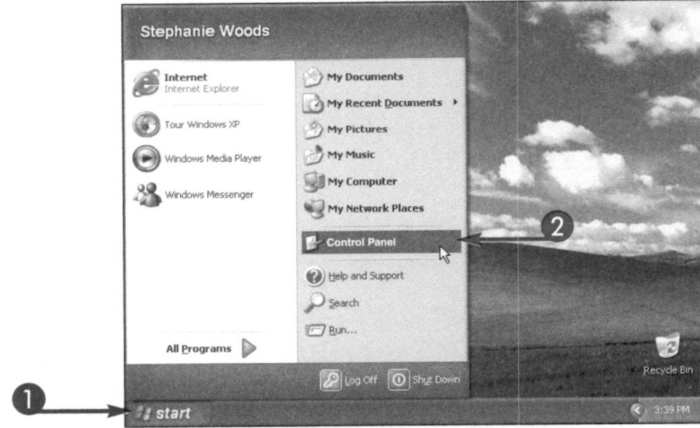

The Control Panel appears.

3. Click Performance and Maintenance.

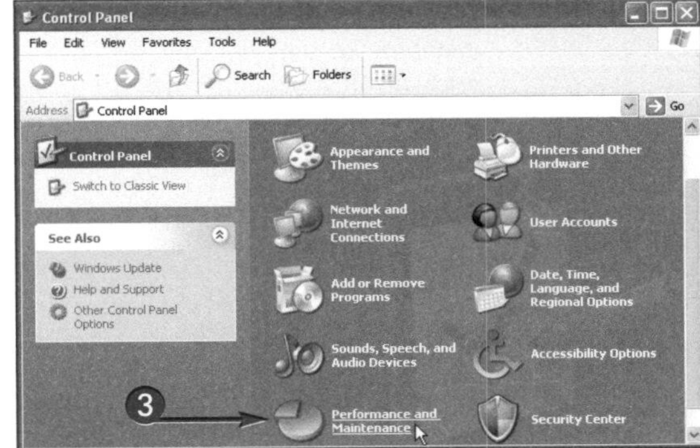

4 Click Power Options.

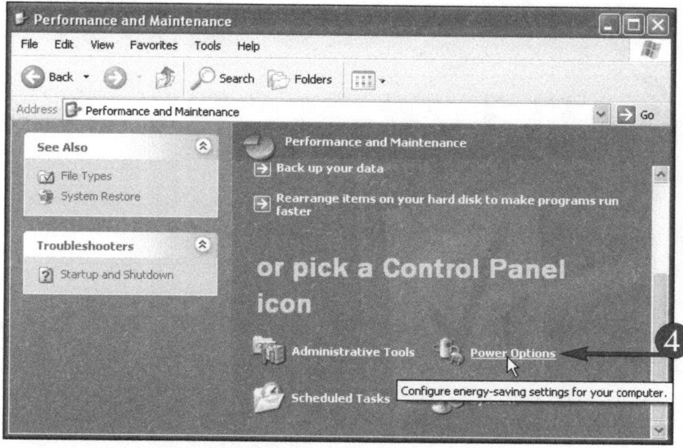

The Power Options Properties dialog box appears.

5 Click here and select Portable/Laptop.

- Select Max Battery if you are going to be without AC power.

6 Click the Alarms tab.

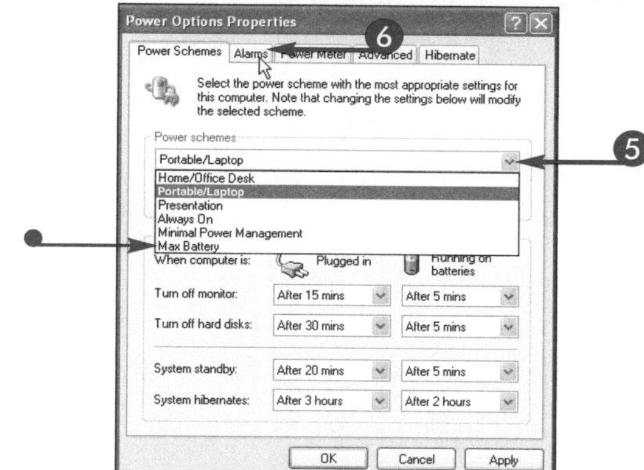

How do I keep my PC from turning off my monitor and hard drive too soon?

▼ You can either select a power scheme that makes minimal or no power saving changes during idle times (such as Always On or Minimal Power Management), or you can create your own scheme with very long time settings and save it by clicking Save As and assigning it a name.

How do I set options for longest battery life?

▼ Select the Max Battery power scheme from the Power Schemes tab of the Power Options Properties dialog box, and set the Turn off monitor and Turn off hard disks settings for as little time as you feel comfortable with. Do the same with system standby and hibernate settings.

continued

Configure Power Management *(Continued)*

You can configure how Windows XP behaves in a low-battery situation on the Alarms tab of the Power Options Properties box. There are two alarms; one notifies you when your PC reaches a low threshold of remaining power (10 percent by default), and another tells you when even less battery power remains (4 percent by default). You can set the type of warning (a sound, a text message, or both) and what occurs next. You can have your PC do nothing, switch to standby or hibernate mode, shut down, or run a program of your choice.

From the Power Meter tab, you can check on the power level of your batteries and determine your current power source (AC or battery). Click the Advanced tab and check the Always show icon on the taskbar option to display a battery icon ( ) with its power level graphically displayed on the taskbar. Move your mouse over the icon to see the power level percentage remaining. If your portable PC is running on AC power, you see a plug icon ( ) instead. Right-clicking this icon (battery or plug) brings up a menu that takes you to the power meter or the Power Options Properties dialog box.

Configure Power Management *(continued)*

7. Click these options to activate low and critical battery alarms.
   - Click and drag these sliders to change the power level percentage that must be reached to make the alarm go off.
   - Click here to change the alarm action.
8. Click the Power Meter tab.

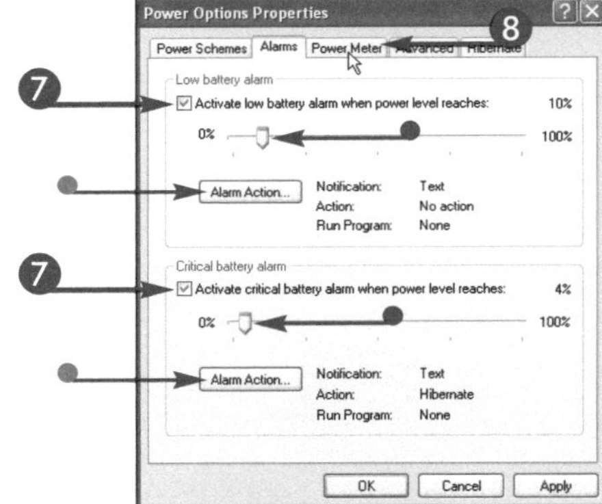

9. Click this option to show battery status.
10. Click the Advanced tab.

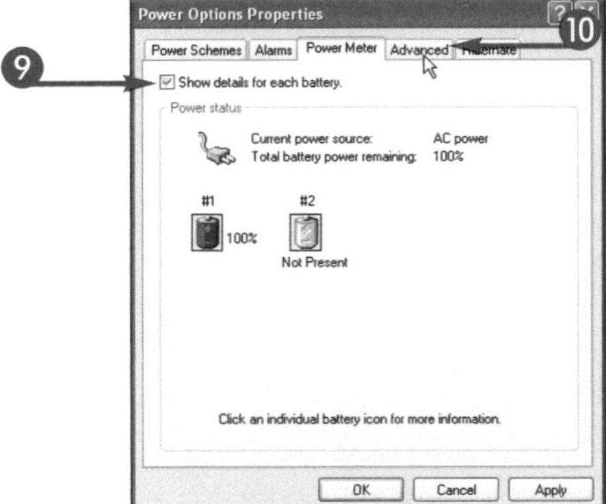

⑪ Click this option to show the power icon (battery or plug) on the taskbar.

⑫ Click OK to accept changes.

⑬ Click ☒ to close the Control Panel.

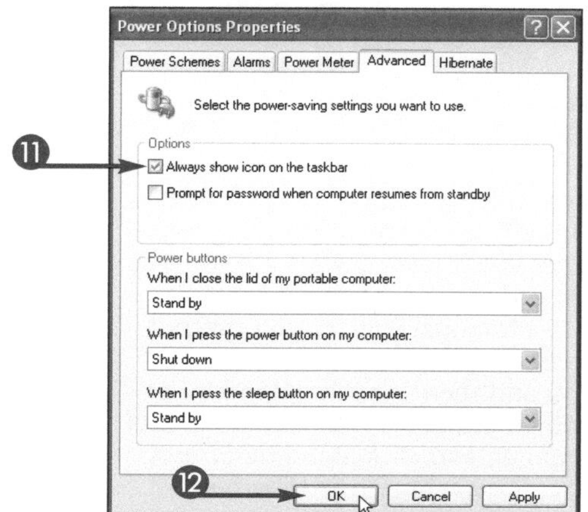

- When running on battery power, the battery icon now appears on the taskbar, showing the percentage of power remaining if you move over it with your mouse. (If running on AC power, a plug icon appears instead.)

PART IV

How do I see if my battery has fully charged yet if my PC is running on AC power?

▼ Click the Advanced tab of the Power Options Properties dialog box, and make sure that the Always show icon on the taskbar option is checked (☑). When you have the icon on the taskbar, you can also get directly to your power meter settings by right-clicking the plug icon ( ) and selecting Power Meter from the menu that appears.

Are there other ways to prolong battery life?

▼ In addition to the power options settings, you can dim your display (how you do this depends on your individual hardware; consult your PC manufacturer's documentation), remove any optional removable drives you are not using, and do not leave floppy disks, CD-ROMs, or DVDs in drives if they are not being used. If you have PCMCIA cards or USB devices that you are not using, remove them from their slots as well.

Configure Standby and Hibernation Modes

You can configure standby and hibernation modes for your PC from the Control Panel. Standby mode puts your computer into a low-power state without turning off the power. You can resume work quickly from this state. In Windows XP Professional Edition, you can put your PC in standby or hibernation mode by selecting Shut Down from the Start menu and then selecting Stand by or Hibernate from the dropdown list. In XP Home Edition, click Start, select Turn Off Computer, and click Stand by or press the Shift key (the Stand by icon becomes the Hibernate icon) and click Hibernate.

To configure standby and hibernation mode settings, open the Control Panel and click Performance and Maintenance and then Power Options. The Power Options Properties dialog box appears. The Advanced tab allows you to require a password upon resume from standby mode, and to select what your PC does when you close the lid, press the power button, or press the sleep button. You can configure your PC to switch to standby and hibernation modes automatically after a certain amount of idle time (see the previous section, "Configure Power Management"). Click the Hibernate tab to enable or disable Hibernate mode.

Configure Standby and Hibernation Modes

1. After clicking Start and Control Panel, click Performance and Maintenance.

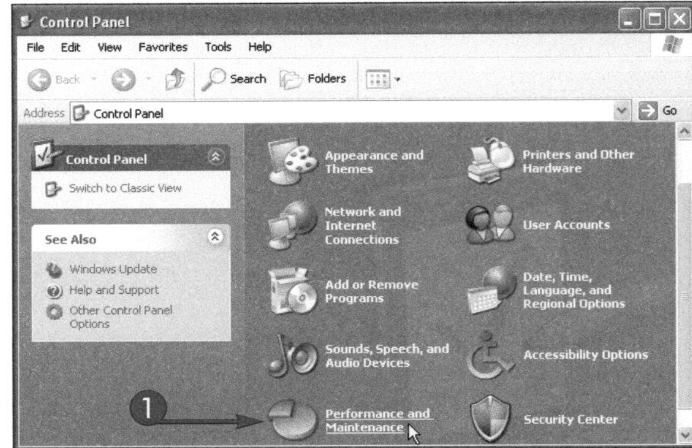

2. Click Power Options.

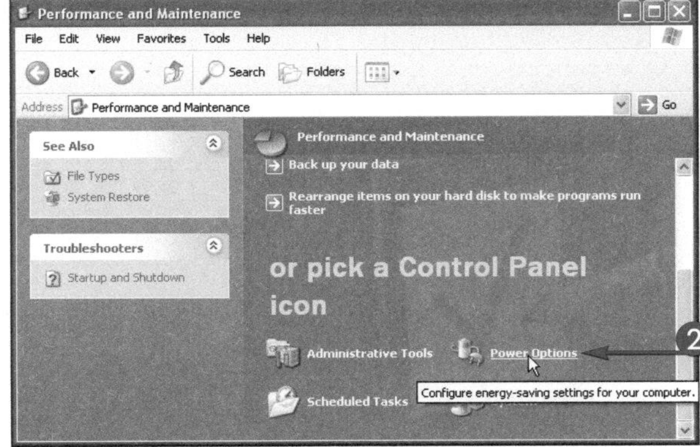

The Power Options Properties dialog box appears.

3. Click the Advanced tab.
4. Click this option to prompt for a password.
5. Click here and select what should happen when you press the power button.
6. Click Apply.
7. Click the Hibernate tab.

- This area indicates free disk space and the amount of disk space required to hibernate.

8. Click this option to enable hibernation.
9. Click OK.
10. Click ☒ to close the Control Panel.

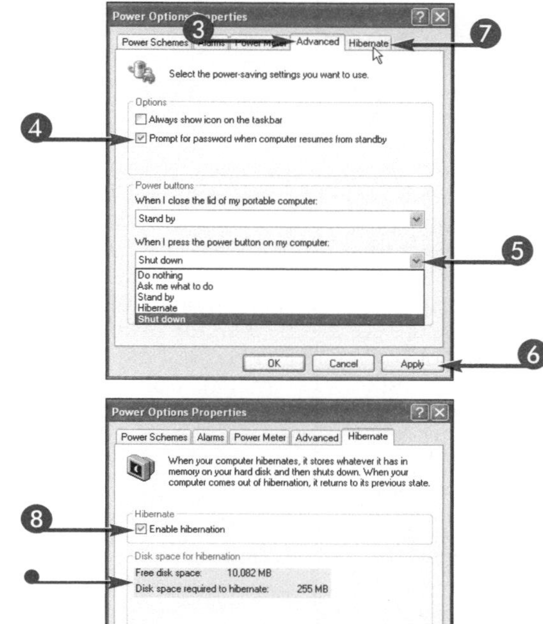

If I choose to have my laptop switch to standby mode when I close the lid when I am running on battery power, could that run my battery down?

▼ Yes. You should avoid having standby mode be the default mode when you close the lid or press the power button, unless you have hibernation enabled and you have your power scheme set to hibernate after a brief period of idle time. See the previous section, "Configure Power Management."

Can I switch to hibernation mode with open applications?

▼ For the most part, yes. However, there is a practical limit. If you are using a network or Web application, although XP attempts to restore network connections, it is dependent on network connectivity, and as a result may not preserve your state exactly. Avoid using hibernation mode in such situations.

Set Up VPN Connections

You can set up Virtual Private Networking (VPN) connections in Windows XP that allow you to take advantage of existing Internet connections to connect securely to a corporate network through a remote access server using encrypted transmissions. VPN connections allow you to work at home or from a remote location and connect directly with the main network. In preparation for setting up a VPN connection, you need to have all the necessary technical data from your network administrator, such as whether to use a Windows domain logon, whether to use a PPTP or L2TP IPSec VPN connection, which user authentication to use, the IP address of the server, and so on. In most situations, the network administrator gives you very specific guidance about which options to set in order to ensure a successful connection.

To set up a new VPN connection, open the Control Panel and click Network and Internet Connections. From the Pick a task section, click Create a connection to the network at your workplace. This launches the Network Connection Wizard. Select the Virtual Private Network connection.

Set Up VPN Connections

1. Click Start.
2. Click Control Panel.

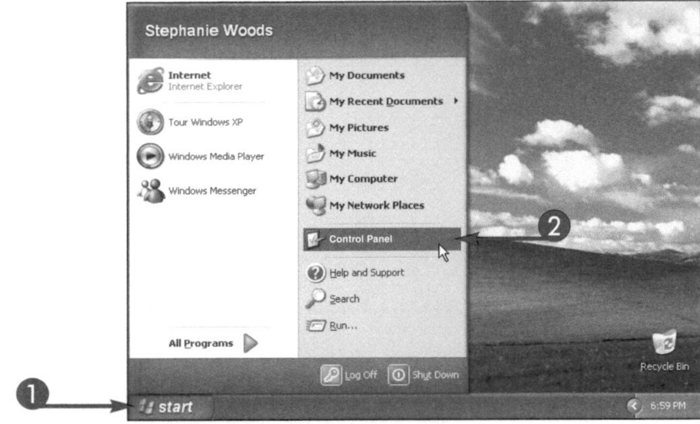

3. Click Network and Internet Connections to create a new connection.

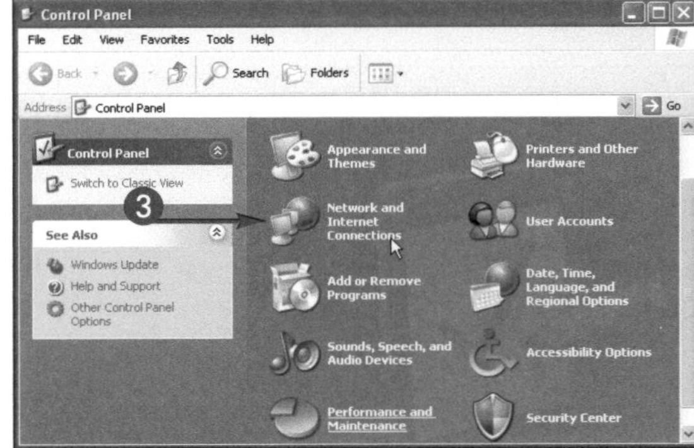

4 Click here to create a new VPN connection.

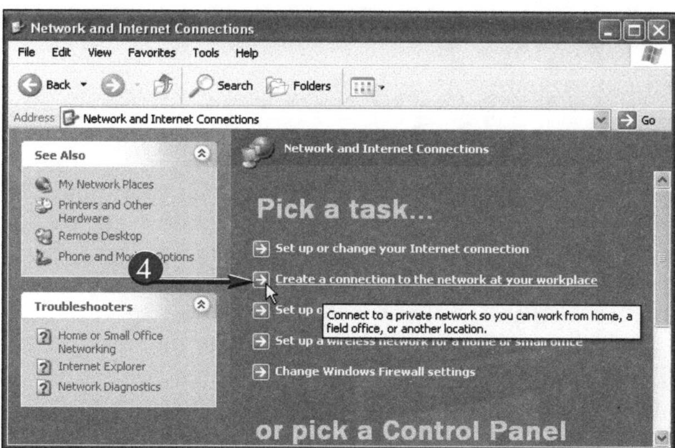

The New Connection Wizard appears.

5 Click this option to select VPN.

6 Click Next.

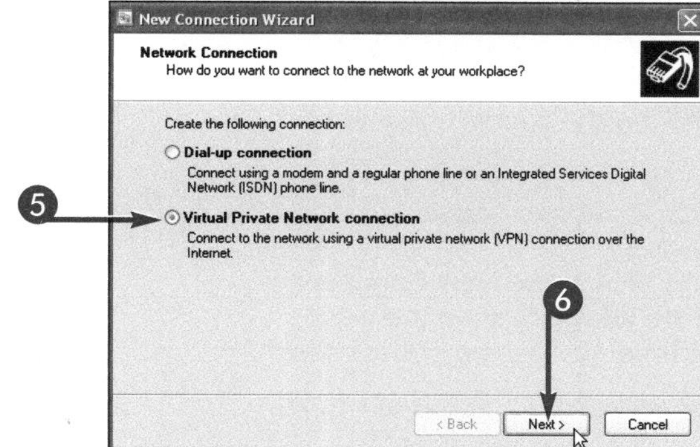

Is there another way to get started?

▼ Yes. If you have chosen to have the Connect To icon ( ) appear on your Start menu, click it and then click Show all connections from the menu that appears. When the Network Connections window appears, click Create a new connection from the Network Tasks pane on the left. This opens the Network Connection Wizard. Click Connect to the network at my workplace.

Can I use a dial-up connection to get to a VPN connection?

▼ Using a dial-up connection to establish your connection to the Internet may be possible but the connection will be very slow. Talk to your network administrator about the availability and feasibility of a dial-up connection to your corporate network.

continued

Set Up VPN Connections *(Continued)*

After you have initiated the New Connection Wizard and selected VPN as your connection type, you are asked to give the VPN connection a name. This name is for your reference; it does not need to be a corporate Web site URL or network server name. Next you are asked to specify a host name (example: microsoft.com) or IP address (four numeric groups separated by dots) of the host server. This concludes the information necessary to do the basic setup of the connection.

When you have a named connection, you can change any settings required by your corporate VPN by selecting the connection and clicking Change settings of this connection (or by double-clicking the connection and clicking Properties). This brings up a properties dialog box for this connection. This is where you need to follow the instructions of your network administrator to make the settings match your corporate VPN's requirements. There are five tabs, General, Options, Security, Networking, and Advanced. Most likely any settings to be changed are in the Security tab, which contains settings such as data encryption, authentication, and IPSec settings.

Set Up VPN Connections *(continued)*

After selecting VPN in the New Connection Wizard, you are asked to name the new connection in the next screen of the wizard.

7. Type a name here (**WILEY** in this example).
8. Click Next.

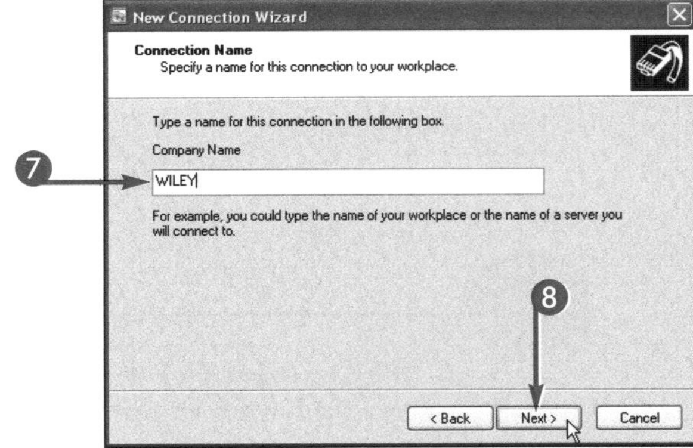

9. Type the host name or IP address here.
10. Click Next.

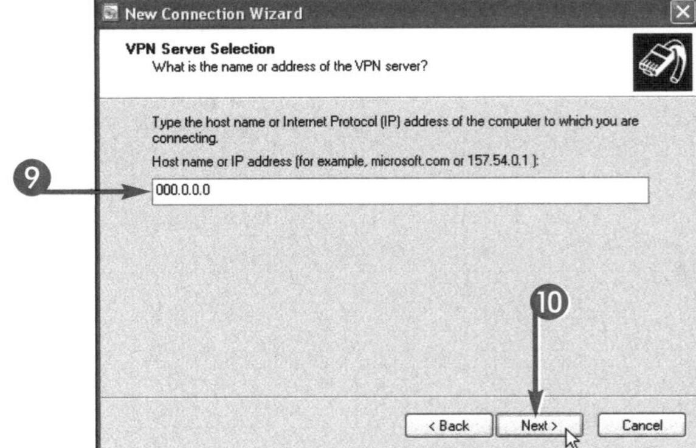

Your VPN connection is now listed.

11 Click Finish.

- Your new VPN connection is listed in the Virtual Private Network category in the Network Connections window. Double-click to connect to your VPN.
- Click here to change additional settings, for example, any settings specified by your network administrator.

12 Click here to close the Control Panel.

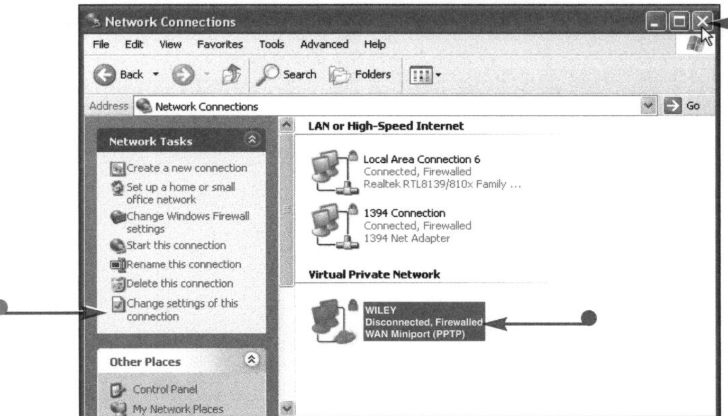

What is the minimum I need to know to get a VPN connection up and running?

▼ You need to know the host name for your corporate VPN or IP address, and authentication (user name, password, or SmartCard).

Can I access my corporate intranet with a VPN connection?

▼ In most cases, yes. Your network administrator needs to assist you with the specifics for your intranet.

Configure Offline File Settings

You can configure files that you work with on a network drive to be available to you when you are offline in Windows XP. After you have modified a file offline, you can synchronize it with the one on the network drive when you next connect to the network. You can make any folder, subfolder, or file available offline, assuming you have the appropriate access rights on the network for that folder or file.

To make a file or folder available offline, go to My Computer and select the network drive where the folder or files reside. Open the network drive and locate the desired folder or file. Right-click the item and select Make Available Offline from the menu that appears. If you are making a large amount of data available offline, you see a synchronization window with a progress bar to indicate where you are in the process. When the process is complete, the icon appears with an added symbol ( ) to indicate that it is a synchronized item. You can elect to synchronize upon connection, or you can force a synchronization by right-clicking the item and then clicking Synchronize from the menu that appears.

Configure Offline File Settings

Make a network item available offline

1. Click Start.
2. Click My Computer.
3. Click Open.

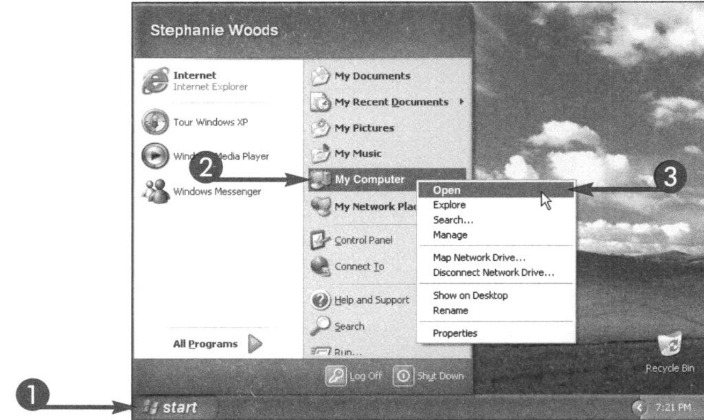

The My Computer window appears.

4. Right-click the network drive.
5. Click Open from the menu that appears.

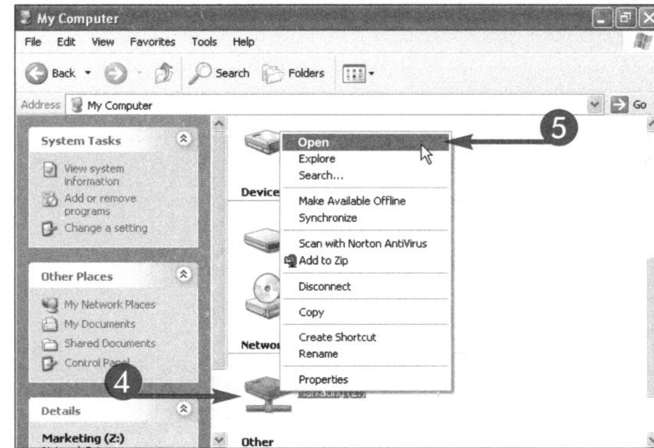

6 Right-click the item you want to make available offline.

7 Click Make Available Offline from the menu that appears.

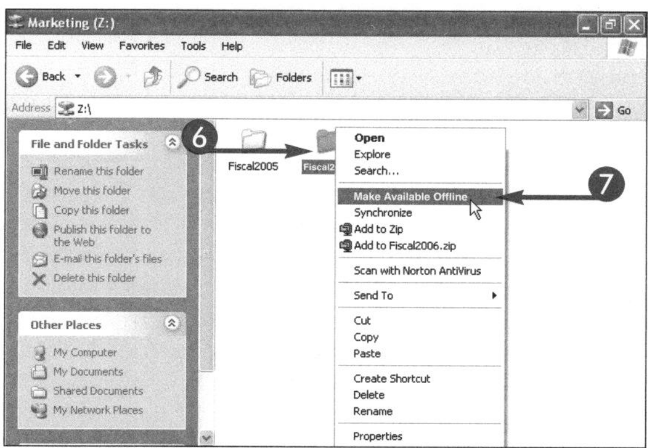

After the synchronization process, the item appears with an added symbol to indicate that it is available offline.

Synchronize the offline item with the network item

8 Right-click the item.

9 Click Synchronize from the menu that appears.

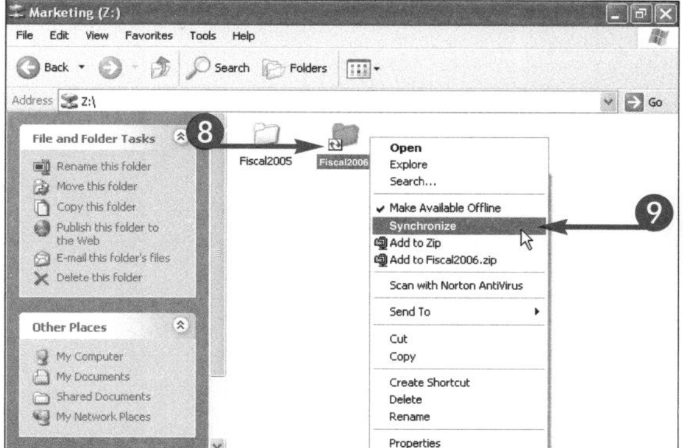

Is there any reason I should not make the whole network drive available offline?

▼ Yes. In order to make an entire mapped network drive available offline, the entire contents must also reside on your local hard drive. When synchronizing, every file is checked. Depending on the size and number of files, this can be a very time-consuming process. Therefore, exercise discretion when deciding what you need to have available offline.

Can I turn off the offline file feature?

▼ Yes. Simply right-click the item and then click the Make Available Offline option again to remove the feature from the item. The icon indicating offline availability and synchronization disappears from the file or folder icon.

Use Disk Cleanup

You can take advantage of Windows XP's Disk Cleanup tool to examine a disk drive and remove old or unwanted files. This is a "housecleaning" process that should be performed periodically. You can avoid clutter and free up disk space. More free space gives you not only more room for new programs and data but also allows your drive to work more efficiently and allows you to more effectively defragment your hard drive (see the next section, "Defragment a Hard Drive," for more information.

To launch Disk Cleanup, click Run from the Start menu, type **cleanmgr**, and click OK. You can also find the Disk Cleanup tool in the System Tools folder of Accessories from the All Programs menu. Once launched, you are asked to choose a drive to clean up. If you have one hard drive, this can have a volume name but usually has the drive listed as (C:). Select the drive you want to clean up from the dropdown list and click OK. The Disk Cleanup tool next scans your disk to determine how much space you can save and to group the files that are candidates for removal or compression into categories.

Use Disk Cleanup

1. Click Start and then Run.

   The Run dialog box appears.

2. Type **cleanmgr**.
3. Click OK.

The Select Drive dialog box appears.

4. Click here and select the drive you want to clean up.
5. Click OK.

You see a progress bar while Disk Cleanup scans your disk.

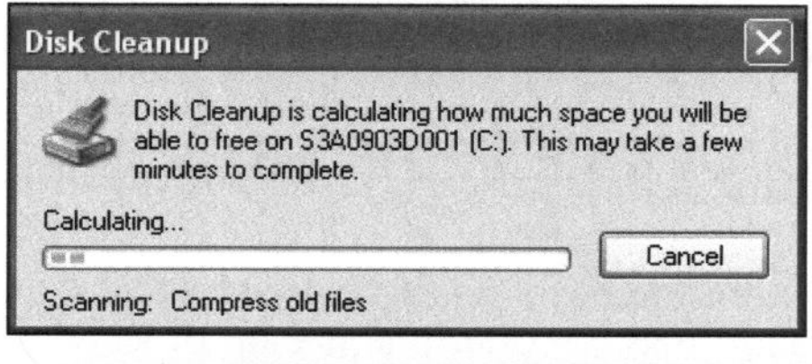

- The Disk Cleanup tool displays selected files as candidates for deletion.
- Click here to view the list of files for a selected category.

6 To delete the list of files suggested, click OK.

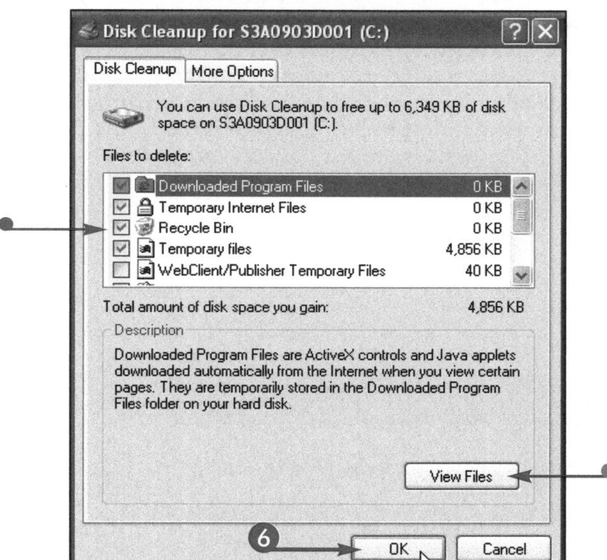

PART IV

How confident can I be that these are not important files that are being deleted?

Windows XP has standardized folders for certain types of files that are necessary but inherently temporary in nature. You can confidently delete any files in categories labeled "temporary." For the Recycle Bin, it is up to you to make sure you have not recently made any accidental deletions. To double-check what is in the Recycle Bin from within the Disk Cleanup tool, select Recycle Bin (☐ changes to ☑) and click View Files.

How does Windows XP determine what "old" means for the Compress old files option?

The default setting is files that have not been accessed in 50 days. You can change the setting by selecting Compress old files and clicking Options in the Files to delete window of the Disk Cleanup dialog box.

continued

Use Disk Cleanup *(Continued)*

After clicking OK to delete temporary files, Disk Cleanup asks to confirm and then proceed with the disk cleanup operation. If after deleting temporary files and compressing old files you still have need of more disk space or simply want to be more thorough, you can take advantage of some additional, discretionary cleanup procedures on the More Options tab of the Disk Cleanup dialog box. From this tab you can remove Windows components that you do not use, remove other applications that you do not use, or remove all but the most recent system restore point.

To access these options, click the More Options tab of Disk Cleanup. Clicking Clean up in Windows components takes you to the Windows Components Wizard. See the section "Add, Remove, and Change Windows Components" in Chapter 3 for more information. Clicking Clean up in Installed programs takes you to Add or Remove Programs in the Control Panel. Select Frequency of use or Date last used in the Sort by list to isolate possible candidates for removal. Click Clean up in System Restore to remove all but the last system restore point (avoid if you have been having system problems).

Use Disk Cleanup *(continued)*

Windows asks you to confirm the deletion.

7 Click Yes to confirm the cleanup operation.

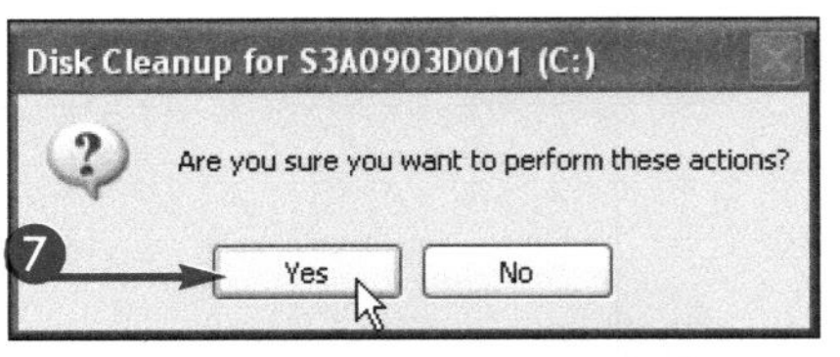

Disk Cleanup shows a progress bar to indicate how far along it is in the operation.

8 Click the More Options tab.

- Click here to remove Windows components.
- Click here to remove programs.

9 Click to remove older system restore points (if you are not having system problems).

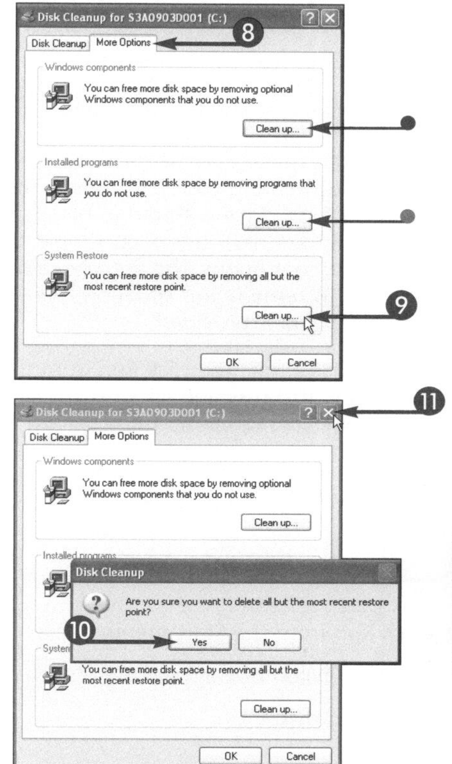

Windows asks you to confirm the deletion.

10 Click Yes to confirm removal of older system restore points.

11 Click here to close Disk Cleanup.

If I click Clean up in Windows components, I notice that some boxes are already checked for removal. Can I rely on these suggestions?

▼ You should review all of them; they are only suggestions and you may intend to use some of the programs that Windows suggests. The games that come with Windows XP are suggested for removal by default, the assumption being that if you need to free up disk space, these would be the first to go.

What are system restore points?

▼ The System Restore tool in Windows XP keeps track of the system configuration at regular intervals and when you do something like make changes to system settings, update a driver, or install a new application. System Restore saves these snapshots of your system settings, called system restore points, so that you can "roll back" to a previous configuration if the new one makes your system unstable. You can also use the System Restore tool to manually create a restore point immediately prior to making a change such as updating a hardware driver.

Defragment the Hard Drive

You can speed up performance by periodically defragmenting your hard drive. The data stored on your hard drive is stored in blocks. If the blocks are *contiguous* (all together), this occurs more quickly. If the blocks are not contiguous, the files are said to be fragmented. To remedy this situation, the Disk Defragmenter tool is provided.

To run Disk Defragmenter, click Run from the Start menu and then type **dfrg.msc** and click OK (or click All Programs and select Disk Defragmenter from System Tools in the Accessories folder). After you select a drive, Disk Defragmenter first analyzes the disk to determine whether a substantial portion of the disk is fragmented. If so, it recommends defragmenting. If the disk is not very fragmented, Disk Defragmenter tells you the disk does not need defragmenting, because disk defragmentation can take a substantial amount of time (from several minutes to several hours) depending on the size and speed of the hard drive and the degree of fragmentation. If Disk Defragmenter recommends defragmenting, you can elect to view the report or immediately proceed to defragmenting.

Defragment the Hard Drive

1. Click Run from the Start menu.

   The Run dialog box appears.

2. Type **dfrg.msc**.
3. Click OK.

   The Disk Defragmenter appears.

4. Click the hard drive to analyze.
5. Click Analyze to analyze the disk.
6. When the analysis is complete, if defragmenting is recommended, click Defragment.

   Click Close if defragmenting is not recommended.

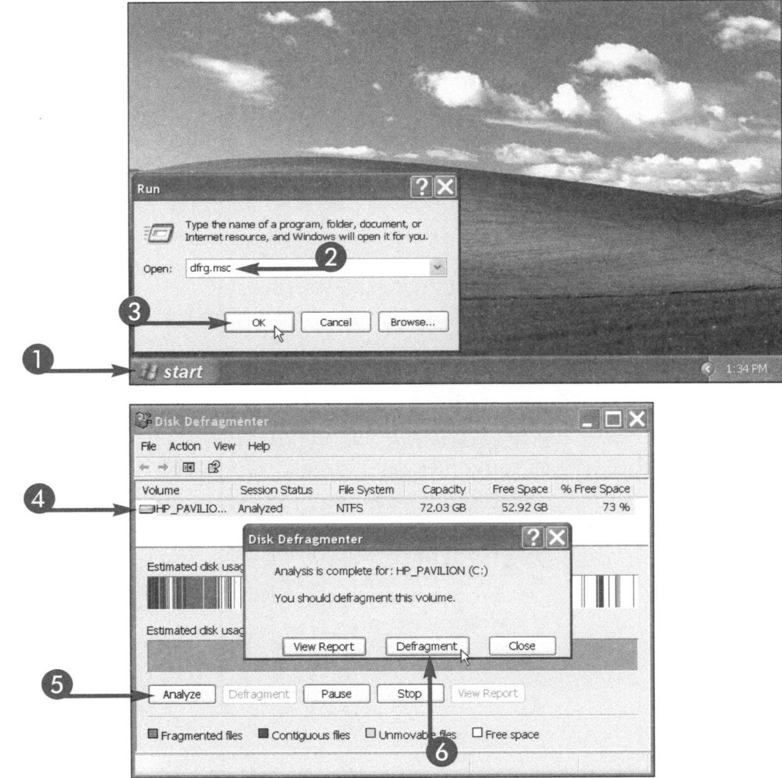

Click View Report to review the defragmentation report.

7. When defragmenting is done, click Close.

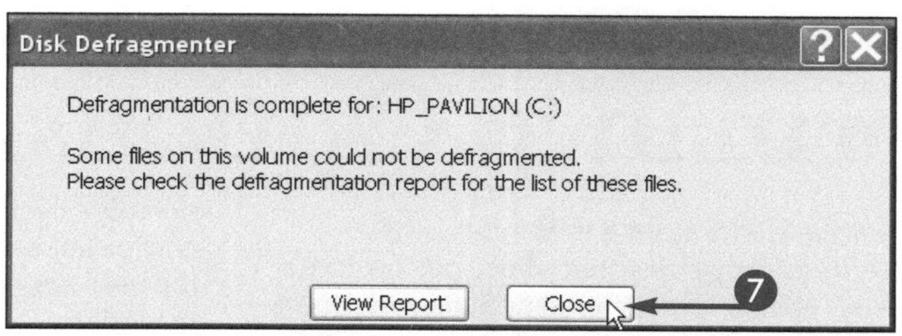

- Note the solid concentration of bars indicating a successfully defragmented hard drive.

8. Click here to close the Disk Defragmenter.

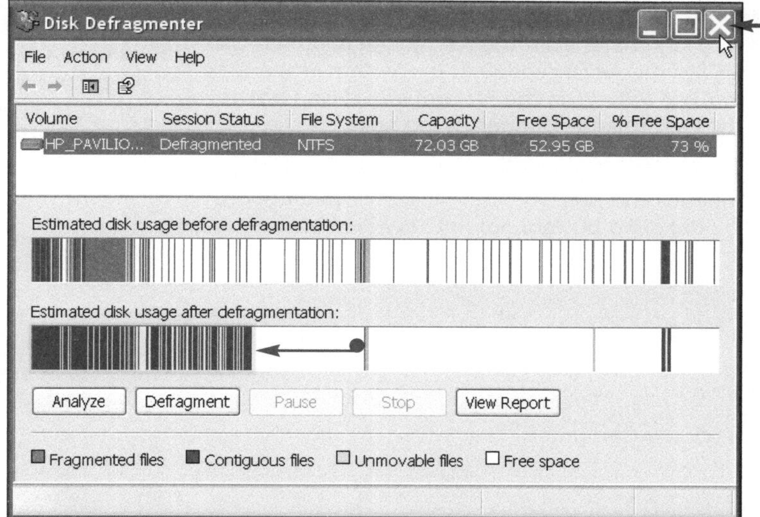

After defragmenting the disk, the Disk Defragmenter tool reports that it was unable to defragment some files. Is something wrong?

Probably not; it is often the case that some files cannot be moved on the hard drive. If a substantial percentage of your hard drive cannot be defragmented, view the report to determine the nature of the files. You many want to uninstall a program and then reinstall it after defragmentation to resolve the problem.

How often should I defragment my hard drive?

This depends on how full your hard drive is and how much data you save to disk. If you use your computer intensively, install and update programs frequently, or use large databases that you store locally on your hard drive, a good rule of thumb would be once a week. You can also use Scheduled Tasks to set this to occur at regular intervals (see the section "Schedule Tasks" in Chapter 14 for more information).

Set Windows Performance Options

You can improve performance in Windows XP by adjusting system properties that affect performance such as visual effects, processor scheduling, memory usage, and virtual memory. (Note: You must be logged on as an administrator to do this.) To access these settings, right-click My Computer from the Start menu and then click Properties. Click the Advanced tab in the System Properties dialog box. Click Settings in the Performance dialog box to bring up the Performance Options dialog box.

The Visual Effects tab allows you to make adjustments based on your priorities and preferences. The preselected options provided by the radio buttons are not very helpful: The default selection, Let Windows choose what's best for my computer, selects all visual effects, as does the option Adjust for best appearance. Going too far in the other direction, the Adjust for best performance option simply removes all the visual effects listed and makes your system look like Windows 98 or Windows 2000 Professional. It makes most sense to select Custom and clear any purely cosmetic visual effects but leave those that aid in using the interface. You can clear all effects from the beginning through the Slide taskbar buttons option with little adverse effect.

Set Windows Performance Options

1. Click Start.
2. Right-click My Computer.

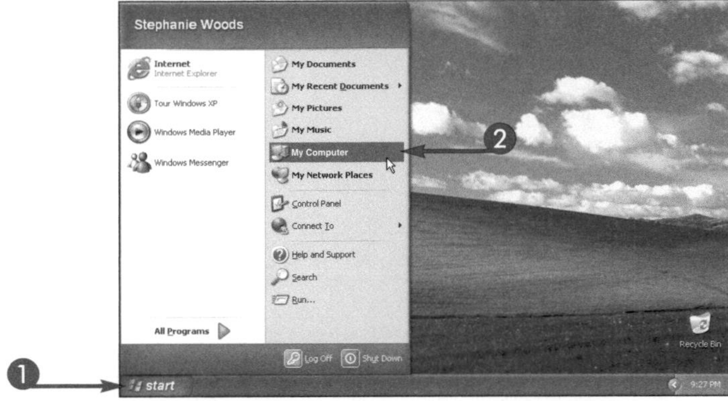

A menu appears.

3. Click Properties.

4 Click the Advanced tab.

5 Click Settings to change performance settings.

The Visual Effects tab of the Performance Options dialog box appears.

- The default setting enables all Windows XP visual effects.

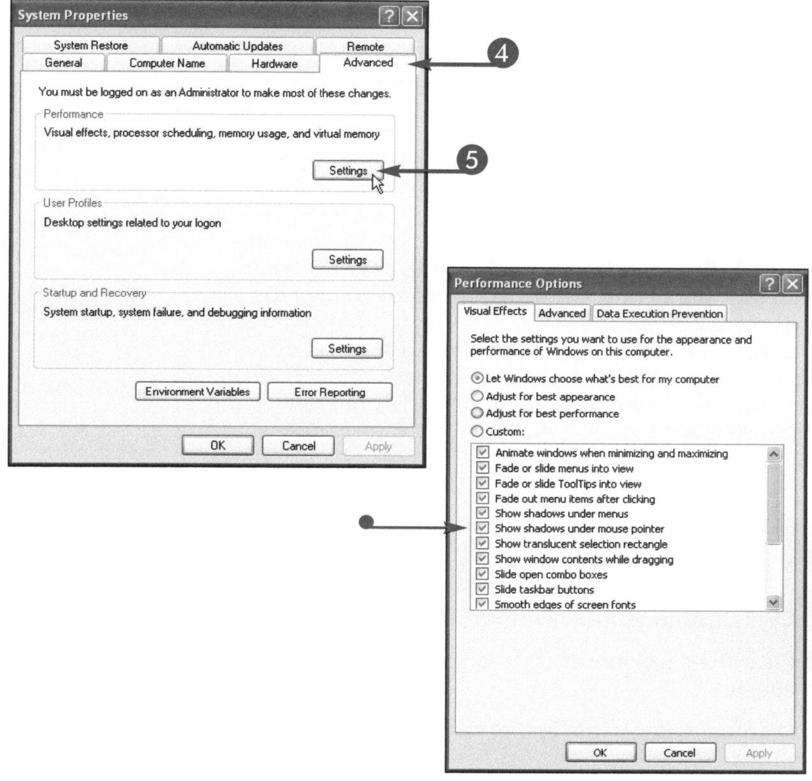

PART IV

Do visual effects really make a difference in system performance?

Yes. One way to test this is to run perfmon (see the section "Monitor Performance" in Chapter 14) and compare processor activity when the Show window contents while dragging effect is turned on to when it is turned off.

I find showing a shadow under my mouse pointer helps me see the mouse. Do I need to turn off that effect?

No. Keep whichever effects you find useful but remember that you are making tradeoffs between visual appeal and performance.

continued

Set Windows Performance Options *(Continued)*

You can make your own decisions about what effects to retain, but some suggestions are to retain those effects that aid in making the user interface readable for you and easier to use, and disable those that are essentially "window dressing." In the example below, screen font smoothing is retained because it makes the words more legible, and smooth-scrolling is preserved for the same reason — without it, scrolling lists flicker as they go by, making them hard to read. The last option is what gives the desktop the XP "look and feel." If you disable this option, your screen will look like an earlier version of Windows.

Besides visual effects, you can assign prioritization of processor scheduling and memory usage. You can also adjust the paging files size for virtual memory. These settings are located on the Advanced tab of Performance Options. In most cases, the Programs option should be selected for both Processor scheduling and Memory usage, giving priority to user applications. The Virtual memory setting allows you to adjust how Windows XP behaves when it switches from RAM to virtual memory (a large file on the hard drive used as if it were RAM).

Set Windows Performance Options *(continued)*

6. Click Custom to make custom changes.
7. Clear the check boxes (☐) for cosmetic visual effects.

   Drag the slider to the end of the list.

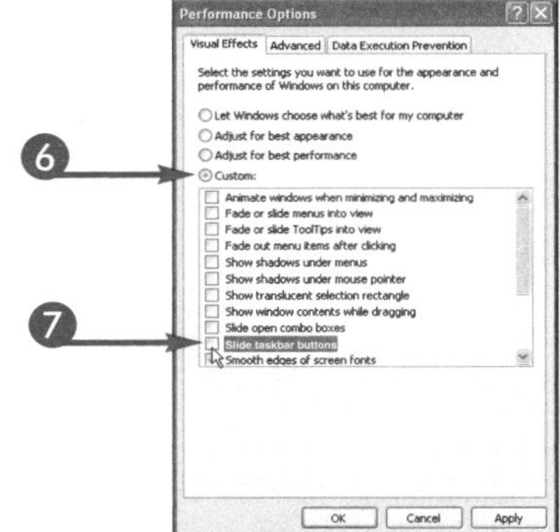

8. Continue to clear check boxes (☐) for any remaining unwanted visual effects.
   - Click this option and the desktop icon label will no longer have a drop shadow.
   - A desktop icon with a drop shadow is shown here.
9. Click Apply.

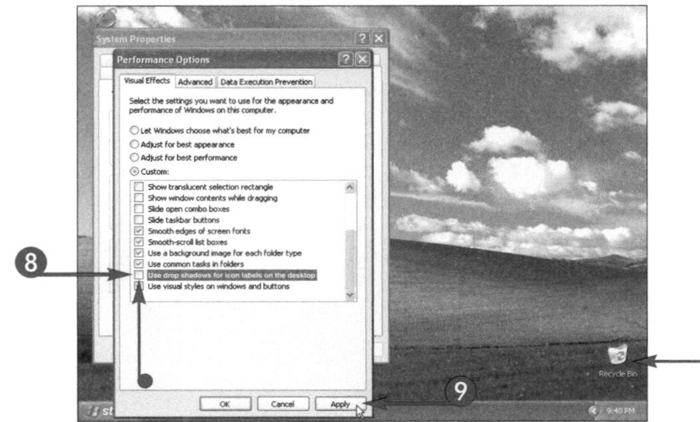

- Disabled visual effects disappear (for example, no drop shadows with desktop icon labels).

⑩ Click the Advanced tab.

⑪ Click Programs to give programs priority in processor scheduling.

⑫ Click Programs to give programs priority in memory usage.

⑬ Click Change to change paging file size for virtual memory.

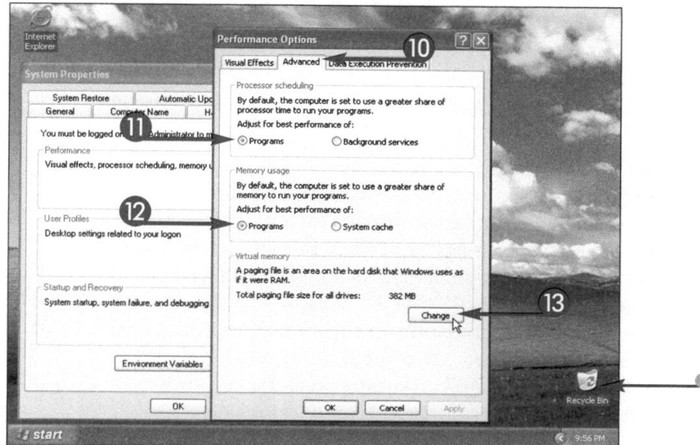

The Virtual Memory dialog box appears.

⑭ Select a hard drive for the paging file.

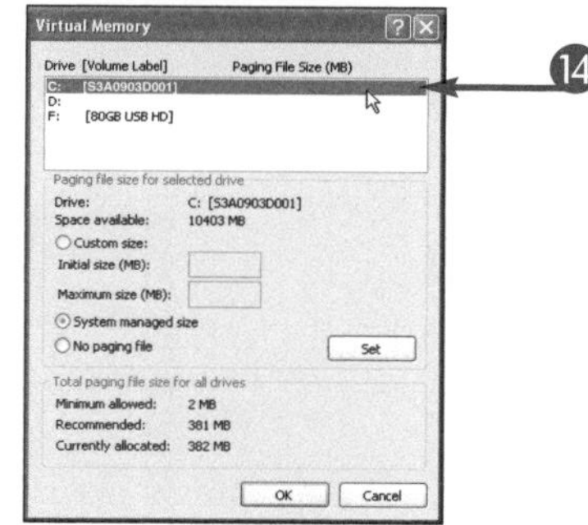

How do I select a hard drive for the paging file?

▼ The default is the C drive that contains your system. If you have more than one local physical drive, however, you may get performance gains by switching the paging file to the other drive (assuming your additional hard drive is as fast as your C drive and assuming it has plenty of free space).

Why should I change from having the system manage the size?

▼ If the system dynamically changes the paging file size, it leads to system slowdowns when the paging file is being changed.

continued

Set Windows Performance Options *(Continued)*

You can set a custom size for your paging file to improve your system's performance when it uses virtual memory (moving from faster RAM to the virtual RAM of hard drive access). After selecting the drive, click Custom size. Check to see your system's current Recommended size. A good rule of thumb is to double that number and type the larger number in both the Initial and Maximum size fields. Next click Set to change the paging file size. The new size in MB (megabytes) appears to the right of the drive letter and volume label. Next click OK and a message appears letting you know that these changes to virtual memory will not take effect until after you restart Windows.

After clicking OK to close Performance Options and again to close System Properties, a message appears asking whether you want to restart your computer. Click Yes to restart and have the changes take effect. Your new changes should help speed performance of your system. For additional ways to optimize performance, check out the Help and Support Center and search for *performance.*

Set Windows Performance Options *(continued)*

15. Click Custom size to enter a custom page size.
16. Type a new page size here (usually twice the recommended size listed below).
17. Type the same new page size again here (usually twice the recommended size listed below).
18. Click Set.

- The new paging file size appears.

19. Click OK to close the Virtual Memory dialog box.

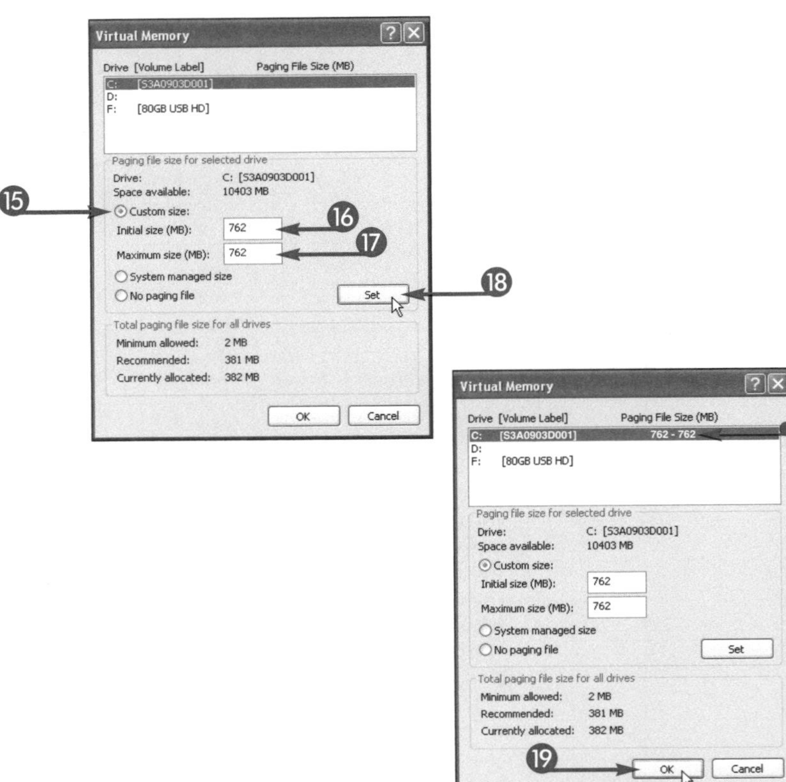

Windows reminds you that you must restart your computer for changes to take effect.

20 Click OK.

21 Click OK to close the Performance Options dialog box.

22 Click OK to close the System Properties dialog box.

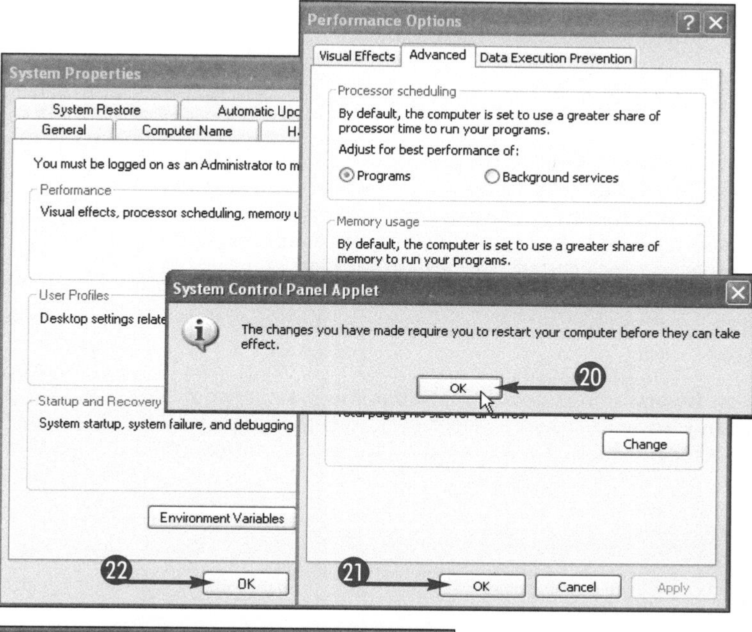

Windows asks you if you want to restart your computer now.

23 Click Yes to do so.

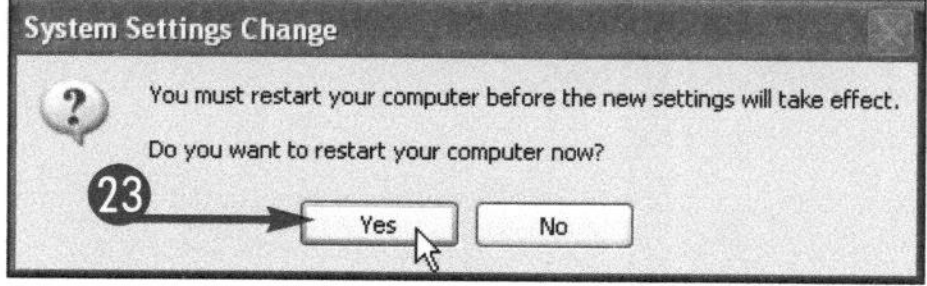

My computer was much faster when I first got it. Why has it slowed down?

- Usually the reason is that you have gradually filled the hard drive with additional programs and data files. Many software products and hardware devices install small helper applications (often referred to as *applets*) that are loaded every time you load Windows.

What can I do to reduce the number of these extra programs?

- The safest way is to use the Add/Remove Programs feature of the Control Panel to review your programs and uninstall and remove any that you do not use. See the section "Add, Remove, and Change Windows Components" in Chapter 3 for more information.

Common Troubleshooting Steps

Although Windows XP has proven to be one of the most stable consumer-oriented operating systems, it is not immune to problems. When problems arise, you want to be able to fix the problems quickly and without losing critical data and important files. One way to minimize downtime and data loss is to have a troubleshooting checklist you can depend on during times of crisis.

One of the first things you should do if you experience a problem is to write down all error messages that appear. These error messages are included by the programmers of Windows and other programs to provide feedback to users (you) and to technical support persons. Some error messages are so generic that they may be of little help to you. Others, however, are specific to the problem, providing error code numbers to help you research and fix the problem.

The following task includes an example of how to diagnose and fix problems with your computer. The other tasks in this chapter show how to deal with common Windows XP troubleshooting situations.

Common Troubleshooting Steps

Document the problem in writing

1. After a problem has occurred, right-click the desktop and click New and then Text File.

   A text file appears.

2. Click Edit and then Time/Date.

   - The current time and date are added to the top of the document.

3. Type a description of the problem.
4. Click File and then save the document to your My Documents folder.

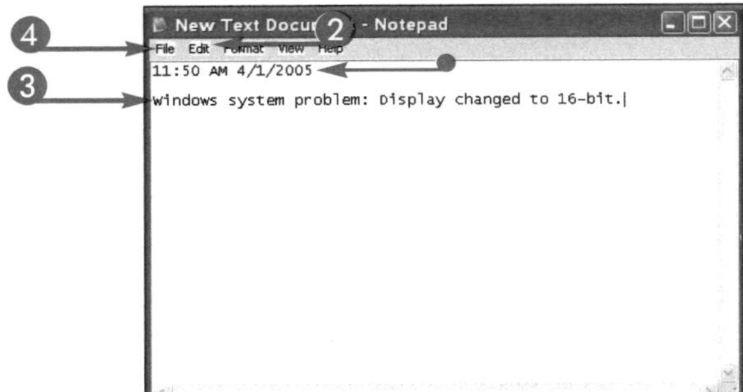

Diagnose hardware problems

1. After a hardware problem has occurred, right-click My Computer.
2. Click Properties from the menu that appears.

   The System Properties dialog box appears.

3. Click the Hardware tab.
4. Click Device Manager.

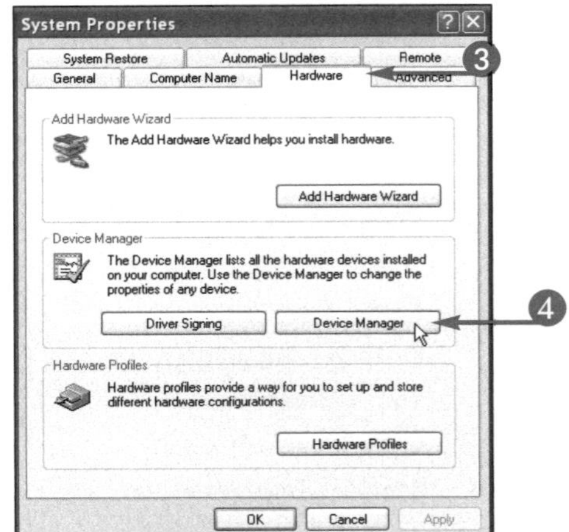

The Device Manager appears, with a list of all the hardware devices on your computer. Devices that are not working correctly show up with a red × or yellow exclamation point.

5 Double-click a device that is showing a problem.

The properties dialog box for the device, a communications port in this example, appears.

- The Device status area usually provides enough information to start diagnosing the problem.

6 Click Troubleshoot.

The Help and Support Center window appears. This utility can guide you through fixing common problems with your hardware.

7 Answer each question as it is presented to you and click Next to work through the problem.

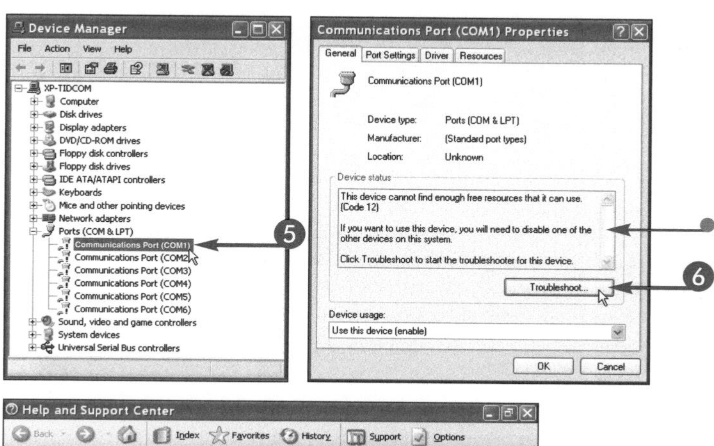

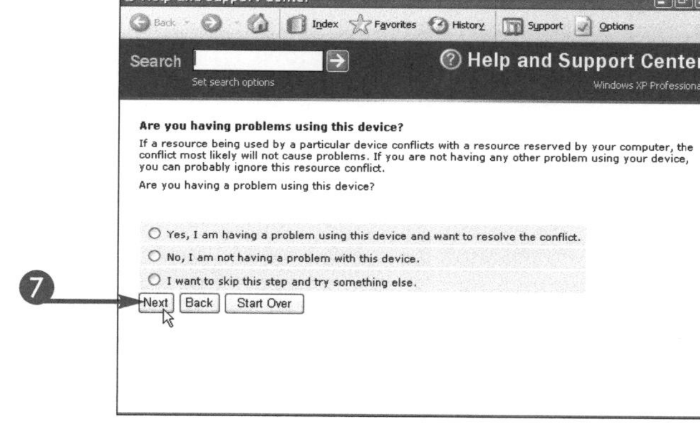

Are there any utilities provided with Windows XP that I can use for troubleshooting problems?

▼ Yes, in fact there are several tools, listed here:

- Dr. Watson
- System Information
- System Restore
- Device Manager
- Event Viewer
- Windows Task Manager
- Scandisk
- Check Disk
- DirectX Diagnostics
- Sound Troubleshooter
- DVD Troubleshooter
- Modem Troubleshooter

I have access to the Internet with another computer. Can you advise me on which sites I should visit for troubleshooting advice?

▼ A number of Web sites, listserves, and newsgroups are available to help you during those times when Windows XP is failing. One of the first places you should consider visiting is the Microsoft Knowledge Base site. The Web site address is http://support.microsoft.com. On this page is a search field into which you can type search words describing the problem you are experiencing with Windows. For example, if an error message appears that includes an error number, such as "Error in Line: 227," enter that information in the search field. Click Run the search. If the search criteria matches documents included in the Microsoft Knowledge Base, a list of those documents is shown. Read the abstracts of each document and click the link to read the entire article. See Chapter 4 for more about Knowlegde Base.

Start Windows in Safe Mode

Windows XP enables you to start in Safe Mode. One way to fix Windows XP is to start it in Safe Mode because this mode uses only the basic drivers and software to get Windows running. You may want to use Safe Mode if you suspect that a specialized driver (such as for a high-end graphics card) or application is causing problems. You can also use Safe Mode to find and destroy spyware files.

When you run Windows in Safe Mode, not all features are functional. One main component that is not functional is printing. Although printing is a critical feature of Windows, Microsoft decided to keep it out of Safe Mode because so many errors are caused by the printing subsystem. If you want to print something, get Windows working correctly and boot into Normal Windows instead of Safe Mode.

Another feature that is not always functional is networking. Safe Mode can be started with or without networking support. You may need networking support to access critical shared folders while you conduct troubleshooting tasks. On the other hand, you may want to disable networking if you think Windows networking support is causing problems with your system.

Start Windows in Safe Mode

1. If still running, shut down Windows.
2. Start your computer.
3. As soon as you see the BIOS information, press F8.

Note: *Make sure to let your computer run a few seconds before pressing F8. Also, you may need to press F8 a few times for the next screen to appear.*

The Windows Advanced Options Menu appears.

4. Use your keyboard up arrow to move to the Safe Mode option.
5. Press Enter.

Windows boots up into Safe Mode.

A message appears informing you that Windows is now in Safe Mode.

6. Click Yes.

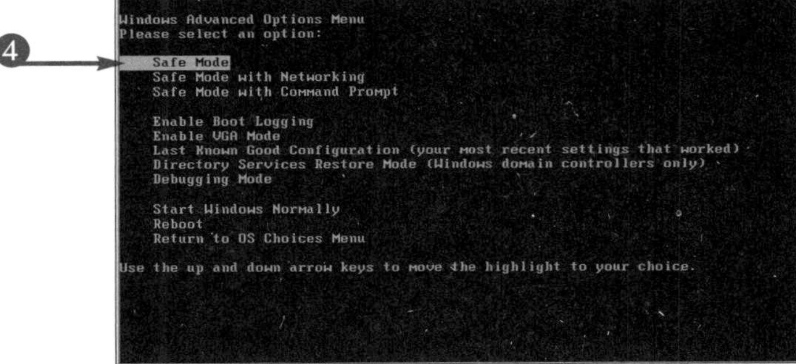

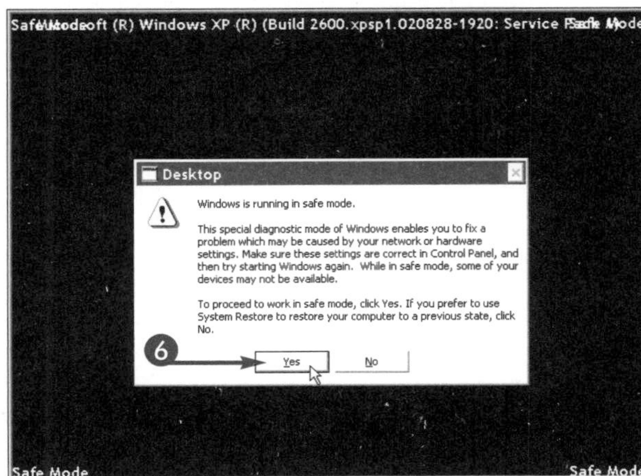

Windows starts in Safe Mode.

Note: *The graphics are not the same as your normal Windows display settings, because Safe Mode uses the default standard VGA setting.*

7. Perform any troubleshooting tasks you need to perform.

For example, you can uninstall a program that may be affecting your computer adversely.

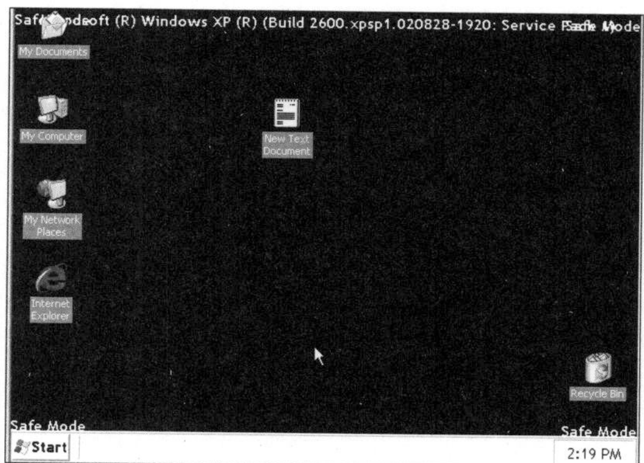

As another example, you can remove a hardware device that is causing a problem.

Note: *Follow the steps in the section "Common Troubleshooting Steps," earlier in this chapter, to access the Device Manager.*

Devices that are not working correctly show up with a red × or yellow exclamation point.

- Double-click a device that is showing a problem.

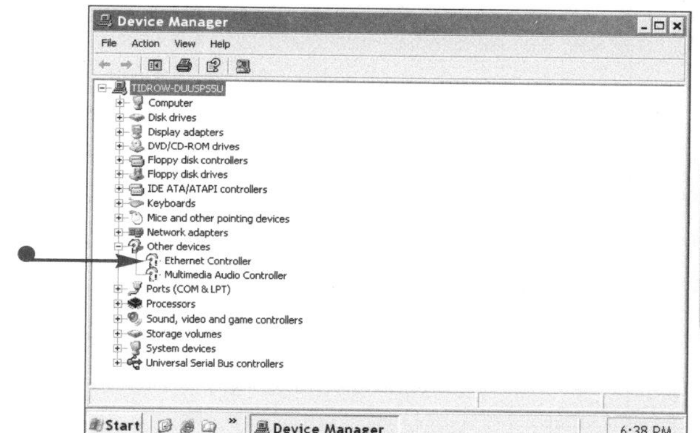

PART IV

When I started Windows today, it said that it was running in Safe Mode. I did not specifically tell it to run in Safe Mode, so why is it running like this?

▼ For a couple of reasons. The main reason for Safe Mode to start after a previous shutdown is that a problem occurred during the last shutdown. You may not have noticed any problem the last time you shut it down because the problem may not have presented an error message. If your computer has started in Safe Mode, sometimes you can correct the problem by shutting down and restarting Windows. If you boot into Windows normally, then your problem was corrected. From the Windows Advanced Options Menu, select Start Windows Normally and press Enter. If Windows starts normally, count your blessings. If not, you are usually given the option of starting in Safe Mode again. Do so and attempt to fix the problem using other means.

I am in Safe Mode. Can I start Windows in Repair Mode from here?

▼ You cannot start Windows in Repair Mode from the Windows Advanced Options Menu. You must have your original Windows XP CD to boot to the Repair Mode. See the section "Repair Windows" for more information.

Restore Windows

Windows XP includes a feature that lets you restore Windows to a previous date. This feature is called System Restore. System Restore is handy if you accidentally make an incorrect change in your system Registry, a virus or spyware has invaded your system, or if Windows just starts acting strangely.

You can restore your computer to a previous date, turning back all changes that have been made to the computer since then. The only thing that does not change are your data files. They are not deleted or lost during the restore process.

Programs, hardware settings, device configurations, and Windows changes are all put back to the date you select. It is like going back in time, only you do not get any younger.

System Restore can be one of your first troubleshooting utilities to help correct Windows problems if Safe Mode does not help. Although System Restore is not perfect, it is very helpful. One thing to keep in mind with System Restore, however, is that you must have a Restore Point — a checkpoint of your system — to go back to. If you ever turn off System Restore, all your old Restore Points are lost for good.

Restore Windows

1. Click Start, All Programs, and then Accessories.
2. Click System Restore.

   The System Restore window appears.
3. Click the option to restore your computer to an earlier time.
4. Click Next.

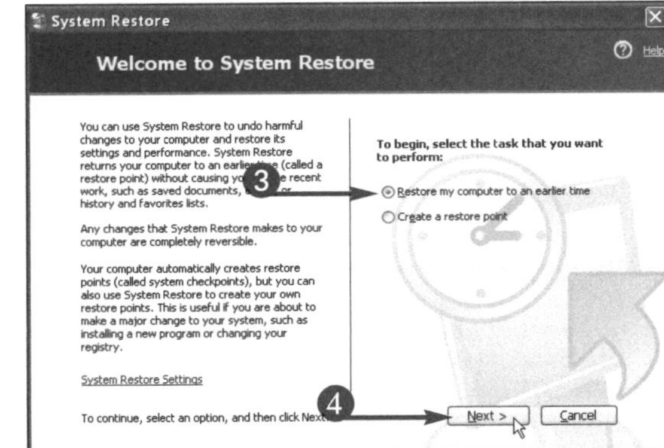

The Select a Restore Point screen appears.

A calendar shows potential restore points in bold.

5. Select a restore point.
   - If a restore point is not available on the calendar showing, click here for previous months. You may find a restore point on these months.
6. In the day list, select a restore point.

Note: *Sometimes only one restore point is available for a chosen day, while others may have several.*

7. Click Next.

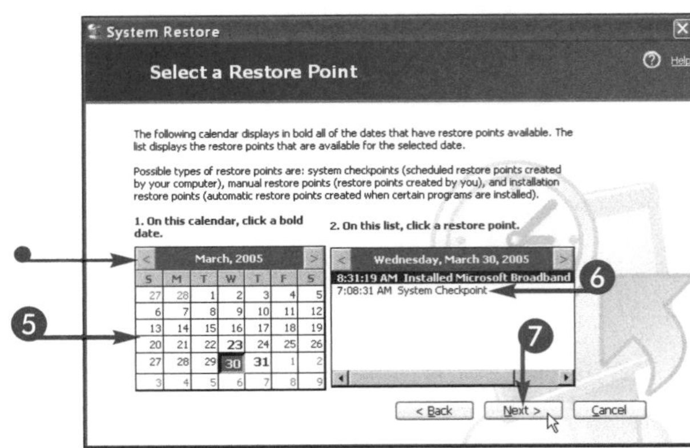

The Confirm Restore Point Selection screen appears.

8 Click Next.

Windows appears to freeze for a moment and then begins the restore process. This can take some time depending on the amount of restore information that was saved in the restore point.

9 After the restore point is restored, Windows shuts down and restarts. Log on to Windows normally.

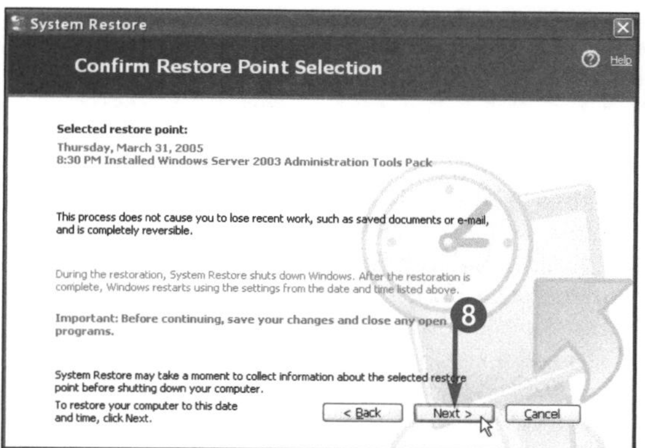

Windows may continue the restore process as it restarts this first time. After it restarts, the Restoration Complete screen appears.

10 Click OK to complete the System Restore process.

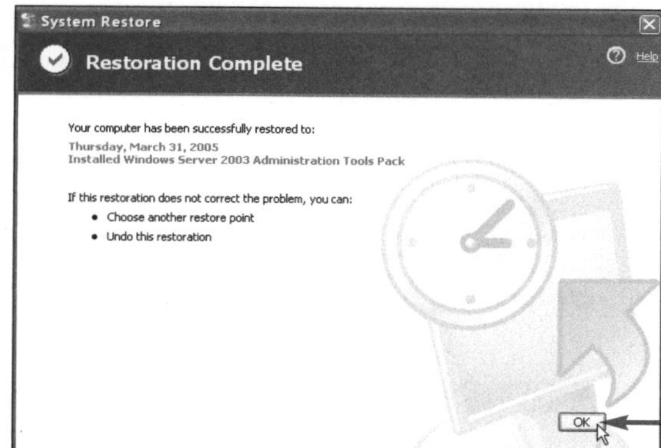

PART IV

I deleted a personal file and emptied the Recycle Bin. Can I use System Restore to get my file back?

▼ If only you could, the system would be almost perfect. However, System Restore is not capable of restoring data files. As soon as you clear your Recycle Bin, your files are gone.

If you have deleted an important file, think about a backup procedure (unrelated to System Restore) to make sure critical data files are backed up and in a secure location so that you can restore them later if you encounter a similar situation.

One reason System Restore does not deal with data files is because of security. Imagine that you delete sensitive files from your computer. You leave the company for another job. The next person who uses your computer could, if System Restore restored data files, access those old files of yours.

Should I create my own Restore Points?

▼ Yes. Any time you make changes to Windows or your computer, such as add new hardware, update new programs, or change Windows in a major way, create a Restore Point. To do this, click Start, then All Programs, then Accessories, then System Tools, and then click System Restore. When the System Restore window opens, click the option to create a restore point (○ changes to ⦿) and click Next. Type a name for your Restore Point, such as the current date or description of the changes you just made. Click Create. Windows XP creates the Restore Point. Click Close to close the screen.

Repair Windows

Sometimes Windows does not start or run correctly even if you have done a System Restore. Or, you may not be able to boot into Windows, in Safe Mode or Normal. During these times your next line of action is to repair Windows. In order to repair Windows, you need to use the setup CD that came with Windows. If you do not have this, purchase or borrow a Windows XP CD.

When you repair Windows, you simply recopy the original Windows files back to their default location. Sometimes this corrects problems you are experiencing if the original files have become corrupted or deleted.

One of the most interesting parts of the repair process is when you first start it. An option you can select is to repair Windows at the Recovery Console. You would think this would be the option to select. It is not.

Instead the Recovery Console is used if you want to use command prompt utilities to work out problems. The one you may want to try is the chkdsk /r command. This runs Check Disk on your hard drive to find and repair (at least attempt to repair) problems with the hard drive.

Repair Windows

1. Insert the Windows CD into the CD drive.
2. Restart your computer.

   As your computer starts, a message appears telling you to press any key to boot to the CD.
3. Press a key to boot to the CD.

   You have only a few seconds to make this choice, so do it quickly.

   - Windows prepares the setup screen.

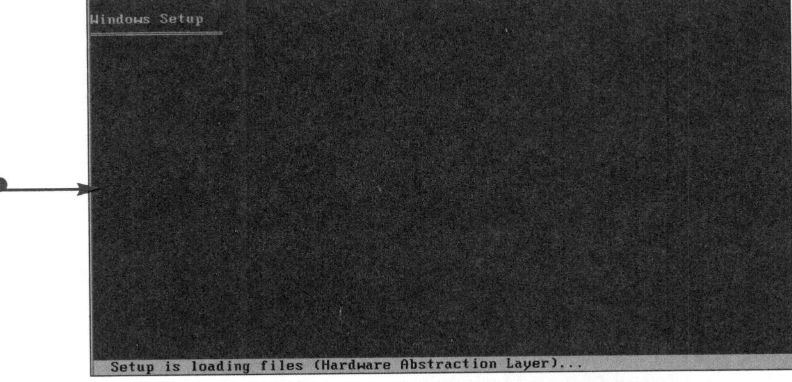

A screen appears showing a list of options from which to choose:

To set up Windows XP now, press Enter.

To repair a Windows XP installation using Recovery Console, press R.

To quit Setup without installing Windows XP, press F3.

4. Choose the first option by pressing Enter.

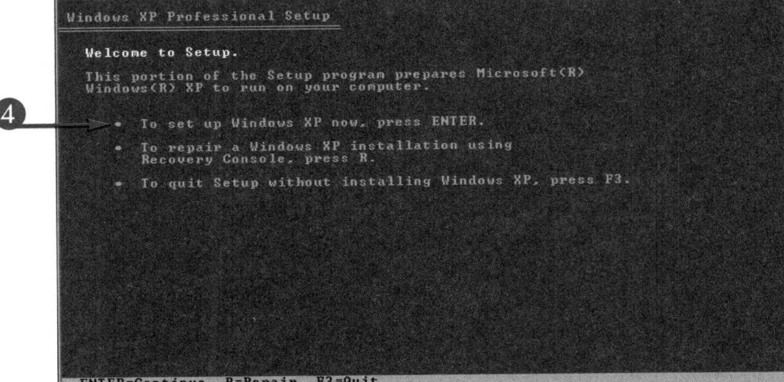

Windows loads the Setup files into memory and displays the EULA window.

5 Press F8 to continue.

Windows searches for any previous installations of Windows and then displays a list of these installations.

6 Select the one you want to repair.

In most cases you have only one version installed.

7 Press R to begin the repair process.

Windows copies files onto your computer.

8 Type **Exit** to restart the computer.

Upon restart, do not press a key to boot from CD, as you did in Step 3. Let this message go by so Windows can continue repairing itself.

Respond to any prompts as you would if this was the initial installation of Windows.

Note: *Your programs all remain intact after the repair is finished.*

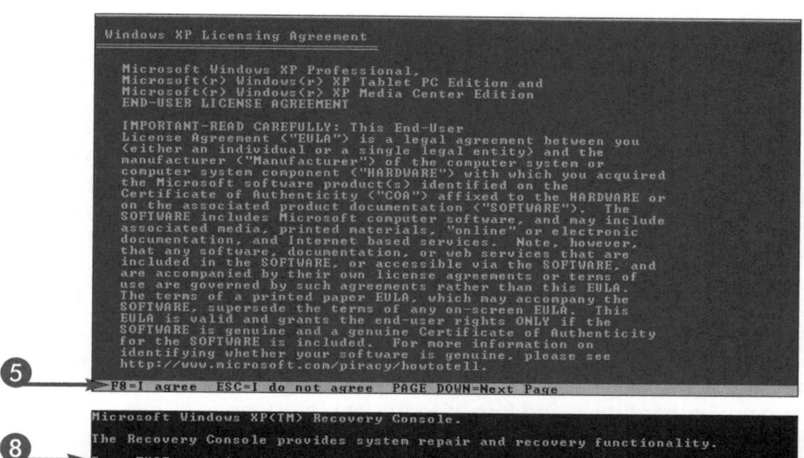

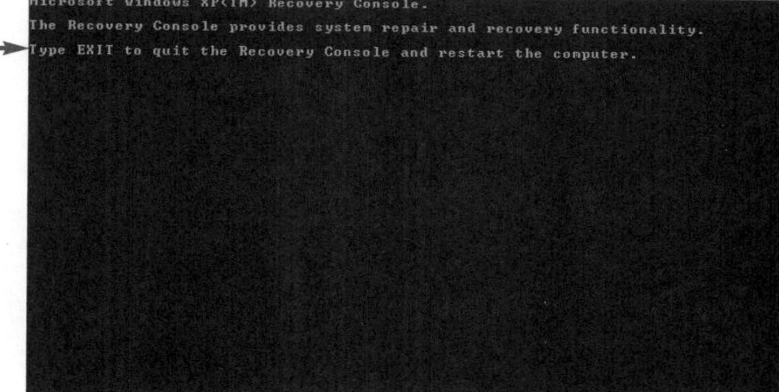

PART IV

I have not deleted any files in my Windows folder. How can they be deleted?

▼ Viruses, spyware (also known as adware or malware), and even some legitimate programs can delete files. Viruses and spyware are created for one use — to cause problems on users' computers. If a virus can delete Windows system files, it will. In the case of legitimate programs, Windows system files can be deleted if the original programmer of the application is not careful in how they name and store files. Other times you may install software not intended for Windows XP (such as programs written for Windows 3.1) that may cause problems with Windows files.

Can I use my friend's copy of Windows to repair my version?

▼ Yes, but you cannot legally use that copy to reinstall Windows on your computer. In fact, because of Windows' activation requirement, you would not be able to activate that copy of Windows because your friend has already done so. However, to repair Windows you can use his copy. Keep this in mind: If his copy is an OEM copy (it will say so on the CD label) and it includes restore information for his computer, do not restore your computer with that CD. You may lose all your data or cause other problems to occur on your system.

Reinstall Windows

You have tried restoring and repairing Windows. You have even called a technical support person, but they charged $60 an hour to walk you through the same processes you just did. You now need to consider reinstalling Windows.

What is involved with reinstalling Windows? It depends on your approach. You can reinstall Windows to the exact same spot it was originally. If you do this, you must reformat your hard drive and lose all your data, program files, device drivers, and so on. Or you can reinstall Windows into a different directory (such as to one called WINXP2) and retain all your data files and any device driver folders already on your system. The downsides, however, are that you still need to reinstall all your programs into the new directory, and that you will have a previous copy of Windows on your system. Also, keep in mind you need at least 1GB of free hard drive space when installing a second copy of Windows on your computer.

The previous copy of Windows, however, can be deleted when you get your computer back up and running. I prefer this approach because you will have your data files still on the computer (just think of all those pictures, videos, and documents you would hate to lose), and you have any preinstalled device driver folders that came with your computer.

Reinstall Windows

1. Insert the Windows CD into your CD drive.
2. Restart your computer.
   - Your computer re-starts.

   A message appears telling you to press any key to boot to the CD.
3. Press a key to boot to the CD.

   You have only a few seconds to make this choice, so do it quickly.

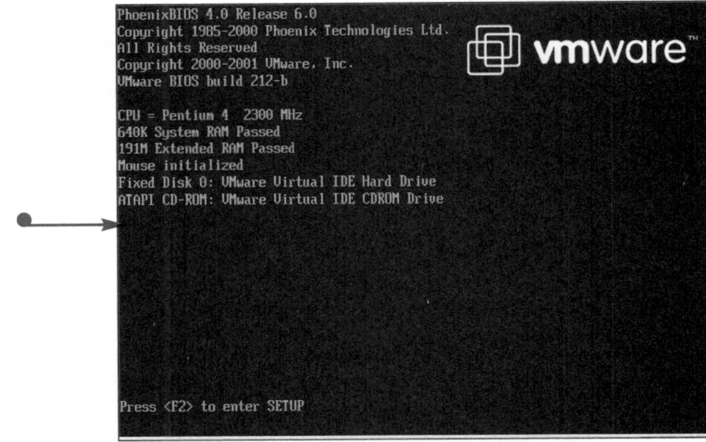

   A screen appears showing a list of options from which you can choose:

   To setup Windows XP now, press Enter.

   To repair a Windows XP installation using Recovery Console, press R.

   To quit Setup without installing Windows XP, press F3.
4. Choose the first option by pressing Enter.

   Windows loads the Setup files into memory and displays the EULA window.
5. Press F8 to continue.

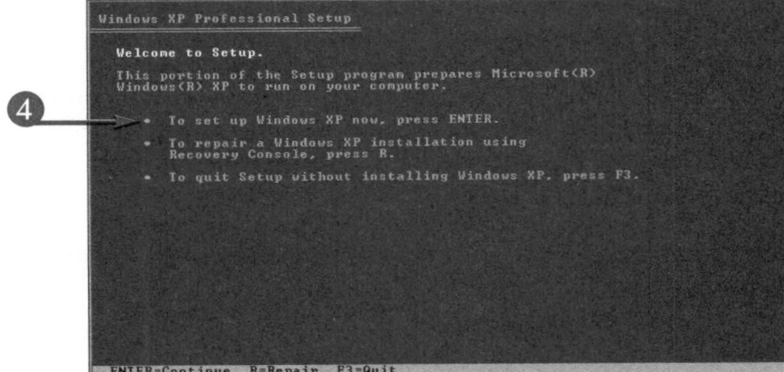

Windows searches for any previous installations of Windows and then displays a list of these installations.

6 Select the partition on which to install Windows.

7 Choose the option to install Windows to a new directory.

If this option is not available, then Windows cannot be reinstalled this way. You will need to reinstall Windows on top of your current installation.

8 Type a name for the new directory.

9 Press Enter to begin the Windows Setup routine.

Windows Setup copies files onto your hard drive, shuts down and restarts Windows, and then continues installing Windows.

As Windows installs, you are prompted for configuration information, such as regional settings, time and date, and network information.

- After Windows is reinstalled, it boots to the desktop.

At this point you need to reinstall all your applications using the Add/Remove Programs icon in the Control Panel, make sure your hardware devices are working (such as testing your sound card, modem, and so on), and customize the Windows environment to your liking.

Note: *You may want to create a System Restore Point in case you need to restore Windows later. See the section "Restore Windows" for more information.*

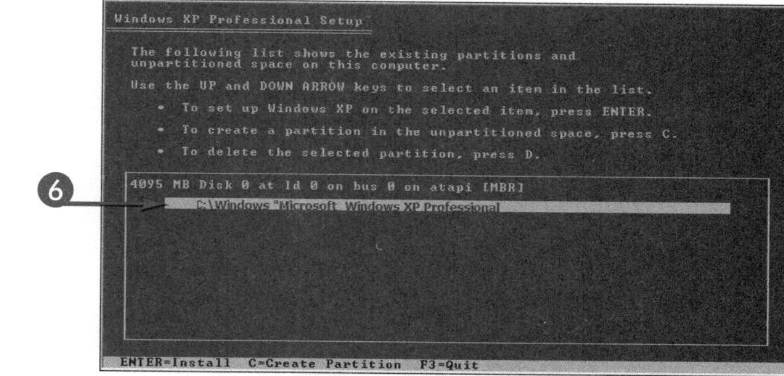

PART IV

MASTER IT

If I reinstall Windows, do I have to reinstall Windows XP SP2?

▼ Yes, you need to obtain a copy of XP SP2 from Microsoft and then reinstall it after you get your Windows SP1 version working again. Again, if you downloaded it originally and stored it on your computer, the file is still there if you use the method of reinstalling Windows to a new directory. If not, you need to obtain SP2 from Microsoft either as a download (it is about 145MB in size) or as a CD ordered from Microsoft.

You mention device drivers as a reason to install Windows to a new directory. What is the big deal about drivers?

▼ Many times when computer manufacturers prepare your computer in the factory, they make a folder called Drivers, INF, or a similar name. The device drivers in this folder are designed to work with the hardware devices — DVD drives, sound cards, network adapters, graphics cards — installed in your computer. If you lose this folder, you may have a difficult time locating all the device drivers for your computer. Even if you contact the manufacturer, they may or may not still have the drivers for your exact computer.

Numbers

A

B

C

E

F

continued

G

H

I

L

M

N

O

P

continued

continued

continued

U

V

W